Taxation of Intellectual Property

First Edition 2011

Taxation of Intellectual Property

First Edition 2011

By

Daniel W. Matthews

VANDEPLAS PUBLISHING

UNITED STATES OF AMERICA

Taxation of Intellectual Property, *First Edition 2011*

Matthews, Daniel W.

Published by:

Vandeplas Publishing – November 2011

801 International Parkway, 5th Floor
Lake Mary, FL. 32746
USA

www.vandeplaspublishing.com

ISBN: 978-1-60042-156-3

ACKNOWLEDGMENTS

Above all, I must acknowledge Professor David Berry's assistance in completing this book. Professor Berry graciously wrote this book's intellectual property overview (Appendix A: An Intellectual Property Primer). He also fielded a seemingly endless stream of questions from me about intellectual property (and did so with great patience). I can say the same for Professor Gerald Tschura, who likewise answered numerous questions about intellectual property, particularly on copyrights and trademarks. I am forever grateful for Professor Paul Marineau's valuable insights about international taxation and for his comments on Chapter 6 of this book. I thank Professor Gina Torielli for giving me the opportunity to teach a course on taxation of intellectual property. Stacie Farina of the Thomas M. Cooley Law School helped me greatly in editing a manuscript of this book. Finally, this book would not be possible without the generous support of the Thomas M. Cooley Law School, its board of directors, and President Don LeDuc.

TABLE OF CONTENTS

Chapter 1: Principles of Federal Income Taxation

1.1 The Importance of Tax Policy

One of the big challenges in studying and understanding tax law is not only to know what the tax law is, but also to know *why the tax law is what it is*. A major mistake in studying tax law is to attempt rote memorization of rules. Rote memorization will not work because tax law is too voluminous to memorize. More importantly, rote memorization causes one to view rules in a vacuum without thinking about the principles that make tax law what it is. Without any context or understanding of the underlying principles, tax law is a vast set of arbitrary and capricious rules without meaning. Believe it or not, there is a rhyme and a reason to the tax laws. Congress does pass tax legislation with some goal in mind. If one knows the policy Congress is trying to promote, one can better understand what the tax law is. When looking at a tax provision, one should ponder why Congress wrote the tax law the way it did. Otherwise, it is very easy to get caught up in and confused by the minutiae of tax law.

For example, one of the great principles of tax law is that certain expenses can be deducted immediately, while other expenses are capitalized and deducted at some later point in time. One can memorize this fact, but why is it the case? As explained in greater detail throughout this Chapter, Congress generally seeks to have taxpayers deduct expenses against the income those expenses help to produce. So, if an expense will produce income over a long period of time, deduction of those expenses right away will result in tax savings today, i.e., tax deferral. Taxpayers desire tax deferral because they want more money in their pockets today so that they can earn interest on that money until such time that they pay the tax. The government obviously wants the opposite to occur. The government seeks to eliminate tax deferral so it can collect more tax currently to use for its own purposes.

If one thinks in terms of tax deferral, one can understand why certain expenses are deducted currently and others capitalized. By understanding what Congress is seeking to accomplish, knowing the rules should follow naturally. So when each new topic is introduced throughout this book, one should consider why the tax law is written the way it is. What policy is Congress trying to accomplish? In the end, understanding the important concepts and principles underlying tax law will do more for one's grasp of the tax law than rote memorization ever can.

1.2 Concepts to Understanding Taxation

Most textbooks on tax law assume that the student is familiar with the basic concepts of tax and finance. This is a faulty assumption. Many intelligent people, including many brilliant law students, may be quite ignorant when it comes to tax and finance. And many bright people are needlessly intimidated by tax and finance because they involve numbers and mathematics. Fortunately, the mathematics necessary to understand tax is that taught in elementary school. Basic arithmetic will do. Addition, subtraction, multiplication, and division are all that is needed, with the occasional fraction thrown in for good measure.

In the real world, tax has everything to do with numbers. The ultimate goal of tax law is come up with a bottom line number, i.e., the amount of tax to be paid to the government or refunded to the taxpayer, but there is more to tax law than the bottom line. Savvy taxpayers view tax in a larger financial context. These taxpayers seek the best way to structure transactions to lower taxes, which in turn, frees up more money that can be used for income-producing purposes. The government, not surprisingly, has the opposite goal in mind. The government would like to collect as much tax as legally possible so that it can use the money for its own purposes. Therefore, any proper instruction in tax, by its very nature, involves the use of numbers. Trying to teach tax without numbers is like trying to teach reading without books. To this end, this Chapter introduces two financial concepts central to the understanding of tax: (1) the value of a deduction and (2) the time value of money.

1.2[1] Value of a Deduction

Nearly everyone has heard of a tax deduction (or has heard of a deduction by its colloquial name, a "write off"). Some taxpayers may seem unconcerned about the cost of an expense because the expense is deductible. After all, "it is deductible," says the taxpayer. Should these taxpayers be more concerned than they are?

Federal income taxation, when broken down to its skeleton parts, is the process of adding up a taxpayer's gross income, then subtracting "deductions." Once a taxpayer subtracts deductions from gross income, the taxpayer calcultates a figure called "taxable income." This is the figure on which the taxpayer calculates tax owed. The taxpayer thereafter applies any credits and determines whether he owes additional taxes or is entitled to a refund.

So what is a deduction worth? A deduction is simply worth the taxpayer's marginal tax rate times the amount of the deduction. A taxpayer's marginal tax rate is a concept often referred to, but rarely explained. Some mistakenly believe that the marginal tax rate applies to all taxable income. This is not true (at least in the case of individuals and some corporations). The marginal tax rate is simply the rate on the last dollar of income the taxpayer earns during the taxable year. Why does the marginal tax rate refer to the last dollar earned? Why not the first dollar earned?

In order to understand marginal tax rates, one must understand that tax rates are graduated. An income tax is graduated when the tax rate increases as the taxpayer's taxable income increases. Consider, for example, the following tax table for married individuals filing jointly:[1]

Table 1 – Married Individuals Filing Joint Returns and Surviving Spouses (2011)	
If Taxable Income Is:	The Tax Is:
Not over $17,000	10% of the taxable income
Over $17,000 but not over $69,000	$1,700 plus 15% of the excess over $17,000
Over $69,000 but not over $139,350	$9,500 plus 25% of the excess over $69,000
Over $139,350 but not over $212,300	$27,087.50 plus 28% of the excess over $139,350
Over $212,300 but not over $379,150	$47,513.50 plus 33% of the excess over $212,300
Over $379,150	$102,574 plus 35% of the excess over $379,150

Suppose a married couple filing jointly knows that their taxable income will greatly exceed $1,000,000. If so, the couple knows they will easily exceed the threshold for landing in the top 35 percent bracket. The couple wants to determine the value of making a $10,000 deductible expense this year. An additional $10,000 deduction in this case will save the couple $3,500 in income taxes (i.e., $10,000 deduction x 35 percent marginal tax rate). In this case, the couple's taxable income will be reduced to $990,000. They will still easily exceed the threshold for the 35 percent bracket. So the $10,000 expense is really being deducted against income that would otherwise be subject to a 35 percent tax. That is why taxpayers use the marginal rate to determine the value of a deduction, rather than any lower tax bracket or average tax rate.

[1] Rev. Proc. 2011-12, 2011-2 I.R.B. 297.

The concept of the average tax rate is worth mentioning. The marginal tax rate is different than the taxpayer's average tax rate. The average tax rate is the total tax paid as a percentage of taxable income. By its very definition, therefore, in a graduated tax system, a taxpayer's average tax rate will always, as a matter of mathematics, be less than the marginal tax rate. What is the average tax rate for the couple with $1,000,000 in taxable income? According to the table above, the couple would pay $319,871.50, which is an average tax rate of 31.99 percent.[2] This shows that although marginal rates go as high as 35 percent, no individual taxpayer will pay 35 percent on all of his taxable income.[3]

A few conclusions can be drawn about the value of deductions:

(1) A deduction is only as valuable as the taxpayer's marginal tax rate. Therefore, the higher the taxpayer's marginal rate, the higher the value of a deduction to the taxpayer. A taxpayer who has no taxable income (because, for instance, deductions are greater than gross income) really has a marginal rate of zero. Therefore, additional deductions to such taxpayer are worth nothing for that particular tax year (in some cases, the excess deductions can be carried forward into future tax years).

(2) Even if an expense is deductible, the taxpayer still has to pay an out of pocket charge. While the deduction and corresponding tax savings effectively acts as a government subsidy, the taxpayer is still picking up most of the tab (assuming the highest marginal tax rate is less than 50 percent). In the above example, the married couple taking a $10,000 deduction saves $3,500 in tax. Another way to look at this is that the married couple is paying $6,500 in after-tax money out of pocket.

(3) While taxpayers focus on the value of the deduction, the government focuses on the cost of the deduction in the form of lost revenue. In the above example, the married couple saved $3,500 in tax on a $10,000

---

[2] According to the table, the couple would pay $102,574 on its first $379,150 and 35 percent over $379,150. Therefore, the calculation is as follows:
Total tax = $102,574 + [($1,000,000 - $379,150) x 35%]
Total tax = $102,574 + $217,297.50 = $319,871.50.
Average tax rate = Total tax ($319,871.50)/Taxable income ($1,000,000) = 31.99%.

[3] The tax brackets for corporate taxpayers contain "bubble" brackets to neutralize the advantages of lower brackets, as explained in the note accompanying Problem 2.1.

deduction. Another perspective is that the government has forgone $3,500 in revenue by allowing the deduction. The cost to the government in permitting a deduction is commonly referred to as a *tax expenditure*.

(4) The higher marginal rates go, the greater the incentive for taxpayers to engage in questionable transactions to produce deductions. Indeed, in the 1970s, high rates (up to 70 percent), coupled with high interest rates, encouraged taxpayers to engage in tax shelters that had little economic significance other than producing deductions to "shelter" high rate income, thereby saving on taxes.[4] While Congress has passed legislation since the 1970s to effectively stop classic tax shelters, the high marginal rates undoubtedly made the classic tax shelters more attractive then.

One final point should be made about the value of a deduction vis-à-vis the value of a credit. Unlike a deduction, a tax credit is a dollar-for-dollar tax savings in the amount of tax owed. So, for example, a $10,000 credit reduces taxes by $10,000. Therefore, a credit (assuming it can be fully used) means the taxpayer has no out of pocket cost. But most federal tax credits are *nonrefundable*, meaning they cannot exceed the amount of tax the taxpayer owes. For example, suppose a taxpayer owing $10,000 in federal tax is entitled to a $15,000 nonrefundable credit. In this case, the credit would be limited to $10,000. Had the credit in this example been a *refundable* credit, the government would have refunded $5,000 to the taxpayer.

The value of deductions and credits are illustrated in the following example:

> **Problem 1.1**: Badger Corporation expects to have $5,000,000 in taxable income for the taxable year. The corporation has the opportunity to make an additional $100,000 deductible expense before the end of the taxable year. The corporation asks you, as its tax counsel, to evaluate the value of a deductible expense of $100,000. What do you advise the corporation? Alternatively, suppose the same $100,000 would qualify as a tax credit. What then? Suppose that the applicable Code provision permitting the credit states that the taxpayer has the option (a) to deduct the expense in full, or (b) take a credit equal to 30 percent of the amount of the expense. Which

---

[4] For an excellent discussion of the 1970s tax shelter craze, see Micheal J. Graetz, *The Decline (and Fall?) of the Income Tax*, 41-51 (W.W. Norton & Co. 1997).

would be better in this instance, the deduction or the credit? In answering these questions, please reference the following corporate income tax table:

Corporate Income Tax Rates[5]

Taxable income over	Not over	Tax rate
$0	$50,000	15%
$50,000	$75,000	25%
$75,000	$100,000	34%
$100,000	$335,000	39%
$335,000	$10,000,000	34%
$10,000,000	$15,000,000	35%
$15,000,000	$18,333,333	38%
$18,333,333	……..	35%

1.2[2] Timing and the Time Value of Money

Once a taxpayer determines that an expense is deductible, should it matter if the expense is deductible now, next year, or five years from now? Much of tax law concerns the issue of timing. Taxpayers and the government have litigated countless cases over the deductibility of expenses. And in many of these cases, the question is not whether the expense is deductible, but *when* the expense is deductible.

An important principle of tax law is to match expenses with the income those expenses help to produce. For instance, a taxpayer may pay or incur an expense for one month's rent of office space. The taxpayer pays one month's rent, but the rent expense has no discernable long-lasting benefit to the taxpayer beyond the month in question. In other words, the office rent helps the taxpayer generate revenue for that month only and will not discernibly help produce income three years later. Accordingly, the taxpayer should have immediate expense recognition and deduct the rent right away.

---

[5] I.R.C. § 11. Corporate income tax brackets, unlike tax brackets for individuals, contain "bubble" brackets of 39 percent and 38 percent to neutralize the advantage of the lower brackets. The 39 percent "bubble" bracket acts as a 5 percent addition to the 34 percent rate, thereby neutralizing the advantage of the 15 percent and 25 percent brackets. The process is complete once taxable income reaches $10 million, so that a corporate taxpayer with $10 million in taxable income pays a flat 34 percent rate. The 38 percent "bubble" bracket acts as a 3 percent addition to the 35 percent rate, thereby neutralizing the advantage of the 34 percent bracket. The process is complete at $18,333,333, so that a corporate taxpayer with taxable income of $18,333,333 pays a flat 35 percent rate.

Compare the rent example with the taxpayer's acquisition of intellectual property by purchase. The intellectual property will help the taxpayer produce income now, next year, and five years from now. So would it be appropriate to allow the taxpayer to deduct the purchase price of the intellectual property right away? Suppose the intellectual property will produce income for 15 years. If so, it would seem appropriate to match the expense and the income by deducting the cost over 15 years. Otherwise, if the taxpayer is able to deduct an expense faster than the income it helps produce, the result is mismatching and tax deferral. In other words, if the taxpayer is allowed to deduct too much, too early, the taxpayer will save on taxes now, but the tax savings are not permanent. By deducting the entire expense currently, the taxpayer will have no deductions with respect to the intellectual property in future years (if the taxpayer had properly matched expenses). Therefore, without these future deductions, the taxpayer will pay more tax in the future than he would have if he had properly matched. So, expensing the intellectual property purchase would save taxes now at the expense of the taxpayer paying more tax in future years.

If the government will eventually receive its revenue, why do the government and the taxpayer care when the tax is paid? The answer has to do with the *time value of money*. The concept of the time value of money is simple. The value of a dollar today is greater than the value of a dollar in the future. This is true because a dollar received (or saved) today can earn interest up until the time a future dollar is received. The taxpayer can invest those saved taxes now and earn interest on them. Therefore, as a general rule of thumb, a taxpayer wants to deduct expenses as soon as possible. Conversely, the government prefers that the taxpayer deduct the expense in the future (or not at all).

In reality, tax deferral can be seen, from the taxpayer's perspective, as an interest-free loan without collateral. From the government's perspective, reducing deferral and collecting taxes today results in the government earning interest on the collected tax. Or more likely, it reduces the amount the government would otherwise have to borrow, thus saving interest the government would otherwise have to pay on the avoided debt.

How can the value of tax deferral be measured? A taxpayer can measure the value of tax deferral many ways, but the most common are (1) interest on the deferred tax, and (2) the present value of the deferred tax. The interest on the deferred tax is the after-tax interest that could be earned on the tax savings. In the case of tax deferral arising from a deduction, the interest on the deferred tax can be expressed by the following financial equation:

$$\text{Interest on deferred tax} = \text{value of deduction} * [(1 + r)^n - 1]$$

The variable "r" is the after-tax interest rate. The variable "n" is the number of years the interest will compound. In the case of tax deferral, the variable "n" would be the number of years the tax is to be deferred.

> **Problem 1.2**: Taxpayer is in the 35 percent marginal bracket and is able to deduct $100,000 immediately. Taxpayer expects to pay the government back in ten years by including $100,000 in income and having it taxed at the same 35 percent marginal tax rate. Assume that Taxpayer will invest the tax savings and earn a five percent after-tax interest on it. What is the interest on the deferred tax in this case?

A second approach to value tax deferral is to calculate the present value of the deferred tax. This approach looks at the amount the taxpayer would have to set aside today to pay taxes in the future. In the case of tax deferral arising from a deduction, the formula for calculating the present value of the deferred tax is stated as follows:

$$\text{Present value of deferred tax} = \text{value of deduction}/(1+r)^n$$

> **Problem 1.3**: Assume the same facts as **Problem 1.2** above. The taxpayer knows that he will have to pay $35,000 tax ten years from now. The taxpayer can invest money in an account that will accrue an after-tax rate of return of five percent. How much would the taxpayer have to set aside today to pay the $35,000 tax in ten years?

Problems 1.2 and 1.3 conveniently assume that the taxpayer will take a deduction today and pay the government back in the form of inclusion at some definite point in the future. The real world, obviously, is more complicated. This is especially true when comparing expensing (i.e., the deduction of the cost of an asset immediately) vis-à-vis amortization or depreciation. With amortization and depreciation, the taxpayer deducts a portion of the cost of the asset today with the remainder of the cost being deducted over a period of years.

The value of expensing is the value of the deduction. But the value of the amortized amount is more complicated. The taxpayer can calculate the present value of the deferred tax for each year of the recovery period. The taxpayer would then take the sum of the present value of the deferred tax for all of the years of the recovery period. The taxpayer would then compare that sum to the value of expensing. Alternately, the taxpayer can calculate the present value of amortization by using the "PV" function in Microsoft Excel®, which is expressed as PV(rate, nper, pmt, fv, type). In this case, "rate" is the after-tax interest rate, "nper" is the number of years the interest will compound, "pmt" is the payment (here, the value of deduction) for each period, and "fv" is the future value (here, "fv" is zero, or "fv" can simply be omitted). The "type" variable should be expressed as "1."[6]

The value of tax deferral when comparing expensing and amortization is illustrated in the following problem:

> **Problem 1.4**: Taxpayer is in the 35 percent marginal tax bracket. Taxpayer purchases for $1,500,000 intellectual property for use in his business. Taxpayer expects the intellectual property to produce an even stream of income for the next 15 years. Compare the consequences to Taxpayer of expensing the $1,500,000 versus amortizing the intellectual property and deducting its cost ratably over 15 years. Assume that Taxpayer's marginal tax rate is 35 percent in all relevant years and that the applicable interest rate is five percent. In answering this question, it may be helpful to create a spreadsheet showing the present value of future deductions for each year of the 15 year amortization period. After completing this spreadsheet, double check your answer by calculating the present value of the amortization deduction using the PV function in Excel®.

Problem 1.4 makes two very big assumptions. First, the example assumes that the taxpayer's marginal tax will remain constant throughout the recovery period. In the real world, Congress could raise or lower tax rates. And the taxpayer's future taxable income could decrease thereby placing the taxpayer in a lower marginal tax bracket. The second major assumption is that the interest rate remains constant. In reality, interest rates are quite volatile.

> **Problem 1.5**: Assume the same facts as Problem 1.4, except that Congress raises tax rates such that Taxpayer is in a 42 percent marginal tax bracket

[6] The "type" can either be expressed as "0" (meaning the value of the deduction is experienced at the end of the period) or "1" (meaning the value of the deduction is experienced at the start of the period). Because the starting reference is the day the deduction is taken in the first year, the value of future deductions are calculated at the start of each yearly interval from the date the first deduction is taken. If "0" is selected as the "type," the value of the deduction in the first year would be calculated at the end of 365 days after the deduction is taken and future deductions would be calculated in yearly intervals from that date.

starting in the second year and continuing through the end of the 15 year amortization period? Alternatively, what would happen if the after-tax interest rate rises to seven percent in the second year and remains constant through the end of the 15 year amortization period?

1.3 The Federal Income Tax

The taxpayer's ultimate goal is to come up with a bottom line number, i.e., the amount the taxpayer owes to the government or the amount the government must refund to the taxpayer. To get there, a taxpayer must first determine amounts included in gross income. Thereafter, the taxpayer subtracts deductions and exemptions to arrive at "taxable income." It is on this "taxable income" figure that the taxpayer applies applicable tax rates to calculate the amount of tax. The taxpayer then applies any applicable credits to arrive at the amount owed or amount to be refunded. Taking this process in mind, federal income taxation can be boiled down into four major subjects, including the following:

1. What items of income are *includible* in gross income?
2. What expenses are *deductible* from gross income?
3. *When* is an item of income includible in gross income and *when* is an expense deductible from gross income?
4. What is the *character* of income or losses?

Each of these topics is addressed separately below.

1.3[1] Income Includible in Gross Income

Gross income is the starting point for calculating tax liability. After filling out one's background information on an income tax return, such as name, address, and taxpayer identification number, the first section with actual dollar figures is gross income. As far as the Code goes, it all starts with Section 61, which states that "[e]xcept as otherwise provided in this subtitle, gross income means all income from whatever source derived."[7] Section 61 then provides a laundry list of fifteen specific items that are includible in gross income. But Congress is careful to point that gross income includes "but is not limited to" the laundry list of the fifteen items.

---

[7] I.R.C. § 61(a).

While Section 61 instructs taxpayers to include "all income from whatever source derived," it does not define what "income" is. In the early years of the income tax, the U.S. Supreme Court struggled with the definition of income. In part, the Court struggled with whether income narrowly encompasses gains derived from capital or labor and from the sale of capital assets, or whether a broader definition should apply.[8] In 1955, the Supreme Court, in *Commissioner v. Glenshaw Glass Co.*,[9] settled on a broad definition of income by stating that income includes "instances of undeniable accessions to wealth, clearly realized, over which the taxpayer has complete dominion." "Undeniable accessions to wealth" not only encompass gains from capital, labor and dealings in property, but it also include things such as prizes, awards, punitive damages, treasure trove, lottery winnings, and the like.[10] Also, the term "undeniable accessions to wealth" is broad enough to cover non-monetary compensation, such compensation paid in property or services.[11]

The proper way to read Section 61 and *Glenshaw Glass Co.* is that all undeniable accessions to wealth, clearly realized, over which the taxpayer has control are includible in gross income, unless Congress has provided an express exclusion in the Code. In other words, a taxpayer should assume an item of income is includible in gross income, unless the taxpayer can point to a specific provision excluding it. Congress has provided for several specific exclusions from gross income, including life insurance proceeds, gifts, bequests and inheritances, compensatory damages for personal physical injury, interest on tax-exempt bonds, certain gains on the sale of a principal residence, and certain fringe benefits, among others.[12] All of these items are income, but they are excludable from gross income, simply because Congress has provided so.

Out of the fifteen specifically enumerated items in Section 61, six are particularly relevant to the taxation of intellectual property. These include compensation for services, gross income derived from business, gain derived from dealings in property, interest, royalties, and

---

[8] *See, e.g.*, *Eisner v. Macomber*, 252 U.S. 189, 206-07 (1920) (defining income as "[t]he gain derived from capital, from labor, or from both combined, provided it be understood to include profit gained through the sale or conversion of capital assets. . . .").

[9] 348 U.S. 42 (1955).

[10] Treas. Reg. § 1.61-14(a).

[11] Treas. Reg. § 1.61-2(d).

[12] *See* I.R.C. §§ 101 (life insurance proceeds), 102 (gifts, bequests, and inheritances), 103 (tax-exempt interest), 104 (compensatory damages for personal, physical injury), 121 (sale of principal residence), and 132 (certain fringe benefits). The exclusion provisions of the Code are generally found in part III of subchapter B, I.R.C. §§ 101-139.

dividends. Compensation for services, gross income derived from business, interest, royalties, and dividends are relatively self-explanatory, so additional mention of them is unnecessary here.[13] But gains from dealings in property are worthy of detailed mention because they are a concept absolutely fundamental to the understanding of federal income taxation.

1.3[1][a] Gains in Dealings in Property

According to Section 1001, a gain from dealing in property is "the excess of the amount realized therefrom over the adjusted basis" of the property sold or exchanged.[14] On the other hand, a loss is the "excess of adjusted basis . . . over the amount realized."[15] A simpler way to think of this is to take the amount realized and subtract the adjusted basis. If the result is a positive number, it is a gain. If the result is a negative number, it is a loss. The formula for calculating gain or loss is as follows:

Amount realized – adjusted basis = gain (positive)/loss (negative)

Most people already intuitively know what the Code says about calculating a gain or loss without having to be familiar with its jargon. In lay terms, Section 1001 really says that gain is where a taxpayer sells or exchanges property for an amount greater than the taxpayer's cost of the property. So if a taxpayer buys low, and sells high, he has a gain derived from dealing in property. And that gain is includible in gross income, unless some provision in the Code provides otherwise.

Section 1001 defines "amount realized" as "the sum of money received plus the fair market value of the property (other than money) received."[16] The "sum of money" does not necessarily mean amounts paid in cash. To illustrate, suppose the taxpayer sells or exchanges property that is subject to a $100,000 mortgage. In this case, the buyer of the property could pay the taxpayer $100,000 cash and the taxpayer could then use the $100,000 cash to pay off the mortgage. Alternatively, the parties may agree that the buyer will simply assume the taxpayer's mortgage to obviate the need to exchange cash. In either case, the end result is the same, i.e., the taxpayer is ultimately relieved of the $100,000 mortgage.

---

[13] However, the issue of whether income is a royalty from a license or a sale of property may have implications as to the character of the income, and has special mention later in this textbook.

[14] I.R.C. § 1001(a).

[15] *Id.*

[16] I.R.C. § 1001(b).

Therefore, relief of liability on a sale or exchange is tantamount to "money received" and is included in amount realized.[17]

The "adjusted basis" of property is its cost plus or minus any adjustments made to the property.[18] A taxpayer's adjusted basis in property is really the taxpayer's *after-tax investment* in the property. Therefore, the key to understanding gain (and loss for that matter) is to understand the difference between *after-tax* and *pre-tax* dollars. After-tax dollars are amounts on which the taxpayer has already paid income tax because at some point the taxpayer has already included these dollars in his gross income (or these dollars were excludable from gross income per a specific Code provision). For example, if a taxpayer uses $100,000 from his bank account to purchase intellectual property, it is assumed that the taxpayer has already paid tax on the $100,000. Similarly, if the taxpayer borrows $100,000 to purchase the intellectual property, it is assumed that the taxpayer will eventually pay off the $100,000 loan with after-tax dollars. Therefore, whether the taxpayer pays for property with cash or borrowed funds, or a combination thereof, such amounts are after-tax and part of the taxpayer's cost in the property.

Pre-tax dollars are obviously the opposite of after-tax dollars. Pre-tax dollars are amounts on which the taxpayer has not yet paid income tax because such dollars have not yet been included in gross income. So when a taxpayer receives pre-tax dollars, such amounts are includible in gross income, unless a specific exclusion applies.

To illustrate the calculation of gain and its relationship to after-tax and pre-tax dollars, consider an example where the taxpayer purchases intellectual property for $100,000 and later sells it for $1,000,000. According to the formula in section 1001, the taxpayer would calculate gain as $1,000,000 (amount realized) less $100,000 (adjusted basis) for a gain of $900,000. Another way to look at this is to ask oneself what the $1,000,000 gross sales price received really represents. The first $100,000 can be viewed as representing a return of the taxpayer's cost, or after-tax investment in the property. The taxpayer has already paid income tax on this $100,000 once and ought not do so again. Therefore, when the taxpayer receives the $1,000,000 from the buyer, the first $100,000 can be viewed as being returned *tax-free* to the taxpayer. The remaining $900,000 represents amounts on which the taxpayer has yet to pay income tax. Therefore, the $900,000 in pre-tax dollars is included in the taxpayer's gross income as gain.

---

[17] Treas. Reg. § 1.1001-2(a).

[18] *See* I.R.C. §§ 1011(a), 1012, & 1016.

The Code uses the term "adjusted basis" because the taxpayer's after-tax investment in property can fluctuate over time. The taxpayer's "cost basis" is the cost to the taxpayer of purchasing the property, which is the amount paid plus any amounts borrowed to purchase the property. The basis can be adjusted upward if the taxpayer adds to or makes an improvement to the property. In this case, basis is adjusted upwards because the taxpayer is increasing his after-tax investment in the property. Suppose a taxpayer purchases a patent for $10,000. A year later, the taxpayer pays $5,000 to settle an infringement suit involving the patent. As explained in greater detail in this Chapter, the $5,000 paid in the infringement settlement is really part of the cost of acquiring the patent. Because the taxpayer is putting another $5,000 after-tax investment in the property, the adjusted basis of the property should be increased to $15,000.

The taxpayer's basis, or after-tax investment, in property can also decrease over time. This is likely to happen with cost-recovery deductions (e.g., depreciation or amortization deductions) associated with the property. Suppose a taxpayer purchases intellectual property for $150,000 that can be amortized over a 15-year period, or $10,000 per year. What happens to the taxpayer's after-tax investment in the intellectual property when the taxpayer is allowed a $10,000 deduction in the first year? When the taxpayer takes $10,000 in amortization deductions from the property, he is effectively sheltering $10,000 from taxable income. So, the $10,000 deduction transforms from after-tax dollars into pre-tax dollars. Thus, the taxpayer's after-tax investment in the intellectual property after one year is reduced to $140,000. Not surprisingly, the Code provides that the taxpayer's adjusted basis is reduced by the $10,000 amortization deduction to $140,000.[19]

> **Problem 1.6**: Taxpayer purchases intellectual property for $1,000,000 used in his business. In making the purchase, Taxpayer paid $200,000 cash and borrowed the remaining $800,000 purchase price secured by a security interest on the intellectual property. Several years later, Taxpayer exchanges the intellectual property for $500,000 cash, real estate worth $2,000,000, and the buyer assumes the $700,000 principal balance then owed on the loan used to acquire the intellectual property. At the time of the exchange, Taxpayer was allowed to deduct $500,000 of the cost of the intellectual property through amortization deductions. What is Taxpayer's gain? In answering this question, determine the amount of after-tax and pre-tax dollars involved.

---

[19] *See* I.R.C. § 1016.

1.3[1][b] The Concepts of Realization and Recognition

Section 1001 provides that a taxpayer *realizes* gain (or loss) upon "the sale or other disposition of property."[20] The Code's realization requirement is consistent with the *Glenshaw Glass* definition of income, which provides that accessions to wealth must be "clearly realized" to be income. Thus, periodic fluctuations in value of intellectual property are not taken into account for tax purposes until realized, which means that the intellectual property has been sold or otherwise disposed of. A taxpayer may hold intellectual property that has wildly appreciated in value since acquired. In this case, the taxpayer has a tremendous amount of "paper gain" from the intellectual property. But as long as the taxpayer continues to hold the appreciated intellectual property, the gain is *unrealized.* Thus, it is the sale or exchange of intellectual property that triggers realization. So the taxpayer must understand that gain or loss is realized any time intellectual property is sold or exchanged.

Section 1001 also provides that the entire amount of realized gain or loss is *recognized,* unless a specific Code provision provides otherwise.[21] *Recognition* is the point in time that realized gain or loss is taken into account for tax purposes. In other words, recognition is when the taxpayer accounts for the realized gain or loss on his tax return. Students new to the study of tax often mistakenly use the terms realization and recognition interchangeably, as if they have the same meaning. Students may confuse the terms because realization and recognition often occur simultaneously, *but this is not always true.* There are instances where gain or loss is realized upon sale or exchange, but all (or part) of that gain or loss is *unrecognized.* An understanding of the distinction between realization and recognition is absolutely fundamental to the understanding of federal income tax law.

Why should there ever be an instance where a realized gain or loss should not be recognized? In many cases, recognition of gain or loss is not proper because the taxpayer maintains *continuity of investment* after an exchange. A taxpayer does not maintain continuity of investment to the extent the taxpayer sells or exchanges property for (1) cash, (2) relief of liabilities (which is tantamount to cash received, as explained above), or (3) property of a different character, or a combination thereof.

Take two examples to illustrate the point. In the first example, the taxpayer realizes gain upon the exchange of intellectual property for a combination of cash and real estate. In this

---

[20] I.R.C. § 1001(a).

[21] I.R.C. § 1001(c).

case, the taxpayer has entirely cashed out and substantially modified his original investment in intellectual property by converting it into cash and real estate – two entirely different things. Because continuity of investment no longer exists, immediate recognition of the realized gain is proper.

In the second example, the taxpayer exchanges appreciated intellectual property for stock in a corporation that the taxpayer controls. In this case, the taxpayer realizes gain upon the exchange, but is recognition of that gain proper? Prior to the exchange, the taxpayer owned the intellectually property individually. After the exchange, the taxpayer maintains control of the intellectual property, albeit through the taxpayer's control of the corporation through stock ownership. Because the taxpayer maintains control of the intellectual property before and after the exchange, the taxpayer maintains continuity of investment. Therefore, recognition of the realized exchange is not proper. For this reason, the Code provides for several instances of *nonrecognition transactions*, including installment sales,[22] like-kind exchanges,[23] transfers to controlled corporations,[24] and transfers to partnerships,[25] among others.

Nonrecognition transfers are sometimes referred to as tax-free because no realized gain is recognized and no tax is paid. While the particular nonrecognition transaction may be tax-free, the unrecognized gain does not permanently escape taxation. The unrecognized gain (or loss) is deferred to a future time when continuity of investment no longer applies, e.g., the taxpayer later cashes out the investment by receiving cash or property in a modified form. So, referring to a nonrecognition transfer as tax-free may be somewhat of a misnomer. Therefore, it is more appropriate to think of nonrecognition transactions as *tax-deferred* exchanges.

1.3[2] Deductible Expenses

Why does the Code provide for deductions from gross income? The concept is simple. According to an old adage, it takes money to make money. In other words, expenses necessary for producing income ought to be deductible. So if a taxpayer has gross income of $1,000,000 but it cost the taxpayer $900,000 to produce that gross income, it naturally follows that the taxpayer should pay income tax on $100,000. In this case, it took $900,000

[22] I.R.C. § 453.

[23] I.R.C. § 1031.

[24] I.R.C. § 351.

[25] I.R.C. § 721.

to produce $1,000,000 for a profit of $100,000. An alternate way of looking at this is in terms of after-tax and pre-tax dollars. The taxpayer had to pay $900,000 in after-tax dollars to create $1,000,000 in pre-tax dollars. The net amount is $100,000 in pre-tax dollars and this is the amount on which the taxpayer should pay income tax.

The U.S. Supreme Court has long held that deductions are a "matter of legislative grace" and that the taxpayer bears the burden of showing the right to the claimed deduction.[26] In contrast to the broad definition of gross income, the courts view deductions narrowly. That is, the taxpayer must be able to point to a specific Code provision allowing the deduction; otherwise an expense is not deductible.

There are two principal limitations on a taxpayer's right to immediately deduct an expense. Generally stated, the first limitation is that the expense must be related to a business or investment. In other words, those expenses that are "personal" in nature are generally nondeductible. The second limitation is that certain expenses are *capital expenditures* because they relate to the acquisition, creation, or improvement of an asset or otherwise provide a significant future benefit. The discussion of business and investment related deductions are addressed in parts 1.3[2][a] and 1.3[2][b], immediately below. The discussion of capital expenditures follows in part 1.3[2][c] below.

1.3[2][a] Trade or Business Expenses – Section 162

The most important Code section for determining the deductibility of an expense is Section 162. Section 162 provides that a taxpayer may deduct "all the ordinary and necessary expenses paid or incurred during the taxable year in carrying on any trade or business. . . ." By requiring the expense to be "ordinary and necessary" and paid or incurred while "carrying on any trade or business," Section 162 implicitly provides that personal expenses are nondeductible. Indeed, Section 262 makes this implication clear by stating that "no deduction shall be allowed for personal, living, or family expenses," unless a specific Code provision provides otherwise.

Section 162 can be broken down into its component parts to provide the following six requirements for deductibility:

(1) the amount the taxpayer pays or incurs must be an *expense*;
(2) the expense must be *ordinary*;

[26] *See e.g. Interstate Transit Lines v. Commr.*, 319 U.S. 590, 593 (1943).

(3) the expense must be *necessary*;
(4) the expense must have been *paid or incurred* during the taxable year;
(5) the expense must relate to the taxpayer's *trade or business*; and
(6) the taxpayer must be *carrying on* any trade or business.

The "expense" requirement means that the amount the taxpayer pays or incurs must not be a capital expenditure.[27] In other words, the amount paid or incurred must be currently deductible. Therefore, if the amount paid relates to the creation, acquisition, or improvement of a long-lasting asset or otherwise provides a significant future benefit, it is not an "expense" within the meaning of Section 162.

The "ordinary" requirement means that the expense must be customary or usual within the experience of a particular industry, business, or trade.[28] An expense can be ordinary if it is common to an industry as a whole, even though the taxpayer has not paid or incurred the expense in the past or on a regular basis. So an ordinary expense need not be habitual or of the type that the taxpayer makes often. A good example is a commercial lawsuit. A taxpayer may be involved in a lawsuit once in the life of a business, but litigated commercial disputes are not unusual for businesses as whole.

The "necessary" requirement means that the expense is "appropriate and helpful" for the taxpayer's business.[29] Courts view the necessary requirement like the business judgment rule of corporate law. That is, the courts will not second guess whether the taxpayer believes the expenses is appropriate or helpful for his business. The courts will, however, second guess whether the expense really relates to the taxpayer's trade or business, or whether it is a disguised personal expense.

The requirement that the expense be "paid or incurred" during the taxable year relates to the taxpayer's method of accounting. As explained in greater detail below, a taxpayer using the cash method of accounting may take a deductible expense in the taxable year paid. In contrast, a taxpayer using the accrual method of accounting may take a deductible expense in the taxable year incurred. Thus, by requiring the expense to be paid or incurred during the taxable year, Section 162 incorporates the principal tenets of the cash and accrual methods of accounting.

---

[27] *See* I.R.C. § 263.

[28] *Welch v. Helvering*, 290 U.S. 111, 114 (1933).

[29] *Id.*

The "trade or business" requirement is critical to deductibility under Section 162, yet neither the Code nor treasury regulations define the term "trade or business." Moreover, the courts have not provided a comprehensive and definitive definition of the term. The U.S. Supreme Court addressed the meaning of a "trade or business" in *Higgins v. Commissioner.*[30] In *Higgins*, the taxpayer paid expenses associated with managing his extensive portfolio of investments in real estate and securities. In an opinion short on analysis, the Court concluded that "[n]o matter how large the estate or how continuous or extended the work required may be" the taxpayer was not engaged in a trade or business.[31] The Court believed that the taxpayer merely kept records and collected the profits from his extensive investment portfolio.

Several decades later, the U.S. Supreme Court revisited Section 162's "trade or business" requirement in *Commissioner v. Groetzinger*,[32] which is included in this Chapter's materials. In reading *Groetzinger*, consider how the Court defines "trade or business." Did the Court provide determinative factors for a trade or business, or is it a factual determination made on an *ad hoc* basis? How does one distinguish a hobby from a trade or business? Must a taxpayer make a profit to be engaged in a trade or business? Can a taxpayer be engaged in more than one trade or business at the same time?

In *Groetzinger*, the court held that "[a] sporadic activity, a hobby, or an amusement diversion" is not a trade or business. The *Groetzinger* holding is consistent with Section 183's prohibition against the deduction of so-called "hobby losses." Section 183 provides that a taxpayer may only deduct expenses associated with a hobby (i.e., an activity not engaged in for profit) to the extent of income from the hobby. In other words, Section 183 prohibits a taxpayer from deducting net losses from the operation of a hobby against other income. Treasury regulations provide nine factors in determining whether an activity is a hobby. These nine factors include (1) the manner in which the taxpayer carries on the activity, (2) the expertise of the taxpayer or his advisors, (3) the time and effort the taxpayer expends in carrying on the activity, (4) the expectation that assets used in the activity will appreciate in value, (5) the success of the taxpayer in carrying on similar or dissimilar activities, (6) the taxpayer's history or income or losses with respect to the activity, (7) the amount of occasional profits, if any, which are earned, (8) the financial status of the

---

[30] 312 U.S. 212 (1941).

[31] *Id.* at 218.

[32] 480 U.S. 23 (1987).

taxpayer, and (9) the elements of personal pleasure or recreation.[33] None of the factors, by itself, is determinative.

In addition to the "trade or business" requirement, Section 162 requires the taxpayer to be "carrying on" a trade or business. This means that expenses paid or incurred *before* a business begins are not deductible under Section 162. Why does Congress require that the taxpayer begin the business? Congress is likely concerned that taxpayer may seek to deduct expenses that are ostensibly personal in nature under the guise that the taxpayer is investigating starting or acquiring a new business. After all, if the taxpayer never begins a trade or business, the expenses must be personal and ought not to be deductible.

Section 162 is clear that the taxpayer must begin a trade or business to deduct expense, but it begs the question of when a business begins. For many businesses, the beginning date is clear. For example, a restaurant begins business the day it begins serving meals to customers. A retail store begins business the day it opens its door and allows customers to shop for its merchandise. On the other hand, the beginning date for some businesses, particularly those heavily involved in the use or production of intellectual property, is much less clear. For instance, when does an inventor begin business, particularly if the inventor is working on his first invention? Must the inventor first complete the invention, patent it, and profit from it? Likewise, when does an aspiring novelist begin business as a professional author? Does the novelist begin business at the time he begins writing the book, at the time when the book is published, or at some other point in time? These issues are addressed in the following problems:

> **Problem 1.7**: Taxpayer is a retired radio technician. One night taxpayer had an epiphany. Through his experience as a radio technician, Taxpayer knew that radio waves were harmless to human tissue. Taxpayer also knew that metal heats up when exposed to radio waves. So Taxpayer came up with an idea. If a cancerous tumor could be injected with metal and then exposed to radio waves, the cancerous tumor could be killed by heat without harming the surrounding healthy tissue. Taxpayer immediately began work on creating a cancer-killing radio-wave machine in his home garage. Eventually, Taxpayer was issued a patent for his machine. Unfortunately, Taxpayer was never able to sell any machines. When Taxpayer attempted to sell the machine to a large medical device manufacturer, he was told that the manufacturer's engineers were already working on a similar machine. Is

[33] Treas. Reg. § 1.183-2(b).

Taxpayer "carrying on" a "trade or business" within the meaning of Section 162? Read *Maximoff v. Commissioner* (included in this Chapter's materials) in connection with this problem.[34]

Problem 1.8: Taxpayer works full-time as an accountant for the U.S. government. Taxpayer sought to create a mobile phone application that measures caloric consumption. The software would work with a mobile phone's GPS system, so that a user could carry the phone on his person while exercising, and the software would measure calories burned over a given period of time. While Taxpayer had dabbled in computer programming in the past, he had never fully developed or sold software. Taxpayer began working on the application on his personal computer in his home office, but he soon discovered that the application was too complicated for his abilities. So Taxpayer hired a programmer to work part-time on the project. Taxpayer and the programmer finished a test version of the application after a year's work. Unfortunately, the application performed poorly and caused a mobile phone to freeze up. At this point, Taxpayer decided to give up on the application without ever having sold a copy of it. Taxpayer never sought copyright protection for the application. Did Taxpayer carry on a trade or business within the meaning of Section 162? Read *Lamont v. United States* (included in this Chapter's materials) in connection with this problem.

Problem 1.9: Taxpayer works full-time as a law school professor. While on sabbatical, Taxpayer decided to write a novel about a U.S. Army Special Forces unit during the invasion of Iraq in 2003. Taxpayer has published articles on legal topics (for free), but has never written a novel (for royalties). Taxpayer began research for his book by traveling around the country to conduct face-to-face interviews with Special Forces veterans. By the end of the tax year, Taxpayer had conducted extensive research for his novel, but had not yet started actually writing it. Additionally, by the end of

[34] This problem is inspired by the true story of John Kanzius (1944-2009). When Mr. Kanzius was diagnosed with leukemia, he sought to develop a machine to kill cancer cells using radio waves. Mr. Kanzius experimented by using the machine on himself. Unfortunately, the machine did not stop Mr. Kanzius's cancer before he passed away, but research on Mr. Kanzius's machine continues. *See* David Templeton, *John Kanzius; Died Feb. 18, 2009; Scientist Who was Trying to Cure Cancer Dies of Leukemia*, Pitt. Post-Gaz. B-1 (Feb. 19, 2009).

> the tax year, Taxpayer had informally talked to a publisher about the novel, but Taxpayer had not yet submitted a formal proposal for publication. Is Taxpayer carrying on a trade or business within the meaning of Section 162? Does it matter if Taxpayer actually finishes the novel? Read *Vitale v. Commissioner* (included in this Chapter's materials) in connection with this problem.

Taxpayers that pay or incur expenses that would be deductible but-for the "carrying on" requirement are not completely out of luck. In 1979, Congress enacted Section 195 to cover so-called "start up expenditures." Under Section 195, certain taxpayers may qualify to currently deduct up to $5,000 in start-up expenditures.[35] Those start-up expenditures not eligible to be currently deducted can be amortized ratably over 180 months beginning in the month the trade or business begins.[36]

1.3[2][b] Investment Expenses – Section 212

As noted above, the Court in *Higgins* held that an "investor" (i.e., a taxpayer managing his own investment portfolio) is not engaged in a trade or business. As such, an "investor" cannot qualify to deduct expenses under Section 162. In some cases, lower courts have distinguished "investors," such as the taxpayer in *Higgins*, from "traders."[37] While investors seek to profit from their portfolio primarily through interest and dividends, "traders" seek to profit through short-term buying and selling. The active short-term trading rises to the level of a trade or business, whereas the collection of interest and dividends does not.

Although investors cannot qualify for Section 162, they are not left completely out of in the cold, so to speak. In direct response to *Higgins*, Congress enacted the predecessor to Section 212 to permit investors to deduct expenses associated with their investment activities.[38] Section 212 provides that *individual* taxpayers may deduct ordinary and necessary expenses paid or incurred "(1) for the production of income; (2) for the management, conservation, or maintenance of property held for the production of income; or (3) in connection with the determination, collection, or refund of any tax."

---

[35] I.R.C. § 195(b).

[36] *Id.*

[37] *See e.g. Moller v. United States*, 721 F.2d 810 (Fed. Cir. 1983); *Purvis v. Commissioner*, 530 F.2d 1332 (9th Cir. 1976).

[38] Revenue Act of 1942, Pub. L. No., 77-619, § 121, 56 Stat. 798, 819 (1942); *see also* H.R. Rpt. 77-2333 at 74-76 (July 14, 1942).

Sections 162 and 212 create parallel universes between those taxpayers engaged in a trade or business and those taxpayers who are merely investors. At first blush, a taxpayer may seem unconcerned whether an expense fits within Section 162 or Section 212, as both sections provide for deductions. But further examination of the Code shows that a taxpayer, given his druthers, would prefer an expense to be deductible under Section 162 than Section 212. This is because Section 162 deductions are taken "above the line,"[39] while Section 212 deductions are taken "below the line" (except for deductions attributable to property held for the production of rents or royalties).[40] The "line" refers to *adjusted gross income*, which is often referred to by its abbreviation, "AGI." "Above the line" means the deduction is taken *before* AGI is calculated. In contrast, "below the line" means that the deduction is taken *after* AGI is calculated. Some the advantages of "above the line" deductions vis-à-vis "below the line" deductions are as follows:

(1) "Below the line" deductions are only available if the taxpayer *itemizes* deductions (i.e., files Schedule A of Form 1040). The Code provides individual taxpayers with a choice; either itemize deductions or claim a standard deduction. So if itemized deductions are less than the standard deduction, they are worthless. In this case, the taxpayer would simply choose the higher standard deduction. Even if itemized deductions exceed the standard deduction, the availability of the standard deduction still lessens the value of itemized deductions. For example, suppose a taxpayer has $10,000 in itemized deductions and the standard deduction is $9,000. In this case, the taxpayer is only deducting $1,000 more than he would have otherwise been entitled to under the standard deduction. So, in essence, only ten percent (i.e., $1,000 out of $10,000) of the itemized deductions provided value to the taxpayer. In contrast, a taxpayer can take all "above the line" deductions and claim a standard deduction at the same time.

(2) Section 212 deductions taken "below the line" are *miscellaneous itemized deductions*, which are only deductible to the extent they exceed two percent of AGI.[41]

---

[39] I.R.C. § 62(a)(1).

[40] I.R.C. §§ 62(a)(4); 63(d).

[41] I.R.C. § 67.

(3) Many states use federal AGI as a starting point for their own income tax. Because an "above the line" deduction has already been subtracted in calculating AGI, the "above the line" deduction is effectively deductible for state income tax purposes. On the other hand, because a "below the line" deduction is not subtracted from AGI, a "below the line" deduction will not reduce most state income taxes.

(4) Because "above the line" deductions reduce AGI, they affect other computations on which AGI depends. For instance, eligibility for certain personal credits and deductions and Roth IRA contributions are dependent on a taxpayer's AGI. In this regard, "above the line" deductions improve the taxpayer's eligibility for these tax benefits, while below the line deductions do not.

1.3[2][c] Capital Expenditures vs. Currently Deductible Expenses

In the prior section, the key was to distinguish business and investment expenses on the one hand, and personal expenses on the other. This distinction is critical because personal expenses are generally *never* deductible. The second limitation on the current deductibility relates to *capital expenditures*. Unlike personal expenses, which are generally never deductible, capital expenditures are *eventually* deductible. Capital expenditures are simply not deductible *immediately*. Therefore, the point in classifying currently deductible expenses and capital expenditures has to do with the issue of *timing*.

As discussed in greater detail above, the goal of the federal income tax is to match expenses with the income that those expenses help to produce. This matching principle lays the foundation for the law on capital expenditures. If a taxpayer is able to currently deduct an expense that will produce income over a long period, the result is *tax deferral*. To illustrate, suppose a taxpayer pays or incurs an expense for the acquisition or creation of intellectual property with a useful life of fifteen years. Under the matching principle, the taxpayer ought not deduct the amount right away. Ideally, the taxpayer ought to match the expense and the income from the expense over the fifteen-year life of the intellectual property acquired or created. In this way, tax deferral is eliminated. The Code accomplishes this by way of depreciation and amortization, which are discussed in detail in Chapter 3. So one way a taxpayer recovers the benefit of a capital expenditure is *over time* through depreciation or amortization.

Even if a capital expenditure is not depreciable or amortizable, a taxpayer will eventually recover a capital expenditure upon sale or exchange. "Capitalization" simply means adding amounts to the basis of an asset created, acquired, or substantially improved. As explained above, a taxpayer calculates gain or loss on a sale or exchange by subtracting adjusted basis from amount realized. When a taxpayer subtracts adjusted basis from amount realized, he is ultimately deducting amounts that were capital expenditures. If the taxpayer has a loss on the sale or exchange, he may be able to recover the remainder of the capital expenditure by taking a loss deduction.[42]

Congress has specifically abandoned the matching principle in certain cases to allow expensing of capital expenditures. In doing so, Congress seeks to encourage certain behavior at the expense of allowing taxpayers the benefits of tax deferral. As discussed in detail in Chapter 2, Congress enacted Section 174 to permit taxpayers to currently deduct certain research and experimentation expenditures. Obviously, Congress wants taxpayers to experiment and innovate and is willing to allow tax deferral as an incentive to encourage it. Another common example is Section 179, which permits taxpayers to expense certain costs of tangible personal property acquired by purchase for use in an active trade or business. Because Section 179 deals with tangible property, it is not covered in detail in this book.

1.3[2][d] Capital Expenditure Defined – Section 263 and Case Law

With an understanding of the matching principle in mind, the next step is to identify capital expenditures. The Code is not entirely helpful in this regard. Section 263 states that capital expenditures include amounts "paid out for new buildings or betterments made to increase the value of any property" and amounts "expended in restoring property or in making good the exhaustion thereof for which an allowance is or has been made."

The U.S. Supreme Court has addressed the issue of capital expenditures many times, but two U.S. Supreme Court cases are particularly relevant in defining capital expenditures. In the first case, *Commissioner v. Lincoln Savings & Loan Assoc.*,[43] federal law required the taxpayer, a saving and loan institution, to pay a premium to the Federal Saving and Loan Insurance Corporation ("FSLIC") to insure its deposits. The FSLIC placed the premium in a reserve account along with premiums from other savings and loan institutions. The taxpayer retained a pro rata interest in the reserve account and could recover its premium in certain

---

[42] I.R.C § 165.

[43] 403 U.S. 345 (1971).

situations. The Court held that the taxpayer had to capitalize the premium because it created a "separate and distinct additional asset" (i.e., the pro rata interest in the reserve account).[44]

In the second case, *INDOPCO, Inc. v. Commissioner*,[45] the taxpayer, a publicly traded corporation, was acquired in a friendly takeover. Prior to the takeover, the taxpayer incurred professional fees to evaluate whether the takeover was fair to its shareholders. The taxpayer relied on the "separate and distinct additional asset" test of *Lincoln Savings* to currently deduct the professional fees. The taxpayer reasoned that the professional fees did not create a new asset of the taxpayer to which the professional fees could attach.

The Court disagreed and held that the "separate and distinct asset" test is not the exclusive test for determining whether an expense is to be capitalized. Instead, the Court adopted a second test for capitalization, which is often referred to as the "significant future benefit" test. The Court stated that "a taxpayer's realization of benefits beyond the year in which the expenditure is incurred is undeniably important in determining whether the appropriate tax treatment is immediate deduction or capitalization."[46] The Court noted that the taxpayer would receive significant future benefits by having access to the acquirer's resources and technology as a result of the takeover. Therefore, the Court held that the professional fees were capital expenditures.[47]

In the aftermath of *INDOPCO*, the "significant future benefit" test created a degree of uncertainty because many expenses previously thought to be currently deductible may provide benefits beyond the current tax year. As a result, the Service issued a series of rulings on *INDOPCO's* impact on certain expenses that taxpayers had routinely deducted prior to *INDOPCO*.[48] For instance, in Revenue Ruling 92-80, the Service addressed whether

---

[44] *Id.* at 354.

[45] 503 U.S. 79 (1992).

[46] *Id.* at 87.

[47] Interestingly, the Court did not indicate to what account the professional fees were to be capitalized or how the taxpayer would recover the fees. Presumably, the taxpayer had to create a new asset for the deferred expenses, which would be recoverable upon the taxpayer's sale or exchange of substantially all of its assets.

[48] *See e.g.* Rev. Rul. 2000-4, 2000-1 C.B. 331 (ruling that costs incurred to obtain, maintain, and renew ISO 9000 certification are currently deductible, except to the extent they result in the creation or acquisition of an asset having a useful life substantially beyond the taxable year (e.g., a quality manual); Rev. Proc. 97-50, 1997-2 C.B. 525 (ruling that costs of Y2K computer compliance are currently deductible, although the Y2K compliance would provide future benefits); Rev. Rul. 94-77, 1994-2 C.B. 19 (ruling that severance payments to ex-employees in a corporate downsizing are

advertising expenses are currently deductible or capital expenditures. Advertising may create goodwill and thus provide benefits to the taxpayer extending beyond the tax year. Does that mean advertising expenses must be capitalized under the "significant future benefit" standard? The Service generally answered "no" to this question. In doing so, the Service ruled as follows:

> The *Indopco* decision does not affect the treatment of advertising costs under section 162(a) of the Code. These costs are generally deductible under that section even though advertising may have some future effect on business activities, as in the case of institutional or goodwill advertising. See section 1.162-1(a) and section 1.162-20(a)(2) of the regulations. Only in the unusual circumstance where advertising is directed towards obtaining future benefits beyond those traditionally associated with ordinary product advertising or with institutional advertising, must the costs of that advertising be capitalized.

In *RJR Nabisco, Inc. v. Commissioner,*[49] the taxpayer, a cigarette manufacturer, deducted expenses relating to the graphic design (i.e., the images, colors, and shapes that make up the visual display) and package design (i.e., physical construction of a package) of its cigarette packages. The Service conceded that "advertising *execution* expenditures," such as amounts paid for radio, newspaper, and TV ads, are currently deductible because they provide short-term benefits. However, the Service argued that "advertising *campaign* expenditures," such as the graphic design and package design, must be capitalized because they provide long-lasting benefits in the form of goodwill and trade dress.

The Tax Court rejected the Service's distinction between "advertising execution expenditures" and "advertising campaign expenditures." The Tax Court noted that the Service's own Revenue Ruling 92-80 ruled that *INDOPCO* did not affect the longstanding rule that advertising is deductible, even where advertising produces future benefits such as

---

currently deductible, although the downsizing may produce long-lasting benefits); Rev. Rul. 94-12, 1994-1 C.B. 36 (ruling that incidental repairs are deductible, even though a repair could provide a long-lasting benefit); Rev. Rul 92-80, 1992-2 C.B. 57 (ruling that advertising expenses are generally deductible even if they produce future benefits).

[49] 76 T.C.M. (CCH) 71 (1998).

goodwill.[50] The court reasoned that the function of graphic and package designs (i.e., campaign expenditures) is similar to that of ordinary product advertising (i.e., execution expenditures). That is, the objective of both is to establish future benefits such as goodwill. Therefore, the court held that the taxpayer could currently deduct the expenses associated with the graphic and package design.[51]

1.3[2][e] Capitalization Regulations Relating to Intangibles

The uncertainty caused by *INDOPCO's* "significant future benefit" test prompted Treasury to propose regulations in 2002 to address the capitalization of expenditures relating to intangible assets. The preamble to the proposed regulations stated:

> A "significant future benefit" standard . . . does not provide the certainty and clarity necessary for compliance with, and sound administration of, the law. Consequently, the IRS and Treasury Department believe that simply restating the significant future benefit test, without more, would lead to continued uncertainty on the part of taxpayers and continued controversy between taxpayers and the IRS. Accordingly, the IRS and Treasury Department have initially defined the exclusive scope of the significant future benefit test through the specific categories of intangible assets for which capitalization is required in the proposed regulations. The future benefit standard underlies many of these categories . . . If an expenditure is not described in one of the categories in the proposed regulations or in subsequent future guidance, taxpayers and IRS field personnel need not determine whether that expenditure produces a significant future benefit.[52]

The regulations were finalized in 2004. The preamble to the final regulations state:

> As in the proposed regulations, the final regulations provide that an amount paid to acquire or create an intangible not otherwise required to be capitalized by the regulations is not required to be capitalized on the ground

---

[50] The court noted that advertising would be capitalized if it takes the form of a physical asset, such as a sign or billboard. *See also Alabama Coca-Cola Bottling Co. v. Commr.*, 28 T.C.M. (CCH) 635 (1969) (holding that cost of advertising in the form of a sign is capitalized).

[51] The Service later issued an "action on decision" announcing its non-acquiescence with the Tax Court's decision. A.O.D. 1999-012 (Oct. 4, 1999).

[52] 67 Fed. Reg. 77701, 77702.

> that it produces significant future benefits for the taxpayer, unless the IRS publishes guidance requiring capitalization of the expenditure.[53]

After *INDOPCO*, capitalization appeared to be the general rule where an expense produced a future benefit. So a taxpayer had to assume that a future benefit had to be capitalized, unless the taxpayer could point to specific authority to the contrary. The proposed and final regulations take a different approach. Under the regulations, if an intangible is not specifically addressed in the regulations or other guidance from the Service, it is currently deductible. So now, under the final regulations, the Service or Treasury must specifically instruct taxpayer to capitalize an intangible, otherwise the taxpayer can rely on the regulations to currently deduct it. The final regulations are extensive and a summary of those regulations pertaining to intellectual property follows below.

Generally, under the final regulations, a taxpayer must capitalize the following:

(1) amounts paid to acquire certain intangibles specifically listed in the final regulations ("acquired intangibles");
(2) amounts paid to create certain intangibles specifically listed in the final regulations ("created intangibles");
(3) amounts paid to create or enhance a separate and distinct intangible asset;
(4) amounts paid to create or enhance a future benefit in future published guidance; and
(5) amounts paid to facilitate an acquisition or creation of an intangible in (1)-(4) above.[54]

1.3[2][e][i] Acquired Intangibles

A taxpayer must capitalize amounts paid to another party to acquire any one of fifteen specifically identified "acquired intangibles."[55] These specifically identified "acquired intangibles" include, among others, the following types of intangibles:

(1) a patent or copyright;[56]
(2) a franchise, trademark, or trade name;[57]

---

[53] 69 Fed. Reg. 436, 436.

[54] Treas. Reg. § 1.263(a)-4(b).

[55] Treas. Reg. § 1.263(a)-4(c)(1).

[56] Treas. Reg. § 1.263(a)-4(c)(1)(vii).

(3) goodwill or going concern value;[58]
(4) a customer list;[59] and
(5) computer software.[60]

Amounts paid to an employee to acquire an intangible from that employee are currently deductible, provided the amounts are includible in the employee's gross income as compensation.[61]

> **Problem 1.10**: Taxpayer is a large automobile manufacturer. Taxpayer employs Employee, an engineer, to work on its car designs. During the scope of his employment, Employee invents a new car part that gives rise to a patent. Employee assigns all rights in the patent to Taxpayer, and in return, Taxpayer pays a $25,000 bonus to the employee. Employee includes the $25,000 bonus in his gross income as compensation. Must Taxpayer capitalize the $25,000 payment to employee? Alternatively, suppose an independent contractor invented the patentable car part while working on a 6-month contract with Taxpayer. In return for assignment of the patent, Taxpayer pays $25,000 to independent contractor. Must Taxpayer capitalize the $25,000 payment to independent contractor? Assume that the independent contractor is not an employee within the meaning of Section 3401(c). *See* Treas. Reg. § 1.263(a)-4(c)(3).

1.3[2][e][ii] Created Intangibles

A taxpayer must capitalize amounts paid to create any specifically identified "created intangible."[62] The lists of "created intangibles" and "acquired intangibles" do not completely overlap. For example, the list of "created intangibles" does not include patents, copyrights, computer software, goodwill, going concern value, customer lists, trademarks, and trade names. However, a taxpayer must capitalize amounts paid to a government agency to

---

[57] Treas. Reg. § 1.263(a)-4(c)(1)(viii). The terms "franchise," "trademark," and "tradename" are defined in Treas. Reg. § 1.197-2(b)(10).

[58] Treas. Reg. § 1.263(a)-4(c)(1)(x). "Goodwill" is defined in Treas. Reg. § 1.197-2(b)(1) and "going concern value" is defined in Treas. Reg. § 1.197-2(b)(2).

[59] Treas. Reg. § 1.263(a)-4(c)(1)(xi).

[60] Treas. Reg. § 1.263(a)-4(c)(1)(xiv).

[61] Treas. Reg. § 1.263(a)-4(c)(3).

[62] Treas. Reg. § 1.263(a)-4(d).

obtain, renew, renegotiate, or upgrade its rights under a trademark, trade name, copyright, license, permit, franchise, or other similar right granted by a government agency.[63] A taxpayer is not required to capitalize an amount paid to a government agency to obtain a patent, if such amount is deductible under Section 174 (covered in detail in Chapter 2).[64]

The final regulations treat amounts paid to another party to defend or perfect title to intangible property as a "created intangible." As such, a taxpayer must capitalize amounts paid to another party to defend or perfect title to intangible property.[65] The rationale is that amounts paid to perfect or defend title are really part of the acquisition or creation cost of the intangible.

> **Problem 1.11**: Buckeye Co. claims to own an exclusive patent on a particular technology. Wolverine Co. brings an action against Buckeye, claiming that Wolverine is the true owner of the patent and that Buckeye stole Wolverine's technology. The action relates solely to the ownership of the patent. Buckeye settles the case by paying Wolverine $1,000,000 in exchange for Wolverine's release of all claims to the patent. Buckeye paid $50,000 to outside counsel for legal representation in the action. Additionally, Buckeye estimates that it paid $40,000 in salary, overhead, and other compensation to its "in house" counsel in connection with the action. What amounts, if any, must Buckeye capitalize? *See* Treas. Reg. § 1.263(a)-4(d)(9); *see also* Treas. Reg. § 1.263(a)-4(e)(4).

1.3[2][e][iii] Separate and Distinct Intangible Assets

An intangible that is not specifically identified as an "acquired intangible" or "created intangible" must nonetheless be capitalized if it is a "separate and distinct intangible asset."[66]

---

[63] Treas. Reg. § 1.263(a)-4(d)(5).

[64] 69 Fed. Reg. 436, 438.

[65] Treas. Reg. § 1.263(a)-4(d)(9); *see also* Treas. Reg. § 1.263(a)-2(c); *Georator Corp. v. United States*, 485 F.2d 283 (4th Cir. 1973) (holding that legal fees incurred in resisting efforts to cancel the registration of a taxpayer's trademark are capital expenditures). The Preamble to the 2002 Proposed Regulations stated that this rule is not intended to require capitalization of amounts paid to recover profits and damages resulting from infringement. 67 Fed. Reg. 77701, 77705. Presumably, therefore, if the suit relates to the profits from intellectual property, rather than the title of such intellectual property, the amounts paid could be currently deducted.

[66] Treas. Reg. § 1.263(a)-4(b)(1)(iii).

A "separate and distinct intangible asset" (1) is a property interest of ascertainable and measurable fair market value in money's worth, (2) subject to protection under applicable state, federal, or foreign law, and (3) capable of being sold, transferred, pledged (ignoring any restrictions on assignability) separate and apart from a trade or business.[67] The final regulations specifically provide that amounts paid to develop computer software do not create a separate and distinct intangible asset.[68] Additionally, the final regulations implicitly adopt the holding of *RJR Nabisco* by stating that amounts paid to develop package designs do not create a separate and distinct intangible asset.[69]

1.3[2][e][iv] Transactional Costs of Acquiring or Creating Intangibles

A taxpayer must capitalize amounts paid to "facilitate" the acquisition or creation of an acquired intangible, created intangible, or separate and distinct intangible asset.[70] An amount "facilitates" the acquisition or creation of an intangible if it is "paid in the process of investigating or otherwise pursuing the transaction."[71] Such transactional costs are really part of the cost of an intangible and thus ought to be capitalized. But the regulations contain two important "simplifying conventions" in applying this rule. The first is that employee compensation and overhead do not facilitate the acquisition or creation of an intangible and need not be capitalized.[72] The second is that "de minimis" costs (amounts not exceeding $5,000) do not facilitate the acquisition or creation of an intangible and need not be capitalized.[73] The purpose of the simplifying conventions is to alleviate the administrative burden of precisely allocating employee compensation, overhead, and minimal costs to each of the taxpayer's transactions.

> **Problem 1.12**: Taxpayer is a manufacturer of dog food. Taxpayer's internal creative arts department developed a new logo for its dog food packaging, which contains a picture of a Yorkshire Terrier named "Ginger." The internal cost (i.e., employee compensation and overhead) to Taxpayer in developing the "Ginger" logo is $250,000. Taxpayer pays $1,000 to the U.S. Patent and Trademark Office to obtain trademark protection on the

---

[67] Treas. Reg. § 1.263(a)-4(b)(3)(i).
[68] Treas. Reg. § 1.263(a)-4(b)(3)(iv).
[69] Treas. Reg. § 1.263(a)-4(b)(3)(v).
[70] Treas. Reg. § 1.263(a)-4(b)(1)(v).
[71] Treas. Reg. § 1.263(a)-4(e)(1)(i).
[72] Treas. Reg. § 1.263(a)-4(e)(4)(i), (ii).
[73] Treas. Reg. § 1.263(a)-4(e)(4)(i), (iii).

"Ginger" logo. Taxpayer also pays $15,000 to its outside counsel to prepare and file the trademark application. What amounts, if any, must Taxpayer capitalize? Also consider the following alternate scenarios:

(a) Suppose Taxpayer's "in house" counsel prepared and filed for trademark protection of the "Ginger" logo. The internal cost (i.e., employee compensation and overhead) to Taxpayer of this matter is $10,000. Must Taxpayer capitalize the $10,000?

(b) Suppose Taxpayer paid an outside consulting firm $250,000 to develop the dog food packaging and the "Ginger" logo. Must Taxpayer capitalize the $250,000?

(c) Suppose Taxpayer acquired the package design and "Ginger" logo (along with applicable trademark rights) from another company for $250,000. Must Taxpayer capitalize the $250,000?

1.3[2][e][v] 12-Month Rule

Another simplification meant to ease the administrative burden on taxpayers is the "12-month rule." Under this rule, a taxpayer need not capitalize amounts paid for a right or benefit that does not extend beyond (1) 12 months from the first date of realizing the right or benefit or (2) the end of the taxable year following the year paid.[74] In determining the duration of a right or benefit, a taxpayer must take into account renewal periods if there is a reasonable expectancy of renewal.[75]

The "12-month rule" reflects the Treasury's adoption of the Seventh Circuit's holding of *U.S. Freightways Corp. v. Commissioner*.[76] In *U.S. Freightways*, the taxpayer, a trucking company, was required to purchase a large number of licenses and permits for its vast trucking fleet. None of these permits or licenses was valid for more than 12 months. But the 12-month period for the permits and licenses did not correspond exactly with the taxpayer's taxable year. As such, the benefit of the permits and licenses extended into the following

---

[74] Treas. Reg. § 1.263(a)-4(f)(1).

[75] Treas. Reg. § 1.263(a)-4(f)(5).

[76] 270 F.3d 1137 (7th Cir. 2001).

taxable year. The Seventh Circuit held that the taxpayer was not required to capitalize the costs of the licenses and permits. The court reasoned that "perfection is a lot to ask for, even in the administration of the tax laws, which we acknowledge endeavor 'to match expenses with the revenues of the taxable period to which they are properly attributable, thereby resulting in a more accurate calculation of net income for tax purposes.'"[77] The court further stated:

> [P]erfection in temporal matching comes at too high a price for these kinds of expenses. At some point the "administrative costs and conceptual rigor" of achieving a more perfect match become too great . . . Here, there is a considerable administrative burden that Freightways and any similarly situated taxpayer will bear if it must always allocate one-year expenses to two tax years, year in and year out . . . the gain in precision for the taxing authorities is far outweighed by the administrative burden [taxpayers] will bear in performing this task.[78]

> **Problem 1.13**: Taxpayer, a calendar year taxpayer, has owned and operated a restaurant for several years. Taxpayer's restaurant has been licensed to sell beer and wine since its opening. Taxpayer recently decided that it should acquire a license to sell liquor as well. Accordingly, under applicable state law, Taxpayer pays a one-time fee of $25,000 to the state to acquire a license to sell liquor. The liquor license is valid indefinitely, provided Taxpayer complies with all applicable state laws regarding the sale of liquor. Taxpayer pays its outside counsel $4,000 to prepare the license application and otherwise represent Taxpayer before the state liquor commission. Additionally, Taxpayer pays an annual fee of $1,000 to maintain its liquor license each year. The annual fee is due on July 1 each year and expires on June 30 the following year. What amounts, if any, must Taxpayer capitalize?

1.3[2][f] Direct and Indirect Acquisition Costs – Section 263A

Acquisition costs are capital expenditures. So, when a taxpayer purchases a patent, copyright, or similar intellectual property, costs of acquiring such property are capitalized. For example, suppose a taxpayer acquires the copyright to a tax treatise written by a

---

[77] *Id.* at 1146.

[78] *Id.*

freelance writer for $10,000. The $10,000 the taxpayer pays for the copyright is capitalized as an "acquired intangible." Should the result be different if the taxpayer pays $10,000 in compensation to one of its employees to write the tax treatise? Under the Section 263 final regulations, the copyright of the tax treatise would be a "separate and distinct intangible" asset. But the taxpayer could rely on the simplifying convention that the $10,000 paid in employee compensation need not be capitalized. It may seem, therefore, that the taxpayer who pays an employee to write the tax treatise could deduct the cost immediately, while a taxpayer who hires an independent contract could not. Though the Section 263 final regulations may produce an anomalous result, another Code section may require capitalization irrespective of whether the tax treatise is written by an employee or freelance writer. That section is Section 263A.

Section 263A requires taxpayers to capitalize direct and indirect expenditures to produce real and "tangible personal property." Section 263A's definition of "tangible personal property" is quite broad and specifically includes "a film, sound recording, video tape, book, or similar property."[79] Section 263A puts a taxpayer who creates its own films, sound recordings, books, and similar properties on parity with a taxpayer who acquires such properties from a third party.

Section 263A(h) provides an exception to the capitalization requirement for "qualified creative expenses" of freelance authors, photographers, and artists. To be within the "qualified creative expense," the expense must (1) be paid or incurred by an individual[80] in the trade or business (other than as an employee) of being a writer, photographer, or artist (as defined in Section 263A(h)(3)); (2) the expense must be deductible, without regard to Section 263A, for the taxable year; and (3) the expense must not be related to printing, photographic plates, motion picture films, video tapes, or similar items.[81]

> **Problem 1.14**: Taxpayer is an individual engaged in the trade or business of being a freelance, independent filmmaker. Taxpayer paid $15,000 in ordinary and necessary expenses in researching and writing his next screenplay called "Toy Dogs of Beverly Hills." Taxpayer copyrighted the screenplay. Thereafter, Taxpayer paid $100,000 in ordinary and necessary expenses to produce "Toy Dogs of Beverly Hills" into a movie. What

[79] I.R.C. § 263A(b), flush language.

[80] A corporation may also qualify, provided the individual and members of his family own substantially all of the corporation's stock. I.R.C. § 263A(h)(3)(D).

[81] I.R.C. § 263A(h)(2).

amounts, if any, must Taxpayer capitalize? Read Technical Advice Memorandum 9643003 (included in this Chapter's materials) in connection with this problem.

1.3[3] Timing of Inclusion and Deduction

The U.S. income tax system is based upon an annual accounting system. This means that taxpayers are required to file income tax returns annually. In most cases, the annual accounting period is the calendar year, but certain taxpayers may report income on a fiscal year basis.[82] Questions may arise as to the proper taxable year for inclusion of income or deduction of an expense, particularly if the transaction giving rise to the income or deduction occurs near the beginning or end of an annual accounting period. In this case, the issue is one of *timing* and whether the income is includible or an expense is deductible in the first or second year. The timing of the inclusion of income or the deduction of an expense often depends upon the taxpayer's method of accounting. Although Congress has provided for several methods of accounting, the "cash method" and "accrual method" are the most common.

A taxpayer may use the "cash method" if it clearly reflects the taxpayer's income.[83] Under the "cash method," a taxpayer must include an item of income in gross income when actually or *constructively* received.[84] The doctrine of constructive receipt provides that a taxpayer can "receive" income without actually possessing it. A taxpayer is in "constructive receipt" of income if it "is credited to his account, set apart for him, or otherwise made available so that he may draw upon it any time. . . ."[85] However, a taxpayer does not constructively receive income "if the taxpayer's control of its receipt is subject to substantial limitations or restrictions."[86] A cash method taxpayer may claim deductions in the tax year actually paid. There is no such thing as constructive payment.

In contrast to the cash method, which focuses on *receipt* for inclusion purposes, the accrual method focuses on *earning* income for inclusion purposes. Similarly, while the cash method focuses on *payment* for deduction purposes, the accrual method focuses on when an expense is *incurred* for deduction purposes. This is why Section 162 deductions are taken in the

---

[82] I.R.C. § 441.

[83] I.R.C. § 446(c)(1).

[84] Treas. Reg. § 1.446-1(c)(1)(i).

[85] Treas. Reg. § 1.451-2(a).

[86] *Id.*

taxable year "paid or incurred." In this case, "paid" refers to cash method taxpayers and "incurred" refers to accrual method taxpayers.

Accrual method taxpayers must apply the "all events test" to determine both the inclusion of income and the deduction of expenses. Under the "all events test," an accrual method taxpayer must include income in the taxable year in which "all the events have occurred that fix the right to receive income and the amount of the income can be determined with reasonable accuracy."[87] Similarly, an accrual method taxpayer deducts expenses in the taxable year in which "all the events have occurred which determine the fact of liability, the amount thereof can be determined with reasonable accuracy, and economic performance has occurred with respect to the liability."[88]

> **Problem 1.15**: Author and Publisher enter an agreement whereby Author grants Publisher the exclusive right to publish Author's book. In return, Publisher agrees to pay Author royalties of 10 percent of the retail sales of the book. But the agreement contains a provision that Publisher will not pay Author more than $100,000 in any one calendar year and sums exceeding $100,000 will be carried over as royalties into subsequent calendar years. In the first calendar year of publication, the retail sales of the book are $1,500,000 giving rise to 10 percent royalties of $150,000. Pursuant to the agreement, Publisher promptly pays $100,000 to author in the first calendar year and carries over $50,000 to the second calendar year. Author is a calendar year, cash method taxpayer. Publisher is a calendar year, accrual method taxpayer. How much income from royalties must Author include in the first calendar year? How much may Publisher deduct in the first calendar year?

1.3[4] Character of Income or Loss

Up to this point, the discussion of income has focused on whether income is includible. It would seem that all includible income would be taxed in the same manner. This is not the case. That is, not all income (and loss for that matter) is created equal. Some income may be taxed at a lower rate than other income. Specifically, long-term capital gains may qualify for a preferential rate, i.e., a rate lower than the taxpayer's marginal rate on ordinary income. Why should this be the case?

---

[87] Treas. Reg. §§ 1.446-1(c)(1)(ii).

[88] Treas. Reg. §§ 1.446-1(c)(1)(ii); 1.461-1(a)(2).

Two primary arguments for allowing preferential rates on long-term capital gains are (1) to alleviate the effects of inflationary gains and (2) to encourage capital investment. The inflationary gain rationale is best explained by way of example. To illustrate, suppose an individual purchases a capital asset for $100,000. Twenty years later, the individual sells the capital asset for $200,000. Clearly, the individual has realized a $100,000 gain. But, if a dollar at the time of purchase is equivalent to two dollars at the time of sale due to inflation, how much economic gain does the individual have? In reality, the individual has no economic gain whatsoever because the gain is entirely inflationary. One way to alleviate the effects of inflationary gain would be to have the taxpayer make inflationary adjustments to basis. But such proposals have been repeatedly rejected as too administratively onerous.

The encouragement of capital investment is the other primary rationale for preferential rates for long-term capital gains. As the rate on long-term capital gains decreases, the after-tax rate of return to taxpayer increases. Thus, preferential rates on long-term capital gains are thought to create an incentive to invest, take risks, and save, thus increasing the capital available for business investment. Stated another way, high taxes on capital gains may be thought to discourage risk-taking and cause taxpayers to remain locked into old investments, thus decreasing the capital necessary for business investment.

In order for a taxpayer to have a capital gain or loss, the taxpayer must execute a "sale or exchange" of a "capital asset."[89] Neither the Code nor Treasury Regulations define the term "sale or exchange." Courts have generally interpreted a "sale or exchange" according to its common meaning.[90] Thus, a "sale or exchange" generally occurs upon any transfer of property for money or the transfer of property for property. But the "sale or exchange" requirement is not satisfied if the transfer is a license (a subject covered in detail in Chapter 4).

The Code defines "capital asset" in the negative. That is, instead of defining what a capital asset is, the Code provides the general rule that all assets are capital assets, unless a specific exception applies.[91] Some of the primary exceptions to the definition of "capital asset" include (1) inventory and inventory-type assets, (2) depreciable property and land used in a trade or business, and (3) self-created copyrights, works of arts, and similar property. The "capital asset" requirement is covered in greater detail in Chapter 4. Additionally, Chapter 4

---

[89] *See generally* I.R.C. § 1222.

[90] *See, e.g., Nahey v. Commissioner*, 111 T.C. 256 (1998).

[91] I.R.C. § 1221.

covers special characterization sections of the Code, such as Section 1231 (relating to quasi-capital assets), Section 1245 (depreciation recapture), Section 1235 (relating to transfers of patents) and Section 1253 (relating to transfers of trademarks and trade names), among others.

Capital gains and losses are classified as "long-term" or "short-term" based on the taxpayer's holding period of the capital asset. If a taxpayer's holding period of a capital asset is *more than one year* at sale or exchange, the capital gain or loss is long-term.[92] Conversely, if the taxpayer's holding period is *one year or less*, the capital gain or loss is short-term.[93] Special rules apply in calculating a taxpayer's holding period of property received by gift, inheritance or devise, or in certain nonrecognition transactions.[94]

To qualify for a preferential rate, a noncorporate taxpayer must have a "net capital gain" for the taxable year. The term "net capital gain" means the amount by which the taxpayer's net long-term capital gain for the year exceeds the net short-term capital loss.[95] Since 1986, the preferential tax rate on a net capital gain has generally been in the range of 15 percent to 28 percent (it has been as low as zero percent for taxpayers in the 15 and 10 percent marginal tax brackets). Congress changes the preferential rate on net capital gain often. If a taxpayer has net short-term capital gain exceeding net long-term capital loss, such excess is treated as ordinary income. Preferential rates for "net capital gain" do not apply to corporate taxpayers.[96]

Problem 1.16: Taxpayer, an individual, sells the following capital assets during the taxable year:

(1) Capital asset #1 sold for $100,000 and originally purchased for $50,000 two years earlier.

(2) Capital asset #2 sold for $250,000 and originally purchased for $200,000 five years earlier.

(3) Capital asset #3 sold for $40,000 and originally purchased six months earlier for $100,000.

---

[92] I.R.C. § 1222(3), (4).

[93] I.R.C. § 1222(1), (2).

[94] I.R.C. § 1223.

[95] I.R.C. § 1222(11).

[96] I.R.C. § 1201.

How much "net capital gain," if any, did the taxpayer recognize for the taxable year?

A noncorporate taxpayer can deduct excess capital losses (i.e., capital losses exceeding capital gains) against ordinary income up to $3,000 (or $1,500 for married individuals filing separately).[97] Any amount exceeding this limit may be carried over indefinitely and used as a capital loss in future tax years.[98] A corporate taxpayer may only deduct capital losses to the extent of capital gains.[99] But a corporate taxpayer may carry back excess capital losses to each of the three preceding taxable years.[100] If net capital loss cannot be applied to carry back years (i.e., there is no net capital gain in those years to offset), a corporate taxpayer can carryover the net capital loss to each of the next five taxable years.

In summary, taxpayers prefer their gains to be long-term capital gains, while the government would prefer gains to be ordinary income. On the other hand, when the taxpayer has a loss, the taxpayer would prefer the loss to be ordinary because ordinary losses do not have limitations placed on them like capital losses do. The government would prefer the taxpayer's loss to be capital so that the loss limitations would apply. So, the position of the taxpayer and government in arguing whether an asset is a capital asset may depend on whether a gain or a loss is involved.

1.4 Materials for Chapter 1

COMMISSIONER v. GROETZINGER

Supreme Court of the United States

480 U.S. 23 (1987)

JUSTICE BLACKMUN delivered the opinion of the Court.

The issue in this case is whether a full-time gambler who makes wagers solely for his own account is engaged in a "trade or business," within the meaning of [Code Section 162].

---

[97] I.R.C. § 1211(b).

[98] I.R.C. § 1212(b).

[99] I.R.C. § 1211(a).

[100] I.R.C. § 1212(a).

I.

There is no dispute as to the facts. The critical ones are stipulated. Respondent Robert P. Groetzinger had worked for 20 years in sales and market research for an Illinois manufacturer when his position was terminated in February 1978. During the remainder of that year, respondent busied himself with parimutuel wagering, primarily on greyhound races. He gambled at tracks in Florida and Colorado. He went to the track 6 days a week for 48 weeks in 1978. He spent a substantial amount of time studying racing forms, programs, and other materials. He devoted from 60 to 80 hours each week to these gambling-related endeavors. He never placed bets on behalf of any other person, or sold tips, or collected commissions for placing bets, or functioned as a bookmaker. He gambled solely for his own account. He had no other profession or type of employment.

Respondent kept a detailed accounting of his wagers and every day noted his winnings and losses in a record book. In 1978, he had gross winnings of $70,000, but he bet $72,032; he thus realized a net gambling loss for the year of $2,032.

Respondent received $6,498 in income from other sources in 1978. This came from interest, dividends, capital gains, and salary earned before his job was terminated.

On the federal income tax return he filed for the calendar year 1978 respondent reported as income only the $6,498 realized from nongambling sources. He did not report any gambling winnings or deduct any gambling losses. He did not itemize deductions. Instead, he computed his tax liability from the tax tables.

Upon audit, the Commissioner of Internal Revenue determined that respondent's $70,000 in gambling winnings were to be included in his gross income and that, pursuant to [Code Section 165] a deduction was to be allowed for his gambling losses to the extent of these gambling gains. But the Commissioner further determined that, under the law as it was in 1978, a portion of respondent's $70,000 gambling-loss deduction was an item of tax preference and operated to subject him to the minimum tax under § 56(a) of the Code, 26 U. S. C. § 56(a) (1976 ed.). At that time, under statutory provisions in effect from 1976 until 1982, "items of tax preference" were lessened by certain deductions, but not by deductions not "attributable to a trade or business carried on by the taxpayer." [Citations omitted].

These determinations by the Commissioner produced a § 56(a) minimum tax of $2,142 and, with certain other adjustments not now in dispute, resulted in a total asserted tax deficiency of $2,522 for respondent for 1978.

Respondent sought redetermination of the deficiency in the United States Tax Court. That court, in a reviewed decision, with only two judges dissenting, held that respondent was in the trade or business of gambling, and that, as a consequence, no part of his gambling losses constituted an item of tax preference in determining any minimum tax for 1978. 82 T.C. 793 (1984). In so ruling, the court adhered to its earlier court-reviewed decision in *Ditunno v. Commissioner,* 80 T.C. 362 (1983). The court in *Ditunno, id., at 371*, had overruled *Gentile v. Commissioner*, 65 T. C. 1 (1975), a case where it had rejected the Commissioner's contention (*contrary* to his position here) that a full-time gambler *was* in a trade or business and therefore was subject to self-employment tax.

The United States Court of Appeals for the Seventh Circuit affirmed. 771 F.2d 269 (1985). Because of a conflict on the issue among Courts of Appeals, we granted certiorari. 475 U.S. 1080 (1986).

Despite the interim reversals by the Second and Sixth Circuits in *Gajewski* and *Cull, supra*, the Tax Court has adhered to its position that a full-time gambler is engaged in a trade or business. See, *e. g., Meredith v. Commissioner,* 49 TCM 318, para. 84,651 P-H Memo TC (1984); *Barrish v. Commissioner,* 49 TCM 115, para. 84,602 P-H Memo TC (1984). It has drawn no distinction between the gambler and the active market trader. See also *Baxter v. United States,* 633 F.Supp. 912 (Nev. 1986).

II.

The phrase "trade or business" has been in § 162(a) and in that section's predecessors for many years. Indeed, the phrase is common in the Code, for it appears in over 50 sections and 800 subsections and in hundreds of places in proposed and final income tax regulations. The slightly longer phrases, "carrying on a trade or business" and "engaging in a trade or business," themselves are used no less than 60 times in the Code. The concept thus has a well-known and almost constant presence on our tax-law terrain. Despite this, the Code has never contained a definition of the words "trade or business" for general application, and no regulation has been issued expounding its meaning for all purposes. Neither has a broadly applicable authoritative judicial definition emerged. Our task in this case is to ascertain the meaning of the phrase as it appears in the sections of the Code with which we are here concerned.

* * *

In *Deputy v. Du Pont,* 308 U.S. 488 (1940), the Court was concerned with what were "ordinary and necessary" expenses of a taxpayer's trade or business, within the meaning of § 23(a) of the Revenue Act of 1928, 45 Stat. 799. In ascertaining whether carrying charges on short sales of stock were deductible as ordinary and necessary expenses of the taxpayer's business, the Court *assumed* that the activities of the taxpayer in conserving and enhancing his estate constituted a trade or business, but nevertheless disallowed the claimed deductions because they were not "ordinary" or "necessary." 308 U.S., at 493-497. Justice Frankfurter, in a concurring opinion joined by Justice Reed, did not join the majority. He took the position that whether the taxpayer's activities constituted a trade or business was "open for determination," *id.,* at 499, and observed:

> "'. . . carrying on any trade or business,' within the contemplation of § 23(a), involves holding one's self out to others as engaged in the selling of goods or services. This the taxpayer did not do. . . . Without elaborating the reasons for this construction and not unmindful of opposing considerations, including appropriate regard for administrative practice, I prefer to make the conclusion explicit instead of making the hypothetical litigation-breeding assumption that this taxpayer's activities, for which expenses were sought to be deducted, did constitute a 'trade or business.'" *Ibid.*

Next came *Higgins v. Commissioner,* 312 U.S. 212 (1941). There the Court, in a bare and brief unanimous opinion, ruled that salaries and other expenses incident to looking after one's own investments in bonds and stocks were not deductible under § 23(a) of the Revenue Act of 1932, 47 Stat. 179, as expenses paid or incurred in carrying on a trade or business. [T]he Court seemed to do little more than announce . . . that the facts in each case must be examined; that not all expenses of every business transaction are deductible; and that "[no] matter how large the estate or how continuous or extended the work required may be, such facts are not sufficient as a matter of law to permit the courts to reverse the decision of the Board." 312 U.S., at 215-218. The opinion, therefore -- although devoid of analysis and not setting forth what elements, if any, in addition to profit motive and regularity, were required to render an activity a trade or business -- must stand for the propositions that full-time market activity in managing and preserving one's own estate is not embraced within the phrase "carrying on a business," and that salaries and other expenses incident to the operation are not deductible as having been paid or incurred in a trade or business. . . . [T]he Court in that case did not even cite *Du Pont* and thus paid no heed whatsoever to the content of Justice Frankfurter's pronouncement in his concurring opinion. Adoption of the Frankfurter gloss obviously would have disposed of the case in the Commissioner's favor handily and automatically, but that easy route was not followed.

* * *

[Upon reviewing the Court's prior decisions regarding the term "trade or business"], we conclude (1) that, to be sure, the statutory words are broad and comprehensive . . .; (2) that, however, expenses incident to caring for one's own investments, even though that endeavor is full time, are not deductible as paid or incurred in carrying on a trade or business . . .; (3) that the opposite conclusion may follow for an active trader . . .; (4) that Justice Frankfurter's attempted gloss upon the decision in *Du Pont* was not adopted by the Court in that case; (5) that the Court, indeed, later characterized it as an "adumbration" . . .; and (6) that the Frankfurter observation, specifically or by implication, never has been accepted as law by a majority opinion of the Court, and more than once has been totally ignored. We must regard the Frankfurter gloss merely as a two-Justice pronouncement in a passing moment and, while entitled to respect, as never having achieved the status of a Court ruling. One also must acknowledge that *Higgins*, with its stress on examining the facts in each case, affords no readily helpful standard, in the usual sense, with which to decide the present case and others similar to it. The Court's cases, thus, give us results, but little general guidance.

III.

* * *

If a taxpayer, as Groetzinger is stipulated to have done in 1978, devotes his full-time activity to gambling, and it is his intended livelihood source, it would seem that basic concepts of fairness (if there be much of that in the income tax law) demand that his activity be regarded as a trade or business just as any other readily accepted activity, such as being a retail store proprietor or, to come closer categorically, as being a casino operator or as being an active trader on the exchanges.

It is argued, however, that a full-time gambler is not offering goods or his services, within the line of demarcation that Justice Frankfurter would have drawn in *Du Pont*. Respondent replies that he indeed is supplying goods and services, not only to himself but, as well, to the gambling market; thus, he says, he comes within the Frankfurter test even if that were to be imposed as the proper measure. "It takes two to gamble." Brief for Respondent 3. Surely, one who clearly satisfies the Frankfurter adumbration usually is in a trade or business. But does it necessarily follow that one who does not satisfy the Frankfurter adumbration is not in a trade or business? One might well feel that a full-time gambler ought to qualify as much as a full-time trader, as Justice Brandeis in *Snyder* implied and as courts have held. The

Commissioner, indeed, accepts the trader result. Tr. of Oral Arg. 17. In any event, while the offering of goods and services usually would qualify the activity as a trade or business, this factor, it seems to us, is not an absolute prerequisite.

We are not satisfied that the Frankfurter gloss would add any helpful dimension to the resolution of cases such as this one, or that it provides a "sensible test," as the Commissioner urges. See Brief for Petitioner 36. It might assist now and then, when the answer is obvious and positive, but it surely is capable of breeding litigation over the meaning of "goods," the meaning of "services," or the meaning of "holding one's self out." And we suspect that -- apart from gambling -- almost every activity would satisfy the gloss. A test that everyone passes is not a test at all. We therefore now formally reject the Frankfurter gloss which the Court has never adopted anyway.

Of course, not every income-producing and profit-making endeavor constitutes a trade or business. The income tax law, almost from the beginning, has distinguished between a business or trade, on the one hand, and "transactions entered into for profit but not connected with . . . business or trade," on the other. See Revenue Act of 1916, § 5(a), Fifth, 39 Stat. 759. Congress "distinguished the broad range of income or profit producing activities from those satisfying the narrow category of trade or business." *Whipple v. Commissioner,* 373 U.S., at 197. We accept the fact that to be engaged in a trade or business, the taxpayer must be involved in the activity with continuity and regularity and that the taxpayer's primary purpose for engaging in the activity must be for income or profit. A sporadic activity, a hobby, or an amusement diversion does not qualify.

It is suggested that we should defer to the position taken by the Commissioner and by the Solicitor General, but, in the absence of guidance, for over several decades now, through the medium of definitive statutes or regulations, we see little reason to do so. We would defer, instead, to the Code's normal focus on what we regard as a common-sense concept of what is a trade or business. Otherwise, as here, in the context of a minimum tax, it is not too extreme to say that the taxpayer is being taxed on his gambling losses, a result distinctly out of line with the Code's focus on income.

We do not overrule or cut back on the Court's holding in *Higgins* when we conclude that if one's gambling activity is pursued full time, in good faith, and with regularity, to the production of income for a livelihood, and is not a mere hobby, it is a trade or business within the meaning of the statutes with which we are here concerned. Respondent Groetzinger satisfied that test in 1978. Constant and large-scale effort on his part was made. Skill was required and was applied. He did what he did for a livelihood, though with a less-than-successful result. This was not a hobby or a passing fancy or an occasional bet for amusement.

We therefore adhere to the general position of the *Higgins* Court, taken 46 years ago, that resolution of this issue "requires an examination of the facts in each case." 312 U.S., at 217. This may be thought by some to be a less-than-satisfactory solution, for facts vary. [Citations omitted.] But the difficulty rests in the Code's wide utilization in various contexts of the term "trade or business," in the absence of an all-purpose definition by statute or regulation, and in our concern that an attempt judicially to formulate and impose a test for all situations would be counterproductive, unhelpful, and even somewhat precarious for the overall integrity of the Code. We leave repair or revision, if any be needed, which we doubt, to the Congress where we feel, at this late date, the ultimate responsibility rests. Cf. *Flood v. Kuhn,* 407 U.S. 258, 269-285 (1972).

The judgment of the Court of Appeals is affirmed.

It is so ordered.

MAXIMOFF v. COMMISSIONER

United States Tax Court

53 T.C.M. (CCH) 423 (1987)

CLAPP, *Judge:*

* * *

FINDINGS OF FACT

Some of the facts have been stipulated and are so found. The stipulation of facts and exhibits attached thereto are incorporated herein by this reference.

Petitioner resided in Los Altos, California when he filed his petition. Petitioner has been an engineer over a period of several years. When petitioner reached the age of 65, he found himself out of work and made various unsuccessful attempts to obtain employment. In 1978, he obtained a job as an engineer at Itek Corporation, Applied Technology Division. His title was Senior Engineer in recognition of his years of experience in the engineering field. The position was initially characterized as temporary of 6 to 9 months duration; nevertheless, petitioner was still working there during the taxable year 1980 and received wages in the amount of $32,588.40 in that year. The firm, for which he did engineering work including detail design, specialized in radar warning receivers.

Because of the uncertainty of his continued employment, petitioner wished to develop his own business in order to ensure an income. Prior to 1980, he had a consulting engineering service which he advertised in several directories. This activity, however, did not generate sufficient income. Sometime in the latter part of 1979, he first began thinking of developing a miles per gallon indicator for passenger automobiles and trucks. In 1980, he commenced development of the indicator. In his opinion, there would be a good market for such a device because of the high price of gasoline at that time. He viewed every owner of a passenger car as well as every automobile manufacturer as a potential customer. He produced a test set-up combined with a miles per gallon indicator for development purposes. Petitioner devoted all his spare time to this activity, approximately 20 to 30 hours a week during 1980. In 1981, petitioner decided to drop any further attempt to develop his device because of several factors. Petitioner began to encounter problems with the design. He realized that because of the required complexity of the design and the cost of installation in the vehicle there would be a limited market due to the cost of the device. Furthermore, when he contacted General Motors regarding his device, he was told that General Motors had started the development of the same device with a team of engineers. Petitioner felt that he would be unable to compete with the corporation's production team. Although petitioner has taken out patents in the past, he did not receive a patent for his miles per gallon indicator. He did not reach a point in the development of the device where marketing or sales activity could be realistically attempted. He generated no income from the project. He was at the time of trial attempting to develop an ultrasonic device to aid blind people in distinguishing obstacles.

On Schedule C of his 1980 Federal tax return, petitioner claimed [$6,137.42 in business expenses].

Offsetting reported income of $390.00, from the claimed business expense deduction of $6,137.42, petitioner reported a loss in the amount of $5,747.42 on his return. The $390.00 of gross income was earned by him for the repair of electrical equipment. The total amount of business expenses claimed by petitioner for 1980 related solely to the development of a new product, a miles per gallon indicator.

* * *

OPINION

* * *

The issue for determination is whether petitioner is entitled to deduct certain expenses incurred in the development of a new product, a miles per gallon indicator. Respondent contends that the expenses are not deductible because petitioner was not engaged in the trade or business of inventing in 1980 pursuant to section 162. . . .

Whether a taxpayer is engaged in a trade or business is a question to be determined by an examination of all the facts in the case. *Higgins v. Commissioner,* 312 U.S. 212 (1941).

> [T]he taxpayer must be involved in the activity with continuity and regularity and * * * the taxpayer's primary purpose for engaging in the activity must be for income or profit. A sporadic activity, a hobby, or an amusement diversion does not qualify. [*Commissioner v. Groetzinger,* 480 U.S. 23 (1987)].

Petitioner's expectation of making a profit need not have been reasonable so long as he had a bona fide objective to realize a profit. *Golanty v. Commissioner,* 72 T.C. 411, 425-426 (1979).

During the taxable year in question, petitioner was employed as a full-time engineer for Itek. It is possible, however, to be engaged in more than one business. Petitioner possessed engineering expertise through his many years of employment as an engineer. He testified that although he was not a believer in patents, he had taken out several patents in the past. Petitioner made a sustained and continuous effort during the year in question to develop his product, devoting 20 to 30 hours a week to this activity in addition to his full-time job. Respondent makes much of the fact that the product was never developed or marketed. Petitioner explained that he dropped the project in 1981 realizing that he could not compete with General Motors research resources and also that the high cost of the indicator he was developing would prohibit successful marketing. We believe that the abandonment of the project at this point shows that petitioner was interested in a money-making activity rather than just a recreational hobby or an activity designed to generate tax losses. The record is clear that petitioner was concerned about his future income in view of his uncertain continued employment due to his post-retirement age and was interested in producing some income. His consulting business prior to 1980 was not generating sufficient receipts and therefore he started on this project. While no income was generated from this project, this factor is not determinative. Experimental activity may yield little, if any, return during the developmental stages although it has the potential of producing significant income. Petitioner was involved in the activity of inventing with continuity and regularity during the taxable year in issue as well as subsequently through at least the time of trial. Accordingly, we find petitioner was engaged in a trade or business pursuant to section 162.

* * *

Decision will be entered under Rule 155.

LAMONT v. UNITED STATES

United States Court of Federal Claims

97-2 U.S. Tax Cas. (CCH) P50,861

* * *

FACTS

Plaintiffs, James W. and Cara M. Lamont, are a husband and wife who reside in Arlington, Virginia. During the 1988 tax year, the only year at issue in this case, Mr. Lamont was employed by the U.S. Department of State as a foreign service officer, and Mrs. Lamont was employed as a teacher. At the same time, James Lamont was the owner of a business known as Interlinguistics Unlimited, Inc. ("Interlinguistics" or "IUI"), a small company that was incorporated by James Lamont under the laws of the State of Virginia in the fall of 1987.

Interlinguistics was incorporated "to develop computer software and systems for helping translators [of foreign languages] and also to provide computer related product[s] and services in that area." (Tr. at 24.) The concept of developing a computer program for translating foreign languages originated with Mr. Lamont's daughter, Monika Lamont, in 1986. Ms. Lamont, who was a college student at the time, was familiar with several foreign languages and had performed various translating jobs. During the course of her translating activities, Ms. Lamont became convinced that there was a need for a computerized method of translating foreign languages. Ms. Lamont proposed the idea to her family, and after some initial investigation, IUI was born.

James Lamont, who was the company's sole shareholder, funded the company's operations through plaintiffs' personal funds, as well as a line of credit secured by a home equity loan. In the fall of 1987, the company acquired two computers and a computer printer from plaintiffs, and in February 1988 the company acquired a second printer. Interlinguistics acquired a third computer, using funds from plaintiffs, in August 1988. The new company operated out of Ms. Lamont's apartment in Philadelphia, Pennsylvania.

In addition to providing funds for the corporation, James Lamont served as Interlinguistics' vice-president. Monika Lamont, served as the company's president, and in this capacity was responsible for the day-to-day management of IUI's affairs. Ms. Lamont was also the company's sole salaried employee. However, neither Monika Lamont, nor James Lamont, possessed the knowledge or skill to develop the computer program that they envisioned when they founded Interlinguistics.[1] Therefore, the Lamonts turned to a number of part-time computer programmers, who worked for IUI as independent contractors, to develop the company's computer translation product. Interlinguistics retained its first programmer, Ralph Nussbaumer, sometime in 1987. Throughout the 1988 tax year, Mr. Nussbaumer worked on a part-time basis to develop Interlinguistics' proposed translation software. In 1988, IUI hired two additional programmers, Mike Warren and Roger Doherty, who also worked on a part-time basis throughout the year to develop the proposed software.

The work of IUI's part-time programmers was directed at the development of a computer program known as the “Interlex system.” The Interlex system was envisioned as a program that would allow users to electronically access various resource materials used in the process of translating foreign languages. As designed by IUI's part-time programmers, the Interlex system consists of two parts -- an “engine” and a “dictionary.” The dictionary component is essentially a database containing a bilingual dictionary. Because Interlinguistics was working to acquire the electronic rights to existing foreign language dictionaries from outside sources, the work of IUI's programmers was aimed primarily, if not solely, at the development of the engine component of the Interlex system.

---

[1] Neither James nor Monika Lamont possesses a degree in computer programming. James Lamont was trained as a computer systems analyst by the U.S. Army, and was involved in the development of computer programs in his work at the Department of State. However, Mr. Lamont's experience involved writing specifications, which were then relayed to programmers who actually wrote the computer programs for Mr. Lamont's review. Monika Lamont took one computer related course in college, but that course concerned teaching children to use computers. Otherwise, Ms. Lamont does not possess any background in computer programming.

The engine component of the Interlex system, which is "truly what the Interlex system is," (Tr. at 59) is designed to provide the user with a means of accessing the information contained in the dictionary/database component. The engine itself consists of two components -- "Trans" and "Editor." The Trans component, which is referred to as a "memory resident look-up program," is designed to permit the user to access the information contained in the database. The Editor portion, on the other hand, is designed to permit the user to modify or expand the database, or to create customized databases such as glossaries.

In February 1988, Interlinguistics received a certificate of copyright registration for the Interlex system from the United States Copyright Office. Even after receiving a copyright registration, however, IUI's programmers continued to revise the Interlex system. As the program evolved throughout the remainder of 1988, Nussbaumer, Warren and Doherty -- IUI's programmers -- forwarded progress reports and new versions of the software to IUI's president, Monika Lamont, for her review. After reviewing each new iteration, Ms. Lamont provided the programmers with detailed comments and criticisms, and suggested new features or enhancements to be incorporated into the nascent Interlex program.

In addition to the efforts of its part-time programmers, IUI retained a software consulting firm, Data & Management Counsel, Inc. ("Data Management"), to assist in the development of the Interlex system. According to William Tripp, a principal of Data Management who worked with IUI in 1988 and 1989, the Interlex program at Interlinguistics was in a very early stage of development when Ms. Lamont first contacted Data Management. Interlinguistics retained Data Management during this early stage of development to conduct focus groups and in-depth interviews with translators, the potential users of the Interlex system, to determine the utility of Interlinguistics' concept.

According to Tripp, IUI was unable to provide Data Management with a fully functional version of the Interlex software that Data Management could demonstrate to potential users. Although Interlinguistics did provide a copy of the Interlex software, Tripp recalled that the software continually "froze up" Data Management's computer. Therefore, Data Management conducted the Interlex focus groups, in August 1988, without the benefit of a working version of the Interlex system.

Throughout 1988, Interlinguistics retained other professionals to assist in the Interlex project. In July 1988, IUI retained a graphic design company, Cloud and Gehshan Associates, to create a corporate identity for Interlinguistics and to design packaging and marketing materials for the Interlex system. In addition, Interlinguistics entered into a preliminary relationship with a marketing firm, TransTech Services USA, in October 1988, whereby TransTech agreed to use its best efforts to assist in the commercialization of the Interlex program.

In the summer of 1988, an associate of Roger Doherty, one of IUI's programmers, introduced Monika Lamont to Charles Ebert. A professor at the Academy of the New Church, a college in Pennsylvania, Ebert has extensive training and experience in computer programming. In addition to teaching courses in mathematics and computer science at the Academy of the New Church, Professor Ebert is the director of the "STAIRS Project," an effort to develop a computerized method of searching academic texts. Professor Ebert learned of Interlinguistics' software, and felt that the company's product might be useful to the STAIRS project. Thus, after viewing a demonstration of the Interlex system conducted by Ms. Lamont in her office/apartment, Professor Ebert purchased the software from IUI for $300 in the summer of 1988.

The record shows that, other than the sale to Ebert in the summer of 1988, Interlinguistics did not make any efforts to market or sell the Interlex program in 1988. Interlinguistics' president, Monika Lamont, was never quite satisfied with the state of the software. She never felt that the program was "finished," and therefore she was not comfortable placing the product on the market in 1988. Thus, the company continued its development efforts, adding enhancements to the program and improving the system's user interface, throughout the remaining months of 1988 and into 1989. Indeed, Ms. Lamont apparently was not satisfied that the Interlex software was "under control," that is, that the system did not require further "enhancements," until sometime at the beginning of 1989. By that time, however, the company had run out of money to complete testing and begin marketing the software. Since that time, the Lamonts have tried, unsuccessfully, to raise the outside capital needed to bring the Interlex program to market.

In 1989, plaintiffs James and Cara Lamont timely filed a joint return for tax year 1988. Plaintiffs' 1988 return indicated that plaintiffs earned $76,317.93 of adjusted gross income, consisting of wages, interest and dividend income. Plaintiffs claimed itemized deductions totaling $9,976.91, which left them with total taxable income of $60,491.22. According to plaintiffs' return, plaintiffs' tax liability for the year in suit totaled $13,070.04, while their income tax withholding totaled $14,279.93. Based on this information, plaintiffs claimed, and later received, a refund of $1,209.89 from the Internal Revenue Service ("IRS").

In 1990, plaintiffs filed an amended return, Form 1040x, for the 1988 tax year. Plaintiffs claimed additional deductions on their amended return, including $79,475 in alleged losses from Interlinguistics. As a result of these losses, plaintiffs' claimed that they owed no federal income tax for tax year 1988, and therefore sought an additional refund of $13,070.04 in alleged overpayment of tax. IRS granted plaintiffs a refund of $1374, but denied the remaining $11,694.04 of their claim. This suit followed.

DISCUSSION

The central issue in this case is whether plaintiffs are entitled to a deduction for the losses generated by Interlinguistics in tax year 1988. Plaintiffs argue that they are entitled to deduct IUI's 1988 expenditures as ordinary and necessary business expenses under [Code Section 162]. . . . Defendant responds that plaintiffs are not entitled to a deduction under [Code Section 162] because IUI was not engaged in an active trade or business in 1988.

* * *

Section 162(a) . . . provides that "there shall be allowed as a deduction all the ordinary and necessary expenses paid or incurred during the taxable year in carrying on any trade or business." 26 U.S.C. § 162(a) (1988). Section 162(a) clearly specifies that a taxpayer must be "carrying on [a] trade or business" during the taxable year in order to deduct expenses under § 162. "This phrase has been held to deny current deductions for startup or preopening costs incurred by taxpayers prior to the beginning of actual business operations." [Citations omitted].

To decide whether a business venture has crossed the line from start-up to active trade or business, thereby enabling the taxpayer to claim a deduction under § 162, courts generally look to determine whether "the business has begun to function as a going concern and performed those activities for which it was organized." [Citations omitted].

Determining whether a business has begun to function as a going concern, in turn, is a question of fact, that depends on the circumstances of each particular case. See *Higgins v. Commissioner,* [312 U.S. 212 (1941)]; see also . . . *Maximoff v. Commissioner*, [1987 T.C. Memo 155] ("Whether a taxpayer is engaged in a trade or business is a question to be determined by an examination of all the facts in the case.").

After examining the evidence in the record, and evaluating the testimony of the witnesses presented at trial, the Court concludes that plaintiffs were engaged in an active trade or business during tax year 1988. According to James Lamont, the sole shareholder and vice-president of Interlinguistics, IUI was organized "to develop computer software and systems for helping translators" and "to provide computer related product[s] and services in that area." As detailed below, the record demonstrates that, throughout tax year 1988, IUI was actively performing activities for which the company was organized -- namely, the corporation was actively engaged in the development of computer software and systems for helping translators.

The idea of organizing a company to develop a computer program for translating foreign languages first came to James Lamont's attention in 1986. In the winter of 1986, Mr. Lamont's daughter, Monika, proposed the idea of developing a computer translation program to her family after she had experienced difficulty performing a translation with books. After hearing his daughter's idea, Mr. Lamont investigated the project's feasibility by consulting with an attorney who was familiar with patent and trademark law. Based on the attorney's investigation, the Lamonts concluded that there were no existing products on the market that performed the functions they envisioned. Therefore, Mr. Lamont formed Interlinguistics in the fall of 1987 to develop a computer program for helping translators.

In late 1987, IUI acquired two computers and a computer printer to be used in the company's operations. The company also hired a programmer, Ralph Nussbaumer, to begin designing the company's proposed translation software in late 1987. Throughout 1988, Nussbaumer worked on a part-time basis to develop the proposed software. Nussbaumer's efforts were supplemented by the efforts of two additional programmers, James Warren and Roger Doherty, who also worked on a part-time basis throughout tax year 1988 to develop Interlinguistics' proposed product.

Through the efforts of its part-time programmers, Interlinguistics developed a program called "Interlex." In February 1988, the company sought and received copyright protection for the Interlex design, which consisted of an "engine" and a "dictionary." However, the company worked throughout 1988 to improve and enhance the constantly evolving Interlex program. Each month, IUI's programmers forwarded their latest refinements of the program to Monika Lamont, the company's president, for her review. After reviewing each new iteration, Ms. Lamont provided comments and suggested new features or enhancements of the program.

In addition to the internal process of review and refinement that took place throughout tax year 1988, Interlinguistics retained an outside firm, Data & Management Counsel, Inc., to evaluate the efficacy of the Interlex design. In the summer of 1988, Data Management conducted focus groups and in-depth interviews with potential users to evaluate the utility of the Interlex system. In addition, Data Management arranged for an independent review of the software. IUI, in turn, used the information it gained from these outside professionals to make modifications to the Interlex system, primarily in the user interface.

In sum, the evidence presented shows that, in tax year 1988, Interlinguistics had progressed beyond the stage of conducting mere start-up or pre-operational activities. Instead, the company was actively working throughout 1988 to develop computer software for translating foreign languages. Because this was precisely the purpose for which the corporation was organized, the Court concludes that IUI was engaged in an active trade or business in tax year 1988.

Defendant expended a great deal of effort at trial to demonstrate that, other than the single unsolicited sale to Professor Ebert, Interlinguistics did not successfully market its product in tax year 1988. However, a company need not make a single sale, or earn a single penny in income, in order to be considered an active trade or business. See *Cabintaxi*, 63 F.3d at 620 ("[Plaintiff] did not have to succeed, even so far as to have a single penny of income, in order to be engaged in a trade or business."); *Jackson,* 864 F.2d at 1526 ("The failure to make sales in a given period does not per se prevent a taxpayer from carrying on a business."); *Maximoff*, 53 T.C.M. (CCH) at 425 ("While no income was generated from this project, this factor is not determinative."). Therefore, IUI's failure to make any additional sales in tax year 1988 does not prevent this Court from concluding that the company was engaged in an active trade or business in tax year 1988.

* * *

CONCLUSION

For the reasons set forth above, the Court concludes that plaintiffs were the owners of an active trade or business, Interlinguistics Unlimited, Inc., in tax year 1988. Plaintiffs are therefore entitled, under 26 U.S.C § 162(a), to deduct $79,475.00 in business losses generated by Interlinguistics from their 1988 income. After deducting these losses, plaintiffs are entitled to a refund of overpayment of income tax totaling $11,696.04, plus interest. The Clerk shall enter judgment accordingly.

VITALE v. COMMISSIONER

United States Tax Court

77 T.C.M. (CCH) 1227 (1999)

FAY, JUDGE:

* * *

The issues for decision are: (1) Whether petitioner was in the trade or business of being an author during the years in issue; if so, (2) whether expenses that petitioner incurred are deductible as ordinary and necessary under section 162. . . .

FINDINGS OF FACT

Some of the facts have been stipulated and are so found. The stipulation of facts and second stipulation of facts, together with the exhibits attached thereto and exhibits offered at trial, are incorporated herein by this reference. Petitioner resided in Arlington, Virginia, when he filed his petition.

Petitioner holds a bachelor's degree in marketing and advertising from the University of Maryland. Towards completion of that degree, he earned more than 24 credit hours of study in English, journalism, and speech. Petitioner worked 40 hours per week for the U.S. Department of the Treasury (hereinafter Treasury) as a budget analyst until January 1997, when he retired after more than 35 years of service. He had been employed at a GS-12 pay grade. As part of his job, he was required to "write budget justifications, procedures, and other written material by applying professional level writing ability to create high quality written work." In an office staffed mostly by accountants, petitioner was often the one delegated to perform writing-based tasks, such as contributing to the Federal Managers' Financial Integrity Act report, in which agencies evaluate their internal control and accounting systems. At some point during his employment, petitioner also served as editor of an in-house newsletter of the Treasury.

In 1992, approximately 2 years before petitioner became eligible to retire, he began writing outside of his full-time job. At trial, petitioner testified that he was "fearful of the concept of retirement" and began writing in 1992 with the hope of making it his second career. The first book-length manuscript he began writing was a fictional piece titled "Lightning at Dawn." Later that same year, petitioner wrote a collection of short stories called "Boys and Girls Together." Before marketing these manuscripts for publication, petitioner had an idea for another book -- a story about the experiences of two men who travel cross-country to patronize a legal brothel in Nevada. In early 1993, petitioner wrote an 18,000-word draft of this basic story line, which he submitted for copyright protection in June. In order to authenticate the story and develop characters for the book, petitioner visited numerous legal brothels in Nevada by acting as a customer for prostitutes.

In a journal describing his experiences at the brothels, petitioner recorded the brothels he visited, the dates (and sometimes the hours) of his visits, the prostitutes he met, and the amount of cash he paid each one. For each entry, petitioner wrote about his visit with the prostitute and about the happenings at brothels in general. For example, he described the manner in which he selected her, the house rules of the brothel, the manner in which he negotiated a price for her time, their dialogue, and the type of clothing worn by her. He also included personal information on the prostitute, including her age, physical characteristics, city or State of residence, religious background, ethnicity, level of education, and the name and age of her offspring, if any. The journal indicates that, at some point during these meetings, petitioner told the prostitutes that he was writing a book about Nevada's legal brothels and that he wished to use them as characters in his book. The journal shows that, during 1993, petitioner spent, on average, 3 days per month (except during the months of February, May, and December) meeting with prostitutes at the brothels.

Using the material that he gathered during these meetings (hereinafter sometimes referred to as interviews), petitioner produced a manuscript called “Searchlight, Nevada” which he submitted for publication. On October 13, 1993, petitioner entered into an agreement for its publication with Northwest Publishing, Inc. (Northwest). In pertinent part, the agreement provided that,

(1) Petitioner was to pay Northwest $4,375 to publish 10,000 copies of his book;

(2) of the 10,000 copies printed, Northwest would (a) give 100 free copies to petitioner; (b) give away 200 copies to major bookstores and book reviewers; (c) sell 2,500 copies through its “test market program”; and (d) sell the remaining books in the retail marketplace;

(3) petitioner would be paid 40% of the retail amount of each book sold through the test market program, and a royalty equal to 15% of the retail price of any remaining books sold to bookstores and wholesalers;

(4) Northwest was to pay royalties on January 31 and July 31 of each year, along with interest penalties for late payments;

(5) Northwest was to do a certain amount of sales promotion, advertising, and publicity; and

(6) Northwest was to have exclusive rights to the book.

Representatives of Northwest had told petitioner that his book would probably earn him at least $20,000 in royalties.

"Searchlight, Nevada" was published by Northwest and released in December 1995 at a retail price of $7.95. The book is 131 pages long and has an international standard book number. It was available for immediate purchase at Barnes & Noble Book-sellers in Boynton Beach, Florida, and Falls Church, Virginia, and at Super Crown Books, store #106. The book could also be purchased by special order at Borders Books and Music in Baileys Crossroads, Virginia.

Prior to the book's being released, petitioner played an active role in all stages of its publication. In 1994, after reviewing the first galley proofs, petitioner inquired about adding two additional chapters to the novel. Then by letter dated February 27, 1995, petitioner made detailed suggestions for the book's cover design and attached pictures of how he thought the characters on the cover should look. Petitioner closed the letter with the following words:

> Any additional assistance I can provide will be done gladly. I realize that the cover design is as important as the story on the inside. It doesn't matter if the story is good if we fail to motivate the reader into purchasing [sic] the book.
>
> * * * * * * *
>
> Perhaps with our joint venture on "Searchlight, Nevada" we can add a hot seller to * * * [Northwest's] catalog. I'd like us to sell over 100,000 copies.

Petitioner also actively participated in the promotion of his book. He provided Northwest's public relations department with mailing lists and telephone numbers of bookstores, newspapers, magazines, and radio and motion picture companies. Petitioner, on his own, mailed about 60 complimentary copies of his book, along with individualized letters, to bookstores, newspapers, magazines, and hotels. He worked with a marketing expert at Northwest to get his book stocked by distributors, and to set up book signings at major bookstores. When petitioner was unhappy with the contents of his press release, he rewrote it and sent his changes to Northwest. Moreover, when petitioner became dissatisfied with

Northwest's marketing efforts, he wrote a letter demanding that the publishing company comply with the terms of its agreement.

In late 1993, after petitioner had signed an agreement with Northwest to have "Searchlight, Nevada" published, he began research on another book, "Nevada Nights, San Joaquin Dawn." He wanted to document the difficulties that women face in their attempt to break free from a life of prostitution, because, as "the story's never been done before to any degree of authenticity", he thought it commercially viable. After discovering that the rooms at the brothels were equipped with listening devices, he began meeting the women at other locations on "out calls," which he paid for by personal credit card. In 1994, during the months of January, February, April, May, June, and July, petitioner spent anywhere from 1 to 6 days per month in Nevada on out calls with prostitutes. He successfully encouraged 10 prostitutes to leave their profession. As of the trial date, petitioner had not yet completed "Nevada Nights, San Joaquin Dawn."

Some time after a contract had been signed for the publication of "Searchlight, Nevada", petitioner submitted another manuscript to Northwest for consideration; i.e., "Lightning at Dawn", which was about 450 pages in length. He was under the impression that Northwest required a joint venture payment for first novels only, and that, if Northwest agreed to publish "Lightning at Dawn", he would have to pay nothing. Petitioner also attempted to market "Boys and Girls Together", but he ceased his efforts when he was told that there was no need or market for short stories at that time.

On May 1, 1996, 4 months after "Searchlight, Nevada" had been on the market, Northwest filed for bankruptcy protection. The corporation had been the subject of a continuing investigation by State authorities. On November 8, 1996, petitioner filed a proof of claim with the U.S. Bankruptcy Court for the District of Utah in the amount of $17,854 for unpaid royalties and breach of contract.

After securing the return of his rights in "Searchlight, Nevada", petitioner began soliciting other publishing houses to have his book published a second time. Petitioner received several responses, including a request by the president of Regnery Publishing, Inc., and an invitation by the editor-in-chief of Farrar, Straus & Giroux, Inc., to submit his manuscript for review. He also began to send letters to literary agents soliciting their interest in his book. At the time of trial, petitioner had since rewritten parts of "Searchlight, Nevada" and had sent his revised manuscript to Paladin Press of Boulder, Colorado, at its request. Petitioner also received a letter from Neal Sperling, a Hollywood script agent, requesting that he submit a plot summary of his book for consideration as a made-for-television movie or feature film. Petitioner is presently a member of Washington Independent Writers, The Authors Guild, Poets and Writers, and Writers Market Book Club. During the years in issue, petitioner spent approximately 25-35 hours per week on his writing activity.

Petitioner did not engage a literary agent for the first publication of "Searchlight, Nevada." Instead, he chose to study the book market and identify publishers which he thought might be interested in his work. For the book's second publication, though, petitioner did attempt to have an agent represent him.

* * *

In 1993, petitioner began treating his writing activity as a trade or business. From that year on, he began filing a Schedule C (Profit or Loss From Business), in which he listed his principal business or profession as author. As of the date of trial, petitioner's writing activity had not resulted in a profit for any year. . . .

For the years in issue, petitioner reported no income from his writing activity but claimed the following as deductible expenses on his Schedules C:

	1993	1994
Advertising	--	$100
Commissions and fees	$40	80
Office expense	420	600
Supplies	150	--
Travel	4,230	9,195
Meals and entertainment	2,520	786
Utilities	--	657
Other expenses	7,830	12,099
Total	15,190	23,517

For 1993, the item denominated "other expenses" consists of a $4,350 joint venture payment to Northwest and $3,480 in cash payments to prostitutes. For 1994, other expenses consist of the following: $2,349 for the purchase of a computer, supplies, and furniture; $480 for mailing expenses; $313 for membership dues; $5,660 for credit card expenses on out calls; $1,295 for tuition and books; $500 for sponsoring a race car team; and $1,502 for miscellaneous other expenses.

Petitioner's travel and meal deductions include expenditures for airfares, rental car expenses, food, and lodging in connection with his travels to Nevada. For the years in issue, the record contains documentary evidence of petitioner's travel and meal expenses; i.e., airline tickets and travel schedules, and hotel, restaurant, rental car, and credit card receipts.

With respect to petitioner's interviews, he characterized the amounts he paid to the prostitutes as business related depending upon whether information gleaned from the interviews was used in his books. Petitioner has personal credit card receipts for 1994 supporting the expenditures he incurred to interview prostitutes away from the brothels. Petitioner does not have receipts of his cash expenditures in 1993 for the interviews that took place at the brothels. Nor does petitioner have records supporting his deductions for advertising, commissions and fees, office expenses, supplies, utilities, or those expenses comprising "other expenses" for 1994 (with the exception of the interviews).

Around the time of the parties' preparation of a stipulation of facts, petitioner prepared a five-page reconstruction of his expenditures, using information reflected on airline tickets and itineraries, hotel and rental car bills, credit card receipts, and petitioner's own memory. This included summary statements for 1993 and 1994, a flight log, and a log of his interviews.

In the notice of deficiency, respondent disallowed under sections 162 and 183 all of the expenses claimed on petitioner's Schedules C for the years in issue because "it has not been shown that * * * [petitioner] either started a trade or business or entered into an activity for profit. * * * [Nor has he] established that any amount was for an ordinary and necessary business expense."

OPINION

Section 162(a) generally allows a deduction for all ordinary and necessary business expenses paid or incurred during the taxable year in carrying on any trade or business. To be engaged in a trade or business within the meaning of section 162, "the taxpayer must be involved in the activity with continuity and regularity and * * * the taxpayer's primary purpose for engaging in the activity must be for income or profit." *Commissioner v. Groetzinger,* 480 U.S. 23, 35, 94 L. Ed. 2d 25, 107 S. Ct. 980 (1987).

We are satisfied that petitioner's writing activity was conducted with continuity and regularity during the years in issue. Nevertheless, in order for an activity to be considered a trade or business within the meaning of section 162, a taxpayer must conduct the activity with the requisite profit motive or intent. See id.

Petitioner argues that he engaged in his writing activity with the intent to make a profit and that his Schedule C expenses for tax years 1993 and 1994 were ordinary and necessary to his endeavor as an author. Respondent does not dispute that amounts were in fact expended, but rather contests their deductibility. Respondent maintains petitioner was not engaged in the trade or business of being an author, and, accordingly, expenses incurred for the writing (and publication of one) of his books are not business expenses deductible under section 162(a). Rather, he argues, they are deductible only to the extent of the income derived from the activity under section 183. . . .

Petitioner bears the burden of proving by a preponderance of the evidence that he was engaged in writing for profit. Rule 142(a). The test of whether a taxpayer engaged in an activity for profit is whether he entered into, or continued, the activity with an actual and honest objective of making a profit. See *Dreicer v. Commissioner,* 78 T.C. 642, 645 (1982), affd. without opinion 702 F.2d 1205 (D.C. Cir. 1983). Although the taxpayer's expectation of profit need not be reasonable, it must be bona fide, as determined from all the surrounding facts and circumstances. See *Keanini v. Commissioner,* 94 T.C. 41, 46 (1990); *Dreicer v. Commissioner, supra at 645.* Thus, whether the requisite profit motive exists is a factual question that must be determined upon the record, see *Benz v. Commissioner,* 63 T.C. 375, 382 (1974), with more weight given to objective facts than to petitioner's statement of intent. See *Engdahl v. Commissioner,* 72 T.C. 659, 666 (1979); sec. 1.183-2(a), Income Tax Regs.

The Treasury regulations list nine factors as an aid in making the profit objective determination. They include: (1) The manner in which the taxpayer carried on the activity; (2) the expertise of the taxpayer or his advisers; (3) the time and effort expended by the taxpayer in carrying on the activity; (4) the expectation that the assets used in the activity may appreciate in value; (5) the success of the taxpayer in carrying on other similar or dissimilar activities; (6) the taxpayer's history of income or loss with respect to the activity; (7) the amount of occasional profits that are earned; (8) the financial status of the taxpayer; and (9) whether elements of personal pleasure or recreation are involved. No one factor is conclusive, and we do not reach our decision herein by merely counting the factors that support each party's position. See sec. 1.183-2(b), Income Tax Regs. Moreover, certain factors are given more weight than others because they are more meaningfully applied to the facts in this case. Respondent concedes that the fourth element, the expectation that assets used in the activity may appreciate in value, is inapplicable to the present case.

Taking into account the above factors and considering the record as a whole, we conclude that, during the years in issue, petitioner had a bona fide intention to derive a profit from his writing activity. In addition to petitioner's testimony, which we found to be credible and forthright, the evidence in the record shows an intent and effort by petitioner to engage in and continue in the writing field with the purpose of producing income and a livelihood.

We first look to the manner in which petitioner carried on the activity. Petitioner managed some aspects of this activity in a businesslike fashion. He kept bills, receipts, and schedules for his traveling expenses, and he kept a contemporaneous journal to substantiate cash expenditures that he incurred to interview prostitutes at the brothels, for which receipts were not available. Petitioner was able to use his records, including credit card statements, to compile logs for 1993 and 1994, showing his travel dates, the dates, times, and places of his interviews, the names of the prostitutes he interviewed, the per hour charges he negotiated, and his method of payment. While petitioner may not have kept a separate checking account or a well-organized set of books, he did attempt to keep an accurate account of the expenses he incurred to research his books.

The record also indicates that, after signing a contract for the publication of "Searchlight, Nevada", petitioner made concerted efforts to promote his book. He took steps to gain maximum personal benefit from Northwest by working closely with its public relations department to ensure that his book was widely advertised and readily available in bookstores. Petitioner then supplemented Northwest's efforts by adopting various methods of his own, while, at the same time, remaining active as an author by writing other manuscripts. Furthermore, when Northwest filed for bankruptcy protection, petitioner did not abandon his writing activity; rather, he sought the return of his rights in "Searchlight, Nevada", and began an extensive search for a new publisher. He had rewritten and revised his manuscript, in an effort to make it more salable to the public, and thus, more attractive to prospective publishers. As an alternative marketing technique, petitioner also made attempts to engage a literary agent. In sum, although petitioner could have been more organized in keeping track of his expenditures, his efforts to make a financial success of his writing activity show a profit objective.

The fact that petitioner did not seek expert advice on how to start or maintain a business as a fiction writer does weigh against his argument that he carried on the activity in a businesslike manner. While petitioner had writing skills, it appears that they were mainly in the technical field of budget analysis. However, it is important to consider that petitioner used his writing skills extensively in his job at Treasury, where he worked for more than 30 years. Moreover, by virtue of his job assignments and performance rating, petitioner was led to believe that writing was his strong point. Although his success at Treasury is not a reasonable predictor of his success as a fiction writer, his prior writing experience is not unrelated to his anticipated performance as a writer in another field. We also note that petitioner has a bachelor's degree in marketing and advertising, which suggests that he has more than a basic familiarity with the business side of his writing activity. It is apparent from the record that petitioner took great interest in the commercial aspects of his endeavor.

The third factor in the regulations focuses on the time and effort expended by the taxpayer in carrying on the activity. There is little question that, during the years at issue, petitioner spent numerous hours per week on his writing activity; i.e., doing research, writing manuscripts, soliciting publishers, and conferring in the early stages of publication. Respondent emphasizes that petitioner worked 40 hours per week as a budget analyst and suggests that his writing activity could not rise to the level of a trade or business because he also had a full-time job. We disagree with respondent. Petitioner's employment at Treasury does not preclude the possibility that his writing activity constituted a separate trade or business. We have recognized that a taxpayer may engage in more than one trade or business at any one time. [Citations omitted]. It is also well settled that the term "trade or business" includes the arts. *Snyder v. United States,* 674 F.2d 1359, 1363 (10th Cir. 1982). Furthermore, as we stated in *Dickson v. Commissioner,* T.C. Memo 1986-182, "[Taxpayer's] maintaining a full-time job * * * in addition to his profit-seeking activities is a positive factor reflecting his motivation, rather than respondent's attempt at negative inference from the fact that petitioner devoted time to other activities."

The fifth factor, the success of the taxpayer in carrying on other similar or dissimilar activities, does not influence our analysis because petitioner has not previously engaged in a writing activity. We accept petitioner's testimony at trial that he was best known at Treasury for his writing ability and that he was often called upon to perform writing-based tasks. This may have contributed to petitioner's belief that he could make money as an author. Moreover, we are convinced that petitioner viewed his agreement with Northwest as offering a real potential for generating profit.

The next two factors, the taxpayer's history of income or losses with respect to the activity and the amount of occasional profits, if any, which are earned, are examined in tandem. Respondent argues that petitioner's continuous record of losses from his activity is persuasive evidence that he was not engaged in this activity for profit. Petitioner argues that, while his efforts as an author have not proved profitable up to this time, his hard work will be rewarded with substantial income when his search for a new publisher proves successful.

It is undisputed that petitioner did report a loss in each year of operation. However, there are two important facts in this case which should be considered with respect to these losses.

First, section 1.183-2(b)(6), Income Tax Regs., states that losses incurred during the startup phase of a business are not necessarily indicative of a lack of profit motive. Because petitioner did not begin treating his writing activity as a trade or business until 1993, the tax years in issue mark the initial stages of his activity. A significant amount of petitioner's total deductions for 1993 and 1994 were travel expenses, which he incurred to collect material for his books. Now that such material has been amassed and incorporated in the manuscripts, petitioner, as a published author, expects his writing activity to be profitable. To remedy the unforeseeable circumstance of his publisher's going bankrupt, petitioner has demonstrated that he has ideas and plans for future publications which would enable him to recoup not only his expenses, but also to make a profit. [Citations omitted].

Second, these losses should be viewed in the context of the nature of petitioner's activity. Works of fiction are difficult to write and to market. We are persuaded by petitioner's statement that first-time authors are not normally offered cash advances. It is not surprising then, that, for the first 2 years of his writing activity, petitioner sustained losses. This field appears to pay large amounts of money to those who succeed in it and "an opportunity to earn a substantial ultimate profit in a highly speculative venture is ordinarily sufficient to indicate that the activity is engaged in for profit even though losses or only occasional small profits are actually generated." Sec. 1.183-2(b)(7), Income Tax Regs. Likewise, we are not inclined to give much weight to the seventh factor, the amount of occasional profits, if any, that are earned, because only the first 2 years of petitioner's writing activity are in issue.

Respondent argues that the next factor, the financial status of the taxpayer, negates petitioner's profit motive because his independent sources of income are such that the writing activity generated tax benefits for him. We disagree with respondent. We do not believe that petitioner's income was so high as to make tax savings his primary objective. We also do not find it unlikely that petitioner, aware of his upcoming retirement and of the change in his pre and postretirement income, would choose to embark on something new. No doubt the fact that he began his writing activity during his preretirement years contributed to his ability to try his hand at it. Nothing in the record, however, indicates that writing then became a hobby for him. Rather, we find it clear from his testimony and from the objective evidence that petitioner was a writer who desired success and who intended to make a profit from his work.

The last factor looks to elements of personal pleasure or recreation. It is obvious that petitioner enjoyed writing and derived personal satisfaction in helping prostitutes seek a new way of life. Nevertheless, "the fact that the taxpayer derives personal pleasure from engaging in the activity is not sufficient to cause the activity to be classified as not engaged in for profit if the activity is in fact engaged in for profit as evidenced by other factors." Sec. 1.183-2(b)(9), Income Tax Regs.

Petitioner has succeeded in proving that he engaged in his writing activity with a profit objective. There are admittedly some factors in this case which indicate the absence of a profit motive: Petitioner has a history of losses, he did not seek any expert advice, and, arguably, there is a recreational element in his writing. These factors, however, are outweighed by the facts demonstrating that petitioner did engage in writing for profit. And though his writing venture may have been speculative and his expectation of profit unreasonable, that alone does not preclude us from finding that petitioner was in the trade or business of being an author during the years before us.

Respondent next asserts that, for 1993 and 1994, petitioner's claimed expenses were not ordinary and necessary business expenses. Section 162(a) allows a deduction for all ordinary and necessary expenses incurred in carrying on a trade or business. Whether an expense is deductible under section 162 is ultimately a question of fact. See *Commissioner v. Heininger, 320 U.S. 467, 475, 88 L. Ed. 171, 64 S. Ct. 249 (1943).* An ordinary and necessary expense is one which is appropriate or helpful to the taxpayer's business and which results from an activity which is a common and accepted practice. See *Boser v. Commissioner,* 77 T.C. 1124, 1132 (1981), affd. by order (9th Cir. 1983). No deduction, however, is allowed for personal, living, or family expenses, even if related to one's occupation. See sec. 262; *Fred W. Amend Co. v. Commissioner,* 55 T.C. 320, 325 (1970), affd. 454 F.2d 399 (7th Cir. 1971).

Deductions are strictly a matter of legislative grace, and petitioner bears the burden of providing supporting evidence to substantiate the claimed deductions. See Rule 142(a); *INDOPCO, Inc. v. Commissioner,* 503 U.S. 79, 84, 117 L. Ed. 2d 226, 112 S. Ct. 1039 (1992). A taxpayer must keep sufficient records to establish their amount. See sec. 6001. Except in the case of expenses subject to section 274, if the taxpayer's records are inadequate or there are no records, the Tax Court may still allow a deduction based on a reasonable estimate, see *Cohan v. Commissioner,* 39 F.2d 540, 543-544 (2d Cir. 1930), provided the taxpayer establishes that he is entitled to some deduction, see *Williams v. United States,* 245 F.2d 559, 560 (5th Cir. 1957); *Vanicek v. Commissioner,* 85 T.C. 731, 743 (1985). In making an estimate, the Court may bear heavily against the taxpayer "whose inexactitude is of his own making." *Cohan v. Commissioner, supra at 544.*

On his Schedules C for the years in issue, petitioner claimed deductions for advertising, commissions and fees, office expense, supplies, and utilities. Petitioner presented no proof, such as bills, receipts, or canceled checks, or offered any testimony to establish that he incurred these expenses. The record does show, however, that, during 1993 and 1994, petitioner completed one manuscript and submitted it for publication. The Court is satisfied that petitioner incurred office expenses in this respect. Applying *Cohan v. Commissioner, supra*, and "bearing heavily" against petitioner, we allow an office expense deduction of $400 for each of the years in question. Petitioner is not entitled to deductions for advertising, commissions and fees, supplies, and utilities for 1993 and 1994.

Petitioner claimed "other expenses" not included above in the amounts of $7,830 and $12,099, respectively, for 1993 and 1994. The amount for 1993 consists of a joint venture payment to Northwest and cash payments to prostitutes at Nevada's legal brothels. Petitioner produced a canceled check reflecting his payment to Northwest and a contemporaneous journal supporting his deductions for amounts paid to prostitutes to research his book. The amount for 1994 consists of a variety of expenses, for which petitioner has provided no documentary or testimonial evidence, with the exception of his expenses to interview prostitutes on out calls, which he substantiated by personal credit card receipts.

We allow petitioner to deduct the joint venture payment of $4,350 for 1993. However, no deduction is allowed for the interview expenses. We find that the expenditures incurred by petitioner to visit prostitutes are so personal in nature as to preclude their deductibility. In evaluating whether certain expenses are personal or qualify as business expenses under section 162, the Court has found that some expenses are so "inherently personal" that they almost invariably are held to come within the ambit of section 262 [providing that "no deduction shall be allowed for personal, living, or family expenses].[17] *Fred W. Amend Co. v. Commissioner, supra.* All the other items constituting "other expenses" for 1993 and 1994 are disallowed for lack of substantiation.

* * *

Decision will be entered under Rule 155.

TECHNICAL ADVICE MEMORANDUM 9643003

July 10, 1996

ISSUE

Are production and engineering costs incurred to produce a sound recording "qualified creative expenses" that are excepted from the general rule of §263A?

FACTS

Taxpayer, who uses the cash receipts and disbursements method of accounting and files returns on a calendar year, is both employed and self-employed as a A. For his Year 1 tax return, Taxpayer filed a Form 1040, U.S. Individual Income Tax Return, with an attached Schedule C (Form 1040), Profit or Loss From Business (Sole Proprietorship) for his self-employment income. In that same year, Taxpayer composed and recorded several songs on a rough-cut "demo" tape hoping that he would find a record company to produce and distribute his music. The production of the tape required Taxpayer to rent a recording studio, and to hire musicians and a recording engineer. The production costs totaled Amount 1, and the sound engineering costs, Amount 2.

Taxpayer deducted the costs of producing the demo tape as a current expense on his return for Year 1, the year the costs were paid. During an examination of Taxpayer's Year 1 return, the examining agent disallowed these deductions, arguing that the demo tape is a sound recording, sound recordings are tangible personal property, and §263A of the Internal Revenue Code and the regulations thereunder require taxpayers to capitalize the costs of producing tangible personal property.

Taxpayer disagrees with the position of the examining agent. Taxpayer correctly notes that §263A(h) excepts the creative expenses incurred by a writer from capitalization, and "writer" is defined to mean an individual whose personal efforts may reasonably be expected to create a literary manuscript, a musical composition (including any accompanying words), or a dance score. Taxpayer argues that he is a writer that has created a musical composition, his musical composition is recorded on the demo tape, and, therefore, the costs he incurred to produce the demo tape are within the exception provided by the Code for the creative expenses of writers.

Furthermore, Taxpayer argues that the examining agent's position does not reflect the reality of the modern process of creating popular music; many composers of popular music can neither read nor write music, and, therefore, "write" their compositions in a recording studio by recording them on magnetic tape. The taxpayer proposes that the Code should be interpreted to accord him the same treatment it allows a free-lance writer who uses an electric word processor to record his literary creations on a floppy disk. That is, the taxpayer should be allowed a current deduction for the recording costs in the year they were paid.

Taxpayer submitted this request for technical advice to resolve what he perceives to be a lack of uniformity in the treatment of creative expenses incurred by free-lance authors using word processors to record their writings and songwriters composing and recording their works on audio tape.

The examining agent did not request, and we do not express, an opinion of whether the costs incurred by Taxpayer in producing the demo tape were costs incurred in an activity not engaged in for profit under §183.

LAW

Section 263A(a) provides in the case of any property to which §263A applies, the direct costs of the property, and such property's proper share of part or all of those indirect costs that are allocable to such property, shall be included in inventory costs in the case of property which is inventory in the hands of the taxpayer, and shall be capitalized in the case of any other property.

Section 263A(b)(1) provides that §263A applies to real or tangible personal property produced by the taxpayer.

Section 263A(b) (flush language) additionally provides that for the purposes of §263A(b)(1), the term "tangible personal property" shall include a film, sound recording, video tape, book, or similar property.

Section 263A(h)(1) provides an exception from the general rule of §263A for any qualified creative expense.

Section 263A(h)(2) provides the term "qualified creative expense" means any expense which is paid or incurred by an individual in the trade or business of such individual (other than as an employee) of being a writer, photographer, or artist, and which without regard to §263A would be allowable as a deduction for the taxable year.

Section 263A(h)(2) (flush language), however, provides the term "qualified creative expense" does not include any expense related to printing, photographic plates, motion picture films, video tapes, or similar items.

Section 263A(h)(3)(A) provides the term "writer" means any individual if the personal efforts of such individual create (or may reasonably be expected to create) a literary manuscript, musical composition (including any accompanying words), or a dance score.

Section 263A(h)(3)(C) provides the term "artist" means any individual if the personal efforts of such individual create (or may reasonably be expected to create) a picture, painting, sculpture, statue, etching, drawing, cartoon, graphic design, or original print edition.

Section 1.263A-1(c)(3) of the Income Tax Regulations provides that "capitalize" means, in the case of property that is inventory in the hands of a taxpayer, to include in inventory costs and, in the case of other property, to charge to a capital account or basis.

Section 1.263A-2(a) provides §263A applies to real property and tangible personal property produced by the taxpayer for use in its trade or business or for sale to its customers.

Section 1.263A-2(a)(1)(i) provides that "produce" includes construct, build, install, manufacture, develop, improve, create, raise, or grow.

Section 1.263A-2(a)(2)(i) provides, in general, §263A applies to the costs of producing tangible personal property, and not to the costs of producing intangible property.

Section 1.263A-2(a)(2)(ii) provides, for the purposes of determining whether a taxpayer producing intellectual or creative property is producing tangible personal property or intangible property, the term tangible personal property includes films, sound recordings, video tapes, books, and other similar property embodying words, ideas, concepts, images, or sounds by the creator thereof.

Section 1.263A-2(a)(2)(ii)(A)(2) lists sound recordings as an example of tangible personal property and defines "sound recording" as a work that results from the fixation of a series of musical, spoken, or other sounds, regardless of the nature of the material objects, such as discs, tapes, or other phonorecordings, in which such sounds are embodied.

ANALYSIS

Section 263A, enacted in the Tax Reform Act of 1986 (Pub. L. No. 99-514), provides uniform capitalization rules that govern the treatment of costs incurred in the production of property or the acquisition of property for resale.

Section 263A(b) provides that tangible personal property produced by a taxpayer is subject to capitalization. Moreover, this section provides, for the purposes of the uniform capitalization rules, the term "tangible personal property" shall include a film, sound recording, video tape, or similar property. See also 2 H.R. Conf. Rep. No. 841, 99th Cong., 2d Sess. II-308 (1986), 1986-3 (Vol. 4) C.B. 302, 308 n.1 (Conference Report) ("[T]angible property includes films, sound recordings, video tapes, books, and other similar property embodying words, ideas, concepts, images, or sounds, by the creator thereof.").

A "sound recording" is defined as a work that results from the fixation of a series of musical, spoken, or other sounds, regardless of the nature of the material objects, such as discs, tapes, or other phonorecordings, in which such sounds are embodied. §1.263A-2(a)(2)(ii)(A)(2).

Thus, the demo tape is a sound recording, is tangible personal property, and is subject to capitalization unless otherwise excepted by the Code.

The Miscellaneous Revenue Act of 1988 (Pub. L. No. 100-647, the "1988 Act") provided an exemption from the capitalization provisions of §263A for "qualified creative expenses" incurred by free-lance authors, photographers, and artists in the trade or business of being a writer, author, photographer or artist. See §263A(h). The exemption is retroactive and effective as if included in the Tax Reform Act of 1986. The exemption does not apply to "any expense that is related to printing, photographic plates, motion picture films, video tapes, or similar items." H.R. Conf. Rep. No. 1104, 100th Cong., 2d Sess. II-145 (1988), 1988-3 C.B. 473, 635 (Conference Report); §263A(h) (flush language).

To be within the "qualified creative expense" exception from §263A, the expense must meet three requirements: (1) the individual or qualified corporation must have paid or incurred the expense while in the trade or business (other than as an employee) of being a writer, photographer, or artist (as defined in §263A(h)(3)), (2) the expense must be allowable as a deduction, without regard to §263A, for the taxable year, and (3) the expense must not be related to printing, photographic plates, motion picture films, video tapes, or similar items ("excluded items").

Our analysis is limited to determining whether the expense of producing the demo tape is included in the term "qualified creative expense," or if it is excluded because it is an expense related to an excluded item.

The expense of recording a musical composition on magnetic tape is not specifically listed in either §263A(h)(3)(A), the paragraph that defines "writer," or as an excluded cost in the flush language of §263A(h)(2). The paragraph that defines "writer," however, does except the expense of creating a musical composition, and the demo tape is a recording of Taxpayer's musical composition.

Section 263A(h)(2) provides exception for any expense that meets certain qualifications; the §263A(h)(2) flush language excludes from the exception the expenses related to certain types of items. Section 263A(h)(3)(A) defines who is a "writer." In defining who is a writer, the paragraph also defines the creative property to which the expense must relate to be excepted from capitalization. The paragraph does not provide that every creative expense of a writer is exempt from capitalization. Together, the flush language and the paragraph limit the forms a writer's creation may take and still be excepted from capitalization.

For example, paragraphs (2) and (3) of subsection (h) provide the expense of a literary manuscript created by a free-lance writer is a qualified creative expense excepted from capitalization, but the flush language provides the term "qualified creative expense" does not include the expenses related to a motion picture film. Thus, if the free-lance writer created a literary manuscript, and then created a motion picture film to express his literary manuscript, the expense of the motion picture film would not be a qualified creative expense because a motion picture film is an excluded item. Similarly, if a writer creates a musical composition, and then creates a sound recording of the musical composition, if the expense of the sound recording is an expense related to a "similar item" (an item that is similar to an excluded item specifically identified in the flush language), the cost of producing the sound recording is not a qualified creative expense.

The plain meaning of §263A(h)(3)(A) is to define a "writer" as a person who creates by writing. Thus, the exception for qualified creative expenses is limited to written creations. This is true even if the creation is a musical composition; the excepted medium for communicating the musical composition is a writing, not a sound recording. The demo tape produced by Taxpayer is an expression of his musical composition, however, it is not a writing that fits within the narrow exception to the general rule.

Furthermore, the demo tape is a "similar item," and the cost of producing the tape is expressly excluded from the definition of a qualified creative expense. Motion picture films and video tapes are specifically identified as examples of both tangible personal property and items that are not qualified creative expenses. A sound recording is specifically identified only as an example of tangible personal property. It is reasonable, however, to conclude that if in one subsection a sound recording is property similar to a film and a video tape, it is an item similar to a motion picture film and a video tape in another subsection of the same section. Thus, our conclusion is based on the similarity of the items specifically identified in the §263A(h)(2) flush language as excluded from the term "qualified creative expenses" to the property specifically identified in §263A(b) as tangible personal property, and the provision in each subsection for "similar property" or "similar items."

Moreover, Notice 89-67, 1989-1 C.B. 723, in its discussion of the amendments to §263A made by the Technical and Miscellaneous Revenue Act of 1988, states "[t]he exemption [for qualified creative expenses] under section 6026(a) of the 1988 Act does not apply to any expense that is related to printing, photographic plates, motion picture films, sound recordings, video tapes, or similar items." Notice 89-67, 1989-1 C.B. at 724 (emphasis added).

CONCLUSION

Production and engineering costs incurred to produce a sound recording are not §263A(h) "qualified creative expenses," and therefore the costs of producing a sound recording are not exempt from the general rule of §263A.

This Technical Advice Memorandum is directed only to the taxpayer who requested it. Section 6110(j)(3) of the Code provides that it may not be used or cited as precedent.

Chapter 2: Taxation of Intellectual Property Development

2.1 Deduction for Research and Experimentation – Section 174

2.1[1] Policy Rationale for the Research and Experimentation Deduction

As explained in detail in Chapter 1, distinguishing between currently deductible expenses and capital expenditures is one of the fundamental topics of federal income tax law. Section 162 provides that a taxpayer may deduct ordinary and necessary expenses paid or incurred during the taxable year in carrying on any trade or business. But if the amount paid relates to the creation, acquisition, or improvement of a long-lasting asset or otherwise provides a significant future benefit, it is not an "expense" within the meaning of Section 162. Generally, such amount is a capital expenditure and must be added to the basis of the asset created, acquired, or improved. The rationale for capitalization is the matching principle, i.e., to properly match expenses with the income that those expenses help to produce. If a taxpayer is able to currently deduct an expense that will produce income over a long period, the result is tax deferral. The purpose of the matching principle is to eliminate tax deferral.

Congress has expressly abandoned the matching principle in certain cases where it believes the cost to the government in allowing tax deferral is outweighed by (1) the incentive to encourage certain behavior and (2) the administrative ease to taxpayers and the government in eliminating uncertainty. One such case is section 174, which permits taxpayers to elect to currently deduct certain research and experimental (R&E) expenditures. R&E expenditures provide long-lasting benefits that would be capital expenditures but for section 174.

The legislative history indicates two reasons for enacting section 174. The first reason is to encourage taxpayers to engage in R&E activities.[101] In other words, if taxpayers can currently deduct research expenditures, they will have a greater incentive to innovate and thereby remain competitive in the global marketplace. The second reason is to eliminate the uncertainty about the tax treatment of R&E activities.[102] In an ideal world, a taxpayer would be able to specifically trace research to the production of an identifiable asset, so that capitalization would be quite easy. In that case, the taxpayer would capitalize such expenditures to the identifiable asset's basis. In reality, however, the taxpayer's research may span several years with different and simultaneous research activities leading in varying

[101] H.R. Rpt. 83-1337 at 28 (Mar. 9, 1954).

[102] *Id.*

degrees to the development of several assets. In that case, how would the taxpayer allocate the R&E expenditures to the several assets produced?

Additionally, much of the taxpayer's research will fail. Under normal capitalization rules, a taxpayer would deduct the failed research expenditures upon abandonment because the research no longer provides long-lasting benefits. But how can a taxpayer prove that research has been completely abandoned? Moreover, how can a taxpayer show that failed research will not eventually lead to long-lasting benefits? Indeed, failure is often a necessary prerequisite to ultimate success. The history of innovation is replete with stories of repeated failure and persistence. For instance, Thomas Edison allegedly made 1,000 unsuccessful attempts before perfecting the incandescent light bulb. Suppose Edison had sincerely believed he was going to quit after his 1,000th attempt, only to change his mind a few years later to continue the research. Would Edison be deemed to have abandoned his research after his 1,000th attempt?

Similarly, James Dyson made 5,126 unsuccessful attempts over a five-year period before perfecting his vacuum cleaner.[103] Ultimately, Dyson's research led to the development of several patents and different vacuum cleaner models. Furthermore, Dyson later used some of his vacuum cleaner research to develop an electric hand dryer. If Dyson was required to capitalize all of his research expenditures, how would Dyson allocate the research between abandoned ideas, his various vacuum models and patents, and his electric hand dryer?

Section 174 eliminates the uncertainty raised in the above questions by allowing the taxpayer to currently deduct R&E expenditures. As explained in Chapter 1, the final regulations under section 263 applied the same rationale in adopting simplifying conventions that generally allow taxpayers to currently deduct employee compensation, overhead, and minimal costs in the creation of an intangible. That is, the simplifying conventions eliminate the uncertainty of precisely allocating employee compensation, overhead, and minimal costs to each of the taxpayer's transactions.

2.1[2] "Research and Experimental Expenditures" Defined

Section 174 provides that a taxpayer may currently deduct "research and experimental expenditures which are paid or incurred by him during the taxable year in connection with his trade or business." The Code contains no definition of the term "research or

---

[103] James Dyson, *How to be Different #4: "Keep Failing" It Works*, The Independent (London) 43 (Dec. 7, 2005).

experimental expenditures." Treasury Regulations define "research and experimental expenditures" as amounts "incurred in connection with the taxpayer's trade or business, which represent research and development costs in the experimental or laboratory sense."[104] The term also includes incidental costs in the development or improvement of a *product*, including costs of obtaining patents and legal fees to perfect patent applications.[105] A "product" is defined as "any pilot model, process, formula, invention, technique, patent, or similar property, and includes products to be used by the taxpayer in its trade or business as well as products to be held for sale, lease, or license."[106]

2.1[2][a] The "Uncertainty" Test

One of the critical requirements for research and experimentation is the element of *uncertainty*. This means that the taxpayer's research must "eliminate uncertainty concerning the development or improvement of a product."[107] Treasury regulations articulate this "uncertainty" test as follows:

> Uncertainty exists if the information available to the taxpayer does not establish the capability or method for developing or improving the product or the appropriate design of the product. Whether expenditures qualify as research or experimental expenditures depends on the nature of the activity to which the expenditures relate, not the nature of the product or improvement being developed or the level of technological advancement the product or improvement represents.[108]

The test for uncertainty is not whether the taxpayer believes the research will result in technical innovation. In fact, the taxpayer may be quite confident of the ultimate success of its research. For instance, many of the scientists on the Manhattan Project were confident that their research would lead to development of an atomic bomb.[109] But the scientists' confidence in the outcome did not detract from the fact that they had to overcome one of the most challenging technical feats in history. After all, no rational taxpayer would engage in research without some rational basis for believing its research might lead to something

[104] Treas. Reg. § 1.174-2(a)(1).

[105] *Id.*

[106] Treas. Reg. § 1.174-2(a)(2).

[107] Treas. Reg. § 1.174-2(a)(1).

[108] *Id.*

[109] *See generally* Richard Rhodes, *The Making of the Atomic Bomb* (Simon & Schuster 1986).

useful. Rather, uncertainty is really the demarcation point between the *research and experimentation stage* of development on the one hand, and the *manufacturing, sale, and marketing stage* on the other. Stated differently, once the taxpayer enters the manufacturing, sale, and marketing stage, there is no longer any uncertainty about how the product will be developed. At that point, the technical innovation stage is complete.

The "uncertainty" test is not strictly a time line test. For instance, a taxpayer may have completed all research on a product's development, yet subsequent costs to obtain a patent on the product are R&E expenditures. Conversely, a taxpayer may conduct market research on a product prior to completion of the technical research, yet market research costs will not be R&E expenditures. Another thing to consider is that technology is continually evolving. So a taxpayer may have a completed product, but thereafter incur research costs to improve that product (or create an entirely new product from the initial research). Research costs to improve the product or create an entirely new product are R&E expenditures.

The "uncertainty" test is consistent with Congress's purposes for enacting section 174. First, the uncertainty principle promotes the underlying rationale to encourage taxpayers to innovate. If a taxpayer already knows how to manufacture a product, the incentive to innovate does not exist. Second, the "uncertainty principle" is consistent with the underlying rationale to eliminate uncertainty about the tax treatment of research and experimentation. During the research stage, the taxpayer is not entirely sure its research activities will be successful. The taxpayer's research may lead in varying degrees of success to several different assets. So the research and experimentation stage is where the complicated tax accounting issues of allocating costs to assets are likely to arise. Conversely, these difficult tax accounting issues are less likely to arise in the manufacturing, sale, and marketing stage because at that point there is an identifiable product to which costs can be capitalized.

> **Problem 2.1**: Taxpayer manufactures bioidentical hormones. A hormone is "bioidentical" if it has the exact same chemical structure as a hormone that is naturally produced in the human body. A bioidentical hormone cannot be patented because the chemical formula occurs naturally. Up to this point, Taxpayer has offered a wide range of bioidentical hormones for manufacture and sale, including bioidentical estrogen and testosterone. Taxpayer seeks to expand its bioidentical hormone inventory by offering bioidentical human growth hormone (HGH) for manufacture and sale. Although the process for creating bioidentical HGH has been widely known for several years, Taxpayer spends $100,000 to perfect its bioidentical HGH manufacturing process. Can Taxpayer treat this $100,000 as R&E

expenditures under section 174? Read *Agro Science Company v. Commissioner* (included in this Chapter's materials) in connection with this problem.

Problem 2.2: Taxpayer develops and manufactures defense systems for the U.S. military. Over the past few years, Taxpayer has incurred $5,000,000 trying to develop an invisibility cloak to make tanks, personnel carriers, and other vehicles appear invisible to the naked eye. Eventually, Taxpayer's scientists and engineers concluded that an invisibility cloak is a technological dead end. From the onset of the project, the general consensus in the scientific community was that an invisibility cloak was technologically impossible. Can Taxpayer treat the $5,000,000 to develop its invisibility cloak as R&E expenditures? Read *Universal Research and Development Partnership No. 1 v. Commissioner* (included in this Chapter's materials) in connection with this problem.

2.1[2][b] Qualifying Expenditures

Treasury regulations clarify that research must be scientific in nature (e.g., physical and biological sciences and engineering) as opposed to research of other types (e.g., marketing, social science, historical, etc.). To this end, the regulations expressly exclude the following from the definition of R&E expenditures:[110]

(1) Ordinary testing or inspection of materials or products for quality control;
(2) Efficiency surveys;
(3) Management studies;
(4) Consumer surveys;
(5) Advertising and promotions;
(6) The acquisition of another's patent, model, production or process; and
(7) Research in connection with literary, historical, and similar projects.

The regulations clarify that "quality control testing" means "testing or inspection to determine whether the particular units of materials or products conform to specific parameters," but "does not include testing to determine if the design of the product is appropriate."[111]

---

[110] Treas. Reg. § 1.174-2(a)(3).

[111] Treas. Reg. § 1.174-2(a)(4).

An expenditure expressly excluded from section 174 "R&E expenditure" definition is not necessarily a capital expenditure. Some of the excluded expenditures may qualify for current deduction under section 162, while others clearly must be capitalized. As explained in detail in Chapter 1, a taxpayer may generally deduct advertising and promotion expenditures, even if relating to package design.[112] Similarly, as explained in Chapter 1, a freelance writer may currently deduct literary or historical research as a "qualified creative expense" within the meaning of section 263A(h). On the other hand, the acquisition of another's patent would be an "acquired intangible" and must be capitalized.[113] Acquisitions of intellectual property are further discussed in Chapter 3.

> **Problem 2.3**: Taxpayer develops, manufactures, and markets pharmaceuticals. Taxpayer recently developed a new drug called "Procore" for the treatment of depression. Taxpayer's development of Procore was comprised of four stages (which is typical for the development of any new drug), including (1) preclinical research, (2) clinical development, (3) regulatory approval, and (4) post marketing. These four stages took 10 years to complete (which is typical).
>
> In the preclinical stage, Taxpayer tested a new compound on animals. Because the animal testing was so promising in the treatment of depression, Taxpayer patented the compound to prevent others from freely using it. Also, during this stage, Taxpayer made an Investigational New Drug Application (IND) with the Food and Drug Administration (FDA), which the FDA approved. In total, Taxpayer incurred the following expenditures during the preclinical stage:
>
> - $10,000,000 on the scientific research to discover the compound and to test it on animals.
> - $150,000 paid to outside counsel in connection with the patent application on the compound.
> - $100,000 paid to outside counsel to prepare the IND and otherwise represent Taxpayer before the FDA.

---

[112] *See* Treas. Reg. § 1.263(a)-4(b)(3)(v).

[113] *See* Treas. Reg. § 1.263(a)-4(c)(1)(vii).

Once the FDA granted the IND, Taxpayer entered the clinical development stage, which was broken up into three phases (i.e., Phases I, II, and III). In Phase I, Taxpayer conducted the first trials on humans to test for safety, tolerance, and pharmacokinetics. In Phase II, Taxpayer conducted testing to evaluate the effectiveness, dosage, and safety on a selected population of patients suffering from depression. In Phase III, Taxpayer conducted large-scale trials on thousands of patients to gather additional evidence to verify dosage, effectiveness, and to better understand side effects. Taxpayer incurred expenditures of $15,000,000 in Phase I, $20,000,000 in Phase II, and $100,000,000 in Phase III.

After Taxpayer completed Phase III trials, it entered the regulatory approval stage. At this point, Taxpayer filed a New Drug Application (NDA) with the FDA to obtain authorization to market its new drug. The FDA granted authorization, thereby allowing Taxpayer to market its drug in the U.S. Taxpayer incurred expenditures of $500,000 in connection with the NDA, which included compensation paid to its own employees, overhead, and amounts paid to outside counsel.

Once the FDA approved the drug, Taxpayer entered the post-marketing stage. Although Taxpayer was able to market its drug to the public at this point, it was required to continue studies on its drug (called "Phase IV" testing). The purpose of Phase IV testing was to determine the incidence of adverse reactions, to determine the long-term effects of the drug, and to study the drug's effects on patient populations not previously studied. During Phase IV, Taxpayer had a continuing obligation to promptly report known post-marketing adverse effects to the FDA. Taxpayer incurred $5,000,000 of expenditures in Phase IV testing.

Also during the post-marketing stage, Taxpayer incurred the following expenditures:

- $5,000,000 to conduct market research and surveys to determine potential consumers' preference regarding the drug, such as its name and the shape, size, and color of the pills. This market testing lead Taxpayer to choose the name "Procore" for the drug.

- $20,000 paid to outside counsel for trademark screening and registering a trademark for "Procore."
- $1,000,000 to outside advertising consultants to develop an advertising campaign for "Procore."

What expenditures described above can Taxpayer treat as R&E expenditures under Section 174? For an expenditure not covered by section 174, determine whether it is deductible under section 162 or a capital expenditure.

2.1[2][b][i] Costs to Acquire or Improve Land or Depreciable Property

Costs to acquire or improve land or depreciable property are classic examples of capital expenditures.[114] Can a taxpayer get around capitalizing such costs by using the acquired or improved land or depreciable property for research and experimentation and deducting them under section 174? The answer is no. Section 174 provides that a taxpayer may not deduct costs to acquire or improve land or property subject to depreciation or depletion, even if the taxpayer uses the land or property for research and experimentation.[115]

Although costs to acquire or improve depreciable property are not R&E expenditures, the *depreciation allowances* on depreciable property used in research and experimentation may be deducted under section 174.[116] The significance of this rule may not be readily apparent. After all, if the taxpayer may deduct depreciation allowances anyway under section 167, what difference does it make that the depreciation allowances are deductible under section 174? The difference relates to characterization of gain upon sale or exchange of the depreciable property. As will be explained in detail in Chapter 4, depreciation allowances deducted under section 167 are recaptured as ordinary income on sale or exchange, whereas there is no ordinary income recapture of prior section 174 deductions.

Problem 2.4: Taxpayer conducts biomedical and pharmaceutical research. In Year 1, Taxpayer places in service in its business a sophisticated electron

---

[114] Treas. Reg. § 1.263(a)-2(a).

[115] I.R.C. § 174(c); Treas. Reg. § 1.174-2(b)(1). In this context, "depreciable property" refers to property subject to an allowance for depreciation under section 167 and "depletable property" refers to property subject to depletion under section 611.

[116] I.R.C. § 174(c); Treas. Reg. § 1.174-2(b)(1). Allowances for depletion on depletable property used for research and experimentation may also be deducted under section 174.

microscope purchased for $1,000,000. Assume that the first year depreciation on the microscope would be $200,000. If the taxpayer uses the microscope exclusively for research and experimentation, how much can the taxpayer deduct under section 174 in Year 1?

An interesting question arises where the taxpayer contracts with another party to conduct research on its behalf, and that other party must acquire or improve land or depreciable property to conduct the research. The questions raised in this situation are twofold. First, can a taxpayer deduct amounts under Section 174 paid to another party to research on its behalf? Second, if so, may the taxpayer deduct amounts under section 174 paid to other party, which the other party uses to acquire land or depreciable property used in the research?

Regarding the first question, the regulations expressly recognize that a taxpayer may deduct under section 174 amounts paid for research and experimentation carried on its behalf by another party (such as a research institute, foundation, engineering company, or similar contractor).[117] Regarding the second question, the taxpayer may deduct under section 174 amounts paid to another party for the acquisition or improvement of land or depreciable property used in the research, provided the other party *retains ownership* of the land or depreciable property. But if the taxpayer acquires rights of ownership to the land or other depreciable property, the taxpayer may not deduct under section 174 amounts paid by the other party to acquire the land or depreciable property.

Problem 2.5: Spartan Corporation manufacturers and distributes fertilizers and pesticides for agricultural use. Spartan engages Gopher University to undertake R&E work in order to create a new, environmentally-friendly pesticide. Spartan pays $2,000,000 to Gopher to conduct the research. Gopher uses $750,000 of these funds to purchase a building to house a laboratory where it will conduct much of the research. Spartan and Gopher agree that Gopher will retain ownership of the laboratory when the research is completed. How much may Spartan treat as R&E expenditures under section 174? How would the answer change if Gopher agrees to transfer ownership of the laboratory to Spartan upon completion of the research?

---

[117] Treas. Reg. § 1.174-2(a)(8).

2.1[2][b][ii] Costs to Create Depreciable Property used in a Trade or Business

Research and experimentation may ultimately lead to the creation or manufacture of depreciable property used in the taxpayer's trade or business. In this case, R&E expenditures do not include the cost for component materials and labor used in the actual construction or installation of the depreciable property.[118] On the other hand, the remaining costs attributable to the design and development of the depreciable property will qualify as R&E expenditures.[119] The regulations provide an example where a taxpayer spends $30,000 to develop a new machine, $10,000 of which is spent on material and labor to construct the machine. The remaining $20,000 spent represents the cost of research and experimentation.[120] While a taxpayer may understand that material and labor to construct the property must be separated from research and experimentation, this may be difficult to do in practice. Is there a bright-line watershed moment where the taxpayer's workers end research and experimentation and begin construction? If no similar prototype of the machine has ever been made, would the actual construction of such a machine itself be experimental? Unfortunately, the regulations and case law provide no additional guidance in this regard.

A taxpayer may also pay another party to create or develop depreciable property to be used in the taxpayer's trade or business. In this situation, amounts paid to the other party qualifies as R&E expenditures only if made (1) upon the taxpayer's order and (2) at the taxpayer's risk.[121] The risk element is important and related to the element of uncertainty. If the taxpayer bears no risk as to the property's development, the taxpayer is really just ordering a finished product from the other party. In this case, the taxpayer is conducting no research and is not motivated by an incentive to innovate. On the other hand, if the taxpayer has a financial risk of loss that the research will lead to nothing useful, the taxpayer is truly engaged in research and experimentation. Therefore, the element of risk draws a line between a taxpayer paying for technology to be created on its behalf (research and experimentation) and a taxpayer who simply acquires another's technology (not research and experimentation).

Problem 2.6: Boilermaker University has a promising research program on a potential drug candidate for the treatment of cancer. Hoosier Corporation

[118] Treas. Reg. § 1.174-2(b)(4).

[119] Treas. Reg. § 1.174-2(b)(2).

[120] Treas. Reg. § 1.174-2(b)(4).

[121] Treas. Reg. § 1.174-2(b)(3).

is a pharmaceutical drug manufacturer and is interested in Boilermaker's research and know-how for the potential cancer drug. Boilermaker and Hoosier enter into a License and Development Agreement for the purpose of developing, marketing, and distributing the potential cancer drug if approved by the FDA. [For background on the FDA approval process, refer to Problem 2.3 above.] Pursuant to the agreement, Hoosier pays a nonrefundable upfront fee of $5,000,000 to Boilermaker as part consideration for rights granted under the agreement. Hoosier will reimburse Boilermaker for research costs up to $10,000,000 per year but no more than the Boilermaker's actual costs in that year. The agreement also calls for Hoosier to make "milestone payments" to Boilermaker contingent on the achievement of certain research goals. For example, Hoosier will pay Boilermaker $10,000,000 upon successful completion of each of Phase I, Phase II, and Phase III drug development. Additionally, Hoosier will pay Boilermaker $5,000,000 upon filing an NDA with the FDA and $100,000,000 upon FDA approval of the cancer drug. What amounts paid to Boilermaker can Hoosier treat as R&E expenditures under Section 174?[122]

2.1[3] "In Connection with" a Trade or Business Requirement

A taxpayer must show that its R&E expenditures are paid or incurred "*in connection with*" its "trade or business" to qualify under section 174. In contrast, section 162 requires expenses to be paid or incurred in "*carrying on*" the taxpayer's "trade or business." As explained in detail in Chapter 1, a taxpayer must actually begin its trade or business to meet the "carrying on" requirement and claim section 162 deductions. So preoperational and investigatory expenses do not qualify under section 162 and are start-up expenditures within the meaning of section 195. Should preoperational and investigatory expenses be treated similarly under section 174, even though section 174 has no "carrying on" requirement? In other words, is there a difference between expenses for "carrying on" a trade or business and those made "in connection with" a trade or business? The U.S. Supreme Court answered this question in *Snow v. Commissioner*.[123]

---

[122] This question is based on issues raised by the Service's Coordinated Issue Paper, *Nonrefundable Upfront Fees, Technology Access Fees, Milestone Payments, Royalties, Deferred Income Under Collaboration Agreement*, LMSB-04-1007-073 (2007).

[123] 416 U.S. 500 (1974).

In *Snow*, the taxpayer invested in a limited partnership formed to develop an unpatented trash incinerator. During the taxable year in question, the partnership built and tested various models of the incinerator, but made no effort to sell any. The partnership obtained a patent on the incinerator four years later and production and sale began shortly thereafter. The Service disallowed the taxpayer's deduction of his distributive share of the partnership's section 174 R&E expenditures because the partnership was not yet engaged in a trade or business.[124]

The Court rejected the Service's claim that a taxpayer must be already engaged in a trade or business to claim the benefits of section 174. The Court noted that Congress specifically used the term "in connection with" a trade or business in section 174, rather than the term "carrying on" a trade or business that it had used in section 162. Legislative history showed Congressional concern that a "carrying on" requirement would limit section 174's availability to established businesses. In part, Congress passed section 174 to encourage innovation and recognized that start up ventures should have as much incentive to innovate as their established counterparts. Therefore, the Court held that Congress adopted the "in connection with" requirement to equalize the tax treatment of R&E expenditures between established businesses and start up ventures.

Although the Court in *Snow* held that preoperational R&E expenditures may be deducted under section 174, it did not eliminate the "trade or business" requirement altogether. The term "trade or business" has the same meaning under section 174 as it does under section 162.[125] As discussed in detail in Chapter 1, neither the Code nor treasury regulations define the term "trade or business." The Supreme Court held in *Commissioner v. Groetzinger*[126] that a trade or business occurs where a taxpayer is "involved in the activity with continuity and regularity and that the taxpayer's primary purpose for engaging in the activity [is] for income or profit."[127] The Court in *Groetzinger* further held that "[a] sporadic activity, a

[124] The taxable year in question was 1966, which predated enactment of passive loss limitations. Thus, if the expenses were allowable under section 174, the taxpayer could deduct his distributable share of those expenses against nonpassive income. Under current law, the taxpayer would not be a material participant in the activity and could only deduct his distributable share of section 174 expenses against income from passive activities. *See* I.R.C. § 469.

[125] *See e.g. Christensen v. Commissioner*, 56 T.C.M. (CCH) 425 (1988) (holding that a taxpayer satisfying the trade or business requirement under Section 162 likewise satisfies the trade or business requirement under section 174).

[126] 480 U.S. 23 (1987).

[127] *Id.* at 35.

hobby, or an amusement diversion does not qualify."[128] Prior to *Groetzinger*, the Supreme Court held in *Higgins v. Commissioner*[129] that management of one's own investments is not a trade or business.

Generally, those taxpayers who conduct their own research on a regular and continual basis with a primary profit motive will meet the "trade or business" requirement. For instance, the courts in both *Maximoff v. Commissioner* and *Lamont v. United States*, included in the Chapter 1 materials, held that a trade or business can exist in the product development stage prior to sale of a product. Importantly, the taxpayers in *Maximoff* and *Lamont*, though unsuccessful in their endeavors, conducted much of the research on their own behalf.

On the other hand, the "trade or business" requirement is more likely to become an issue where an investment partnership engages another party to conduct research on its behalf. As discussed above, a taxpayer may treat amounts paid to another party to conduct research on its behalf as R&E expenditures. This, of course, assumes that the research and experimentation is done in connection with the taxpayer's trade or business. After *Snow* broadly interpreted "in connection with" a trade or business to include preoperational R&E expenditures, some taxpayers incorrectly believed they could claim section 174 deductions by simply investing in another's research. Unfortunately, *Snow* set off a wave of tax shelter formation in its wake.

In the typical tax shelter scenario, individuals formed a partnership to fund research and experimentation undertaken by an unrelated party. Although the partnership would purport to own the developed technology, it would license the technology back to the third party. Thus, the third party would actually produce and market the finished product. The individual partners of the partnership generally had no technical expertise and had no day-to-day involvement in the R&E activities. The individual partners would deduct their distributive share of partnership loss created by large R&E expenditures.

The Service successfully attacked these tax shelters by arguing that the partnerships did not satisfy the "trade or business" requirement. In adopting the Service's position, many courts have held that a taxpayer must have a *realistic prospect* of engaging in a trade or business *at some point*.[130] The key is to determine if the taxpayer truly intends to exploit the research in

---

[128] *Id.*

[129] 312 U.S. 212 (1941).

[130] *See, e.g.*, *Lewin v. Commissioner*, 335 F.3d 345 (4th Cir. 2003); *LDL Research & Dev. II, Ltd. v Commissioner*, 124 F.3d 1338 (10th Cir. 1997); *Harris v. Commissioner*, 16 F.3d 75 (5th Cir. 1994);

its own business or is simply an investor in another party's research (which is not a trade or business per *Higgins*). The Service's Field Attorney Advice 20055203F, included in this Chapter's materials, contains an excellent overview of the case law in this regard.

Many tax shelter cases involved tax years predating adoption of the passive loss limitations of section 469, which became effective in 1987. Under current law, even if an R&D partnership can show a realistic prospect of engaging in a trade or business, its partners must still overcome the passive loss limitations to deduct section 174 expenditures. Generally, under section 469, a taxpayer may only offset losses from passive activities (including section 174 deductions) against income from passive activities.[131] A passive activity includes any research and experimentation activity (within the meaning of section 174) in which the taxpayer does not materially participate.[132] Generally, an interest in an R&D partnership as a limited partner is not an activity in which the taxpayer materially participates.[133] Therefore, passive investors in R&D partnerships may only deduct their distributive share of section 174 expenditures to the extent they have income from passive activities. If the post-*Snow* case law did not stymie R&D tax shelter formation, the passive loss limitations of Section 469 certainly did.

> **Problem 2.7**: Taxpayer is a corporation formed as a joint venture between Hawkeye Corporation and Wildcat Corporation. Hawkeye and Wildcat each own 50 percent of Taxpayer's outstanding shares. Both Hawkeye and Wildcat manufacture and sell semiconductors. Hawkeye and Wildcat formed Taxpayer for the purpose of undertaking semiconductor R&E and to commercialize any successful results. Hawkeye and Wildcat collectively contributed capital, certain in-process R&E and other intangible assets to the Taxpayer for this purpose. Taxpayer's board of directors is comprised of six members, three from Hawkeye and three from Wildcat. Each director has

---

Kantor v. Commissioner, 998 F.2d 1514 (9th Cir. 1993); *Diamond v. Commissioner*, 930 F.2d 72 (4th Cir. 1991); *Zink v. U.S.*, 929 F.2d 1015 (5th Cir. 1991); *Spellman v. Commissioner*, 845 F.2d 148 (7th Cir. 1988); *Green v. Commissioner*, 83 T.C. 667 (1984).

[131] I.R.C. § 469. Any excess passive loss is disallowed in the current year and is carried over as a passive loss in succeeding years. I.R.C. § 469(a), (b). Suspended passive losses may be deducted in full in the year the taxpayer disposes of his entire interest in the passive activity in a fully taxable transaction. I.R.C. § 469(g).

[132] I.R.C. § 469(c)(1), (c)(5). A taxpayer materially participates in an activity only if he does so in a regular, continuous, and substantial basis. I.R.C. § 469(h)(1).

[133] I.R.C. § 469(h)(2).

extensive experience in the semiconductor industry. Taxpayer has no employees and no offices. Instead, employees of Hawkeye and Wildcat perform all R&E on Taxpayer's behalf. Hawkeye and Wildcat each charge Taxpayer a fee for all services provided based on the actual hours worked by their employees. Additionally, Taxpayer reimburses Hawkeye and Wildcat for actual R&E expenditures incurred. Taxpayer licenses successful inventions to Hawkeye and Wildcat for manufacture and sale in their respective territories in exchange for royalties. Taxpayer does not license successful inventions to any other parties. Can Taxpayer treat amounts paid to Hawkeye and Wildcat as section 174 R&E expenditures?

2.1[4] Election to Amortize R&E Expenditures

In most cases, a taxpayer will elect to currently deduct R&E expenditures to benefit the most from tax deferral. The taxpayer may elect, however, to treat R&E expenditures as deferred expenses that may be deducted ratably over a period not less than 60 months (beginning with the month in which the taxpayer first realizes benefits from the expenditures).[134] If the taxpayer does not elect to currently deduct or amortize the R&E expenditures over 60 months, it must treat the R&E expenditures as capital expenditures.[135]

Why would a taxpayer elect amortization over current deduction? In some cases, the alternative minimum tax (AMT) may reduce the tax benefit of currently deducted R&E expenditures. A taxpayer must calculate income tax liability under the "regular" tax and the AMT and pay the higher amount. For AMT purposes, noncorporate taxpayers who do not materially participate in the R&E activity must treat currently deducted R&E expenditures as a tax preference item (thereby increasing the amount of AMT).[136] On the other hand, if the taxpayer elects the 60-month amortization method, R&E expenditures are not AMT tax preference items.[137] As noted above, a noncorporate taxpayer who does not materially

---

[134] I.R.C. § 174(b).

[135] Treas. Reg. § 1.174-1.

[136] I.R.C. § 55(b)(2).

[137] To avoid treating currently deducted R&E expenditures as an AMT tax preference item, a taxpayer has the option to amortize the R&E expenditures ratably over 10 years in the year they were paid or incurred. I.R.C. § 59(e). The 10-year amortization for AMT purposes begins in the year paid or incurred, while the 60-month amortization begins the month in which the taxpayer first realizes benefits from the expenditures. Thus, if the taxpayer realizes benefits many years after R&E expenditures are paid or incurred, the 10-year amortization may actually provide a faster recovery.

participate in the R&E activity must overcome passive loss limitations to deduct R&E expenditures in the first place. Therefore, the AMT issue likely applies in the limited cases where a passive investor can offset R&E expenditures against income from passive activities.[138]

2.2 Special Discussion of Computer Software Development

The development of computer software merits special discussion because, as explained below, the Service has issued specific advice on computer software development and its relation to section 174. As explained in Chapter 1, a taxpayer must capitalize amounts paid (1) to acquire certain listed intangibles ("acquired intangibles"), (2) to create certain listed intangibles ("created intangibles"), and (3) to create or enhance a separate and distinct intangible asset.[139] Canned computer software (i.e., readily available to the general public and not substantially modified) is specifically listed as an "acquired intangible" and amounts paid for it must be capitalized.[140] But computer software is not listed as a "created intangible" and the regulations specifically provide that amounts paid to develop computer software do not create a separate and distinct asset.[141] Therefore, while amounts paid to purchase canned computer software are capitalized (as further discussed in Chapter 3), amounts paid to create, develop, or substantially modify computer software are not.

If costs of creating computer software are not capitalized, the taxpayer must determine what Code section permits current deduction. Assuming the taxpayer is *carrying on* a trade or business, it may conceivably deduct computer software development costs under either section 162 (ordinary and necessary business expenses) or section 174 (R&E expenditures). At first blush, a taxpayer may not care, as both section 162 and section 174 provide for

---

[138] In addition to the AMT issue, a taxpayer may also prefer amortization if (1) it will be several years before the taxpayer anticipates having income against which to apply the R&E expenditures, or (2) the taxpayer prefers to show a stronger financial position, e.g., higher profits and more assets on its balance sheet.

[139] Treas. Reg. § 1.263(a)-4(b).

[140] Treas. Reg. § 1.263(a)-4(c)(1)(xiv), (c)(2). A taxpayer may elect to expense all or part of the purchase of canned software under Section 179, if eligible to do so.

[141] See Treas. Reg. § 1.263(a)-4(d) (list of created intangibles do not contain computer software); Treas. Reg. § 1.263(a)-4(b)(3)(iv) (providing that created computer software is not a separate and distinct intangible asset).

current deduction. However, as discussed above, section 174 deductions can be a tax preference item for AMT purposes, whereas section 162 deductions are not.[142]

In *Lamont v. United States*,[143] included in the Chapter 1 materials, the court allowed the taxpayer (a new venture) to deduct under section 162 expenses paid to develop language translation software. The court held that the taxpayer's expenses were paid for carrying on a trade or business because they were incurred after the preoperational stage. Because the court found section 162 to apply, it did not address deductibility under section 174. The court in *Lamont* never addressed the issue of capitalization, possibly because the taxpayer abandoned the software development project. Therefore, it is not clear if *Lamont* is limited to its facts, but it is worth bearing in mind for software development costs.

The Service's preference for deductibility of software creation costs appears to be section 174. In Revenue Procedure 2000-50, included in this Chapter's materials, the Service announced that "costs of developing computer software (whether or not the particular software is patented or copyrighted) in many respects so closely resemble the kind of [R&E] expenditures that fall within the purview of [section] 174 as to warrant similar accounting treatment." Revenue Procedure 2000-50 applies to software for internal use and software that is to be sold or licensed to third parties. "Computer software" is defined as:

> any program or routine (that is, any sequence of machine-readable code) that is designed to cause a computer to perform a desired function or a set of functions, and the documentation required to describe and maintain that program or routine. It includes all forms and media in which the software is contained, whether written, magnetic, or otherwise. Computer programs of all classes, for example, operating systems, executive systems, monitors, compilers, and translators, assembly routines, and utility programs as well as application programs, are included. Computer software also includes any incidental and ancillary rights that are necessary to effect the acquisition of the title to, the ownership of, or the right to use the computer software, and that are used only in connection with that specific computer software. Computer software does not include any data or information base described in § 1.197-2(d)(4) of the Income Tax Regulations (for example, data files, customer lists, or client files) unless the database or item is in the public

[142] Additionally, costs under section 174 (but not under section 162) may have to be allocated between the United States and foreign sources.

[143] 97-2 U.S. Tax Cas. (CCH) P50,861.

> domain and is incremental to a computer program. Nor does it include any cost of procedures that are external to the computer's operation.[144]

In Revenue Procedure 2000-50, the Service never says that software creation costs are R&E expenditures per se. Rather, the Service indicates that software creation costs "*so closely resemble*" R&E expenditures such that they should be treated in the similar manner as R&E expenditures under section 174 (i.e., currently deducted or amortized over 60-months). If software development is to be treated in a similar manner as R&E expenditures, many of the principles applicable to R&E expenditures should likewise apply to software development. As such, software development costs incurred in the research and development stage may be deducted, but costs incurred in the manufacturing and sale stage ought to be capitalized. Similarly, the more lenient "in connection with" a trade or business test should apply to software development, which could be helpful for start up ventures that cannot satisfy the stricter "carrying on" a trade or business test. Additionally, taxpayers should be able to deduct amounts paid to other parties to develop software, so long as the software development is at the taxpayer's order and at the taxpayer's risk.

As discussed earlier in this Chapter, R&E expenditures must be scientific and technical in nature. If the Service analogizes software development to R&E, does this mean that the developed software has to be scientific and technical in its application to fall within Revenue Procedure 2000-50? Or is the development of the software itself technical and scientific in a manner similar to R&E expenditures? As an example, suppose an accounting firm incurs costs to develop tax preparation software for internal use and for sale to third parties. Can the accounting firm rely on Revenue Procedure 2000-50 to deduct the costs in developing the tax preparation software? The answer is probably yes. While preparation of tax returns may not be scientific or technical, the development of the tax preparation software should be.

> **Problem 2.8**: Taxpayer is a large player in the entertainment business. Taxpayer produces, among other things, motion pictures, television programs, music, and video games. Taxpayer incurred $40,000,000 in expenses to produce an action movie called "Andromeda." The movie was groundbreaking in its visual and digital effects. In addition to the $40,000,000 to actually produce the movie, Taxpayer incurred $5,000,000 in costs to create sophisticated computer software that could produce digital scans to precisely capture the shape, shine, color and texture of an actor's

144 Rev. Proc. 2000-50, 2000-2 C.B. 601.

face down to the level of each fine pore and wrinkle. Taxpayer used the detailed scans to create Andromeda's photorealistic digital humans and creatures, which many critics lauded as a groundbreaking achievement in the evolution of digital filmmaking. Taxpayer plans to use the computer software in future movies. Taxpayer also paid $1,000,000 to an outside consultant to produce a website to promote Andromeda and paid $50,000 to purchase the website's domain name from a third party. Because Andromeda was a smash hit, Taxpayer sought to further cash in by internally developing a video game based on Andromeda. The cost for developing the computer program for the video game was $3,000,000. Additionally, Taxpayer paid $100,000 to thoroughly test the video game once produced to ensure that there were no glitches in the program. How should Taxpayer treat the above expenses?

2.3 Research and Development Credit – Section 41

Congress enacted section 174 to encourage innovation by allowing taxpayers to currently deduct R&E expenditures that would otherwise be capitalized. But by 1981, Congress determined that a tax credit would provide an additional incentive for taxpayers to innovate. To this end, Congress enacted a research and development (R&D)[145] credit to "encourage business firms to perform the research necessary to increase the innovative qualities and efficiency of the U.S. economy."[146]

The computation of the R&D credit is quite complex and is not covered in detail in this Chapter. The R&D credit is intended to apply to incremental expenditures over prior years, although special rules apply to start up ventures. Generally stated, the R&D credit is a nonrefundable 20 percent credit for certain increases for scientific and technological expenditures conducted in the United States.[147] A taxpayer claiming the R&D credit must

---

[145] Section 174 generally refers to research and experimental (R&E) expenditures, whereas the Section 41 credit is generally referred to as the research and development (R&D) credit. The terms R&E and R&D are often used interchangeably.

[146] Sen. Rpt. 99-313 at 694 (May 29, 1986); H. R.. Rpt. 99-426 at 177 (Dec. 7, 1985).

[147] I.R.C. § 41(a). The R&D credit is actually is the sum of (1) 20 percent of the excess (if any) of "qualified research expenses" over a base amount (defined in section 41(c)), (2) 20 percent of "basic research payments" (as defined in section 41(e)), and (3) 20 percent of the taxpayer's share of the energy research expenses of an "energy research consortium." *Id.*

reduce its deduction of Section 174 R&E expenditures by the amount of the credit claimed.[148]

Since it was first enacted in 1981, the R&D credit has never been a permanent fixture of the Code, as Congress has always set an expiration date on the credit's availability. While the R&D credit has expired on several occasions, Congress has typically retroactively extended it, although on one occasion Congress let the credit expire for a 12-month period.[149] At the time this Chapter is written, it is not apparent whether Congress will make the credit permanent, continue to extend it on a year-to-year basis, or simply let it expire. Furthermore, Congress has continually tinkered with the R&D credit in the past and may substantially modify it in the future (e.g., to make it simpler or more complex, to make broader or narrower, or to provide for additional special exceptions, etc.). Therefore, this Chapter will not delve too deeply into the R&D credit, especially computational issues. Instead, because the R&D credit applies to "qualified research," this Chapter focuses on how "qualified research" for the R&D credit compares to section 174 R&E expenditures.

One component of the R&D credit applies to incremental "qualified research expenses."[150] A taxpayer's "qualified research expenses" include "in-house research expenses" (i.e., wages, supplies, and certain charges for the research use of computers and laboratory equipment) and 65 percent of "contract research expenses" (i.e., certain amounts paid to research firms, universities, etc.).[151] The term "qualified research expenses" incorporates by

---

[148] I.R.C. § 280C(c). Alternatively, a taxpayer may elect to claim a reduced credit and deduct the full amount of the R&E expenditures. I.R.C. § 280C(c)(3).

[149] For example, when Congress passed the Tax Relief and Health Care Act of 2006, the R&D credit was set to expire after December 31, 2007. *See* Tax Relief and Health Care Act of 2006, Pub. L. No. 109-432, § 104(a)(1), 120 Stat. 2922, 2934 (2006). In October 2008, Congress passed the Tax Extenders and Alternative Minimum Tax Relief Act of 2008, which retroactively extended the credit from January 1, 2008 through December 31, 2009. *See* Tax Extenders and Alternative Minimum Tax Relief Act of 2008, Pub. L. No. 110-343, § 301(a)(1), 122 Stat. 3765, 3865 (2008). The R&D credit expired from July 1, 1995 to June 30, 1996. *See* Omnibus Budget Reconciliation Act of 1993, Pub. L. No. 103-66, § 13111(a), 107 Stat. 312, 420 (1993) (setting a June 30, 1995 expiration date on the R&D credit); Small Business Job Protection Act of 1996, Pub. L. No. 104-188, § 1204, 110 Stat. 1755, 1773 (1986) (extending R&D credit from July 1, 1996 to May 31, 1997, but not making it retroactive to July 1, 1995). In December 2010, Congress retroactively extended the credit through December 31, 2011. *See* Tax Relief, Unemployment Insurance Reauthorization and Job Creation Act of 2010, Pub. L. No. 111-312, § 731(a), 124 Stat. 3296, 3317 (2010).

[150] I.R.C. § 41(a)(1).

[151] I.R.C. § 41(b).

reference the definition of "qualified research" in section 41(d) and consists of the following three requirements:

(1) the research expenses must qualify as section 174 R&E expenditures;

(2) the research must be undertaken for the purpose of *discovering information that is technological in nature* that is intended to be useful in the development of a new or improved business component of the taxpayer (the "discovery" requirement); and

(3) substantially all of the research activities of must be a *process of experimentation* relating to a new or improved function, performance, reliability, or quality (the "process of experimentation" requirement).[152]

In other words, the activities encompassed by the term "qualified research" include section 174 R&E expenditures as further restricted by the "discovery" and "process of experimentation" requirements of section 41(d). Therefore, the expenses giving rise to the R&D credit must be section 174 R&E expenditures, but not all section 174 R&E expenditures will qualify for the R&D credit (whether this is of any practical significance is discussed below). A taxpayer seeking to utilize the R&D credit must first test its expenses under section 174, and if section 174 is satisfied, the taxpayer must then satisfy the "discovery" and "process of experimentation" requirements.

2.3[1] The "Discovery" Requirement

The interpretation of the discovery requirement has been a source of considerable controversy. At issue is whether the discovery requirement adds an additional test to the section 174 requirements or whether it simply restates them. At one point, Treasury issued regulations (now suspended) that created a "discovery test" that required a taxpayer to undertake research "to obtain knowledge that exceeds, expands, or refines the common knowledge of skilled professionals in a particular field of science or engineering."[153] This discovery test went beyond what section 174 requires. Some courts adopted a similar discovery test.[154]

---

[152] I.R.C. § 41(d).

[153] Treasury issued these regulations as "final" regulations in January 2001, but they were later suspended. *See* Notice 2001-19, 2001-10 I.R.B. 784. The quoted material is found in the January 2001 suspended regulations at Treas. Reg. § 1.41-4(a)(3) (suspended).

[154] *See e.g. United Stationers v. Commissioner*, 163 F.3d 440 (7th Cir. 1998); *Norwest Corp. v. Commissioner*, 110 T.C. 454 (1998).

At first blush, it would seem that Congress intended a discovery test that added to the section 174 requirements. After all, why would Congress require the research to qualify under section 174 *and* impose a discovery requirement that is exactly the same as the section 174 requirements? In other words, a discovery requirement that merely restates the section 174 requirements would seem to make it superfluous. Nevertheless, several commentators argued the discovery test of the R&D credit added nothing to the section 174 requirements. These commentators noted that the discovery requirement was added to the R&D credit prior to issuance of regulations under section 174 that clarified that R&E expenditures must be "intended to discover information that would eliminate the uncertainty concerning the development or improvement of a product" (i.e., the uncertainty test, discussed above).[155] In other words, the section 174 regulations were clarified to bring R&E expenditures in line with the discovery requirement of the R&D credit. As such, these commentators argued that the discovery requirement of the R&D credit is the same as the uncertainty test under section 174. Additionally, many commentators criticized the "discovery test" as too administratively burdensome because it required complex factual determinations of what is "common knowledge" and who is a "skilled professional."[156]

Treasury was ultimately persuaded by these criticisms and suspended the regulations that imposed a discovery test requiring taxpayers to expand upon the common knowledge of skilled professionals.[157] Instead, Treasury determined that the discovery requirement does not create a test separate and distinct from the section 174 requirements.[158] Accordingly, current regulations adopt the uncertainty test of section 174 by stating that the R&D credit discovery requirement is satisfied if the taxpayer undertakes research "to eliminate uncertainty concerning the development or improvement of a business component."[159] Taxpayers are no longer required to undertake research that exceeds, expands, or refines the common knowledge of skilled professionals.[160] The current regulations further state that

---

[155] *See* 66 Fed. Reg. 66362, 66363. The discovery requirement was added to section 41 in 1986. *See* Tax Reform Act of 1986, Pub. L. No. 99-514, § 231(b), 100 Stat. 2085 (1986). The "uncertainty test" was added to the section 174 regulations in 1994. *See* 59 Fed. Reg. 50159 (promulgating the "uncertainty test" of section 174 in Treas. Reg. § 1.174-2(a)(1)).

[156] *See* 66 Fed. Reg. 280, 283.

[157] 66 Fed. Reg. 66362 (replacing suspended regulations issued in January 2001 with new proposed regulations in December 2001).

[158] *See* 66 Fed. Reg. 66362, 66363.

[159] Treas. Reg. § 1.41-4(a)(3)(i).

[160] Treas. Reg. § 1.41-4(a)(3)(ii).

"information is technological in nature if the process of experimentation used to discover such information fundamentally relies on principles of the physical or biological sciences, engineering, or computer science."[161] Taxpayers may rely upon a "patent safe harbor" whereby issuance of a patent "is conclusive evidence that a taxpayer has discovered information that is technological in nature that is intended to eliminate uncertainty concerning the development or improvement of a business component."[162]

2.3[2] The "Process of Experimentation" Requirement

Like the "discovery" requirement, the "process of experimentation" requirement has also been a source of controversy. As is the case with the discovery requirement, the issue is whether the process of experimentation requirement adds to the section 174 requirements or merely restates them. As discussed above, a taxpayer's research can qualify under section 174 even if the taxpayer is confident its research objectives can be achieved, provided there is uncertainty as to the capability or method. Treasury issued regulations (now suspended) stating that "[a] process of experimentation does not include the evaluation of alternatives to establish the appropriate design of a business component, if the capability and method for developing or improving the business component are not uncertain."[163] Essentially, Treasury took the position that the process of experimentation requirement meant that the feasibility of the research had to be in doubt at the outset. Treasury later abandoned this view, yet maintained that the process of experimentation requirement adds to the section 174 requirements. In the preamble of new regulations addressing the process of experimentation requirement, Treasury stated:

> Treasury and the IRS continue to believe that the requirements for a process of experimentation under section 41 are more stringent than the requirements for research and development in the experimental or laboratory sense under § 1.174-2(a)(1) [i.e., the "uncertainty" test]. However, Treasury and the IRS have determined that a process of experimentation may exist if

---

[161] Treas. Reg. § 1.41-4(a)(4).

[162] Treas. Reg. § 1.41-4(a)(3)(iii). Issuance of a patent is not a precondition for credit eligibility. *Id.* Not all research succeeds in achieving its objective and not all research intended to discover technical information results in a patent. Therefore, the absence of a patent has no bearing on credit eligibility. *Id.*

[163] Treasury issued these regulations as "final" regulations in January 2001, but they were later suspended. *See* Notice 2001-19, 2001-10 I.R.B. 784. The quoted material is found in the January 2001 suspended regulations at Treas. Reg. § 1.41-4(a)(5)(i) (suspended).

> a taxpayer performs research to establish the appropriate design of a business component when the capability and method for developing or improving the business component are not uncertain. . . . [But] not all research to arrive at the appropriate design of a business component will be credit eligible.[164]

Treasury further clarified that "merely demonstrating that uncertainty has been eliminated (e.g., the achievement of the appropriate design of a business component when such design was uncertain as of the beginning of the taxpayer's activities) is insufficient to satisfy the process of experimentation requirement."[165] The taxpayer must also (1) identify one or more alternatives to eliminate the uncertainty and (2) identify a process of evaluating the alternatives (e.g., modeling, simulation, or a systematic trial and error methodology).[166]

Treasury's insistence that the requirement to test and evaluate one or more alternatives makes R&D credit eligibility more stringent than section 174 may have little practical significance. After all, can a taxpayer engage in research to eliminate uncertainty without testing and evaluating one or more alternatives? The uncertainty test of section 174 is the demarcation point between the research and development stage on the one hand and the manufacturing and marketing stage on the other. If a taxpayer is certain how its research will turn out and therefore need not test and evaluate one or more alternatives, the taxpayer is probably already in the manufacturing stage of the process. In that case, the taxpayer's expenses at that point are not section 174 R&E expenditures. While Treasury claims that not all section 174 R&E expenditures are "qualified research" for R&D credit purposes, its regulations are lacking in clear examples of situations where this would occur.

2.3[3] Activities Specifically Excluded from "Qualified Research"

Section 41(d)(4) lists several activities that are excluded from "qualified research" for purposes of the R&D credit, including research relating to:

(1) activities commencing after commercial production;
(2) the adoption or duplication of an existing business component;

---

[164] 66 Fed. Reg. 66362, 66364. *See also* Treas. Reg. § 1.41-4(a)(5)(i).

[165] 69 Fed. Reg. 22, 24.

[166] Treas. Reg. § 1.41-4(a)(5)(i). The "substantially all" requirement is satisfied only if 80 percent or more of a taxpayer's research activities, measured on a cost or other consistently applied reasonable basis constitute elements of a process of experimentation. Treas. Reg. § 1.41-4(a)(6).

(3) ordinary tests and surveys relating to efficiency or marketing;
(4) the development of certain computer software for internal use;
(5) activities conducted outside the U.S., its possessions, or Puerto Rico;
(6) the social sciences, arts, or humanities; and
(7) activities funded by another person or government entity.[167]

2.3[3][a] Internal-use Computer Software

The exception for the development of computer software deserves special consideration because it has also been a source of controversy. Treasury issued proposed regulations on internal-use computer software in 2001 but has yet to finalize them.[168] In the meantime, taxpayers may rely on the proposed regulations.[169]

The proposed regulations presume that all software is "internal-use," unless the taxpayer develops it to be commercially sold, leased, licensed, or otherwise marketed for separately stated consideration to unrelated third parties.[170] Additionally, internal-use software does not include a new or improved package of computer software and hardware that the taxpayer develops as a single product.[171]

2.3[3][b] "High Threshold of Innovation" Test

The development of internal-use software is *not per se* ineligible for the R&D credit. Generally, the development of internal-use software is qualified research if it satisfies both the general requirements for credit eligibility under section 41 and an additional, three-part

---

[167] I.R.C. § 41(d)(4).

[168] 66 Fed. Reg. 66632 (proposed regulations issued December 2001). Treasury issued final regulations on internal-use computer software in January 2001, but later suspended them. *See* 66 Fed. Reg. 280 (suspended by Notice 2001-19, 2001-10 I.R.B. 784). Treasury finalized regulations on "qualified research" in January 2004 without addressing internal use computer software. *See* 69 Fed. Reg. 22. Treasury noted that it would issue finalized regulations on internal-use computer software at a later date. *See* 69 Fed. Reg. 43.

[169] 69 Fed. Reg. 43, 47. Treasury stated that taxpayers may also rely upon the suspended regulations issued in January 2001. The suspended regulations create a higher threshold for taxpayers to satisfy. Thus, taxpayers meeting the proposed regulations will likely satisfy the suspended regulations. To reduce confusion, only the proposed regulations on internal-use computer software are addressed in this chapter.

[170] Prop. Reg. § 1.41-4(c)(6)(iv) (December 2001 proposed regulations).

[171] Prop. Reg. § 1.41-4(c)(6)(iii) (December 2001 proposed regulations).

"high threshold of innovation" test. The "high threshold of innovation" test generally requires that:

(1) the internal-use software be innovative;

(2) the development of the internal-use software involve significant economic risk; and

(3) the internal-use software not be commercially available.[172]

Software is "innovative" if it "is intended to be unique or novel and is intended to differ in a significant and inventive way from prior software implementations or methods."[173] Software involves "significant economic risk" if the taxpayer "commits substantial resources to the development and there is substantial uncertainty, because of technical risk, that such resources would be recovered within a reasonable period."[174] The high threshold of innovation test, however, does not apply to the development of software (1) for use in conducting qualified research, (2) for use in a production process, and (3) for use in providing computer services to customers.[175]

> **Problem 2.9**: Reconsider the facts of **Problem 2.8**. Would the taxpayer's development of sophisticated digital effects software be "qualified research" for purposes of the R&D credit?

2.4 Cost Recovery of Capitalized Amounts

A taxpayer must capitalize the creation costs of intellectual property that cannot be currently deducted under section 162 (e.g., by way of a simplifying convention of the section 263 regulations) or section 174. As explained in Chapter 1, although capital expenditures are not immediately deductible, they are *eventually* deductible. Therefore, capitalization of expenditures really has to do with *timing* deductions.

Based on the matching principle, capitalized amounts that provide benefits over a determinable life (i.e., because the benefits are exhausted or become obsolete) ought to be written off over that determinable life. In that way, the taxpayer can properly match deduction of its expenses to the income those expenses help to produce. The deduction of

[172] Prop. Reg. § 1.41-4(c)(6)(vi) (December 2001 proposed regulations).

[173] Prop. Reg. § 1.41-4(c)(6)(iv)(A) (December 2001 proposed regulations).

[174] Prop. Reg. § 1.41-4(c)(6)(iv)(B) (December 2001 proposed regulations).

[175] Prop. Reg. § 1.41-4(c)(6)(ii) (December 2001 proposed regulations).

capital expenditures over time to reflect exhaustion or obsolescence is referred to as *amortization* or *depreciation*. Amortization and depreciation are similar concepts. The Code, regulations, and courts sometimes use the terms interchangeably. But for the most part, amortization refers to the deduction for the decline in value due to obsolescence or exhaustion of *intangible* assets, while depreciation is the counterpart for *tangible* assets.

The amortization of intangibles is governed primarily by sections 167 and 197. Section 197, to the extent applicable, trumps section 167, so a taxpayer should first check if section 197 applies.[176] Section 197 provides that the capitalized costs of an "amortizable section 197 intangible" may be amortized and deducted ratably over a 15-year period beginning with the month in which it was acquired.[177]

While many *acquired* intangibles are "amortizable section 197 intangibles" (as discussed in detail in Chapter 3), most *self-created* intangibles are not. In general, section 197 specifically excludes a self-created intangible from the definition of an "amortizable section 197 intangible."[178] A self-created intangible generally means an intangible created by the taxpayer that is not created in connection with the acquisition of a trade or business (those intangibles created in connection with a business acquisition are really "acquired"). An important exception for self-created intangibles applies to franchises, trademarks, or trade names created by the taxpayer.[179] Thus, self-created trademarks and trade names are "amortizable section 197 intangibles" subject to 15-year amortization. Other types of self-created intellectual property, such as patents, trade secrets, computer software, and copyrights are not "amortizable section 197 intangibles."

> **Problem 2.10**: In **Problem 2.3** above, Taxpayer paid $20,000 to outside counsel for trademark screening and registering a trademark for "Procore," a new drug that Taxpayer developed. Assume Taxpayer paid and incurred the $20,000 in March 2011 and began using the "Procore" trademark immediately thereafter. What are the tax consequences to the taxpayer?

---

[176] I.R.C. § 197(b).

[177] I.R.C. § 197(a). The intangible must be held in connection with a trade or business or an investment activity. I.R.C. § 197(c)(1)(B). Otherwise, the cost of the intangible would be a nondeductible personal expense.

[178] I.R.C. § 197(c)(2); Treas. Reg. § 1.197-2(d)(2)(i).

[179] I.R.C. § 197(c)(2)(A); Treas. Reg. § 1.197-2(d)(2)(iii)(A).

If section 197 is not applicable, the taxpayer must look to section 167 or an administrative pronouncement to amortize capitalized costs of a created intangible. Section 167 provides for amortization deductions for the exhaustion, wear, tear, and obsolescence of property used in a trade or business or for the production of income.[180] Treasury regulations provide as follows:

> If an intangible asset is known from experience or other factors to be of use in the business or in the production of income for only a limited period, the length of which can be estimated with reasonable accuracy, such an intangible asset may be the subject of a depreciation allowance. Examples are patents and copyrights. An intangible asset, the useful life of which is not limited, is not subject to the allowance for depreciation. No allowance will be permitted merely because, in the unsupported opinion of the taxpayer, the intangible asset has a limited useful life. No deduction for depreciation is allowable with respect to goodwill.[181]

Therefore, a taxpayer may amortize capitalized costs of a created intangible over its determinable useful life. In certain cases, a taxpayer can apply a 15-year amortization "safe-harbor" rule.[182] Section 167 and the regulations provide for alternative methods of amortization, including the "straight-line method," the "income forecast method," and the "variable contingent payment method" – all of which are discussed in detail in Chapter 3. For those intangible assets that are non-amortizable (i.e., because they do not exhaust or have a determinable useful life, such as stock and equity interests in businesses), the taxpayer writes off the capitalized amount by offsetting its adjusted basis against the amount realized upon sale or other disposition.

2.5 Materials for Chapter 2

AGRO SCIENCE COMPANY v. COMMISSIONER

United States Tax Court

58 T.C.M. (CCH) 1093 (1989)

[For the 1982 and 1983 taxable years, the Service disallowed Section 174 deductions taken by Argo Science Company and two other partnerships (collectively the "Partnerships").

---

[180] I.R.C. § 167(a).

[181] Treas. Reg. § 1.167(a)-3(a).

[182] Treas. Reg. § 1.167(a)-3(b).

Each of the Partnerships] were organized to engage in research and development activities in connection with the development, production, licensing, and marketing of diagnostic health care products utilizing monoclonal antibody conjugates. To accomplish these purposes, [the Partnerships] entered into research and development agreements with [a company called "Coral"].

In 1982 Mr. Allen Campbell formed Coral under the laws of Brazil. . . . Campbell formed Coral to perform the laboratory work needed to make monoclonal antibody conjugates for the Partnerships. Coral had limited laboratory facilities and offices in Sao Paulo, Brazil. No meaningful research or development activities for the Partnerships took place in the Sao Paulo offices. The laboratory work that is the subject of this litigation was performed in Coral's laboratory facilities in Cambridge, England. The staff and equipment in Cambridge were competent and adequate to perform the monoclonal antibody research contracted for by the Partnerships. The laboratory included animal facilities, cell culture facilities, bacterial facilities, immunology facilities, microbiology facilities, and facilities for the purification of antibodies.

Dr. Fred Stark was employed by Coral to set up and manage the Coral laboratory. He had been Assistant Chief of Medicine and Chief of Infectious Disease Service at Letterman Army Medical Center, Associate Clinical Professor of Medicine at the University of California, and a Fellow in Infectious Diseases and Immunology at Walter Reed General Hospital. The full-time researchers at the Coral laboratory in Cambridge included among others, Bruce Wright, who had worked as senior research officer in charge of the tissue culture facilities of Dr. Milstein who had been awarded a Nobel Prize for the discovery of monoclonal antibodies. By late 1984, Coral employed approximately 100 people. Coral sold approximately 170 monoclonal antibody production projects to United States investment groups and succeeded in producing monoclonal antibody conjugates for approximately 70 percent of the projects undertaken.

An antibody is a disease fighting component found in the body. When a human's body is invaded by a pathogen (e.g., a bacterium or virus), the body normally responds by making a variety of antibodies to destroy the invading organism by binding to the antigens of the organism. Each monoclonal antibody developed by Coral was a laboratory copy of an antibody designed to bind with a single antigen of an organism.

The source of antibodies is B-lymphocytes ("B-cells"). B-cells cannot grow in culture; so to produce a monoclonal antibody, a B-cell producing a particular antibody is fused with a cancer cell (a myeloma). The cancer cell confers the ability to grow permanently in cell culture and to support unlimited antibody production. The B-cell contributes gene coding for the specific antigen to which the antibodies will react. The fused B-cell and cancer cell is called a "hybridoma."

In general, the steps of Coral's production of monoclonal antibodies were as follows: (1) obtain a purified antigen, a potentially toxic substance; (2) inject the purified antigen into a laboratory mouse to invoke an immune response in the mouse (usually through the release of B-cells into the blood) directed to a particular antigen; (3) sacrifice the mouse and fuse the sacrificed mouse's antibody-producing cells with a cancer cell to form the hybridomas; (4) place the resulting hybridomas in a cell culture medium for growth or cloning; and (5) test the resulting clones for production of the desired antibody. Each antibody in a mouse has several subclasses of antibody. Coral produced a single subclass of each monoclonal antibody.

Coral would then conjugate the monoclonal antibody. "Conjugation" of a monoclonal antibody refers to the process of coupling the antibody with a substance which allows the antibody to produce a "signal." A monoclonal antibody conjugate is a monoclonal antibody linked to a label or tag, such as an enzyme, capable of providing a signal (such as a simple color change) which indicates a particular antigen/antibody reaction. The Partnerships hoped that a conjugated monoclonal antibody particular to a specific antigen would have potential usefulness (either alone or in combination with other antibodies) in connection with human or animal diagnostics, epidemiology, serological classification or identification, animal therapeutics, and general medical and scientific research.

Coral maintained laboratory notebooks for each monoclonal antibody project at issue. The lab books were divided into sections and contained blank forms to fill in with the project results. The lab books were not complete. Most of the forms were not filled in. Some sections contained only pages of computer printouts with no explanation.

* * *

In December 1982 the Partnerships entered into . . . research and development agreements with Coral. . . . Pursuant to the agreements, Coral was to diligently conduct for 12 months or until completion of the project, whichever first occurred, the "research and experimentation" necessary for the development of a particular monoclonal antibody conjugate. The agreements did not require that Coral produce more than one subclass of the monoclonal antibody or specify which subclass of monoclonal antibody Coral would produce. Coral at its option could extend the term of the agreement with each partnership for two additional 12-month periods.

The research agreement between [the first of the three Partnerships] and Coral describes the product to be developed by Coral as:

> A conjugate of Alkaline phosphatase and a monoclonal antibody which is produced by a single mouse/mouse hybrid cell line and which combines specifically in an immunological manner with the characteristic antigen of Escherichia coli K99.

* * *

The research agreement between [the second of the three Partnerships] and Coral describes the product to be developed by Coral as:

> A conjugate of Alkaline phosphatase and a monoclonal antibody which is produced by a single mouse/mouse hybrid cell line and which combines specifically in an immunological manner with the characteristic antigen of Shigella K7.

Coral subsequently redesignated the target antigen as Shigella boydii OC7, in a memorandum dated December 2, 1983. . . .

The research agreement between [the third of the three Partnerships] and Coral describes the product to be developed by Coral as:

> A conjugate of Alkaline phosphatase and a monoclonal antibody which is produced by a single mouse/mouse hybrid cell line and which combines specifically in an immunological manner with the characteristic antigen of Pseudomonas aeruginosa 6.

* * *

[By] January 1988. . . . [a]lthough provisional patent applications were filed by [the "Partnerships"] covering the research Coral had done for the Partnerships, no patents were granted.

On May 20, 1985, Coral successfully completed for [the first of the three Patnerships] development of a conjugate of alkaline phosphatase and a monoclonal antibody which combines in an immunological manner with Shigella boydii OC7. On November 27, 1985, Coral successfully completed for [the second of the three Partnerships] the development of a conjugate of alkaline phosphatase and a monoclonal antibody which combines in an immunological manner with Escherichia coli K-99. On November 27, 1985, Coral successfully completed for [the third of the three Partnerships] the development of a conjugate of alkaline phosphatase and monoclonal antibody which combines in a immunological manner with Pseudomonas aeruginosa 6.

The Coral projects had the stated goal of using monoclonal antibody conjugates to develop more rapid and accurate identification and diagnosis of disease in clinical laboratories, hospitals, and research laboratories, and in doctors' offices. . . .

[The Partnerships] at all times relevant maintained their books and records and filed their Federal income tax returns on the basis of a calendar year using the accrual method of accounting. The Partnerships elected to treat research and development expenditures as expenses not chargeable to capital accounts pursuant to section 174.

* * *

OPINION

[A portion of the Opinion describes how the Partnerships were formed as tax shelters. Although the Partnerships paid some cash to Coral under their respective agreements, a sizable portion of the amounts to be paid to Coral were in the form of promissory notes payable in Brazilian currency. The interest rates on the notes were unreasonably low given the hyperinflation of Brazilian currency at that time. At the time the notes were signed, the face amounts of the notes in Brazilian currency could be exchanged into a relatively high amount of U.S. dollars. And the Partnerships sought deductions based on these relatively high amounts of liabilities stated in U.S. dollars. But the Partnerships could reasonably expect to repay the notes with hyper inflated Brazilian currency that would have a nominal value in U.S. dollars. The court held that the notes lacked economic substance and denied any deductions relating to liabilities from these notes.]

* * *

Next we consider whether petitioners are entitled to any deduction for R&E expenditures pursuant to section 174 in connection with the development of monoclonal antibody conjugates by Coral on behalf of the Partnerships. Section 174(a)(1) provides that research or experimental expenditures paid or incurred during the taxable year in connection with a taxpayer's trade or business may at the taxpayer's election be deducted currently rather than capitalized. The term "research or experimental expenditures" is defined in the regulations as

> expenditures incurred in connection with the taxpayer's trade or business which represent research and development costs in the experimental or laboratory sense. The term includes generally all such costs incident to the development of an experimental or pilot model, a plant process, a product, a formula, an invention, or similar property, and the improvement of already existing property of the type mentioned. * * * [Sec. 1.174-2(a)(1), Income Tax Regs.]

We have found this definition to be "consistent with the intent of the statute to limit deductions to those expenditures of an investigative nature expended in developing the concept of a model or product." (Emphasis omitted.) *Mayrath v. Commissioner,* 41 T.C. 582, 590 (1964), affd. 357 F.2d 209 (5th Cir. 1966).

Section 174 requires that the taxpayer's expenditure is for *research* or for *experimental* purposes. Scientific research and development costs for purposes of section 174 includes an attempt to discover or develop a product, or to develop a new technique or procedure. The goal of the research must be scientifically reasonable, but research is more than repeating what has already been done. It requires some element of experimentation.

Petitioner presented one expert witness at trial to testify about the scientific aspects of the transactions, Henry D. Isenberg, Ph.D. Dr. Isenberg has a Ph.D. degree in Microbiology. He is a microbiologist and the Chief of the Division of Microbiology at Long Island Jewish Medical Center. He is also a clinical professor in Medical Microbiology and Immunology at the University of South Florida College of Medicine. Dr. Isenberg is a member and officer of many professional societies and has received many honors in microbiology. He has been the editor of a variety of medical journals and has published numerous articles on topics related to microbiology and health. His field of concentration is epidemiology.

Respondent presented two expert witnesses at trial with regard to the scientific aspects of the transactions, Michael V. Norgard, Ph.D., and Milton R. Tam, Ph.D. Dr. Norgard has a Ph.D.

degree in Microbiology and is an Associate Professor of Microbiology at the University of Texas, Southwestern Medical Center at Dallas. He runs a microbiology research program and teaches microbiology and infectious diseases. Dr. Norgard is a member of scientific societies related to microbiology and disease, has lectured on microbiology, and has received many honors in his area of expertise. Dr. Norgard has published numerous articles on microbiology, including several articles on E. coli.

Dr. Tam has a Ph.D. degree in Immunology. He is a Program Manager for Bacteriology and a Senior Scientist with Genetic Systems Corp. He has published many articles on immunology and monoclonal antibodies. At Genetic Systems Corp., he manages, directs, and supervises programs associated with the development of monoclonal antibodies, and their use for immunological assays and diagnostic tests.

Roger H. Kennett, Ph.D., was a neutral, court-appointed expert witness. Dr. Kennett has a Ph.D. degree in Biochemical Sciences from Princeton University and is an Associate Professor of Human Genetics at the University of Pennsylvania School of Medicine. Dr. Kennett has published extensively, including three books and many articles about monoclonal antibodies.

All of the experts were very well-qualified in their respective specialties. Petitioner's expert, Dr. Isenberg, testified to the importance of the monoclonal antibody production in epidemiology, the transfer of disease. Dr. Isenberg is a leading authority on the subject of epidemiology. He does not, however, have the expertise to comment on the particular scientific processes at issue in this case. We, therefore, do not give much weight to Dr. Isenberg's testimony on monoclonal antibodies. We relied heavily on the opinions of Drs. Kennett, Norgard, and Tam to analyze the scientific aspects of the monoclonal antibody conjugate production.

We hold that Coral's development of monoclonal antibody conjugates on behalf of [the Partnerships] does not qualify as "research or experimental expenditures" as defined in section 1.174-2(a)(1), Income Tax Regs. Producing the monoclonal antibody conjugates was clearly scientific work. The projects required a laboratory and trained scientists and technicians. The Coral laboratory in Cambridge was adequate, and the Coral staff in Cambridge was qualified for producing the monoclonal antibody conjugates. The services Coral performed, however, were not investigative in nature. Rather, as Dr. Kennett's testimony reveals, the projects undertaken by Coral were routine. Our discussion at trial was as follows:

> *THE COURT*: If somebody had come to you in 1982 and said, I would like you to produce for me what is asked for in the research contracts here for Shigella, Pseudomonas and E. coli * * * what would you have said about the likelihood of being able to produce the monoclonal antibody?
>
> * * *
>
> *THE WITNESS*: There are few sure things in research, but this is so sure that I could say that we can do it. I can almost assure them that we would be able to do it within a year. And we will probably get it done much sooner than that.

The contracts here in question did not require Coral to invent or to develop the concept or design of any product. These contracts rather were merely production contracts under which Coral agreed to manufacture or produce certain monoclonal antibody conjugates. *Mayrath v. Commissioner, supra.* Dr. Kennett and Dr. Tam believed that the monoclonal antibodies sold as projects to investors were those that were easy to produce, rather than those that could be useful for any of the Partnerships' hoped-for purposes, such as diagnostics.

The primary stated purpose for producing the monoclonal antibody conjugates was for diagnostics. A panel of the monoclonals was proposed for use in a kit to test for the presence of a particular organism in urine, blood, or stool samples. A simple color change would indicate that the organism was present. Campbell testified that a large number of monoclonal antibodies was needed for this purpose.

Dr. Kennett and Dr. Tam testified, however, that the Coral antigens were not obviously useful for diagnostics. Even if the monoclonal antibodies selected were appropriate, Dr. Tam testified that the ability to test for a specific antigen of the organism does not help the physician prescribe treatment for a patient because the serotype (the antigen pattern of the organism) does not determine the antibiotic susceptibility of a particular bacterium. The physician needs to know only that the organism is, for example, E. coli. When the physician suspects an E. coli infection, he will prescribe initially an antibiotic that he believes to be active against a broad group of organisms, depending on the patient's condition and using his best guess. He will then determine the actual antibiotic susceptibility of that organism by isolating it, growing it on media, and testing it with individual antibiotics to determine to which antibiotic it is sensitive. Based on the results of this testing, which takes 24 to 48 hours, the physician will alter the initial antibiotic prescribed if necessary.

Another problem with the Coral approach is that to test for the presence of one of the organisms, each antigen of that organism must be tested for. E. coli has more than 160 "O" antigens, more than 50 "H" antigens, and more than 100 "K" antigens. Shigella boydii has 15 antigens and Pseudomonas aeruginosa has 17 antigens. To test for the presence of the organism, all of the monoclonal antibodies against each antigen of the organism would have to be grouped into one kit. Dr. Tam and Dr. Kennett both testified that if more than four or five antibodies are grouped in one solution, the antibodies begin to interfere with each other, affecting the outcome of the test. Of course, each antigen could be tested for separately. In the case of E. coli, however, that would involve 160 different tests just to cover the "O" antigens, which would be both time-consuming and costly. Coral, therefore, was not "researching" to develop a practical commercial test kit.

Even if it was feasible to combine the monoclonals for all antigens of each organism, Coral could not have done so because only some of the antigens for each organism had been sold as projects to investors. Because monoclonals are antigen specific, using only a single monoclonal as the Partnership had planned could have been misleading. A negative report would indicate the absence of that particular antigen while the bacterium with other antigens was present. In short, Coral's research and development plans could not under any circumstances have created a useful testing kit for any of the organisms at issue.

Dr. Tam believed that a viable approach to using monoclonal antibodies for diagnostics would be to search for a single monoclonal antibody that reacts to all antigens or serotypes of the target pathogen. Coral, however, was only locating monoclonal antibodies against each single antigen of the organism. Coral was not researching to find a monoclonal antibody suitable for diagnostics. Instead, Coral was merely producing monoclonal antibodies against single antigens that were not particularly important.

Another weakness in Coral's approach was that its contracts did not specify for what use the monoclonal antibody was being produced. As a result, Coral's production of monoclonals was necessarily incomplete in every project. Coral produced only one of the several subclasses of antibody in a mouse. Some subclasses of the antibodies are more suited to particular types of assays or tests. For example, one subclass would be suitable for a blood test, another for a urine test. Dr. Kennett testified that because Coral did not know what the antibodies would be used for, it should have provided several classes of the antibodies. Coral in fact produced only a single subclass of each monoclonal antibody for each antigen.

Coral kept laboratory notebooks for each of the projects at issue. The state of Coral's lab books, however, evidences the lack of serious research in these cases. A scientist keeps a lab book so that another scientist can follow the steps taken and reproduce the work or experiment. In other words, another scientist should be able to follow the trail laid out in the lab book and duplicate the experiment. The lab books in this case were sloppy and casual, both in the way they were assembled and in the way the information was recorded. The lab books were divided into sections and contained forms to fill in with the results of Coral's efforts to produce monoclonal antibodies. Although the forms if filled in would have provided a lot of necessary information, most of the forms were not filled in. Some sections contained only pages of computer printouts with no explanation.

From the condition of the lab books, we conclude that Coral's investigations were not organized or well supervised. Coral produced the monoclonal antibodies in a haphazard manner without adequate scientific technique. Coral's substandard effort in keeping the lab books reinforces our view that producing the monoclonal antibody conjugates did not involve "research or experimental expenditures" within the meaning of section 174.

* * *

Decisions will be entered for the respondent.

UNIVERSAL RESEARCH AND DEVELOPMENT PARTNERSHIP NO. 1 v. COMMISSIONER

United States Tax Court

62 T.C.M. (CCH) 661 (1991)

[R]espondent determined adjustments to the 1982, 1983, and 1984 partnership returns of Universal Research and Development Partnership No. 1 (hereinafter Universal No. 1). . . .

[W]e must decide . . . whether Universal No. 1 incurred research and development expenses pursuant to section 174.

FINDINGS OF FACT

* * *

Universal No. 1 [was] formed effective December 1, 1982 . . . to "engage in research, experimentation, and development work" and to "manufacture, sell, distribute, put into use, lease, license, and exploit such technology resulting therefrom." Kenneth A. Duncan (Duncan), a business and tax attorney, was [Universal No. 1's] initial partner and managing agent.

In the spring of 1982, Duncan met Richard McDonald (McDonald) while soliciting advice concerning what turned out to be unsuccessful commodities futures trading activities. McDonald was a nonworking certified public accountant who, like Duncan, had held a wide variety of investments in various enterprises. During the course of their contact, McDonald told Duncan about a research and development (R&D) company he was forming called Omega.

In August 1982, McDonald incorporated Omega "to raise funds for research and development in various fields of development" using a "foreign currency incentive technique." Omega developed a list of R&D projects that it had determined were feasible. Omega then offered for sale investment interests in each of these projects at a set fee and offered to assist in forming Texas partnerships through which to make the investments. The development fee was payable one-eighth in cash and seven-eighths in a promissory note payable in U.S. dollars or Brazilian cruzeiros, at the option of the debtor, 7 to 10 years after the date on which the note was executed.[5]

Universal No. 1

McDonald and Duncan agreed in late September 1982 that Duncan was to form a Louisiana general partnership, rather than a Texas partnership, to invest in and acquire technology from Omega. From October through December 1982 they negotiated the terms of an R&D agreement and a technology transfer agreement between Omega and what became Universal No. 1.

On McDonald's advice, Duncan selected a pattern recognition project, designated Project A-40 (A-40), to automatically identify and monitor ingress and egress from large parking facilities. Omega set a research fee of $3,000,000 for A-40, with $375,000 of that amount payable in cash and the balance in the form of a promissory note. . . .

* * *

---

[5] McDonald incorporated Omega after reviewing a prospectus on Coral Sociedade Brasileira de Pesquisas e Desenvolvimento Ltda. (Coral). For a more complete description of Coral see *Agro Science Co. v. Commissioner,* T.C. Memo 1989-687, *affd.* 934 F.2d 573 (5th Cir. 1991).

Project A-40

Of the $375,000 cash paid to Omega by Universal No. 1, $75,000 of this amount was paid to Duncan for setting up the contract between them. On December 31, 1982, Omega entered into an R&D subcontract with Alpha Research and Development Corporation (Alpha). Alpha agreed to provide R&D services with respect to A-40 in exchange for $225,000 cash and four additional payments . . . to be made between December 30, 1989, and December 30, 1992. Alpha then entered into an R&D subcontract with R. A. McDonald, Inc. (RAMCO). RAMCO agreed to provide R&D services to Alpha with respect to A-40 in exchange for two cash payments totaling $202,500, as well as additional compensation, payable as royalties if the project were successfully marketed. . . .

Omega agreed to use its reasonable best efforts to complete A-40 within 1 year, and that its obligations were to expire 1 year from the date of the agreement. The R&D agreement required Omega to keep a record of progress and costs, and to limit its expenditures to those deductible under section 174. Otherwise, Omega had complete discretion over the conduct of its R&D activities. Omega projected A-40 could be developed for approximately $355,000, but with risks this figure could exceed $800,000. RAMCO did not keep separate records of actual project costs for each of the projects on which it was working.

Beginning in January 1983, implementation of A-40 and four or five other projects was begun under the supervision of Daniel L. Dunn (Dunn) at RAMCO's facilities in Chatsworth, California. Dunn was an engineering consultant whose wholly owned consulting firm was being paid $6,000 per month by Alpha for his services. Dunn had a wide range of experience in systems engineering and pattern recognition. It was Dunn who had developed the A-40 idea, investigated its feasibility, and researched its market potential by contacting an airport parking lot consultant.

Through April 1983, little progress was made on A-40 other than locating and purchasing equipment and finding engineers qualified to work on Omega's projects. Several of the engineers throughout the years at issue worked on more than one of Omega's projects, splitting their time between them. In addition to their salaries, these engineers had a "Compensation/Income Agreement" stating that they would be paid additional amounts . . . in the event that certain projects, including A-40, were successful.

Dunn envisioned A-40 as a computer system which, upon a vehicle entering a parking lot, would record a visual image of the license plate, then "read" the numbers into a digital format from the image so that the numbers, rather than a picture of them could be stored in the computer memory. Then when the vehicle left the parking lot, the system would again photograph the license plate, "read" the license plate number, and match it to the computer records corresponding to when the vehicle entered the lot. To be feasible, the system needed to "search, find, and read" the number in less than 5 seconds.

A digital picture of the rear end of an automobile amounts to a quarter of a million pieces of information, with approximately 1,000 bits of this information relating to the license plate. Because computer memory was limited, RAMCO wanted to isolate the information it wanted, and discard the rest. Between June and July 1983, personnel working on A-40 met with a vision imaging specialist from the University of Southern California (USC), who suggested that RAMCO record the visual image of the license plate using a computer program to generate a line drawing from a digital scan of a photograph, and then use character recognition software to extract from the line drawing an actual digital number. The vision imaging specialist then produced in 17 minutes a line drawing from a photograph of a license plate using USC's sophisticated and expensive equipment.

Through July and August 1983, RAMCO tried, without success, to develop software to find the center of a license plate, locate the numbers, and identify them. RAMCO's engineers abandoned those efforts when they realized they had reached a "technological dead end."

After abandoning its software research, RAMCO developed a hardware-based line drawing technique which produced, in less than 5 seconds, a simplified computer-generated line drawing of the number on a license plate. The line drawing system was not what RAMCO had set out to do inasmuch as it could not produce "a hard digital number that you could put in a computer." Because of this, personnel in the parking lot business would not buy or test the project. For this reason, and because the cost of development was prohibitive, the line drawing system was not marketable.

During RAMCO's work on A-40, McDonald and Dunn occasionally sent written status reports to Universal No. 1. By letter dated February 29, 1984, Omega advised Universal No. 1 that the project had been completed. On March 2, 1984, Omega informed Universal No. 1 that it was exercising its option to obtain a review license. By letter dated May 1, 1985, McDonald notified Duncan that Omega would not exercise its option to acquire a permanent license in the A-40 technology. McDonald concluded that "the 'Pattern Recognition Technology,' although unique and possibly patentable was not sophisticated enough to meet our minimum requirement for Universal's parking lot application."

* * *

OPINION

* * *

The . . . issue that we decide is whether Universal No. 1 incurred research or experimental expenditures within the meaning of section 174. While section 174 does not define the term "research or experimental expenditures," we have approved of the definition found in section 1.174-2(a)(1), Income Tax Regs., limiting the expenditures to "research and development costs in the experimental or laboratory sense." *Mayrath v. Commissioner,* 41 T.C. 582, 590 (1964), affd. 357 F.2d 209 (5th Cir. 1966). Included in this definition are:

> all such costs incident to the development of an experimental or pilot model, a plant process, a product, a formula, an invention, or similar property, and improvement of already existing property of the type mentioned. [Sec. 1.174-2(a)(1), Income Tax Regs.]

In *Agro Science Co.* we stated that "The goal of the research must be scientifically reasonable, but research is more than repeating what has already been done." *Agro Science Co. v. Commissioner,* T.C. Memo 1989-687, 1989 Tax Ct. Memo LEXIS 687, 58 T.C.M. (CCH) 1093, 1102, T.C.M. (RIA) 89687 at 3551.

Initially, respondent claims that the work done on A-40 through August 1983 did not qualify as research or experimental expenditures because Omega's attempt to "search, find, and read" the license plate on the rear of an automobile was not scientifically reasonable. Respondent presented expert evidence and argues that if Omega and Universal No. 1 had done more research into the area, they would have realized that the project was not feasible because it required too much computer capacity.

Section 174 does not limit deductions for expenditures to those which result in successful R&D projects. In addition, there is no indication in the statute that the deduction is available only if the taxpayer's investigation determines that success is probable. Prior to September 1983, Universal No. 1 was not merely purchasing another's process or product. Based on the facts and circumstances of this case we are not persuaded that expenditures for A-40 were scientifically unreasonable. Omega made investigations and believed A-40 was feasible.

Respondent next argues that costs incurred by Omega after it abandoned its software approach in August 1983 were not deductible because Omega was merely "repeating what has already been done." See *Agro Science Co. v. Commissioner, supra.* In support, respondent presented evidence that police officers in Germany were using hard-drive technology to catch speeders similar to that which Omega developed. We are not persuaded that A-40 was not an improvement on any foreign technology. See sec. 1.174-2(a)(1), Income Tax Regs. The German technology took 2 weeks to determine the characters on a license plate while A-40 took less than 5 seconds.

Universal No. 1 incurred expenditures for the R&D of a project scientific in nature. The project involved unique processes, or the improvement of existing processes, which Omega reasonably believed could result in a patentable invention. While we make no intimations on how we would decide this issue if any of the facts were changed, or if the burden of proof were different, in the instant matter respondent has failed to persuade us that the costs actually incurred for the development of A-40 were not deductible under section 174, and having raised the issue by amended answer, the burden of proof was on him. Rule 142(a).

Respondent next argues that the record does not show that Omega incurred $3,000,000 worth of research or experimental expenditures in developing A-40, and that Universal No. 1 should therefore not be entitled to a section 174 deduction in that amount. We agree that the $75,000 used by Omega to pay Duncan for negotiating the R&D agreement was not deductible by Universal No. 1 under section 174. If Universal No. 1 had paid that amount to Duncan directly, Universal No. 1 would have had to capitalize it. The expense could not be transformed into a current deduction merely because Omega paid it. See sec. 1.174-2(a)(2), Income Tax Regs. [In an omitted portion of the opinion, the court ruled that the $2,625,000 promissory noted lacked economic substance because it was stated in foreign currency that was reasonably expected to rapidly deflate in relation to the U.S. dollar. As such, the court disallowed deduction of $2,625,000 in expenses relating to the note].

We believe that the $300,000 of cash which Universal No. 1 paid Omega to undertake development of A-40 was reasonable based on the facts known by the parties at the time of contracting. While Omega may have spent less than $300,000 in developing A-40, respondent has not persuaded us that this difference was anything other than Omega's compensation for undertaking the project's development on Universal No. 1's behalf. We need not determine whether this difference could have been deductible under section 162, since section 174 clearly contemplates that it was deductible under its provisions. See sec. 1.174-2(a)(3), Example (1), Income Tax Regs. We hold that in 1982 Universal No. 1 incurred a $300,000 expense deductible under section 174.

Based on the foregoing,

Decisions will be entered under Rule 155.

FIELD ATTORNEY ADVICE 20055203F

Office of Chief Counsel, Internal Revenue Service

December 30, 2005

[The taxpayer was a U.S. corporation formed as a joint venture between a U.S. corporation (50 percent shareholder) and a foreign corporation (50 percent shareholder). The taxpayer's purpose was to undertake R&E regarding specific inventions and to commercialize any successful results. The taxpayer's board of directors was comprised of six members, three from the U.S. shareholder and three from the foreign shareholder. Both corporate shareholders provided contract R&E and administrative services to the taxpayer under two respective services agreements. The taxpayer, itself, had no employees and no offices. As such, employees of the U.S. shareholder and foreign shareholder performed all R&E and other services (e.g., legal, financial, planning, personnel, and public relations) on the taxpayer's behalf. The U.S. shareholder and foreign shareholder each charged the taxpayer for all services provided based on the number of actual hours their employees worked. Additionally, the taxpayer reimbursed its shareholders for actual R&E expenditures incurred. Although the taxpayer owned all of the products created by the R&E, it granted exclusive licenses to its products to its shareholders. The shareholders then manufactured and sold the products in their respective territories and paid royalties back to the taxpayer. In territories not covered by the license agreements with its shareholders, the taxpayer licensed its products to third parties in exchange for royalties.]

[Upon audit of the taxpayer, the Service's audit team initially denied Section 174 deductions on the basis that the taxpayer's licensing activities did not qualify as a trade or business. The audit team reasoned that the taxpayer's activities were passive, like those of an investor (and unlike those of a manufacturer). The audit team pointed out that the joint venture had no employees and no office space and that it merely hired its own shareholders and licensed the results back to them. The Service's Office of Chief Counsel issued the following advice on the issue of whether the taxpayer's R&E expenditures were in connection with a trade or business within the meaning of Section 174.]

LAW AND ANALYSIS

Section 174(a)(1) provides that a taxpayer may treat R&E expenditures paid or incurred during the taxable year "in connection with a trade or business" as expenses that are not chargeable to capital account. Accordingly, a taxpayer may claim a deduction for such expenditures.

* * *

[W]e will analyze whether Taxpayer's activities constitute a trade or business under section 174 case law.

B. Trade or Business Determination for Licensing Activities

Taxpayer engaged in licensing activities. In the section 174 context, the Tax Court has held that licensing activities can constitute a trade or business, provided that the taxpayer has established a profit motive and conducts its activities in a regular and continuous manner. For example, in *Louw v. Commissioner,* 30 T.C.M. (CCH) 1421 (1971), the issue was whether certain R&E expenses incurred by an individual taxpayer were in connection with a trade or business of being an inventor and therefore deductible under section 174. Although the taxpayer had not yet received any income from his inventions, the court noted that he devoted his time regularly and continuously to free-lance inventive work for several years. The court concluded that the taxpayer was engaged in a trade or business, even though he did not expect to use the fruits of his R&E to manufacture products and his purpose was to "sell, lease, or license the patent or design to others." *Id.* at 1423. Under these circumstances, the court found that the taxpayer "is not merely preparing to enter a business; he is already engaged in it." *Id.* Under the Tax Court's holding, a taxpayer is not required to manufacture products in order to satisfy section 174's trade or business test; it is sufficient for the taxpayer to have a purpose of selling, leasing or licensing the patent or design to others, as long as he has the requisite profit motive and conducts his activities with regularity and continuity.

In *Kilroy v. Commissioner,* 41 T.C.M. (CCH) 292 (1980), the Tax Court reiterated its position that the "exploitation of inventions through royalties, sales of patents, or otherwise may constitute a business." *Id.* at 295 (citation omitted). In noting that the concept of a "trade or business" under section 174 is similar to that in section 162, the Court opined that "whether a [taxpayer] is engaged in a trade or business . . . is a matter of intent to be determined from the facts." *Id.*

While acknowledging that licensing can constitute a trade or business, courts have found that not all taxpayers that receive royalty income and have a profit motive are necessarily engaged in a trade or business. For example, a taxpayer with a profit motive may be receiving a royalty as a return on its investment in another person's business. Under these circumstances, the taxpayer, although possessing a profit motive, is truly an investor in the R&E activities rather than engaged in the trade or business of conducting R&E and commercially exploiting the resulting intangible property. *See e.g., Green v. Commissioner,* 83 T.C. 667, 689 (1984) (taxpayer's royalty interest in the development and commercialization of certain intangibles was analogous to that of an investor in securities, in part because the taxpayer had no ownership interest in the inventions and no control over their actual development, production, or marketing); see also *I-Tech Ltd. Research P'ship v. Commissioner,* 81 T.C.M. (CCH) 1012 (2001) (management of investments held not to rise to the level of a trade or business). Additionally, a taxpayer that concludes only one licensing transaction rather than regularly engaging in licensing activities for profit may not be engaged in a trade or business because the licensing activity is not conducted with regularity and therefore fails to rise to the level of a trade or business. *See Harris v. Commissioner,* 16 F.3d 75, 81-82 (5th Cir. 1994) (the action of disposing of all inventions in one transaction, instead of regularly licensing inventions for profit, did not possess the indicia of continuity and regularity necessary to endow an activity with trade or business status).

Here, Taxpayer engaged in licensing the intangible property it developed. As determined in the cases discussed above, licensing intangible property can constitute a trade or business for purposes of section 174, so long as the facts of the case establish that the taxpayer is in fact conducting a trade or business. Thus, the key to determining whether Taxpayer's licensing activities constitute a trade or business is to examine the facts and circumstances of its activities. Taxpayer must show that it had a profit motive and that it engaged in its activities in a continuous and regular manner.

We think it is clear based on these facts that Taxpayer's formation and ongoing operations were for the purpose of making a profit by conducting a business. Taxpayer had the requisite profit motive. Foreign Shareholder and U.S. Shareholder formed Taxpayer for the purpose of going into business with each other through the joint development and commercialization of certain Inventions. For the years at issue, Taxpayer carried on such business by contracting with Foreign Shareholder and U.S. Shareholder to provide R&E and other services on Taxpayer's behalf, and by licensing the results to others and receiving an income stream in return. Taxpayer commercially exploited the intangible property; it held the ownership interest in the results of the R&E, and it had control over the actual development and marketing.

Taxpayer also conducts its activities in a substantial, continuous and regular manner and has done so since Year 1. Taxpayer's R&E and licensing activities are not limited to isolated instances. During the years at issue, Taxpayer oversaw the joint R&E process by holding regular board and Science Meetings, engaged outside contractors to perform R&E and administrative services, and received royalty income pursuant to multiple license agreements with Foreign Shareholder and U.S. Shareholder as well as with third parties. Taxpayer's revenue stream from multiple sources indicates that its activities are substantial and conducted with continuity and regularity.

Under our analysis of section 174, we conclude that Taxpayer conducted a trade or business for the years at issue. Thus, Taxpayer qualifies for the section 174 deduction.

C. Lack of Employees and Lack of Office Space

[The audit team] focused in part on the lack of employees and absence of office space as evidence that Taxpayer does not conduct business activities. Although the existence of employees and office space are relevant factors to consider in determining whether a taxpayer has a profit motive and conducts its activities with continuity and regularity, we are not aware of any authority that would deny a taxpayer trade or business status just because the taxpayer chooses to conduct its day-to-day activities through contractors, particularly if there are other factors tending to establish the taxpayer's profit motive.

In *Kilroy, supra,* the court held that the taxpayer was carrying on a trade or business, despite that fact that the taxpayer and his limited partnership hired outside consultants, such as attorneys, economists, and engineers, to perform activities on the taxpayer's and the partnership's behalf. The Tax Court found these facts to be favorable for the taxpayer because it supported his claim that he engaged in his activities with a profit motive. *Kilroy,* 41 T.C.M. (CCH) 292 at 293, 295 (1980).

Congress enacted section 174 to put all businesses (and potential businesses) conducting R&E on an equal footing. *See* Hearings on H.R. 8300 Before the Senate Committee on Finance, 83d Cong., 2d Sess., pt.19, p.105 (1954) (statement of Marion B. Folsom, Under Secretary of the Treasury). The courts interpret section 174 as allowing a deduction prior to the commencement of a trade or business to give effect to Congress' intent to stimulate the search for new products and new inventions, particularly by small and new enterprises, and to place them on an equal footing with established businesses. *See e.g.*, *Snow,* 416 U.S. at 503-04.

To treat the hiring of employees and the leasing of office space as determinative factors would violate Congressional intent, since taxpayers engaged in legitimate joint business ventures that choose for business reasons not to hire separate employees or to lease separate office space would be treated differently from other businesses. The form in which a taxpayer chooses to operate its business, either through employees or outside contractors, should have no bearing on the availability of the section 174 deduction once a taxpayer has established it is in fact carrying on a trade or business. Thus, although Taxpayer's lack of employees and absence of office space should be considered in light of all the facts and circumstances, these facts are not dispositive. Weighing the totality of all the facts, Taxpayer conducted a trade or business for the years at issue and qualifies for the section 174 deduction.

D. Case Law Under Section 174

In addition to its focus on the lack of employees and absence of office space, [the audit team] identified several court cases disallowing the section 174 deduction that it believes are on point. The following discussion presents an in depth analysis of the section 174 case law, including those cases cited by [the audit team] as well as other cases, and the application of the law to the facts of this case. This analysis further supports our conclusion that Taxpayer operates a trade or business for section 174 purposes.

1. *Cases Disallowing the Section 174 Deduction*

The cases in which the section 174 deduction was denied follow a general pattern. Individuals generally contributed cash to a partnership and the partnership used the cash to fund R&E undertaken by an unrelated business enterprise. Although the partnership purported to own all the rights to the fruits of the R&E, it was required through either a pre-existing legal agreement or otherwise to license all those rights back to the enterprise actually conducting the R&E. In one case, the enterprise conducting the R&E held an option to acquire these rights at a later date for a nominal sum. In virtually all the cases, the partnership and the partners had little or no technical knowledge of the specific R&E endeavors and no expertise in the particular industry, were not generally involved with the day-to-day R&E activities, had no rights to control the R&E process, and did not oversee the R&E activities.

The issue in these cases was whether the individual limited partners of the subject partnerships were entitled to deduct their distributive share of the losses created by the R&E expenditures deducted under section 174 at the partnership level. The partnerships argued that they were entitled to deduct these expenses as incurred in connection with a trade or business. The courts carefully reviewed the facts of each case and universally held that the partnership's activities did not rise to the level of operating a business in connection with such R&E. Rather, the partnerships were merely investment vehicles by which the individuals invested in the R&E activities of someone else's business.

For example, in *Green v. Commissioner,* 83 T.C. 667 (1984), the taxpayers invested cash in a partnership. The partnership's stated purpose was to acquire four inventions for investment and income-producing purposes. The partnership used cash obtained from several investors to fund four R&E projects undertaken by different inventors. Although a legal agreement conveyed to the partnership all the rights, title and interest to the inventions, a simultaneously executed agreement granted the inventors the exclusive, worldwide licensing rights to manufacture, use and sell any resulting inventions for the duration of the inventions' patent term. The Tax Court held that the partnership's activity constituted a management of investments, not a trade or business. The partnership's activities were limited and purely ministerial. The partnership had no right to control the R&E results and relinquished all its interests in the four R&E projects at the outset of the endeavor.

In *Kantor v. Commissioner,* 998 F.2d 1514 (9th Cir. 1993), *aff'g* 60 T.C.M. (CCH) 225 (1990), the facts were slightly different in that the general partner of the partnership was involved to some extent with the R&E activities conducted on the partnership's behalf by a research firm. At the outset of the endeavor, however, the partnership granted to the corporation conducting the R&E the option to acquire the exclusive marketing rights to the R&E results for a nominal sum of $5,000, even though the partnership advanced $3.15 million to fund the R&E expenditures. The Ninth Circuit held that the partnership effectively relinquished any possibility of conducting a business in connection with the research results by issuing the option at a nominal sum, making it more probable than not that the option holder would exercise the option. Thus, not only was the partnership merely an investment vehicle that is not engaged in a trade or business currently, it did not have a realistic prospect of ever conducting a business with the research results. The fact that the general partner was involved with the R&E activities did not change this result, because these activities constituted the promotion and protection of an investment, not a business.

In *Harris v. Commissioner,* 16 F.3d 75 (5th Cir. 1994), *aff'g* 58 T.C.M. (CCH) 1441 (1992), two individual inventors formed a partnership for purposes of obtaining capital to fund the

R&E to be performed by a wholly owned corporation of the inventors. The partnership used cash from unrelated investors to fund the R&E conducted by the corporation and granted the corporation an option of obtaining a perpetual exclusive license for the resulting technology. The license called for very large royalty payments, which the taxpayer argued made it unlikely that the corporation would exercise the option, thereby leaving the partnership with no choice but to market the technology on its own. Thus, the taxpayer argued that it possessed a realistic prospect of entering its own trade or business with the technology. The Fifth Circuit affirmed the Tax Court's finding that the parties intended at a later date to renegotiate the option to a lower level of royalty payments, thus allowing the corporation to license the technology at a reasonable price. Under these circumstances, the Court held that the partnership was not engaged in a trade or business and had no realistic prospect of doing so since the parties intended for the corporation, and not the partnership, to engage in the business. Thus, the partnership was truly an investor. In reaching its holding, the Court observed, "In our view, those cases in which a *section 174* deduction was upheld may be distinguished by one dispositive factor: in each of the cases allowing the deduction, the entity that incurred the research expenses actually managed and actually controlled the use or marketing of the research results." *Id.* at 80.

In *Levin v. Commissioner,* 832 F.2d 403 (7th Cir. 1987), *aff'g* 87 T.C. 698 (1986), several partnerships funded R&E projects to be conducted by a corporation for the development of food machinery equipment. On paper, each partnership appeared to have significant rights and interests such that it would be possible for the partnership to use the technology to manufacture and market the food machines. Nonetheless, the facts and circumstances of the case led the Seventh Circuit to affirm the Tax Court's holding that the parties did not reasonably anticipate availing themselves of the privileges they possessed on paper and that each partnership's role was restricted to that of a passive investor. The Court observed that "legal entitlements, divorced from economic incentives and business probabilities, are not enough" to create a realistic prospect that the taxpayer will enter a trade or business in connection with the R&E. *Id.* at 407.

In *Zink v. Commissioner,* 929 F.2d 1015 (5th Cir. 1991), a partnership was not involved. Rather, two individuals, husband and wife, entered into a purported purchase agreement with two unrelated companies to purchase the R&E results (plans and specifications for airplane component parts) from these two companies. As part of the purchase agreement, the taxpayers agreed to grant a license to each company for the nonexclusive right to use, employ and exploit all the R&E results in exchange for fixed royalty payments per each airplane sold that contained the respective component parts. The two unrelated companies then contracted with other research firms to engage in the actual R&E. Under these circumstances, the Fifth Circuit found that the taxpayers were merely investors and that the activities they conducted, including receiving reports, keeping apprised of R&E developments, visiting a research plant on one occasion, and attending an exhibition in their hometown, were insufficient, as a matter of law, to rise to the level of a trade or business.

In other cases with similar fact patterns, the courts reached the same conclusion: taxpayers who are investors in the R&E activities of another enterprise's business are not themselves engaged in a trade or business. *See e.g., LDL Research & Dev. II, Ltd. v. Commissioner,* 124 F.3d 1338 (10th Cir. 1997); *Diamond v. Commissioner,* 930 F.2d 372 (4th Cir. 1991); *Spellman v. Commissioner,* 845 F.2d 148 (7th Cir. 1988); *I-Tech Ltd. Research P'ship v. Commissioner,* 81 T.C.M. (CCH) 1012 (2001).

In each of these cases, the common factors weighing against the taxpayers included the lack of technical expertise on the part of the person claiming to have a trade or business; the lack of oversight or control over the R&E process; and the lack of management and control over the R&E results since the rights to those results were relinquished (or effectively relinquished) at the outset of the endeavor. These factors and the economic realities of the transactions demonstrated that the taxpayers were merely investors funding R&E, rather than incurring R&E expenditures in connection with a trade or business. The taxpayers were not substantively operating a trade or business, even if they purported to do so in form. *See Harris,* 167 F.3d at 80 (stating that the court cases "interpret the . . . 'in connection with' language using the economic realities, or substance over form, doctrine."). Further, the facts and circumstances of each case demonstrated that the taxpayer did not have a realistic prospect of subsequently entering into its own trade or business with the R&E results, either because the financial arrangements made it improbable that the taxpayer would do so or the taxpayer effectively relinquished all rights, title and interest to the R&E results.

* * *

2. *Cases Upholding the Section 174 Deduction*

In contrast to the cases where the section 174 deduction was denied, the cases upholding the deduction presented very different fact patterns. For example, in *Snow, supra,* the individual taxpayer was a limited investor in a partnership. The partnership, through its general partner, actually conducted a significant amount of R&E and also contracted R&E out to others. Eventually, the R&E proved fruitful and the partnership incorporated. The taxpayer became a board member of the incorporated entity. The corporation manufactured products and sold the products to customers. The Supreme Court permitted the taxpayer a section 174 deduction even though the partnership was not yet selling goods in the year at issue. *Snow,* 416 U.S. at 503-04.

Under these circumstances, the Court found that the partnership was precisely the type of small and pioneering venture that section 174 was designed to benefit. Although the opinion is silent on whether the Court's holding was based on a finding that the partnership was not an investment vehicle, we believe the Court's holding is premised on the same principles articulated by subsequent courts. The Snow facts indicate clearly that the partnership was formed for the purpose of making a profit by conducting a business and even though the Court found that the business had not yet commenced, the partnership had a realistic prospect of conducting a business with the R&E results in the future given the economic realities of the current arrangement.

A key distinction between Snow and the other cases where the section 174 deduction was denied is that Snow did not involve outside investors funding the R&E activities of another business. Rather, the partnership that undertook and funded the R&E expenditures did so for the purpose of developing an asset that it intended to exploit in its own business.

Another case upholding the section 174 deduction is *Cleveland v. Commissioner,* 297 F.2d 169 (4th Cir. 1961), *aff'g in part, rev'g in part* 34 T.C. 517 (1960). In that case, the court held that the taxpayer, who provided funding for R&E conducted by an inventor, was an equal participant in a joint business venture with the inventor. Although the relationship between the parties started off as one of investor and inventor, the court found that the relationship evolved over time into a joint business venture.

A written agreement executed between the parties a few years after their relationship began clearly set forth the parties' intent that the taxpayer's advances were "no longer loans but were made strictly at the risk of the venture with the expectation of profiting therefrom." *Id.* at 173. Furthermore, the taxpayer acted as a business and legal advisor for the venture and was responsible for developing business contacts for the purpose of finding a commercial use for the invention. The inventor's R&E activities, conducted on behalf of the joint venture, were attributable to the joint venture and the taxpayer was allowed to deduct expenditures under section 174.

Although *Cleveland* was decided before *Snow*, the Cleveland court applied similar principles to determine the taxpayer's intent and motive, as evidenced by the attendant circumstances. It found based on the evidence that while the taxpayer was initially an investor in the R&E

activities, he subsequently incurred R&E expenses in his capacity as an equal participant in a joint business venture and not as an investor.

In another case upholding the section 174 deduction, *Scoggins v. Commissioner,* 46 F.3d 950 (9th Cir. 1995), *rev'g* 61 T.C.M. (CCH) 2859 (1991), two inventors with significant technical knowledge and expertise formed both a partnership and a corporation. These inventors were the sole partners of the partnership and collectively owned 75% of the corporation's stock. The partnership's purpose was to engage in R&E to develop a new type of epitaxial reactor, which is a type of semiconductor equipment used to apply layers of silicon on substrate silicon wafers for the purpose of manufacturing computer chips. The two inventors, through the partnership, advanced $500,000 for the corporation to conduct the R&E. The inventors themselves actually conducted R&E as employees of the corporation. The partnership granted to the corporation a 15-month nonexclusive license to exploit the resulting technology (which the corporation was not obligated to exercise) and thereafter an option to purchase the rights to the technology for $5 million, which the corporation would be entitled to exercise three months after the conclusion of the 15-month license period. Thus, even if the corporation exercised the option at its earliest opportunity, the partnership still had an 18-month period during which it could market and sell the reactor.

The Ninth Circuit, taking great care to distinguish this case from its earlier decision in *Kantor*, held that the partnership had a realistic prospect of entering into a trade or business of its own with the technology. The Court noted several distinctions between the partnership in *Kantor* and the *Scoggins* partnership. First, the partnership in *Kantor* was composed entirely, with only one exception, of investors with no technical expertise of the product that was to be developed and the research firm conducting the R&E was completely independent from the partnership. Second, the *Kantor* partnership granted the independent research firm an option to acquire the exclusive technology rights for a nominal sum of $5,000 as compared with the $3.15 million it funded in R&E, making it "unrealistic to conclude that if the $3.15 million expended in research were successful in producing a marketable product, the research corporation would not expend the $5,000 to obtain exclusive marketing rights." *Id.* at 955.

In contrast to *Kantor*, the $5 million option at issue in *Scoggins* is a significant amount when compared to the $500,000 in R&E expenditures to be funded by the partnership. Accordingly, the corporation holding the option would be required to raise a significant amount of capital to exercise that option. The Court found it significant that the partnership and the corporation in *Scoggins* were controlled and financed by the same individuals and that it would be these individuals who would decide whether it would be more fruitful to raise $5 million on behalf of the corporation to exercise its option, or to manufacture and sell the product through the partnership without raising this capital.

Thus, the Court appears to suggest that regardless of how the two individuals would choose at a later date to conduct their business, it does not change the fact that they possessed the good faith intent to enter the business of marketing the reactor if the R&E efforts proved successful and that there exists a realistic prospect that such business may be conducted through the partnership. The partnership was certainly capable of entering into a business with the R&E results given the expertise and experience of its partners, and would have the financial capacity to do so since it possessed the right to market the product for 18 months and for the indefinite future if the corporation did not choose to exercise its option. *Id.* at 953. Under these circumstances, these two individuals, through their partnership, "are among the class of taxpayers Congress intended to encourage and reward by enacting section 174." *Id.* at 956.

3. *Application of Case Law to the Facts of this Case*

To determine whether a section 174 deduction is available, the courts have applied the substance over form doctrine and examined the true economic realities. *See Harris,* 167 F.3d at 80. Despite the varied fact patterns and the different financial arrangements at issue, the court cases we have discussed in this memorandum all have a common theme. The distinguishing factor has been whether the true substance of the case revealed that the taxpayer was an investor in another person's business, or revealed that the taxpayer exhibited a good faith intent to use the fruits of the R&E in a business venture of its own.

In the cases where the deduction was denied, that good faith intent did not exist and the attendant circumstances made it clear that the taxpayers were merely investors that did not possess the objective intent, or the capability, of entering into a business of their own with the fruits of the R&E. These cases disallowing the section 174 deduction do not control the outcome here since the facts of this case are distinguishable in several key respects.

First, Taxpayer is a combined business operation, not an investment vehicle. Unlike the partnerships in the court cases, which merely functioned as a vehicle for injecting risk capital into another person's existing business, Taxpayer was formed by its shareholders to undertake a new and separate business of engaging in the joint development and commercialization of certain Inventions. . . . In our view, the fact that Taxpayer operates a different business than the business carried on separately by either Foreign Shareholder or U.S. Shareholder is clear evidence that Taxpayer is not an investment vehicle attempting to disguise itself as a business -- it is a true business. Taxpayer funds its own R&E efforts at its own risk with the intention of making a profit. Further, unlike the partnerships that lacked business and technical expertise, Taxpayer possesses significant business experience and expertise . . . by virtue of its officers and directors.

Second, in the cases where the section 174 deduction was disallowed, the research firms conducting R&E were generally independent from the partnerships (or individuals) that provided funding for the R&E. Thus, the person purporting to incur R&E expenditures in connection with a trade or business generally had no power to direct or control the R&E process. Even where such persons were involved to some extent in the R&E process, the court found that these activities did not rise to the level of a trade or business because they were undertaken to protect and promote the partnership's investment. This is not the case with Taxpayer, which exercises significant control over the R&E process in connection with its business. Through its officers and directors, Taxpayer decides which R&E projects it will undertake and oversees the R&E process undertaken by the employees of Foreign Shareholder and U.S. Shareholder. Taxpayer's management has the power to direct the R&E process and actually exercised that power by sponsoring regular Science Meetings, where the research scientists at both Foreign Shareholder and U.S. Shareholder met to address both technical and operational matters. Thus, Taxpayer exercises management and control over the R&E process.

Third, unlike the partnerships in the court cases that relinquished management and control over the right to market the R&E results, Taxpayer retains significant legal rights to market its R&E results and actually did market such results (and continues to do so) through its licensing activities. Although Taxpayer relinquished its rights to exploit the R&E results in territories covered by Foreign Shareholder and U.S. Shareholder, it retained rights for all other markets. A significant percentage of Taxpayer's income for the years at issue . . . is derived from third party licenses. This fact is significant because it establishes not only that Taxpayer had management and control over a significant portion of the research results, but that Taxpayer actually exercised that control by choosing to license to third parties. As observed by the Harris court, management and control over the R&E results is a dispositive factor in determining whether a taxpayer has a trade or business. *See Harris, supra,* 16 F.3d at 80.

* * *

CONCLUSION

Based on the court cases in this area, we conclude that the term "in connection with a trade or business" means that a taxpayer's contract R&E expenditures must be paid or incurred in connection with the taxpayer's own trade or business, rather than in connection with the taxpayer's investment in the trade or business of another person. The facts and circumstances of this case demonstrate that Taxpayer incurred R&E expenditures in connection with its own business, and did not incur such expenditures in connection with an investment in another person's business.

We wish to emphasize that our conclusion does not create a bright line test for every joint venture. Although joint ventures are often created with the intent of carrying on a business, it is possible for taxpayers to create joint ventures with the intent to invest in the business (or businesses) of another person(s). Each case must be examined based on its own facts and circumstances to determine the true substance of the activity. That is, the economic realities of each particular case must be evaluated to determine whether the activity is undertaken with the requisite profit motive and carried on in a manner to endow it with trade or business status, or whether the activity is merely an investment purporting to be a business and the taxpayer has no realistic prospect of entering into a business of its own in the future with the R&E results.

* * *

REVENUE PROCEDURE 2000-50

December 26, 2000

SECTION 1. PURPOSE

This revenue procedure provides guidelines on the treatment of the costs of computer software.

SECTION 2. DEFINITION

For the purpose of this revenue procedure, "computer software" is any program or routine (that is, any sequence of machine-readable code) that is designed to cause a computer to perform a desired function or set of functions, and the documentation required to describe and maintain that program or routine. It includes all forms and media in which the software is contained, whether written, magnetic, or otherwise. Computer programs of all classes, for example, operating systems, executive systems, monitors, compilers and translators, assembly routines, and utility programs as well as application programs, are included. Computer software also includes any incidental and ancillary rights that are necessary to effect the acquisition of the title to, the ownership of, or the right to use the computer software, and that are used only in connection with that specific computer software. Computer software does not include any data or information base described in § 1.197-2 (b) (4) of the Income Tax Regulations (for example, data files, customer lists, or client files) unless the data base or item is in the public domain and is incidental to a computer program. Nor does it include any cost of procedures that are external to the computer's operation.

* * *

SECTION 4. SCOPE

This revenue procedure applies to all costs of computer software as defined in section 2 of this revenue procedure. This revenue procedure does not apply to any computer software that is subject to amortization as an "amortizable section 197 intangible" as defined in § 197 (c) and the regulations thereunder, or to costs that a taxpayer has treated as a research and experimentation expenditure under § 174.

SECTION 5. COSTS OF DEVELOPING COMPUTER SOFTWARE

.01 The costs of developing computer software (whether or not the particular software is patented or copyrighted) in many respects so closely resemble the kind of research and experimental expenditures that fall within the purview of § 174 as to warrant similar accounting treatment. Accordingly, the Service will not disturb a taxpayer's treatment of costs paid or incurred in developing software for any particular project, either for the taxpayer's own use or to be held by the taxpayer for sale or lease to others, where:

(1) All of the costs properly attributable to the development of software by the taxpayer are consistently treated as current expenses and deducted in full in accordance with rules similar to those applicable under § 174 (a); or

(2) All of the costs properly attributable to the development of software by the taxpayer are consistently treated as capital expenditures that are recoverable through deductions for ratable amortization, in accordance with rules similar to those provided by § 174 (b) and the regulations thereunder, over a period

of 60 months from the date of completion of the development or, in accordance with rules provided in § 167 (f) (1) and the regulations thereunder, over 36 months from the date the software is placed in service.

* * *

Chapter 3: Taxation of Intellectual Property Acquisitions

A taxpayer can acquire intellectual property either (1) by purchase or (2) by license. As discussed in this Chapter, the acquisition of intellectual property by purchase may have completely different tax consequences than a license. This Chapter will first address acquisition by purchase and its tax consequences. This is followed by a discussion of acquisition of intellectual property by license and its tax consequences.

3.1 Acquisition of Intellectual Property by Purchase

As explained in Chapter 1, a taxpayer must capitalize amounts paid to another party to acquire any of one of fifteen "acquired intangibles." These specifically identified "acquired intangibles" include the following:[183]

(1) ownership interests in business entities;
(2) debt instruments;
(3) financial instruments;
(4) endowment, annuity, and insurance contracts;
(5) non-functional currency;
(6) leases;
(7) patents and copyrights;
(8) franchises, trademarks, and trade names;
(9) assembled workforces;
(10) goodwill;
(11) customer lists;
(12) servicing rights;
(13) customer-based and supplier-based intangibles;
(14) computer software;
(15) agreements for the right to use, possess, or use an intangible described in (1)-(5) above.

Acquired intangibles are capitalized due to the matching principle. Each acquired intangible represents the acquisition of a new asset that will provide long-lasting benefits to the taxpayer. As such, if a taxpayer was able to deduct the cost of an acquired intangible immediately, the taxpayer would have mismatching of expenses to the income those

[183] Treas. Reg. § 1.263(a)-4(c)(1).

expenses help to produce. For this reason, a taxpayer is required to capitalize the cost to the adjusted basis of the acquired intangible.

3.1[1] Ways Intellectual Property can be Acquired

Intellectual property can be purchased separately and disconnected from the acquisition of a trade or business. Alternatively, intellectual property can be acquired as a part of a larger transaction representing the acquisition of a trade or business. For instance, a large automobile manufacturer may purchase a patent from a small automobile supplier. The supplier would continue its independent existence and continue to operate after the purchase. In this case, the patent would be an acquired intangible and its cost would be capitalized to the adjusted basis of the patent.

The tax consequences are more complicated if intellectual property is acquired as part of taxable acquisition of a trade or business (i.e., a "taxable asset acquisition"[184]). For instance, the automobile manufacturer could acquire the desirable patent by acquiring the supplier's business along with all other intellectual property of the supplier (e.g., other patents, trademarks, etc.) as well as its tangible assets (e.g., equipment, buildings, and machinery). In a taxable asset acquisition, the taxpayer must allocate the purchase price between the acquired intangibles and other acquired assets. The issue of allocation is critical because the taxpayer must determine the adjusted basis of each acquired asset and whether it is amortizable.

---

[184] For purposes of this Chapter, a "taxable asset acquisition" is a transfer of assets constituting a trade or business where the transferee's basis in the acquired assets is determined wholly by reference to the consideration paid for them. *See* I.R.C. § 1060(c). The term "taxable asset acquisition" encompasses certain stock acquisitions and mergers that are treated as taxable asset acquisitions for tax purposes. For instance, a taxable stock acquisition where a section 338 election is in effect is treated for tax purposes as a taxable asset acquisition. I.R.C. § 338(a). Additionally, certain taxable mergers (e.g., a direct merger with taxable consideration or a forward triangular merger with taxable consideration) are treated as taxable asset acquisitions. *See* Rev. Rul. 69-6, 1969-1 C.B. 104. The requirements of a Section 338 election are very technical and beyond of scope of this book. For an excellent discussion of Section 338, *see* Thomas T. Chudy et al., "Stock Purchases Treated as Asset Acquisitions—Section 338," 788-2d Tax. Mgmt. (BNA) U.S. Income. For an excellent discussion of taxable mergers, see Barnet Phillips, IV et al., "Structuring Corporate Acquisitions—Tax Aspects," 770-3rd Tax Mgmt. (BNA) U.S. Income.

3.1[2] The Residual Method

In a taxable asset acquisition, the taxpayer must allocate the purchase price to the acquired assets under the *residual method.*[185] Under the residual method, the parties to an applicable asset acquisition[186] must allocate the purchase price among seven classes of assets in the following order:

Class I: Cash and cash equivalents;
Class II: Certain actively traded personal property (including publicly-traded stock), certificates of deposit, and foreign currency;
Class III: Accounts receivable, mortgages, and credit card receivables, which arise in the ordinary course of business;
Class IV: Inventory and certain inventory-type assets;
Class V: All assets not included in Classes I-IV and VI-VII;
Class VI: All section 197 intangibles except goodwill and going concern value; and
Class VII: Goodwill and going concern value.[187]

An allocation to any particular asset cannot exceed that asset's fair market value (other than goodwill and going concern value).[188] Generally, the Service will respect a purchase price allocation between the contracting parties, particularly where the parties negotiated at arm's length. While the contracting parties are bound by their agreed-upon allocation, the Service may challenge the parties' allocation if it not appropriate.[189]

Congress enacted the residual method to prevent abuses that occurred where the parties to an asset acquisition provided no specific allocation of the purchase price in their agreement.[190]

---

[185] I.R.C. § 1060(a), (c). The residual method applies to taxable asset acquisitions (as opposed to nontaxable asset acquisitions) constituting the acquisition of a trade or business. I.R.C. § 1060(c). Nontaxable asset acquisitions are beyond the scope of this Chapter.

[186] An applicable asset acquisition essentially means a taxable asset acquisition of a trade or business. I.R.C. § 1060(c).

[187] Treas. Reg. § 1.1060-1(a) (incorporating by reference the residual method of Treas. Reg. § 1.338-6(b)(1)). Treasury regulations define "goodwill" as "the value of a trade or business attributable to the expectancy of continued customer patronage." Treas. Reg. § 1.1060-1(b)(2)(ii). "Going concern value" is defined as "the additional value that attaches to property because of its existence as an integral part of an ongoing business activity." *Id.*

[188] Treas. Reg. § 1.1060-1(a) (incorporating by reference Treas. Reg. § 1.338-6(c)(1)).

[189] I.R.C. § 1060(a).

[190] Sen. Rpt. 99-313, at 253-54 (May 29, 1986).

Prior to the residual method requirement, sellers tended to allocate more of the purchase price to appreciated capital assets such as goodwill in order to maximize capital gain on the sale. Conversely, the buyer tended to allocate less to goodwill (prior to the enactment of section 197, goodwill was non-amortizable) and more to depreciable assets. In other words, parties to an asset acquisition often took inconsistent positions with each party allocating the purchase price in the most tax favorable manner to it, resulting in a "whipsaw" to the government. Congress added the residual method to the Code to prevent this "whipsaw" effect.[191]

> **Problem 3.1**: Nittany Lion Corporation purchases all of the assets of Illini Corporation in a taxable acquisition. The purchase price is $10,000,000 and the fair market value of the acquired assets is as follows:

Equipment and machinery	$5,000,000
Building and Land	$4,000,000
Patent	$1,000,000

> How much, if any, of the purchase price may the parties allocate to goodwill and going concern value?

> **Problem 3.2**: How would the answer to **Problem 3.1** change if the equipment and machinery had a fair market value of $4,000,000?

3.2 Recovery of Capitalized Amounts

As discussed in Chapter 2, once the taxpayer determines that it must capitalize the costs of acquired intellectual property, it must then determine how that capitalized amount is recovered. Based on the matching principle, capitalized amounts that provide benefits over a determinable life (i.e., because the benefits are exhausted or become obsolete) ought to be written off over that determinable life. In that way, the taxpayer can properly match deduction of its expenses to the income those expenses help to produce. The deduction of capital expenditures over time to reflect exhaustion or obsolescence is referred to as *amortization* or *depreciation*.

Many acquired intangibles are "amortizable section 197 intangibles," which are amortized over a 15-year period beginning in the month they are acquired. Those acquired intangibles

[191] *Id.*

excluded from amortization under section 197 may be eligible for amortization pursuant to section 167. Because section 197, to the extent it is applicable, trumps section 167, this Chapter discusses section 197 first. Before delving into the detail of section 197, a discussion of the rationale and purpose of section 197 is necessary.

3.2[1] Section 197 Amortization

Prior to the enactment of section 197 in 1993, goodwill and going concern value were non-amortizable because they did not have a determinable useful life.[192] Consequently, buyers often sought minimal allocation to those assets and instead sought to maximize allocations to amortizable and depreciable assets. Conversely, sellers often sought to maximize allocations to capital assets like goodwill and going concern value to generate capital gain and sought minimal allocations to ordinary assets that generated ordinary income. In many cases, buyers and sellers agreed to "carve out" certain "customer-based intangibles," such as subscription lists, customer lists, workforce in place, and other similar items, from goodwill and going concern value. By "carving out" these separate "customer-based intangibles," buyers were able to allocate the purchase price to amortizable intangibles with limited useful lives while providing capital gain to sellers.[193]

Another area of controversy was allocation of purchase price to covenants not to compete. Buyers often sought to maximize amounts allocated to covenants not to compete because covenants have limited useful lives (typically three years or less) and thus were amortizable over a relatively short period. On the other hand, sellers sought minimal allocation to covenants not to compete because amounts received for covenants generated ordinary income.

Congress enacted section 197 to reduce allocation controversies by requiring a broad range of intangibles, including goodwill, going concern, and covenants not to compete, to be amortized over 15 years.[194] As such, section 197 eliminates the incentive to "carve out" intangibles from goodwill and going concern because amounts allocated to goodwill, going concern, or any other "carve out" will be amortized over the same 15-year period.

---

[192] Treas. Reg. § 1.167(a)-3 (prior to amendment by T.D. 8865, 65 Fed. Reg. 3820 (2000)).

[193] For instance, in *Newark Morning Ledger Co. v. U.S.*, 507 U.S. 546 (1993), the Supreme Court upheld a carve-out allocation to a newspaper subscription list separate and apart from goodwill and going concern. The Court held that the subscription list was amortizable because it could be readily valued and that it had a limited useful life that could be reasonably estimated.

[194] H.R. Rpt. 103-111 (May 25, 1993).

Additionally, because amounts allocated to covenants not to compete are amortized over the same 15-year period as other section 197 intangibles, buyers have less incentive to maximize allocations to covenants not compete. But section 197 did not completely eliminate the historical tension between buyers and sellers over allocations. Buyers continue to have the incentive to maximize allocations to depreciable assets with shorter recovery periods (e.g., 3-, 5-, and 7-year property), such as equipment and machinery. Sellers, meanwhile, generally try to minimize amounts allocated to depreciable assets with shorter recovery periods (because they often trigger ordinary income through depreciation recapture as discussed in Chapter 4).

3.2[1][a] "Amortizable Section 197 Intangibles"

The Code defines a "section 197 intangible" to include the following:[195]

(1) goodwill;
(2) going concern value;
(3) workforce in place;
(4) information base (such as business books and records)
(5) know-how and similar items (including patents, copyrights, formulae, processes, designs, package designs, certain computer software, films, sound recordings, video tapes, and books);[196]
(6) customer-based intangibles;[197]
(7) supplier-based intangibles;[198]
(8) intangibles similar to (3)-(7) above;
(9) licenses and permits granted by governmental units;
(10) covenants not to compete, *but only if* entered into in connection with the direct or indirect acquisition of a business or a substantial portion thereof;
(11) franchises, trademarks, and trade names; and
(12) contracts or licenses for the use of any of the above intangibles.[199]

---

[195] I.R.C. § 197(d)(1).

[196] *See also* Treas. Reg. § 1.197-2(b)(5).

[197] "Customer-based intangibles" include composition of market, market share, and any other value resulting from the future provision of goods or services pursuant to contractual or noncontractual relationships with customers in the ordinary course of business. I.R.C. § 197(d)(2).

[198] "Supplier-based intangibles" are the value resulting from the future acquisition of goods or services used or sold by the taxpayer pursuant to contractual or noncontractual relationships with suppliers. I.R.C. § 197(d)(3).

A "section 197 intangible" listed above must be "amortizable" to qualify for the 15-year write off. First, in order to be amortizable, the "section 197 intangible" must be held in connection with a trade or business or an investment-activity.[200] Second, the manner in which the taxpayer acquired the "section 197 intangible" is important in determining whether it is "amortizable." Congress's primary concern in enacting section 197, i.e., to alleviate allocation disputes, does not arise when an intangible is self-created. For this reason, self-created assets are generally *not* amortizable section 197 intangibles (with an important exception for self-created franchises, trademarks and trade names, as discussed in Chapter 2).[201] Likewise, allocation issues are less of a concern where assets are separately acquired, so the following intangibles, if separately acquired, are *not* "amortizable" section 197 intangibles:[202]

(1) films, sounds recordings, video tapes, books, or similar properties;
(2) rights to receive tangible property or services under a contract or granted by a governmental unit or agency;
(3) patents or copyrights;
(4) certain rights under a contract granted by a governmental unit that (i) has a fixed duration less than 15 years or (ii) is fixed in amount and would otherwise be amortizable under a method similar to the unit-of-production method; and
(5) computer software.[203]

Whether an asset is acquired separately or as part of a taxable asset acquisition is a factual question based on the nature and amount of assets acquired compared to the nature and amount of assets the transferor retained.[204] The relative value of the asset acquired vis-à-vis the assets retained is not determinative.[205]

---

[199] Treas. Reg. § 1.197-2(b)(11).

[200] I.R.C. § 197(c)(1). The taxpayer must also acquire the intangible after the enactment of section 197, which was August 10, 1993. I.R.C. § 197(c)(1)(A).

[201] I.R.C. § 197(c)(2); Treas. Reg. § 1.197-2(d)(2).

[202] I.R.C. § 197(e)(4).

[203] *See* Treas. Reg. § 1.197-2(c)(4)(ii).

[204] Treas. Reg. § 1.197-2(e)(4).

[205] *Id.*

As a general rule, the acquisition of a franchise, trademark, or trade name is, in and of itself, the acquisition of a trade or business.[206] But there are three exceptions to this general rule. First, a franchise, trademark, or trade name is disregarded if its value is nominal or the taxpayer irrevocably disposes of it immediately after its acquisition.[207] Second, the acquisition of a right or interest in a trademark or trade name is disregarded if it is merely a license under the principles of section 1253 (discussed later in this Chapter).[208] Finally, a trademark or trade name is disregarded if it is included in computer software or in an interest in a film, sound recording, video tape, book, or other similar property.[209]

Computer software's treatment under section 197 deserves special mention. While computer software is generally listed as a section 197 intangible under the umbrella of "know-how," significant exceptions apply. First, separately acquired computer software is not subject to section 197.[210] Second, "off-the-shelf" computer software that is (i) readily available for purchase to the general public, (ii) is subject to a nonexclusive license, and (iii) and is not substantially modified is not a section 197 intangible.[211] Third, computer software that is bundled together with hardware is tangible property and outside the scope of section 197.[212] Therefore, section 197 should apply to computer software that is "custom" (as opposed to "off-the-shelf"), stand alone (as opposed to bundled with hardware), and acquired in a taxable asset acquisition.

> **Problem 3.3**: Smith and Johnson formed Gopher Corporation as equal shareholders to provide information technology consulting services in the greater Minneapolis-St. Paul area. While Gopher's business was highly successful for many years, Smith and Johnson had personal disagreements and mutually decided to go their separate ways. As such, Smith agreed to "buy out" Johnson. The parties structured the "buy out" as a stock redemption where Gopher redeemed all of Johnson's stock for adequate consideration. After the redemption, Smith was Gopher's sole shareholder. Additionally, Johnson agreed not to compete with Gopher for a period of five years in exchange for $100,000. Must Gopher treat Johnson's covenant

---

[206] Treas. Reg. § 1.197-2(e)(2)(i).

[207] Treas. Reg. § 1.197-2(e)(2)(ii)(B).

[208] Treas. Reg. § 1.197-2(e)(2)(ii)(C).

[209] Treas. Reg. § 1.197-2(e)(2)(ii)(A).

[210] I.R.C. § 197(e)(3)(B).

[211] I.R.C. § 197(e)(3)(A).

[212] Treas. Reg. § 1.167(a)-14(b)(2).

not to compete as an "amortizable section 197 intangible?" Read *Frontier Chevrolet Co. v. Commissioner* (included in this Chapter's materials) in connection with this problem.

Problem 3.4: Buckeye Corporation, a large pharmaceutical manufacturer, acquired substantially all of the assets of its chief competitor, Wolverine Corporation, in a taxable asset acquisition. Buckeye acquired Wolverine, in part, to market, sell, and distribute Wolverine's highly successful depression medication called "Procore." The purchase agreement allocated $100,000,000 to the patent protecting the medication's chemical compound. Patent protection on the compound will continue for another 10 years. The purchase agreement also allocated $20,000,000 to the "Procore" trademark, $1,000,000 to the domain name "procore.com," and $500,000 to the generic domain name "drugs.com." Assume that the allocations made in the purchase agreement are appropriate and will be respected by the Service. Which, if any, of the acquired intangibles are "amortizable section 197 intangibles?"

How would your answer change, if at all, if Buckeye had only acquired the patent, the "Procore" trademark, and the "procore.com" and "drugs.com" domain names from Wolverine? In answering this question, you may assume that Buckeye did not acquire Wolverine's goodwill and that Wolverine continued to operate as large pharmaceutical business separate from Buckeye after the acquisition. *See* Treas. Reg. § 1.197-2(c)(7) & 2(e).

Problem 3.5: Spartan Corporation acquired all of the assets of Badger Corporation in a taxable asset acquisition. Among the assets Spartan acquired from Badger were the following:

- 200 copies of stand alone word processing software that Badger had used under a nonexclusive license with the developer. The word processing software was not modified and was widely sold to the general public.
- 500 desktop computers, each of which came preloaded with the latest operating system software from the world's largest software developer.

- One copy of computer software Badger used to maintain a comprehensive accounting system, including general and subsidiary ledgers, payroll, accounts receivable and payable, cash receipts and disbursements, fixed asset accounting, and inventory cost accounting controls. The software was a modified version of the software the developer sold to the general public (the unmodified version sells for $500). The cost of the modifications made to the software was $5,000.

Which, if any, of the above assets are "amortizable section 197 intangibles?"

3.2[1][b] Section 197 Amortization Calculation

Section 197 provides that the capitalized costs of an "amortizable section 197 intangible" may be amortized and deducted ratably over a 15-year period beginning with the month in which it was acquired.[213] Amortization is only available for those section 197 intangibles held "in connection with" a trade or business or an investment-activity.[214] The "in connection with" language of section 197 is also used in section 174 dealing with research and experimental expenditures. As discussed in Chapter 2, the Supreme Court in *Snow v. Commissioner*[215] interpreted the "in connection with" language to allow deduction of preoperational expenses under section 174. Does the *Snow* holding on preoperational expenses likewise apply to section 197? Treasury regulations say no and provide that the 15-year recovery period under section 197 cannot begin prior to the first day of month in which the taxpayer's trade or business or investment-activity begins.[216]

A taxpayer may purchase an amortizable section 197 intangible for an amount that is measured, at least in part, by some future contingency. In such case, the taxpayer generally adds contingent payments to the adjusted basis of the intangible at the beginning of the month when the contingency is satisfied. If the taxpayer makes a contingent payment during the 15-year amortization period, the contingent payment is amortized ratably over the

[213] I.R.C. § 197(a). The taxpayer may disregard estimated salvage value, so the entire capitalized cost (adjusted basis) of an "amortizable section 197" can be written off over the 15-year period. Treas. Reg. § 1.197-2(f)(1)(ii). The taxpayer cannot claim amortization in the month of disposition. Treas. Reg. § 1.197-2(f)(1)(iii).

[214] I.R.C. § 197(c)(1).

[215] 416 U.S. 500 (1974).

[216] Treas. Reg. § 1.197-2(f)(1)(i)(B).

remaining 15-year period.[217] If the taxpayer makes the contingent payment after the end of the 15-year period, the contingent payment is immediately deducted in full.[218]

> **Problem 3.6**: Hawkeye Corporation, a calendar-year taxpayer, acquired all of the assets from Boilermaker Corporation in a taxable asset acquisition on February 26, Year 1. Among the assets Hawkeye acquired from Boilermaker was a patent on an herbicide. The parties agreed to allocate \$1.8 million of the purchase price to the herbicide patent with additional payments to be made in future years contingent upon Hawkeye's sales of the herbicide. Pursuant to the agreement, Hawkeye made contingent payments to Boilermaker of \$500,000 on December 10, Year 11 and \$500,000 on August 4, Year 16. Assume that the amount allocated to the patent and the contingent payments are appropriate and will be respected by the Service. What are the tax consequences to Hawkeye?

A taxpayer may not recognize a loss on disposition of an amortizable section 197 intangible if the taxpayer retains other amortizable section 197 intangibles acquired in the same transaction.[219] Instead, the loss is allocated among the retained intangibles, thereby increasing their adjusted bases.[220] Without this rule, a taxpayer could artificially inflate the amount allocated to a certain amortizable section 197 intangible it intends to sell shortly after acquisition. Because the intangible's adjusted basis would be artificially inflated, the intangible would likely be sold at a loss. If the taxpayer could deduct this loss, it would effectively accelerate the 15-year amortization period of section 197.

3.2[2] Recovery of Capitalized Costs Excluded from Section 197

If an acquired intangible is not amortizable under section 197, the taxpayer must look to section 167 or published guidance to amortize its capitalized costs. Section 167 provides for amortization deductions for the exhaustion, wear, tear, and obsolescence of property used in a trade or business or for the production of income.[221] Treasury regulations provide that a taxpayer may amortize any intangible that "is known from experience or other factors to be of use in the business or in the production of income for only a limited period, the length of

217 Treas. Reg. § 1.197-2(f)(2)(i).

218 Treas. Reg. § 1.197-2(f)(2)(ii).

219 I.R.C. § 197(f)(1)(A)(i).

220 I.R.C. § 197(f)(1)(A)(ii)

221 I.R.C. § 167(a).

which can be estimated with reasonable accuracy. . . ."[222] Treasury regulations specifically cite patents and copyrights as examples. Those intangibles that do not have a determinable useful life, such as stock and equity interests in businesses, are non-amortizable. Section 167 and its regulations provide for alternative methods of amortization of intangibles. Three of these methods, i.e., the "straight-line method," the "income forecast method," and the "variable contingent payment method," are discussed in this Chapter.

3.2[2][a] "Straight-line" Method

The straight-line method is the default method for amortizing intangibles that are not covered by section 197. Under the straight-line method, a taxpayer calculates the annual amortization deduction by dividing the capitalized cost of the amortizable intangible (less salvage value) by its useful life.[223] Treasury regulations define useful life as "the period over which the asset may reasonably be expected to be useful to the taxpayer in his trade or business or in the production of income."[224]

Because the useful life of an asset may often be difficult to measure, Treasury regulations provide a 15-year "safe-harbor" rule. Under the safe-harbor rule, a taxpayer may amortize an intangible ratably over 15 years beginning on the first day of the month in which the intangible is placed in service (the same manner as an "amortizable section 197 intangible").[225] A taxpayer may not use the safe-harbor if the intangible's useful life can be estimated with reasonable accuracy or is specifically provided for in the Code, regulations, or published guidance.[226]

The Code specifically provides that computer software excluded from section 197 is amortized under the straight-line method over 36 months.[227] The 36-month amortization

[222] Treas. Reg. § 1.167(a)-3(a).

[223] Treas. Reg. § 1.167(b)-1(a).

[224] Treas. Reg. § 1.167(b)-1(b).

[225] Treas. Reg. § 1.167(a)-3(b)(3).

[226] Treas. Reg. § 1.167(a)-3(b)(1). Additionally, a taxpayer may not use the safe harbor for intangibles described in Treas. Reg. § 1.263(a)-4(c) (relating to certain acquired intangibles), Treas. Reg. § 1.263(a)-4(d)(2) (relating to certain created financial interests), or Treas. Reg. § 1.263(a)-4(d)(8) (relating to certain benefits arising from the provision, production, or improvement of real property). *Id.*

[227] I.R.C. § 167(f)(1)(A). Additionally, "off-the-shelf" computer software is "section 179 property" and may be expensed (at least in part) if the taxpayer is eligible to make a section 179 election. I.R.C.

period applies to computer software that is "unbundled" from hardware. Computer software bundled with hardware is simply part of the hardware and depreciated along with the hardware.[228]

> **Problem 3.7**: Same facts as **Problem 3.6** except that Hawkeye separately acquired all substantial rights to the herbicide patent and did not acquire a trade or business from Boilermaker. Hawkeye paid a fixed amount of $1 million for the patent, and the purchase was completed on March 1, Year 1. The patent is due to expire on April 30, Year 5 at which point the patent's useful life is reasonably expected to end. Is the patent an "amortizable section 197 intangible?" If not, is the patent amortizable, and if so, how should Hawkeye amortize its adjusted basis? *See* Treas. Reg. § 1.167(a)-14(c)(4).

3.2[2][b] "Income Forecast" Method

The straight-line method properly matches expenses to income if an intangible produces a relatively even income stream over its useful life. In other words, an even recovery of an intangible's adjusted basis over its useful life would match an even stream of income over useful life. But what if the intangible is reasonably expected to produce an uneven stream of income over its useful life? Use of the straight-line method in such a case would cause a mismatching of expenses and income.

For example, a film studio may reasonably expect its movie to generate more income earlier in its useful life (i.e., during theatrical release) than later (i.e., through DVD sales). If the film studio uses the straight-line method to amortize the movie, it will write off a lower portion of the movie's total capitalized cost in early years relative to the portion of income received in early years to total income. To illustrate this with numbers, suppose the movie has a five-year useful life. Straight-line method amortization of the movie would result in a 20 percent write off each year. But if the movie is reasonably expected to generate 50

---

§ 179(a), (d)(1)(A)(ii). Section 179 expensing of "off-the-shelf" computer software was scheduled to expire after 2010, but may be extended by future legislation.

[228] Rev. Rul. 71-177, 1971-1 C.B. 5. Computer hardware is "section 179 property" and may be expensed (at least in part) if the taxpayer is eligible to make a section 179 election. I.R.C. § 179(a), (d)(1)(A)(i). Any remaining portion of the capitalized cost of computer hardware is depreciated under the modified cost recovery system (MACRS) with a 5-year recovery period. *See generally* I.R.C. § 168, Rev. Proc. 87-56, 1987-2 C.B. 674.

percent of its total income in the first year, a 20 percent write off would be mismatched with 50 percent of total income.

To alleviate the effects of such mismatching, the Service has permitted use of the income forecast method for certain intangibles since the 1960s.[229] Congress later codified the income forecast method in section 167(g) in 1996.[230] A taxpayer using the "income forecast method" recovers the adjusted basis of an intangible in proportion to anticipated income to be earned from the intangible over its useful life. In this way, the "income forecast method" is meant to more clearly match the expense of the intangible with the income that it produces.

The Code limits the availability of the income forecast method to films (including TV shows), videotapes, sound recordings, copyrights, books, and patents.[231] The "income forecast method" is appropriate for these types of intangibles because their usefulness and earning potential are tied to variables such as popularity and audience appeal rather than the mere passage of time. A taxpayer may not use the income forecast method for any "amortizable section 197 intangible."[232]

In 2002, Treasury proposed regulations on the income forecast method.[233] The proposed regulations are too lengthy and comprehensive to cover in detail, so a summary of the proposed regulations is discussed in this Chapter. The proposed regulations require a taxpayer to calculate the annual recovery under the income forecast method according to the following formula:[234]

$$\text{Depreciable basis of intangible} \times \frac{\text{Current year income}}{\text{Forecasted total income}}$$

---

[229] *See* Rev. Rul. 60-358, 1960-2 C.B. 68 (permitting use of income forecast method for TV shows); Rev. Rul. 64-273, 1964-2 C.B. 62 (movies); Rev. Rul. 79-285, 1979-2 C.B. 91 (books, patents, and sound recordings); Rev. Rul. 89-62, 1989-1 C.B. 78 (videocassettes); Priv. Ltr. Rul. 85-01-006 (Sept. 24, 1984) (copyrights).

[230] Small Business Job Protection Act of 1996, Pub. L. No 104-188, § 1604(a), 110 Stat. 1755, 1836 (1996).

[231] I.R.C. § 167(g)(6).

[232] *Id.*

[233] 67 Fed. Reg. 38025 (2002).

[234] Prop. Reg. § 1.167(n)-4(a).

An intangible's initial "depreciable basis" includes amounts paid or incurred as of the year it was placed in service.[235] A taxpayer may not include contingent payments (e.g., payments to actors based on a percentage of a film's gross income) in depreciable basis until such payments are actually paid or incurred.[236] If a contingent payment is paid or incurred after the year the intangible is placed in service, the taxpayer may either (i) depreciate the contingent payment separately under the income forecast method or (ii) calculate depreciation using a "redetermined basis," which accounts for the contingent payment.[237]

As a general rule, "current year income" includes all income earned (less distribution costs) in the current year.[238] A taxpayer computes current year income with its regular accounting method (e.g., cash or accrual method).[239] Current year income does not include income from the sale or disposition of the intangible.[240]

A taxpayer determines "forecasted total income" at the end of the year in which the intangible is placed in service based on all the information available at that time.[241] "Forecasted total income" includes the sum of the following:[242]

(i) income for year the taxpayer places the intangible in service;

(ii) income attributable from any prior year; and

(iii) all income estimated from the intangible for the 10 years after the year the intangible was placed in service.

Therefore, a taxpayer includes a total of 11 years of actual or estimated income in "forecasted total income." A taxpayer may deduct any remaining depreciable basis in the tenth taxable year following the taxable year the intangible is placed in service.[243] The taxpayer may deduct the remaining depreciable basis earlier if the intangible ceases to produce income and is reasonably expected to generate no future income.[244]

---

[235] Prop. Reg. § 1.167(n)-2(a).

[236] Prop. Reg. § 1.167(n)-2(a)(2), (d).

[237] Prop. Reg. § 1.167(n)-2(b), (4)(c).

[238] Prop. Reg. § 1.167(n)-3(a).

[239] *Id.*

[240] Prop. Reg. § 1.167(n)-3(d).

[241] Prop. Reg. § 1.167(n)-3(b).

[242] *Id.*

[243] I.R.C. § 167(g)(1)(C); Prop. Reg. § 1.167(n)-4(d)(1)(ii).

[244] Prop. Reg. § 1.167(n)-4(d)(1)(i).

How is a taxpayer prevented from grossly underestimating forecasted total income in order to increase the amortization fraction and thereby accelerate depreciation? The proposed regulations address this issue in two ways. First, a taxpayer is required to revisit its forecasted total income annually. If "revised forecasted total income" is either less than 90 percent, or more than 110 percent of the forecasted total income used in the preceding year, a taxpayer must use a *revised computation* to calculate depreciation for the year in question and in future years.[245] A taxpayer may elect to use the revised computation even if it is not required.[246] A taxpayer calculates the revised computation as follows:

$$\text{Unrecovered depreciable basis} \quad \text{x} \quad \frac{\text{Current year income}}{\text{[“Revised forecasted total income” – current income from prior years]}}$$

The "revised forecasted total income" is the sum of (i) actual income from current and prior years, and (ii) all future income the taxpayer reasonably estimates will be earned from the intangible through the tenth year after it was place in service.[247]

Second, a taxpayer must generally test a "look-back" provision in the third and tenth years after the intangible was placed in service or in the year the intangible is disposed of or ceases to generate income.[248] The "look-back" provision generally applies if actual income from the intangible for each preceding year is less than 90 percent or more than 110 percent of the estimated income taken into account in determining the depreciation deduction for the intangible.[249] If the "look-back" provision is triggered, a taxpayer may be required to pay interest to the government where depreciation was accelerated (or a taxpayer may receive interest if depreciation was delayed).[250]

> **Problem 3.8**: In Year 1, Taxpayer, a large movie studio, purchased for $1 million all rights to a documentary film on climate change. Taxpayer

[245] Prop. Reg. § 1.167(n)-4(b)(2).

[246] Prop. Reg. § 1.167(n)-4(b)(1).

[247] Prop. Reg. § 1.167(n)-3(c).

[248] Prop. Reg. § 1.167(n)-6(a). The "look-back" provision does not apply to an intangible with an unadjusted basis of $100,000 or less. Prop. Reg. § 1.167(n)-6(f).

[249] Prop. Reg. § 1.167(n)-6(e)(2)(i). The taxpayer treats actual income and estimated income as equal in years where the "look-back" provision previously applied. Prop. Reg. § 1.167(n)-6(e)(2)(ii).

[250] *Id.*

immediately placed the documentary in service in Year 1 by releasing it in theaters in select cities. In Year 1, Taxpayer grossed $1 million from the film and the distribution costs totaled $500,000. Based on all available information at the end of Year 1, Taxpayer estimated that the film would earn an additional $1,500,000 (net of distribution costs) over the next 10 years, mostly through DVD sales and sales through other electronic media. How much depreciation can Taxpayer claim on the film in Year 1 under the income forecast method?

In Year 2, Taxpayer released the film on DVD and grossed $2 million from the film. The film's distribution costs for Year 2 totaled $1 million. Based on all available information at the end of Year 2, Taxpayer estimated that the film would earn an additional $500,000 (net of distribution costs) over the next nine years. How much depreciation can Taxpayer claim on the film in Year 2 under the income forecast method?

In Year 3, Taxpayer grossed $500,000 from the film and the distribution costs totaled $200,000. Based on all available information at the end of Year 3, Taxpayer reasonably estimated that the film would earn (net of distribution costs) an additional $500,000 in Years 4 through 11. Is Taxpayer required to use a revised computation to calculate depreciation in Year 3 under the income forecast method? How much depreciation can Taxpayer claim in Year 3 under the income forecast method?

Year 4 was an unexpectedly poor year for the film. In Year 4, Taxpayer's gross from the film equaled distribution costs. Nevertheless, based on all available information at the end of Year 4, Taxpayer reasonably believed that the film would earn (net of distribution costs) an additional $500,000 in Years 5 through 11. How much depreciation can the Taxpayer claim in Year 4 under the income forecast method?

When the film was released in Year 1 climate change was a hot topic (no pun intended) that interested much of the public. But by Year 5, the public's interest in climate change had waned substantially. And scientific studies released in Year 5 proved many of the film's claims to be inaccurate. As a result, taxpayer's gross from the film equaled distribution costs in Year 5. Based on all available information at the end of Year 5, taxpayer reasonably estimated that the film would no longer generate income exceeding distribution costs. How much depreciation can the taxpayer claim in Year 5 under the income forecast method?

In 2005, Congress created a temporary elective rule (effective through 2010) to exempt certain musical compositions and copyrights from the income forecast method.[251] The election allows a taxpayer to amortize "applicable musical property" ratably over five years beginning with the month in which the property was placed in service.[252] "Applicable musical property" includes any musical composition (including any accompanying words) or any copyright covering a musical composition.[253] The election is not available for any section 197 intangible or any "qualified creative expense" under section 263(h) (discussed in Chapter 1).[254]

3.2[2][c] "Variable Contingent Payment" Method

In many cases, the purchase price for a separately-acquired intangible, particularly a patent or copyright, is not fixed. Instead, the purchase price may be entirely contingent upon the buyer's usage of the acquired intangible. Because neither the straight-line method nor income forecast method work well without a fixed basis, a taxpayer may use the "variable contingent payment" method to amortize intangibles excluded from section 197 purchased for contingent payments.[255]

Calculation of amortization under the variable contingent payment method is simple. The taxpayer merely adds a contingent payment to the acquired intangible's basis as paid or incurred and then deducts that amount as an amortization deduction in the same year.[256] Thus, amortization deductions under the variable contingent payment method work the same way as current expensing under sections 162 and 174 *with one major difference.* As discussed in Chapter 4, amortization deductions may be recaptured as ordinary income upon disposition of the intangible, whereas deductions under sections 162 and 174 do not trigger ordinary income recapture.

---

[251] Tax Increase Prevention and Reconciliation Act of 2005, Pub. L. No. 109-222, § 207, 120 Stat. 345, 350-51 (2005).

[252] I.R.C. § 167(g)(8)(A), (E).

[253] I.R.C. § 167(g)(8)(C)(i).

[254] I.R.C. § 167(g)(8)(C)(ii).

[255] *Associated Patentees, Inc. v. Commr.*, 4 T.C. 979 (1945); Treas. Reg. § 1.167(a)-14(c)(4); Rev. Rul. 67-136, 1967-1 C.B. 58.

[256] *Id.*

Problem 3.9: Wildcat Corporation acquired all substantial rights to a patent on a blood pressure medicine from Hoosier Corporation. Wildcat did not acquire a trade or business from Hoosier. In exchange for the patent, Wildcat agreed to pay Hoosier 5 percent of the gross sales of the blood pressure medicine payable annually for the next 10 years (the remaining useful life of the patent). In the first year, Wildcat paid a royalty of $1,000,000 to Hoosier pursuant to their agreement. Is the patent an "amortizable section 197 intangible?" How should Wildcat amortize the $1,000,000 payment it made to Hoosier in the first year? Would amortization of the $1,000,000 payment ratably over the patent's remaining useful life of 10 years more properly match expenses and income than the variable contingent payment method? Read *Associated Patentees, Inc. v. Commissioner* and Rev. Rul. 67-136 (both included in this Chapter's materials) in connection with this problem.

3.3 Acquisition of Intellectual Property by License

As mentioned earlier in this Chapter, a taxpayer may acquire intellectual property in two primary ways: (1) by purchase or (2) by license. The tax consequences of a license vis-à-vis a purchase (sale) can vary. So distinguishing between a license and a sale is necessary. In many cases, the line between a license and sale can be a fine one. Parties to an agreement may label a transaction as a "license" when, in fact, the transaction is a sale for tax purposes. As discussed in greater detail in Chapter 4, a sale generally occurs where the transferor transfers *all substantial rights* in the property to the transferor.[257] A license, therefore, occurs where a transferee receives less than all substantial rights to the property from the transferor. Treasury regulations caution that licenses will be closely scrutinized to determine if a license is really a sale because all substantial rights have been transferred.[258] Once a

---

[257] Treasury regulations dealing with section 197 incorporate the "all substantial rights" standard from section 1235, which distinguishes between sales and licenses of patents. *See* Treas. Reg. § 1.197-2(f)(3)(iii). Section 1253, which distinguishes between sales and licenses of franchises, trademarks and trade names, uses a slightly different standard. Under section 1253, a sale (or exchange) occurs where the transferor does not retain any significant right or continuing interest in the franchise, trademark, or trade name. *See* I.R.C. § 1253(a). Chapter 4 addresses the sale versus license issue from the transferor's perspective because a sale may generate capital gain while a license does not.

[258] Treas. Reg. § 1.197-2(f)(3)(iii). The "all substantial rights" standard comes from section 1235, which distinguishes between sales and licenses of patents.

taxpayer determines that a transaction is truly a license, the next step is to determine how the taxpayer recovers the cost of license.

3.3[1] License for the Use of Intellectual Property

A contract or license for the use of a section 197 intangible *is itself a section 197 intangible.*[259] This rule is meant to prevent taxpayers from avoiding section 197 by licensing rather than purchasing section 197 intangibles. At first blush, one might conclude that this rule has a great impact on the licensing of intellectual property. But the rule is subject to caveats and exceptions that effectively exempt most licenses of intellectual property from section 197.

To be an "amortizable section 197 intangible," a license must be acquired as part of the acquisition of a trade or business (i.e., acquired in a taxable asset acquisition).[260] This rule makes sense because the very purpose of section 197 is to alleviate allocation disputes in taxable asset acquisitions. And if there is no taxable asset acquisition, there will be no allocation dispute to trigger section 197's purpose. Therefore, a license for the use of intellectual property that is not acquired as part of a trade or business is not subject to section 197.[261]

Even if a license is acquired as part of a trade or business, it may nonetheless fall outside the scope of section 197 if either of two exceptions applies. First, a license for any information base (other than a customer-related information base), patent, copyright, formula, process, know-how, format, package design, computer software, film, sound recording, video, book, or similar property is not subject to section 197 if the taxpayer can establish the following:

(1) the license is truly a license and not a sale (because the taxpayer has not acquired all substantial rights to the intellectual property), and

(2) the license is transferred for arm's length consideration.[262]

Second, a license of a franchise, trademark, or trade name is not subject to section 197 if it is truly a license (and not a sale or exchange) under the principles of section 1253.[263] Section

[259] Treas. Reg. § 1.197-2(b)(11).

[260] Treas. Reg. § 1.197-2(f)(3)(ii)(A).

[261] Treas. Reg. § 1.197-2(f)(3)(iii).

[262] Treas. Reg. § 1.197-2(f)(3)(ii)(B).

[263] Treas. Reg. § 1.197-2(e)(2)(ii)(C).

1253 provides that a sale or exchange occurs where the transferor retains no "significant power, right, or continuing interest" in the franchise, trademark, or trade name.[264] Stated differently, a license occurs where the transferor does retain a significant power, right, or continuing interest" in the franchise, trademark, or trade name. Section 1253 specifically provides that a taxpayer can currently deduct "contingent serial payments" made on a license of a franchise, trademark, and trade name.[265] "Contingent serial payments" are payments (1) contingent on the productivity or usage of the franchise, trademark, trade name, (2) made at least annually, and (3) substantially equal in amount (or payable under a fixed formula).[266]

> **Problem 3.10**: Gopher Corporation is an automobile manufacturer that produces, in separate divisions, passenger automobiles, heavy-duty trucks, industrial equipment (e.g., forklifts), and agricultural equipment (e.g., tractors, combines, and the like). Gopher sold its agricultural equipment division to Hawkeye Corporation in a taxable asset acquisition, except that Gopher retained certain patents and customer lists that are also used by its other divisions. Gopher licensed these patents and customer lists to Hawkeye in exchange for royalties based on usage. The licenses are arm's length, reasonable in amount, and are licenses (not sales) under the principles of section 1253. Are the licenses of the patents and customer lists "amortizable section 197" intangibles?

3.3[2] Cost Recovery of a License that is not Subject to Section 197

The length of a license that is not subject to section 197 is critical in determining whether its cost is currently deductible or capitalized. As discussed in Chapter 1, the 12-month rule that provides a taxpayer may currently deduct a right or benefit that does not extend beyond (1) 12 months from the first date of realizing the right or benefit, or (2) the end of the taxable year following the year paid.[267] Therefore, payments on licenses that fit within the 12-month

---

[264] I.R.C. § 1253(a). A "significant power, right, or continuing interest" is defined in section 1253(b)(2) and discussed in greater detail in Chapter 4. One such "significant power, right, or continuing interest" is the right to receive "contingent serial payments" based on the productivity or usage of the transferred franchise, trademark, or trade name. I.R.C. § 1253(b)(2)(F).

[265] I.R.C. § 1253(d)(1).

[266] I.R.C. § 1253(d)(1)(B).

[267] Treas. Reg. § 1.263(a)-4(f)(1); *see also U.S. Freightways Corp. v. Commr.*, 270 F.3d 1137 (7th Cir. 2001).

rule should qualify for current deduction. Conversely, payments on licenses that fall outside the 12-month rule should be capitalized (and amortized over their useful lives).[268]

3.4 Materials for Chapter 3

FRONTIER CHEVROLET CO. v. COMMISSIONER

United States Tax Court

116 T.C. 289 (2001)[269]

RUWE, Judge

Respondent determined deficiencies in petitioner's Federal income taxes as follows:

Year	Amount
1994	$28,996
1995	135,880
1996	110,320

After concessions, the issue for decision is whether petitioner must amortize noncompetition agreement payments over 15 years pursuant to section 197.

BACKGROUND

The parties submitted this case fully stipulated. The stipulation of facts, stipulation of settled issues, and the attached exhibits are incorporated herein by this reference. Petitioner is a corporation that had its principal place of business in Billings, Montana, at the time it filed its petition.

Petitioner is engaged in the trade or business of selling and servicing new and used vehicles. Roundtree Automotive Group, Inc. (Roundtree), is a corporation engaged in the trade or

---

[268] Treas. Reg. § 1.263(a)-4(d)(6)(i)(A). Generally, a license for the use of an intangible is a "created intangible" that must be capitalized. *Id.* Exceptions to capitalization apply if the amount paid on the license is "de minimis" ($5,000 or less) or the 12-month rule applies. Treas. Reg. §§ 1.263(a)-4(d)(1) (providing that a taxpayer need not capitalize a created intangible if the 12-month rule applies) & 1.263(a)-4(d)(6)(v) (providing for the "de minimis" rule).

[269] The Ninth Circuit affirmed the Tax Court's decision in 329 F.3d 1131 (9th Cir. 2003).

business of purchasing and operating automobile dealerships and providing consulting services to these dealerships. Frank Stinson (Mr. Stinson) was involved in the operations of Roundtree during the years 1987 through 1994.

Roundtree originally purchased all the stock of petitioner in August of 1987. Consistent with Mr. Stinson's and Roundtree's policy of management, petitioner filled the position of executive manager of its dealership with one of Mr. Stinson's long-term employees, Dennis Menholt (Mr. Menholt). As part of his employment by petitioner, Mr. Menholt was allowed to purchase, from 1987 through 1994, 25 percent of the stock of petitioner.

In 1994, Mr. Menholt was the general manager of petitioner's automobile dealership located in Billings, Montana, and Mr. Stinson was the president of Roundtree. Mr. Stinson participated in the management of petitioner's business, particularly in advertising and sales training. Roundtree received monthly payments of $22,000 for management services it performed for petitioner. Prior to August 1, 1994, Roundtree owned 75 percent of the stock in petitioner, and Mr. Menholt owned the remaining 25 percent.

Petitioner entered into a "Stock Sale Agreement" with Roundtree. Effective August 1, 1994, petitioner redeemed all its stock owned by Roundtree for $3.5 million. The funds to redeem the stock were borrowed from General Motors Acceptance Corporation (GMAC), with liens placed on all tangible assets of petitioner. After the stock sale agreement, Mr. Menholt was the sole remaining shareholder of petitioner.

Petitioner also entered into a "Non- Competition Agreement" (noncompetition agreement) with Mr. Stinson and Roundtree, effective August 1, 1994. The noncompetition agreement stated:

> To induce *** [petitioner] to enter into and consummate the Stock Sale Agreement and to protect the value of the shares of stock being purchased, Roundtree and [Mr.] Stinson covenant, to the extent provided in Section 1 hereof, that Roundtree and [Mr.] Stinson shall not compete with *** [petitioner's] automobile dealership, stock of which was sold to *** [petitioner] pursuant to the Stock Sale Agreement.

Section 1, entitled "Covenant Not to Compete", provided that Roundtree and Mr. Stinson would not compete with petitioner in the car dealership business within Yellowstone County for a period of 5 years. The agreement stated that the competition restrictions against Mr. Stinson and Roundtree "are reasonable and necessary to protect the business and interest which *** [petitioner] under the Stock Sale Agreement is acquiring pursuant to the Stock Sale Agreement." As consideration for the obligations of Roundtree and Mr. Stinson, petitioner agreed to pay Roundtree and Mr. Stinson $22,000 per month for 60 months. The consideration under the noncompetition agreement was in addition to the consideration petitioner paid to redeem its stock. In the event petitioner defaulted on the noncompetition agreement payments, the entire amount of the remaining payments would immediately become due and collectible, and the covenant not to compete would terminate 90 days after such default. If Roundtree and Mr. Stinson breached their obligations under the agreement, petitioner was entitled to one-half of the net profits for 5 years of any business conducted which breached the covenant not to compete.

Due to the GMAC loan, petitioner was leveraged with large interest expenses. In the summer of 1994, petitioner was below the minimum working capital requirements of its franchisor and had to obtain a special waiver of working capital requirements in order to continue holding its franchise. There was no known alternative to the noncompetition agreement with Roundtree and Mr. Stinson in order to protect petitioner from their competition in the Billings market. Without the agreement, it would have been difficult for petitioner to raise capital or to pay its loan from GMAC.

On its Federal income tax returns for the years 1994 through 1996, petitioner amortized the noncompetition agreement payments over 15 years. In 1999, petitioner filed a claim for refund for the taxable years 1995 and 1996 on the basis that the noncompetition agreement payments should be amortized over 60 months, the life of the agreement. In its amended petition, petitioner claims that it is entitled to a deduction for the years 1995 and 1996 for the same reasons set forth in its claim for refund.

DISCUSSION

The issue for decision is whether petitioner must amortize noncompetition agreement payments to Roundtree and Mr. Stinson over 15 years pursuant to section 197.

Section 197(a) provides that "A taxpayer shall be entitled to an amortization deduction with respect to any amortizable section 197 intangible." The deduction is determined by amortizing the adjusted basis of the intangible ratably over a 15-year period beginning with the month in which such intangible was acquired. *See* sec. 197(a). An "amortizable section 197 intangible" is any section 197 intangible acquired by a taxpayer after August 10, 1993, and held in connection with the conduct of a trade or business. Sec. 197(c)(1). A covenant not to compete entered into in connection with a direct or indirect acquisition of an interest in a trade or business is a section 197 intangible. *See* sec. 197(d)(1)(E).

Petitioner argues that it did not acquire any interest in a trade or business; therefore, the covenant not to compete is not a section 197 intangible and petitioner is permitted to amortize the payments over 60 months, the life of the covenant. This is the first instance in which we have the opportunity to consider the statutory requirements of section 197 as they relate to a covenant not to compete.

Petitioner entered into a stock sale agreement with Roundtree. Under the terms of that agreement, petitioner redeemed 75 percent of its stock from Roundtree for $3.5 million. Petitioner also entered into a noncompetition agreement with Roundtree and Mr. Stinson. A purpose of the noncompetition agreement was:

> To induce *** [petitioner] to enter into and consummate the Stock Sale Agreement and to protect the value of the shares of stock being purchased, Roundtree and [Mr.] Stinson covenant, to the extent provided in Section 1 hereof, that Roundtree and [Mr.] Stinson shall not compete with *** [petitioner's] automobile dealership, stock of which was sold to *** [petitioner] pursuant to the Stock Sale Agreement.

The noncompetition agreement prohibited Roundtree and Mr. Stinson from competing with petitioner in the car dealership business within Yellowstone County for a period of 5 years. The facts establish, and petitioner does not dispute, that the noncompetition agreement was entered into "in connection with" the stock sale agreement.

Petitioner argues that it did not acquire an interest in a trade or business pursuant to the stock transaction because, both before and after the transaction, petitioner was engaged in exactly the same trade or business and it acquired no other new assets. Respondent argues that petitioner's redemption of its stock was an "acquisition" of an interest in a trade or business within the meaning of section 197.

Normally, we look to the plain language of a statute to interpret its meaning. *See Consumer Prod. Safety Commn. v. GTE Sylvania, Inc.*, 447 U.S. 102, 108 (1980); *Union Carbide Foreign Sales Corp. v. Commissioner*, 115 T.C. 423, 430 (2000). When a statute is clear on its face, we require unequivocal evidence of legislative purpose before interpreting the statute to override the plain meaning of the words used therein. *See Hirasuna v. Commissioner*, 89 T.C. 1216, 1224 (1987); *Huntsberry v. Commissioner*, 83 T.C. 742, 747-

748 (1984). The legislative history of section 197 contains no evidence that Congress intended a purchase of stock to be excluded from the meaning of the term "acquisition" simply because the purchase occurred in the form of a redemption.

The term "acquisition" is defined as "The gaining of possession or control over something" and "Something acquired." Black's Law Dictionary 24 (7th ed. 1999). The term "redemption" is defined as "The act or an instance of reclaiming or regaining possession by paying a specific price." *Id.* at 1282. Redemption, in the context of securities, is defined as "The reacquisition of a security by the issuer." *Id.* In the instant case, petitioner entered into a stock sale agreement in which it redeemed 75 percent of its outstanding stock from Roundtree. As a result of the stock sale agreement, petitioner regained possession and control over its stock. On the basis of the plain meaning of the statute, we conclude that the redemption was an "acquisition" within the meaning of section 197 because petitioner received 75 percent of its stock as a result of the transaction with Roundtree.

In order for section 197 to apply, petitioner must have directly or indirectly acquired an "interest in a trade or business." The relevant legislative history of section 197 provides:

> The term "section 197 intangible" also includes any covenant not to compete (or other arrangement to the extent that the arrangement has substantially the same effect as a covenant not to compete) entered into in connection with the direct or indirect acquisition of an interest in a trade or business (or a substantial portion thereof). For this purpose, an interest in a trade or business includes not only the assets of a trade or business, *but also stock in a corporation that is engaged in a trade or business* or an interest in a partnership that is engaged in a trade or business. [H. Rept. 103-111, at 764 (1993), 1993-3 C.B. 167, 340; emphasis added.]

See also H. Conf. Rept. 103-213, at 677 (1993), 1993-3 C.B. 393, 555 (using language nearly identical to that used in the House report). The legislative history explains that an "acquisition of stock that is not treated as an asset acquisition" is treated as "an indirect acquisition of a trade or business." *Id.* at 694, 1993-3 C.B. at 572. Thus, the legislative history indicates that an interest in a trade or business includes not only the direct acquisition of the assets of the trade or business but also the acquisition of stock in a corporation that is engaged in a trade or business.

The noncompetition agreement provides that the covenant not to compete was "reasonable and necessary to protect the business and interest which *** [petitioner] under the Stock

Sale Agreement is acquiring pursuant to the Stock Sale Agreement." Petitioner acquired 75 percent of its stock when it entered into the stock sale agreement with Roundtree. Petitioner is a corporation engaged in the trade or business of selling and servicing new and used vehicles. Thus, when petitioner executed the stock sale agreement it indirectly acquired an interest, in the form of stock, in a corporation engaged in a trade or business.

Petitioner agrees that section 197 might apply if it had acquired a new trade or business, but it contends that the statute does not apply in the instant case because petitioner continued the operation of its own existing business. Neither the statute nor the legislative history contains any indication that an interest in a new trade or business must be acquired in order for section 197 to apply. Accordingly, we find that petitioner acquired an "interest in a trade or business" within the meaning of section 197 when it redeemed its stock from Roundtree.

Finally, petitioner appears to argue that even if there was an acquisition of an interest in a trade or business, it was by a shareholder and not petitioner. Both the stock sale agreement and the noncompetition agreement identify petitioner, Roundtree, and Mr. Stinson, as the parties involved in the agreements. Under the terms of the stock sale agreement, Roundtree agreed to transfer the stock directly to petitioner, not to any shareholders of petitioner. In its brief, petitioner states that the noncompetition agreement was not entered into by any shareholders of petitioner. Accordingly, petitioner's argument lacks merit.

We find that the noncompetition agreement was entered into in connection with an acquisition of an interest in a trade or business. Therefore, we hold that petitioner must amortize the noncompetition agreement payments to Roundtree and Mr. Stinson over 15 years pursuant to section 197.

Decision will be entered under Rule 155.

ASSOCIATED PATENTEES, INC. v. COMMISSIONER

United States Tax Court

4 T.C. 979 (1945)

Memorandum findings of fact and opinion was entered in this proceeding on August 31, 1943. The deficiencies involved arose wholly from the disallowance by respondent of a deduction of $42,209.76 taken by petitioner for the calendar year 1940 as patent royalties paid in that year by it to four individuals. Our conclusion was that this payment was a capital expenditure by petitioner in the acquisition of the patents from those individuals and as such was not deductible. Decision was entered for the respondent.

Thereafter, petitioner filed timely motions to vacate the decision, to reconsider the opinion, and for rehearing or new trial. On October 20, 1943, we entered an order, upon petitioner's motions, vacating our decision and opinion theretofore entered, and granted petitioner's motion for rehearing, directing that such rehearing be limited to the question of the depreciation to which petitioner would be entitled in the taxable year in question for exhaustion of its capital investment in view of our holding that the expenditures deducted by petitioner were capital in character. Petitioner, by our order, was permitted to file an amended petition raising the issue as to allowance of depreciation. Such amended petition was duly filed.

The rehearing as directed by our order was held May 8, 1944. Certain evidence was introduced, without objection, bearing upon the question of the value of the patents in question. We make the following findings of fact.

FINDINGS OF FACT

The petitioner is a business corporation organized in 1933 under the laws of the State of New Jersey. Its principal place of business was in East Orange, New Jersey. Its authorized capital stock consisted of 100 shares of common without par value. All shares were issued. In about 1928 or 1929, Alwyn E. Borton, Frederick Koch, and Walter P. Powers, all inventors and holders of patent rights, together with Cecil Todd, a financier, entered into an oral agreement to pool the patents and inventions on an equal share basis of one-quarter to each. They caused the petitioner to be formed. Each became an officer and director of the corporation. At the first meeting of the directors, held on January 14, 1933, the aforementioned individuals made an offer to sell, assign, and transfer to the petitioner all of their right, title, and interest in and to 20 patents in exchange for the 100 shares of the capital stock of the petitioner. The directors, by resolution, accepted the offer. On January 16, 1933, these individuals executed and delivered to the petitioner a written assignment of 20 patents, designated therein by number, date of issue, and a brief description thereof. Thereupon the petitioner caused to be issued to each of these assignors 25 shares of its capital stock of no par value.

* * *

The following instrument was executed by the petitioner and the four individuals:

Whereas, since January 14, 1933, C. Todd, A. E. Borton, F. Koch and W. P. Powers have made certain inventions and have obtained numerous patents, and

Whereas, the said C. Todd, A. E. Borton, F. Koch and W. P. Powers are now working on numerous inventions and are applying for and seeking numerous patents, and

Whereas, the patents as obtained have been turned over to Associated Patentees, Inc., from time to time without any arrangement being made as to compensation, and

Whereas, the understanding was that the parties would arrive at the matter of compensation in due time, and

Whereas, Associated Patentees, Inc., have licensed certain patents and inventions to others, and are obtaining certain royalties from time to time, and

Whereas, almost the entire income of Associated Patentees, Inc., consists of royalties received from licensing others to use these patents and inventions, and

Whereas, a verbal arrangement was made earlier this year to the effect that the Associated Patentees, Inc., would pay to each C. Todd, A. E. Borton, F. Koch, and W. P. Powers 20% of all royalties received for the use of the patents and inventions turned over by them since January 14, 1933, to Associated Patentees, Inc., and

Whereas, it is thought wise, because of the volume of business being done, and for other reasons, to reduce the whole arrangement to writing,

Now This Contract Witnesseth:

That in consideration of one dollar, and other good and valuable considerations, the receipt whereof is hereby acknowledged, and in consideration of the use of numerous patents and inventions as listed on

> attached Schedule A, and in further consideration of the premise on the part of C. Todd, A. E. Borton, F. Koch, and W. P. Powers to keep such patents and inventions current in so far as they can do so, and in further consideration of the promise on the part of C. Todd, A. E. Borton, F. Koch, and W. P. Powers to turn over any inventions they may make to the Associated Patentees, Inc., the Associated Patentees, Inc., this 31st day of December, 1940, agrees to pay to each of the said C. Todd, A. E. Borton, F. Koch, and W. P. Powers, as royalties for the use of the patents and inventions turned over to Associated Patentees, Inc. since January 14, 1933, as shown in Exhibit A attached, an amount of cash equal to twenty (20) per cent of all royalties received by the said Associated Patentees, Inc.; and
>
> Further, the Associated Patentees, Inc. agrees to pay to each of the said C. Todd, A. E. Borton, F. Koch and W. P. Powers as royalties for the use of the patents and inventions turned over to the Associated Patentees, Inc., since January 14, 1933, as shown on Exhibit A attached, and as royalties for the use of patents and inventions to be turned over by the said C. Todd, A. E. Borton F. Koch, and W. P. Powers, to the Associated Patentees, Inc. in the future, an amount of cash equal to twenty (20) per cent of all royalties that Associated Patentees, Inc. hereafter receives.
>
> This contract shall continue in full force and effect during the entire life of said patents and inventions, including the life of any patents and inventions that may be turned over to the Associated Patentees, Inc., in the future.

* * *

Prior to the end of 1940 petitioner paid $42,209.76 to the four individuals in equal amounts.

The value of the patents in question was far in excess of $42,209.76, the amount of the payments made by petitioner to the individuals for the calendar year 1940. These payments were capital expenditures in acquisition of legal and equitable title to the patents.

OPINION

Petitioner asks us to find from the evidence introduced upon the rehearing that the patents in question had a cost to it of $3,000,000. This we can not do. That evidence was directed to the question of value, whereas the question we have is one of cost. Moreover, that evidence consists of an opinion based upon such uncertain factors that we do not think it carries weight in determining the value of the patents. We are convinced, however, from the testimony that the patents had great value, largely in excess of the total amounts paid by petitioner in the year 1940, and have so found.

Petitioner acquired the patents from four individuals. The patents had varying lives. The consideration to be paid for the patents was 80 percent of the yearly income received by petitioner from licenses granted by it to use the patents. The four individual further contracted, in consideration of petitioner's agreement to make these annual payments, to perform services in keeping up the patents, all improvements thereon invented by them to become the property of the petitioner.

Thus the amount of $42,209.76, paid in 1940 by petitioner under the contract, in no sense constitutes the total cost of the patents. This cost includes the future payments which will be made and can not be determined until the expiration of the patents, at which time their value passes out. Of course, it is unquestioned that petitioner is entitled to recover this total cost through reasonable deductions for exhaustion over the period of their lives. The obstacle to computation of depreciation over the term of the lives of the patents in the ordinary way by a proration of total cost is the fact that we have here the first year of the term. It is impossible to determine in this year what the total cost will be, since it will include a percentage of earnings of petitioner in each year of that term. These earnings can not now be determined.

Under these conditions, it is respondent's contention that for the year 1940 there should be allowed as depreciation only a proportionate part of the $42,209.76 paid in that year, the balance of that cost to be prorated over the succeeding years of the lives of the patents, and that in each succeeding year there should be allowed depreciation upon payments made therein based upon the then remaining lives of the patents, petitioner to be allowed this amount plus the amount of depreciation allocated to such succeeding year from prior payments.

It will readily be seen that although this method of computation will give to the petitioner aggregate theoretical deductions for depreciation equaling the total ultimate cost, its practical result will be an entirely inadequate allowance for depreciation at the beginning of the term and excessive allowances for depreciation at the end. Actually, in the later years, the depreciation allowances would largely exceed income from the patents. Under such a method of computation the petitioner might not, in fact, recover its cost from income.

Petitioner's contention is that the cost payment made each year is subject to depreciation in its full amount because it is a cost pertaining to that year alone and measured by income over that period. It is argued that, with an allowance so made, at the close of the lives of the patents the petitioner will have recovered the amount of their cost prorated equitably over their lives.

Section 23(l) [now Section 167(a)] provides for "a reasonable allowance" for depreciation. It provides no specific method for its computation. Respondent's regulations recognize the fact that there is not fixed rule, but that the cost should be apportioned over the useful life in such ratable amount as may reasonably be considered necessary to recover during the remaining useful life of the property the unrecovered cost or other basis. The situation here is unusual. But we think that the method for computing depreciation for which petitioner argues gives it a reasonable, and not more than a reasonable, allowance, whereas the method urged by respondent might deny petitioner the recovery of its cost and would unquestionably result in a distortion of income.

Accordingly, we have found here, as we did in our earlier opinion, that petitioner acquired legal and equitable title to the patents in question prior to the tax year. But we now hold that in computing its contested taxes for that year petitioner is entitled to a deduction for exhaustion of the patents equal to the total payments of $42,209.76 made in that year.

Decision will be entered for the petitioner.

REVENUE RULING 67-136

1967-1 C.B. 58

A taxpayer-purchaser may deduct, as an allowance for depreciation under section 167 of the Internal Revenue Code of 1954, an amount equal to the payments made during the taxable year on the purchase price of United States patents and United States patent applications, where the invention covered by the patent application is one for which a patent will be issued in the normal course, if the purchase price is fixed by the contract of sale as a reasonable percentage of the annual return derived by the taxpayer-purchaser from the use or exploitation of the patents and patent applications over the period of their remaining lives.

Advice has been requested whether, under the circumstances described below, a taxpayer may deduct as an allowance for depreciation of property under section 167 of the Internal

Revenue Code of 1954, an amount which equals the annual payments made on the purchase price of certain patents and patent applications where the invention covered by the patent application is one for which a patent will be issued in the normal course.

The taxpayer, who is engaged in the business of purchasing patents and patent applications and licensing their use to third persons, entered into a contract with an individual who owned certain United States patents and United States patent applications relating to inventions on which a patent will be issued in the normal course. The agreement provided that the seller would convey to the taxpayer all his right, title, and interest in these patents and patent applications.

As consideration for the transfer, the taxpayer agreed to pay to the seller each year a reasonable percentage of all royalties or other consideration which he received from any licenses of the patents and patent applications. The agreement provides for termination of the contract if the taxpayer becomes bankrupt, in which case all rights transferred by the contract will revert to the seller.

Section 167(a) of the Code provides, in part, that as a general rule there shall be allowed as a depreciation deduction a reasonable allowance for the exhaustion, wear and tear (including a reasonable allowance for obsolescence), of property used in the trade or business, or of property held for the production of income.

In accordance with section 1.167(a)-3 of the Income Tax Regulations, if an intangible asset is known from experience or other factors to be of use in the business or in the production of income for only a limited period, the length of which can be estimated with reasonable accuracy, such an intangible asset may be the subject of an allowance for depreciation. Examples are patents and copyrights. An intangible asset, the useful life of which is not limited, is not subject to an allowance for depreciation.

A depreciation deduction is designed, generally, to allow a taxpayer to recover his cost or other basis in assets over the period of their usefulness in his trade or business. Similarly, by the terms of the contract in the instant case, the price of the assets is tied to the benefits the taxpayer derives from them; as the assets produce income their cost or basis increases and their period of usefulness to the taxpayer is proven. The use of the amounts which the taxpayer in this case is contractually obligated to pay on the price as the measure of the allowance for depreciation assures minimum distortion of income. The contrary would be the case if the taxpayer were required to delay recapturing his capital investment in the assets until their total price is established.

Accordingly, since the invention covered by each of the applications is one for which a patent will be issued in the normal course and the purchase price of the patents and patent applications is contractually fixed as a reasonable percentage of the annual earnings from such patents and patent applications over the period of their remaining lives, the taxpayer-purchaser may deduct a sum equal to the payments made during the taxable year on the purchase price of such patents and patent applications as an allowance for depreciation under section 167 of the Code. *See Associated Patentees, Inc. v. Commissioner,* 4 T.C. 979 (1945), acquiescence, C.B. 1959-2, 3.

Chapter 4: Sales, Exchanges, and Licenses of Intellectual Property

4.1 Transfers of Intellectual Property – General

If one word could summarize the taxation of intellectual property transfers, that word would be *characterization*. As discussed in Chapter 1, taxpayers generally prefer their gains to be capital (as opposed to ordinary) because capital gains may qualify for preferable tax rates. On the other hand, transferors generally prefer losses to be ordinary (as opposed to capital) because ordinary losses are not limited. A transfer of intellectual property that is a *sale or exchange* may give rise to a capital gain (or loss) to the transferor. And a sale or exchange has the added benefit of allowing the transferor to offset the adjusted basis of the transferred property against the amount realized. Conversely, a transfer of intellectual property that is a *license* gives rise to ordinary income (i.e., royalty income) to the transferor.[270] And the transferor of a license may not offset the adjusted basis of the transferred property against the royalty payments. Therefore, the distinction between a sale or exchange, on the one hand, and a license, on the other, is critical in determining the character of gain or loss on the transfer.

4.1[1] Transfers Qualifying for Capital Gain (or Loss) Treatment

In order for a taxpayer to have a capital gain or loss, the taxpayer must execute (1) a "sale or exchange" (2) of a "capital asset."[271] Satisfying the "sale or exchange" and "capital asset" requirements, by themselves, does not qualify the taxpayer for preferential rates. As explained in Chapter 1, to qualify for a preferential rate, a noncorporate taxpayer must have a "net capital gain" for the taxable year. The term "net capital gain" means the amount by which the taxpayer's net long-term capital gain for the year exceeds the net short-term capital loss.[272] In other words, preferential rates are reserved for those capital assets held for *more than one year*, i.e., long-term capital gains.

---

[270] I.R.C. § 61(a)(6).

[271] *See generally* I.R.C. § 1222.

[272] I.R.C. § 1222(11). Capital gains and losses are classified as "long-term" or "short-term" based on the taxpayer's holding period of the capital asset. If a taxpayer's holding period of a capital asset is *more than one year* at sale or exchange, the capital gain or loss is long-term. I.R.C. § 1222(3), (4). Conversely, if the taxpayer's holding period is *one year or less*, the capital gain or loss is short-term. I.R.C. § 1222(1), (2). Special rules apply in calculating a taxpayer's holding period of property received by gift, inheritance or devise, and in certain nonrecognition transactions. I.R.C. § 1223.

4.1[1][a] "Sale or Exchange" vs. License – Definitions

Neither the Code nor Treasury Regulations define the term "sale or exchange." Courts have generally interpreted "sale or exchange" according to its common meaning.[273] Thus, a "sale or exchange" generally occurs upon any transfer of property for money or the transfer of property for property. But the "sale or exchange" requirement is not satisfied if the transfer is a license.

The courts often seek to ascertain whether the parties intended to create a sale or a license. While the terminology of the contract is of great importance in establishing the parties' intent, it is not necessarily determinative.[274] For example, a transfer labeled as a "sale" may be treated as a license if the parties really intended the transfer to create a license.[275] And a transfer labeled a "license" will be treated as a sale if the substance of the transfer is a sale.[276]

As discussed in detail later in this Chapter, Congress has specifically adopted an "all substantial rights" standard in section 1235 to distinguish between sales and licenses of patents. That is, a sale or exchange occurs where the taxpayer transfers "all substantial rights" and a license occurs where the taxpayer does not. Courts have often applied the "all substantial rights" standard by analogy to other types of intellectual property to determine whether a transfer is a "sale or exchange" or a license.[277]

4.1[1][b] "Sale or Exchange" vs. License – Factors

The courts generally look to three factors to ascertain the intent of parties to create a "sale or exchange" or a license. The first factor is the *duration* of the agreement. A sale or exchange is a transfer of property for an unlimited duration. A license, conversely, is a transfer for a limited duration. Therefore, a transfer for a period less than the intellectual property's useful

---

[273] *See e.g. Nahey v. Commr.*, 111 T.C. 256 (1998).

[274] *See e.g. Waterman v. Mackenzie*, 138 U.S. 252, 256 (1891) ("Whether a transfer of a particular right or interest under a patent is [a sale] or a license does not depend upon the name by which it calls itself, but upon the legal effect of its provisions."); *Pickren v. U.S.*, 378 F.2d 595, 600 (5th Cir. 1967) (In distinguishing between a sale and a license, "the terminology used may be of great importance.").

[275] *See e.g. Juda v. Commr.*, 90 T.C. 1263 (1988), *aff'd*, 877 F.2d 1075 (1st Cir 1989).

[276] *See e.g. Watson v. Commr.*, 222 F.2d 689 (10th Cir. 1955).

[277] *See e.g. Pickren v. U.S.*, 378 F.2d 595 (5th Cir. 1967); *Henry Vogt Mach. Co. v. Commr.*, 66 T.C.M. (CCH) 426 (1993).

life or a transfer that is terminable at will by the transferor before the end of its useful life is a license and not a sale or exchange.[278]

The second factor is the right to prevent unauthorized disclosure. In a sale or exchange, a transferee receives all substantial rights to the intellectual property and one of these rights is the transferee's right to prevent the transferor from disclosing the intellectual property to others. In other words, a sale or exchange involves the *exclusive* right to the intellectual property. A transfer of a nonexclusive right to intellectual property (i.e., the transferor is not legally prevented from disclosing the intellectual property to others) is a license.[279]

The third factor is *geographic limitations* placed on the transferee's use of the intellectual property. A sale or exchange clearly occurs if the transferee receives unlimited and exclusive worldwide rights to the transferred intellectual property. But does a sale or exchange occur if the transferee receives an unlimited and exclusive right to intellectual property only in a particular geographic region? A transfer of an unlimited and exclusive right to intellectual property in *all* of the territory of a particular country is sale or exchange.[280] But it is less clear if a sale or exchange can occur where a transfer is limited to a particular geographic region *within* a country. As discussed later in this Chapter, a transfer limited to a particular geographic region within a country is not a transfer of "all substantial rights" under section 1235. Because courts often apply section 1235's "all substantial rights" test to intellectual property transfers outside section 1235's scope, a transfer limited to a region within a country is likely a license and not a sale or exchange.[281]

---

278 *See e.g. Pickren v. U.S.*, 378 F.2d 595 (5th Cir. 1967); *Henry Vogt Mach. Co. v. Commr.*, 66 T.C.M. (CCH) 426 (1993); Rev. Rul. 60-226, 1960-1 C.B. 26; Rev. Rul. 71-564, 1971-2 C.B. 179.

279 *See e.g. E. I. du Pont de Nemours & Co. v. U.S.*, 153 Ct. Cl. 274 (1961); *Taylor-Winfield Corp. v. Commr.*, 57 T.C. 205 (1971); *Henry Vogt Mach. Co. v. Commr.*, 66 T.C.M. (CCH) 426 (1993).

280 *See e.g.* Rev. Rul. 64-56, 1964-1 C.B. 133 (an unlimited and exclusive transfer of a secret process or know-how "within all the territory of a country" constitutes a sale).

281 There is some authority holding that a sale can occur even if the transfer covers a limited geographic portion of a country. For instance, in *Marco v. Commissioner*, 25 T.C. 544 (1955), a pre-section 1235 case, a taxpayer was able to create a sale of a patent for the region west of the Mississippi River and a separate sale for east of the Mississippi River. Similarly, in *Rodgers v. Commissioner*, 51 T.C. 927 (1969), a case decided under section 1235, a taxpayer was able to create a sale of a patent to an almond variety in one region of California and a separate sale of the patent in the remaining portion of California (but California was the only U.S. state in which almonds were grown, so the division of California into two parts was effectively a split of the entire U.S. into two parts). The Tax Court later announced that it would no longer follow *Rodgers* in section 1235 cases. *Kueneman v. Commr.*, 68 T.C. 609 (1977). Because the Tax Court did not specifically repudiate the

The existence of contingent payments (i.e., payments based on the transferee's productivity, use, or disposition of the transferred property) will not negate "sale or exchange" treatment.[282] The transferor can "sell" intellectual property while retaining reasonable restrictions to secure future payments (contingent or installment). For instance, a transferor can take a security interest in the transferred intellectual property to secure future payments without adversely affecting "sale or exchange" treatment.[283] Likewise, a transferor may restrict the transferee from assigning or sublicensing the transferred property, if such restriction is meant to secure future payments.[284]

> **Problem 4.1**: Taxpayer is the world's leading manufacturer of hypodermic needles and syringes. The key to Taxpayer's success is that its needles are sharper than its competitors. Sharper needles more easily penetrate skin than blunt needles, thereby providing more comfort for the patient. The sharpness of Taxpayer's needles is attributable to an unpatented process that shapes the tip of its needles as finely as possible. Taxpayer has taken steps to maintain the secrecy and confidentiality of its process and technology. Taxpayer's competitors have unsuccessfully attempted to replicate taxpayer's secret process for manufacturing sharper needless.
>
> Taxpayer granted Yamada Corporation, a Japanese competitor, the exclusive right to use the secret process to manufacture and sell needles in Japan. Yamada agreed to maintain the secrecy of the process and was strictly prohibited from using it to produce needles for sale outside Japan. Yamada agreed to pay Taxpayer $10 million in cash plus a 3 percent royalty

---

holdings of *Marco* and *Rodgers* in non-section 1235 cases, some commentators suggest that the more lenient limited geographic region standard still applies to non-section 1235 transfers. *See e.g.* Joseph E. Olson, *Federal Taxation of Intellectual Property Transfers*, § 5.07 (Richard E. Kaye ed., 11th ed., L. J. Press 2009). But in *Marco* and *Rodgers*, the taxpayer effectively sold its entire rights to the patent in the U.S., albeit to two separate buyers (in *Rodgers*, the sale of the patent in California effectively covered the entire U.S.). In neither case did the taxpayer transfer rights to a region of a country while retaining rights to other parts of the country. Therefore, taxpayers who transfer intellectual property to a limited region within a country and seek "sale" treatment do so at their own peril.

[282] Rev. Rul. 60-226, 1960-1 C.B. 26.

[283] *See e.g. Mros v. Commr.*, 493 F.2d 813 (9th Cir. 1974); *see also* Treas. Reg. § 1.1235-2(b)(2)(ii) (a security interest is not the retention of a "substantial right").

[284] *See e.g. Rollman v. Commr.*, 244 F.2d 634 (4th Cir. 1957).

on the net sales of needles sold under the agreement. The agreement was effective for 10 years, and at the end of the initial 10-year term, either party could terminate the agreement upon 180 days written notice. Upon termination, Yamada was prohibited from using or disclosing the taxpayer's secret process. Was the transfer of the secret process to Yamada a sale or a license and why does it matter? Read *Henry Vogt Machine Co. v. Commissioner* (included in this Chapter's materials) in connection with this problem.

Problem 4.2: Five years ago, Taxpayer purchased for $1,000,000 all rights (including copyright) to a novel called "Beverly Hills Yorkie" from its author. Since that time, Beverly Hills Yorkie has become a best-seller and Taxpayer has earned substantial royalties on its sale. To cash in further on the novel's success, Taxpayer transferred the exclusive motion picture rights to the novel to a large Hollywood studio. Taxpayer retained all rights to the novel in all media of publication other than motion pictures. The studio paid taxpayer $5,000,000 plus a percentage of gross sales of any motion picture based on the novel. The transferred motion picture rights are perpetual and cover the entire life of the novel's copyright. Was the transfer of motion picture rights to the novel a sale or a license? Read *Herwig v. United States* and Revenue Ruling 60-226 (both included in this Chapter's materials) in connection with this problem.

4.2 Capital Asset Defined

The Code defines "capital asset" in the negative. That is, instead of defining what a capital asset is, the Code provides the general rule that all assets are capital assets, unless a specific exception applies.[285] The Code contains eight categories of assets that are excluded from the definition of a capital asset. Three of these exceptions are particularly relevant to the taxation of intellectual property, including the following:

(1) stock-in-trade, inventory, and property held by the taxpayer primarily for resale to customers in the ordinary course of a trade or business ("inventory and inventory-type" assets);[286]

---

[285] I.R.C. § 1221.

[286] I.R.C. § 1221(a)(1).

(2) property used in a trade or business that is subject to an allowance for depreciation under section 167 ("depreciable trade or business" property);[287] and

(3) copyrights, literary, musical, and artistic compositions held by the creator (a taxpayer whose personal efforts created it) or by a taxpayer whose adjusted basis is carried over from the creator ("self-created copyrights and similar property").

Although an asset may fall within one of these exceptions, capital gain treatment may still be available to the taxpayer under a special provision, such as section 1231 (quasi-capital assets) or section 1235 (sales and exchanges of patents). On the other hand, a taxpayer may be required to characterize gain that would normally be capital as ordinary income under a special provision, such as section 1245 (depreciation recapture) and section 1239 (sales of depreciable property to a related party). These special provisions are discussed in detail later in this Chapter.

4.2[2][a] "Inventory and Inventory-type" Exception

The "inventory and inventory-type exception" denies capital asset status to stock in trade of the taxpayer, inventory, and other property held primarily for resale in the ordinary course of the taxpayer's trade or business.[288] This exception ensures that taxpayers who are in the business of selling inventory treat their gains and losses as ordinary, just as any other business would treat its operating income. Historically, courts have held that a "professional" inventor holds a patent as an "inventory or inventory-type" asset, while an "amateur" inventor does not. For instance, in *Lockhart v. Commissioner*,[289] the court found an inventor who was granted 37 patents over a 19-year period to be a "professional," so that the gain on the sale of his patents was denied capital gain treatment. *First National Bank of Princeton v. United States*[290] involved an inventor who was a physics professor specializing in the field of optics and acoustics. While the inventor had been granted 19 patents in the field of optics and acoustics (12 of which he sold), he also held and later sold a patent

---

[287] I.R.C. § 1221(a)(2). This exception also includes real property used in a trade or business. Because the subject of this textbook is intellectual property, discussion of real property is intentionally omitted.

[288] I.R.C. § 1221(a)(1).

[289] 258 F.2d 343 (3rd Cir. 1958).

[290] 136 F. Supp. 818 (D.N.J. 1955).

relating to a toothbrush. While the inventor might have been a "professional" in the field of optics and acoustics, the court ruled him to be an "amateur" in the field of toothbrushes. So the court allowed capital gain treatment on the sale of the toothbrush patent.

The distinction between a "professional" and "amateur" inventor became less important with the introduction of section 1235 in 1954. As discussed later in this Chapter, section 1235 generally characterizes gain on the sale or exchange of a patent as long-term capital gain, irrespective of whether the inventor is a professional or amateur. But if section 1235 is not applicable (e.g., sale to a related party or the taxpayer is not a "holder"), a taxpayer must test the transfer under general capital gain principles to characterize gain or loss. So the distinction between a professional and an amateur may arise today in such an instance.

The "inventory and inventory-like" exception probably applies even less to trademarks, trade names, and copyrights than it does to patents and other technological intellectual properties. Only in the rarest cases (if at all) would a taxpayer hold a trademark or trade name as inventory or as property held primarily for resale in the ordinary course of business. In the context of copyrights, the "inventory and inventory-like" exception became largely irrelevant with the addition of the "self-created copyright and similar property" exception (discussed below) in 1950. The "inventory and inventory-like" exception could possibly arise in the context of a noncreator. But it is unlikely that a noncreator, such as a publisher, would hold a copyright as inventory or as property held primarily for resale in the ordinary course of business. More likely, a noncreator would hold the copyright in its trade or business and fall under the "depreciable trade or business property" exception (discussed below).

4.2[2][b] "Depreciable Trade or Business Property" Exception

The "depreciable trade or business exception" denies capital asset status to property used in a trade or business that is subject to an allowance for depreciation under section 167.[291] The exception is comprised of two parts, both of which must be met: (1) the taxpayer must use the property in a trade or business and (2) the property must be depreciable under section 167. With respect to the first part, the distinction between a "trade or business" activity and an investment activity is a subject covered in detail in Chapters 2 and 3. So intellectual property held as an investment, even if depreciable under section 167, does not fall within the "depreciable trade or business property" exception.

---

[291] I.R.C. § 1221(a)(2). The exception also covers real property used in a trade or business. *Id.*

The second part is widely applicable to intellectual property because many forms of intellectual property are depreciable under section 167. Patents and copyrights are specifically listed in the regulations as examples of depreciable property under section 167.[292] "Amortizable section 197 intangibles" (discussed in Chapters 2 and 3) are treated as property depreciable under section 167.[293] Nondepreciable intellectual properties, such as self-created trade secrets and know-how, even if used in a trade or business, do not fall within the "depreciable trade or business property" exception. Because many types of intellectual property fall within the "depreciable trade or business property" exception, it may appear, at first blush, that sales of intellectual property would rarely qualify as capital gains. Although depreciable trade or business property is not a capital asset, it may nonetheless qualify for capital gain treatment under section 1231 (discussed later in this Chapter).

4.2[2][c] "Self-created Copyrights and Similar Property" Exception

The "self-created copyrights and similar property" exception denies capital asset status to a "copyright, a literary, musical, or artistic composition, a letter or memorandum, or similar property" held by any one of the following:[294]

(1) a taxpayer whose personal efforts created such property;

(2) in the case of a letter, memorandum, or similar property, a taxpayer for whom such property was prepared or produced; or

(3) a taxpayer in whose hands the basis of such property is determined, for purposes of determining gain from a sale or exchange, in whole or in part by reference to the basis of such property in the hands of a taxpayer described in (1) or (2) above.

Prior to the addition of the "self-created copyrights and similar property" exception in 1950, courts distinguished between professional and amateur authors. Professional authors were denied capital gains on the grounds that their works fell within the "inventory and inventory-like" exception.[295] Amateur authors, however, received capital gain treatment.[296] In 1948, the press reported that Dwight Eisenhower claimed "amateur" author status to report long-

---

[292] Treas. Reg. § 1.167(a)-3.

[293] I.R.C. § 197(f)(7).

[294] I.R.C. § 1221(a)(3).

[295] *E.g. Fields v. Commr.*, 14 T.C. 1202 (1950), *aff'd*, 189 F.2d 950 (2d Cir. 1951).

[296] *E.g. Herwig v. U.S.*, 105 F. Supp. 384 (Ct. Cl. 1952).

term capital gain on the sale of his World War II memoirs, *Crusade in Europe*, thereby saving him over $500,000 in taxes compared to what he would have paid had he been a "professional" author.[297] Reports of the Eisenhower story prompted Congress to plug the amateur author loophole by adding the "self-created copyright and similar property" exception in 1950. Congress reasoned that an author, whether professional or not, is really being compensated for his personal efforts upon sale of a copyright or similar property.[298] And compensation, in whatever form it takes, ought to be ordinary income.

The term "similar property" includes "a theatrical production, a radio program, a newspaper cartoon strip, or any other property eligible for copyright protection (whether under statute or common law)."[299] But "similar property" does not include "a patent or an invention, or a design which may be protected only under the patent law and not under the copyright law."[300] An unresolved issue in these definitions is the characterization on the sale of intellectual property, such as computer software, that can be both copyrighted and patented. For example, if a taxpayer creates computer software that is subject to copyright and patent protection, is such software denied capital asset treatment under the "self-created copyright and similar property" exception? Or is the computer software eligible for capital gain treatment under section 1235?[301]

> **Problem 4.3**: Author wrote the best-selling novel, "Beverly Hills Yorkie." The novel's principal character is a lovable little Yorkie named "Ginger." Author sold all exclusive and perpetual motion picture rights in the novel to a movie studio. And, for separately stated consideration, Author sold to the studio the exclusive and perpetual right to use the "Ginger" character in additional motion pictures. Author recognized a substantial gain on both the sale of the motion picture rights to the novel and on the "Ginger" character. What are the tax consequences to Author? Read *Stern v. United States* (included in this Chapter's materials) in connection with this problem.

---

297 *Eisenhower to Pay Tax as an 'Amateur' Writer*, N.Y. Times 31 (Jun. 2, 1948).

298 H.R. Rpt. 81-2319 at 54 (Jun. 23, 1950).

299 Treas. Reg. § 1.1221-1(c)(1).

300 *Id.*

301 In *Levy v. Commr.*, 64 T.C.M. (CCH) 534 (1992), the Tax Court held that an uncopyrighted computer program eligible for copyright protection was not a capital asset in the hands of its creators. The court did not, however, address whether the computer program was eligible for patent protection.

> Alternatively, assume Author gifted all rights (including copyright) in the novel to her Daughter. A few years later, Daughter sold all rights (including copyright) to the novel to an unrelated party for a substantial gain. What are the tax consequences to Daughter? How would your answer change if, instead of gifting the novel to Daughter, Author died and devised all rights (including copyright) in the novel to Daughter?

In 2006, Congress amended the Code to provide a tax break for the sale or exchange of self-created musical works.[302] This provision allows a taxpayer to elect to have the "inventory and inventory-like" and "self-created copyright and similar property" exceptions *not* apply to self-created "musical compositions" and "copyrights in musical works."[303] The election is also available to a taxpayer who received a transferred basis in the property from the creator.[304] This provision effectively allows a taxpayer to elect capital gain treatment on the sale or exchange of self-created musical compositions and copyrights in musical works. This elective provision is largely a result of the lobbying efforts of the Nashville Songwriters Association International ("NSAI").[305] The NSAI convinced Congress that songwriters deserved a special tax break based, in part, on the substantial loss in revenue to the music industry due to piracy and illegal digital file-sharing.[306] Query: Are creators of musical works more deserving of a tax break than other creators of copyrightable works? What is a "musical composition" and "copyrights in musical works?" If a taxpayer writes a screenplay for a musical, which includes accompanying dialogue, music, and lyrics, has he sold a "musical composition?"

> **Problem 4.4**: Composer created a musical composition, which he held for several years before selling it to Publisher for a substantial gain. After holding the musical composition in its trade or business for over a year, Publisher resold it to an unrelated party for a substantial gain. Assume that

---

[302] Tax Increase Prevention and Reconciliation Act of 2005, Pub. L. No. 109-222, § 204(a), 120 Stat. 345, 350 (2006) (enacted May 17, 2006). As originally enacted, the provision was scheduled to expire at the end of 2010. But Congress later made the provision permanent. Tax Relief and Health Care Act of 2006, Pub. L. No. 109-432, § 412(a), 120 Stat. 2922, 2963 (2006). As explained later in this Chapter, for charitable deduction purposes, the taxpayer's deduction is limited to the taxpayer's adjusted basis in the musical work, rather than its fair market value.

[303] I.R.C. § 1221(b)(3).

[304] *Id.*

[305] *See generally* Spencer Anastasio, *Copyright Law in the New Millennium: TIPRA and the Songwriter's Capital Gains Equity Act*, 25 Ent. & Sports Law. 1 (2008).

[306] *Id.*

the sales by Composer and Publisher constitute a "sale or exchange" of the musical composition. May Composer elect to treat the musical composition as a capital asset? Was the musical composition a capital asset in the Publisher's hands? If not, may Publisher likewise make the capital asset election?

4.3 Special Characterization Provisions

4.3[1] "Quasi-Capital Assets" (Section 1231)

As discussed above, the "depreciable trade or business" exception denies capital asset status to property used in a trade or business that is subject to an allowance for depreciation under section 167.[307] But for section 1231, any gain or loss recognized on the disposition of such property would be ordinary. Stated another way, section 1231 provides that a recognized gain on the sale or exchange[308] of such property may be characterized as capital gain, while a recognized loss remains ordinary. Because section 1231 may provide capital gain treatment to noncapital assets, those assets subject to section 1231 are sometimes referred to as "quasi-capital assets."

The first step in applying section 1231 is to identify the transactions to which section 1231 applies. By its own terms, section 1231 applies to recognized gain and loss on the sale or exchange of "property used in the trade or business."[309] The term "property used in the trade or business" includes those assets falling within the "depreciable trade or business" exception to capital asset status that are held for more than one year.[310] Thus, those assets held for one year or less are not "quasi-capital assets" (there is no such thing as a "short-term" section 1231 gain or loss). The term "property used in the trade or business" does not

---

[307] I.R.C. § 1221(a)(2). The exception also covers real property used in a trade or business. *Id.*

[308] Section 1231 also applies to recognized gain or loss on the involuntary conversion of "depreciable trade or business" property (or any capital asset held for more than one year held in connection with a trade or business or transaction for profit). *See* I.R.C. § 1231(a)(3)(A)(ii); (a)(3)(B). The specific reference in section 1231 to involuntary conversions is necessary because an involuntary conversion is typically not treated as a "sale or exchange." Because the involuntary conversion of intellectual property is rare, the interplay between section 1231 and involuntary conversions is not covered in detail in this Chapter.

[309] I.R.C. § 1231(a)(3)(A)(i), (a)(3)(B). Section 1231 also applies to the involuntary conversion of "property used in the trade or business" and capital assets held for more than one year in a trade or business or in a transaction for profit. I.R.C. § 1231(a)(3)(A)(ii).

[310] I.R.C. § 1231(b)(1).

include any asset falling within the "inventory and inventory-like" or "self-created copyright and similar property" exceptions.[311]

The second step in applying section 1231 is to "net" the taxpayer's "section 1231 gains" against "section 1231 losses."[312] A net positive number renders all gains and losses as long-term capital gains and long-term capital losses.[313] On the other hand, a net negative number renders all gains and losses as ordinary.[314] A faulty assumption is to assume that a "section 1231 gain" is automatically a long-term capital gain. A taxpayer must apply the netting procedure first, and a section 1231 gain is treated as a long-term capital gain only if the netting produces a positive number. A taxpayer could have a section 1231 gain, yet a negative number in the netting procedure, in which case the section 1231 gain would not be a long-term capital gain.

4.3[2] Depreciation Recapture (Section 1245)

Depreciation recapture is another special provision that may affect characterization of a taxpayer's gain. Under the depreciation recapture rule, a gain on the disposition of "section 1245 property" is characterized as ordinary income to extent is it attributable to depreciation or amortization deductions taken on the property.[315] "Section 1245 property" includes intellectual property that is or has been subject to an allowance for depreciation under section 167.[316] Thus, depreciation recapture applies to depreciable intellectual property, including "amortizable section 197 intangibles" (recall that an amortizable section 197 intangible is treated as a section 167 depreciable asset). Section 1245 does not apply to that portion of gain exceeding prior depreciation (i.e., true economic appreciation of the property). Therefore, gain attributable to depreciation is recaptured as ordinary income, while true economic appreciation may qualify for capital gain treatment under section 1231 or general capital gain provisions.

---

[311] I.R.C. § 1231(b)(1)(A)-(C). Those assets denied capital asset status under section 1221(a)(5) (certain government publications) are also excluded from the definition of "property used in the trade or business" for section 1231 purposes. I.R.C. § 1231(b)(1)(D).

[312] I.R.C. § 1231(a)(1)-(2).

[313] I.R.C. § 1231(a)(1).

[314] I.R.C. § 1231(a)(2).

[315] I.R.C. § 1245(a).

[316] I.R.C. § 1245(a)(3)(A).

The rationale for depreciation recapture is simple. But for deprecation recapture, gain attributable to depreciation might qualify as long-term capital gain under section 1231 or general capital gain provisions. So, without depreciation recapture, a taxpayer could offset depreciation deductions against income that would otherwise be taxed at ordinary rates, yet pay back excess depreciation at preferential rates upon disposition. Section 1245 prevents this tax arbitrage by requiring a taxpayer to "recapture" as ordinary income that amount previously deducted against ordinary income.

> **Problem 4.5**: Assume the same facts of **Problem 4.2**. Further assume that Taxpayer's transfer of motion picture rights was a sale for a lump sum of $5,000,000 and that Taxpayer held the copyright to the novel in its trade or business (Taxpayer did not hold the copyright primarily for resale to customers in the ordinary course of its trade or business). Taxpayer elected to depreciate the copyright using the income forecast method and was allowed $300,000 depreciation at the time of sale. In connection with the sale, Taxpayer hired a qualified appraiser to value the motion picture rights vis-à-vis the remaining copyright retained by the taxpayer. The appraiser opined that the motion picture rights represent 90 percent of the total value of the copyright. How much gain does Taxpayer realize on the sale and what is the character of such gain? In calculating Taxpayer's adjusted basis on sale, it may be helpful to review Treas. Reg. § 1.61-6(a).

> **Problem 4.6**: Taxpayer, an individual, paid $250,000 in costs to produce a patentable invention. Taxpayer deducted all $250,000 of his costs under section 174 as R&E expenditures. If Taxpayer sells all rights to the patentable invention for $250,000 to an unrelated party, how much gain, if any, must Taxpayer recapture as ordinary income under section 1245? Read Revenue Ruling 85-186 (included in this Chapter's materials) in connection with this Problem.

4.3[3] Sale or Exchange of Depreciable Property to Related Persons (Section 1239)

As explained above, gain attributable to the economic appreciation of depreciable property may be eligible for capital gain treatment (either under section 1231 or general capital gains provisions). But favorable treatment under section 1231 (and general capital gains provisions) is not available upon sale or exchange of depreciable property to certain "related persons" (such as a taxpayer and a corporation where the taxpayer's ownership exceeds 50 percent).[317] Instead, section 1239 provides that *any* gain on such a sale or exchange is ordinary income, even if attributable to economic appreciation.[318] The section 1239 ordinary income rule applies to intellectual property that is or has been subject to an allowance for depreciation under section 167. So an "amortizable section 197 intangible" is subject to section 1239.[319] While a patent application is nondepreciable, it is treated as depreciable property subject to section 1239.[320]

Without section 1239, a taxpayer could sell depreciable intellectual property to a controlled entity, claim capital gain treatment on the economic appreciation, and then "redepreciate" the intellectual property through the controlled entity. Given the differential between capital gains and ordinary rates, the controlled entity may save more tax from depreciation deductions than the individual paid on the sale. Section 1239 prevents "redepreciation" by requiring the individual to report all gain as ordinary income.

4.3[4] Sale or Exchange of a Patent (Section 1235)

As discussed above, self-created copyrights and similar property are denied capital asset status because a creator is really being compensated for his personal efforts upon sale of a copyright or similar property. One might think the same rationale ought to apply to self-created patents. After all, proceeds on the sale of a self-created patent compensate the inventor for his personal efforts in developing the patent. Indeed, when Congress added the "self-created copyright and similar property" exception to the Code in 1950 it also considered denying capital asset status to self-created patents.[321] But Congress declined to do so, reasoning that the benefit of fostering technical innovation outweighed the revenue to be raised by denying capital asset status to self-created patents.[322] Instead, at that time, Congress left intact the historical distinction between professionals and amateur inventors (discussed above). That is, professional inventors were denied capital asset status on their patents under the "inventory and inventory-like" exception, while amateurs could claim their

---

[317] I.R.C. § 1239(a). "Related persons" generally include a taxpayer and "controlled entities," a taxpayer (or taxpayer's spouse) and trust where the taxpayer is a beneficiary (except for a remote contingent beneficiary), and an executor and an estate, expect where the transfer satisfies a pecuniary bequest. I.R.C. § 1239(b).

[318] *Id.*

[319] I.R.C. § 197(f)(7).

[320] I.R.C. § 1239(e).

[321] Sen. Rpt. 81-2375 at 44 (Aug. 22, 1950).

[322] *Id.*

patents as capital assets. Later, in 1954, Congress enacted section 1235 to provide capital treatment to certain patent sales, irrespective of professional or amateur status.[323] Section 1235 generally provides as follows:

> [a] transfer (other than by gift, inheritance, or devise) of property consisting of all substantial rights to a patent . . . by any holder [is] the sale or exchange of a capital asset held for more than 1 year, regardless of whether [the consideration is] (1) payable periodically [during] the transferee's use of the patent, or (2) contingent on the productivity, use, or disposition of the property transferred.[324]

Section 1235, if applicable, provides all the necessary elements for long-term capital gain treatment on the sale or exchange of a patent. First, a transfer of "all substantial rights" meets the "sale or exchange" requirement, irrespective of the existence of contingent payments. So section 1235 trumps the traditional tendency of the Service to associate contingent payments with licenses, rather than sales or exchanges.[325] Congress recognized that contingent payments may be the most practical way to set a purchase price for a new invention.[326] Second, section 1235 confers capital assets status on applicable patent transfers. So the question of whether the inventor is a professional or amateur is no longer an issue if section 1235 applies. Third, section 1235 provides the one-year holding requirement for long-term capital gain, irrespective of the actual holding period of the patent. So an inventor could sell a patent actually held for less than a year and still qualify for long-term capital gain.

Section 1235 has a number of definable terms, including "patent," "transfer," "holder," and "all substantial rights." Additionally, section 1235 does not apply to certain related party transfers. The definable terms and related party transfers are discussed below.

---

[323] H.R. Rpt. 83-1337 at 82 (Mar. 9, 1954). At the same time, Congress sought to encourage innovation by allowing current deductibility of R&E expenditures under section 174, as discussed at length in Chapter 2.

[324] I.R.C. § 1235(a).

[325] Mim. 6490, 1950-1 C.B. 9, *rev'd*, Rev. Rul. 58-353, 1958-2 C.B. 408.

[326] Sen. Rpt. 83-1622 at 439 (Jun. 18, 1954).

4.3[4][a] "Patent" Defined

Section 1235, by its very terms, applies to a transfer of a "patent." While section 1235 does not define "patent," regulations define a patent as "a patent granted under the provisions of title 35 of the United States Code, or any foreign patent granting rights generally similar to those under a United States patent."[327] Treasury regulations further state that "[i]t is not necessary that the patent or patent application for the invention be in existence" for qualification under section 1235.[328] Rather, the *patentability* of an invention, as opposed to its formal status as a patent, is the key for qualification under section 1235. An inventor need never apply for a patent for an invention, so long as the inventor can establish patentability. For instance, in *Gilson v. Commissioner*,[329] the court held that section 1235 applied to a professional inventor's sale of 82 unpatented industrial designs because the designs were patentable.

4.3[4][b] Qualifying Transfers

Section 1235 requires a "transfer" of a patent to qualify for long-term capital gain treatment.[330] The "transfer" requirement is most likely an issue where an employer makes payments to an employee for the employee's invention. Treasury regulations provide that "[p]ayments received by an employee as compensation for services rendered as employee are not attributable to a transfer to which section 1235 applies."[331] In making this determination, consideration is given to the facts and circumstances of the employment relationship and to whether the payments are based upon "the production, sale or use by, or the value to, the employer of the patent rights transferred."[332]

Courts have applied a "hired to invent" rule to distinguish between compensation and payments for the sale of a patent.[333] For instance, in *Downs v. Commissioner*[334] (included in

---

[327] Treas. Reg. § 1.1235-2(a).

[328] *Id.*

[329] 48 T.C.M. (CCH) 922 (1984).

[330] Gifts, inheritances, and devises are not section 1235 transfers because they do not give rise to recognition of gain or loss. I.R.C. § 1235(a).

[331] Treas. Reg. § 1.1235-1(c)(2).

[332] *Id.*

[333] The hired to invent rule only applies to employees, not independent contractors. Therefore, in *Gilson v. Commissioner*, 48 T.C.M. (CCH) 922 (1984), an independent contractor specifically engaged to create industrial designs could characterize payments received from customers for his patentable designs as long-term capital gains under section 1235.

this Chapter's materials), the court held that an employee specifically "hired to invent" an electric hospital bed made no section 1235 "transfer" when assigning his invention to his employer because he had no rights in an invention to sell (it already rightfully belonged to his employer). Conversely, in *Chilton v. Commissioner*[335] (included in this Chapter's materials), the court held that an employee who was not specifically hired to invent a particular product could make a section 1235 "transfer" to his employer regarding inventions made during the scope of his employment. In reading *Downs* and *Chilton*, consider how they are factually different. Was the employee in each case contractually obligated to assign his inventions to the employer? If so, was the employer required to pay separate consideration to the employee for the invention's assignment? Was the amount payable to the employee irrespective of his inventive success? Consider *Downs* and *Chilton* in connection with the following problems.

> **Problem 4.7**: Taxpayer has been employed for several years by Spartan University as a chemistry professor. Taxpayer's responsibilities have involved teaching, conducting research, and conducting administrative tasks in varying degrees, with 50 to 100 percent of the taxpayer's efforts devoted to research during any given academic term. Under the University's academic policies and procedures, a professor must report any invention made during the course of his employment to a Patents Committee, which then decides whether to assert the University's rights in the invention. If the University wishes to own the invention, the University may apply for a patent in the professor's name (the professor must then assign the patent application to the University) and the professor and the University must execute a written agreement relating to the division of royalties generated by the patent's licensing. If the University decides not to exercise its rights, the invention becomes the sole property of the professor.
>
> In the course of his research for the University (no part of which was federally funded), Taxpayer developed a compound called Carboplatin, which is a platinum-based chemotherapy drug used to treat various types of cancer. Taxpayer reported the invention to the University's Patents Committee, which decided to assert the University's ownership of the invention. The University filed a patent application for Carboplatin on Taxpayer's behalf (Taxpayer simultaneously assigned the patent application

[334] 49 T.C. 533 (1968).

[335] 40 T.C. 552 (1963).

to the University, and a patent for Carboplatin was ultimately issued). Taxpayer and the University executed a written agreement whereby the University agreed to pay Taxpayer royalties resulting from the licensing of Carboplatin. The University licensed the patent to a large pharmaceutical manufacturer, who then produced Carboplatin for sale. Can Taxpayer characterize royalties he receives from Spartan University as long-term capital gains under section 1235?[336]

Problem 4.8: Taxpayer was an engineer employed by an automobile manufacturer. Taxpayer's employment agreement required Taxpayer to assign all inventions created during the scope of his employment to the manufacturer for no additional consideration. In accordance with his employment agreement, Taxpayer assigned to the manufacturer all rights to a patent for an automobile part that Taxpayer invented during the course of his employment. Ten years later (the manufacturer still employed Taxpayer), the manufacturer adopted an incentive award plan to "recognize employee achievements of significant or outstanding value, especially those that are beyond the levels of expected performance in assigned jobs." The amount to be paid under the incentive award plan was in the manufacturer's absolute discretion and was not necessarily tied to the sale or licensing of an employee's invention. Pursuant to this incentive award plan, the manufacturer paid $100,000 to Taxpayer in recognition of the patent he had assigned to the manufacturer ten years earlier. Can Taxpayer treat the $100,000 as long-term capital gain under section 1235?[337]

Alternatively, assume the manufacturer's incentive award plan provided that amounts paid to employees (1) were based on specified percentage of the income the manufacturer generated from the sale or licensing of the employee's invention, (2) would continue to be paid, even if the manufacturer later discontinued the plan, (3) would continue to be paid if the employee terminated his employment, and (4) would be paid to the employee's estate if he died. Would these additional facts change your answer?[338]

---

[336] This problem is loosely based on Tech. Adv. Mem. 2002-49-002 (Dec. 6, 2002).

[337] This problem is loosely based on *Lehman v. Commr.*, 835 F.2d 431 (2d Cir. 1987).

[338] This problem is loosely based on *McClain v. Commr.*, 40 T.C. 841 (1963).

4.3[4][c] "Holder" Defined

Section 1235 only applies to transfers of patent rights by a "holder" to an unrelated person. A "holder" is typically an individual whose efforts created the invention.[339] But a "holder" can also be an individual (other than the creator's employer or a person "related" to the creator) who acquired an interest in the invention prior to its actual reduction to practice in exchange for adequate consideration paid to the creator (so called "financial backers").[340] By extending "holder" status to financial backers, Congress recognized that the "seed" money of financial backers can be as crucial in promoting innovation as the creators themselves. But Congress also wanted to make sure financial backers also bear the same technological risk of failure that creators do. For this reason, a financial backer must provide adequate consideration for his interest prior to the actual reduction of the invention to practice, which occurs when the invention "has been tested and operated successfully under operating conditions."[341]

Because a "holder" must be an individual, entities (e.g., corporations, partnerships, or trusts) do not qualify under section 1235. Although a partnership cannot be a holder, each individual partner may qualify as a holder as to his share of a patent owned by the partnership.[342] For example, suppose a partner of a partnership comprised solely of individuals uses partnership property to develop an invention with the understanding that the patent, when issued, would become partnership property. In this case, each of the individual partners would qualify as a holder.[343] But if the partnership is not composed solely of individuals, each of the individual partner's distributive shares of income attributable to the transfer of the patent can qualify as long-term capital gain under section 1235.[344]

Even if the taxpayer is a "holder," a transfer cannot qualify under section 1235 if it occurs directly or indirectly between "related persons."[345] A "related person" has the same meaning as it does in sections 267(b) and 707(b), except that (1) "25 percent or more" is substituted for "50 percent or more" in each place it appears in sections 267(b) and 707(b) and (2)

---

[339] I.R.C. § 1235(b)(1).

[340] I.R.C. § 1235(b)(2).

[341] Treas. Reg. § 1.1235-2(e).

[342] Treas. Reg. § 1.1235-2(d)(2). This rule likewise applies to limited liability companies that are taxed as partnerships. *E.g.* Priv. Ltr. Rul. 2005-06-008 (Oct. 20, 2004).

[343] *Id.*

[344] *Id.*

[345] I.R.C. § 1235(d).

siblings are not treated as related persons.[346] The purpose of the "related person" rule is to prevent related parties from lowering their overall tax burden through clever planning. Without the "related person" rule, a corporation could intentionally overpay for a related holder's patent. By doing so, the corporation would increase its depreciation deductions thereby decreasing its profit. The profit the corporation would have recognized had it not overpaid for the patent would be effectively shifted to the related holder and converted into long-term capital gain.

If a transfer does not qualify under section 1235 (e.g., it violates the "holder" requirement or the "related person" rule), it may still qualify for capital gain treatment under the general principles apart from section 1235 (e.g., the transfer meets the capital asset, sale or exchange, and one-year holding period requirements).[347] In other words, the mere fact that a patent transfer does not qualify under section 1235 will not prevent it from qualifying for long-term capital treatment under general capital gain principles.

> **Problem 4.9**: Taxpayer, an individual, sold to Cornhusker Corporation all substantial rights to a patent relating to genetically modified corn. Taxpayer is not an employee of Cornhusker and did not use Cornhusker's facilities or materials in developing the patent. Cornhusker's outstanding stock is owned 20 percent by Taxpayer, 10 percent by Taxpayer's father, and 70 percent by Taxpayer's paternal uncle. May Taxpayer's sale of the patent to Cornhusker qualify for long-term capital gain treatment under Section 1235? How would your answer change if Taxpayer's sister owned 10 percent of Cornhusker's outstanding stock instead of Taxpayer's father? Alternatively, how would your answer change if Taxpayer was not a professional inventor and had held the patent for more than one year?

---

[346] I.R.C. § 1235(d)(1), (2).

[347] *Cascade Designs, Inc. v. Commr.*, 79 T.C.M. (CCH) 1542 (2000); Rev. Rul. 69-482, 1969-2 C.B. 164. *See also* Treas. Reg. § 1.1235-1(b) (If a transaction falls outside section 1235, then "section 1235 shall be disregarded in determining whether or not such transfer is the sale or exchange of a capital asset. For example, a transfer by a person other than a holder or a transfer by a holder to a related person is not governed by section 1235. The tax consequences of such transfers shall be determined under other provisions of the internal revenue laws.").

4.3[4][d] Transfer of "All Substantial Rights"

Section 1235 only applies to a transfer "of all substantial rights to a patent" or "an undivided interest therein."[348] The adoption of an "all substantial rights" standard ensures that the transfer is in the form of a sale or exchange, rather than a license. Regulations define "all substantial rights" as "all rights (whether or not then held by the grantor) which are of value at the time the rights to the patent (or an undivided interest therein) are transferred."[349] Regulations also provide that a transfer of "all substantial rights" does not occur if:

(1) the transfer is *limited geographically* within the country of issuance;[350]

(2) the transfer is *limited in duration* to a period less than the patent's remaining life;[351]

(3) the transfer is *limited to fields of use* within trades or industries, which are less than all the rights the patent covers and exist and have value at the time of the grant;[352] or

(4) the transfer *grants less than all the claims or inventions* the patent covers (which exist and have value at the time of the transfer);[353] or

(5) the transfer is *terminable at will* by the transferor.[354]

The geographic and field of use limitations require additional discussion. Prior to the adoption of section 1235, an exclusive geographic transfer could be a "sale or exchange," even if the exclusive territory covered only a limited portion of a country. For instance, in *Marco v. Commissioner*,[355] a pre-section 1235 case, a taxpayer was able to create a sale of a patent for the region west of the Mississippi River and a separate sale for east of the

---

[348] I.R.C. § 1235(a).

[349] Treas. Reg. § 1.1235-2(b)(1).

[350] Treas. Reg. § 1.1235-2(b)(1)(i).

[351] Treas. Reg. § 1.1235-2(b)(1)(ii).

[352] Treas. Reg. § 1.1235-2(b)(1)(iii).

[353] Treas. Reg. § 1.1235-2(b)(1)(iv).

[354] Treas. Reg. § 1.1235-2(b)(4).

[355] 25 T.C. 544 (1955).

Mississippi River. After Congress enacted section 1235, Treasury effectively overruled *Marco* by adopting the regulation that a transfer limited geographically within a country is not a transfer of "all substantial rights."

In *Rodgers v. Commissioner*,[356] the Tax Court held the "limited geographic transfer" regulation to be invalid. The court reasoned that Congress did not intend section 1235 to be more restrictive than the Code's general capital gain provisions. Because the court in *Marco* had allowed an exclusive geographic transfer within a country to be a "sale," the court ruled that the regulation improperly altered prior law. Therefore, the court held that section 1235 applied to exclusive transfers of a patent to an almond variety in one region of California and another in the remaining portion of California (California was the only region in the U.S. where almonds were grown, so the division of California into two parts was effectively a split of the entire U.S. into two parts).

In *Kueneman v. Commissioner*,[357] the Tax Court announced that it would no longer follow *Rodgers*. The court in *Kueneman* reasoned that if a "patent can be sliced into smaller segments, and the all-substantial-rights test satisfied merely be transferring all substantial rights with respect to the segment, capital gain treatment would be allowed, even though the patent holder retains very substantial rights to the patent."[358] Consequently, the taxpayer in *Kueneman* could not apply section 1235 to the transfer of an exclusive right to use a patent in only a limited portion of the U.S.

"Field of use" restrictions are also worthy of special mention because the treatment of such restrictions under section 1235 mirrors that of geographic restrictions. Clearly, the regulations provide that a "limited field of use transfer" is not a transfer of all substantial rights. But prior to the regulation's adoption, the Tax Court in *Rouverol v. Commissioner*[359] held that a taxpayer could make a section 1235 transfer of all substantial rights notwithstanding a field of use restriction. Even after the regulation's adoption, the Tax Court, in two cases, allowed transfers with field of use restrictions to qualify under section 1235 (thereby invalidating the regulation), but both cases were reversed on appeal.[360]

---

[356] 51 T.C. 927 (1969).

[357] 68 T.C. 609 (1977).

[358] *Id.* at 618.

[359] 42 T.C. 186 (1964), *nonacq.*, 1965-2 C.B. 7.

[360] *Fawick v. Commr.*, 52 T.C. 104 (1969), *rev'd*, 436 F.2d 655 (6th Cir. 1971) (transfer of exclusive rights in patents relating to drive clutches and power transmissions in marine applications only); *Mros v. Commr.*, 30 T.C.M. (CCH) 519 (1971), *rev'd*, 493 F.2d 813 (9th Cir. 1974) (transfer of exclusive

Eventually, the Tax Court in *Kueneman* conceded that the "limited field of use transfer" regulation was based on sound reasoning, and its validity has not since been placed in doubt.

Although transfers limited geographically within a country or fields of use fail to qualify under section 1235, a question remains whether such transfers can still satisfy the "sale or exchange" requirement under the Code's general capital gains provisions. If the taxpayer can also meet the "capital asset" and "one-year holding" requirements, he could qualify for long-term capital gain treatment despite failing section 1235. Indeed, the regulations specifically provide that if section 1235 does not apply to a transfer, then "section 1235 shall be disregarded in determining whether or not such transfer is the sale or exchange of a capital asset."[361] And *Kueneman* held that section 1235 changed "the tests for qualification" for long-term capital gain, thereby suggesting that the "sale or exchange" requirement and "all substantial rights" standard are not the same.[362] Nevertheless, several cases decided since *Kueneman* have applied the "all substantial rights" by analogy to "sale or exchange" cases.[363] Against this backdrop, is the "sale or exchange" requirement more lenient than the "all substantial rights" standard in allowing field of use restrictions or geographic limits within a country?[364]

---

rights in patent relating to gear reduction device for hoists, winches, boat accessory devices, and air motor power drives only).

[361] Treas. Reg. § 1.1235-1(b).

[362] *Kueneman*, 68 T.C. at 618.

[363] *E.g. Henry Vogt Mach. Co. v. Commr.*, 66 T.C.M. (CCH) 426 (1993).

[364] As discussed *supra* at n. 281 and accompanying text, a transfer limited geographically within a country may not be treated as "sale or exchange." On the other hand, a field of use restriction may not necessarily nullify "sale or exchange" treatment, provided the transfer is exclusive and perpetual. For instance, copyrights may be divided between different media of publication, so that a taxpayer may make a "sale" of motion pictures rights while retaining the copyright for all other media of publication. Rev. Rul. 60-226, 1960-1 C.B. 26. But it is unclear whether similar field of use fragmentation of a patent can qualify as a "sale or exchange." In *E.I. du Pont de Nemours & Co. v. U.S.*, 432 F.2d 1052 (3d Cir. 1970), a non-section 1235 case (the taxpayer was a corporation), the taxpayer transferred four process patents relating to the manufacture of nylon fibers for exclusive use in Brazil. Use of transferred process patents was restricted to the manufacture of nylon only, although such patents could also be used in the manufacture of Dacron. The Third Circuit applied the "all substantial rights" standard by analogy to determine whether the transfer was a "sale or exchange." In doing so, the court concluded that the transfer was a "sale" because the retained field of use (manufacture of Dacron) had no substantial value. Had the retained field of use (manufacture of Dacron) had a substantial value, the Third Circuit likely would have ruled the transfer a license. In *Vision Info. Servs., L.L.C. v. Commr.*, 419 F.3d 554 (6th Cir. 2005), the Sixth Circuit, in dicta,

Problem 4.10: Taxpayer, an individual, is the owner and developer of a patented compound that has proven effective in treating cancerous tumors. Taxpayer transferred to Gopher Corporation the exclusive right to practice under the patent in the field of veterinary medicine. Gopher will pay Taxpayer a 2½ percent royalty on the net sales of any product utilizing the patent. May Taxpayer treat the royalties he receives from Gopher as long-term capital gain under section 1235? If not, may Taxpayer qualify for long-term capital gain treatment under the Code's general capital provisions, assuming Taxpayer is not a professional inventor and has held the patent for more than one year before the transfer?

A few years after the transfer to Gopher, Taxpayer transferred to Wolverine Corporation all remaining rights he owned in the compound patent. Wolverine agreed to pay Taxpayer a 4½ percent royalty on the net sales of any product utilizing the patent. May Taxpayer treat the royalties it receives from Wolverine as long-term capital gain under section 1235? Read *Blake v. Commissioner* (included in this Chapter's materials) in connection with this problem.

After using the compound patent in its business for two years, Wolverine transferred all rights it owned in the compound patent to Buckeye Corporation for a gain of $1 million. At the time of the transfer, Wolverine had been allowed $200,000 in depreciation deductions with respect to the compound patent. What is the character of Wolverine's gain on the transfer to Buckeye? Read Revenue Ruling 78-328 (included in this Chapter's materials) in connection with this problem.

In determining whether a transfer is of "all substantial rights," the key is to examine what rights the taxpayer retains after the transfer and whether such rights are substantial. Treasury regulations specifically allow a taxpayer to retain legal title or a security interest in the transferred patent to secure performance because the retention of such right is not substantial.[365] The regulations further provide that (1) retention of the right to prohibit sublicensing and (2) failure to convey to the transferee the right to use or sell the patent

---

suggested that a field of use restricted transfer that fails the "all substantial rights" standard should likewise fail the "sale or exchange" requirement.

[365] Treas. Reg. § 1.1235-2(b)(2).

property may or may not be the retention of a substantial right, depending on the facts and circumstances of the whole transaction.[366] Query: In what instances would a retained right to prohibit sublicensing or assignment not be a substantial right?

4.3[4][e] Tax Consequences to the Transferee

A transfer qualifying under section 1235 also has important tax consequences to the *transferee*. That is, if section 1235 applies to a transfer, the transferee must treat the payments as the cost of acquiring the patent rather than as royalties.[367] The consequence is that the transferee must capitalize its payments and amortize them[368] (as opposed to currently deducting royalties paid).

4.3[5] Sale or Exchange of a Franchise, Trademark, or Trade name (Section 1253)

Prior to the enactment of section 1253, there was a split of authority whether a transfer of a franchise was a sale or a license under general capital gain principles. Five appellate cases involving Dairy Queen franchise transfers are particularly emblematic of this split (the "Dairy Queen cases").[369] The Dairy Queen cases involved franchise transfers based on similar terms. In each case, the taxpayer transferred perpetual and exclusive territorial rights to a Dairy Queen franchise in exchange for fixed and contingent consideration. The taxpayer also retained rights to maintain quality and uniformity and to ensure contingent payments were paid timely and in the right amount. One court ruled the transfers to be "licenses," such that all payments, whether fixed or contingent, were ordinary income.[370] Three courts ruled the transfers to be "sales," but differed on the treatment of fixed and contingent consideration. One of these courts allowed capital gain as to both the fixed and

---

[366] Treas. Reg. § 1.1235-2(b)(3).

[367] Treas. Reg. § 1.1235-1(d).

[368] If the patent is acquired as part of the acquisition of a trade or business, it would be an "amortizable section 197 intangible" and amortized over 15 years. Otherwise, if the patent is separately-acquired, it would be depreciated over its remaining useful life. *See* Chapter 3.

[369] *Estate of Gowdey v. Commr.*, 307 F.2d 816 (4th Cir. 1962); *Moberg v. Commr.*, 365 F.2d 337 (5th Cir. 1966) (involving Vern Moberg, brother of the taxpayer in the 9th Circuit case); *Wernentin v. Commr.*, 354 F.2d 757 (8th Cir. 1965); *Moberg v. Commr.*, 310 F.2d 782 (9th Cir. 1962) (involving Theodore Moberg, brother of the taxpayer in the 5th Circuit case); *Diary Queen of Okla., Inc. v. Commr.*, 250 F.2d 503 (10th Cir. 1957).

[370] *Werentin*, 354 F.2d at 766. The court in *Werentin* was silent on the issue of whether the taxpayer was able to offset its adjusted basis against the payments received.

contingent consideration,[371] while the other two courts allowed capital gain as to the fixed consideration only and held that the contingent consideration generated ordinary income.[372] The final court (a case involving four types of franchise agreements) found transfers under one type of franchise agreement to be a "sale" generating capital gain as to fixed and contingent consideration, while finding transfers under the other three types of franchise agreements to be "licenses" generating ordinary income (because the taxpayer retained too much operational control under these agreements).[373]

Suffice it to say, the Dairy Queen cases created an unacceptable amount of confusion, thereby prompting Congress to enact section 1253 to provide certainty to the tax treatment of franchise transfers. Because Congress found trademarks and trade names to be similar to franchises, it extended section 1253 to cover trademark and trade name transfers as well.[374]

Section 1253 does two things from the transferor's perspective. First, section 1253 denies capital gain treatment to contingent consideration received on the transfer of a franchise, trademark, or trade name. Specifically, section 1253 states that "[a]mounts received or accrued on account of a transfer, sale, or disposition of a franchise, trademark, or trade name which are contingent on the productivity, use, or disposition of the franchise, trademark, or trade name transferred shall be treated as amounts received or accrued from the sale or other disposition of property which is not a capital asset."[375] If the franchisor operated the franchise itself, Congress reasoned that a franchisor would have treated profits based on productivity as ordinary income. So Congress felt that the franchisor should likewise treat as ordinary income those amounts based on productivity received from its franchisee.[376]

Second, section 1253 denies capital gain treatment where the taxpayer retains "any significant power, right, or continuing interest" in the transferred franchise, trademark, or trade name.[377] The Code provides six examples of a retained "significant power, right, or continuing interest," including (but not limited to) the following:[378]

---

[371] *Dairy Queen of Okla., Inc.*, 250 F.2d at 506.

[372] *Estate of Gowdey*, 307 F.2d at 820; *Moberg*, 365 F.2d at 339-40.

[373] *Moberg*, 310 F.2d at 783-84.

[374] Sen. Rpt. 91-552 at 208 (Nov. 21, 1969).

[375] I.R.C. § 1253(c).

[376] H.R. Rpt. 91-413 at 163 (Aug. 2, 1969).

[377] I.R.C. § 1253(a).

[378] I.R.C. § 1253(b)(2).

(1) a right to disapprove any assignment of the transferred interest, or any part thereof;

(2) a right to terminate at will;

(3) a right to prescribe standards of quality of products used or sold, or of services furnished, and of the equipment and facilities used to promote such products or services;

(4) a right to require the transferee to sell or advertise only the transferor's products or services;

(5) a right to require the transferee to purchase substantially all of its supplies and equipment from the transferor; and

(6) a right to payments contingent on the productivity, use, or disposition of the subject matter of the interest transferred, if such payments constitute a substantial element under the transfer agreement.[379]

Would a taxpayer's retention of any of the rights enumerated above be significant as a matter of law? For example, if a taxpayer transfers exclusive and perpetual rights to a trademark, but retains a right for 30 days to terminate the transfer at will, has the taxpayer retained a significant right? Is the list of enumerated rights above exhaustive? If not, under what standard is an *unenumerated* right judged to be significant? Read *Stokley USA, Inc. v. Commissioner,*[380] which is included in this Chapter's materials, to answer these questions and the following problem.

> **Problem 4.11**: For several years, Taxpayer owned the trademark "Five O'clock," which it used in the manufacture, marketing, and sale of distilled liquors and spirits. Taxpayer transferred to Purchaser all rights to the "Five O'clock" trademark (together with all associated goodwill) subject to two restrictions. First, Taxpayer retained the right to disapprove any assignment of the "Five O'clock" trademark for five years after the transfer. Second, the Purchaser could not use the "Five O'clock" trademark in connection with the sale of whiskey for 20 years after the transfer. Taxpayer insisted on

[379] In *Nabisco Brands, Inc. v. Commr.*, 69 T.C.M. (CCH) 2230 (1995), the Tax Court found contingent payments comprising 25 percent of the total consideration to be a "substantial." Treasury proposed regulations (now withdrawn) that would treat contingent payments comprising more than 50 percent of total estimated consideration to be substantial. Prop. Reg. § 1.1253-2(d)(6) (withdrawn on Apr. 27, 1993 due to expiration of a "sunset" provision placed on the regulations when originally proposed in 1971).

[380] 100 T.C. 439 (1993).

> this restriction because it believed Purchaser's sale of whiskey would adversely affect Taxpayer's sale of its "Happy Hour" whiskey brand. Purchaser agreed to pay Taxpayer $1,000,000 in a lump sum at closing plus a 3½ percent royalty on the net sales of any product utilizing the "Five O'clock" trademark for the next 20 years. The parties reasonably estimated that Taxpayer's 20-year right to royalties had a present value of $4,000,000 at the time of transfer. Taxpayer's adjusted basis in the transferred trademark was $0 at the time of transfer. What are the tax consequences to Taxpayer upon the transfer of the "Five O'clock" trademark?

If a taxpayer retains a "significant right, power, or continuing interest" in the transferred property, may the taxpayer treat the transfer as a "sale or other disposition" for section 1001 purposes and recover its adjusted basis? In other words, must a taxpayer retaining a significant right in the transferred property treat all payments received as ordinary income without offset of adjusted basis (i.e., a license)? On the one hand, if the taxpayer retains a significant right in the transferred property, section 1253(a) states that the transfer "shall not be treated as a sale or exchange." And if the transfer is not a sale or exchange, one might conclude that such a transfer is to be treated as a license with no offset of adjusted basis. Indeed, while the legislative history to section 1253 does not specifically address the issue of basis offset, it repeatedly states that section 1253 is meant to distinguish "sales" from "licenses."[381] On the other hand, one could argue that section 1253 was enacted for the sole purpose of determining characterization and does not affect whether a transfer is a sale or other disposition allowing recovery of basis under section 1001. For instance, in *Tomerlin Trust v. Commissioner*,[382] the Tax Court held, for purposes of the personal holding company tax, section 1253 does not deem a transfer a license or a sale, but only characterizes certain payments as ordinary.

4.3[6] Installment and Contingent Payment Sales (Section 453)

Section 1001 provides that the entire amount of realized gain or loss is *recognized* (i.e., taken into account for tax purposes), unless a specific Code provision provides an exception.[383] Section 453 provides one such exception by instructing taxpayers to generally recognize gain (but not loss) from an "installment sale" under the "installment method." An "installment sale" is "a disposition of property where at least 1 payment is to be received

---

[381] *E.g.* Sen. Rpt. 91-552 at 207-11 (Nov. 21, 1969); H.R. Rpt. 91-413 at 160-64 (Aug. 2, 1969).

[382] 87 T.C. 876 (1986).

[383] I.R.C. § 1001(c).

after the close of the taxable year" of disposition.[384] The "installment method" prorates the taxpayer's total gain over the total payments to be received, irrespective of whether the taxpayer is on the cash or accrual method. The rationale for the installment method is simple: the taxpayer ought to recognize gain and pay the associated tax liability as the taxpayer receives payments. In this way, the installment method ensures that the taxpayer has sufficient liquidity to pay the tax liability.

Under the installment method, the taxpayer calculates recognized gain for the tax year by multiplying the payment received that year by the "gross profit ratio."[385] The "gross profit ratio" is expressed by a fraction, i.e., "gross profit" realized divided by total "contract price."[386] The "gross profit" is generally the selling price less adjusted basis (i.e., realized gain).[387] And the total "contract price" is generally the selling price less any qualifying indebtedness the buyer assumes or takes the property subject to (but only to the extent it does not exceed the taxpayer's adjusted basis of the property).[388] Therefore, a taxpayer calculates recognized gain as follows under the installment method:

$$\text{Payment for tax year} \times \frac{\text{Gross profit realized}}{\text{Total contract price}} = \text{Gain recognized for tax year}$$

The installment method is not available for certain "dealer dispositions," sales of inventory of personal property, and sales of publicly-traded property.[389] Additionally, a taxpayer must immediately recognize recapture income in the year of disposition.[390] But the taxpayer may continue to report on the installment method that portion of the realized gain that is not recapture. In doing so, the taxpayer must add the recapture income to his adjusted basis of the property sold for purposes of calculating "gross profit" (such that "gross profit" becomes that portion of gain realized that is not recapture).[391] Without such an adjustment to basis, the taxpayer's gross profit ratio would be too high and cause the taxpayer to over report gain.

---

[384] I.R.C. § 453(b)(1).

[385] I.R.C. § 453(c).

[386] *Id.*

[387] Treas. Reg. § 15A.453-1(b)(2)(v).

[388] Treas. Reg. § 15A.453-1(b)(2)(iii).

[389] I.R.C. § 453(b)(2)(A), (b)(2)(B) & (k).

[390] I.R.C. § 453(i). "Recapture income" includes amounts that sections 1245 and 1250 would characterize as ordinary income if all payments to be received were received in the year of disposition. I.R.C. § 453(i)(2).

[391] *See* Sen. Rpt. 98-169 at 466 (Apr. 2, 1984).

Recognition of gain under the installment method is automatic, unless the taxpayer elects out.[392] A taxpayer may elect out of the installment method for various reasons. But two commons reasons are (1) the taxpayer believes future tax rates will increase, such that current payment of tax outweighs the benefit of tax deferral, and (2) the taxpayer has sufficient losses to offset the gain recognized from the disposition.

Calculation of recognized gain on the "installment method" is relatively straightforward when payments are fixed. In such case, the taxpayer can easily determine "gross profit" and total "contract price." But when all or part of the consideration is contingent, "gross profit" and total "contract price" cannot be readily determined at the time of sale. In such case, how and when does the taxpayer recognize gain?

One approach would be to leave the transaction "open" until all contingent payments are made. This approach, adopted in *Burnet v. Logan*,[393] would allow the taxpayer to first offset payments against adjusted basis and recognize gain only after full basis recovery. Because the "open" transaction maximizes tax deferral, Congress instructed Treasury to provide regulations to account for a ratable basis recovery upon receipt of contingent payments.[394] So the "open" transaction has limited applicability today and a taxpayer must recognize gain from contingent payment sales on the "installment method" (unless the taxpayer elects out).[395]

Under the regulations, a taxpayer must first determine whether the contingent payment sale is subject to a "stated maximum selling price." If so, the taxpayer must generally use the "stated maximum selling price" as the "selling price" for purposes of calculating the gross profit ratio.[396] If there is no "stated maximum selling price," the taxpayer must next determine if the contingent payment sale is for a fixed period. If so, the taxpayer generally

---

[392] I.R.C. § 453(d).

[393] 283 U.S. 404 (1931).

[394] I.R.C. § 453(j)(2).

[395] Treas. Reg. § 15A.453-1(c)(1). If the taxpayer "elects out," gain (or loss) is calculated under ordinary rules (amount realized less adjusted basis) and the fair market value of the contingent payment obligation is included in amount realized. Treas. Reg. § 15A.453-1(d)(2)(i). The contingent payment obligation cannot be valued less than the fair market value of the transferred property. Treas. Reg. § 15A.453-1(d)(2)(iii). Only in "rare and extraordinary cases" where fair market value cannot be ascertained may a taxpayer apply the "open" transaction rule (but the transfer will be closely scrutinized to determine if it is really a sale). *Id.*

[396] Treas. Reg. § 15A.453-1(c)(2)(i).

allocates his adjusted basis over that fixed period in equal annual amounts.[397] But the taxpayer generally cannot claim a loss until the final payment year.[398] If contingent payments in a year are less than the basis allocated in that year, the taxpayer must carry forward the unrecovered basis to the next year.[399]

If there is neither a "stated maximum selling price" nor a fixed period, the Service will closely scrutinize whether the transfer is really a sale.[400] If deemed to be a sale, the taxpayer must allocate basis equally over a 15-year period and carry forward any unrecovered basis to the next year.[401] The taxpayer cannot claim a loss for unrecovered basis until the contingent payment obligation is deemed worthless.[402]

> **Problem 4.12**: On January 1, Year 1, Taxpayer purchased a trademark (and all associated goodwill) for a lump sum payment of $1,500,000. Taxpayer immediately used the trademark to promote its products. On January 1, Year 6, Taxpayer transferred to Purchaser all rights to the trademark (and all associated goodwill). In return, Purchaser agreed to pay Taxpayer 5½ percent of the net sales of products using the trademark for the next five years. The parties agreed, however, that in no event would Purchaser be required to pay more than $2 million for the trademark. Pursuant to the agreement, Purchaser paid Taxpayer $400,000 in Year 6, $500,000 in Year 7, $600,000 in Year 8, $300,000 in Year 9, and $200,000 in Year 10. Based on the foregoing, what are the tax consequences to Taxpayer? Alternatively, how would your answer change if the parties had not set a maximum selling price of $2 million?

---

397 Treas. Reg. § 15A.453-1(c)(3)(i).

398 *Id.*

399 *Id.*

400 Treas. Reg. § 15A.453-1(c)(4).

401 *Id.*

402 *Id.*

4.4 Materials for Chapter 4

HENRY VOGT MACHINE COMPANY v. COMMISSIONER

United States Tax Court

66 T.C.M. (CCH) 426 (1993)

* * *

After concessions by the parties, the sole issue for decision is whether payments received by petitioner under an agreement to transfer technical information and know-how to a Japanese corporation qualify for treatment as long-term capital gains under section 1222.

FINDINGS OF FACT

Some of the facts have been stipulated and are found accordingly. The stipulation of facts and attached exhibits are incorporated by this reference. Petitioner, a corporation organized under the laws of Kentucky, had its principal office located at Louisville, Kentucky, at the time the petition herein was filed. For the years in issue, petitioner reported its income based on the accrual method of accounting and filed Federal income tax returns (Form 1120) on the basis of a fiscal year ended August 31.

At all relevant times, petitioner's principal business activity was the design, manufacture, and sale of heat recovery equipment and products related thereto; petitioner was not in the trade or business of selling technology. One of the products manufactured and sold by petitioner was a heat recovery steam generator (HRSG). A HRSG is a generator installed behind a gas turbine to recover the heat from the turbine's exhaust to produce steam. Because the steam produced is of high quality, it can be converted into electrical power or used in various industrial and commercial processes.

Petitioner developed the technology to manufacture HRSG's in the 1960s and has owned the technology ever since. With the exception of a licensing agreement with Standard Fasel of Holland, the HRSG technology has at all times been confidential to petitioner, and petitioner has taken steps to maintain such confidentiality. Although an incidental portion of the HRSG technology was the subject of a U.S. patent, the HRSG technology consists of essentially unpatented engineering and manufacturing know-how. Through 1985, petitioner had manufactured and sold HRSG's for use in 79 projects worldwide. Although all such HRSG's were manufactured by petitioner in the United States, and many were installed in the United States, a small number were installed abroad in Iran, Korea, Holland, the United Kingdom, and Brunei.

Until 1985, petitioner did not actively pursue business in the Far East. In January 1985, petitioner and Kawasaki Heavy Industries (KHI), entered into a written agreement (the Yamada agreement) whereby petitioner granted KHI a 10-year license to use petitioner's HRSG technology in certain geographical areas. KHI is a Japanese corporation engaged in the design, manufacture, and sale of combustion boiler generators and other energy related products. (A combustion boiler generator is a different type of generator from a HRSG.) KHI unsuccessfully attempted to market its own HRSG, but it did not manufacture and sell HRSG's prior to the execution of the Yamada agreement in 1985.

Pertinent terms of the Yamada agreement are as follows:

> WHEREAS, VOGT has for many years been engaged in designing, engineering, and manufacturing certain Products (as defined hereinafter) and has acquired considerable experience therein; and
>
> WHEREAS, VOGT is carrying on research and development work on said Products; and
>
> WHEREAS, KHI intends to undertake the manufacture of said Products and wishes to secure Vogt's know-how therefor; and
>
> WHEREAS, VOGT is willing to grant the right to use this know-how to KHI on the conditions set forth hereinafter;
>
> NOW IT IS AGREED AS FOLLOWS:
>
> CLAUSE 1
> *Definitions:*
>
> a. Products shall mean Henry Vogt type, natural circulation, water tube, horizontal gas flow type Waste Heat Steam Generator for Gas Turbine Exhaust Recovery, except those for use in the thermal enhanced oil recovery applications and those for marine use. * * *

b. Technical Information shall mean certain information relating to Products in VOGT's possession, to the extent of VOGT's right by law thereto. * * *
c. Technology Transfer Fee shall mean payment received by VOGT for the transfer of Technical Information * * *
d. Territory shall mean the whole world except the United States of America and its protectorates, Canada and Mexico * * *

* * * *

CLAUSE 3
Manufacturing and Selling Rights

a. VOGT grants to KHI manufacturing and selling rights as provided hereunder:

1) Manufacturing Right

An exclusive right and license to manufacture Products in Japan.

2) Selling Right

1. An exclusive right and license to offer and sell Products for installation in Japan.
2. A non-exclusive right and license to offer and sell Products in:
    A. The Asian countries, the Oceanian countries, the Middle East countries, and the Union of Soviet Socialist Republic except U.S.A.'s Protectorates (American Samoa, Guam and Wake I.)
    B. Any other countries of [sic] Territory as defined in Clause 1(d) whenever principally Japanese financing is a requirement by the customer or the Product is incorporated into a plant which will be supplied by a Japanese company, except for installation in Western Europe. * * *

* * *

CLAUSE 6
Secrecy

All data, drawings and other Technical Information supplied under this Agreement are for the exclusive use of KHI and KHI agrees that same will not be given, sold or made available in any fashion to any other firm, company or person and KHI shall not permit any other firm, company or person to use the Technical Information, directly or indirectly, or permit such activities as aforesaid, except for use in sub-contracting of any components of Products. All Technical Information supplied by VOGT pursuant to this Agreement shall remain the property of VOGT, and KHI shall not use any Technical Information supplied under this Agreement for any purpose except the design, manufacture, quotation, sale, erection and operation of Products within the territory during the term of this Agreement.

During the term of this Agreement, KHI will hold in confidence and not disclose any Technical Information furnished by VOGT hereunder without a prior written consent of VOGT except as necessary for the proper performance of this Agreement and excepting the following information which:

1. at the time of disclosure to KHI is known to the public;
2. after the time of disclosure to KHI becomes known to the public through no fault of KHI;
3. at the time of disclosure to KHI was in the possession of KHI; or
4. after the time of disclosure to KHI is lawfully received by KHI from a third party.

CLAUSE 7
Compensation

In consideration of grant of right and license, supply of Technical Information * * * and supply of technical assistance * * *, KHI shall pay to VOGT:

a. *Technology Transfer Fee* - A single payment of US $500,000 (U.S. Dollars Five Hundred Thousand) will be paid within forty-five (45) days after execution of this Agreement.

b. *Royalties* - * * * KHI will pay to VOGT a royalty, which shall be computed at three percent (3%) of Net Selling Price of each Product manufactured and sold by KHI under this Agreement.
c. In no event shall VOGT ever receive * * * as total compensation under this Agreement, an amount less than the minimum yearly Royalty fee of $60,000, except that the minimum yearly Royalty shall be exempted for the first half of the first Contract Year.
d. The compensation rates herein provided for shall continue for the duration of this Agreement, unless altered in accordance with the terms of Clause 21 hereof.

* * *

CLAUSE 16
Duration of Agreement

a. This Agreement will be in effect for the term of TEN (10) YEARS from the effective date hereof, unless terminated earlier under the terms provided for.
b. After the expiration of the initial TEN (10) YEAR TERM, this Agreement will be continued from year to year, in accordance with the terms and conditions to be agreed upon by both parties unless notice is given in writing by one party to the other at least sixty (60) days before the expiration of the original or extended period that the notifying party does not intend to review or extend this Agreement.
c. In the event that either of the parties hereto, at anytime during the term of this Agreement, commits the breach of any provision hereunder, and fails to rectify such breach within ninety (90) days from the receipt of written notice thereof from the other party hereto, such other party may, at its sole option, and in addition to any other remedies that it may be entitled to, terminate this Agreement forthwith by notice in writing to the breaching party to such effect within thirty (30) days from the end of the above ninety (90) days [sic] period. This agreement may be terminated forthwith at any time by either party upon the bankruptcy, dissolution of either KHI or VOGT; provided further that this Agreement may be terminated forthwith by either party if there should occur a substantial change in the management, operation or control of KHI or VOGT.

CLAUSE 17

Obligations of KHI After Termination of Agreement

a. After any termination of this Agreement as herein above provided, KHI will no longer have the right to manufacture Products, and to use Technical Information supplied to KHI by VOGT under this Agreement.
b. Any notice of termination, or any termination, of this Agreement will not prevent KHI from completing manufacture and delivering Products which were ordered before the date of said notice; provided, however, that KHI will have the duty to make the Royalty payment required * * *, provided further, that KHI will have the duty to maintain Secrecy of all Technical Information * * *, and KHI will have the duty to return to VOGT all designs, drawings and other physical materials comprising the Technical Information within thirty (30) days after termination.

* * *

CLAUSE 24

Integration, Merger and Waiver

a. The terms and provisions contained on this and the foregoing pages of this Agreement, are the full agreement of the parties * * *, no prior understanding or obligation not expressly set forth herein shall be binding upon the parties to this Agreement, and no subsequent modification of this Agreement shall be binding upon the parties unless negotiated upon the terms herein provided and executed with the same formalities as this Agreement.
b. It is expressly understood that all prior negotiations pertaining to the subject matter of this Agreement are merged into this Agreement, and this Agreement contains the full agreement between the parties.

* * *

Petitioner reported all payments received under the Yamada agreement as ordinary income. One such payment was the $500,000 "Technology Transfer Fee" paid by KHI to petitioner during fiscal year 1985.

At an unspecified date in 1985, petitioner's officers were informed that the payments from KHI could be taxable as long-term capital gain, rather than ordinary income, if petitioner conveyed to KHI the exclusive and perpetual right to use its HRSG technology to manufacture, use, and sell HRSG's and products derived therefrom in Japan. In this respect, an internal memorandum dated September 13, 1985, captioned Taxation of License Agreements, sent to the officers of petitioner, stated:

> Subsequent to a discussion about the DISC with an attorney at the Chicago Law Firm of Baker & McKenzie we were sent the attached report on taxation of foreign license agreements and technology transfer fees as capital gains. Long terms [sic] capital gains are taxable at a rate of 20% versus ordinary income at 50%. This differential in taxation could save the company over $150,000 in taxes in fiscal 1985 alone.
>
> While there are no guarantees that we will be able to recover excess taxes due on income from current license agreements, there is a distinct possibility that future taxes may be reduced by a significant amount. John Ryan reviewed the attached article and sees no conflicts other than perhaps the word "perpetual."
>
> I feel that we should consider engaging Baker & McKenzie to explore this possible opportunity. It may also behove us to run our current license agreements past them for review as we already are aware of some errors and ommissions [sic] in them.

A subsequent memorandum, dated October 30, 1985, stated:

> Attached please find a listing of only the changes which must take place in order to allow the KHI-VOGT agreement to qualify for capital gains. Anything not mentioned on these pages will remain exactly as it was written in the original document.
>
> Sorry about the Chicago lawyers changing minor wording throughout the agreement. Most of their changes improve the document but have little bearing on capital gains treatment. The new Clause 25 is necessary unless you want the risk of a jail term or fine for not complying with U.S. export licensing laws.

> Please present these documents, along with the enclosed Baker & McKenzie letter of explaination [sic] and the HVHjr letter I sent to Tokyo earlier. Do not present KHI with the fully revised agreement, we will send them a fresh copy after they agree to the revisions.
>
> All we need are the changes on these pages. Please try to get a feel for their willingness to proceed with the revision on timely basis.
>
> Our position remains that we would like to grant KHI additional rights in order to receive better treatment under U.S. tax laws.

* * *

Ultimately, an agreement (the Kubota agreement) was executed in late January or early February 1986. The Kubota agreement purportedly canceled and superseded all prior agreements between KHI and petitioner regarding the HRSG technology, including the Yamada agreement.

In several respects the Yamada agreement and the Kubota agreement are indistinguishable; in fact 19 of the Kubota agreement's 26 clauses are identical to those in the Yamada agreement. Each agreement controls the transfer of the same HRSG technology and each has identical compensation and termination clauses. Pertinent terms of the Kubota agreement that differ from those in the Yamada agreement are as follows:

> CLAUSE 1
> *Definitions:*
>
> d. "Exclusive Territory" shall mean Japan. "Non-Exclusive Territory" shall mean the countries listed in Clause 3.a.2) 2. hereof.
>
> * * *
>
> CLAUSE 3
> *Manufacturing and Selling Rights*
>
> a. VOGT hereby grants to KHI Manufacturing and selling rights as provided hereunder:

1) Manufacturing right

An exclusive and perpetual right and license to utilize the Technical Information for KHI's manufacture and use of the Products in Japan.

* * *

CLAUSE 6
Secrecy

a. All of the Technical Information supplied by VOGT under this Agreement shall be for the exclusive use of KHI and KHI agrees that same shall not be given, sold, or otherwise made available in any fashion to any other firm, company, or person except with the prior written consent of VOGT in accordance with the provisions of Clause 3 hereof, and KHI shall not permit any other firm, company or person to use the Technical Information, directly or indirectly, or to permit such activities as aforesaid, except as expressly permitted in accordance with the provisions of Clause 3 hereof. KHI shall not use any of the Technical Information supplied by VOGT under this Agreement for any purpose except the design, manufacture, quotation, sale, erection, and operation of the Products within the Exclusive Territory and the sale of the Products within the Non-Exclusive Territory during the term of this Agreement.
b. During the term of this Agreement, KHI will hold in confidence and not disclose any Technical Information furnished by VOGT hereunder without a prior written consent of VOGT except as necessary for the proper performance of this Agreement and excepting the following information which:

1. at the time of disclosure to KHI is known to the public;
2. after the time of disclosure to KHI becomes known to the public through no fault of KHI;
3. at the time of disclosure to KHI was in the possession of KHI; or
4. after the time of disclosure to KHI is lawfully received by KHI from a third party.

* * *

> [Note: Clause 16, regarding the agreement's duration, was unchanged from the prior Yamada agreement]
>
> CLAUSE 17
> *Obligations After Termination of Agreement*
>
> a. After any termination of this Agreement by VOGT in accordance with the provisions of Clause 16.c. hereof, KHI shall no longer have the right to manufacture the Products and to use the Technical Information supplied to KHI by VOGT under this Agreement. KHI shall have the duty to return to VOGT all of the design, drawings, and other physical materials comprising the Technical Information within thirty (30) days after such termination.
> b. Not withstanding [sic] the provisions as set forth in the above Clause 17.a., after the expiration or termination of this Agreement due to breach by VOGT * * *, KHI shall have the right to retain any Technical Information supplied by VOGT hereunder and shall have the right to manufacture and sell the Products in Japan without payment by KHI to VOGT.
> c. Any notice of termination, or any termination, of this Agreement will not prevent KHI from completing manufacture and delivering Products which were ordered before the date of said notice; provided, however, that KHI will have the duty to make the Royalty payment required * * *, provided further, that KHI will have the duty to maintain Secrecy of all Technical Information * * *.
>
> * * *
>
> [Clause 25 dealt with compliance with U.S. export licensing laws.]

Under each agreement (Clause 7 in both the Yamada and Kubota agreements), KHI was required to pay petitioner a "Technology Transfer Fee" as follows:

> A single payment of US $500,000 (U.S. Dollars Five Hundred Thousand) will be paid within forty-five (45) days after the execution of this Agreement.

KHI paid the "Technology Transfer Fee" under the Yamada agreement during fiscal year 1985; there is no evidence that KHI paid such fee at any time thereafter. No explanation was offered as to why KHI failed to remit the required $500,000 fee under the Kubota agreement, nor did petitioner explain why it did not seek enforcement of KHI's obligation to remit the $500,000 fee.

KHI manufactured and sold three HRSG's during the years in issue for final installation in the country of India; each was manufactured in Japan, sold to a Japanese company, and shipped to an end user in India. KHI did not play a role in shipping the three HRSG's (which were shipped FAS Yokohama, Japan); it did, however, send supervisors to oversee the installation.

During fiscal year 1986, KHI paid petitioner $80,000 (2 semi-annual minimum royalty payments of $30,000 each, and a $20,000 computer program maintenance fee); petitioner reported the $80,000 as long-term capital gain.

During fiscal year 1987, KHI paid petitioner $267,623 (a single semi-annual minimum royalty payment of $30,000, 2 semi-annual computer program maintenance fees of $5,000 each and royalty payments of $37,546.20 and $190,076.50); petitioner reported the $267,623 as long-term capital gain.

Respondent determined that both the $80,000 and $267,623 payments reported as long-term capital gain for fiscal years 1986 and 1987, respectively, were taxable as ordinary income.

OPINION

Petitioner contends that it is entitled to treat the payments received from KHI during fiscal years 1986 and 1987 as long-term capital gain under section 1222(3) because: (1) The HRSG technology is a capital asset under section 1221; (2) petitioner's transfer of the HRSG technology to KHI under the Kubota agreement was a sale or exchange under section 1222(3); and (3) petitioner held the HRSG technology for the requisite holding period under section 1222(3). In support of its contention that there was a sale or exchange of the HRSG technology, petitioner asserts that under the Kubota agreement, which canceled and superseded the Yamada agreement, it transferred all substantial rights of value in its HRSG technology to KHI for KHI's exclusive and perpetual use thereof in Japan (the exclusive territory). Not surprisingly, respondent disagrees.

Respondent maintains that the payments received by petitioner from KHI during the years in issue are royalty payments earned under a license agreement, and therefore such payments are taxable as ordinary income under section 61(a)(6). In support of its position, respondent makes the following three alternative arguments as to why all payments received by petitioner from KHI are taxable as ordinary income: (1) because the Kubota agreement should not be recognized for tax purposes; (2) if the Kubota agreement is recognized for tax purposes, then because the Kubota agreement is not supported by adequate consideration; and (3) if the Kubota agreement is recognized for tax purposes and supported by adequate consideration, then because petitioner retained certain substantial rights of value after the purported sale. We agree with respondent's third alternative argument; i.e., petitioner retained substantial rights of value after the purported sale of the HRSG technology to KHI. As a result, we need not, and do not, decide whether the Kubota agreement should be recognized for tax purposes or whether it is supported by adequate consideration.

To be entitled to long-term capital gains treatment, petitioner must establish: (1) That the technology in question constituted a capital asset; (2) that there has been a sale or exchange of such technology; and (3) that petitioner held such technology for [the requisite holding period] prior to the "sale or exchange." [Citations omitted].

Petitioner has established the first and third stated requirements. First, it is well settled that confidential, unpatented technology or technical know-how is property. Here, petitioner was not engaged in the trade or business of selling technology during the years in question; thus, it is clear that the HRSG technology constitutes a capital asset. [citations omitted]. Additionally, the record indicates that the HRSG technology was held [for the requisite holding period for long-term capital gain treatment]. Thus, the only question remaining is whether there was a "sale or exchange" of the HRSG technology, as contended by petitioner, or a mere license thereof, as urged by respondent.

The taxation of transfers of unpatented technical data, secret processes, and trade secrets is a subject not specifically covered by statute or regulation. It is well settled, however, that unpatented technology, such as know-how, can be the subject of a sale and that the transfer of technical data and know-how is sufficiently akin to patents to warrant the application, by analogy, of the tax law that has been developed relating to the transfer of patent rights. [Citations omitted].

In order for the transfer of the HRSG technology to be deemed a sale for tax purposes, petitioner must establish that it surrendered all substantial rights of value in the HRSG technology in Japan; otherwise, the transfer is deemed to be a license. [Citation omitted].

Where an agreement transferring technical data or know-how is terminable at will by the transferor before the end of the remaining life of the technical data or know-how, the transferor is deemed to have retained substantial rights of value if subsequently it has the right to disclose the technical data or know-how to others in the transferee's exclusive territory. [Citations omitted]. However, the fact that the agreement transferring technical data or know-how does not require the know-how to be returned to the transferor upon termination of the agreement is not determinative as to whether the transferor actually retained the right to disclose such information (since obviously, the transferee cannot eradicate knowledge gained via the transfer upon termination of the agreement). [Citations omitted].

Thus, the character of the payments received by petitioner from KHI under the Kubota agreement depends upon: (1) Whether the Kubota agreement was terminable by petitioner at will before the end of the remaining life of the HRSG technology, and (2) if so, whether petitioner has the right to disclose the HRSG technology to others in the exclusive territory upon termination of the agreement. An ancillary determination as to whether the HRSG technology has a practical or material value to petitioner at the time when petitioner is able to terminate the Kubota agreement at will must also be made.

In determining whether an agreement was a license or a sale for tax purposes, the Court of Appeals for the Fifth Circuit in *Pickren v. United States* [378 F.2d 595, 599 (5th Cir. 1967)] stated:

> The cardinal rule in the interpretation of contracts is to ascertain the mutual intention of the parties and then, so far as it is possible so to do consistently with legal principles, give effect to that intention. * * *

We, therefore, shall start our deliberation by examining the terms of the Kubota agreement in order to ascertain whether petitioner and KHI intended that there be a transfer to KHI of all substantial rights of value in the HRSG technology. We are mindful that the terminology used in the agreement may be of significance. However, the label or name the agreement bears is not determinative, nor is the form thereof conclusive. [Citations omitted].

Upon examining the terms of the Kubota agreement, we conclude the parties did not intend that petitioner transfer to KHI all substantial rights of value in the HRSG technology within the exclusive territory. We base our conclusion on the fact that petitioner had the right to terminate the Kubota agreement at will at the end of the 10-year term and thereafter petitioner retained the right to disclose the HRSG technology to others in the exclusive territory.

In the instant case, the agreement contains an integration clause stating that it represents the full agreement between the parties and contains no language preventing petitioner from disclosing the technical data or know-how to other persons or entities in the exclusive territory after the termination of the agreement.

To support its claim that the Kubota agreement effected a complete transfer of the HRSG technology to KHI in the exclusive territory, petitioner directs our attention to Clause 3.a.2. of the agreement which uses the word "perpetual" to describe KHI's exclusive right and license. Petitioner contends that clause 3.a. specifically limits the non-exclusive license to the "term of this Agreement," whereas no such explicit limitation is stated with regard to the exclusive right and license. Further, petitioner points out that whereas the phrase "All Technical Information * * * shall remain the property of VOGT"; was included in clause 6 of the Yamada agreement, such phrase is not contained in the Kubota agreement. We do not deem the factors which petitioner calls to our attention persuasive.

To begin with, when viewed in the context of the entire Kubota agreement, we do not believe the use of the term "perpetual" in clause 3.a. transforms the Kubota agreement into a sale or exchange. In cases where the terms "perpetual" or "irrevocable" appear in a know-how transfer agreement, but are incompatible with other provisions of the agreement, we have rejected arguments made by other taxpayers that the presence of those terms is determinative. [Citations omitted].

Clause 16 of the Kubota agreement, which is identical to clause 16 of the Yamada agreement, provides in part as follows:

> a. This Agreement will be in effect for the term of TEN (10) YEARS from the effective date hereof, unless terminated earlier under the terms provided for.
>
> b. After the expiration of the initial TEN (10) YEAR TERM, this Agreement will be continued from year to year, in accordance with the terms and conditions to be agreed upon by both parties unless notice is given in writing by one party to the other at least sixty (60) days before the expiration of the original or extended period that the notifying party does not intend to review or extend this Agreement.

* * *

In the instant case, clauses 16.a. and b. of the Kubota agreement give petitioner the absolute right to terminate the Kubota agreement at will after 10 years. Such termination right, together with the fact that the Kubota agreement does not expressly prohibit petitioner from disclosing the HRSG technology to others within Japan upon termination of the agreement, persuades us that petitioner retained the right to sell or license the HRSG technology to others in Japan after termination of the Kubota agreement. And, because petitioner has not established that the HRSG technology will lack practical or material value in the exclusive territory at the time when petitioner is able to terminate the Kubota agreement at will, we conclude that petitioner's right to sell or license the HRSG technology thereafter is a substantial right of value.

Our decision follows a line of cases which hold that where a transfer of a patent or technical data is terminable by the grantor not on the happening of a future event beyond his control but at his own discretion before the expiration of a patent or during the useful life of technical data, the grantor is deemed to have retained substantial rights of value in the technology or patent transferred. [Citations omitted].

* * *

In view of our conclusion, it is not necessary for us to consider the remaining arguments asserted by petitioner or respondent.

To summarize, we hold that the transfer of rights in the unpatented HRSG technology for a limited period of time did not constitute a sale or exchange of such property under section 1222(3); consequently, the payments received by petitioner from KHI under the Kubota agreement are taxable as ordinary income.

To reflect concessions by the parties,
Decision will be entered under Rule 155.

HERWIG v. UNITED STATES

United States Court of Claims

105 F. Supp. 384 (Ct. Cl. 1952)

[Note: *Herwig* preceded enactment of the "self-created copyright" exception to capital asset status, which is currently provided in section 1221(a)(3). Thus, at the time this case was decided, an "amateur" author could claim capital gain treatment upon the "sale or exchange" of a self-created copyright. The portion of the opinion addressing whether the taxpayer was a "professional" or an "amateur" is omitted.]

Plaintiffs seek to recover a portion of federal income taxes paid by them in the year 1945 on the proceeds received by plaintiff [Kathleen Winsor][*] from the Twentieth Century-Fox Film Corporation for the sale of the exclusive motion picture rights to her book "Forever Amber."

* * *

In 1943 Kathleen Winsor completed the novel originally entitled "Wings of the Morning" which was later changed to "Forever Amber." On March 2, 1944, Miss Winsor entered into a contract with The Macmillan Company for the publication of her book. The terms of that contract reserved to her the motion picture and certain other specified rights to the literary work. On January 8, 1945, Miss Winsor entered into a contract with Twentieth Century-Fox Film Corporation, designated as "Purchaser" under the contract, in which she as owner did "grant, convey and assign" the exclusive motion picture rights in and to her literary property for $125,000 in cash plus additional payments not to exceed $75,000. After the deduction of certain commissions she received the net amount of $165,000 for these rights.

The principal issue before us is whether her profit from this transaction was taxable as long-term capital gain. That in turn depends upon whether the transaction constituted a sale of capital assets held for [for the requisite holding period].

From the chronology of dates above set forth, it is obvious that the motion picture rights, having been reserved under the publishing contract entered into March 1944, had been held considerably in excess of six months at the time of their disposition in January 1945.

However, in order to ascertain whether the movie rights were a capital asset we must first determine whether the transaction between Miss Winsor and the Twentieth Century-Fox

[*] During the tax years in question, Ms. Winsor was married to Robert Herwig (they later divorced). Hence, the name "Herwig" in the case name. Ms. Winsor's novel *Forever Amber* was the top bestselling U.S. novel of the 1940s. The 1947 film adaptation of *Forever Amber*, directed by Otto Perminger, was less successful. Ms. Winsor died on May 26, 2003 at the age of 83. Although Ms. Winsor wrote seven more novels, she never again achieved the success of *Forever Amber*. *See* Eric Homberger, *Obituary: Kathleen Winsor: Forever Amber Author who Launched the Bodice-Ripper Boom*, The Guardian (London) at 25 (Jun. 4, 2003).

Film Corporation, disposing of her motion picture rights in "Forever Amber" constituted a "license" or a "sale." * * *

The contract with Twentieth Century-Fox Film Corporation provided in part:

> FIRST: The owner does hereby grant, convey and assign unto the Purchaser, its successors and assigns forever:
> (a) The sole and exclusive motion picture rights and motion picture copyright throughout the world in and to said literary property.
> (b) The sole and exclusive right, throughout the world, to mechanically produce, reproduce and license the reproduction of * * * all or a part of the theme, text and/or dialogue contained in said literary property.
> (c) The sole and exclusive right to make, produce, adapt, sell, lease, rent, exhibit, perform and generally deal in and with and copyright motion picture versions of said literary property, * * * to add to and subtract from the literary property, * * * and to register and obtain copyright therein, throughout the world * * *.

A separate assignment simultaneously executed also contained these provisions.

The contention of the plaintiff that the above language clearly expresses an intent to sell the motion picture rights is met by the defendant's contention based upon the indivisibility of a copyright as an individual thing which cannot be split up and partially assigned either as to time, place, or particular rights or privileges, in less than the sum of all the rights comprehended in the copyright; and that while exclusive rights may, however, be granted, limited as to time, place, or extent of privileges which the grantee may enjoy, such limited rights operate merely as licenses.

This concept of the indivisibility of a copyright has been embodied in a ruling of the Commissioner of Internal Revenue in I. T. 2735, XII-2 Cum. Bull. 131 (1933) in which he ruled in substance that a copyright constituted a single unit of property and that any rights granted thereunder by the author were merely licenses and that amounts paid for the rights granted constituted royalties which were taxable as ordinary income.

The copyright act provides that a person entitled to a copyright by complying with the provisions for registration, including the deposit of copies (17 U.S.C. §§ 5, 10, 11, 12), shall have several "exclusive rights" which are specifically enumerated in the five subsections of Section 1 of the statute (17 U S.C. § 1). They include the right to print, publish, and sell copies (subsection (a)), the right to translate, dramatize, convert into a novel (subsection (b)), to perform publicly (subsection (c)), to make transcriptions or records, to exhibit (subsection (d)), and to reproduce mechanically (subsection (e)). The "one package rule" of the tax law is said to have been used to rationalize the conviction that a transfer of less than all the rights conferred under Section 1 of the copyright act makes the transferee "a mere licensee" entitled to less judicial aid than an "assignee" - proprietor. [Citation omitted].

* * *

Modern business and commercial practices connected with the various rights enumerated in Section 1 of the Copyright Act, 35 Stat. 1075, 1088, 17 U.S.C. § 1, *e. g.*, right to print, dramatize, record, etc., are inherently and essentially different. They can be exercised or purchased by different persons, *Ford v. Charles E. Blaney Amusement Co.,* 148 Fed. 642, and include a variety of industries such as the book publishing trade, the newspaper, magazine publishing industry, the legitimate stage, the motion picture industry, and the television industry. It has been pointed out that the value of each one of these rights can be separately computed, *Interstate Hotel Company of Nebraska v. Remick Music Corp.,* 157 F.2d 744, and the copyright owner can dispose of such portion of his copyright as he desires. Furthermore, many of the separate rights of a copyright owner may be used as the basis for securing new and separate copyrights, *e. g.*, copyright owner of a novel has the right to dramatize it, and he may secure a copyright of the dramatic version. He may also write a motion picture scenario based upon the copyright. [Citation omitted].

Since the basic nature of copyrights, patents and trademarks is the same, *i.e.,* grants of monopolies for a fixed period of time by the Government as a reward for the particular genius of the one receiving the grant, it would seem that the rights granted in connection with any one of them should be treated the same under the law. In *Parke, Davis & Co.,* 31 B. T. A. 427, the Board of Tax Appeals considered the patent cases which had held that a "licensee" who acquired less than all the rights in a patent could not obtain legal title and hence could not sue for infringement. The Board pointed out that a right to maintain a suit at law is controlled by the question of the possession of the "naked, legal title" and deemed that question to be "entirely different" from the tax problem presented, saying that the "legal title" is of little consequence, and the inquiry is as to the ownership of the beneficial interest. The solution was determined solely by the fact that the "licensor" had "divested itself irrevocably of certain capital investments in consideration of the payment made to it."

In the field of trademarks, see *Rainier Brewing Co.,* 7 T. C. 162, aff'd. per curiam, 165 F. 2d 217, and *Seattle Brewing & Malting Co.,* 6 T. C. 856, aff'd. per curiam, 165 F. 2d 216, wherein the court cited . . . its own opinion in *Parke, Davis & Co., supra,* and pointed out that an owner of a trademark or tradename, like the owner of a copyright or patent, has a monopoly which is a property right and which he may assign or transfer even in a limited territory. The court concluded by saying that: "If such grant is exclusive and perpetual, its characteristics more resemble a sale than a license, * * *." *(ibid.,* 869). The retention of the naked, legal title by the grantor was held to be immaterial.

While it has been suggested that the splitting up of the right on a geographical basis appears less feasible with respect to a copyright than with respect to patents or trademarks, even in the copyright field an agreement of this kind would be possible; *e. g.,* a grant of the rights to dramatize productions limited to certain cities. Fulda, *Copyright Assignments and the Capital Gains Tax* (1949), 58 Yale L. J. 245, 261. To such a geographical limitation might also be added a language limitation.

Lest there be any concern with a multiplicity of suits which might result from such a split up of the "bundle of rights" in violation of the theory of indivisibility, we observe that the modern rules of civil practice and procedure and the interest of the parties concerned would undoubtedly insure a final and conclusive judgment in each case involving the "naked, legal title" and the "equitable interests" as they might appear. Furthermore, it is customary to include in the licensing agreement a specific provision regarding the rights of the parties to institute proceedings to enjoin and restrain any infringement of the rights granted. For example, in the agreement between Kathleen Winsor and the Twentieth Century-Fox Film Corporation . . . there is contained the following paragraph:

> FOURTH: The Owner does hereby grant unto the Purchaser the free and unrestricted right, but at the Purchaser's own cost and expense, to institute in the name and on behalf of the Owner any and all suits and proceedings in law or in equity, to enjoin and restrain an infringements of the rights herein granted, and does hereby assign and set over unto the Purchaser any and all cause and causes of action arising or resulting by reason of or based upon such infringement or infringements, and does hereby assign and set over unto the Purchaser any and all recoveries obtained in any such action. The Owner agrees that she will not compromise, settle or in any manner interfere with such litigation, if brought, and the Purchaser does hereby agree to indemnify and save harmless the said Owner from any costs or damages that may arise by reason of any such suits or proceedings.

We believe that it is not only logical but also practical and just to consider the exclusive and perpetual grant of any one of the "bundle of rights" which go to make up a copyright as a "sale" of personal property rather than a mere "license."

We, therefore, hold that the agreement between Kathleen Winsor and the Twentieth Century-Fox Film Corporation constituted a sale of all her motion picture rights in and to "Forever Amber."

* * *

It is so ordered.

REVENUE RULING 60-226

1960-1 C.B. 26

The consideration received by a proprietor of a copyright for a grant transferring the exclusive right to exploit the copyrighted work in a medium of publication throughout the life of the copyright shall be treated as proceeds from a sale of property, regardless of whether the consideration received is measured by a percentage of the receipts from the sale, performance, exhibition, or publication of the copyrighted work, or is measured by the number of copies sold, performances given, or exhibitions made of the copyrighted work, or whether such receipts are payable periodically over a period generally coterminous with the grantee's use of the copyrighted work.

Revenue Ruling 54-409, C.B. 1954-2, 174, modified.

In view of the revocation of Mimeograph 6490, C.B. 1950-1, 9, and Revenue Ruling 55-58, C.B. 1955-1, 97, which dealt with the Federal income tax treatment of amounts received by inventors from the assignment or exclusive licensing of their patents, the Internal Revenue Service has given further consideration to the position stated in Revenue Ruling 54-409, C.B. 1954-2, 174, with respect to the tax treatment of amounts received by a copyright proprietor for a grant of the exclusive right to exploit a copyrighted work.

Revenue Ruling 54-409 deals generally with the circumstances under which a grant of a copyright proprietor's right may confer a license or constitute a transfer of property. The Revenue Ruling holds, in pertinent part, that when the proprietor of a copyright grants the exclusive right to exploit the copyrighted work throughout the life of the copyright in a medium of publication or expression for a consideration which is not measured by a percentage of the receipts from the sale, performance, exhibition, or publication of the copyrighted work, is not measured by the number of copies sold, performances given or exhibitions made of the copyrighted work, and is not payable periodically over a period generally coterminous with the grantee's use of the copyrighted work, the consideration is to be treated as the proceeds of a sale of property and not as rentals or royalties.

Mimeograph 6490 held that, effective for taxable years beginning after May 31, 1950, payments received by inventors from the assignment of a patent or the license of the exclusive right to make, use and sell a patented article under an agreement whereby payments are measured by production, sale, or use by the transferee, or are payable periodically over a period generally coterminous with the transferee's use of the patent, constitute ordinary income. Revenue Ruling 55-58 announced that the Internal Revenue Service would continue to apply the rule of Mimeograph 6490 in cases where section 1235 of the Internal Revenue Code of 1954 was not applicable.

By Revenue Ruling 58-353, C.B. 1958-2, 408, the Service revoked Mimeograph 6490 and Revenue Ruling 55-58 and announced acquiescence in the decisions of the Tax Court of the United States in *Edward C. Myers v. Commissioner,* 6 T.C. 258, *Leonard Coplan et ux. v. Commissioner,* 28 T.C. 1189, and *Roy J. Champayne v. Commissioner,* 26 T.C. 634. This action means that the consideration received by the owner of a patent for the assignment of the patent, or the granting of an exclusive license to such patent, may be treated as the proceeds of a sale of property, for Federal income tax purposes, even though the consideration received by the transferor is measured by production, use, or sale of the patented article.

Since the property rights of patents and copyrights are similar in substance, it is concluded that the Service should adopt, in the case of copyrights, the position that is being taken in the case of patents.

Accordingly, it is held that the consideration received by a proprietor of a copyright for a grant transferring the exclusive right to exploit the copyrighted work in a medium of publication throughout the life of the copyright shall be treated as proceeds from a sale of property, regardless of whether the consideration received is measured by a percentage of the receipts from the sale, performance, exhibition, or publication of the copyrighted work, or is measured by the number of copies sold, performances given, or exhibitions made of the copyrighted work, or whether such receipts are payable over a period generally coterminous with the grantee's use of the copyrighted work.

The modification, here announced, of Revenue Ruling 54-409, *supra,* is to the effect that assignments of copyrights will not be denied treatment as sales solely because of the form which purchase price takes. In cases where interests resembling royalties are retained by the copyright proprietor along with other rights in the transferred interest, the transaction may under some conditions fail to have the required characteristics of a sale. See Revenue Ruling 58-353, *supra.*

It should be noted that whether a copyright is a capital asset within the meaning of section 1221 of the Code and when the provisions of section 1302 of the Code with respect to copyrights would apply are separate and distinct questions which are not considered in this ruling.

Revenue Ruling 54-409, *supra,* is modified to the extent that it holds that the consideration received by the proprietor of a copyright for a grant of the exclusive right to exploit the copyrighted work in a medium of publication is to be treated as proceeds from a sale of property only if the consideration received is not measured by the publication, use, or sale of the copyrighted work, and is not payable over a period generally coterminous with the grantee's use of the copyrighted work.

STERN v. UNITED STATES

United States District Court, Eastern District of Lousiana

164 F. Supp. 847 (E.D. La. 1958)

This case concerns "Francis," the talking mule. Francis is a product of World War II. It was created by a lonely second lieutenant in the Pacific theater of operations who sometimes wondered whether there was anything in the Army lower than a second lieutenant. Francis convinced him there was. Now, seven motion pictures later, that second lieutenant, the taxpayer here, is claiming that the income from "Francis" is entitled to capital gains treatment under the Internal Revenue laws.

In 1933, after attending Harvard University, David Stern, III, was employed as a dramatic critic for the Philadelphia Record, a newspaper owned by his father. Beginning four months later, he became successively comptroller of the Record, classified advertising salesman, assistant classified manager, classified manager, promotion manager, and general manager. During the time that Stern was learning the business, he continued to serve the Record as part-time dramatic critic. In 1938 he became publisher of the Courier-Post newspapers in

Camden, New Jersey. Throughout the prewar years, when Stern was a newspaper business executive, his hobby was writing. He wrote some stories and articles in his spare time, but he was unable to sell any of them.

In the spring of 1943, Stern enlisted as a private in the United States Army. He was later commissioned as a second lieutenant, and subsequently became co-officer in charge of the Central Pacific Edition of Stars and Stripes. While in the Pacific, Stern wrote some imaginary dialogue between a second lieutenant and an old Army mule, some of which he sold to Esquire for approximately $200. He also wrote several short stories while in the Army which he sold to magazines for $50 to $250.

After his release from the Army in 1946, Stern returned to Camden as publisher of the Courier-Post newspapers. In 1947 Stern's connection with the Courier-Post newspapers was terminated. He immediately entered negotiations to purchase a newspaper. While so doing and at the suggestion of a book publisher, he rewrote in book form all of the episodes about the talking mule, Francis. During this period he also wrote a sequel to "Francis," called "Francis Goes to Washington." It, too, was published by Farrar-Strauss, publisher of "Francis." In July 1949 Stern completed negotiations for the purchase of The New Orleans Item and took over the controlling interest and active management of the newspaper as its publisher. Since that date, he has devoted virtually his full time to the newspaper business as publisher.

On June 2, 1950 Stern sold to Universal Pictures Co., Inc., all of his "right, title and interest * * * in and to * * * that certain character known as "Francis" conceived and created by" him, together with all of his rights to the two novels mentioned above and all of his rights to any contracts with respect to the properties conveyed. In consideration of this transfer, Universal agreed to pay him $50,000 plus 5% of the net profits from photoplays based on the character Francis, and 75% of all sums received by Universal under contracts for the use of licensing of the property. Payment of the $50,000 entitled Universal to a "commitment period" of two years within which to make a motion picture. Thereafter, and following release of each picture, Universal was entitled to additional commitment periods by paying a similar fixed consideration of $50,000 as to each picture or period. The contract further provided that "if purchaser shall elect not to pay fixed consideration with respect to any next succeeding commitment period * * * the property shall revert to the seller," all rights in motion pictures produced to remain in Universal. Under this agreement, Universal produced six additional motion pictures in which the character Francis was used. Stern prepared the screen play for the first of these pictures but has had no connection whatever with the writing or production of subsequent pictures except occasionally and incidentally as a consultant. The novel, "Francis Goes to Washington," was not used for screen material.

Plaintiffs have reported as ordinary income for tax purposes all amounts received by them from the sale of the motion picture and publishing rights to the novel "Francis," for preparing a short screen treatment of the book, "Rhubarb," and income received under the agreement for writing screen plays. Only those amounts received from Universal for the character Francis have been treated by plaintiffs as capital gains, accrued during the years received. For the year 1950, the Internal Revenue Service originally accepted plaintiffs' treatment of this income as capital gains from the sale of the character Francis. In considering subsequent years, the Appellate Division of the Internal Revenue reopened the return for the year 1950 and ruled that income from the character Francis was not subject to capital gains treatment for the reason that the contract with Universal was not a sale of the character Francis, that if it were, Francis was property held by the taxpayer primarily for sale to customers in the ordinary course of his business and, further, under [the "self-created copyrights and similar property" exception] the character Francis was similar to a copyright, a literary or artistic composition and, therefore, not a capital asset.

* * *

The question as to whether the taxpayer's contract with Universal Pictures is a sale will be considered first because if it is not a sale, it will be unnecessary to consider the other objections to capital gains treatment of the income made by the Government. It will be noted in the contract that Stern sold all of his interest in the books "Francis," and "Francis Goes to Washington," the character Francis, and all rights and pending contracts concerning them. The agreement makes reference to "the full and complete ownership in the property sold, transferred and granted to (Universal) hereunder." It declares that Stern "hereby sells, transfers and conveys * * * all right, title and interest" in the property to Universal and guarantees "the full benefit of (Universal's) full and complete ownership in the property." Obviously, the draftsmen of this contract intended that it be a sale and called it such. Apparently they were familiar also with the one case, *Cory v. Commissioner of Internal Revenue,* 2 Cir., 230 F.2d 941, which the Government cites as authority for its contention that this agreement is not a sale, because the language of the agreement leaves no doubt that Stern transferred his entire bundle of rights in all the Francis properties, together with rights of future exploitation, to Universal Pictures. Thus this agreement is different from the agreement under consideration in *Cory v. Commissioner, supra*, because there the agreement provided for "a transfer of a part of the cluster of rights" inhering in the taxpayer. *Cory v. Commissioner, supra,* at page 944.

The Government's suggestion, without citation of authority, that the contract in suit is not a sale because it provided for contingent payments of indeterminate sums similar to royalties, and because the property reverted back to Stern if the fixed consideration for any period is not paid, cannot convert this contract of sale into a licensing agreement. Perhaps a sale which provides for contingent payments of indeterminate sums and reversion does violence to the doctrinaire concepts of what a sale should be. But [courts] have so long and so consistently held such contracts to be sales that the Internal Revenue Service itself in [Revenue Ruling 58-353] is now indicating its acquiescence in this classification.

[The court ruled that the taxpayer did not create "Francis" to hold as "property held by the taxpayer primarily for sale to customers in the ordinary course of his trade or business."]

* * *

Finally, and unfortunately for the taxpayer, the Government's position on the 1950 amendment to the 1939 Code is well taken. That amendment excludes from capital gains treatment income from the sale of "a copyright; a literary, musical, or artistic composition; or similar property" held by "a taxpayer, whose personal efforts created such property." The purpose of this amendment is obvious. It is intended to deny capital gains treatment to income from the sale, by their creator, of literary, musical, or artistic compositions, or similar property. Prior to 1950, various rulings of the Internal Revenue Service had approved capital gains treatment of various literary, musical and artistic compositions, including books and radio programs. Congress determined to eliminate such treatment for such compositions. Hence the amendment.

The taxpayer contends that the character "Francis" is not covered by the amendment, that it is not subject to copyright, that it is not a literary, musical or artistic composition or similar property. He argues that he has paid his taxes at the regular rates on all his income from his writings. He states that the character "Francis" is an "intellectual conception" and that as such the income from the sale thereof is entitled to capital gains treatment.

The taxpayer cites several cases in support of his position that the character Francis is not subject to being copyrighted. And he spends much time in his brief arguing that the Internal Revenue Service itself has limited the words of the statute "or similar property" to property capable of being copyrighted. It is not necessary for this Court to appraise the taxpayer's citations, his argument on this point, or the counter citations and argument of the Government. It is this Court's view that the character Francis, irrespective of its susceptibility to copyright, is "a literary composition" and as such the income from the sale thereof is not entitled to capital gains treatment. The taxpayer concedes, as he must, that the novel, "Francis," in which the character Francis is the leading figure, is a literary composition, but he argues that Francis, the principal characterization in the book, is not. In this he is mistaken. The character Francis gets its definition and its delineation from the book. The literary description in the book composes the character. How can it be said that the book is a literary composition yet the main character delineated therein is not? A slice of the loaf is still bread. It would be absurd to attribute to Congress the intention, under the 1950 amendment, of covering whole literary compositions but not parts thereof, particularly in view of the catchall, "or similar property," which appears at the end of the amendment.

Without the literary description of Francis, his mannerisms and his manifestations, Francis would cease to exist. In any event, an amorphous Francis could hardly be called "property held by the taxpayer," the sale of which is entitled to capital gains treatment. [Citation omitted]. If Francis is, as taxpayer suggests, an "intellectual conception," sans form and substance, existing in the mind alone, it is incapable of ownership and, therefore, of being "property held by the taxpayer." [Citations omitted]. If Francis has sufficient form and substance to be considered property capable of ownership, this is so because of its literary composition. [Citation omitted].

The taxpayer is entitled to capital gains treatment on the income from the contract in suit for the year 1950 because the 1950 amendment to the Code does not apply to income received during that year. As to subsequent years, however, capital gains treatment of the income from the contract must be denied as proscribed by that amendment.

REVENUE RULING 85-186

1985-2 C.B. 84

Research or experimental costs previously deducted pursuant to section 174(a) of the Code are not subject to recapture upon the subsequent sale of the resulting technology. Rev. Rul. 72-528 revoked.

ISSUE

Whether "tax benefit" recapture as ordinary income of research or experimental expenditures previously deducted pursuant to section 174(a) of the Internal Revenue Code is required upon subsequent sale of the resulting technology.

FACTS

The principal business activity of the taxpayer is the manufacture and sale of consumer products. Since commencing trade or business activity in 1960, the taxpayer has engaged in extensive in-house research and experimental activities directed at the development of patented and unpatented technology to be used in the manufacture of products sold in the ordinary course of taxpayer's trade or business. The taxpayer has consistently deducted all qualifying research or experimental expenditures pursuant to section 174(a) of the Code, and no portion of these deductions failed to effect a reduction of the taxpayer's federal income tax liability. In 1985, the taxpayer decided to discontinue a product line to better conform its product offerings to its marketing strategy. As a result of the decision, the taxpayer sold certain patented and unpatented technology that had resulted from qualifying expenditures properly deducted in prior tax years pursuant to section 174(a) of the Code.

LAW AND ANALYSIS

Section 174(a) of the Code and section 1.174-3(a) of the Income Tax Regulations provide that a taxpayer may treat research or experimental expenditures that are paid or incurred during the tax year in connection with the taxpayer's trade or business as expenses that are not chargeable to capital account. Section 1.174-2(a)(1) of the regulations provides that the term "research or experimental expenditures" as used in section 174 means expenditures incurred in connection with the taxpayer's trade or business that represent research and development costs in the experimental or laboratory sense.

The tax benefit rule requires the inclusion in income of certain amounts that were deducted in a prior tax year and that generated a tax benefit to the taxpayer through a reduction in the amount of tax liability in the prior tax year. [Citations omitted]. In appropriate circumstances, if a deduction reduces ordinary income in the year the amount is paid or incurred, and if an event in a subsequent taxable year triggers application of the tax benefit doctrine, the amount of the prior deduction will be included in gross income and characterized as ordinary income. [Citation omitted]. In *Hillsboro National Bank v. Commissioner*, 460 U.S. 370, 75 L. Ed. 2d 130, 103 S. Ct. 1134 (1983), 1983-1 C.B. 50, the

United States Supreme Court stated that, in order for the tax benefit doctrine to be invoked, an event must occur in a subsequent year that is "fundamentally inconsistent" with the premise or premises on which the prior year deduction was based. The *Hillsboro* standard requires an analysis of whether the prior year deduction would have been allowed if the subsequent year event had occurred in the prior year, considering the purpose and the function of the provision allowing the prior year deduction.

To determine the applicability of the tax benefit doctrine to previously deducted research or experimental expenditures, *Hillsboro* requires a determination of the purpose and the function of the provision permitting the prior year deduction. The legislative history of section 174 of the Code indicates two purposes for enacting section 174(a): (1) to encourage research and experimental activities and (2) to eliminate the uncertainty as to the tax treatment of research or experimental expenditures. H.R. Rep. No. 1337, 83rd Cong., 2d Sess. 28 (1954).

To encourage research or experimental activities, section 174(a) permits the deduction of research or experimental expenditures during the tax year such expenditures are paid or incurred. This rule of section 174(a) represents a deviation from the general rules governing the deductibility of expenditures. Under the general rules, expenditures otherwise deductible under section 162 are not deductible to the extent attributable to the acquisition or creation of assets having a useful life extending substantially beyond the tax year. See sections 1.263(a)-2(a) and 1.461-1(a) of the regulations. However, section 174(a) allows a current deduction for research or experimental expenditures even though such expenditures may lead to the creation of assets having a useful life that extends substantially beyond the tax year.

To eliminate uncertainty as to the tax treatment of research or experimental expenditures, section 174 (a) relieves taxpayers of the obligation, imposed by the rules that ordinarily govern the deductibility of expenditures, to allocate costs between amounts currently deductible and amounts required to be capitalized.

In the present situation, both purposes underlying section 174(a) were accomplished by allowing the taxpayer a current deduction for the research or experimental expenditures paid or incurred. The legislative purpose of encouraging research or experimental activity was accomplished in the year of the deduction because that is the year the research or experimental expenditures were paid or incurred. The legislative purpose of relieving the taxpayer of the obligation to allocate costs between amounts currently deductible and amounts required to be capitalized was accomplished in the year of the deduction because the taxpayer was allowed a deduction in that year for all research or experimental expenditures paid or incurred. It would be inconsistent with this legislative purpose to relieve the taxpayer of the obligation to allocate costs in the year of the deduction only to impose the obligation in the year of disposition of the resulting technology.

Because the two legislative purposes for enacting section 174(a) were accomplished in the year of the deductions, the subsequent sale of the resulting technology had independent significance and was not fundamentally inconsistent with the prior section 174(a) deductions. Accordingly, the tax benefit doctrine as articulated in *Hillsboro* does not apply to the research or experimental expenditures previously deducted by the taxpayer pursuant to section 174(a).

HOLDING

Under the facts set forth above, disposition of the technology resulting from previously deducted section 174(a) expenditures is not fundamentally inconsistent with the prior year deduction of such expenditures. Accordingly, under these facts, the tax benefit doctrine does not apply to the disposition of the resulting technology.

* * *

DOWNS v. COMMISSIONER

United States Tax Court

49 T.C. 533 (1968)

FINDINGS OF FACT

Some of the facts have been stipulated and are found accordingly.

William Tiffin Downs (herein referred to as petitioner) and Helen C. Downs, husband and wife, were residents of Detroit, Mich., at the time their petition herein was filed. They filed a joint Federal income tax return, and subsequently an amended return, with the district director of internal revenue at Detroit, Mich.

Petitioner is a graduate mechanical engineer who has practiced professionally since 1932. He has worked primarily as an inventor and has acquired a specialized knowledge of hospital equipment. Several patents have been issued for devices of which petitioner was sole or joint inventor.

The American Metal Products Co. (sometimes referred to herein as American Metal) became interested in developing an automatic electric hospital bed after it was approached with the idea by representatives of the University of Michigan Medical Center. Petitioner was recommended to American Metal officials as experienced in this field and, after discussions of the project, was offered a position with American Metal. A contract was executed on October 5, 1956, which provided as follows:

> I, W. Tiffin Downs, hereby agree with American Metal Products Company (hereinafter referred to as A.M.P.) that in consideration of the payment of one thousand dollars ($1,000.00) Dollars per month, and the continuation of such payment on a monthly basis, I promise the following:
>
> I agree to abide by A.M.P. employee rules and regulations, but it is understood that I am an Engineering Consultant on a contractual basis, and as such I do not have any additional benefits due me from A.M.P. other than the monthly consultant fee, for which I shall render monthly statements.
>
> I further agree to render my services to A.M.P. beginning September 12, 1956, from 8:00 A.M. to 12:15 P.M., and from 1:00 P.M. to 6:00 P.M. daily, five days a week, until September 28, 1956, after which time I will render my services from 8:00 A.M. to 12:00 noon, and 1:00 P.M. to 5:30 P.M. daily, five days a week, plus working Saturdays from 8:00 A.M. until 12:00 noon.
>
> I do further covenant and agree to and do hereby assign, transfer and convey to said A.M.P., its successors and assigns, for the term of this agreement and for six (6) months following termination of my services, the entire title, right and interest in and to any and all inventions which during my employment with said A.M.P., its successors and assigns, are conceived and reduced to practice by me, either solely or jointly with others, that shall be within the contemplated scope of the Company's business with the exception of surgical tools and instruments and air conditioning units during the time I am in its employ, as well as the entire right, title and interest in and to any and all United States and foreign Letters Patent and applications for Letters Patent covering any and all said inventions, and I further agree to promptly

> and fully disclose said inventions to said A.M.P. and to perform all acts and execute and deliver upon request, without further consideration, but without expense to me, any and all papers and documents, including applications for patents and assignments of the same as may be deemed necessary or desirable by the said A.M.P., its successors or assigns, to secure and enjoy full benefits and advantages thereof, and it is specifically understood by me that I will receive reasonable and adequate compensation, consistent with royalty or licensing policies now practiced by A.M.P. for any and all inventions reduced to practice before entry upon employment with A.M.P., and I will, upon demand by A.M.P., disclose any patent improvements or inventions reduced to practice before entering the employ of A.M.P. which is within the scope of the Company's business. That this agreement shall be binding upon me only upon its acknowledgement and acceptance by A.M.P.

The agreement was amended twice: in March 1964 to increase the monthly consideration to $1,100, and in May 1965 to increase the monthly consideration to $1,200. Sales of the subsequently completed electric bed increased during this period but not in the same proportion as the monthly payments to petitioner. As of November 14, 1966, petitioner was still associated with American Metal under the amended 1956 agreement.

Petitioner had not worked on an electric bed prior to his association with American Metal, but had ideas from other inventions that would be adaptable to such a bed. He began work on the bed project in September 1956 under the direct supervision of Richard J. Williams and Russell G. Heyl, Jr., who were the heads of research and engineering at American Metal. His design activities were carried on at American Metal facilities, at a tool and engineering shop, and occasionally at his own home. Petitioner did not work the regular hours called for in the agreement, nor was he requested to do so by his supervisors.

Petitioner's efforts resulted in the development of a bed which contained several unique features, including a longitudinal-beam structure, a steel panel in lieu of springs, storage safety sides, and telescopic legs. A major component of the bed was a spinning nut which was developed by American Metal before petitioner became associated with the company. Since a patent cannot be issued in the name of a corporation, a patent application was submitted, on April 2, 1959, for the motor-operated hospital bed in the names of William T. Downs, Richard J. Williams, and Russell G. Heyl, Jr. On March 30, 1959, all rights to the invention, the patent application, and any resulting patents were assigned to American Metal for the consideration of $1.

American Metal began production of the bed, then sold all its rights in the bed to the Simmons Co. (herein referred to as Simmons) in 1960. After that time, petitioner continued to work on improvements to the bed, and American Metal continued to produce parts for it. The parts and improvements were then sold to Simmons. To date, approximately 25,000 of the beds, manufactured by both American Metal and Simmons, have been sold.

During the calendar year 1959 the petitioner received a total of $12,900 from all sources. Of this sum, $150 was received from the Michigan Drilling Co. as director's fees. Under the 1956 agreement, American Metal paid petitioner $12,150 and an additional $600 Christmas bonus distributed to all employees. To receive his payments from American Metal petitioner submitted 24 bimonthly vouchers which read: "To bill you for services rendered under contract." Petitioner did not participate in American Metal's employee pension or group insurance plans. Petitioner reported on his Federal income tax returns the payments received from American Metal in 1956, 1957, and 1958 as ordinary income.

* * *

OPINION

The principal issue in this case is whether payments of $12,750 received by petitioner in 1959 from American Metal were consideration for the transfer of all substantial rights to a "patent" within the provisions of section 1235, as contended by petitioner, or were compensation for services rendered within the meaning of section 61(a)(1), as asserted by respondent.

Briefly stated, section 1235 provides that a transfer of property consisting of all substantial rights to a patent by an individual whose efforts created the property is treated as the sale of a capital asset held for more than 6 months. Section 1.1235-2(a), Income Tax Regs., clarifies the use of the word "patent" by declaring it unnecessary for the patent or patent application for the invention to be in existence if the requirements of section 1235 are otherwise met.

A determination of ownership of the patent rights in an invention is critical to the application of section 1235. *Roland Chilton*, 40 T.C. 552 (1963). On the facts of this case it is plain that American Metal held the patent rights to the electric hospital bed at all times and did not receive such rights by transfer from petitioner.

The concept of the electric hospital bed originated, for the purposes of this record, with the personnel of the University of Michigan Medical Center and was adopted by American Metal. American Metal then began to search for a mechanical engineer with experience in related areas who could reduce the idea to a tangible, workable form. American Metal's interviews with petitioner about the project, and petitioner's work exclusively on it after becoming associated with the company, demonstrate clearly that petitioner was retained for the purpose of bringing the electric hospital bed concept into fruition. Working with two supervisors of American Metal, petitioner accomplished this purpose and, pursuant to the terms of the 1956 contract, assigned all his rights in the invention to American Metal.

In the benchmark case of *United States v. Dubilier Condenser Corporation,* 289 U.S. 178, 188 (1933), the Supreme Court stated:

> [An invention] is the result of an inventive act, the birth of an idea and its reduction to practice; the product of original thought; a concept demonstrated to be true by practical application or embodiment in tangible form. [Citations omitted.]
>
> Though the mental concept is embodied or realized in a mechanism or a physical or chemical aggregate, the embodiment is not the invention and is not the subject of a patent. This distinction between the idea and its application in practice is the basis of the rule that employment merely to design or to construct or to devise methods of manufacture is not the same as employment to invent.

Since petitioner was paid to reduce to practical application a concept originated by American Metal, the patent application in his name and in the names of two other employees of American Metal was held for American Metal. *Standard Parts Co. v. Peck,* 264 U.S. 52 (1924). The assignment provisions in the 1956 contract merely affirmed American Metal's preexisting patent rights in the subsequently developed invention. No substantive rights were "transferred" by the 1956 contract or the assignment executed on March 30, 1959.

Our conclusion that there was no "transfer" within the meaning of section 1235 is reinforced by the provisions of section 1.1235-1(c) (2), Income Tax Regs. Whether the payments received by petitioner were "compensation for services rendered as an employee" is a question of fact. That petitioner was considered an employee by American Metal is shown by the requirement that petitioner submit bimonthly vouchers, "To bill you [American Metal] for services rendered under contract," in order to receive his payments, by its characterization of him as an "Engineering Consultant," and by its payment to him, along with its other employees, of a $600 Christmas bonus. Indeed, the fact that petitioner reported the payments as ordinary income in 1956, 1957, and 1958 is some evidence that he also considered the payments as compensation for services rendered.

But the terms of the 1956 contract are the strongest evidence that the payments were made under a "contract of employment." The contract, under which petitioner agreed to abide by American Metal's employee rules and regulations, refers to petitioner's "employment" and "employ" with American Metal. The payments of $1,000 per month were not dependent upon the sale or use by American Metal of any patent rights resulting from petitioner's efforts. His association with American Metal, and consequently the payment made in consideration for his labors, could be terminated at the will of the company. Finally, petitioner convenanted to assign all rights he might have in inventions developed by his efforts "without further consideration." This last provision clearly reveals that the development of a patentable invention, an electric hospital bed, was the principal object of petitioner's employment.

Since section 1235 is inapplicable, we must determine the tax consequences of the contractual arrangement between petitioner and American Metal under the general provisions of the Code. Sec. 1.1235-1(b), Income Tax Regs. With regard to facts similar to those in the present case, this Court stated in *Arthur N. Blum,* 11 T.C. 101, 108, 110 (1948), affd. 183 F. 2d 281 (C.A. 3, 1950), a case decided under the Internal Revenue Code of 1939, which had no special provision for patent transfers comparable to section 1235:

> The answer to this controversy involves a determination of the ownership of the patents. * * *
>
> * * * *
>
> In the instant case, one of the terms of employment was that petitioner was to devote his attention to the adaptation of the chain saw which the company hoped to manufacture and sell. * * *
>
> * * * *
>
> Applying the established law relative to the rights of employer and inventor to the specific employment contract in question, we conclude that the patents involved were the exclusive property of the company. Petitioner's

> only interest therein was to receive the compensation provided in such employment agreement. No sale of patents or other capital assets was included.

On facts distinguishable from those present here, this Court in *Roland Chilton, supra at 562*, declared the established law to be:

> If a person is employed by another "to invent" a specific product or specific products, the fruits of the employee's labor, the invention, belongs to his employer. [Citations omitted.]
>
> The payment to the employee is for his labor, not for the product, "the invention." The payment is therefore compensation for services and taxable as such. * * *

Accordingly, we conclude on this record that petitioner was employed "to invent a specific product" and that the payments he received were compensation for services rendered, and taxable as ordinary income under section 61(a)(1).

* * *

CHILTON v. COMMISSIONER

United States Tax Court

40 T.C. 552 (1963)

The issue for decision is whether amounts received in the years here involved by Roland Chilton pursuant to contracts with his employers constitute ordinary income as compensation or long-term capital gains from the sale or exchange of patents.

FINDINGS OF FACT

* * *

Roland Chilton (hereinafter referred to as petitioner) is an engineer. He was educated in England.

Prior to 1918 petitioner had been employed as an engineer successively by the Sunbeam Motor Car Co., D. Napier & Sons, J. B. Ferguson, and Crane Simplex Corp. In 1918 petitioner became employed as chief engineer by the Aeromarine Plane and Motor Co. (hereinafter referred to as Aeromarine). He remained employed by this company until September 1929, when he became employed by Wright Aeronautical Corp. Petitioner's work at Aeromarine consisted primarily of designing and supervising the construction and testing of aircraft engines. During the time petitioner was employed by Aeromarine, he made approximately 50 patentable inventions, although only a relatively small part of his time was devoted to making inventions. An important area of petitioner's inventive activities at Aeromarine was in the field of variable speed transmissions and starter devices, particularly the inertia starter. Petitioner had no specific agreement with Aeromarine in regard to his inventions. Aeromarine claimed that it owned all inventions made by petitioner by virtue of the fact that petitioner was its employee. Before petitioner's employment with Aeromarine was terminated, he had obtained an agreement from Aeromarine to pay royalties to him on the inventions and patents covering the inertia starter.

While petitioner was employed by Aeromarine, he had extensive sales contacts on behalf of that company with the Bureau of Aeronautics of the U.S. Navy Department and particularly with an employee of that bureau who subsequently became vice president of sales and service at Wright Aeronautical Corp. (hereinafter referred to as Wright). It was this officer of Wright who suggested that petitioner be employed by Wright. At that time Wright was having serious operating difficulties with one of its engines, which had failed to meet a test established by the U.S. Navy Department which had been successfully met by Aeromarine.

Early in 1928, Wright entered into negotiations looking toward the employment of petitioner. Wright had a compelling need at that time to strengthen its engineering department and the officers of Wright knew of petitioner's ability and experience as a skilled engineer and troubleshooter. The officers of Wright also knew of petitioner's reputation as an inventor. Wright was primarily interested in acquiring petitioner's services as an engineer and initially submitted to him a contract which simply provided for payment to him of an annual salary of $15,000. Because of petitioner's prior disputes with Aeromarine with respect to that company's obligation to pay royalties for his inventions, petitioner insisted upon a contract with Wright which would make special provision with respect to his inventions. On September 3, 1929, petitioner and Wright entered into a contract which provided in part as follows:

> I. The Company shall employ Chilton and Chilton shall enter the employ of the Company.
>
> II. Chilton shall be known under the title of "Consulting Engineer."

III. The Company shall pay Chilton as compensation at the rate of Fifteen thousand dollars ($15,000.00) per year, payable in semi-monthly installments during the term of Chilton's employment.

IV. The term of Chilton's employment shall be from the date of the execution of this contract to the date of its termination as hereinafter provided.

V. The services that Chilton shall render to the Company shall consist in engineering work relating to the improvement of existing types of aircraft engines and other products of the Company or products similar to the products of the Company and to the development of new types and in allied engineering activities. Chilton shall during business hours devote his whole time and apply his experience and his inventive ability to the problems, improvements, and developments relating to the Company's products and products similar to the Company's products, referred to him by the Company.

VI. (A) Chilton shall assign to the Company the entire right, title, and interest in and to all inventions and improvements made by him during his employment by said Company relating to aircraft engines and other products manufactured by the Company or products similar thereto, and all said inventions and improvements shall belong to and be the sole and exclusive property of said Company in and for all countries of the world, and Chilton hereby acknowledges that all said inventions and improvements shall be made for and in the interest and for the account of said Company and he hereby expressly transfers and assigns all said inventions and improvements to said Company in and for all countries of the world.

(B) Chilton shall disclose promptly to the Company all inventions and improvements which he may make relating to or upon aircraft engines and other products manufactured by the Company, or products similar thereto, during the term of this contract.

VII. (A) The Company shall pay for the preparation, filing, and prosecution of all applications for Letters Patent which the Company desires to be filed in its behalf on the inventions or improvements of Chilton.

(B) Chilton shall do all acts and things and execute and deliver all application papers, assignments, and other instruments in writing that may be necessary to secure to and vest in the Company the entire right, title, and interest in and to said inventions and improvements, in and to all applications for Letters Patent covering said inventions and improvements, and in and to all Letters Patent of the United States and of all other countries that may be granted for said inventions and improvements.

VIII. Chilton shall furnish the Company, with such assistance as the Company can give him, complete copies of detailed working drawings covering all inventions and improvements and shall furnish the Company with such information as he may have available with respect to the construction of any products covered by said inventions and improvements.

IX. The Company shall have 90 days after completion of a development test on any invention or improvement to determine whether or not it will accept any such invention or improvement offered to it by Chilton, and unless within said 90 days the Company gives Chilton written notice that it accepts said invention or improvements, Chilton shall be at liberty to file applications on his own behalf and at his own expense on any of such inventions which have not so been accepted by the Company.

X. Chilton shall have and retain full rights in and shall be free to file in his own behalf applications for patents on any and all of his inventions not directly relating to aircraft engines or other products of the Company or products similar thereto, and, in addition thereto, Chilton shall have and retain full rights in and to any and all inventions in or directly relating to engine starting devices and shall be at liberty to file in his own behalf applications for patents on said inventions.

XI. As additional compensation, the Company shall pay Chilton:

> (a) Two and one-half percent (2 1/2%) royalty on the published list price, * * *

XII. The employment of Chilton by the Company may be terminated by either of the parties hereto upon thirty (30) days' notice in writing each to the other, such notice to be by registered mail, addressed to the last known address of the party who receives such notice. Upon the termination of the employment by such written notice, the payment of the compensation herein provided shall terminate. The Company, however, shall continue to make the payments to Chilton in accordance

> with subdivisions (a) and (b) of paragraph XI hereof, said payments to continue with respect to each invention or improvement during the life of the Letters Patent granted thereon.
>
> XIII. The Company shall keep complete books of account and records respecting the manufacture and sale of all devices, components, assemblies, or parts hereunder and shall give Chilton or his duly authorized representative the privilege of inspecting or examining the Company's books in his behalf at all reasonable times, not to exceed four such inspections or examinations per year.
>
> * * *
>
> XV. Chilton shall assist the Company to prosecute infringers of any of the Letters Patent included within this agreement and also to defend any action instituted against the Company by reason of its manufacture, sale, and/or use of any products in accordance with the provisions of this contract; if as the result of the decision of a court of last resort in any suit brought on a patent assigned by Chilton to the Company, or by the decision of an inferior court from whose decree no appeal is taken within the time provided by law, such patent is declared either invalid or an infringement, or for any reason whatsoever, then the payments by the Company to Chilton with respect to such patent shall cease and terminate and there shall be no further liability on the part of the Company to Chilton thereunder.
>
> XVI. This agreement shall be binding upon the heirs and assigns of Chilton and upon the successors and assigns of the Company.

The contract between petitioner and Wright was terminated on December 31, 1934, at which time petitioner was employed by Reed Propeller Co., Inc. (hereinafter referred to as Reed). Reed and Wright were both subsidiaries of Curtiss-Wright Corp. (hereinafter referred to as Curtiss-Wright). The contract dated December 31, 1934, between petitioner and Reed, insofar as here pertinent, contained provisions identical to those of petitioner's contract of September 3, 1929, with Wright. On December 31, 1934, Wright assigned to Reed all its right, title, and interest in the patents and patent applications in which it had an interest. Petitioner remained employed by Reed under this contract until June 30, 1938, when his employment was terminated, and he simultaneously entered the employ of Wright under a contract dated June 30, 1938, which insofar as here pertinent, contained substantially the same provisions as the September 3, 1929, contract between petitioner and Wright except that paragraph 6(a) thereof provided only:

> 6. (a) CHILTON shall assign to WRIGHT the entire right, title and interest in and to all inventions and improvements made by him during his employment by WRIGHT directly relating to aircraft engines and/or their accessories, and all said inventions and improvements shall belong to and be the sole and exclusive property of WRIGHT in and for all countries of the world.

Reed on June 30, 1938, assigned to Wright all the right, title, and interest it had in patents and patent applications. At no time was petitioner represented by counsel in connection with the preparation or execution of the 1929, 1934, or 1938 contracts.

The 1938 contract between petitioner and Wright was amended several times, primarily to provide for limitation of the amount of royalties which petitioner might be entitled to receive in view of the greatly increased demand for Wright's products caused by war conditions during the period 1941 to 1945. On October 12, 1949, Wright notified petitioner that his employment under the agreement dated June 30, 1938, would terminate on November 15, 1949. Petitioner has not been an employee of Wright, Reed, or Curtiss-Wright since November 15, 1949.

During the period from September 3, 1929, through November 15, 1949, whenever petitioner developed an invention covered by his contract with Wright or Reed, he offered such invention to his employing company. In each instance the company notified petitioner in writing whether or not it was interested in acquiring the invention. Whenever the company indicated its desire to acquire an invention, a formal application for patent and an assignment by petitioner to the company were prepared by the employer's attorneys and executed by petitioner. If petitioner's employing company did not indicate a desire to acquire the invention, no instrument of transfer from petitioner to Wright or Reed was executed.

During petitioner's association with Wright he devoted the major portion of his time to the diagnosis of problems involving the functioning and development of Wright's products in a manner not designed to and in fact not resulting in patentable inventions. Among his duties were giving advice and counsel to layout men, supervising test operations, analyzing and screening inventions submitted by outside inventors, traveling for inspection and other business purposes, serving as a member on Wright's engineering council, handling problems with the U.S. Government, and preparation of service reports. A relatively minor portion of petitioner's time at Wright was spent in inventing. However, petitioner did obtain 91 patents which were assigned to Wright, Reed, or Curtiss-Wright pursuant to these contracts. During this same period petitioner applied for and obtained 27 patents which were not assigned to

Wright, Reed, or Curtiss-Wright. Wright and Reed did not use all the patents assigned to them by petitioner in their manufacture of aircraft engines and accessories.

Subsequent to 1949 the Wright Aeronautical Division of Curtiss-Wright assumed the obligations of Reed and Wright under the contracts of these companies with petitioner. During the taxable years 1954 through 1957 Curtiss-Wright paid to petitioner [$168,851.41 in 1954, $71,285.46 in 1955, $13,771.33 in 1956, and $4,883.33 in 1957] with respect to the patents. . . .

During the period that petitioner was associated with Wright or Reed he conducted extensive design and patent activities away from the premises of these corporations and outside his regular employment hours. The office and drafting facilities used by petitioner in his independent research were maintained at his own expense and he paid the compensation of his associates and assistants for the work they performed for him. As a result of this work away from Wright's or Reed's premises petitioner developed a number of patents or inventions, some of which were sold to parties other than Wright or Reed, and some to Wright outside of the contract between petitioner and Wright.

Petitioner at no time owned any stock in Wright and never had more than a nominal interest in any corporation affiliated with Wright.

Wright, on its books and income tax returns, treated the $15,000 a year paid to petitioner from September 3, 1929, through November 15, 1949, as a salary payment, and the remaining payments to petitioner as royalty payments. No deduction was made from the amounts treated as royalty payments for income tax or social security tax and such payments were not included in the base for determination of petitioner's pension rights. During the period of World War II, the Salary Stabilization Unit of the Bureau of Internal Revenue issued a ruling to Wright that the amount paid to petitioner which it designated as royalties did not constitute salary within the meaning of the applicable salary stabilization regulations.

At the time of petitioner's original employment by Wright in 1929, Wright's treasurer and chief engineer received less salary than petitioner, and its factory manager, the same salary as petitioner. This situation generally prevailed until around 1941 when Wright made a general salary adjustment and most of its employees' salaries were increased, the salary of the vice president and general manager going up to $60,000 a year. There was no increase in petitioner's salary (except for a small increase for a period of about a year) from 1929 until the termination of his employment with Wright on November 15, 1949.

Other employees of Wright who made inventions were required to assign such inventions to the company for only a nominal consideration. Most of these employees received salary increases during the period in which petitioner received no such increase.

Petitioner usually received 5-percent royalty on inventions he assigned to parties other than Wright as compared to the 2 1/2 percent on inventions assigned to Wright.

On petitioner's income tax returns for the years 1939 to 1953, he reported the payments received from Wright, Reed, or Curtiss-Wright in respect of the inventions made during his employment by Wright and Reed as ordinary income from a business or profession. On his income tax returns for the years 1954, 1955, 1956, and 1957 he reported the payments received from Curtiss-Wright in respect to such inventions as capital gains.

Respondent, in his notice of deficiency, determined that the payments received by petitioner from Curtiss-Wright during the years 1954, 1955, 1956, and 1957, pursuant to his contracts with Reed and Wright, constituted ordinary income and gave the following explanation in each of these years:

> The grounds for this determination are: (1) the amount constitutes compensation for personal services; (2) you have failed to establish that said amount qualifies for treatment as long-term capital gain.

OPINION

Section 1235 of the Internal Revenue Code of 1954 provides that a transfer of property consisting of all substantial rights to a patent by the person whose efforts produced such patent shall be considered the sale or exchange of a capital asset held for more than 6 months,* regardless of whether or not payments in consideration of such transfer are contingent on the productivity, use, or disposition of the property transferred and regardless of the taxable year in which such transfer occurred. The amounts received by petitioner during the years here involved were with respect to patents produced by his efforts. Therefore, under section 1235 these amounts are capital gains from the sale or exchange of a capital asset if at any time petitioner made a transfer of all substantial rights to these patents.

---

* The requisite holding period for long-term capital gain was 6 months at the time this case was decided.

It is respondent's position that petitioner never made a transfer of all substantial rights to any of the patents with respect to which the payments during the years in issue were received. Respondent takes the position that petitioner never owned any substantial rights in such patents and therefore his assignment of the patents to Wright or Reed did not transfer to those companies any substantial rights. Respondent contends that under petitioner's contracts with Wright and Reed those companies owned the inventions which petitioner made at all times from the discovery leading to the inventions. In support of his position, respondent relies primarily upon his regulations[2] which provide that payments received by an employee as compensation for services rendered as an employee under an employment contract requiring the employee to transfer to the employer the right to any invention by such employee are not attributable to a transfer to which section 1235 applies, and the case of *Arthur N. Blum,* 11 T.C. 101 (1948), affd. 183 F. 2d 281 (C.A. 3, 1950).

Petitioner contends that under the facts here present, he was not employed to invent so as to make his inventions the property of Wright or Reed. Petitioner distinguishes the *Blum* case on the basis of the differences in the facts in that case and the instant case. He also contends that the controlling law is different in the instant case since no provisions similar to section 1235 were applicable to the years involved in the *Blum* case.

It is clear from the contracts between petitioner and Reed and Wright that petitioner was obligated to disclose to Wright and Reed all inventions or improvements which he made relating to aircraft engines and their accessories. If within 90 days after completion of development tests, Wright or Reed notified petitioner in writing that it accepted the invention, petitioner was obligated by his contract to execute and deliver all application papers, assignments, and other writings necessary to secure to Reed or Wright the entire

---

[2] Income Tax Regs., sec. 1.1235-1(c)(2). *Payments to an employee.* Payments received by an employee as compensation for services rendered as an employee under an employment contract requiring the employee to transfer to the employer the rights to any invention by such employee are not attributable to a transfer to which section 1235 applies. However, whether payments received by an employee from his employer (under an employment contract or otherwise) are attributable to the transfer by the employee of all substantial rights to a patent (or an undivided interest therein) or are compensation for services rendered the employer by the employee is a question of fact. In determining which is the case, consideration shall be given not only to all the facts and circumstances of the employment relationship but also to whether the amount of such payments depends upon the production, sale, or use by, or the value to, the employer of the patent rights transferred by the employee. If it is determined that payments are attributable to the transfer of patent rights, and all other requirements under *section 1235* are met, such payments shall be treated as proceeds derived from the sale of a patent.

right, title, and interest in and to the inventions relating to aircraft engines and their accessories and all letters patent that might be granted for such inventions, developments, or improvements.

Respondent argues that these provisions of the contract made Wright or Reed the equitable owners of any inventions with respect to aircraft engines and their accessories made by petitioner. Respondent states that had petitioner refused to assign any rights in any inventions which he made or applications for patents or patents on such inventions to Wright or Reed, these companies could have obtained such an assignment by an action in equity for specific performance. Petitioner does not contend that Wright and Reed could not under the contracts have enforced specific performance of his agreement to transfer to them his inventions and patents. Petitioner argues that this right created by the contracts did not, itself, constitute the transfer of the patents and that when the transfer occurred the companies acquired "all substantial rights" to the patents. Petitioner relies on a number of cases involving executory contracts to assign patents including *Carl G. Dreyman,* 11 T.C. 153, 161 (1948); *Briggs v. Hofferbert,* 85 F. Supp. 941 (D. Md. 1949), affd. 178 F. 2d 743 (C.A. 4, 1949); and *Becker v. United States,* 161 F. Supp. 333 (W.D. Pa. 1958). The facts in each of these cases differ from those in the instant case but in each case a sale was held to have been made at the time of the assignment of the patent even though prior to such assignment a contract to assign had been executed.

Petitioner further points out that even if an executory contract to assign an invention is construed as transferring all rights to such invention immediately upon the conception of the invention, section 1235 makes the transfer of the invention at that time the sale of a capital asset held for more than 6 months. [Citation omitted]. Respondent's regulations do not state that all payments to an employee who is required to assign his inventions to his employer are compensation for services. These regulations refer to compensation for services rendered "as an employee."

We agree with petitioner that his agreement with Wright and Reed to assign to them the rights to his inventions, standing alone, would not cause section 1235 to be inapplicable to the payments received by him in the years here in issue pursuant to these contracts.

The real question in issue here is whether petitioner was "hired to invent" aircraft engines and accessories or assigned the duties of devoting himself to such specific inventions. If a person is employed by another "to invent" a specific product or specific products, the fruits of the employee's labor, the invention, belongs to his employer. *United States v. Dubilier*

Condenser Corp., 289 U.S. 178 (1933); and *Marshall v. Colgate-Palmolive-Peet Co.*, 175 F. 2d 215 (C.A. 3, 1949).

The payment to the employee is for his labor, not for the product, "the invention."[3] The payment is therefore compensation for services and taxable as such. [Citations omitted].

The nature of the relationship between petitioner and his employers must be determined from the contracts between them and the conduct of the parties. [Citation omitted]. If the provisions of the contract were unambiguous, it might be unnecessary to consider other facts. However, these provisions are not clear as to the nature of petitioner's employment. [Citation omitted]. Petitioner agreed to apply his "inventive ability" to his employers' products. However, preceding the sentence referring to petitioner's "inventive ability" is a sentence classifying petitioner's services as "engineering work." There is a similar inconsistency between the reference in the contracts to all petitioner's aircraft engine inventions being the property of Wright or Reed and the provision that if written notice were not given to petitioner within 90 days after the completion of development tests, all rights to the inventions shall belong to petitioner.

Turning to the other evidence, we think it clear that petitioner was not "hired to invent" aircraft engines, improvements thereon, or accessories thereto. Such, in substance, was the testimony of several witnesses. The actions of the parties support this testimony. Wright at the time it hired petitioner had not proposed to have the contract make provision for his inventions. From at least 1939 petitioner on his income tax returns reported the amounts received with respect to the patents assigned to Wright or Reed as income from his business of inventing. When these returns were filed, this income was taxable as ordinary income. There existed no self-serving reason for petitioner to report the payments as income from a business or profession as distinguished from compensation for services. Reed, Wright, and

---

[3] In *United States v. Dubilier Condenser Corp.*, 289 U.S. 178, 187, the Court stated:

> One employed to make an invention, who succeeds, during his term of service, in accomplishing that task, is bound to assign to his employer any patent obtained. The reason is that he has only produced that which he was employed to invent. His invention is the precise subject of the contract of employment. A term of the agreement necessarily is that what he is paid to produce belongs to his paymaster. *Standard Parts Co. v. Peck*, 264 U.S. 52. On the other hand, if the employment be general, albeit it cover a field of labor and effort in the performance of which the employee conceived the invention for which he obtained a patent, the contract is not so broadly construed as to require an assignment of the patent. *Hapgood v. Hewitt*, 119 U.S. 226; *Dalzell v. Dueber Watch Case Mfg. Co.*, 149 U.S. 315. * * *

Curtiss-Wright each on their books and records and Federal income tax returns, treated the payments to petitioner with respect to the patents as royalties and not as compensation. These facts and others in the record indicate that none of the parties to these contracts considered the payments with respect to the patents to be compensation to petitioner for services as an employee.

Since the payments petitioner received with respect to the patents in accordance with his contracts with his employers were not compensation for services rendered "as an employee," the amounts were payments to petitioner for transfer to his employers of his inventions and patents. This is the very type of payment which section 1235 states shall be considered as received from the sale or exchange of a capital asset. We sustain petitioner in his contention that the payments he received from Curtiss-Wright during the years here involved are taxable as gain from the sale of a capital asset held for over 6 months.

BLAKE v. COMMISSIONER

United States Court of Appeals, Sixth Circuit

615 F.2d 731 (6th Cir. 1971)

The principal issue raised by this appeal is whether the royalties paid by a licensee to the taxpayer-appellee as holder of a patent were long term capital gain to taxpayer under § 1235 of the Internal Revenue Code of 1954 or were ordinary income. The Commissioner of Internal Revenue found that such royalties were ordinary income and determined an income tax deficiency; on a petition to redetermine the deficiency, the Tax Court held (67 T.C. 7 (1976)) that such royalties were long term capital gain and the Commissioner brought this appeal. * * *

I.

The relevant facts as stipulated or as found by the Tax Court (and which are not in dispute) can be rather briefly summarized.

A. Factual background of capital gain issue.

Taxpayers are David R. Blake (hereafter referred to as "Taxpayer") and his wife Betty H. Blake, who filed joint returns for the years 1969 and 1970. It was on these returns that taxpayer, the holder of the patent, reflected the royalties received as long term capital gain.

In 1948, taxpayer filed for a patent on a leveling device for tables and chairs (referred to as a "glide") and a patent was issued in 1955. In 1954, taxpayer entered into a license agreement with American Seating Company (American Seating) whereby it was granted the right, for the life of the patent, to make, have made, use and sell glides but only in the public seating field, i. e. furniture and equipment for schools, churches, courtrooms, theatres and hospitals but excluded furniture designed for restaurant and cafeteria use. The royalty to be paid was eight-tenths of a cent on each glide sold.

In 1960, taxpayer entered into an exclusive license agreement with Ever-Level Glides, Inc. (Ever-Level) to make, have made, use and sell glides for the life of the patent, subject, however, to the American Seating license. It is agreed that the only commercially worthwhile use of the patent outside of the public seating field (covered by the American Seating license) is the restaurant field and is agreed that, upon the license to Ever-Level, taxpayer, as holder of the patent, retained no commercially worthwhile rights that could be the subject of further licensing.

Taxpayer reported royalties payable by both American Seating and Ever-Level as long term capital gain. The Commissioner disagreed. The Tax Court held that royalties payable by American Seating were ordinary income, and taxpayer did not appeal this holding. However, as before indicated, the Tax Court held that the royalties payable by Ever-Level were long term capital gain from which holding the Commissioner has appealed.

* * *

II.

It is taxpayer's position, succinctly stated, that since he, as the patent holder, in 1960 transferred to Ever-Level all of his remaining substantial rights to the patent, this was a transfer to Ever-Level of "property consisting of all substantial rights to a patent" within the meaning of § 1235 of the Code. On the other hand, it is the position of the Commissioner that, since taxpayer had, prior to 1960, transferred substantial rights to the patent to American Seating, taxpayer's transfer to Ever-Level in 1960 was not a transfer of "property consisting of all substantial rights to a patent" within the meaning of § 1235. Taxpayer, therefore, contends that the royalties received from Ever-Level should be afforded long term capital gain treatment under § 1235 since he transferred to Ever-Level all of the patent rights that he had at the time of the transfer. The Commissioner contends, on the other hand, that this transfer to Ever-Level did not satisfy the requirements of § 1235 because all patent rights in existence at the time of the transfer were not transferred to Ever-Level.

We conclude that, under the reasoning of this court in *Fawick v. Commissioner,* 436 F.2d 655 (6th Cir. 1971), the Commissioner was correct and the Tax Court was in error and therefore we reverse the Tax Court. Indeed, the Tax Court, in its opinion, recognized that it was refusing to follow the reasoning of this court in *Fawick*, and it also in effect held to be invalid a Treasury Regulation that had been specifically upheld in *Fawick*.

Section 1235 of the Code provides in relevant part as follows:

> *SEC. 1235.* SALE OR EXCHANGE OF PATENTS.
>
> (a) General. A transfer . . . of property consisting of all substantial rights to a patent, or an undivided interest therein which includes a part of all such rights, by any holder shall be considered the sale or exchange of a capital asset held for more than 6 months, regardless of whether or not payments in consideration of such transfer are
>
> > (1) payable periodically over a period generally coterminous with the transferee's use of the patent, or
> >
> > (2) contingent on the productivity, use, or disposition of the property transferred.

The Treasury Regulation (1954 Code) § 1.1235-2 provides in relevant part:

> § 1.1235-2 Definition of terms.
>
> (b) All substantial rights to a patent. (1) The term "all substantial rights to a patent" means all rights (whether or not then held by the grantor) which are of value at the time the rights to the patent (or an undivided interest therein) are transferred. The term "all substantial rights to a patent" does not include a grant of rights to a patent.
>
> > (i) Which is limited geographically within the country of issuance;

> (iii) Which grants rights to a grantee, in fields of use within trades or industries, which are less than all the rights covered by the patent, which exist and have value at the time of the grant; or
>
> (iv) Which grants to the grantee less than all the claims or inventions covered by the patent which exist and have value at the time of the grant.

Thus under the plain words of the statute and certainly under the Regulation, the transfer by taxpayer to Ever-Level of his remaining rights to the patent, after having transferred substantial rights to American Seating, simply does not satisfy the test established by § 1235 for long term capital gain treatment.

This court, in *Fawick*, in tracing the history that lead to the enactment of § 1235, pointed out that prior thereto only amateur inventors could obtain capital gain treatment for royalty payments (since otherwise the patent would not be a capital asset in the hands of the inventor) and even an amateur inventor's right to treat his receipt of royalty as capital gain was questioned unless he received it in a lump sum. Thus the purpose in enacting § 1235 was twofold: to allow professional as well as amateur inventors an opportunity to enjoy long term capital gain treatment for their royalties and to allow such treatment even though royalties are payable periodically and even though payment is contingent on the productivity or use of the patent. Even so, as the *Fawick* court pointed out, long term capital gain treatment of royalties is afforded to the holder of the patent if and only if the transfer of rights in the patent that produces such royalties is a transfer of all existing substantial rights which have commercial value. In this respect the *Fawick* court said:

> With the above cited legislative history as background, it is our opinion that a two prong inquiry is necessary to determine if a transaction qualifies for special treatment under § 1235. The initial inquiry for determining whether or not there has been a transfer by the holder of "property consisting of all substantial rights to a patent" requires consideration of what the holder has left after the transfer. If he retains any substantial rights to the patent, then he has not transferred the property that comprises all those rights.
>
> If the taxpayer can show that he has no substantial rights in the patent after the transfer, as a second inquiry we must look at what he actually relinquished to the transferee. It is our opinion that the phrase "all substantial rights to a patent" is a reference to the monopoly right for which

> the patent stands. The monopoly right granted by the patent is the right to exclude others from making, using, or selling the invention. This necessarily encompasses the right to exclude others from any particular industrial field in which those others might choose to use the invention. This is the right that must be sold to the transferee, and the transfer must cover all practical fields-of-use for the invention. (Footnote omitted).

It is true that, in *Fawick*, the precise question presented here was not before the court; the question presented there was the question before the Tax Court in the instant case with respect to the tax treatment of the American Seating royalties. Nevertheless, as stated, the reasoning of *Fawick* applies here and the Regulation held to be valid in *Fawick* clearly applies here.

The Tax Court initially got off the track in applying § 1235 in *William S. Rouverol,* 42 T.C. 186 (1964) and has stayed off the track in spite of a series of reversals in: *Fawick v. Commissioner,* 52 T.C. 104 (1969), rev'd, 436 F.2d 655 (6th Cir. 1971); Mros v. Commissioner, 1971 P.H.T.C. Memo. No. 71, 123, rev'd, 493 F.2d 813 (9th Cir. 1974); and *Klein v. Commissioner,* 61 T.C. 332 (1973), rev'd, 507 F.2d 617 (7th Cir. 1974), cert. denied, 421 U.S. 991, 95 S. Ct. 1998, 44 L. Ed. 2d 482 (1975). Thus it appears that not only is the holding here required by the holding of this court in *Fawick* but is also consistent with the holdings of other courts of appeal that have dealt with this issue.

* * *

REVENUE RULING 78-328

1978-2 C.B. 215

A corporation that is not a dealer in patents sold all its rights to a patent used in its manufacturing business subject to a nonexclusive, royalty-free license granted by its predecessor transferor. The sale was a sale of property used in a trade or business within the meaning of section 1231 of the Code.

Advice has been requested whether the sale of all rights to a patent by a corporation that is not a dealer in patents is the sale of property used in its trade or business within the meaning of section 1231 of the Internal Revenue Code of 1954 when the rights transferred are all the then existing rights to the patent except for a nonexclusive, royalty-free license acquired by an unrelated party from the corporation's predecessor transferor.

In 1974 *X* corporation developed a device and secured a patent on it. In 1975 *X* assigned to *Y* corporation a royalty-free, nonexclusive license for the sale or use of the device and sold its remaining rights in the patent to Z corporation. Z used the patent in its manufacturing business. Z depreciated the cost of the patent over its remaining useful life under the provisions of section 1.167(a)-6 of the Income Tax Regulations.

In 1976, more than 6 months after acquiring the patent rights, Z sold all the rights it ever held in the patent (although not all the existing rights) and realized a gain on the sale. Z realized no losses from the sale of other property during 1976. The consideration for this transfer was a lump-sum of 100,000x dollars and certain additional amounts to be paid in the future based on a percentage of gross sales from marketing the device.

The question presented is whether the gain from the transaction is income to Z attributable to the sale of property used in the trade or business within the meaning of section 1231 of the Code.

Although section 1235 of the Code is inapplicable to this case because that section only applies to transfers of patents by individuals, Rev. Rul. 69-482, 1969-2 C.B. 164, states that when holders make transfers of patents that do not meet the requirements for capital gains treatment under section 1235, the tax consequences of such transfers will be determined under other sections of the Code.

Section 1231(a) of the Code provides, in part, that if, during the taxable year, the recognized gains on sales of property used in the trade or business held for more than 6 month (9 months for taxable years beginning in 1977; 1 year for taxable years beginning after 1977), exceed the recognized losses from such sales, such gains and losses shall be considered as gains and losses from sales of capital assets held for more than 6 months (9 months for taxable years beginning in 1977; 1 year for taxable years beginning after 1977).

Section 1231 (b) of the Code provides, in part, that the term "property used in the trade or business" means property used in the trade or business of a character that is subject to the allowance for depreciation provided in section 167, and that is held for more than 6 months (9 months for taxable years beginning in 1977; 1 year for taxable years beginning after 1977).

Section 167(a) (1) of the Code provides that there shall be allowed as a depreciation deduction a reasonable allowance for the exhaustion, wear, and tear of property used in the trade or business.

Section 1.167 (a)-6 of the regulations provides that the cost or other basis of a patent shall be depreciated over its remaining useful life.

In *MacDonald v. Commissioner,* 55 T.C. 840 (1971), *acq.,* 1973-1 C.B. 2, a case in which section 1235 of the Code did not apply, the United States Tax Court concluded that the sale of all the rights a taxpayer ever held in a patent, but which rights did not include all existing rights in the patent because the patent was already subject to a nonexclusive license, may qualify for capital gains treatment under section 1231.

In *MacDonald,* the court questioned the validity of section 1.1235-2 (b) of the regulations. The issue in *MacDonald* was whether the sale of less than all the then existing, substantial rights to a patent was nevertheless the sale of a capital asset within the meaning of sections 1221 or 1231 (as the case may be) of the Code when the taxpayer transferred all the rights the taxpayer had. The Service's acquiescence in *MacDonald* merely indicates that the Service agrees with the court that the sale of the patent in question qualifies for capital gain treatment. No inference should be drawn from the Service's acquiescence in *MacDonald* that the regulations under section 1235 are not controlling for purposes of section 1235. In addition, the Tax Court indicated in *Kueneman v. Commissioner,* 68 T.C. 609 (1977), taxpayer on appeal to 9th Cir., that it will no longer follow the cases of *Rodgers v. Commissioner*, 51 T.C. 619 (1977), and *Fawick v. Commissioner, 52 T.C. 104 (1969), rev'd* 436 F.2d 655 (6th Cir. 1971), which were cited in *MacDonald* as the authority for the invalidity of the section 1235 regulations.

In the present case, Z acquired the patent already subject to a license and transferred no interest in the patent prior to its sale. Therefore, Z transferred all the rights it had ever held in the patent.

Consequently, because Z transferred all the rights it had ever held in the patent and because these rights are depreciable property used in Z's business, the sale of the patent rights is considered the sale of property used in the trade or business within the meaning of section 1231(a) of the Code.

Accordingly, except to the extent provided in section 1245 of the Code, the income from the sale of all the rights the taxpayer had in the patent will be treated as long term capital gain.

STOKLEY USA, INC. v. COMMISSIONER

United States Tax Court

100 T.C. 439 (1993)

* * *

Petitioner is in the business of processing, canning, and marketing canned and frozen vegetables, fruits, tomato products, and juices. Its principal products are canned corn, beans, peas, and beets.

* * *

Petitioner and Quaker Oats . . . agreed to the transfer of certain trademarks owned by Quaker Oats. On November 5, 1984, Quaker Oats transferred to the Quaker Oats Foundation (the Foundation), a private foundation controlled by Quaker Oats, the trademarks that it intended to transfer to petitioner. On November 15, 1984, the Foundation and petitioner entered into a trademark transfer agreement pursuant to which, for a lump-sum payment of $1,584,500, the Foundation:

> [transferred], [sold] and [assigned] to * * * [petitioner] * * * THE FOUNDATION'S right, title and interest, both statutory and at common law, in The Trademarks and the registrations thereof, subject to * * * [certain restrictions] * * * including the right to sue for and collect damages for any past infringement * * *.

The trademarks referred to in the agreement were Stokely's, Shellie, Bavarian Style, and the two Stokely's Finest trademarks (the Stokely trademarks). The agreement . . . contained the following restrictions:

> 2.1 * * * [Petitioner] shall not use The Trademarks on * * * [pork and beans, and products containing beans and wieners (such wieners being composed of either beef, pork, chicken or poultry or a combination thereof) for] * * * [20 years].

> 2.2 * * * [Petitioner], and its successors and assigns shall never use the trademark "VAN CAMP" on any products either as part of or apart from The Trademarks.
>
> * * *
>
> 2.4 The FOUNDATION shall have the right to disapprove any assignment of [Petitioner's] right, title and interest in the Trademarks for a period of five years.

* * *

[The sole issue was whether the petitioner could amortize the $1,584,500 lump sum payment it made to the Foundation for the Stokely trademarks. Under the law as it existed at the time, a taxpayer could amortize the cost of a trademark over 10-years, if the transfer was *not* treated as a sale or exchange of a capital asset under section 1253(a). On the other hand, the cost to purchase a trademark (i.e., a sale or exchange) was a non-amortizable capital expenditure because trademarks do not have determinable useful lives. Under current law, the lump sum paid for the trademarks would be amortizable over 15-years under section 197 (as discussed in Chapter 3). Although the law has changed, the opinion is nonetheless instructive because it addresses whether the transferor (the Foundation) retained "any significant power, right, or continuing interest" in the Stokely trademarks.]

* * *

There is no question that the Stokely trademarks were transferred to petitioner. Therefore, whether the transfer of the Stokely trademarks is to be treated as the sale or exchange of a capital asset under section 1253(a) depends upon (1) whether the Foundation retained any "power, right, or continuing interest with respect to the subject matter" of the Stokely trademarks and, if so, (2) whether one or more of these rights was "significant."

1. Did the Transferor Retain Any Power, Right, or Continuing Interest in the Subject Matter of the Trademarks?

Petitioner contends that the Foundation's 5-year right to disapprove any assignment of petitioner's right, title, and interest in the trademarks and the 20-year prohibition on petitioner's use of the trademarks with respect to pork and beans (the pork and beans restriction), represent powers, rights, or continuing interests retained by the Foundation. We agree with petitioner that the Foundation's right to disapprove transfer of the trademarks by petitioner during the first 5 years after the transfer constitutes a retained power, right, or continuing interest with respect to the subject matter of the trademarks. Respondent does not dispute this. Respondent's only argument with respect to this retained power, right, or interest is that it is not "significant" within the meaning of section 1253(a).

Respondent argues, however, that the pork and beans restriction does not constitute a retained power, right, or continuing interest, but rather, merely defines the assets that petitioner purchased. In essence, respondent contends that petitioner simply did not purchase the right to use the Stokely trademarks for pork and beans. According to respondent, petitioner purchased the right to use the Stokely trademarks on everything except pork and beans, and the Foundation retained no right to use the Stokely trademarks. Respondent, therefore, concludes that the pork and beans restriction did not give the Foundation a retained power, right, or continuing interest over what petitioner purchased.

Respondent's analysis begs the question. It is clear that petitioner did not "purchase" the right to use the Stokely trademarks on pork and beans (for 20 years). It is equally clear that the Foundation retained no right to continue to use the specific trademarks that were transferred to petitioner. However, the relevant statutory language of section 1253 refers to neither of these factors. Rather, section 1253(a) refers to a "transfer of a * * * trademark." This reference to the transfer of a trademark contemplates all transfers, including those with substantial restrictions and limited durations.

Section 1253(a) states that such "transfer" "shall not be treated as a sale or exchange of a capital asset if the transferor retains any significant power, right, or continuing interest with respect to the subject matter of the * * * trademark." The subject matter of the Stokely trademarks included the ability to use them in the marketing of food products. Trademarks and trade names represent goodwill. [Citation omitted]. Goodwill is characterized as "the expectancy of continued patronage, for whatever reason." [Citations omitted]. Petitioner purchased the Stokely trademarks with the expectation that potential customers would be more likely to purchase petitioner's products if they were identified by the Stokely trademarks. Stokely trademarks could have been used to market pork and beans. Registration number 277,037 (one of the Stokely's Finest trademarks) expressly includes pork and beans within the products for which the trademark is to be used. The other two transferred trademarks have less detailed usage descriptions, but both could be used for pork and beans products. While petitioner acquired less than the full use of the Stokely trademarks, this was the direct result of the pork and beans restriction, through which the Foundation was able to prevent petitioner from using the trademarks on pork and beans products.

The statute contains examples that show the error of respondent's reliance on the fact that petitioner did not purchase the right to use the trademarks on pork and beans. Section 1253(b)(2) lists several significant retained powers, rights, or continuing interests. One of these is the right of the transferor to disapprove any transfer. Sec. 1253(b)(2)(A). The purchaser of a trademark encumbered by this type of restriction clearly does not "purchase" the unencumbered right to transfer the trademark. Nevertheless, it is clear that this type of restriction was to qualify as a retained power within the meaning of section 1253. Another example is the "right to prescribe the standards of quality of products used or sold." Sec. 1253(b)(2)(C). A transferee subject to such a right clearly does not purchase the right to use a trademark with respect to any product that it wishes. Yet, in this situation, the statute states that the transferor retains a significant power, right, or continuing interest. Sec. 1253(b)(2)(C).

Respondent argues that the pork and beans restriction is not a power, right, or continuing interest retained by the "transferor," since the Foundation itself did not market pork and beans products. In the trademark transfer agreement, petitioner specifically acknowledged that its use of the trademarks for pork and beans products during the 20-year period would result in irreparable injury to the Foundation and that injunctive relief for the Foundation would be appropriate if petitioner violated this restriction. The Foundation is a private entity controlled by Quaker Oats. Quaker Oats' control over the Foundation also indicates that the restriction on petitioner's use of the Stokely trademarks on pork and beans products was a genuine restriction designed to protect Quaker Oats and the Foundation.

Based on the foregoing factors, we find that the pork and beans restriction was a retained power, right, or continuing interest with respect to the subject matter of the Stokely trademarks.

2. Were the Retained Powers, Rights, or Continuing Interests "Significant?"

Petitioner's primary argument is that the Foundation's right to disapprove assignment of the Stokely trademarks for 5 years is, as a matter of law, "significant." Section 1253(b)(2) states:

> The term "significant power, right, or continuing interest" includes, but is not limited to, the following rights with respect to the interest transferred:
>
> > (A) A right to disapprove any assignment of such interest, or any part thereof.

> (B) A right to terminate at will.
>
> (C) A right to prescribe the standards of quality of products used or sold, or of services furnished, and of the equipment and facilities used to promote such products or services.
>
> (D) A right to require that the transferee sell or advertise only products or services of the transferor.
>
> (E) A right to require that the transferee purchase substantially all of his supplies and equipment from the transferor.
>
> (F) A right to payments contingent on the productivity, use, or disposition of the subject matter of the interest transferred, if such payments constitute a substantial element under the transfer agreement.

The powers, rights, or continuing interests specified in section 1253(b)(2) are deemed significant by the terms of the statute. If a retained power, right, or continuing interest falls within the rights listed in section 1253(b)(2), no further inquiry is necessary. This list, however, is nonexclusive and does not preclude the possibility that other retained powers, rights, or continuing interests may be "significant."

Petitioner contends that the Foundation's right to disapprove assignment of the Stokely trademarks for 5 years is "a right to disapprove any assignment of such interest, or any part thereof" within the meaning of subparagraph (A) of section 1253(b)(2). Respondent counters by pointing out that the Foundation's right to disapprove assignments was limited to the 5-year period following the transfer, whereas petitioner's rights in the transferred trademarks were for an unlimited duration. Respondent therefore argues that the Foundation's disapproval rights did not extend to "any assignment" within the meaning of the statute. In essence, the parties ask us to decide whether the words "any assignment" in the statute mean *all* assignments (suggested by respondent), or *some* assignments (suggested by petitioner).

Respondent argues that "any assignment" means "all assignments" because any other interpretation would mean that every transitory right to disapprove an assignment would be deemed significant regardless of how short (or insignificant) the period during which the disapproval right could be exercised. In response, petitioner contends that if the period during which a transferor retains the right to disapprove an assignment is so short as to be meaningless, the courts could treat such a right as a sham and disregard it.

The parties' arguments present us with a conundrum. Subparagraph (A) refers to "*any* assignment of such interest, or *any* part thereof." (Emphasis added.) The second "any" in subparagraph (A) can only mean "some." It would be arguably inconsistent to interpret the first "any" in a single sentence to mean "all" and the second "any" to mean "some." Yet, if the first "any" means "some", the interpretative problems noted by respondent arise.

The better course, and the one we adopt, is to interpret subparagraph (A) in light of the statute as a whole. Section 1253(b)(2) contains a list of retained rights upon which Congress conferred significance as a matter of law. Once a right falls within one of the specifically enumerated rights in subsection (b)(2), Congress intended that there should be no further inquiry into its significance. However, unless the retained rights listed in subsection (b)(2) are coextensive in duration with the interest transferred, it can readily be seen that any one of them could be objectively insignificant if the time period during which the transferor could exercise such right was restricted. Courts would then be faced with the dilemma of either interpreting the statute in a way that would produce absurd results or making a case-by-case determination of the actual significance of whatever temporal limits had been placed on the retained right. Neither approach is satisfactory or in keeping with the legislative objective of subsection (b)(2). We believe, therefore, that the retained rights enumerated in subsection (b)(2) must be exercisable for a period of time that is coextensive with the duration of the interest that was transferred. This interpretation is consistent with the language in section 1253, the legislative history, and the objective of the statute.

The language of section 1253 makes a literal distinction between the object of a significant retained right referred to in subsection (a) and the object of the specifically described rights in subsection (b)(2). Section 1253(a) refers to retained rights "with respect to the *subject matter* of the franchise, trademark, or trade name." (Emphasis added.) While a transferred interest in a franchise, trademark, or trade name may itself have a specifically limited duration, the "subject matter" of these intangibles, including the goodwill associated with them, would not likely have an ascertainable limit. In contrast, *section 1253(b)(2)*, which lists specifically defined rights, refers to rights retained "with respect to the *interest* transferred." (Emphasis added.) The "interest transferred" can encompass less than the subject matter of a franchise, trademark, or trade name. The "interest transferred" can be, and often is, for a limited period. See S. Rept. 91-552 (1969), *1969-3 C.B. 423, 557* ("For purposes of this provision, a transfer is to include a transfer of *any interest* (*i.e., a part*) in a franchise, trademark or trade name."). (Emphasis added.) Thus, the duration of a retained right takes on added importance "with respect to the *interest* transferred" under subsection (b)(2). Our interpretation of the statute recognizes that importance.

The legislative history of section 1253 also emphasizes the importance of duration in regard to the retained rights enumerated in subsection (b)(2). It states:

> If the transfer agreement includes significant conditions or restrictions which are subject to the transferor's approval on a *continuing* basis, this power to exercise *continuing*, active, operational control over the transferee's business activities *is* to be considered as a retention by the transferor of a significant power, right, or continuing interest.

The legislative history then lists six retained rights (found in section 1253(b)(2)) that, in the view of Congress, meet the above standards without question. The focus of the legislative history on *continuing* control supports our interpretation that retained rights listed in subsection (b)(2) must be coextensive with the duration of the interest transferred.

One of the objectives of Congress in enacting section 1253 was to provide a simple, uniform method for determining whether the transfer of a trademark, franchise, or trade name should receive capital gains treatment. Courts had previously conducted detailed factual analyses of such transfers to determine the significance of rights retained by the transferor. These factual analyses led to divisions of authority among courts about the significance of many retained rights. Subsection (b)(2) was intended to end this diversity. If, as suggested by petitioner, the duration of the retained rights listed in subsection (b)(2) need not be coextensive with the duration of the interest transferred, two potential interpretative scenarios follow.

Under the first scenario, a retained right listed in subsection (b)(2) would be deemed significant regardless of its duration. If we were to adopt this approach, a 1-month or 1-week right to disapprove the assignment of a 20-year franchise would, as a matter of law, be considered significant for purposes of section 1253(b)(2). The same problem exists with respect to the other six rights enumerated in section 1253(b)(2). For example, restaurant franchises are typically granted for a limited period. [Citation omitted]. If such a franchise gave the transferor a right to terminate at will that could only be exercised in the first month of a 20-year franchise, such a right would probably be objectively insignificant but would nonetheless automatically qualify as significant if we adopted petitioner's approach. This is clearly not what Congress intended, S. Rept. 91-552, *supra*, 1969-3 C.B. at 555-556, and could easily lead to absurd results. [Citations omitted].

Under the second scenario, a retained right listed in subsection (b)(2) might or might not have significance, depending upon an analysis of the facts and circumstances in order to determine whether its duration was adequate. This type of analysis leads directly back to the problems and resulting uncertainty that existed prior to the enactment of section 1253, and therefore, subverts the intent of Congress. See S. Rept. 91-552, *supra*, 1969-3 C.B. at 555.

Based on the foregoing analysis, we hold that those powers, rights, or continuing interests retained by a transferor that are enumerated in subsection (b)(2) must be coextensive with the duration of the interest transferred. It follows that the Foundation's 5-year transfer disapproval right is not a significant right within the meaning of section 1253(b)(2).

This does not mean that the Foundation's disapproval right is not significant for purposes of section 1253(a). The list in subsection (b)(2) is nonexclusive, and therefore, retained rights not included in subsection (b)(2) may still qualify under subsection (a) so as to entitle petitioner to amortize its payment. Whether a retained right not specifically enumerated in section 1253(b)(2) is "significant" for purposes of section 1253(a) must be determined in light of all the facts and circumstances at the time of the transfer.

There is very little evidence regarding the impact on petitioner as a result of the 5-year disapproval right. The parties presented no evidence regarding the circumstances that supplied the motivation for including the 5-year disapproval right in the transfer agreement. Absent such evidence, we are unprepared to find that this disapproval right, on its own, should be characterized as a significant power, right, or continuing interest for purposes of section 1253(a).

Petitioner next argues that the 20-year restriction on using the Stokely trademarks on pork and beans products is itself a "significant" retained power, right, or continuing interest. Respondent contends that this restriction is not significant for two reasons. First, respondent asserts that the name "Stokely" is barely visible on Quaker Oats' well-known line of Van Camp's pork and beans products. This, according to respondent, belies the claim that the Stokely trademarks could have been used by petitioner to successfully market pork and beans products. Second, respondent notes that petitioner was not in the business of producing pork and beans products at the time it entered the transaction to acquire the trademarks. From this, respondent argues that the restriction had no significance for petitioner's business or its use of the Stokely trademarks. We disagree.

The restriction clearly had significance for Quaker Oats. The specific reason for its inclusion in the contract was to protect the company's Van Camp's line. Because of the close connection in the public mind between the Van Camp's and Stokely names, Quaker Oats' management believed that the Van Camp's mark would be "seriously diluted," and Quaker Oats' sales of pork and beans products materially and adversely affected, if petitioner were allowed to use the Stokely trademarks for these products. On brief, respondent agrees that the Stokely and Van Camp's names have been associated with one another in the minds of the public. Thus, it is probable that the use of the Stokely trademarks on pork and beans products would have had considerable importance in any effort by petitioner to market such products.

Moreover, petitioner wanted to enter into the market for pork and beans. Petitioner initially approached Quaker Oats regarding the purchase of the Stokely-Van Camp's trademark, but was rejected. Petitioner wanted to use the Stokely trademarks on pork and beans products and would have done so but for the restriction. Despite the restriction, petitioner attempted to sell pork and beans for a short period under another label. Petitioner was forced to abandon its plans for that market due to the lack of a strong brand name. Stokely could have been that name.

* * *

In light of these facts, the pork and beans restriction carried undoubted significance for the Foundation, Quaker Oats, and petitioner. The trademark transfer agreement states this clearly:

> [Petitioner] recognizes and acknowledges that such use of The Trademarks before expiration of the applicable time period would result in immediate and irreparable injury to the FOUNDATION, which could not be adequately compensated by payment of money damages, and hence injunctive relief would be appropriate in favor of the FOUNDATION or its designees to prevent use of The Trademarks in such manner.

* * *

Respondent points to the Senate Finance Committee report and its reference to powers, rights, or interests allowing the transferor "active, operational control" and argues that, in contrast to this language, the pork and beans restriction does not grant such control to the Foundation. However, the Senate Finance Committee report also indicates that "any general control of the transferee's activities and operations by the transferor," S. Rept. 91-552, *supra*, 1969-3 C.B. at 555, can be significant. We believe the pork and beans restriction allows the Foundation control of the transferee's activities and operations in that it prevents petitioner from using its trademarks for a significant market that petitioner could have and would have otherwise entered. This constitutes a "significant [condition] or [restriction]." See *id.*, 1969-3 C.B. at 556.

We recognize that the pork and beans restriction is not coextensive with the duration of petitioner's rights in the trademarks. The restriction lasts for 20 years, whereas petitioner acquired its right, title, and interest in the trademarks in perpetuity. Section 1253(a) provides that a transfer "not be treated as a sale or exchange of a capital asset if the transferor retains any significant power, right, or continuing interest with respect to the *subject matter of the franchise, trademark, or trade name*." (Emphasis added.) As previously noted, the subject matter of a trademark may be broader than the "interest transferred" referred to in section 1253(b)(2). Section 1253(a) is therefore distinguishable from section 1253(b)(2). Unlike section 1253(b)(2), section 1253(a) contains no specifically enumerated criteria for determining the significance of a retained right. While the duration of a restriction may be an important factor, the ultimate determination of whether a retained right is "significant" for purposes of section 1253(a) must be based on all the facts and circumstances. In the context of petitioner's business, 20 years is a significant period.

We have examined all the facts and circumstances regarding the Stokely trademarks and the pork and beans restriction and conclude that the pork and beans restriction qualifies as a "significant power, right, or continuing interest with respect to the subject matter of the * * * [trademarks]" within the meaning of section 1253(a). As a result, petitioner is entitled to deductions that it claimed under section 1253(d)(2).

Chapter 5: Holding Companies and State Tax Minimization

You have probably heard of the "Delaware Holding Company" (DHC), but may have been unaware of one of its primary purposes. You may suspect that a DHC was formed to take advantage of Delaware's favorable corporate governance laws. While corporate governance may be important, state tax minimization may be another equally important reason for the DHC's existence.

In order to understand how a DHC can minimize state taxes, one must understand how state corporate income taxes work. In this regard, this Chapter first provides a brief introduction of state corporate income taxes [this introduction is not intended to be a comprehensive review of state corporate income taxes]. Thereafter, this Chapter discusses how a DHC can be used to minimize state tax and how states have responded to DHCs.

5.1 Overview of State Corporate Income Taxes

5.1[1] State Tax Base

As of 2011, nearly all of the states and the District of Columbia place a tax on corporate income.[403] While each state's corporate income tax has its own idiosyncrasies, state corporate income taxes generally have one thing in common: the *state tax base*. The state tax base is the starting point for calculating the state tax. Almost all states, in some form or another, "piggy back" on the federal corporate income tax. That is, most states incorporate the Internal Revenue Code by reference and use federal taxable income (before apportionment) as the state tax base. Incorporating federal taxable income by reference is administratively convenient because the states need not enact complicated rules similar to those found in Subchapter C of the Code (i.e., rules dealing with corporate formation, distributions, reorganizations, and liquidations). States generally make some modifications from federal taxable income, such as requiring taxpayers to add back certain deductions, such as net operating loss carrybacks and other special deductions.[404] But it is generally safe to say that an expense deductible for federal income tax purposes is similarly deductible for state tax purposes.

---

[403] *See* Shirley Sicilian, *State Business Taxes*, § 2.01[2] (Walter Nagel ed., 2d. ed., Law J. Press 2010). Nevada, Washington, and Wyoming do not have direct taxes on corporate income or a franchise tax. *Id.* South Dakota imposes a franchise tax on financial institutions only. *Id.*

[404] Other common examples include adjustments to reflect differences in the treatment of depreciation, state and local taxes, and interest from government bonds.

5.1[2] Apportionment and Allocation

Suppose a corporate taxpayer does business in every state and the District of Columbia. Would it be fair to require the taxpayer to pay income tax in each state based on its entire taxable income? Of course not. The taxpayer will invariably have a greater presence in some states over others. For instance, the taxpayer may have all of its employees and all of its property in one state. Because the taxpayer would use more of its home state's services (roads, fire, police, and other state services) than others, the home state ought, in this case, to require a greater inclusion of a portion of taxpayer's taxable income than the others. The division of a taxpayer's taxable income among the several states is called *apportionment*. In *Complete Auto Transit v. Brady,*[405] the Supreme Court held that fair apportionment of state income tax is constitutionally mandated under the Commerce Clause.

Seeing the need for uniformity in the apportionment of state corporate income tax, the National Conference of Commissioners on Uniform State Laws, in 1957, promulgated the Uniform Division of Tax Purposes Act (UDITPA).[406] UDITPA serves two primary purposes. First, UDITPA defines "business income" and provides a three-factor formula for its *apportionment*.[407] Second, UDITPA defines "nonbusiness income" and provides for its *allocation* to the proper state.[408] Several states adopt the rules of UDITPA and non-adopting states generally adopt UDITPA's principles and then make state specific modifications. Discussion and explanation of the various state specific changes to UDITPA is far beyond of this Chapter's scope (in fact, it could form the basis of its own book). For this reason, this Chapter simplifies matters by focusing primarily upon the rules of UDITPA.

UDITPA defines "business income" as "income arising from transactions and activity in the regular course of the taxpayer's trade or business and includes income from tangible and intangible property if the acquisition, management, and disposition of the property constitute integral parts of the taxpayer's regular trade or business operations."[409] Once a taxpayer identifies its business income based on the foregoing definition, UDITPA requires the

[405] 430 U.S. 274 (1977).

[406] Unif. Div. of Income for Tax Purposes Act (UDITPA). UDITPA does not apply to financial organizations and public utilities. UDITPA § 2.

[407] *Id.* §§ 1(a), 9.

[408] *Id.* §§ 1(e), 4-8.

[409] *Id.* § 1(a).

taxpayer to apportion that business income based on an equally weighted average of three factors, (1) *property*, (2), *payroll*, and (3) *sales*.

The *property factor* is the "average value of the taxpayer's real and personal property owned or rented in the state during the tax period" divided by "the average value of all the taxpayer's real and tangible personal property owned or rented and used during the tax period."[410] In the other words, the property factor is expressed by the following fraction:

$$\text{Property factor} = \frac{\text{Property (real or tangible personal, owned or rented) in state}}{\text{Property (real or tangible personal, owned or rented) everywhere}}$$

The property factor raises a number of interpretive issues. How is property to be valued? Is value based on original cost, depreciated cost, appraised value, or some other figure? The location of property is easily determined for real property and heavy equipment, but where is moveable property located?

UDITPA generally values property based on its original cost.[411] An exception is made for inventory, which is valued according to the same method the taxpayer uses for federal income tax purposes.[412] A taxpayer values rented property at eight times its net annual rental rate.[413] To account for acquisitions and dispositions of property throughout the year, a taxpayer determines the value of property by averaging the values at the beginning and ending of the tax period.[414] While the drafters of UDITPA admit that valuation based on original cost and eight times net annual rent is somewhat arbitrary, they justify it based on administrative convenience.[415]

In determining whether property is used "in state," moveable property's value is generally assigned to the state based on the portion of time used in that state.[416] UDITPA does not take intangible property into account in the property factor. This is likely due to the fact that

---

[410] *Id.* § 10.

[411] *Id.* § 11.

[412] MTC Reg. § IV.11.(a)(1). The Multistate Tax Commission (MTC) has issued regulations interpreting UDITPA.

[413] UDITPA § 11.

[414] *Id.* § 12.

[415] *Id.* § 11, comment.

[416] MTC Reg. § IV.10.(d).

UDITPA does not apply to financial organizations. For this reason, many states have enacted special rules regarding the property factor of financial organizations.[417]

The *payroll factor* is the compensation paid in the state during the tax period divided by the total compensation paid everywhere during the tax period.[418] Thus, the payroll factor is expressed by the following fraction:

$$\text{Payroll factor} = \frac{\text{Compensation paid in state}}{\text{Total compensation paid everywhere}}$$

Like the property factor, the payroll factor also raises interpretive issues. What is includible as compensation? Does a taxpayer include amounts paid to independent contractors? In what state is compensation paid if an employee travels frequently for work?

UDITPA defines compensation as "wages, salaries, commissions and any other form of remuneration paid to employees for personal services."[419] Compensation does not include amounts paid to independent contractors.[420] Generally, UDITPA assigns compensation to the state in which the employee performs services (incidental services performed outside the state are disregarded).[421] If an employee performs substantial services both inside and outside a state, then compensation is assigned to the employee's base of operation.[422] If the employee has no base of operation, then compensation is assigned to the state where the employee's services are directed or controlled (and if none, then to the employee's state of residence).[423]

The *sales factor* is the taxpayer's in state sales during the tax period divided by the taxpayer's total sales everywhere during the tax period.[424] Therefore, the sales factor is expressed as follows:

---

[417] In 1994, the MTC proposed a recommended formula for the apportionment and allocation of the net income of financial institutions.

[418] UDITPA § 13.

[419] *Id.* § 1(c).

[420] MTC Reg. § IV.13.(a)(3).

[421] UDITPA § 14; MTC Reg. § IV.14.

[422] *Id.*

[423] *Id.*

[424] UDITPA § 15.

$$\text{Sales factor} = \frac{\text{Sales in state}}{\text{Total sales everywhere}}$$

The sales factor also raises several interpretive issues. For instance, what is included in "sales?" How does a taxpayer account for the sale of its services? Where is a sale located?

UDITPA defines sales as nonallocable "gross receipts" (i.e., business income).[425] Therefore, sales generally include gross sales less returns and discounts and receipts from sales of services (including fees and commissions).[426] Sales of tangible personal property are generally sourced to a state based on the "destination principle." That is, the sale is generally sourced to the state where goods are delivered "regardless of the f.o.b. point or other conditions of the sale."[427] There are two exceptions where sales are sourced back to the state of origination. The first exception is the sale of goods to the U.S. government.[428] The second exception applies where the taxpayer is not taxable in the destination state (e.g., the taxpayer does not have nexus with the destination state).[429] This second exception is often called the "throwback rule" because sales are "thrown back" from the destination state to the state of origin.

Once a taxpayer has determined its payroll, property, and sales factors, it must calculate its apportionment percentage. Because the UDITPA's three-factor formula is equally weighted, the taxpayer must divide the sum of the three factors by three:

$$\text{Apportionment percentage} = \frac{\text{Property factor + payroll factor + sales factor}}{3}$$

Theoretically, the equally-weighted three-factor formula measures a multistate corporation's in state activities or "presence" in a particular state. When UDITPA was initially proposed in 1957, the U.S. economy was much more manufacturing-based than it is today. In a manufacturing-based economy, many multistate corporations own heavy machinery, factories, warehouses, and the like, so that the property factor, in particular, is a decent measure of presence. With a service-based economy, ownership of tangible property may

---

425 *Id.* § 1(g).

426 UDITPA § 15, comment; MTC Reg. § IV.15.(a).

427 *Id.* § 16(a).

428 *Id.* § 16(b).

429 *Id.*

not be as accurate of an indicator of "presence." So the recent trend is to weigh the sales factor more heavily than property and payroll. For instance, some states employ a double-weighted sales factor, such that sales are weighted 50 percent and property and payroll are weighted 25 percent each.[430] Some states have gone further by relying entirely on the sales factor.[431] Another reason for heavier reliance on the sales factor is to deflect tax away from taxpayers based in-state (because their in state property and payroll is less a factor) onto taxpayers based out-of-state.[432] Query: a single-weighted sales factor is tempting for states because it is thought to benefit in-state businesses at the expense of out-of-state businesses. But is there a downside to relying entirely on a sales factor?

In theory, a multistate corporation ought to apportion exactly 100 percent of its taxable income among the several states in which it does business. Because states adopt inconsistent formulas for apportionment, the practical result is that taxpayers may pay tax on more or less than 100 percent of its business income. In some cases, a multistate corporation may include less than 100 percent of its business income in state income. In other cases, the multistate corporation may include more than 100 percent of its business income in the various state tax bases. Not surprisingly, multistate corporations employ tax professionals to legitimately plan to minimize the amount includible among the various states.

While a taxpayer's business income is apportioned among several states, a taxpayer's "nonbusiness income" is *allocated* to a specific state. UDITPA defines nonbusiness income as "all other income other than business income."[433] Nonbusiness income typically includes passive-type income, such as interest, dividends, rents, royalties, and capital gains. But it would be incorrect to assume that interest, dividends, rents, royalties, and capital gains are nonbusiness income *per se*. If such income is generated as an integral part of the taxpayer's regular business operations, such income would be business income subject to

---

[430] *See* Sicilian, *supra* note 403, at § 2.06[2].

[431] *Id.*

[432] The constitutionality of a single-weighted sales factor is not entirely clear. In *Moorman Mfg. Co. v. Bair*, 437 U.S. 267 (1978), the Supreme Court upheld the constitutionality of Iowa's single-weighted sales factor based, in part, on the taxpayer's evidentiary failure to show that sales sourced to Iowa were attributable to activities in another state. Presumably, in a future case, if a taxpayer can present such evidence, the Supreme Court might hold differently. For additional discussion, *see* Mark L. Nachbar & Brian L. Browdy, *The Single Sales Factor Apportionment Method and Developments*, J. St. Taxn. 35 (July/Aug. 2009).

[433] UDITPA § 1(e).

apportionment. Thus, it is the income's relationship to the taxpayer's regular business, rather than the type of income, that determines whether income is apportioned or allocated.

UDITPA generally allocates nonbusiness net rents and royalties of real and tangible personal property to the state where the property is located.[434] Similarly, nonbusiness capital gains and losses from sales of real and tangible personal property are allocated to the state where the property is located.[435] A taxpayer must allocate nonbusiness interest and dividends to the state of its commercial domicile.[436] Nonbusiness royalties from patents and copyrights are generally allocated to the state where the patent or copyright is utilized.[437] A patent is utilized in a state if it is "employed in production, fabrication, manufacturing, or other processing in state or to the extent that a patented product is produced in the state."[438] A copyright is utilized in a state "to the extent that the printing or publication originates in the state."[439] If the taxpayer is not taxable in the state where the patent or copyright is utilized (e.g., due to lack of nexus), royalties from the patent or copyright are "thrown back" and allocated to the taxpayer's state of commercial domicile.[440]

Once a taxpayer determines its apportionable and allocable income, it can then calculate its state taxable income. In most states, a taxpayer generally calculates its state taxable income in the following steps:

Step 1. Determine State Tax Base. Federal taxable income ± state adjustments = state tax base (before apportionment and allocation)

Step 2. Determine Apportionable Income. State tax base – nonbusiness income = apportionable income (business income)

Step 3. Determine Income Apportioned to State. Apportionable income x apportionment percentage = state apportioned income.

---

[434] *Id.* § 5.

[435] *Id.* § 6.

[436] *Id.* § 7.

[437] *Id.* § 8(a)(1).

[438] *Id.* § 8(b).

[439] *Id.* § 8(c).

[440] *Id.* § 8(a)(2).

Step 4. Determine State Taxable Income. State apportioned income + nonbusiness income allocated to state = state taxable income.

Problem 5.1: Taxpayer is a multistate corporation domiciled in State X. Taxpayer does not have any subsidiaries or affiliates. During its most recent tax year, Taxpayer had $10 million of federal taxable income, which included $9 million of taxable income attributable to general operations and a $1 million capital gain on the sale of an asset unrelated to its regular business.

Taxpayer has established nexus with State Y and must file a corporate income tax return there for the tax year. State Y has adopted UDITPA and uses federal taxable income as its state tax base. The average value of Taxpayer's real and personal property owned or rented in State Y during the tax year was $5 million; while the average value of all Taxpayer's real and tangible personal property owned or rented and used during the tax year was $100 million. Taxpayer paid $2 million in compensation in the State Y during the tax year compared to $40 million in compensation paid everywhere during the tax year. Taxpayer's sales in State Y were $40 million in State Y compared to total sales of $200 million everywhere.

What is Taxpayer's apportionment percentage and state taxable income in State Y during the tax year? How would your answer change if State Y adopted a single-weighted sales factor for apportionment?

5.1[3] Separate Filing and Combined Reporting

A multistate corporation might choose to operate its business through one or more divisions of a single entity. A similarly situated corporation may choose to operate its business through one or more subsidiaries or affiliates. For instance, a multistate manufacturer could operate its production, warehousing, and distribution in one corporation. Or a multistate manufacturer could operate its production in one corporation, warehousing in a second corporation, and distribution in a third corporation. There may be several reasons why a multistate business may choose to operate a unitary business through various subsidiaries and affiliates. As discussed in this Chapter, one reason for operating through affiliates may be to minimize state taxes.

A state can take two basic approaches in the income taxation of a unitary business operated through two or more affiliates. A state could treat all affiliates as separate legal entities and require each (assuming nexus is established) to account for its own taxes based on its own business income. This basic approach is generally referred to as *separate filing*. The other basic approach requires an affiliate to pay tax on its apportioned share of the unitary business's combined business income. This second basic approach is generally referred to as *combined reporting*. Essentially, the goal of combined reporting is to replicate what would happen if the unitary business were operated in a single entity.

A state's adoption of combined reporting vis-à-vis separate filing is, on its face, revenue neutral. That is, combined reporting is not inherently more tax burdensome than separate filing, and vice versa. In some cases, a state's adoption of combined reporting may increase the overall tax a unitary business pays compared to separate filing. Sometimes the opposite will occur. For instance, suppose a unitary business is operated through two affiliated corporations. Suppose the in state affiliate is profitable, while the out of state affiliate is losing money. In separate filing, the profitable in state affiliate would file its own return and pay taxes on those in state profits without offset of losses from the out-of-state affiliate. And if the out-of-state affiliate has no in state nexus, then it would have no reporting requirement at all in state. In combined reporting, the in state profits would be offset by the out-of-state loses, so that the unitary business would have less state taxable income and pay less overall tax in comparison to separate filing.

In other cases, combined reporting may generate more revenue for a state because combined reporting generally ignores *intercompany transactions* of a unitary business. Because the business income of a unitary business is combined before apportionment, intercompany transactions essentially "wash out" (i.e., a deduction to one affiliate is canceled out by income to the other). Query: In what ways could a unitary business exploit separate filing requirements by using intercompany transactions to reduce overall tax on the unitary business?

5.1[4] Requirements for Combined Reporting

The rules for combined reporting vary somewhat from state to state. But combined reporting states generally have two requisites for combined reporting: (1) the satisfaction of common ownership requirements and (2) the existence of a unitary business. The common ownership requirement is typically satisfied if there is common ownership (either directly or indirectly) of more than 50 percent of the voting stock of each corporation in the group.[441] The Multistate Tax Commission's regulations define a unitary business as follows:

> A unitary business is a single economic enterprise that is made up either of separate parts of a single business entity or of a commonly controlled group of business entities that are sufficiently interdependent, integrated and interrelated through their activities so as to provide a synergy and mutual benefit that produces a sharing or exchange of value among them and a significant flow of value to the separate parts.[442]

The Supreme Court, in *Mobil Oil Corp. v. Vermont*,[443] held that a unitary business is evidenced by three factors, including (1) functional integration, (2) centralization of management, and (3) and economies of scale. Functional integration typically includes "transfers or pooling with respect to the unitary business's products or services, technical information, marketing information, distribution systems, purchasing, and intangibles such as patents, trademarks, service marks, copyrights, trade secrets, know-how, formulas, and processes."[444] Centralization of management "exists when directors, officers, and/or other management employees jointly participate in the management decisions that affect the respective business activities and that may also operate to the benefit of the economic enterprise."[445] Economies of scale "refers to a relation among and between business activities resulting in a significant decrease in the average per unit cost of operational or administrative functions due to the increase in operational size."[446]

In addition to the common ownership and unitary business requirements, most states either limit their combined reporting to those affiliates within the "water's edge" or allow taxpayers to make a "water's edge" election.[447] "Water's edge" means that taxpayers combine the business income of domestic affiliates only. Similarly, for purposes of apportionment, water's edge reporting only requires inclusion of domestic affiliates in the appointment factors. In contrast, worldwide combined reporting requires combination of all

---

[441] *E.g.* MTC Reg. § IV.1(b)(4).

[442] MTC Reg. § IV.1(b)(1)(A).

[443] 445 U.S. 425 (1980).

[444] MTC Reg. § IV.1(b)(1)(B)(1).

[445] *Id.* § IV.1(b)(1)(B)(2).

[446] *Id.* § IV.1(b)(1)(B)(3).

[447] *See e.g.* Michael J. McIntyre et al., *Designing a Combined Reporting Regime for a State Corporate Income Tax: A Case Study of Louisiana*, 61 La. L. Rev. 699, 733 (2001).

commonly-owned affiliates of a unitary business, whether domestic or foreign. While the Supreme Court has upheld the constitutionality of worldwide combined reporting,[448] states have generally been unwilling to make it mandatory. Combined reporting is generally unpopular with the business lobby and worldwide combined reporting is even more so.

5.1[5] Combined Reporting Compared to Federal Consolidated Returns

Combined reporting is often confused with the federal consolidated return requirements. Yet combined reporting and consolidated returns are two entirely different things. Consolidated returns aim to tax a group as a single unit, so that one return is filed and a single tax is remitted. On the other hand, the purpose of combined reporting is to apportion unitary income among the separate corporations of the unitary business having nexus in the state. As such, in combined reporting, each corporation with nexus in state typically files its own tax return and is responsible for its own taxes. Therefore, it is helpful to think of combined reporting as a way of *apportioning unitary income* of corporations engaged in a unitary business to the states, rather than the consolidation of those entities into one taxpayer. Another difference is that combined reporting generally requires more than 50 percent common ownership, while the threshold for federal consolidated returns is 80 percent. Finally, combined reporting only applies if there is a unitary business, whereas returns are consolidated if the common ownership is met, irrespective of whether a unitary business exists.

5.1[6] Unitary Income Apportionment under Combined Reporting

Once a taxpayer determines that combined reporting is required, the next step is to apportion the unitary income to each of the corporations of the unitary group. Only those corporations having nexus with the state are required to file. The most common method for apportionment under combined reporting, often called the *Joyce* method,[449] requires a

---

[448] *See Container Corp. of America v. Franchise Tax Board*, 463 U.S. 159 (1983); *Barclays Bank P.L.C. v. Franchise Tax Board*, 512 U.S. 298 (1994).

[449] The *Joyce* method is named for the California administrative appeal that approved its use. *Appeal of Joyce, Inc.*, No. 66-SBE-070, 1966 W.L. 1411, (Cal. State Bd. of Equal. Nov. 23, 1966). Another less commonly applied method is the *Finnigan* method, which is also named for a California administrative appeal. *Appeal of Finnigan Corp.*, No. 88-SBE-022, 1990 W.L. 15164, (Cal. State Bd. of Equal. Jan 24, 1990). The *Finnigan* method differs from the *Joyce* method in that the *Finnigan* method treats the unitary group as a single taxpayer for *apportionment purposes only*. Once the unitary group's income is apportioned to the state, the *Finnigan* method then requires that income to

taxpayer to include in the numerator of its apportionment factors only its own property, payroll, and sales (just as it would under separate filing). But the denominator of its property, payroll, and sales factors includes the figures from the *entire unitary group*. Therefore, under combined reporting, a taxpayer calculates its property, payroll, and sales factors as follows under combined reporting:

$$\text{Combined property factor} = \frac{\text{Taxpayer's own in state property}}{\text{Total property of unitary group}}$$

$$\text{Combined payroll factor} = \frac{\text{Taxpayer's own in state payroll}}{\text{Total payroll of unitary group}}$$

$$\text{Combined sales factor} = \frac{\text{Taxpayer's own in state sales}}{\text{Total sales of unitary group}}$$

The taxpayer multiplies its apportionment percentage by the combined business income of the unitary group to calculate state apportioned income. Therefore, under combined reporting, the state apportioned income of a corporation is calculated as follows (assuming UDITPA's equally weighted three-factor formula applies):

$$\text{State apportioned income} = \text{Business income of unitary group} \times \frac{\text{Combined property factor} + \text{Combined payroll factor} + \text{Combined sales factor}}{3}$$

Problem 5.2: Badger Co., Gopher Corp., and Cornhusker, Inc. are commonly-controlled U.S. corporations that conduct a unitary business. Badger and Gopher have nexus with State X and must file corporate income tax returns there. On the other hand, Cornhusker has no nexus with State X. Assume State X adopts UDITPA's equally-weighted three factor formula

---

be intrastate apportioned among those taxpayers with nexus in the state. The practical difference between *Joyce* and *Finnigan* relates to the inclusion of certain sales in the *numerator* of the sales factor. In some cases, a member of a unitary business can have in state sales, but not be required to file a return in that state (most likely due to Public Law 86-272, discussed later in this Chapter). Under the *Joyce* method, such sales do not get taken into account in the sales factor numerator (because each corporation with nexus in state includes only its own sales in its sales factor numerator). In contrast, under the *Finnigan* method, such sales do get taken into account in the sales factor numerator.

for apportionment. The corporations have the following business income, property, payroll, and sales:

(Dollars in thousands)

Badger Co.	**U.S. Wide**	**State X**
Business income	$4,000	
Property	$20,000	$2,000
Payroll	$40,000	$10,000
Sales	$100,000	$10,000
Gopher Corp.		
Business income	$4,000	
Property	$10,000	$1,000
Payroll	$50,000	$1,000
Sales	$200,000	$30,000
Cornhusker, Inc.		
Business income	$2,000	
Property	$10,000	$0
Payroll	$10,000	$0
Sales	$50,000	$0

If State X requires separate filing, what is the state apportioned income of Badger, Gopher, and Cornhusker in State X?

Alternatively, if State X requires combined reporting, what is the state apportioned income of Badger, Gopher, and Cornhusker in State X? If Badger, Gopher, and Cornhusker operated together as one corporation, what would be the state apportioned income of that one corporation in State X?

Problem 5.3: Hoosier Corp. is a multistate corporation domiciled in Indiana. Hoosier has no affiliates or subsidiaries. For purposes of this problem, assume that Indiana is a separate filing state that adopts UDITPA's equally-weighted three factor formula for apportionment. Hoosier has the following business income, property, payroll, and sales:

(Dollars in thousands)

Hoosier Corp.	**U.S. Wide**	**Indiana**
Business income	$100,000	
Property	$500,000	$2,000
Payroll	$300,000	$10,000
Sales	$1,000,000	$10,000

What is the state apportioned income of Hoosier in Indiana?

Alternatively, suppose Hoosier had transferred its trademarks and trade names to a wholly-owned subsidiary (SubCo) formed in Delaware. Pursuant to a licensing agreement between Hoosier and SubCo, Hoosier pays an annual royalty to SubCo equal to one percent of its gross sales in exchange for use of the trademarks and trade names. SubCo's royalty income is exempt from corporate income tax in Delaware. In the most recent tax year, Hoosier paid a $10 million royalty to SubCo, which it deducted as an ordinary and necessary expense on its federal income tax return. If Indiana's state tax base is tied to federal taxable income, what impact does Hoosier's payment of the royalty to SubCo have on its business income in Indiana? In answering this question, assume Hoosier's business income is $100 million (as noted in the above table) *before* giving effect to the royalty paid to SubCo.

If the licensing agreement between Hoosier and SubCo is respected and SubCo has no nexus in Indiana, what is Hoosier's state apportioned income in Indiana (assume Hoosier's property, payroll, and sales are the same as noted in the above table)? How would your answer to this question change if Indiana required combined reporting?

Alternatively, suppose Indiana requires combined reporting, but limits combined reporting to those unitary affiliates within the "water's edge." Instead of forming SubCo in Delaware, Hoosier forms SubCo in a foreign country that imposes no corporate income tax. How would that change your answer, if at all?

Problem 5.3 demonstrates how holding companies can be used strategically to minimize state taxes. Essentially, the holding company exploits separate filing by deflecting revenue away from a high tax state to a state that has no tax at all. In other words, the goal is to create "*nowhere income*" that is not subject to state tax.[450] Delaware is a favored source state because it does not tax royalties generated on the licensing of intellectual property.[451] But any other state that does not impose a corporate income tax would work as well, such as Nevada, South Dakota, or Wyoming.[452] Because Delaware is known for its favorable governance laws and is familiar to corporate attorneys nationwide, Delaware is the most popular state for holding companies. Hence, the term "DHC" is used generically to refer to holding companies in general, even though a unitary business might choose another tax haven. Businesses are then careful to ensure that their DHC does not establish nexus outside Delaware. In this way, the revenue of the DHC is entirely sourced to Delaware, which does not tax such revenue at all.[453] Does this sound too good to be true? To answer this question, one must consider the various ways states have attacked the DHC strategy, which forms the discussion in the next subsection of this Chapter.

5.1[7] The Importance of Nexus

Before discussing ways in which states have attacked the DHC strategy, one must understand the importance of nexus. Under the Commerce Clause of the U.S. Constitution, a state may only impose a tax on those taxpayers having "substantial nexus" with that state.[454] In the seminal case of *Quill Corp. v. North Dakota*,[455] the Supreme Court held that a state could not impose a *use tax* on an out-of-state taxpayer whose only in state contact was

---

[450] The licensing of intellectual property, shown in Problem 6.3, is merely one of many strategies multistate corporations use to exploit separate filing. Other strategies include payment of rent to related real estate investment trusts (REITs) and payment of insurance to captive insurance companies. For an excellent discussion of such strategies, see Michael Mazerov, *State Corporate Tax Shelters and the Need for Combined Reporting*, 46 St. Tax Notes 621 (2007).

[451] Del. Code Ann tit. 30, § 1902(b)(8) (2010).

[452] *See* Sheldon H. Laskin, *Only a Name? Trademark Royalties, Nexus, and Taxing that which Enriches*, 22 Akron Tax. J. 1, 6 (2007).

[453] Instead of forming a holding company in Delaware or Nevada (which are reputed tax havens), a multistate corporation could form a holding company in a combined reporting state where it already has a substantial presence. This strategy works because the multistate corporation's unitary income stays the same in the combined reporting state, yet royalties paid to the combined reporting state shift income away from separate filing states. Formation of a holding company in a tax haven, such as Delaware or Nevada, is sometimes referred to as "first generation" holding company planning. And the formation of a holding company in a combined reporting is sometimes referred to as second generation" holding company planning.

[454] *Complete Auto Transit, Inc. v. Brady*, 430 U.S. 274, 279 (1977).

[455] 504 U.S. 298 (1992).

shipping goods to in state customers via common carrier. Thus, with respect to a *sales and use tax*, a taxpayer must have *physical presence* in state to create substantial nexus under the Commerce Clause.[456] *Quill* leaves open the question of whether a physical presence standard similarly applies in the context of a *corporate income tax*. As of 2011, the U.S. Supreme Court has not definitively answered this question. But not surprisingly, state courts have typically limited *Quill* to sales and use taxes only, so that physical presence is not constitutionally required for a corporate income tax. The cases included in this Chapter's materials address *Quill*. Do you agree with the courts' rationale?

Another limitation on a state's right to tax corporate income is Public Law 86-272,[457] which Congress passed in 1959. Public Law 86-272 prevents a state from taxing the income of a corporation whose only in state contact is the "solicitation of orders" for tangible goods, provided the following two requirements are met:

(1) orders must be sent out of state for approval; and

(2) the goods must be shipped from outside the state.[458]

5.1[8] State Challenges to the DHC Strategy

5.1[8][a] Judicial responses

Beginning in the early 1990s, state taxing authorities in separate filing jurisdictions began an assault against DHCs. DHCs typically did not file returns outside Delaware on the claim that they lacked nexus with any other state. Thus, states had to overcome the legal hurdle of establishing "substantial nexus" on the part of the DHC. The seminal case in this regard is *Geoffrey, Inc. v. South Carolina Tax Commn.*,[459] which is included in this Chapter's materials. The South Carolina Supreme Court decided *Geoffrey* a year after *Quill* and held that the *Quill's* physical presence nexus standard does not apply to corporate income

---

[456] While the Supreme Court in *Quill* imposed a physical presence standard, the Court did not clearly define what constitutes physical presence. The Court stated in a footnote that the slightest physical presence is insufficient, such as the in state presence of taxpayer's floppy disks licensed to an in state customer. *Quill*, 504 U.S. at 315 n. 8. States typically adopt their own standards for the required amount of employees or property in state or the required length of time that the employees or property must be located in state to constitute physical presence.

[457] 15 U.S.C. § 381.

[458] *Id.*

[459] 437 S.E.2d 13 (S.C. 1993).

taxes.[460] Thus, *Geoffrey* introduced the concept of "economic nexus." That is, without the necessity of physical presence, a holding company's in state economic presence (i.e., the licensing of intangibles in South Carolina) can create substantial nexus. In *Kmart Properties, Inc. v. Taxation and Revenue Dept.*,[461] also included in this Chapter's materials, the court attributed the physical presence of the in state affiliate to the out-of-state holding company (so called "attribution nexus").

> **Problem 5.4**: Read *Geoffrey, Inc. v. South Carolina Tax Commn.* and *Kmart Properties, Inc. v. Taxation and Revenue Dept.* included in this Chapter's materials. In *Geoffrey* and *Kmart Properties*, the courts found nexus on part of an out-of-state holding company thereby subjecting the holding company to tax in the taxing state. Assuming the holding company's receipt of royalties is business income, how should the holding company apportion that business income? If the holding company has no property and no payroll in the taxing state, and its receipt of royalties is sourced to Delaware for purposes of the sales factor, what is its apportionment percentage in the taxing state? Did the South Carolina Supreme Court address this issue in *Geoffrey*? How did New Mexico Court of Appeals address this issue in *Kmart Properties*? Do you agree with the result?

States have also attacked the holding company strategy by arguing that the royalty payment should be disregarded as a sham lacking economic substance. By denying deduction of royalties paid as a sham, a state effectively taxes the in state affiliate on the income of the holding company. In this way, the taxing state avoids the issue of the out-of-state holding company's nexus. Two Massachusetts cases included in this Chapter's materials, *Syms Corp. v. Commissioner of Revenue*[462] and *Sherwin-Williams Co. v. Commissioner of Revenue*,[463] address the sham transaction issue. The court in *Syms* disregarded royalty payments to the holding company as a sham. Conversely, the court in *Sherwin-Williams*

---

[460] Other states have followed suit (some of these cases involved the same "Geoffrey, Inc." holding company at issue in the South Carolina case). *See e.g. Bridges v. Geoffrey, Inc.*, 984 So.2d 115 (La. Ct. App. 2008); *Geoffrey, Inc. v. Commr. of Revenue*, 899 N.E.2d 87 (Mass. 2009); *Lanco, Inc. v. Dir., Div. of Taxn.*, 879 A.2d 1234 (N.J. Super. App. Div. 2005), *aff'd*, 908 A.2d 176 (N.J. 2006); *A&F Trademark, Inc. v. Tolson*, 605 S.E.2d 187 (N.C. App. 2004); *Geoffrey, Inc. v. Okla. Tax Commn.*, 132 P.3d 632 (Okla. Ct. App. 2005).

[461] 131 P.3d 27 (N.M. App. 2001), *rev'd on other grounds*, 131 P.3d 22 (N.M. 2005).

[462] 765 N.E.2d 758 (Mass. 2002).

[463] 778 N.E.2d 504 (Mass. 2002).

respected the royalty payments to the holding company.[464] Query: What factual differences between the transactions in *Syms* and *Sherwin-Williams* lead the courts to their differing conclusions?

5.1[8][b] Statutory responses

The primary statutory response to combat the DHC strategy is to adopt mandatory combined reporting. In 2004, Vermont became the first state in over 20 years to switch from separate filing to combined reporting.[465] Several other states followed suit in the next few years.[466]

Additionally, several states have adopted "add back" statutes whereby royalties paid to a related company for the use of intangibles may be added back to the income of the payor. The practical result of an "add back" statute is the same as the result in *Syms*. That is, while the holding company's income remains non-taxable, the in state affiliate's payments to the holding company are no longer deductible thereby eliminating the tax savings. "Add back" statutes generally contain exceptions for legitimate business transactions. Although "add back" statutes vary from state to state, common exceptions to "add back" of royalties paid include the following:

(1) payments to the related company are subject to tax in another jurisdiction;
(2) the transaction has a valid business purpose unrelated to tax savings;
(3) the related company is merely a conduit for passing through the payment to an unrelated party; and
(4) the transaction is "arm's length."[467]

---

[464] Apparently, the Massachusetts Commissioner of Revenue did not assert that Massachusetts had nexus over the holding company. Subsequently, the Massachusetts Commissioner of Revenue changed course and successfully litigated the holding company's in state nexus. *See Geoffrey, Inc. v. Commr. of Revenue*, 899 N.E.2d 87 (Mass. 2009).

[465] Mark J. Cowan & Clint Kakstys, *A Green Mountain Miracle and the Garden State Grab: Lessons from Vermont and New Jersey on State Corporate Tax Reform*, 60 Tax Law. 351, 390 (2007).

[466] Combined reporting became effective in New York in 2007, Michigan in 2008, and in Massachusetts, West Virginia, and Wisconsin in 2009.

[467] Cowan & Kakstys, *supra* note 465, at 361-62.

5.1[8][c] Future Status of the DHC Strategy

States have been relatively successful in challenging the DHC strategy in recent years. Whether states will continue to have success could depend on future decisions of the U.S. Supreme Court and acts of Congress. The Supreme Court will likely address the physical presence issue at some point. Additionally, Congress could also step in and pass federal legislation to require physical presence for corporate income taxation. If the Supreme Court rules physical presence is required, the *Geoffrey* and *Kmart Properties* cases become obsolete, and taxpayers may constitutionally challenge *Syms* and "add back" statutes as taxing income that has no nexus to a state. Such a result may push the remaining separate filing states to adopt mandatory combined reporting (and the recent trend has certainly gone that way already). At some point in the future, multinational corporations may place additional emphasis on paying royalties to offshore holding companies (an issue discussed in greater detail in the next Chapter) to save tax in "water's edge" combined reporting jurisdictions.

5.2 Materials for Chapter 5

GEOFFREY, INC. v. SOUTH CAROLINA TAX COMMISSION

Supreme Court of South Carolina

437 S.E.2d 13 (S.C. 1993)

HARWELL, Chief Justice:

Geoffrey, Inc. (Geoffrey), a foreign corporation, appeals from a ruling that requires it to pay South Carolina income tax and business license fees. We affirm.

I. *FACTS*

Geoffrey is a wholly-owned, second-tier subsidiary of Toys R Us, Inc. (Toys R Us) incorporated in Delaware with its principal offices in that state. It has no employees or offices in South Carolina and owns no tangible property here.

In 1984, Geoffrey became the owner of several valuable trademarks and trade names, including "Toys R Us." Later that year, Geoffrey executed a License Agreement (Agreement) that allows Toys R Us to use the "Toys R Us" trade name, as well as other trademarks and trade names, in all states except New York, Texas, Pennsylvania,

Massachusetts, and New Jersey. The Agreement further grants Toys R Us a right to use Geoffrey's merchandising skills, techniques, and "know-how" in connection with marketing, promotion, advertising, and sale of products covered by the Agreement.

As consideration for the licenses granted by the Agreement, Geoffrey receives a royalty of one percent "of the net sales by [Toys R Us], or any of its affiliated, associated, or subsidiary companies, of the Licensed Products sold or the Licensed Services rendered under the Licensed Mark." Toys R Us reports the aggregate sales of all stores to Geoffrey in a single figure on a monthly basis. The royalty payment is made annually via wire transfer from a Toys R Us account in Pennsylvania to a Geoffrey account in New York.[1]

Toys R Us began doing business in South Carolina in 1985 and has since then made royalty payments to Geoffrey based on South Carolina sales. In 1986 and 1987, Toys R Us deducted the royalty payments made to Geoffrey from its South Carolina taxable income. The South Carolina Tax Commission (Commission) initially disallowed the deduction, but later took the position that Toys R Us was entitled to the deduction and that Geoffrey was required to pay South Carolina income tax on the royalty income. The Commission also held that Geoffrey was required to pay the South Carolina corporate license fee.

Geoffrey paid the taxes under protest and filed this action for a refund, claiming, among other things, that it did not do business in South Carolina and that it did not have a sufficient nexus with South Carolina for its royalty income to be taxable here. The trial judge upheld the Commission's assessment of taxes against Geoffrey. Geoffrey appealed.

II. *DISCUSSION*

S.C.Code Ann. § 12-7-230 (Supp.1992), pursuant to which both foreign and domestic corporations are taxed, provides:

---

[1] The net effect of this corporate structure has been the production of "nowhere" income that escapes all state income taxation. *See* Rosen, *Use of a Delaware Holding Company to Save State Income Taxes,* 20 Tax Adviser 180 (1989). One commentator has recognized such income as the "product of a divide and conquer strategy that some members of the corporate world have exercised effectively for decades." Corrigan, *Interstate Corporate Income Taxation-Recent Revolutions and a Modern Response,* 29 Vand. L. Rev. 423, 429 (1976). The strategy's effectiveness is unquestionable. In 1990, Geoffrey, without any full-time employees, had an income of approximately $55 million and paid no income taxes to any state.

> [E]xcept as otherwise provided, every foreign corporation transacting, conducting, doing business, or having an income within the jurisdiction of this State, whether or not the corporation is engaged in or the income derived from intrastate, interstate, or foreign commerce, shall make a return and shall pay annually an income tax equivalent to five percent of a proportion of its entire net income, to be determined as provided in this chapter. The term "transacting," "conducting," or "doing business," as used in this section, includes the engaging in or the transacting of any activity in this State for the purpose of financial profit or gain.

Section 12-7-230 levies a tax on the income of foreign corporations "transacting, conducting, doing business, or having an income *within the jurisdiction of this State,*" which "includes," but is not limited to, "the engaging in or the transacting of any activity in this State for the purpose of financial profit or gain." We construe this language as extending to the limits of the constitution South Carolina's authority to tax foreign corporations. Here, Geoffrey contends that the Due Process Clause, U.S. Const. amend. XIV, § 1, and the Commerce Clause, U.S. Const. art. I, § 8, cl. 3, prohibit the taxation of its royalty income by South Carolina. We disagree.

A. *Due Process*

The Due Process Clause requires "some definite link, some minimum connection, between a state and the person, property or transaction it seeks to tax," and that the "income attributed to the state for tax purposes must be rationally related to values connected with the taxing State." *Quill Corp. v. North Dakota*, 504 U.S. 298, 112 S.Ct. 1904, 1909-10, 119 L.Ed.2d 91, 102 (1992). Geoffrey argues that the Commission has failed to satisfy both of these requirements. We disagree.

The nexus requirement of the Due Process Clause can be satisfied even where the corporation has no physical presence in the taxing state if the corporation has purposefully directed its activity at the state's economic forum. *Quill*, 112 S.Ct. at 1909-10, 119 L.Ed.2d at 104. Geoffrey asserts that it has not purposefully directed its activities toward South Carolina. To support its position, Geoffrey points out that Toys R Us had no South Carolina stores when it entered into the Agreement and urges, therefore, that Toys R Us's subsequent expansion into South Carolina was unilateral activity that cannot create the minimum connection between Geoffrey and South Carolina required by due process.

In our view, Geoffrey has not been unwillingly brought into contact with South Carolina through the unilateral activity of an independent party. Geoffrey's business is the ownership, licensing, and management of trademarks, trade names, and franchises. By electing to license its trademarks and trade names for use by Toys R Us in many states, Geoffrey contemplated and purposefully sought the benefit of economic contact with those states. Geoffrey has been aware of, consented to, and benefited from Toys R Us's use of Geoffrey's intangibles in South Carolina. Moreover, Geoffrey had the ability to control its contact with South Carolina by prohibiting the use of its intangibles here as it did with other states. We reject Geoffrey's claim that it has not purposefully directed its activities toward South Carolina's economic forum and hold that by licensing intangibles for use in South Carolina and receiving income in exchange for their use, Geoffrey has the "minimum connection" with this State that is required by due process. [Citations omitted].

In addition to our finding that Geoffrey purposefully directed its activities toward South Carolina, we find that the "minimum connection" required by due process also is satisfied by the presence of Geoffrey's intangible property in this State. Geoffrey's Secretary, a certified public accountant, agreed during cross examination that sales by Toys R Us in South Carolina create an account receivable for Geoffrey. In addition, the trial judge found that Geoffrey had a franchise in South Carolina. That the presence of these intangibles is sufficient to sustain a tax is settled law. In *Virginia v. Imperial Coal Sales Co., Inc.*, 293 U.S. 15, 20, 55 S.Ct. 12, 14, 79 L.Ed. 171, 175 (1934), the United States Supreme Court stated:

> It is not the character of the property that makes it subject to such a tax, but the fact that the property has a situs within the state and that the owner should give appropriate support to the government that protects it. That duty is not less when the property is intangible than when it is tangible. Nor are we able to perceive any sound reason for holding that the owner must have real estate or tangible property within the state in order to subject its intangible property within the state to taxation.

Geoffrey asserts that under the doctrine of *mobilia sequuntur personam,* the situs of its intangibles is its corporate headquarters in Delaware, not South Carolina. However, in *Mobil Oil Corp. v. Comm'r of Taxes of Vermont*, 445 U.S. 425, 100 S.Ct. 1223, 63 L.Ed.2d 510 (1980), the United States Supreme Court rejected the view that the constitution requires taxation of intangibles by allocation to a *single* situs, finding no adequate justification for preferring that rule over taxation by apportionment. The High Court concluded that:

> [a]lthough a fictionalized situs of intangible property sometimes has been invoked to avoid multiple taxation of ownership, there is nothing talismanic about the concepts of "business situs" or "commercial domicile" that automatically renders those concepts applicable when taxation of income from intangibles is at issue. The Court has observed that the maxim *mobilia sequuntur personam,* upon which these fictions of situs are based, "states a rule without disclosing the reasons for it." ... The Court has also recognized that "the reason for a single place of taxation no longer obtains" when the taxpayer's activities with respect to the intangible property involve relations with more than one jurisdiction.... Even for property or franchise taxes, apportionment of intangible values is not unknown.... Moreover, cases upholding allocation to a single situs for property tax purposes have distinguished income tax situations where the apportionment principle prevails. (Citations omitted).

Id. at 445, 100 S.Ct. at 1235, 63 L.Ed.2d at 525-26. *See also Wheeling Steel Corp. v. Fox,* 298 U.S. 193, 56 S.Ct. 773, 80 L.Ed. 1143 (1936) (intangibles may acquire a situs for taxation other than at the domicile of the owner if they have become integral parts of some local business); *Southern Express Co. v. Spigener*, 118 S.C. 413, 110 S.E. 403 (1920) (the situs of intangible property is within this State if the right afforded by it is exercised here); Dexter, *Taxation of Income from Intangibles of Multistate-Multinational Corporations,* 29 Vand.L.Rev. 401 (1976); J. Hellerstein & W. Hellerstein, *State Taxation,* Para. 9.08-.09 (2d ed. 1992). We reject Geoffrey's claim that its intangible assets are located exclusively in Delaware. Accordingly, we find that Geoffrey's purposeful direction of activity toward South Carolina as well as its possessing intangible property here provide a definite link between South Carolina and the income derived by Geoffrey from the use of its trademarks and trade names in this State.

We also find that the second prong of *Quill* test has been met. Contrary to Geoffrey's assertion, South Carolina has conferred benefits upon Geoffrey to which the challenged tax is rationally related. As the United States Supreme Court recognized in *Curry v. McCanless,* 307 U.S. 357, 365-66, 59 S.Ct. 900, 905, 83 L.Ed. 1339, 1347 (1939):

> Very different considerations, both theoretical and practical, apply to the taxation of intangibles, that is, rights which are not related to physical things. Such rights are but relationships between persons, natural or corporate, which the law recognizes by attaching to them certain sanctions enforceable in courts. The power of government over them and the

> protection which it gives them cannot be exerted through control of a physical thing. *They can be made effective only through control over and protection afforded to those persons whose relationships are the origin of the rights....* Obviously, as sources of actual or potential wealth—which is an appropriate measure of any tax imposed on ownership or its exercise—*they cannot be dissociated from the persons from whose relationships they are derived.* (Citations omitted). (Emphasis added).

The real source of Geoffrey's income is not a paper agreement, but South Carolina's Toys R Us customers. [Citation omitted]. By providing an orderly society in which Toys R Us conducts business, South Carolina has made it possible for Geoffrey to earn income pursuant to the royalty agreement. *See, e.g., Allied-Signal v. Comm'r of Finance*, 79 N.Y.2d 73, 580 N.Y.S.2d 696, 588 N.E.2d 731 (1991) (benefits afforded to an in-state corporation inure to non-resident shareholders). That Geoffrey has received protection, benefits, and opportunities from South Carolina is manifested by the fact that it earns income in this state. [Citation omitted]. That the tax is rationally related to these protections, benefits, and opportunities is evidenced by the fact that the State seeks to tax only that portion of Geoffrey's income generated within its borders. Based on the foregoing reasons, we hold that the Due Process Clause does not prohibit South Carolina's taxation of Geoffrey's royalty income.

B. *Commerce Clause*

A tax will survive challenge under the Commerce Clause so long as it 1) is applied to an activity with a substantial nexus with the taxing state, 2) is fairly apportioned, 3) does not discriminate against interstate commerce, and 4) is fairly related to the services provided by the State. *Complete Auto Transit, Inc. v. Brady*, 430 U.S. 274, 279, 97 S.Ct. 1076, 1079, 51 L.Ed.2d 326, 331 (1977). Relying on *Nat'l Bellas Hess, Inc. v. Dep't of Revenue of Ill.*, 386 U.S. 753, 87 S.Ct. 1389, 18 L.Ed.2d 505 (1967), Geoffrey contends that it does not have a substantial nexus with South Carolina because it is not physically present in this state. In our view, Geoffrey's reliance on the physical presence requirement of *Bellas Hess* is misplaced.[4]

It is well settled that the taxpayer need not have a tangible, physical presence in a state for income to be taxable there. The presence of intangible property alone is sufficient to

[4] The U.S. Supreme Court recently revisited the physical presence requirement of *Bellas Hess* and, while reaffirming its vitality as to *sales and use taxes*, noted that the physical presence requirement had not been extended to other types of taxes. *Quill*, 112 S.Ct. at 1914, 119 L.Ed.2d at 108.

establish nexus. *American Dairy Queen*, 93 N.M. at 747, 605 P.2d at 255. *See also Int'l Harvester Co. v. Wisconsin Dep't of Taxation,* 322 U.S. 435, 441-442, 64 S.Ct. 1060, 1063-64, 88 L.Ed. 1373, 1379 (1944) (a state may tax such part of the income of a non-resident as is fairly attributable either to property located in the state or to events or transactions which, occurring there, are within the protection of the state and entitled to the numerous other benefits which its confers); J. Hellerstein & W. Hellerstein, *supra*, at 6.08 (any corporation that regularly exploits the markets of a state should be subject to its jurisdiction to impose an income tax even though not physically present). A taxpayer who is domiciled in one state but carries on business in another is subject to taxation measured by the value of the intangibles used in his business. *Curry*, 307 U.S. at 368, 59 S.Ct. at 906, 83 L.Ed. at 1348. We hold that by licensing intangibles for use in this State and deriving income from their use here, Geoffrey has a "substantial nexus" with South Carolina.[5]

Geoffrey finally contends that even if it is subject to South Carolina income tax, all of its royalty income would be allocated or apportioned to Delaware pursuant to S.C.Code Ann. §§ 12-7-1120(5) or 12-7-1140 (1977 and Supp.1992). These statutes are inapplicable to the income received by Geoffrey. Section 12-7-1120(5) allocates gains or losses from the sale of intangible personal property not connected with the business of the taxpayer, other than any intangible personal property held for sale to customers in the regular course of business. Section 12-7-1140 apportions the income of taxpayers whose principal business in this State is (a) manufacturing or any form of collecting, buying, assembling or processing goods and materials within this State, or (b) selling, distributing or dealing in tangible personal property within this State.

In conclusion, we hold that the taxation of Geoffrey's royalty income pursuant to section 12-7-230 is not prohibited by the Due Process Clause or the Commerce Clause of the United States Constitution. Our finding that Geoffrey may be taxed pursuant to section 12-7-230 settles the question whether Geoffrey must pay the corporate license fee. All corporations subject to section 12-7-230 are required to do so. *See* S.C.Code Ann. §§ 12-19-20, 12-19-70 (1977 & Supp.1992).

The order of the trial judge is **AFFIRMED.**

---

[5] Further discussion of the remaining requirements of the Commerce Clause is unnecessary. Our Due Process analysis of the benefits conferred upon Geoffrey applies with equal force here and need not be repeated. Moreover, Geoffrey raised no constitutional claim that the challenged tax is not fairly apportioned or discriminates against interstate commerce.

KMART PROPERTIES, INC. v. TAXATION AND REVENUE DEPART. OF NEW MEXICO

Court of Appeals of New Mexico

131 P.3d 27 (N.M. App. 2001)

BOSSON, Chief Judge.

Kmart Properties, Incorporated (KPI), a wholly owned Michigan subsidiary of Kmart Corporation, owns and manages trademarks previously developed by Kmart Corporation. KPI challenges New Mexico's assessment of state income taxes and gross receipts taxes upon royalties paid by Kmart Corporation to KPI. KPI bases its challenge upon the following grounds: (1) New Mexico's assertion of jurisdiction to tax KPI violates the Due Process Clause of the United States Constitution; (2) New Mexico's assessment of each tax against KPI is prohibited by the Commerce Clause of the United States Constitution; (3) New Mexico's tax on KPI's gross receipts is not authorized by state law; (4) the method for apportioning KPI's income for income tax purposes violates state law; and (5) the hearing officer was not independent and impartial, and his decision was not timely as required by state law. In affirming both taxes, we address matters of first impression regarding the constitutional limits imposed on New Mexico in its efforts to tax income and gross receipts in light of the physical-presence standard of *Quill Corp. v. North Dakota,* 504 U.S. 298, 112 S. Ct. 1904, 119 L. Ed. 2d 91 (1992) (Quill).

BACKGROUND

In the fall of 1991 Kmart Corporation created KPI for the purpose of holding title to and managing the trademarks, trade names, and service marks (collectively referred to as the "marks") that Kmart Corporation had developed and used in the United States over the years. Those marks include such well known trade names as "Blue Light Special," and "At Home with Martha Stewart," among many others, as well as the trade name "Kmart" that appears on Kmart stores, signs, products, and employee apparel throughout the United States. When creating KPI, Kmart Corporation followed a plan, developed by Price Waterhouse, entitled "Utilization of an Investment Holding Company to Minimize State and Local Income Taxes." Under this plan, Kmart Corporation infused KPI with assets by transferring ownership of all its domestic marks and their associated goodwill to KPI, in exchange for all of KPI's stock. An independent appraiser estimated that the marks were worth between $2,734,100,000 and $4,101,200,000. Both companies were incorporated in

Michigan, as were their headquarters and principal places of business. KPI rented an office suite located one block from Kmart Corporation's corporate headquarters, where KPI housed a total of five employees who were transferred from Kmart Corporation, including two intellectual property lawyers and support staff.

On October 30, 1991, Kmart Corporation transferred ownership of the marks to KPI, and the two corporations entered into a licensing agreement whereby KPI granted Kmart Corporation the exclusive right to use the marks in the United States and its territories, thereby allowing Kmart Corporation the continued use of the "Kmart" name. In exchange for Kmart Corporation's exclusive right to use the marks, the licensing agreement required Kmart Corporation to make royalty payments to KPI, based on 1.1 percent of Kmart Corporation's gross sales throughout the United States. The licensing agreement was negotiated, drafted, and signed by the parties in Michigan.

The creation of KPI dramatically affected Kmart Corporation's tax liability within New Mexico. New Mexico income tax laws allow Kmart Corporation to take a business deduction for royalty payments made to KPI. With this deduction, Kmart Corporation was able to reduce significantly and, in some years, eliminate altogether its New Mexico income tax liability. Meanwhile, KPI paid state taxes only in Michigan, which does not tax income from royalty payments. Thus, income formerly attributed to Kmart Corporation's operations in New Mexico and taxed in New Mexico was shifted to KPI, a corporation with no formal operations in the state, which paid no state income taxes on that income.

In 1997 an auditor for the New Mexico Taxation and Revenue Department (the Department) inquired about Kmart Corporation's royalty deduction, and requested from Kmart a copy of the licensing agreement. By applying the 1.1 percent royalty rate to the relevant New Mexico sales revenues, the Department determined that, during the tax assessment period, KPI earned royalty income in excess of $2,000,000 per year from conducting business within New Mexico. Using that information, the Department then audited KPI, which resulted in the assessment of income taxes and gross receipts taxes upon KPI. Assessment No. 2134646 assessed corporate income tax in the amount of $758,392, apportioned to reflect the royalty income from February 1991 through January 1996 that KPI derived from Kmart Corporation's operations in New Mexico. Assessment No. 2134647 assessed gross receipts taxes in the amount of $478,099.55 for royalty payments during this same period. Additionally, each assessment included penalties and interest for the failure to pay these taxes in a timely manner. KPI timely filed a written protest of all assessments. *See* NMSA 1978, § 7-1-24(B) (2000).

KPI's protest was heard by a Department hearing officer who affirmed the assessment of income and gross receipts taxes plus interest, but reversed the assessment of a penalty. KPI appealed the hearing officer's decision to this Court. *See* NMSA 1978, § 7-1-25(A) (1989); Rule 12-601 NMRA 2001. The Department did not appeal the hearing officer's decision to eliminate the penalty.

DISCUSSION

This appeal requires us to examine whether the federal constitution prohibits New Mexico taxation of a non-domiciliary company under these circumstances. A state's ability to tax a non-domiciliary company may be limited by the Due Process Clause or the Commerce Clause. *See* U.S. Const. art. I, § 8, cl. 3 & amend. XIV, § 1. In the past, courts analyzed these clauses with little differentiation between the two, in part because they both address a non-domiciliary company's nexus with the taxing state. *See Burger King Corp. v. Rudzewicz,* 471 U.S. 462, 475, 105 S. Ct. 2174, 85 L. Ed. 2d 528 (1985) ('Jurisdiction is proper, however, where the contacts proximately result from actions by the defendant *himself* that create a 'substantial connection' with the forum State."); *cf. Complete Auto Transit, Inc. v. Brady,* 430 U.S. 274, 279, 97 S. Ct. 1076, 51 L. Ed. 2d 326 (1977) (Complete Auto Transit) (holding that a state must demonstrate that the "tax is applied to an activity with a substantial nexus with the taxing State"); *Nat'l Geographic Soc'y v. Cal. Bd. of Equalization, 430 U.S. 551, 558, 97 S. Ct. 1386, 51 L. Ed. 2d 631 (1977)* (same). Historically, courts treated the nexus requirement of Commerce Clause jurisprudence as though it were similar, if not identical, to that found in the *Due Process Clause. See Quill,* 504 U.S. at 325-27 (White, J., concurring in part and dissenting in part); *Nat'l Bellas Hess, Inc. v. Dep't of Revenue,* 386 U.S. 753, 756, 87 S. Ct. 1389, 18 L. Ed. 2d 505 [***32] [*182] (1967) (Bellas Hess) (stating that the "same principles" of minimum contacts guide the state's power to tax under each, after observing that the two clauses share a "similar" test), *overruled on other grounds by Quill, 504* U.S. at 301-02; *Trinova Corp. v. Mich. Dep't of Treasury,* 498 U.S. 358, 373, 111 S. Ct. 818, 112 L. Ed. 2d 884 (1991); *Memphis Natural Gas Co. v. Stone,* 335 U.S. 80, 96-97, 68 S. Ct. 1475, 92 L. Ed. 1832 (1948) (Rutledge, J., concurring).

However, in 1992 while reviewing a state's ability to impose a use tax on an out-of-state mail order company, which had no stores or sales staff in the taxing state, the United States Supreme Court held that the nexus requirements of the two constitutional clauses were distinct. *Quill,* 504 U.S. at 313-14. After stating that "a corporation may have the 'minimum contacts' with a taxing State as required by the Due Process Clause, and yet lack the 'substantial nexus' with that State as required by the Commerce Clause," *id.* at 313, the

Court fashioned a bright-line test to determine the constitutional validity of sales and use taxes under the Commerce Clause, *id.* at 314. To justify a sales and use tax, this bright-line test required a taxpayer's physical presence in the taxing state. *Id.* at 315-17.

There has been a split among state courts regarding whether *Quill's* presence requirement was intended as a broad, Commerce Clause principle, applicable to all state taxes, or whether physical presence was limited to sales and use taxes. *See J.C. Penney Nat'l Bank v. Johnson,* 19 S.W.3d 831, 839 (Tenn. Ct. App. 1999) (requiring physical presence beyond sales and use taxes to satisfy Commerce Clause); *cf. Geoffrey, Inc. v. S.C. Tax Comm'n,* 313 S.C. 15, 437 S.E.2d 13, 18 n.4 (S.C. 1993) (articulating the court's understanding that the physical-presence requirement is limited to sales and use taxes under the Commerce Clause). Additionally, states have grappled with determining what satisfies *Quill*'s physical-presence test for the Commerce Clause, beyond the minimum contacts of due process that are shown when a taxpayer purposefully conducts economic activity within a state. *See, e.g., J.C. Penney Nat'l Bank,* 19 S.W.3d at 840 (holding that the physical presence of 11,000 to 17,000 accounts of the bank's credit cards failed to satisfy the physical-presence requirement of the Commerce Clause under *Quill*).

In this appeal, KPI contends that neither the minimum-contacts requirement of due process nor the substantial nexus and physical-presence requirements of the Commerce Clause are satisfied with respect to either the state's income tax or its gross receipts tax. We discuss, in turn, each constitutional argument as it is applied to each tax assessed against KPI.

Due Process Minimum Contacts Nexus

When a state asserts its jurisdiction to tax, the Due Process Clause "'requires some definite link, some minimum connection, between a state and the person, property or transaction it seeks to tax.'" *Quill,* 504 U.S. at 306 (quoting *Miller Bros. Co. v. Maryland*, 347 U.S. 340, 344-45, 74 S. Ct. 535, 98 L. Ed. 744 (1954)). The fundamental concern of due process is fairness: whether a foreign corporation's contacts with the taxing state are sufficient to put the foreign corporation on notice that the taxing state will exercise power over it. *Quill,* 504 U.S. at 312. Due process does not require that the taxpayer be physically present within the taxing state. *Id.* at 308.

KPI contends that it lacked any connection to New Mexico, and argues that its corporate business was conducted solely within the territorial boundaries of Michigan. KPI emphasizes that the licensing agreement was executed in Michigan, between two Michigan corporations, and was to be performed within Michigan. KPI arranged its corporate structure so that its employees did not leave Michigan. KPI has no tangible property or formal KPI representatives located in New Mexico, or apparently in any state other than Michigan. Accordingly, KPI argues that it does not have the minimum contacts with New Mexico that would justify the imposition of any state tax consistent with the Due Process Clause.

We disagree. KPI takes a narrow view of its licensing agreement with Kmart Corporation that ignores its substance. The licensing agreement ties KPI to New Mexico, and to other states outside of Michigan where Kmart has its stores. The agreement grants to Kmart the "exclusive right, license and privilege to use the Marks in the United States." (Emphasis added.) As consideration for that right, Kmart made quarterly royalty payments to KPI, calculated at 1.1 percent of the gross sales generated by the "Hardlines, Fashions and Reader's Market Divisions" from all "Kmart stores in the United States." The parties have stipulated that, at the time KPI signed the licensing agreement, Kmart owned and operated approximately twenty-two stores in New Mexico. On October 30, 1991, when Kmart transferred ownership of its marks to KPI and KPI licensed its use back to Kmart, those marks continued to be used, much as before, at the same Kmart stores in New Mexico. Certainly KPI, as owner of the marks, took no action to prevent its licensee from using the marks in New Mexico. *See Geoffrey,* 437 S.E.2d at 16 (noting that trademark licensing company had the ability to control its contact with the state by prohibiting the use of its intangible).

KPI allowed Kmart Corporation to use its marks in New Mexico, in exchange for 1.1 percent of a specific revenue stream generated in New Mexico. That revenue gave KPI, as the recipient of a direct pecuniary benefit, a clear stake in New Mexico's consumer market. By allowing its marks to be used in New Mexico to generate income, KPI "purposefully availed itself of the benefits of an economic market in the forum State." *Quill,* 504 U.S. at 307; *see also Burger King Corp.,* 471 U.S. at 476 (due process is satisfied "so long as a commercial actor's efforts are 'purposefully directed' toward residents of another State"). Thus, New Mexico satisfies the traditional due process standard, which is universally used to evaluate whether an out-of-state business has established and maintained minimum contacts within a taxing state.

This holding should come as no surprise to KPI. New Mexico courts have long held that the Due Process Clause permits the state to tax a foreign corporation that allows its intangible trademarks to be used in New Mexico. *See, e.g., Aamco Transmissions, Inc. v. Taxation & Revenue Dep't,* 93 N.M. 389, 392, 600 P.2d 841, 844 (Ct. App. 1979) (holding that gross receipts tax on a franchise fee paid to out-of-state franchiser did not violate due process when trademarks were used in New Mexico); *Am. Dairy Queen Corp. v. Taxation &*

Revenue Dep't, 93 N.M. 743, 746, 605 P.2d 251, 254 (Ct. App. 1979) (same). In a case almost identical to this one, the Supreme Court of South Carolina held that an out-of-state trademark holding company, similar to KPI, was subject to the state's taxing jurisdiction because its parent company, Toys-R-Us, used those trademarks under license in the course of its retail sales business in South Carolina. *See Geoffrey,* 437 S.E.2d at 18. The court specifically held that the tax was consistent with due process because the trademark holding company "purposefully directed its activities toward South Carolina," and because of the "presence of Geoffrey's intangible property in [the] State." *Id.* at 16. Likewise, United States Supreme Court precedent has consistently upheld the taxation of intangibles employed within the taxing state despite due process concerns. *See Int'l Harvester Co. v. Wis. Dep't of Taxation,* 322 U.S. 435, 441, 64 S. Ct. 1060, 88 L. Ed. 1373 (1944); *Wis. v. J.C. Penney Co.,* 311 U.S. 435, 450-52, 61 S. Ct. 246, 85 L. Ed. 267 (1940) (Roberts, J., dissenting); *Curry v. McCanless,* 307 U.S. 357, 365-66, 59 S. Ct. 900, 83 L. Ed. 1339 (1939); *Wheeling Steel Corp. v. Fox,* 298 U.S. 193, 209-11, 56 S. Ct. 773, 80 L. Ed. 1143 (1936).

Accordingly, we hold that KPI has established and maintained sufficient minimum contacts with New Mexico to satisfy all due process concerns. This holding applies equally to New Mexico income tax and its gross receipts tax.

Commerce Clause Substantial Nexus

As we have seen, the Commerce Clause imposes a more demanding standard than that required by due process. In the words of the United States Supreme Court, "Although [we] might suggest that every tax that passes contemporary Commerce Clause analysis is also valid under the Due Process Clause, it does not follow that the converse is as well true: A tax may be consistent with due process and yet unduly burden interstate commerce." *Quill,* 504 U.S. at 313-14 n.7. We turn now to that more exacting standard to determine if either the state income tax or the gross receipts tax unduly burdens interstate commerce.

The framers of the federal constitution expressly reserved to Congress the authority to "regulate Commerce with foreign Nations, and among the several states." U.S. Const. art. I, § 8, cl. 3. In what has become known as the "negative" or "dormant" *Commerce Clause* jurisprudence, the Commerce Clause has been interpreted as implicitly "prohibiting certain state actions that interfere with interstate commerce." *Quill,* 504 U.S. at 309. Under the dormant Commerce Clause, state taxes that fail to meet the four-part test of *Complete Auto Transit,* 430 U.S. at 279, interfere unconstitutionally with interstate commerce. That *Complete Auto Transit* test upholds a state tax as long as it "'[1] is applied to an activity with a substantial nexus with the taxing State, [2] is fairly apportioned, [3] does not discriminate against interstate commerce, and [4] is fairly related to the services provided by the State.'" *Quill,* 504 U.S. at 311 (quoting *Complete Auto Transit*, 430 U.S. at 279). The *Complete Auto Transit* analysis does not require physical presence in the taxing state. *Quill,* with its physical-presence standard for sales and use taxes, was decided after the Court adopted the four-part Commerce Clause test outlined in *Complete Auto Transit.* As an initial matter, we must determine whether *Quill*'s physical-presence component of the Commerce Clause analysis is limited to the sales and use taxes that were at issue in *Quill,* or whether it applies to income taxes as well.

Quill's Physical-Presence Requirement Does Not Apply to the State Income Tax

In *Quill,* 504 U.S. at 311, the Supreme Court affirmed the Commerce Clause holding of *Bellas Hess,* 386 U.S. at 753-60, a twenty-five-year-old opinion at the time, which held that an Illinois sales and use tax imposed upon an out-of-state mail-order company that lacked physical presence in the taxing state violated both the Due Process Clause and the Commerce Clause. *Quill* involved an interstate mail-order business similar to *Bellas Hess* whose only nexus to the taxing state was by way of interstate mails or common carrier. *Quill,* 504 U.S. at 302. Whereas both *Quill* and *Bellas Hess* involved sales and use taxes, neither case involved a state income tax.

In considering the scope of *Quill,* we turn first to the text of the opinion. The Supreme Court repeatedly emphasized a narrow focus upon sales and use taxes and the need to retain a bright-line test of physical presence for the benefit of an interstate mail-order industry that had relied upon such a test for sales and use taxes. *Quill,* 504 U.S. at 315-17. The Court stated,

> *Bellas Hess* . . . created a safe harbor for vendors "whose only connection with customers in the [taxing] State is by common carrier or the United States mail." Under *Bellas Hess*, such vendors are free from state-imposed duties to collect sales and use taxes. . . . Such a rule firmly establishes the boundaries of legitimate state authority to impose a duty to collect sales and use taxes and reduces litigation concerning those taxes. . . . Moreover, a bright-line rule in the area of sales and use taxes also encourages settled expectations and, in doing so, fosters investment by businesses and individuals. . . . We have never intimated in our review of sales or use taxes that *Bellas Hess* was unsound.

Id. (footnotes omitted).

In that same text, the Court leaves the clear impression that it was not applying the *Bellas Hess* physical-presence requirement to any other taxes. The Court acknowledged that it had "not, in our review of other types of taxes, articulated the same physical-presence requirement that *Bellas Hess* established for sales and use taxes." *Quill,* 504 U.S. at 314. The Court also stated,

> Although in our cases subsequent to *Bellas Hess* and concerning other types of taxes[,] we have not adopted a similar bright-line, physical-presence requirement, our reasoning in those cases does not compel that we now reject the rule that *Bellas Hess* established in the area of sales and use taxes. To the contrary, the continuing value of a bright-line rule in this area [of sales and use taxes] and the doctrine and principles of *stare decisis* indicate that the *Bellas Hess* rule remains good law.

Quill, 504 U.S. at 317. While acknowledging that "contemporary Commerce Clause jurisprudence might not dictate the same result were the issue to arise for the first time today," *Quill,* 504 U.S. at 311, the Court, nonetheless, retained the physical-presence test for sales and use taxes to establish stability for a particular industry faced with the burdens of a particular kind of tax. *See id.* at 317 ("The *Bellas Hess* rule has engendered substantial reliance and . . . therefore counsels adherence to settled precedent.").

It is also evident from *Quill* that a sales and use tax can impose a special burden on interstate commerce beyond just the payment of money. Unlike an income tax, a sales and use tax can make the taxpayer an agent of the state, obligated to collect the tax from the consumer at the point of sale and then pay it over to the taxing entity. Whereas, a state income tax is usually paid only once a year, to one taxing jurisdiction and at one rate, a sales and use tax can be due periodically to more than one taxing jurisdiction within a state and at varying rates. *See id.* at 313 n.6. Thus, collecting and paying a sales and use tax can impose additional burdens on commerce that the Supreme Court has repeatedly identified in prior opinions. *See, e.g., Nat'l Geographic Soc'y,* 430 U.S. at 558; *Bellas Hess,* 386 U.S. at 759-60; *Scripto, Inc. v. Carson,* 362 U.S. 207, 211, 80 S. Ct. 619, 4 L. Ed. 2d 660 (1960).

New Mexico gross receipts tax is similar in structure to the sales and use tax at issue in *Quill.* New Mexico income tax is not. Considering this difference and the Supreme Court's narrow focus on the sales and use tax in *Quill,* we believe that *Quill*'s physical-presence requirement was intended to apply to sales and use taxes only; it was not intended to apply to other taxes such as a state income tax. In coming to this conclusion, we join other state courts that have applied an identical rationale to uphold the constitutionality of other state taxes in a similar context. *See Geoffrey,* 437 S.E.2d at 18 (upholding the constitutionality of an income tax on royalty payments to a wholly-owned, out-of-state trademark holding company on the basis that, even after *Quill*, "the taxpayer need not have a tangible, physical presence in a state for income to be taxable there"); *Gen. Motors Corp. v. City of Seattle,* 107 Wn. App. 42, 25 P.3d 1022, 1028 (Wash. Ct. App. 2001) (declining "to extend [*Quill*'s] physical presence requirement in the context of [Seattle's business and occupation tax]"); *see also Borden Chems. & Plastics, L.P. v. Zehnder,* 312 Ill. App. 3d 35, 726 N.E.2d 73, 80, 244 Ill. Dec. 477 (Ill. App. Ct. 2000) ("The *Quill* court merely carved out a narrow exception in the area of use tax collection duties. Moreover, the court's decision was based upon considerations that have no bearing upon the facts of this case."); *cf. J.C. Penney Nat'l Bank,* 19 S.W.3d at 839 ("Both *Bellas Hess* and *Quill* are clear in their holding that in the context of a use tax, physical presence is required in order to satisfy the substantial nexus requirement of *Complete Auto.*"). We also observe that applying a physical-presence requirement to state income taxes would be a marked departure from established precedent. *See, e.g., New York ex rel. Whitney v. Graves,* 299 U.S. 366, 372, 57 S. Ct. 237, 81 L. Ed. 285 (1937); *Int'l Harvester Co.,* 322 U.S. at 441-42. *See generally* Jerome R. Hellerstein & Walter Hellerstein, *State Taxation: Constitutional Limitations and Corporate Income and Franchise Taxes* P6.08 (3d ed. 1907-2000) (stating a corporation that regularly exploits state markets should be subject to its state income tax whether or not it is physically present); Michael T. Fatale, *State Tax Jurisdiction and the Mythical "Physical Presence" Constitutional Standard,* 54 Tax Law. 105, 131 ("In general, the state court cases determine that, when a taxpayer has income derived from a state's economic market, the taxpayer is subject to that state's income tax.").

Accordingly, we conclude that the Commerce Clause analysis of New Mexico income tax is controlled, not by *Quill*'s physical presence, but by the overarching substantial nexus test announced in *Complete Auto Transit.* Although *Quill* did establish that "substantial nexus" under *Complete Auto Transit* has more than the minimum contacts required of due process, *Quill, 504 U.S. at 313,* we need not quantify that difference here. In whatever manner that difference may be measured, the use of KPI's marks within New Mexico's economic market, for the purpose of generating substantial income for KPI, establishes a sufficient nexus between that income and the legitimate interests of the state and justifies the imposition of a state income tax. *See Complete Auto Transit, 430 U.S. at 279*; *Geoffrey, 437 S.E.2d at 18.* Accordingly, we hold that the Department's assessment of state income tax on KPI's royalty revenues is not an undue burden on interstate commerce within the meaning of the United States Constitution.

The Gross Receipts Tax Does Not Unduly Burden Interstate Commerce Where There Is Physical Presence or Its Functional Equivalent

The Department acknowledges that KPI does not have any of its own employees, operations, offices, or facilities physically located within New Mexico. Thus, this case lacks the usual indicia of physical presence described in *Quill.* If the Department is to satisfy the *Quill* standard, it must demonstrate something special about the nature of trademarks and KPI's relationship with Kmart Corporation within New Mexico that constitutes physical presence or its functional equivalent. Any such showing must also satisfy *Quill*'s fundamental concern of avoiding an undue burden on interstate commerce. We also keep in mind the statutory presumption that the New Mexico Legislature intends "to extend the reach of the [Gross Receipts and Compensating Tax] Act to its constitutional limits." *Sonic Indus., Inc. v. State,* 2000 NMCA 87, P14, 129 N.M. 657, 11 P.3d 1219, *cert. granted*, 129 N.M. 519, 10 P.3d 843 (2000) (Sonic).

We begin by recognizing that KPI, not Kmart Corporation, is the true owner of all of KPI's domestic marks and the goodwill represented by them, which includes the trademark name "Kmart." Ownership of those marks brings with it the complexities of trademark law and one of its abiding principles: that a trademark, and its goodwill, are inseparable property rights that, as a practical matter, are bound to the business that generates the goodwill. "Unlike patents or copyrights, trademarks are not separate property rights. They are integral and inseparable elements of the goodwill of the business or services to which they pertain." *Visa, U.S.A., Inc. v. Birmingham Trust Nat'l Bank,* 696 F.2d 1371, 1375 (Fed. Cir. 1982). A trade name or mark "is merely a symbol of goodwill; it has no independent significance apart from the goodwill it symbolizes." *Marshak v. Green,* 746 F.2d 927, 929 (2d Cir. 1984). "Good will and its trademark symbol are as inseparable as Siamese Twins who cannot be separated without death to both." 2 J. Thomas McCarthy, *McCarthy on Trademarks and Unfair Competition* § 18:2, at 18-5 (4th ed. 2001).

When a company acquires trademarks and goodwill, the essence of what it obtains "is the right to inform the public that it is in possession of the special experience and skill symbolized by the name of the original concern, and of the sole authority to market its products." *Levitt Corp. v. Levitt,* 593 F.2d 463, 468 (2d Cir. 1979). The value of what it obtains is tied to the underlying business that generates the goodwill associated with the trademarks. "If there is no business and no good will, a trademark symbolizes nothing." McCarthy, *supra*, § 18:2, at 18-5 to 18-6. Goodwill is bound to the business with which it is associated, and "can no more be separated from a business than reputation from a person." *Id. at 18-7* (citing *Webster Investors, Inc. v. Comm'r,* 291 F.2d 192 (2d Cir. 1961)). *See generally* Jerome Gilson, *Trademark Protection and Practice* § 1.03[7][b] (2001) ("Since there can be no goodwill for the trademark to symbolize without such a going business and corresponding use of the trademark, trademark rights in the United States, at least, are wholly dependent upon actual use.").

When Kmart Corporation created KPI and transferred ownership of the "Kmart" name, it legally separated the trademark and its goodwill from the actual business upon which that goodwill depends. As a practical matter, KPI and Kmart Corporation then became, to paraphrase McCarthy, corporate "Siamese Twins," inextricably bound to each other. McCarthy, *supra*, § 18:2, at 18-5. For KPI, the trademark right to inform the public that they would have a "Kmart shopping experience" would be meaningless without access to Kmart retail outlets that actually provide that experience. Kmart Corporation, in turn, needed continued access to the trademark "Kmart" name so that it could differentiate its retail outlets from other general merchandising stores.

Thus, for the mutual benefit of both companies, Kmart Corporation's retail outlets in New Mexico continued to use the KPI-owned, trademark name, "Kmart," on the storefront. According to the record below, KPI's trademark on the storefront told New Mexico citizens that they would have a "Kmart shopping experience" at that store. Upon entering a Kmart store, a New Mexico consumer will find Kmart Corporation employees bearing the trademark "Kmart" name on their store uniforms. The use of the "Kmart" name has informed customers that they will find products and services associated only with the Kmart name, such as the "Blue Light Special" and "At Home with Martha Stewart," a shopping experience that, because of KPI's marks, could only happen within the confines of a "Kmart" store.

The use of KPI's marks in this fashion has allowed Kmart Corporation to personify the goodwill owned by KPI to facilitate merchandise sales in New Mexico. In this manner, Kmart employees, wearing KPI's trademarks and working at stores with KPI's trademark on the marquee, have acted to represent and promote the goodwill of KPI's marks to the New Mexico consuming public. The value of that goodwill in New Mexico depended, at least to some extent, on how well or how poorly those employees and products performed in New Mexico. Kmart customers, of course, have had no way of knowing that they were dealing with representatives of KPI's goodwill; apparently few people were actually aware that KPI, and not Kmart Corporation, owned the marks and associated goodwill. But, nonetheless, the use of those marks in New Mexico by Kmart Corporation employees promoted the good business reputation associated with KPI's property.

The licensing agreement further demonstrates that Kmart Corporation represented KPI's goodwill in New Mexico by requiring Kmart employees, at least in some form, to act on behalf of KPI's interests. Under the licensing agreement, Kmart Corporation's use of the "Kmart" name was to be "consistent with the high standards of quality and excellence established over the years." The licensing agreement obligated Kmart Corporation to refrain from activities that would "injure or diminish the image or reputation" of KPI's goodwill. More to the point, to ensure that Kmart Corporation would "maintain and enhance the goodwill and image of quality associated by the public with the Marks," Kmart Corporation could only use the "Kmart" name on "establishments maintaining a good business reputation." Kmart Corporation could not use the trademark name in association with "any illegal, vulgar, obscene, immoral, unsavory or offensive activities." Thus, this licensing agreement empowered KPI to dictate a standard of conduct that governed Kmart's employees in New Mexico, so that Kmart stores could maintain a good business reputation in the local community.

The Department argues that the use of Kmart Corporation stores and employees in New Mexico, to represent KPI's goodwill, gives KPI a "physical presence" in New Mexico under the analysis of *Tyler Pipe Industries, Inc. v. Washington Department of Revenue,* 483 U.S. 232, 107 S. Ct. 2810, 97 L. Ed. 2d 199 (1987) (Tyler Pipe) and *Scripto,* 362 U.S. at 211. In each of these cases, the United States Supreme Court upheld the constitutionality, under the Commerce Clause, of state sales or use taxes imposed on out-of-state companies that did business in the taxing state *solely* through independent representatives. These representatives were local people who were *not* employees or agents of the taxpayer. In each case, the out-of-state taxpayers had *none* of their own employees or facilities in the taxing state. The Supreme Court considered sufficient, for Commerce Clause purposes, the physical presence of local jobbers, wholesalers, and independent contractors who assumed the job of promoting or aiding the taxpayers' interests within the taxing state. *See Tyler Pipe,* 483 U.S. at 251 (holding that "the activities of Tyler's sales representatives adequately support the State's jurisdiction to impose its wholesale tax"); *Scripto,* 362 U.S. at 209 (finding that each independent sales representative was engaged as "a representative of 'Scripto'").

Importantly, the Supreme Court regarded the label or technical legal status of the representative within the taxing state as "without constitutional significance." *Scripto,* 362 U.S. at 211. What mattered was a physical presence, within the taxing state, of someone acting on the company's behalf. Even though *Scripto* and *Tyler Pipe* preceded *Quill*, the Supreme Court in *Quill* reconfirmed that the presence of independent representatives within the taxing state satisfies the physical-presence test. *Quill,* 504 U.S. at 314 (observing that cases such as *Tyler Pipe* "involved taxpayers who had a physical presence in the taxing State" through local independent representatives).

Tyler Pipe and *Scripto* provide a close analogy for purposes of analyzing Commerce Clause concerns and physical presence. As the Department argues, the record below supports a conclusion that Kmart Corporation used its stores and employees in New Mexico as local representatives of KPI's goodwill, under a licensing agreement with KPI, to promote both its own sales and the goodwill of KPI's marks. However, there is a difference. Unlike *Tyler Pipe* and *Scripto*, KPI is not engaged in the retail sales of a product. Its sole function is to hold title to marks and associated goodwill that are under license to Kmart Corporation. The question is whether this distinction, with respect to the kind of business and the nature of the intangible property interests being promoted, requires any different result. We think not. Being intangible property, a trademark can only have "physical presence," beyond the state of its creation, in those locales where it is put to tangible use. *See Geoffrey,* 437 S.E.2d at 17-18. When Kmart Corporation uses KPI's marks in a highly visible and commercially purposeful fashion in New Mexico, it logically follows that those marks are physically present during their period of use. Otherwise, trademarks could never be physically present anywhere other than where the taxpayer designates for its own tax purposes. *See id.* (rejecting similarly restrictive argument regarding use of intangible trademarks in taxing state). The Constitution does not impose such a taxpayer-driven restriction on New Mexico's taxing policy. *See Sonic,* 2000 NMCA 87, P13, 129 N.M. 657, 11 P.3d 1219; *Am. Dairy Queen Corp.,* 93 N.M. at 746, 605 P.2d at 254.

KPI counters that, if we attribute physical presence for Commerce Clause purposes, based *solely* on the tangible manifestation of KPI's marks in New Mexico, then the State's taxing jurisdiction would become boundless. KPI poses a hypothetical dilemma that any out-of-state third-party, such as a national book author or a holding company for the trademarks of an international sports or entertainment personality, would have to pay gross receipts tax to New Mexico simply for allowing its trademark to appear on products held for sale on Kmart's shelves. Under that hypothetical, New Mexico would be allowed to extend its reach to tax the out-of-state author for each book sold and the international sports star for each pair of sports paraphernalia sold in a Kmart store without any other connection to this state. KPI contends that this would be gross overreaching on the state's part without precedent anywhere in the country.

We agree that such a result would be unprecedented. However, we disagree that our opinion opens the door to any such hypothetical tax. We have no indication on this record that New Mexico intends to impose its gross receipts tax upon national book authors or sports celebrities merely because merchandise bearing their trademark names is sold in New Mexico stores. We emphasize that we do not decide such a question in the abstract.

The case before us presents far more than just merchandise bearing out-of-state trademarks for sale in New Mexico stores. An extensive apparatus of Kmart stores, signs, and employees are also physically present in New Mexico to work on behalf of KPI's goodwill and associated interests. That apparatus represents KPI's property interests in New Mexico, pursuant to a licensing agreement that requires Kmart Corporation to act on KPI's behalf.

Considering the *Quill* standard in the context of this case, we conclude that the combination of Kmart Corporation's activities in New Mexico, together with the tangible presence of KPI's marks, constitutes the functional equivalent of physical presence as afforded by the independent representatives in *Scripto* and *Tyler Pipe*. As the Supreme Court implicitly acknowledges in the *Quill* opinion, by citing *Scripto* in the context of its physical presence discussion, an independent representative present in the taxing state satisfies the physical presence test and Commerce Clause concerns. *Quill,* 504 U.S. at 314. Here, as in *Tyler Pipe*, Kmart employees were instrumental in "'maintaining and improving the name recognition, market share, goodwill, and individual customer relations'" associated with valuable property owned by KPI. *Tyler Pipe,* 483 U.S. at 249.

We also note that the gross receipts tax in this instance appears to be less of a burden on interstate commerce than the use tax in *Quill*. Because KPI is not engaged in retail sales, it does not have to collect a separate tax from each consumer and then pay it at varying rates according to each local governmental entity in which it is present. As we have previously noted, KPI pays one tax, at a uniform rate, to a single entity based solely on the royalty payment from Kmart Corporation to KPI. This is significantly different from the burden threatened in *Quill* upon the interstate mail-order industry.

KPI also contends that Kmart Corporation cannot be a representative of KPI because Kmart Corporation sells general merchandise, whereas KPI sells only trademarks. Yet, the licensing agreement undercuts this claim. Having granted Kmart Corporation "the exclusive right, license and privilege to use the Marks in the United States," KPI no longer has the capacity to sell its trademarks in the United States. KPI's business purpose, under the terms of the licensing agreement, is to pursue the "further protection and enhancement of its uniquely valuable trademarks and service marks." In other words, KPI is in the business of protecting the goodwill and reputation of the "Kmart" name. This includes ensuring that New Mexico's consumers can continue to rely on the quality that the "Kmart" name has come to represent. *See Dawn Donut Co. v. Hart's Food Stores, Inc.,* 267 F.2d 358, 367 (2d Cir. 1959).

For purposes of clarity, we wish to emphasize that our holding today does *not* make Kmart Corporation or any of its employees the agents of KPI, and it does *not* purport to establish a legal relationship of agency, respondeat superior, or premises liability. *See Oberlin v. Marlin Am. Corp.*, 596 F.2d 1322, 1327 (7th Cir. 1979). Nothing in this opinion should imply vicarious liability in KPI for the tortious acts of Kmart Corporation and its personnel. *See Ciup v. Chevron U.S.A., Inc.*, 1996 NMSC 62, P8, 122 N.M. 537, 928 P.2d 263. As the Supreme Court emphasized in *Scripto*, representatives for purposes of establishing Commerce Clause physical presence do not need legal authority to bind the out-of-state taxpayer, contractually or otherwise. *Scripto,* 362 U.S. at 209 (noting that orders collected by the sales representatives were sent "directly to the Atlanta office for acceptance or refusal").

* * *

Apportionment of KPI's Income for Income Tax Purposes Based on Income Generated From Use of the Marks in New Mexico Complies With State Law

KPI files an additional protest against the state income tax on the ground that the tax is not properly apportioned between this state and Michigan as provided by New Mexico law. KPI relies on the Uniform Division of Income for Tax Purposes Act (UDITPA), NMSA 1978, §§ 7-4-1 to -21 (1965, as amended through 2001), a widely-used, uniform system of apportioning and allocating the income of taxpayers who operate in multiple states. In an effort at fair and uniform allocation of taxable income among the states, UDITPA apportions business income among the states based upon the amount and location of three factors regarding the taxpayer's business: real and tangible personal property, employee payroll, and sales. *See* §§ 7-4-10, -11, -14, -16.

It is undisputed that KPI has no real or tangible personal property in New Mexico nor any employees, and it is also settled that KPI never consummated any of its own sales in New Mexico. Therefore, KPI argues that application of the UDITPA formula should result in none of its income being subject to tax in New Mexico and all of its income subject to tax in Michigan. In short, KPI charges that the State of New Mexico is breaking faith with a kind of national compact by imposing its income tax on revenues that should rightly be taxed elsewhere.

The Department responds by citing to Section 7-4-19, a section of UDITPA [Ed.: section 18] that allows New Mexico, as with other states, to modify an apportionment formula that "does not fairly represent the extent of the taxpayer's business activity in this state." That section reads,

> 7-4-19 Equitable adjustment of standard allocation or apportionment.
>
> If the allocation and apportionment provisions of [UDITPA] do not fairly represent the extent of the taxpayer's business activity in this state, the taxpayer may petition for, or the department may require, in respect to all or any part of the taxpayer's business activity, if reasonable:
>
> A. separate accounting;
> B. the exclusion of any one or more of the factors;
> C. the inclusion of one or more additional factors which will fairly represent the taxpayer's business activity in this state; or
> D. the employment of any other method to effectuate an equitable allocation and apportionment of the taxpayer's income.

The Department specifically relied upon Section 7-4-19 to fashion a modified formula that would fairly represent the extent of KPI's "business activity" in New Mexico. The Department applied the sales factor, finding that KPI had a business presence in New Mexico directly related to Kmart's use of KPI's marks and goodwill to produce a revenue stream of sales from New Mexico's markets that translated into royalties paid to KPI. However, the Department excluded the property and payroll factors from the formula pursuant to Section 7-4-19(B), because those factors were de minimis compared to the sales factor in both amount and significance in terms of KPI's business activity. The Department concluded that property and payroll played little or no role in how KPI generated its income, and that inclusion of those factors would distort the economic reality of KPI's business presence.

KPI objects that Section 7-4-19 should be used only under unusual circumstances, and that the Department is simply changing the rules to unfairly increase its revenues. KPI also cites out-of-state case law for the universally accepted propositions that UDITPA, Section 7-4-19, should be used sparingly and that the Department has a heavy burden of persuasion to justify any modification of the UDITPA formula. *See Roger Dean Enters., Inc. v. Dep't of Revenue,* 387 So.2d 358, 363 (Fla. 1980); *Donald M. Drake Co. v. Dep't of Revenue,* 263 Ore. 26, 500 P.2d 1041, 1044 (Or. 1972) (in banc).

We agree that, by definition, modification of the standard formula should be the exception, not the rule. However, we are also aware that the Department did establish a case below to carry its burden in support of exceptional circumstances. The Department presented evidence sufficient to persuade the hearing officer that use of the standard formula in this instance "distorts" the economic reality of KPI's income. The hearing officer concluded that, "in this case, the Department has met its burden of proving that the three-factor formula does not fairly represent KPI's business activity in the state." Although there was evidence on both sides of the proposition, the hearing officer's conclusion finds support in the evidentiary record. It also has support in case law and treatise materials. *See, e.g., Twentieth Century-Fox Film Corp. v. Dep't of Revenue,* 299 Ore. 220, 700 P.2d 1035, 1043 (Or. 1985) (in banc) (describing criteria for adjustment of UDITPA formula); Hellerstein, *supra,* P9.09[4], at 9-44 (suggesting that attribution of income to the place where the intangible asset is being exploited would be "likely to reflect, realistically and equitably, the legitimate competing claims of the states involved in the taxation of income").

The hearing officer's determination is also supported by a Department regulation, adopted in 1974 pursuant to Section 7-4-19, providing that where the income producing activity producing business income from intangibles can be readily identified, that income should be sourced to that state and not the state with the greatest cost of production. *See* 3 NMAC 5.19.11(A)(3). Application of that regulation and Section 7-4-19 to the specific circumstance of taxing KPI's royalties generated in New Mexico is supported, in this case, by an amicus curiae brief from the Multistate Tax Commission, "the organization primarily responsible for promoting uniformity of taxation in member states." *Twentieth Century-Fox Film Corp.,* 700 P.2d at 1041. Finally, even with the adjusted formula, it bears repetition that New Mexico is only taxing revenues (royalties) from sales attributable to New Mexico; the Department is not trying to tax income generated beyond its borders. We conclude that the Department sustained its burden to justify a modified formula under Section 7-4-19.

* * *

CONCLUSION

We affirm the decision and order of the hearing officer upholding the taxes imposed.

IT IS SO ORDERED.

SYMS CORP. v. COMMISSIONER OF REVENUE

Supreme Judicial Court of Massachusetts

765 N.E.2d 758 (Mass. 2002)

CORDY, J.

Syms Corp. (Syms) appeals from a decision of the Appellate Tax Board (board) affirming the refusal by the Commissioner of Revenue (commissioner) to abate $291,571 in corporate excise taxes assessed against it for the tax years 1986, 1987, 1989, 1990, and 1991. The assessments resulted from the commissioner's disallowance of deductions Syms had taken for royalty payments it had made to its wholly owned subsidiary, SYL, Inc. (SYL). The royalties were paid to SYL for the use of certain trade names, trademarks, and service marks (marks), which Syms had transferred to SYL in December, 1986.

After an evidentiary hearing, the board found that Syms had not sustained its burden of establishing its entitlement to an abatement, and that the commissioner had properly disallowed the deductions on three alternative grounds: (1) the transfer and leaseback of the marks was a sham and could be disregarded under the "sham transaction doctrine";[1] (2) the royalty payments were not deductible as ordinary and necessary business expenses where there was no valid business purpose justifying the expense and SYL added little or no value to the marks; and (3) G. L. c. 63, § 39A, permitted the commissioner to eliminate the royalty payments from the calculation of net income because they were made between affiliated corporations and were in excess of fair value.

On appeal, Syms claims that the board's findings are not supported by the record, that G. L. c. 63, § 39A, only permits the elimination of payments between subsidiaries and not from a parent corporation to its subsidiary, and that the disallowance of the deductions violates the due process and commerce clauses of the United States Constitution. Syms also challenges the board's refusal to abate the penalties assessed against it by the commissioner. We conclude that the board's findings are supported by substantial evidence in the record and that the disallowances do not violate the United States Constitution. We need not and therefore do not reach the question of the applicability of G. L. c. 63, § 39A, to the payments in this case.

---

[1] A "sham transaction" in this context means a transaction that in fact occurred in an effort to exploit a feature of the tax laws, not a transaction that did not occur, or did not occur as reported.

1. *Background.* Syms is a New Jersey corporation engaged in "off-price" retailing, which is the retail sale of brand name clothing at prices lower than those in department stores. It was founded in 1959 by Sy Syms. It operates two stores in the Commonwealth and therefore is subject to Massachusetts corporate excise tax.

During the years in question, Sy Syms was the chairman of the board of directors and the dominant shareholder, owning fifty-six per cent of the stock and controlling the votes for another twenty-four per cent held in trust for family members. His daughter, Marcy Syms, was the president of the company.

Syms used several marks in its business, including the "Syms" name, a "multiple 'S' logo" that it placed on its own brands of clothing, and the slogan, "An Educated Consumer is Our Best Customer." Prior to December, 1986, Syms owned these marks.

The idea of a trademark holding subsidiary was first brought to the attention of Syms in early 1986 by Irv Yacht, a consultant with a company called Coventry Financial Corporation. Yacht broached this idea in a letter to Syms's chief financial officer, Richard Diamond, in which he promised that he "had a method of saving state taxes." Immediately after their first meeting in the spring of 1986, Yacht and Diamond signed an agreement, which recited that Coventry "has developed a program . . . for reducing [Syms's] income taxes by reorganizing the business activities of [Syms] in certain areas." Yacht's proposal was for Syms to form a Delaware subsidiary, transfer the marks to that subsidiary, and then execute a license agreement under which Syms would continue to use the marks as it had before the transfer (Coventry plan).

Under the license agreement, Syms would pay a large royalty to the subsidiary, thereby generating a deduction for Syms on its State excise taxes. The subsidiary, however, would not pay any State tax on the royalty income because, under Delaware law, corporations that hold intangible assets are exempt from income tax. Syms was to pay Coventry twenty-five percent of the tax savings realized in the first year, with a declining percentage for the next four years.

In considering whether to engage in the Coventry plan, Syms recognized the risk of a tax audit. In a memorandum to Sy Syms, Diamond wrote, "There have been cases when corporations attempted to do this and did not do it properly and thus had problems in various states. It is everyone[']s feeling that New York is the most sophisticated state in terms of tax audits and most other states will not even realize the impact of the transactions." As a precaution, Syms held part of Coventry's compensation in escrow in case the hoped-for tax savings were disallowed in an audit.

Syms also consulted its trademark attorneys about risks attendant to the transfer of the marks under trademark law, and was advised that the transfer would be valid as a matter of trademark law because "Syms Corp. will own and control the subsidiary. Whether or not the subsidiary is an active entity, its assets (consisting of the trademarks) belong to the parent company. Syms Corp. will, in fact, continue to stand behind the goods and services identified by these marks."

Syms decided to proceed with the Coventry plan and SYL was incorporated in Delaware on December 4, 1986, as Syms's wholly owned trademark holding company. Its board of directors and officers were Sy Syms, Marcy Syms, Richard Diamond, and Edward Jones, a partner in a Delaware accounting firm. SYL and Syms executed a license agreement on December 18, 1986. SYL, acting as the owner of the marks, granted to Syms the right to use the marks nationally for a royalty equal to four per cent of Syms's annual net sales. The marks were transferred from Syms to SYL the next day, December 19, 1986.

For the calendar year 1986, Syms paid SYL a royalty for the marks that constituted four percent of its annual net sales from October 1, 1986, until the end of December. The 1986 royalty was approximately $2.8 million. In subsequent years, the royalty amount increased from nearly $10 million in 1987 to $12.7 million in 1991. In each of these years SYL received one annual royalty payment from Syms, which it held in Delaware for a few weeks before paying it back to Syms, with interest (minus expenses) as a tax-free dividend. SYL's only income came from Syms's annual royalty payments, and its expenses amounted to approximately one-tenth of one percent of its income.

SYL's corporate "office" consisted of an address rented from Jones's Delaware accounting firm, for an annual fee of $1,200. The accounting firm provided this same service to "a couple of hundred" other corporations that used Delaware subsidiary corporations to hold their intangible assets. Jones was not only a partner of the accounting firm, he was SYL's only employee, serving in a part-time capacity for which he was paid $1,200 per year.

The business operations of Syms did not change after the transfer and license-back of the marks. All of the work necessary to maintain and protect the marks continued to be done by the same New York City trademark law firm that had previously performed those services, and Syms (not SYL) continued to pay all the expenses attendant thereto. All efforts to maintain the good will and thus to preserve the value of the marks were undertaken by Syms, and all advertising using the marks was controlled and paid for by Syms or by a wholly owned Syms subsidiary formed solely to do advertising. The choice of which products would be sold under the marks, as well as the quality control of those products, remained the responsibility of the same persons who had done that work before the transfer – Sy Syms himself, and the Syms staff of buyers.

2. *Sham transaction.* Syms does not contest the validity of the "sham transaction doctrine" and the commissioner's authority under that doctrine to disregard, for taxing purposes, transactions that have no economic substance or business purpose other than tax avoidance. It is a doctrine long established in State and Federal tax jurisprudence dating back to the seminal case of *Gregory v. Helvering*, 293 U.S. 465, 79 L. Ed. 596, 55 S. Ct. 266 (1935). It works to prevent taxpayers from claiming the tax benefits of transactions that, although within the language of the tax code, are not the type of transactions the law intended to favor with the benefit. *Horn v. Commissioner of Internal Revenue*, 296 U.S. App. D.C. 358, 968 F.2d 1229, 1236-1237 (D.C. Cir. 1992). "Usually, transactions that are invalidated by the doctrine are those motivated by nothing other than the taxpayer's desire to secure the attached tax benefit," and are structured to completely avoid economic risk. *Id.* at 1236.

Syms contends that the doctrine does not apply in this case because it had business purposes, other than tax avoidance, for incorporating SYL and then transferring to it and licensing back the marks which it previously owned. It complains that the board ignored the "uncontroverted" evidence of these other business purposes, and based its decision on the record in another case litigated shortly after this one,[9] and on an across-the-board policy of the "disallowance of deductions for all related trademark protection companies."

The question whether or not a transaction is a sham for purposes of the application of the doctrine is, of necessity, primarily a factual one, on which the taxpayer bears the burden of proof in the abatement process. *Koch v. Commissioner of Revenue*, 416 Mass. 540, 556, 624 N.E.2d 91 (1993).

The board's decision is final as to findings of fact. G. L. c. 58A, § 13. See *Commissioner of Corps. & Taxation v. J.G. McCrory Co.*, 280 Mass. 273, 278, 182 N.E. 481 (1932). This means that the board's "findings have the same force and effect as the verdict of a jury or the finding of a judge sitting without a jury in an action at law or the finding of a judge or master in equity upon unreported evidence." *Id.* Accordingly, our review of the board's factual

---

[9] *Sherwin-Williams Co. vs. Commissioner of Revenue*, Appellate Tax Board No. F233560 (SJC-08516). [Ed.: The appellate decision in *Sherwin-Williams Co.* is included in this Chapter's materials].

findings is limited to whether, as a matter of law, the evidence is sufficient to support them. *Olympia & York State St. Co.* v. *Assessors of Boston*, 428 Mass. 236, 240, 700 N.E.2d 533 (1998). "Our review of the sufficiency of the evidence is limited to 'whether a contrary conclusion is not merely a possible but a necessary inference from the findings.'" *Id.*, quoting *Kennametal, Inc. v. Commissioner of Revenue*, 426 Mass. 39, 43, 686 N.E.2d 436 (1997), cert. denied, 523 U.S. 1059 (1998). If supported by sufficient evidence, we will not reverse a decision of the board unless it is based on an incorrect application of the law. See *Koch v. Commissioner of Revenue, supra* at 555.

The board found that the transfer and license back transaction had no practical economic effect on Syms other than the creation of tax benefits, and that tax avoidance was the clear motivating factor and its only business purpose.[11] See *Casebeer v. Commissioner of Internal Revenue*, 909 F.2d 1360, 1365 (9th Cir. 1990) (taxpayer must show both that transaction was supported by business purpose other than tax avoidance and had economic substance other than creation of tax benefit); *James v. Commissioner of Internal Revenue*, 899 F.2d 905, 908-909 (10th Cir. 1990) (consideration of business purpose and economic substance are factors in determining whether transaction had any practical effect other than creation of income tax losses). The board rejected the other business purposes claimed by Syms during the hearing, finding them to be "illusory, not supported by the evidence, or contrary to the weight of the evidence."[12]

Our review of the record of the proceedings before the board confirms that it rejected the purported business purposes not by ignoring "strong, uncontested, evidence" of their

---

[11] The board appropriately looked beyond the issue whether SYL was a validly constituted separate corporate entity and focused on whether the transfer and license-back transaction was a sham.

[12] Syms proffered, and the board rejected, almost a dozen nontax business purposes to support its claim that the transfer and license-back was not intended solely to avoid taxation. For example: Syms's assertion that the transfer would protect the marks from claims of Syms's creditors was rejected by the board, because creditors could reach assets of Syms's wholly owned subsidiary; Syms's claim that the transfer would protect the marks from a hostile takeover was rejected, because Syms could only have achieved that goal by transferring the marks to an independent third party, and with eighty per cent of the stock controlled by the company founder, such a takeover was hypothetical at best; Syms's claim that the transfer would result in better management of the marks was rejected because Syms retained the same responsibilities for managing and maintaining the marks after the transfer; and Syms's assertion that the formation of the subsidiary would enhance Syms's ability to borrow funds was rejected because creditors would have viewed the two entities as intermingled and would not have offered any different financing arrangements, Syms's founder strenuously opposed borrowing money, and the subsidiary never borrowed any money.

existence, but after carefully examining and weighing the evidence proffered as to each of them. Its detailed findings on these matters are supported by substantial evidence, and Syms's allegation that the board's decision was based on the record of another case is without foundation. While there may be many important business purposes attendant to the transfer and licensing back of intangible assets within corporate families, to be viable for the purposes claimed by Syms, they must be more than theoretical musings, concocted to provide faint cover for the creation of a tax deduction.

3. *Ordinary and necessary expense.* General Laws c. 63, § 1 ("net income"), provides that corporations may take business deductions allowable under the Internal Revenue Code (Code). Under the Code, only "ordinary and necessary" business expense deductions are allowable. I.R.C. § 162. Deductions are not permitted if the expense was "created solely for the purpose of effectuating a camouflaged assignment of income." *United States v. Estate Preservation Servs.*, 202 F.3d 1093, 1101 (9th Cir. 2000), quoting *Audano v. United States*, 428 F.2d 251, 256-257 (5th Cir. 1970). As an alternative ground for the disallowance of Syms's deduction for royalty expense, the board concurred with the commissioner's position that the royalty payments were not an "ordinary and necessary" business expense.
The board found that the value of the marks had been created entirely by Syms, and, even after their transfer and the payment of the royalties, Syms continued to pay the expenses associated with owning them, including the legal expenses incurred in maintaining them. It concluded that, in such circumstances, Syms's royalty payments to SYL for the use of the marks was unnecessary. In effect, Syms was paying twice for their use. The board further reasoned that it was irrelevant that the measure of royalty payments might have been equivalent to what would have been paid in an arm's-length transaction where, as here, the payments were not for services provided by SYL but rather part of a contrived mechanism by which affiliated entities shifted income, tax free, between themselves in a circular transaction for the benefit of Syms.

Syms counters that, having validly transferred the trademarks to SYL in consideration for receipt of SYL stock, it was required to pay royalty fees, and, therefore, they were a necessary business expense. It also argues that there is no requirement that owners add value to assets before allowing their use by another entity, and that the sole test whether the royalty payments are deductible is whether they were made at "arm's length."

These arguments closely mirror those made on the question whether the transfer and license back of the marks constituted a "sham" transaction. The central issue for the court to decide is whether the board's finding that there was no business reason for Syms to incur the expense of millions of dollars in royalties other than to create tax deductions is supported by the record. As we have already concluded, it is. The royalty expense to Syms "resulted not as an ordinary, necessary incident in the conduct of the taxpayer's business, but instead was created solely for the purpose of effectuating a camouflaged assignment of income." *United States v. Estate Preservation Servs., supra* at 1101, quoting *Audano v. United States, supra.* It was properly disallowed.

4. *Due process and commerce clause.* Syms's perfunctory constitutional argument does nothing but restate its earlier arguments under a new label. Because Syms had two stores in Massachusetts, the minimal constitutional "nexus" requirement was met. *Becton, Dickinson & Co.* v. *Department of Revenue*, 383 Mass. 786, 788, 422 N.E.2d 1350 (1981). Hence, the only question for the board to decide was whether Syms could reduce its taxable income by deducting the royalties. By disallowing those deductions, the board did not apply a "unitary" theory of taxation to reach the non-Massachusetts income. Rather, it simply rejected "a deduction which is not justifiable under the facts of a particular transaction." *Id.* It based this conclusion on evidence received at a fair hearing. Syms's disappointment that the board did not find the facts the way it would have liked does not rise to a constitutional question.

5. *The commissioner's policy.* Finally, Syms claims that its royalty deduction was disallowed pursuant to "an across-the-board policy for the arbitrary, automatic, disallowance of deductions for all related trademark protection companies," allegedly adopted by the commissioner. It points to no evidence of such a policy. Without a factual basis on which to support its claim that such a policy exists, the claim fails of its own weight.

* * *

Decision of the Appellate Tax Board affirmed.

THE SHERWIN-WILLIAMS COMPANY v. COMMISSIONER OF REVENUE

Supreme Judicial Court of Massachusetts

778 N.E.2d 504 (Mass. 2002)

CORDY, J.

The Sherwin-Williams Company (Sherwin-Williams) appealed from a decision of the Appellate Tax Board (board) upholding the denial by the Commissioner of Revenue (commissioner) of its request to abate $59,445.40 in corporate excise taxes assessed for tax year 1991 and we transferred the case to this court on our own motion. The contested assessment was the result of the commissioner's disallowance of approximately $47 million that Sherwin-Williams had deducted from its taxable income for royalty payments to two wholly owned subsidiaries, Sherwin-Williams Investment Management Company, Inc. (SWIMC), and Dupli-Color Investment Management Company, Inc. (DIMC) (collectively referred to as the subsidiaries), for the use of certain trade names, trademarks, and service marks (marks), that Sherwin-Williams had transferred to the subsidiaries and licensed back as part of a corporate reorganization of its intangible assets in January, 1991. The commissioner also disallowed $80,000 that Sherwin-Williams had deducted for interest payments to SWIMC, in connection with a $7 million loan made to it by SWIMC in the fourth quarter of 1991, which was repaid in the first quarter of 1992.

After a protracted evidentiary hearing, the board found that Sherwin-Williams had not sustained its burden of establishing its entitlement to an abatement, and that the commissioner had properly disallowed the deductions on three alternative grounds: (1) the transfer and license back of the marks was a sham and could be disregarded under the "sham transaction doctrine"; (2) the royalty payments were not deductible as ordinary and necessary business expenses when there was no valid business purpose justifying the expense; and (3) G. L. c. 63, § 39A, permitted the commissioner to adjust the taxable income of Sherwin-Williams by eliminating the royalty payments because they were not made at arm's length and distorted the actual income of Sherwin-Williams. The board also affirmed the elimination of the interest expense deduction based on the commissioner's contention that Sherwin-Williams should never have paid the royalties that generated both the need to borrow money from SWIMC, and the source of the funds loaned to it.

We conclude that the board erred when it found that the transfer and licensing back transactions between Sherwin-Williams and its subsidiaries were without economic substance and therefore a sham. We also conclude that: the payment of royalties and interest to SWIMC and DIMC were properly deductible by Sherwin-Williams because obtaining licenses to use the marks was necessary to the conduct of its business; even assuming G. L. c. 63, § 39A, empowers the commissioner to eliminate payments made between a foreign parent corporation and its subsidiaries, it does so only to the extent that such payments are in excess of fair value, and in light of the substantial evidence that the royalties paid by Sherwin-Williams reflected fair value, there is no basis to support the elimination of these payments; and, because the transactions were not a sham, and the loan between SWIMC and Sherwin-Williams was genuine, interest was properly chargeable to Sherwin-Williams when it borrowed the funds and was, accordingly, properly deductible.

1. *Background.* From the uncontested evidence presented at the evidentiary hearing, we set forth the following backdrop to the issues presented for decision. Sherwin-Williams is a corporation that has manufactured, distributed, and sold paints and related products for more than 125 years. It was incorporated under the laws of the State of Ohio, and has its principal place of business in Cleveland. It manufactures and sells its products under many brand names, including its own signature brand, "Sherwin-Williams," and other brands, including "Dutch Boy," "Martin-Senour," "Kem-Tone," "Dupli-Color," and "Krylon." Sherwin-Williams also uses hundreds of marks, including the "Sherwin-Williams" trademark, several "Dutch Boy" trademarks, and "The Look that Gets the Look" slogan.

In June, 1990, one of Sherwin-Williams's attorneys suggested to Robert E. McDonald, Sherwin-Williams's senior corporate counsel for patents and trademarks, the idea of forming two subsidiary companies to hold and manage the Sherwin-Williams marks and to invest and manage royalty proceeds earned therefrom. McDonald discussed this idea with other senior corporate officials, who asked him to evaluate the potential benefits and risks of establishing such subsidiaries and transferring the Sherwin-Williams marks to them. After concluding that the potential benefits would be substantial, McDonald traveled to Delaware, along with another Sherwin-Williams employee, to meet with individuals who had experience in the management of intangible asset holding companies there. They met with lawyers, bankers, and investment managers, including Donald J. Puglisi.

Puglisi was a professor of business and finance at the University of Delaware, the founder and owner of an investment management and services firm (Puglisi and Associates), and a member of the board of directors of many investment companies and Delaware subsidiaries of foreign corporations. His expertise was principally in business management, portfolio management, and corporate finance. Puglisi and McDonald discussed how intangible asset subsidiaries might be created in Delaware to manage and protect Sherwin-Williams's marks, increase their value, and maximize the investment of royalty income. They also discussed Puglisi's expertise and interest in assisting the companies if Sherwin-Williams decided to create the Delaware subsidiaries.

Delaware was a jurisdiction with which Sherwin-Williams was very familiar, having previously established a number of corporate subsidiaries there. It afforded significant legal and tax advantages to corporations that confined their activities to holding, maintaining, and managing intangible assets. In particular, under Delaware law, royalties and other income earned by such corporations were exempt from State taxation. Del. Code Ann. tit. 30, § 1902(b)(8) (1997). These advantages were known and considered by McDonald and Sherwin-Williams in evaluating the trademark subsidiary plan.

On his return from Delaware, McDonald had further meetings with senior corporate officials, including Sherwin-Williams's chief financial officer and its general counsel, to discuss and evaluate the benefits of transferring the company's marks into separate corporations. McDonald also assessed the legal risks attendant to the transfer of the marks to ensure that it could be done without jeopardizing their continued validity. He further directed an effort to fully identify, catalogue, and document properly the hundreds of marks that Sherwin-Williams had developed or acquired during its many years of operation, including common-law trademarks that had never been recorded with the United States Patent and Trademark Office. These efforts continued over many months, culminating in the preparation by McDonald and others of a business plan for consideration by senior management, and ultimately the Sherwin-Williams board of directors, in January, 1991.

On January 23, 1991, the Sherwin-Williams board of directors voted to form SWIMC and DIMC under Delaware law, and to transfer to them all of Sherwin-Williams's domestic marks. The minutes of the January 23, 1991, board meeting set forth the reasons for the board vote, including:

> (1) improvement of quality control oversight and increased efficiencies with regard to the marks by virtue of having profit centers separate from Sherwin-Williams;
>
> (2) easier profit analysis of Sherwin-Williams by having profit centers for the marks that were separate from it;
>
> (3) enhanced ability to enter into third-party licensing arrangements at advantageous royalty rates;
>
> (4) increased over-all profitability because of the availability of Delaware's corporate income tax exemption for investment management and trademark holding companies;
>
> (5) maximized investment returns associated with the marks due to separate and centralized investment management;
>
> (6) enhanced borrowing capabilities;
>
> (7) subsidiaries could be used in certain instances to acquire businesses;

(8) provided ability to take advantage of the well-developed body of corporate law and expeditious legal system in Delaware;

(9) insulated the marks from Sherwin-Williams's liabilities;

(10) provided flexibility in preventing a hostile takeover; and

(11) increased liquidity.

Under the board-approved plan, all of the marks affiliated with aerosol products were assigned to DIMC, and all of the marks affiliated with non-aerosol products were assigned to SWIMC. These assignments were recorded in the United States Patent and Trademark Office, and SWIMC and DIMC became the owners of the marks. Sherwin-Williams also contributed $50,000 and $42,000 respectively to SWIMC and DIMC to help finance the startup of the companies. In return, Sherwin-Williams and another of its subsidiaries, Dupli-Color Products Company, received one hundred per cent of the stock of both subsidiaries, and agreements that licensed most, but not all, of the marks back to Sherwin-Williams for ten-year terms on a nonexclusive basis. Under the licensing agreements Sherwin-Williams agreed to pay royalties to the subsidiaries quarterly, based on a percentage of the sales of the products bearing those marks. The value of the marks transferred to the subsidiaries, and fair market royalty rates, were to be determined by an independent appraisal company.

SWIMC and DIMC were incorporated in Delaware seven days after the January 23 vote. Their boards of directors first met on February 1, 1991, in Delaware. The original boards of directors of each subsidiary were comprised of the same three individuals. John Ault, the controller of Sherwin-Williams, served as chairman of both boards. Conway Ivy, a vice-president and then treasurer of Sherwin-Williams, served as the second board member. Donald Puglisi, who was not affiliated with Sherwin-Williams, served as the third member. Puglisi was elected president and treasurer. Gordon Stewart, a partner in the Delaware office of Duane, Morris, & Heckscher (who had been retained as corporate counsel to the subsidiaries), was elected secretary of both companies. At their second set of board meetings in the spring of 1991, Stewart was elected to each of the boards of directors as a fourth member. SWIMC and DIMC each agreed to pay Puglisi a salary of $18,000 annually, and each agreed to pay Stewart $500 annually. The subsidiaries had no other employees during 1991.

SWIMC and DIMC jointly executed a lease agreement with the Bank of Delaware for an office that the subsidiaries used to store records. Puglisi conducted his work as president of the subsidiaries, as well as work in connection with his other businesses, from his own office in Newark, Delaware. Puglisi and Associates charged rent to each subsidiary for the use of his office. The subsidiaries each opened bank accounts with the Bank of Delaware, and arranged for the bank to take physical custody of the marks on transfer from Sherwin-Williams. In addition to retaining independent corporate legal counsel (Stewart), the subsidiaries also retained an independent auditing firm. Routine accounting work was done by Puglisi and Associates.

The articles of organization of both SWIMC and DIMC provided that their activities would "be confined to the maintenance and management of its intangible investments." The articles also placed restrictions and prohibitions on the subsidiaries, providing that neither SWIMC nor DIMC could "lease, sell, exchange, transfer, license, assign (except to affiliates), or dispose of any of the assets of the Corporation (except for assets having a value under $2,000)," in the absence of approval by the holder of the majority of shares. In addition, neither subsidiary could pledge any of its assets without the approval of a majority of stockholders. These restrictions were reiterated in the bylaws for both corporations. The articles and bylaws were subsequently amended to eliminate stockholder approval for the licensing of the marks to conform with the subsidiaries' practice of entering license agreements without securing stockholder approval.

Once the subsidiaries had been formed, Sherwin-Williams engaged American Appraisal Associates (AAA) to appraise the value of the marks that it was transferring to the subsidiaries in exchange for their stock, and to help establish an arm's-length royalty rate for the license back of the marks it intended to use. AAA appraised the value of the marks to be $328,000,000, and recommended royalty rates ranging from one per cent to four and one-half per cent for each of Sherwin-Williams's product divisions.

After their formation SWIMC and DIMC operated as ongoing businesses, entering into nonexclusive licensing agreements with Sherwin-Williams and other unrelated licensees, receiving substantial royalty payments (principally from Sherwin-Williams), setting their own investment policies, investing their royalty income and earning a return on those investments greater than that earned on comparable funds by their parent, paying taxes, and hiring and paying professionals to audit the companies and to perform occasional quality control testing on Sherwin-Williams's products. They also hired and paid their own lawyers to represent them in multiple trademark proceedings. To assist them with the filings necessary to maintain the marks, both companies contracted with Sherwin-Williams and paid market rates on periodic invoices for the services they received. All corporate formalities were meticulously observed.

Sherwin-Williams's senior management had concerns dating as far back as 1983 regarding the maintenance and effective management of its marks because one of its marks, the "Canada Paint Company," which was to be used in a Canadian joint venture had been lost. The corporate official who had been most vocal in expressing these concerns, Conway Ivy, was put on the boards of SWIMC and DIMC when they were formed in 1991. The testimony of senior corporate managers further established that before 1991, the multiple divisions of Sherwin-Williams, its decentralized management and culture, and the use of many of the marks across divisions, created uncertain authority and diffuse decision-making regarding the maintenance and exploitation of the marks, contributing to their ineffective and inadequate management as a company asset. Finally, board members of SWIMC and DIMC and Sherwin-Williams's associate general counsel for patents and trademarks testified that these concerns had been effectively addressed by the transfer of the marks to the subsidiaries whose sole focus was on their maintenance and management.

In the proceedings before the board, the commissioner offered evidence from several experts who testified that the many nontax business reasons proffered by Sherwin-Williams for the transfer and licensing back of the marks were either illusory, unrealistic, contradictory, not achievable, or could have been better achieved by internal business adjustments rather than by creating subsidiaries and transferring valuable assets to them to be licensed back. Sherwin-Williams contested the testimony of the commissioner's experts through the testimony of its own experts. None of the commissioner's experts contended that the subsidiaries were not ongoing, profit-making businesses, engaged in business activities including and apart from the licensing of their marks to Sherwin-Williams, or that the royalty rates paid by Sherwin-Williams were outside the range of royalties that would be paid by parties acting at arm's length.

2. *Sham transaction.* Massachusetts recognizes the "sham transaction doctrine" that gives the commissioner the authority "to disregard, for taxing purposes, transactions that have no economic substance or business purpose other than tax avoidance." *Syms Corp.* v. *Commissioner of Revenue*, 436 Mass. 505, 509-510, 765 N.E.2d 758 (2002) (*Syms*). The doctrine generally "works to prevent taxpayers from claiming the tax benefits of transactions that, although within the language of the tax code, are not the type of transactions the law intended to favor with the benefit." 436 Mass. at 510, citing *Horn v. Commissioner of Internal Revenue*, 296 U.S. App. D.C. 358, 968 F.2d 1229, 1236-1237 (D.C. Cir. 1992).

"The question whether or not a transaction is a sham for purposes of the application of the doctrine is, of necessity, primarily a factual one, on which the taxpayer bears the burden of proof in the abatement process." *Syms*, 436 Mass. at 511. Our review of the board's factual findings is limited to whether, as a matter of law, the evidence is sufficient to support them. *Olympia & York State St. Co. v. Assessors of Boston*, 428 Mass. 236, 240, 700 N.E.2d 533 (1998). If supported by sufficient evidence, we will not reverse a decision of the board unless it is based on an incorrect application of the law. *Koch v. Commissioner of Revenue*, 416 Mass. 540, 555, 624 N.E.2d 91 (1993).

In *Syms*, we upheld a finding of the board that a transfer and licensing back of trademarks between a parent and its newly formed subsidiary was a sham transaction for taxing purposes. There, the evidence that the transaction was specifically designed as a tax avoidance scheme; royalties were paid to the subsidiary once a year and quickly returned to the parent company as dividends; the subsidiary did not do business other than to act as a conduit for the circular flow of royalty money; and the parent continued to pay all of the expenses of maintaining and defending the trademarks it had transferred to the subsidiary, fully supported the board's findings that the transaction had no practical economic effect other than the creation of a tax benefit and that tax avoidance was its motivating factor and only purpose.

The facts of the present case are substantially different. There is no evidence that the transfer of the marks to the subsidiary corporations and their licensing back to Sherwin-Williams was specifically devised as a tax avoidance scheme. The revenue earned by the subsidiaries, including the proceeds from the royalty payments made by Sherwin-Williams, was not returned to Sherwin-Williams as a dividend but, rather, was retained and invested as part of their ongoing business operations, earning significant additional income. The subsidiaries entered into nonexclusive license agreements not only with Sherwin-Williams, but also with unrelated parties. The subsidiaries assumed and paid the expenses of maintaining and defending their trademark assets. Whether the board properly applied the sham transaction doctrine to these facts requires a more rigorous analysis of the origin and purposes of that doctrine than was necessary in *Syms*.

We start with two principles first articulated by Judge Learned Hand in *Helvering v. Gregory*, 69 F.2d 809 (2d Cir. 1934), the seminal case establishing the sham transaction doctrine. The first principle is: "Any one may so arrange his affairs that his taxes shall be as low as possible; he is not bound to choose the pattern which will best pay the Treasury; there is not even a patriotic duty to increase one's taxes." *Id.* at 810. Or, as stated by the United States Supreme Court in its affirmance of Judge Hand's decision: "The legal right of a taxpayer to decrease the amount of what otherwise would be his taxes, or altogether avoid them, by means which the law permits, cannot be doubted." *Gregory v. Helvering*, 293 U.S. 465, 469, 79 L. Ed. 596, 55 S. Ct. 266 (1935) (*Gregory*). See *Knetsch v. United States*, 364 U.S. 361, 365, 5 L. Ed. 2d 128, 81 S. Ct. 132 (1960), quoting *Gregory*, *supra*; *Yosha v. Commissioner of Internal Revenue*, 861 F.2d 494, 497 (7th Cir. 1988) ("There is no rule against taking advantage of opportunities created by [the Legislature or revenue service] for beating taxes"). The second principle is that a transaction "does not lose its [tax] immunity, because it is actuated by a desire to avoid, or, if one chooses, evade, taxation." *Helvering v. Gregory*, *supra* at 810. In other words, our tax system is a rule-based system, objective in nature, that places principal importance on what taxpayers do and the economic consequences attached to those actions, not on what may have subjectively motivated them to act in the first place.

Based on these two principles, Sherwin-Williams, on initially going into business, could have organized itself in such a way that its intangible assets (e.g., its marks) were held in a corporation separate from the corporations holding its production facilities and sales operations; the corporation owning the marks could have licensed those marks to its sister corporations; and this arrangement would have been respected by taxing authorities even if the structure were motivated entirely by a desire to minimize Sherwin-Williams's over-all tax burdens. Although motivated by tax considerations, such a structure would not have been an uncommon way of doing business nor an artificial construct whose only possible effect was the avoidance of taxes. Against this backdrop, we decide what an established business enterprise must prove when it undertakes to reorganize itself to effectuate a more efficient tax structure in order that the taxing authorities recognize the reorganization for tax purposes, rather than disregard it as a sham.

The facts and holding in the *Gregory* decision are instructive on this question. In that case, the taxpayer owned all the stock of a corporation, which in turn owned 1,000 shares of a second corporation. *Gregory*, 293 U.S. at 467. "For the sole purpose of procuring a transfer of these shares to herself in order to sell them for her individual profit, and, at the same time, diminish the amount of income tax which would result from a direct transfer [of the stock] by way of dividend," the taxpayer sought to bring about a business "reorganization" under the tax code. *Id.* To that end, the corporation set up a subsidiary to which the 1,000 shares of stock were transferred. All of the stock of the subsidiary were then transferred to the taxpayer on a tax free basis. Three days later, the taxpayer dissolved the subsidiary and distributed the 1,000 shares to herself on a reduced tax basis. *Id.* As the Supreme Court noted, "no other business was ever transacted, or intended to be transacted, by [the subsidiary]." *Id.*

In setting aside the transaction as a sham for taxing purposes, the United States Court of Appeals for the Second Circuit and subsequently the Supreme Court disregarded the question of taxpayer's motive, focusing instead on whether the transactions were a business reorganization as contemplated by the reorganization statute or "an elaborate and devious form of conveyance masquerading as a corporate reorganization, and nothing else." 293 U.S. at 470. Both courts concluded that it was the latter. Although the transactions met the technical requirements of the reorganization statute, the evidence demonstrated that there was "no business or corporate purpose," and that the "sole object and accomplishment . . . was the consummation of a preconceived plan, not to reorganize a business or any part of a business, but to transfer a parcel of corporate shares to the petitioner." 293 U.S. at 469. Consequently, "the transaction upon its face [lay] outside the plain intent of the [reorganization] statute," and did not qualify for the favorable tax treatment available to such reorganizations under the statute. 293 U.S. at 470.

The Supreme Court further elaborated on the sham transaction doctrine in *Frank Lyon Co. v. United States*, 435 U.S. 561, 55 L. Ed. 2d 550, 98 S. Ct. 1291 (1978) (*Lyon*), in which it concluded that a sale and leaseback of real property needed to be respected for tax purposes. In *Lyon*, a bank sold a building that it was constructing to the Frank Lyon Company (company), which simultaneously leased the building back to the bank for its own use. *Id.* at 566. After the purchase and completion of construction, the company became liable on the permanent financing loan for the building, which was secured by an assignment of the bank's lease. *Id.* at 568. The company took various tax deductions and depreciation allowances premised on its ownership of the building. *Id.* The Commissioner of Internal Revenue challenged the company's right to those deductions and allowances, asserting, inter alia, that the bank was the owner of the building and the sale and leaseback should be disregarded as a sham for taxing purposes. *Id.* at 568-569. The Supreme Court concluded that the sale and leaseback had economic substance and was therefore not a sham because the obligation to repay the loan fell squarely on the company, and that "so long as the lessor retains significant and genuine attributes of the traditional lessor status, the form of the transaction adopted by the parties governs for tax purposes." *Id.* at 583-584.

Taken together, the *Gregory* and *Lyon* decisions suggest that for a business reorganization that results in tax advantages to be respected for taxing purposes, the taxpayer must demonstrate that the reorganization is "real" or "genuine," and not just form without substance. Stated otherwise, the taxpayer must demonstrate that the reorganization results in "a viable business entity," that is one which is "formed for a substantial business purpose or actually engages in substantive business activity." *Northern Ind. Pub. Serv. Co.* v.

Commissioner of Internal Revenue, 115 F.3d 506, 511 (7th Cir. 1997), quoting *Bass v. Commissioner of Internal Revenue*, 50 T.C. 595, 600 (1968).

Sham transaction cases most often involve discrete transactions by businesses or individuals rather than business reorganizations. In determining whether a transaction is real or just form over substance, a number of Federal courts have adopted a "two prong" sham transaction inquiry. *Rice's Toyota World, Inc.* v. *Commissioner of Internal Revenue*, 752 F.2d 89 (4th Cir. 1985) (*Rice's Toyota*). The first prong of the inquiry examines whether the transaction has economic substance other than the creation of a tax benefit, which has been labeled the "objective" economic substance test. The second prong examines whether the transaction was motivated by any business purpose other than obtaining a tax benefit, which has been labeled the "subjective" business purpose test. While often using similar language, courts have applied this "two prong" inquiry in different ways. In *Rice's Toyota*, 752 F.2d at 91, the court concluded that "to treat a transaction as a sham, the court must find that the taxpayer was motivated by no business purposes other than obtaining tax benefits in entering the transaction, *and* that the transaction has no economic substance because no reasonable possibility of a profit exists" (emphasis added). According to *Rice's Toyota* and its progeny, if a taxpayer's transaction satisfies the requirements of *either* prong of the test it must be respected for taxing purposes. See *Horn v. Commissioner of Internal Revenue*, 296 U.S. App. D.C. 358, 968 F.2d 1229 (D.C. Cir. 1992); *United States v. Wexler*, 31 F.3d 117 (3d Cir. 1994); *Boca Investerings Partnership v. United States*, 167 F. Supp. 2d 298 (D.D.C. 2001).

Other courts have rejected a rigid two-step analysis, opting instead to treat economic substance and business purpose as "more precise factors to consider in the application of [the] traditional sham analysis; that is, whether the transaction had any practical economic effects other than the creation of income tax losses." *Sochin v. Commissioner of Internal Revenue*, 843 F.2d 351, 354 (9th Cir.), cert. denied, 488 U.S. 824, 102 L. Ed. 2d 49, 109 S. Ct. 72 (1988). See *ACM Partnership v. Commissioner of Internal Revenue*, 157 F.3d 231 (3d Cir. 1998); *Casebeer v. Commissioner of Internal Revenue*, 909 F.2d 1360, 1363 (9th Cir. 1990); *James v. Commissioner of Internal Revenue*, 899 F.2d 905 (10th Cir. 1990); *Shriver v. Commissioner of Internal Revenue*, 899 F.2d 724, 726 (8th Cir. 1990); *Rose v. Commissioner of Internal Revenue*, 868 F.2d 851, 854 (6th Cir. 1989). See also *Bergman v. United States*, 174 F.3d 928, 932 (8th Cir. 1999) ("a transaction must have a purpose, substance, or utility beyond creating a tax deduction for it to have . . . effect").

We agree with those courts that have concluded that whether a transaction that results in tax benefits is real, such that it ought to be respected for taxing purposes, depends on whether it has had practical economic effects beyond the creation of those tax benefits. In the context of a business reorganization resulting in new corporate entities owning or carrying on a portion of the business previously held or conducted by the taxpayer, this requires inquiry into whether the new entities are "viable," that is, "formed for a substantial business purpose or actually engaging in substantive business activity." *Northern Ind. Pub. Serv. v. Commissioner of Internal Revenue*, 115 F.3d at 511. In making this inquiry, consideration of the often interrelated factors of economic substance and business purpose, is appropriate.

We turn now to the questioned transactions in this case. The board found that none of the transactions at issue, however defined, had either economic substance or business purpose other than tax avoidance. The board also found that, even if the transactions had had a business purpose other than tax avoidance, their lack of economic substance was fatal to Sherwin-Williams's claim. We disagree. These transactions (the transfer and license back of property) are a product and intended part of a business reorganization, and their economic substance and business purpose must be assessed not in the narrow confines of the specific transactions between the parent and the subsidiaries, but in the broader context of the operation of the resultant businesses. See *Northern Ind. Pub. Serv. Co. v. Commissioner of Internal Revenue*, 115 F.3d at 512 (newly created subsidiary's existence, transactions with parent, and other economic activities all relevant to sham transaction analysis). After applying the proper legal standards to the evidence, we conclude that the reorganization, including the transfer and licensing back of the marks, had economic substance in that it resulted in the creation of viable business entities engaging in substantive business activity.

The evidence of economic substance, or substantive business activity, beyond the creation of tax benefits for Sherwin-Williams, was substantial. Legal title and physical possession of the marks passed from Sherwin-Williams to the subsidiaries, as did the benefits and burdens of owning the marks. The subsidiaries entered into genuine obligations with unrelated third parties for use of the marks. The subsidiaries received royalties, which they invested with unrelated third parties to earn additional income for their businesses. The subsidiaries incurred and paid substantial liabilities to unrelated third parties and Sherwin-Williams to maintain, manage, and defend the marks. In sum, the subsidiaries became viable, ongoing business enterprises within the family of Sherwin-Williams companies, and not businesses in form only, to be "put to death" after exercising the limited function of creating a tax benefit. *Gregory v. Helvering*, 293 U.S. 465, 470, 79 L. Ed. 596, 55 S. Ct. 266 (1935). See *Bass v. Commissioner of Internal Revenue*, 50 T.C. 595, 600 (1968) (taxpayers' newly formed subsidiary engaged in "substantive business activity" when it held title to working interests in oil and gas leaseholds; assumed and paid its share of expenses for the operation of those leaseholds; collected income from the leaseholds and invested its excess funds; signed contracts regarding the management of the properties; and filed income tax returns).

In the face of this substantial evidence, the board rested its finding that the reorganization and consequent transactions were without economic substance, principally on subsidiary findings that after the reorganization (1) Sherwin-Williams owned the stock of, and therefore controlled, the subsidiaries; (2) Sherwin-Williams (and not the subsidiaries) expended the money to advertise the products that carried the marks; and (3) Sherwin-Williams's employees continued to provide the services necessary to maintain the marks. While these subsidiary findings are supported in the record, they do not support the board's ultimate finding that the reorganization was without economic substance or effect and therefore a sham.

The separate corporate identities of Sherwin-Williams and the subsidiaries must be respected for tax purposes (where they conduct equivalent of business activity), see *Moline Props.* v. *Commissioner of Internal Revenue*, 319 U.S. 436, 438-439, 87 L. Ed. 1499, 63 S. Ct. 1132 (1943), regardless of their stock ownership. While transactions that occur between related companies require close scrutiny to ensure that they have substance as well as form (and that they are valued at levels neither artificially inflated nor deflated because of the interrelated nature of their ownership), the fact that Sherwin-Williams owned the stock of the subsidiaries does not mean that the reorganization had no economic substance or effect on its business. It no longer owned the marks. Instead, it owned stock in the companies that do. It no longer had the exclusive right to use the marks. Instead, it had nonexclusive and time-limited licenses to most but not all of them. The new owners of the marks were free, under their amended bylaws, to enter into licensing agreements with companies other than Sherwin-Williams without shareholder approval, and the subsidiaries did so. In addition, Sherwin-Williams relinquished control over monies it previously retained but now paid to the subsidiaries as royalties. These monies were not returned to it as dividends. They were invested (and therefore placed at risk) by the subsidiaries, under their own investment guidelines and with third parties outside of Sherwin-Williams's control. These changes resulted from the reorganization and have legal, practical, and economic effects on Sherwin-Williams regardless of its stock ownership position. More importantly, they are ample evidence of a reorganization that has resulted in the creation of new, viable business enterprises.

Sherwin-Williams incurred advertising expenses to sell its products not to promote or strengthen the marks. While the marks undoubtedly benefited from the advertising and sale of Sherwin-Williams products bearing their names, such benefits are secondary to the principal purpose of the expenditures. Sherwin-Williams properly expended and expensed these advertising costs against its sales. In this regard, the board's finding that Sherwin-Williams and not the subsidiaries incurred the costs of advertising its products is inconsequential to the ultimate question whether the reorganization was real.

Finally, that the subsidiaries contracted with Sherwin-Williams for professional services necessary to maintain the marks bears little relationship to whether the reorganization had economic substance. What is relevant is whether the subsidiaries paid the expenses of running their businesses (with whomever they may have contracted) or whether those expenses continued to be paid by the parent company, as they were in the *Syms* case. Here, those expenses were paid by the subsidiaries to Sherwin-Williams and, in significantly greater amounts, to other unrelated professionals.

We turn next to the board's assessment of business purpose about which there was a great deal of contested evidence. Applying our limited scope of review to the evidence before the board, we conclude that there was sufficient evidence to support the board's finding that Sherwin-Williams failed to prove that it undertook the reorganization for any of the reasons adopted by its board of directors on January 23, 1991, other than reducing its State tax burden. This finding is of course not conclusive on the ultimate question whether the reorganization was real. Indeed, the board found that, even if the reorganization and the consequent transfer and licensing transactions had been motivated by nontax reasons, or served other business purposes, they would still be a sham because they lacked economic substance beyond the creation of tax benefits.

We embrace the reasoning of courts that have concluded that tax motivation is irrelevant where a business reorganization results in the creation of a viable business entity engaged in substantive business activity rather than in a "bald and mischievous fiction." *Moline Props. v. Commissioner of Internal Revenue*, 319 U.S. at 439. See *Northern Ind. Pub. Serv. Co.* v. *Commissioner of Revenue*, 115 F.3d 506, 512 (7th Cir. 1997) (public utility's formation of wholly owned Netherlands subsidiary to borrow money for parent overseas without triggering Federal withholding tax requirement not a sham, in spite of tax avoidance motive, where subsidiary engaged in substantive business activity); *Stearns Magnetic Mfg. Co.* v. *Commissioner of Internal Revenue*, 208 F.2d 849, 852 (7th Cir. 1954) (corporate taxpayer who transferred patents to stockholder partnership as dividend and licensed them back, may convert form of business as it wishes, even though motive is to reduce taxes; conversion must be accorded recognition unless it is a change in form only, without substance); *Bass v. Commissioner of Internal Revenue*, 50 T.C. 595, 600 (1968) (tax avoidance purpose for reorganizing business into foreign corporate form irrelevant where form adopted was viable business entity, i.e., one which "actually engaged in substantive business activity"). See, e.g., *United Parcel Serv.* v. *Commissioner of Internal Revenue*, 254 F.3d 1014, 1019 (11th Cir. 2001) (when dealing with "going concern," a restructuring has adequate "business purpose" so long "as it figures in a bona fide, profit-seeking business," regardless of tax motivation). Because the record in this case establishes that the reorganization and subsequent transfer and licensing transactions were genuine, creating viable businesses engaged in substantive economic activities apart from the creation of tax benefits for Sherwin-Williams, they cannot be disregarded by the commissioner as a sham regardless of their tax-motivated purpose.

3. *Ordinary and necessary business expenses.* General Laws c. 63, § 1 ("net income"), provides that corporations may take such deductions as are allowable under the Internal Revenue Code (IRC). See G. L. c. 63, § 1. Under the IRC, only "ordinary and necessary" business expenses are allowable deductions. 26 U.S.C. § 162 (2000). The determination whether an expenditure satisfies the requirements for deductibility under § 162 is a question of fact. See *Commissioner of Internal Revenue v. Heininger*, 320 U.S. 467, 475, 88 L. Ed. 171, 64 S. Ct. 249 (1943).

To qualify as an allowable deduction under § 162, a taxpayer must demonstrate that an expenditure satisfies five requirements: (1) it was paid or incurred during the taxable year, (2) it was used to carry on a trade or business, (3) it was an expense, (4) it was a necessary expense, and (5) it was an ordinary expense. See *Commissioner of Internal Revenue v. Lincoln Sav. & Loan Ass'n*, 403 U.S. 345, 352, 29 L. Ed. 2d 519, 91 S. Ct. 1893 (1971). The issue here is whether the royalty payments for the use of the marks were ordinary and necessary business expenses.

Exactly what constitutes an "ordinary and necessary" business expense has been the subject of much discussion over the years. In *Welch v. Helvering*, 290 U.S. 111, 115, 78 L. Ed. 212, 54 S. Ct. 8 (1933), United States Supreme Court Justice Cardozo noted: "The standard set up by the statute is not a rule of law; it is rather a way of life. Life in all its fullness must supply the answer to the riddle." In *Deputy v. DuPont*, 308 U.S. 488, 495-496, 84 L. Ed. 416, 60 S. Ct. 363 (1940), Justice Douglas emphasized that "ordinary has the connotation of normal, usual, or customary," and that each case "turns on its special facts." And in *Commissioner of Internal Revenue v. Tellier*, 383 U.S. 687, 16 L. Ed. 2d 185, 86 S. Ct. 1118 (1966), Justice Stewart observed: "Our decisions have consistently construed the term 'necessary' as imposing only the minimal requirement that the expense be 'appropriate and helpful' for 'the development of the [taxpayer's] business.'" *Id.* at 689, quoting *Welch v. Helvering*, 290 U.S. 111, 113, 78 L. Ed. 212, 54 S. Ct. 8 (1933).

As an alternative ground for the disallowance of Sherwin-Williams's deduction of royalty payments, the board concluded that Sherwin-Williams's payment of royalties to its wholly owned subsidiaries was not deductible as an ordinary and necessary business expense because "the transfer and license-back transactions between Sherwin-Williams and its subsidiaries should have been royalty-free." It based this conclusion on its findings that Sherwin-Williams maintained the value of the marks after the transfer (by way of advertising and services), and that the subsidiaries "had not developed the marks in any way, or built any goodwill, or created anything of value that could be licensed back to the parent."

We disagree with the board's analysis. As noted earlier, advertising costs were incurred for the purpose of selling products not maintaining the value of the marks, and any services provided by Sherwin-Williams to maintain the marks were paid for by the subsidiaries. More fundamentally, however, the board misconstrues the nature of the reorganization. While Sherwin-Williams may have voluntarily conveyed the marks to its newly formed subsidiaries, it received full consideration for the conveyance, i.e., one hundred per cent of their stock. The relevant question is not who created the value in the marks, but who had the right to that value, at the time the royalty payments were made. Once conveyed, Sherwin-Williams had no legal right or claim to the marks absent licensing agreements. Moreover, the subsidiaries were not required to add value to what they had acquired from Sherwin-Williams in order to get fair market royalty rates from it or from the unrelated third-party licensees with whom they did business. If the subsidiaries had used some of their stock (or cash) to acquire marks from another company and in turn licensed them to Sherwin-Williams, there would be no need for them to "add value" in order properly to demand the payment of royalty fees, and none is required in these circumstances. As the commissioner's expert, Professor Alan L. Feld, conceded on cross-examination, "In the corporate world . . . a company does have the right to make a bona fide complete transfer of a tree . . . and then whoever owns the tree, they get the fruit."

Because we have concluded that the reorganization of Sherwin-Williams's intangible assets was not a sham, the answer to the question who had the right to the value of the marks, as a matter of law and substance, is the subsidiaries. The deductibility of the royalty payments between Sherwin-Williams and the subsidiaries must therefore be treated as the deductibility of any other expense incurred in a bona fide transaction between related entities.

The payment of the royalties was a necessary expense because Sherwin-Williams had "irrevocably divested itself of all title [to the marks] and had a right to enjoy the property thereafter only upon payment of reasonable rental." *Stearns Magnetic Mfg. Co. v. Commissioner of Internal Revenue*, 208 F.2d 849, 853 (7th Cir. 1954). Once the marks had been transferred to the subsidiaries, the royalty payments were necessary so that Sherwin-Williams could use the marks to advertise and sell its products. One of the commissioner's experts testified about the importance of the marks: "I think the trademarks at Sherwin - Williams are very important to its business. . . . Their trademarks are very intertwined with the rest of their business." We agree, and conclude that the royalty payments were "'appropriate and helpful' for 'the development of [Sherwin-Williams's] business.'" *Commissioner of Internal Revenue v. Tellier, supra* at 689, quoting *Welch v. Helvering, supra* at 113.

The payment of royalties was also an ordinary expense. "Ordinary has the connotation of normal, usual, or customary." *Deputy v. DuPont, supra* at 495. Although "the transaction which gives rise to [the expense] must be of common or frequent occurrence in the type of business involved . . . the fact that a particular expense would be an ordinary or common one in the course of one business and so deductible . . . does not necessarily make it such in connection with another business." *Id.* In finding that the expense was not "ordinary," the board credited and relied on the testimony of one of the commissioner's witnesses who testified in general terms, and without specifics, that license back arrangements between parent and subsidiary corporations are quite typically "royalty free." He also testified, however, that he was personally aware of instances where companies licensed intangible assets to affiliates and charged them royalties for their use. Puglisi testified that when Sherwin-Williams once asked him for a royalty-free license, he turned them down. Based on the particular facts of this case in all their fullness, we conclude that there was not substantial evidence before the board to support its finding that the royalty payments were not ordinary expenses.

4. *Reasonableness of the royalty payments.* Although we have concluded that the royalty payments that Sherwin-Williams made to the subsidiaries were ordinary and necessary expenses, we must also consider whether the amount of the royalty payments was reasonable. "Inherent in section 162(a)'s concept of 'ordinary and necessary' expenses is the requirement that any payment asserted to be allowable as a deduction . . . be reasonable in relation to its purpose. 'An expenditure may be, by its nature, ordinary and necessary, but at the same time it may be unreasonable in amount." *Audano v. United States*, 428 F.2d 251, 256 (5th Cir. 1970), quoting *United States v. Haskel Eng'g & Supply Co.*, 380 F.2d 786, 788 (9th Cir. 1967).

The agreements under which payments are made will be given effect "if the arrangement is fair and reasonable, judged by the standards of a transaction entered into by parties dealing at arm's length." *Stearns Magnetic Mfg. Co. v. Commissioner of Internal Revenue*, 208 F.2d 849, 852 (7th Cir. 1954). See *Audano v. United States, supra* at 256 (if agreement was such as "reasonable men dealing at arm's length" would have made, it should be valid for tax purposes). A common method for establishing reasonableness is the use of professional appraisers who can look broadly at related industries and practices and estimate a proper royalty rate. The AAA report appraised the value of the marks and recommended royalty rates ranging from one per cent to four and one-half per cent for each of Sherwin-Williams's product divisions. We are satisfied from our review of the record that this report established royalty rates that represented arm's-length transactions, and the commissioner's experts did not testify otherwise.

5. *General Laws c. 63, § 39A.* General Laws c. 63, § 39A, provides that the commissioner may determine the "net income of a foreign corporation which is a subsidiary of another corporation or closely affiliated therewith by stock ownership" by "eliminating all payments to the parent corporation or affiliated corporations in excess of fair value." The purpose of the statute is to give the commissioner the "authority to make adjustments to correct the effect of less than arm's length transactions," between closely affiliated companies, *Commissioner of Revenue v. AMIWoodbroke, Inc.*, 418 Mass. 92, 97, 634 N.E.2d 114 (1994), quoting *Polaroid Corp.* v. *Commissioner of Revenue*, 393 Mass. 490, 500, 472 N.E.2d 259 (1984) and thereby address concerns that "tax evasion by means of intercorporate transactions . . . would depress the . . . income of corporations subject to taxation in Massachusetts." *Id.*

The board found that the transfer and license back of the marks in exchange for royalty payments were not arm's-length transactions because Sherwin-Williams controlled the subsidiaries and there was never a question that the marks would be licensed back to Sherwin-Williams because its existence depended on their use. It further found that the royalty payments had no economic purpose because Sherwin-Williams had itself created the obligation by transferring the marks, and the subsidiaries did nothing to add value to them which would justify such payments. Consequently, it concluded that any payments were in excess of fair market value.

Sherwin-Williams contends that § 39A does not apply to it because it is a parent corporation, not a subsidiary. It also contended that the royalty payments reflected fair value and arm's-length rates as evidenced by the AAA appraisal report, the testimony of its own witnesses, and the testimony of the commissioner's experts. Consequently, there were no payments to eliminate.

Although we agree with the board that the transactions were not entered into at arm's length, the relevant inquiries are whether the transfers were bona fide (which we have concluded they were) and if so, whether the royalty rates paid were in excess of fair market value (which we have concluded they were not).

Assuming that § 39A, construed to give effect to its broad remedial purpose, permits the commissioner to eliminate payments made by a parent to a subsidiary corporation, it does so only to the extent that those payments are in excess of fair value. Having concluded that the board was in error in concluding that the payments were in excess of fair value, we hold that the commissioner's adjustment to Sherwin-Williams's income could not have been made pursuant to Section 39A.

6. *Interest expense.* The commissioner disallowed a deduction for interest that Sherwin-Williams paid SWIMC in connection with a short-term loan of $7 million. The rationale for the disallowance was that, because the royalty payments from Sherwin-Williams to SWIMC were unnecessary, the loan back to Sherwin-Williams and the interest on that loan were also unnecessary. The board affirmed the disallowance. We reverse. Because we have concluded that the transfer and license back of the marks was not a sham and the royalty payments were necessary and ordinary expenses of Sherwin-Williams, and because there is no dispute that the loan was actually made, the interest paid to secure it was deductible.

7. *Conclusion.* The decision of the Appellate Tax Board is reversed.

Chapter 6: International IP Transactions of U.S. Corporations

The "global economy" is one of the ubiquitous buzzwords of the 21st Century. While the term "global economy" is a cliché, it does reflect modern reality and has very important tax consequences. The world is more global today than it was years ago and certainly more global than it was when many of the current rules of the Code were enacted. In this "global economy," more so than at any time in history, nations need clear and effective rules for the income taxation of cross-border transactions, including those transactions involving intellectual property (IP).

Chapter 5 introduced the idea of IP transactions in a multi-jurisdictional context. That Chapter discussed how transfers of IP across state borders might minimize state corporate income taxes. This Chapter likewise has a multi-jurisdictional focus, except the focus is "global" rather than domestic. As discussed in this Chapter, the location and licensing of intangibles across international borders may have significant tax consequences for multinational companies. Therefore, this Chapter focuses on how multinational U.S. corporations can minimize U.S. tax exposure through the development, transfer, and licensing of IP in international transactions.

Indeed, tax minimization through international IP transactions is very important to U.S. multinationals. One can look to numerous, widely-reported examples as proof. The business press is replete with articles about U.S. multinationals shifting intangibles around the globe in the most tax favorable manner. For instance, Google allegedly reduced its effective tax rate to 2.4 percent by employing a series of international IP licensing and development agreements.[468]

One must have a modicum of knowledge about international tax to understand the tax issues involved in international IP transactions. Therefore, this Chapter first presents a brief introduction to the Code's foreign income rules. This Chapter is not a comprehensive review of international tax (an incredibly comprehensive and complicated subject in its own right) and focuses primarily on U.S. multinational corporations and their foreign affiliates. After this introduction, this Chapter covers how the cross-national development, transfer, and licensing of IP can used in a tax advantageous way. This Chapter then concludes with an introduction to the transfer pricing rules (another vast and complex subject) as they affect intercompany IP transactions.

---

[468] Jesse Drucker, *Google 2.4% Rate Shows How $60 Billion Lost to Tax Loopholes*, Bloomberg (Oct. 21, 2010).

6.1 The International Tax Base – The Big Picture

Chapter 5 discussed how the states determine the taxable income of corporations subject to income tax there. The states typically incorporate federal taxable income by reference then apportion business income and allocate nonbusiness income among the several states. In other words, in the state corporate income tax concept, the issue is the sharing of income among the several states. A similar issue applies to the U.S. and all foreign nations. The nations must develop rules to share the tax bases of multinational corporations among the several nations. So the goal of international income taxation, like the goal of multistate income taxation, is really about the sharing of the income. This Chapter focuses on the U.S. system of international income taxation. Most developed nations follow a similar model (although they may not tax domestic corporations on worldwide income).

While a *multistate* corporation generally determines its state tax base by apportionment and allocation, a *multinational* corporation generally determines its international tax base by *residency* and *source*. A corporation's residency is generally its place of incorporation, so that a corporation incorporated in a U.S. State or the District of Columbia is a U.S. corporation and a corporation incorporated elsewhere is a foreign corporation.[469] Residency is significant because U.S. corporations are generally taxable on their *worldwide* income.[470] Therefore, the income taxation of U.S. corporations is often referred to as "residence-based" taxation. Because a U.S. corporation's worldwide income may also be taxed in another country, the Code provides a *foreign tax credit* for taxes paid to foreign countries on foreign source income.[471] Additionally, a U.S. corporation may qualify to reduce or exclude its foreign based income under a tax treaty between the U.S. and the foreign source country.

Conversely, foreign corporations are generally taxable on their *U.S. source income* only. Thus, the Code's treatment of foreign corporation is often referred to as "source-based" taxation. A foreign corporation's income from a U.S. trade or business (called "effectively connected income" or U.S. business income) is taxed under the normal Code provisions (unless a tax treaty provides otherwise).[472] In this way, the Code treats U.S. corporations and foreign corporations the same with respect to their U.S. sourced business income. On the other hand, the Code generally subjects a foreign corporation's nonbusiness income (e.g.,

[469] I.R.C. § 7701(a)(4)-(5), (9).

[470] I.R.C. § 11.

[471] I.R.C. §§ 901-908.

[472] I.R.C. §§ 871(b); 882.

nonbusiness dividends, interests, rents, and royalties) from U.S. sources to a flat 30 percent tax.[473] But this 30 percent flat tax may be reduced (or eliminated altogether) under a tax treaty between the U.S. and the foreign corporation's country.

International tax experts often refer to cross-border transactions of multinational corporations as either "outbound" or "inbound." Generally speaking, outbound transactions refer to U.S. corporations doing business or investing *outside* the U.S. Conversely, inbound transactions refer to foreign corporations doing business and investing *inside* the U.S. Because this Chapter discusses a U.S. corporation's transfer, development, and licensing of IP outside the U.S., this Chapter will address the outbound rules more than the inbound rules.

U.S. corporations can conduct their outbound transactions in two basic ways. First, a U.S. corporation may operate its foreign business directly through a foreign branch. Because a U.S. corporation is taxed on its worldwide income, the foreign branch's income is immediately included in the U.S. corporation's gross income. But the U.S. corporation may qualify for a foreign tax credit for taxes paid to foreign countries on its foreign branch's income.

Second, a U.S. corporation may choose to operate its foreign business indirectly through a foreign subsidiary. As a general rule, the foreign subsidiary's foreign income is not subject to U.S. tax until it is *repatriated* to the U.S. (e.g., through payment of a dividend or liquidating distribution to the U.S. parent). In other words, the Code generally respects the foreign subsidiary as a separate legal entity, so that it is not subject to U.S. tax on its foreign activities. If the foreign country has a lower tax rate than the U.S., a U.S parent has an incentive to keep the profits of its foreign subsidiary offshore as long as possible. The result is *deferral* of U.S. taxes.

6.1[1] Tax Deferral and Prevention of its Abuse

The Code permits deferral of foreign subsidiary income to provide U.S. corporations competitive footing with their foreign competitors.[474] For instance, suppose a U.S. parent operates a business in a low-tax foreign country (Country X) through a foreign subsidiary.

---

[473] I.R.C. § 871(a). The Code generally refers to a foreign person's nonbusiness income as "fixed or determinable annual or periodical" income. *Id.*

[474] *See generally* U.S. Treasury Dept., *The Deferral of Income Earned Through U.S. Controlled Corporations: A Policy Study* (Dec. 2000).

Further assume that the foreign subsidiary has the same pre-tax profit in Country X as a local competitor. The local competitor would pay a relatively low-tax rate in Country X on its profits and pay no U.S. tax. But the foreign subsidiary would pay the same low-tax in Country X, and without a deferral system, the U.S. parent would also pay U.S. tax on the same income (after application of the foreign tax credit, U.S. parent and its foreign subsidiary would incur an effective tax rate on the foreign income equal to the higher U.S. rate). While the local competitor and the foreign subsidiary have the same pre-tax profit, the local competitor's *after-tax profit* would be greater, thereby placing the U.S. parent and its foreign subsidiary at a competitive disadvantage. Thus, Congress finds deferral in such a case as being done for legitimate business reasons.

On the other hand, if the competitiveness of U.S. corporations is not an issue, the deferral of U.S. tax is not legitimate and Congress has enacted anti-deferral provisions to prevent it. The most important anti-deferral provisions are contained in Subpart F dealing with a "controlled foreign corporations" (CFCs). The Subpart F provisions are among the most complicated in the Code, and a full discussion of such rules is beyond the scope of this Chapter. But a broad overview of Subpart F is needed to dispel the notion that tax deferral of foreign subsidiary profits is automatic. Broadly stated, Subpart F's prevents a U.S. corporation from deferring U.S. tax on certain types of income earned through a foreign subsidiary located in a low-tax (or no tax) country (i.e., a tax haven). Generally, Subpart F generally targets the following two categories of income that are easily shifted to offshore tax havens: (1) passive investment income,[475] and (2) income generated through certain related party transactions.[476] Conversely, Subpart F generally does not apply to income of a foreign subsidiary generated from an active business.

---

[475] To illustrate how passive investment income is easily deflected offshore, consider an example of a U.S. corporation seeking to create a "rainy day" fund consisting of cash or cash equivalents. The U.S. corporation could invest its rainy day fund onshore and pay current U.S. tax on its earnings (e.g., interest and dividends). Without Subpart F, the U.S. corporation could invest its rainy day fund offshore in a foreign subsidiary located in a tax haven and pay no current U.S. or foreign tax on the earnings. Subpart F prevents this by making the U.S. corporation pay current U.S. tax on the interest and dividends. For this same reason, a U.S. corporation cannot create a purely passive IP holding company in a tax haven, accumulate royalties in the IP holding company from worldwide licensing, and avoid current U.S. current tax.

[476] To illustrate how income from related party transactions is easily deflected offshore, consider an example where a U.S. parent sells products to a foreign subsidiary located in a tax haven. The foreign subsidiary then resells the products to end users in other countries. In this case, the U.S. parent and its foreign subsidiary may try to isolate some of the profit in the foreign subsidiary. The Service could invoke Code section 482 (discussed later in this Chapter) to reallocate income between the U.S. parent

6.1[2] Controlled Foreign Corporations and Subpart F income

A foreign corporation must be a CFC to trigger Subpart F. A CFC is a foreign corporation in which "U.S. shareholders" own more than 50 percent of the foreign corporation's stock, either by vote or value.[477] A "U.S. shareholder" is a U.S. person owning at least 10 percent or more of the foreign corporation's total combined voting stock.[478] The Code imposes attribution rules such that a U.S. person constructively owns the stock of certain related parties.[479] Under these rules, eleven unrelated U.S. persons can equally own a foreign corporation without creating a CFC (because none of the U.S. persons is a "U.S. shareholder"). A foreign corporation owned equally by a U.S. corporation and an unrelated foreign person is not a CFC (because U.S. shareholders do not own more than 50 percent of the foreign corporation's stock by vote or value). The combinations of ownership between U.S. persons and foreign persons are endless. Suffice it to say, a foreign subsidiary wholly-owned by a U.S. parent is a CFC (as is the case in most of this Chapter's problems). Because a wholly-owned foreign subsidiary is a CFC, the U.S. parent seeking to defer U.S. tax must ensure that the CFC's income is not included in "Subpart F income." Otherwise, if a CFC has Subpart F income, each U.S. shareholder must currently include its pro rata share of that income in its gross income (even if the CFC does not distribute that income).[480]

As noted above, Subpart F income generally applies to income that is easily shifted offshore, such as passive investment income and income from related party transactions. The Code accomplishes this task by defining the most important category of Subpart F income as "foreign base company income."[481] "Foreign based company income" is, in turn, divided into three primary subcategories including (1) foreign personal holding company income (FPHCI), (2) foreign base company sales income, and (3) foreign base company services income.[482] FPHCI is meant to catch passive investment income, while foreign base company

---

and the foreign subsidiary (i.e., transfer pricing). But Subpart F obviates the need for transfer pricing analysis because the foreign subsidiary's income is currently taxable to the U.S. parent as Subpart F income, even if the transactions between the U.S. parent and the foreign subsidiary are arm's length.

[477] I.R.C. § 957(a).

[478] I.R.C. § 951(b).

[479] I.R.C. § 958(b).

[480] I.R.C. § 951(a).

[481] I.R.C. § 952. Subpart F income also includes certain insurance income, certain income from countries engaged in international boycotts, and certain illegal payments. *Id.*

[482] I.R.C. § 954(a). There is a fourth subcategory that covers "foreign base company oil related income." I.R.C. § 954(a)(5). Additionally, the Code contains a "de minimis" rule that exempts

sales income and foreign base company service income are meant to catch sales and services income from related party transactions.[483] FPHCI is the subcategory most relevant to the taxation of IP. FPHCI generally includes passive investment income, such as interest, dividends, rents, royalties, and net gains from the sale of passive investments.[484] So royalties a CFC receives from the licensing of IP, for example, are generally FPHCI and included as Subpart F income.

An important exception to FPHCI is the "active royalties" exception. This exception exempts from FPHCI royalties a CFC receives (1) from an unrelated person (2) in the active conduct of the CFC's business.[485] A CFC derives royalties from an active business if the CFC performs extensive production activities or extensive marketing activities in connection with the licensing of property.[486] Even if the CFC receives royalties from a related person, such royalties are exempt from FPCHI if received for the use of property in the country where the CFC is organized.[487] This exception is referred to as the "related party same country" exception.[488]

> **Problem 6.1**: USCo, a U.S. corporation, is in the business of developing, manufacturing and marketing pharmaceuticals. Recently, USCo developed a new drug called "Obliviotol" for the treatment of depression. USCo owns

---

foreign base company income (and certain insurance income) from Subpart F income if it is lower than the lesser of (a) 5 percent of the CFC's gross income or (b) $1 million. I.R.C. § 954(b)(3)(A).

[483] "Foreign base company sales income" generally includes income from the sale of property purchased from (or sold to) a related person, provided the property is manufactured and sold for use outside the CFC's country of organization. I.R.C. § 954(d)(1). "Foreign base company services income" generally includes income from services performed outside the CFC's country of organization for (or on behalf of) a related person. I.R.C. § 954(e). Detailed discussion of foreign base company sales income and foreign base company services income is beyond the scope of this Chapter.

[484] I.R.C. § 954(c)(1). FPHCI also includes income from annuities, certain currency gains, certain commodities transactions, and certain income that is equivalent to interest. *Id.*

[485] I.R.C. § 954(c)(2)(A).

[486] Treas. Reg. § 1.954-2(d).

[487] I.R.C. § 954(c)(3).

[488] In 2006, Congress provided a temporary "look through" exception. Under the "look through" exception, royalties a CFC received from a related CFC are exempted from FPHCI to the extent attributable to the payor's income that is neither (1) Subpart F income nor (2) effectively connected with a U.S. trade or business. I.R.C. § 954(c)(6). The "look through" exception expired on December 31, 2009.

the U.S. and various foreign patents on the drug's compound and has trademarked the "Obliviotol" brand name in the U.S. and overseas. Additionally, USCo has obtained the necessary regulatory approvals to sell Obliviotol in the U.S. and foreign countries. Obliviotol is very popular in the U.S., and USCo recently expanded its sales overseas. In doing so, USCo manufactured Obliviotol in the U.S. and sold it to overseas customers through a foreign branch located in Europe. USCo made a $100 pretax profit on each box of Obliviotol it sold overseas. Assume USCo is subject to 35 percent U.S. corporate income tax rate on its taxable income. What are the U.S. tax consequences from USCo's overseas sales of Obliviotol through its foreign branch (ignore application of the foreign tax credit)? What is USCo's after-tax profit on each box of Obliviotol it sold through its foreign branch?

Problem 6.2: Assume the same facts as **Problem 6.1**, except USCo forms a wholly-owned subsidiary incorporated in Ireland ("Ireland Co."). Instead of selling Obliviotol through a foreign branch, USCo grants a nonexclusive license to Ireland Co. to manufacture and sell Obliviotol in markets outside the U.S. Under their licensing agreement, Ireland Co. pays a $10 royalty to USCo for each box of Obliviotol it sells (assume U.S. and Irish taxing authorities respect this royalty as "arm's length"). Ireland Co.'s employees, based in Ireland, perform all manufacturing, testing, quality control, and packaging of Obliviotol for sales outside the U.S. Additionally, Ireland Co. is responsible for all marketing and distribution of Obliviotol to non-U.S. customers. Ireland Co. makes a $100 pretax and preroyalty profit of $100 on each box of Obliviotol it sells. For purposes of illustration and simplicity, assume that Ireland Co. is subject to a 10 percent effective tax rate in Ireland on its sales of Obliviotol. What are the tax consequences to USCo and Ireland Co. from the licensing and sale of Obliviotol? How does the effective tax rate on sales of Obliviotol in this problem compare to **Problem 6.1**?

6.1[3] Use of Existing IP in a Foreign Subsidiary

Problems 6.1 and 6.2 demonstrate how a U.S. multinational corporation might utilize its IP through foreign subsidiaries (as opposed to foreign branches) to defer U.S. income tax. In addition to Subpart F, U.S. multinationals must overcome two other major hurdles to exploiting existing IP developed in the U.S. through foreign subsidiaries. The first is section

367(d), which denies nonrecognition treatment to a U.S. corporation's transfer of IP to a foreign subsidiary. The second is section 482 transfer pricing, which allows the Service, among other things, to adjust royalties paid on the transfer of IP between related parties to an "arm's length" price. Section 367(d) and section 482 transfer pricing, respectively, are discussed below.

6.1[3][a] Outbound IP Transfers to Foreign Corporations – Section 367(d)

An IP holding company formed domestically (like those discussed in Chapter 5) is relatively easy to form because the transfer of IP to a domestic subsidiary is typically nontaxable. In other words, the transfer of IP to a domestic corporation is nontaxable if the transferor receives a controlling interest in the transferee corporation (at least 80 percent of its stock) in the exchange (i.e., a "section 351 exchange").[489] Similarly, the transfer of IP to a domestic subsidiary in a section 368 reorganization is nontaxable under section 361 (a "section 361 exchange").[490]

Should the same result apply if the IP holding company is a foreign corporation, rather than a domestic one? To answer this question, consider the result if the Code's normal rules of nonrecognition apply. In that case, a U.S. parent could transfer highly appreciated IP to a foreign subsidiary in exchange for all of the subsidiary's stock (or transfer the IP to a foreign subsidiary in a nontaxable reorganization). Under the Code's normal rules of nonrecognition, the exchange between U.S. parent and foreign subsidiary would be nontaxable. The foreign subsidiary may then generate substantial income from exploiting the IP, and at some later date, it may sell the transferred IP at a substantial gain. If the foreign subsidiary is not engaged in a U.S. trade or business, income from the IP's exploitation and gain from the IP's sale might not be subject to U.S. tax, even though much of the IP's appreciation occurred while the U.S. parent held it.[491] Additionally, if the transferred IP is a manufacturing intangible (such as a patent), the U.S. parent may have deducted its research and development costs against U.S. tax.[492] Likewise, if the transferred IP is a marketing intangible, the U.S. parent may have deducted its developmental costs as

---

[489] I.R.C. §§ 351(a), 368(c).

[490] I.R.C. §§ 361(a), 368(a).

[491] I.R.C. § 865(d).

[492] *See* I.R.C. § 174. Section 174 and research and experimental expenditures are discussed in detail in Chapter 2.

advertising or graphic design costs.[493] If the gain is held offshore indefinitely (and Subpart F is not triggered[494]), the U.S. will not be able to recapture these deductions.

In summary, U.S. corporations might exploit the normal rules of nonrecogntion to avoid U.S. tax upon outbound IP transfers. Recognizing this potential for U.S. tax avoidance, Congress enacted section 367(d) to deny nonrecognition to outbound IP transfers to foreign corporations. Generally speaking, if a U.S. person transfers intangibles to a foreign corporation in either a section 351 or 361 exchange, section 367(d) treats the transfer as a *sale* for royalty payments over the transferred intangible's useful life (not to exceed 20 years).[495] Section 367(d) *deems* these royalties to be paid to the U.S. transferor, regardless of whether the foreign transferee actually pays them.[496]

The deemed royalty must be "commensurate with the income attributable to the intangible."[497] This "commensurate with income" standard is determined under section 482's "arm's length" transfer pricing rules, discussed later in this Chapter.[498] "Intangible property" for section 367(d) purposes is broadly defined to encompass various types of IP, including patents, inventions, formulae, processes, designs, copyrights, trademarks, trade or brand names, and franchises, among others.[499] But section 367(d) intangible property does

---

[493] *See* Chapter 1 for detailed discussion of the deduction of advertising and graphic design costs.

[494] As discussed earlier in this Chapter, the foreign IP holding company would, in most cases, need to conduct an active trade or business to avoid generating Subpart F income to the U.S. parent.

[495] I.R.C. § 367(d); Treas. Reg. § 1.367(d)-1T(c). Regulations allow the U.S. transferor to elect to treat the transfer as an immediate sale (with immediate gain recognition rather annual inclusion of deemed royalties) in three very limited circumstances: (1) the U.S. transferor makes an outbound transfer of certain "operating" intangibles (generally long-term purchase or supply contracts, surveys, and customer lists); (2) the government where the foreign subsidiary is organized requires the U.S. transferor to make the transfer as a condition of doing business there; or (3) certain joint ventures. Treas. Reg. § 1.367(d)-1T(g)(2).

[496] Treas. Reg. § 1.367(d)-1T(a). The decision whether the foreign transferee actually makes payments is typically dependent on the foreign country's rules for withholding taxes and deductions. A deemed royalty (as opposed to one actually paid) may not be subject to a withholding tax in the foreign subsidiary's country. On the other hand, a deemed royalty will not generate a deduction in the foreign country, while a royalty actually paid likely would.

[497] I.R.C. § 367(d)(2)(A).

[498] Treas. Reg. § 1.367(d)-1T(c)(1).

[499] I.R.C. § 367(d)(1). Section 367(d) incorporates by reference the definition of "intangible property" in section 936(h)(3)(B), which includes any:

(1) patent, invention, formula, process, design, pattern, or know-how;

not include foreign goodwill or going concern value of a business conducted outside the U.S.[500] Special gain acceleration rules may apply where the transferee foreign corporation later directly or indirectly transfers the IP a second time. Generally, deemed royalty payments continue if the IP is transferred to a related person, while gain is immediately recognized if the IP is transferred to an unrelated person.[501]

> **Problem 6.3**: Assume the same basic facts of **Problem 6.1**. USCo deducted its costs in developing Obliviotol as section 174 research and experimental expenditures. Once Obliviotol receives the necessary regulatory approvals and is ready to market, USCo transfers U.S. and foreign patents (and related trademarks) relating to Obliviotol to Ireland Co., an Irish corporation, in exchange for all of Ireland Co.'s stock. Ireland Co.'s employees, based in Ireland, will perform all manufacturing, testing, quality control, and packaging of Obliviotol for sales outside the U.S. Ireland Co. will make no royalty payments to USCo for sales of Obliviotol. Based on the foregoing, what are the tax consequences to USCo?

6.1[3][b] Transfer Pricing – Section 482

Problem 6.2 introduced the importance of intercompany (transfer) pricing of royalties for intangibles. The facts of Problem 6.2 specifically assumed that the royalty paid from an Irish subsidiary to its U.S. parent was "arm's length." Why does the Service insist that transfer pricing of the royalty be "arm's length"? In answering this question, imagine what would happen if the Service had no ability to challenge intercompany pricing. In Problem 6.2, the U.S. parent (subject to a 35 percent effective tax rate) has a strong incentive to shift more profit to its Irish subsidiary (subject to a 10 percent effective tax rate). Without any transfer pricing restrictions, the U.S. parent would purposely cause its Irish subsidiary to pay back the lowest possible royalty. In this way, more profit from product sales would be

---

(2) copyright, literary, musical, or artistic composition;

(3) trademark, trade name, or brand name;

(4) franchise, license, or contract;

(5) method, program, system, procedure, campaign, survey, study, forecast, estimate, customer list, or technical data; or

(6) any similar item, which has substantial value independent of the services of any individual.

[500] Treas. Reg. § 1.367(d)-1T(b).

[501] *See* Treas. Reg. § 1.367(d)-1T(d)-(f).

earned in low-tax Ireland rather than the high-tax U.S. In theory, if no transfer pricing rules applied at all, the U.S. parent would license its product royalty-free to its Irish subsidiary, so the entire profit from product sales would be taxed at the lower Irish tax rate. So long as the profits are not repatriated to the U.S. and Subpart F is avoided, the corporate group, as a whole, would have more after-tax working capital for its use.

Congress is fully aware that multinational corporations can manipulate cross-border intercompany prices to shift profit away from the U.S. to lower tax countries. To this end, section 482 gives the Service broad latitude to allocate gross income, deductions, and credits between related parties to the extent necessary "to prevent the evasion of taxes" or to clearly reflect the income of any related taxpayers.[502] In the case of the transfer (or license) of IP, the Service can adjust royalties "commensurate with the income attributable to the intangible."[503]

Section 482 is all encompassing because it covers all sorts of intercompany transactions, including, among other things, intercompany sales of goods, intercompany services, interest charged on intercompany loans, and the intercompany transfers (and licensing) of intangibles. Whole treatises are dedicated exclusively to transfer pricing. Many professionals dedicate their entire careers to transfer pricing issues and make their livelihood doing so. Suffice it to say, this Chapter cannot comprehensively cover transfer pricing in great detail. Instead, this Chapter's goal is to give a general overview of the transfer pricing issues specifically relating to intercompany transfer (and licensing) of intangibles.

Section 482 does not include much text, so most of the transfer pricing rules are left to the section 482 regulations. The principle underlying the section 482 regulations is that related party transactions should be "*arm's length.*"[504] The regulations typically refer to related party deals as "controlled transactions" and unrelated party deals as "uncontrolled transactions." So when a U.S. parent transfers IP to a foreign subsidiary (a "controlled transaction"), that transfer must be made on substantially similar terms to a transfer to an unrelated party (an "uncontrolled transaction") to be "arm's length." Section 482 only gives to Service the right to adjust the terms of controlled transactions, not the taxpayers involved.

[502] I.R.C. § 482.

[503] *Id.*

[504] Treas. Reg. § 1.482-1(b)(1).

The regulations generally provide three[505] methods for determining the "arm's length" price for the transfer of IP between related parties, including:

(1) the comparable uncontrolled transaction method (the "CUT" method);
(2) the comparable profits method; and
(3) the profit split method.[506]

6.1[3][b][i] Comparable Uncontrolled Transaction (CUT) Method

Under the CUT method, a related party IP transfer is arm's length if the royalty charged equals that of a comparable uncontrolled (unrelated) transaction.[507] The CUT method makes a distinction between *exact* comparables and *inexact* comparables. An "exact comparable" exists if the transferor transferred the *same* intangible to an unrelated party under the *same or substantially similar* circumstances.[508] Same or substantially similar circumstances means "there are at most only minor differences that have a definite and reasonable ascertainable effect on the amount charged and for which appropriate adjustments are made."[509] An exact comparable generally provides the most reliable measure of an arm's length transfer.[510]

But exact comparables may not exist. In that case, regulations allow an inexact comparable to be used under the CUT method. An "inexact comparable" exists if the transferor transferred a *comparable* intangible under *comparable* circumstances. Not surprisingly, regulations state that inexact comparables are less reliable than exact comparables. An intangible is comparable to the one transferred if it is used within the same general industry and has a "similar profit potential."[511] Regulations provide a number of factors to weigh in determining whether the circumstances are comparable, including the licensing terms, economic risks, and the product's stage of development, among others.[512]

---

[505] Regulations also provide a fourth alternative for certain unspecific methods described in Treas. Reg. § 1.482-4(d). These "unspecified" methods are used sparingly and are not discussed in this Chapter.

[506] Treas. Reg. § 1.482-4(a).

[507] Treas. Reg. § 1.482-4(c)(1).

[508] Treas. Reg. § 1.482-4(c)(2)(ii).

[509] *Id.*

[510] *Id.*

[511] Treas. Reg. § 1.482-4(c)(2)(iii)(B)(1).

[512] Treas. Reg. § 1.482-4(c)(2)(iii)(B)(2).

Problem 6.4: USCo, a U.S. corporation, is in the business of developing, manufacturing, and marketing pharmaceuticals. Recently, USCo developed a new drug (Zymbol) for the treatment of lung cancer. USCo has obtained U.S. and foreign patents on Zymbol and all necessary regulatory approvals for its sale. USCo licenses Zymbol to an unrelated party, Austria Co., for Zymbol's manufacture and sale in Austria. In exchange for the license, Austria Co. agrees to pay USCo a five percent royalty based on gross sales. At the same time, USCo licenses Zymbol to its wholly-owned foreign subsidiary, Swiss Co, for its manufacture and sale in Switzerland. Because USCo contemporaneously licensed Zymbol for five percent to unrelated Austria Co., USCo uses the same five percent royalty for its license to Swiss Co. (all other terms of the Swiss Co. license are substantially similar to the Austria Co. license).

Austria and Switzerland are neighboring countries with highly developed economies. Both countries have similar laws protecting intellectual property rights. Austria's population (8.2 million people) is slightly more than Switzerland (7.6 million people). Per capita income in Switzerland ($42,000 US) is slightly more than Austria ($40,000 US). The incidence of smoking in Switzerland (25 percent of adult populations) and Austria (25 percent of adult population) is equal. And the incidence of lung cancer in Switzerland is about the same as it is in Austria.

Based on the foregoing, can USCo use its license with Austria Co. as an "exact comparable" in setting the royalty rate on the Swiss Co. license? Can you think of any additional facts that would greatly impact your answer?

At the same time, suppose USCo also licenses Zymbol to its wholly-owned subsidiary, Japan Co., for Zymbol's manufacture and sale in Japan. Japan has a population of 125 million people. While a greater percentage of Japanese (35 percent of adult population) smoke than Austrians (25 percent of adult population), the incidence of lung cancer in Japan is only marginally greater than it is in Austria. Japan has a highly developed economy and has laws similar to Austria that protect intellectual property rights. Can USCo use its license with Austria Co. as an "exact comparable" in setting the royalty rate on the Japan Co. license? In answering these questions, read the examples contained in Treas. Reg. § 1.482-4(c)(4).

6.1[3][b][ii] Comparable Profits Method (CPM)

The principle underlying the CPM is that similarly situated taxpayers will earn similar profits over a reasonable period of time. To this end, the CPM evaluates an "arm's length" royalty by comparing the profitability of a "tested party" (typically, the IP licensee) with the profitability of "uncontrolled taxpayers that engage in similar business activities under similar circumstances."[513] For instance, the royalty Swiss Co. pays to USCo in Problem 6.4 would be evaluated by comparing the profitability of Swiss Co. with the profitability of unrelated pharmaceutical manufacturers engaged in similar licensing transactions. If Swiss Co.'s profitability differs meaningfully (i.e., outside an "arm's length range") from the profitability of similar uncontrolled taxpayers, the Service can adjust the royalty Swiss Co. pays to USCo to bring Swiss Co's profitability within an acceptable "arm's length range."[514] In effect, the CPM limits a licensee's retained profit to that of a similarly situated uncontrolled taxpayer. So the licensee must pay any excess profit (outside the arm's length range) to the licensor as additional royalties.

6.1[3][b][iii] Profit Split Method

The profit split method typically applies where related parties each own valuable IP that significantly contributes to their combined profit (or loss). The purpose of the profit split method is to allocate or "split" this combined profit between the related parties.[515] The regulations provide two alternative profit split methods: (1) the "comparable profit split method" and (2) the "residual profit split method." The comparable profit split method relies exclusively on external market data (similar transactions between unrelated parties) to calculate the appropriate profit split. So the combined profits of related parties are split between them in the same proportion as profits are split between unrelated parties engaging in similar transactions.[516] Because reliable external market data may not be available, the comparable profit split method is used sparingly.

The residual profit split method employs a two-step process to allocate profit between related parties.[517] Under the first step, the Service allocates a market return to each party's

[513] Treas. Reg. § 1.482-5(a).

[514] *See generally* Treas. Reg. § 1.482-5(b).

[515] Treas. Reg. § 1.482-6(a).

[516] Treas. Reg. § 1.482-6(c)(2).

[517] Treas. Reg. § 1.482-6(c)(3).

"routine" contributions (assets and liabilities) and allocates profit accordingly.[518] Under the second step, the Service allocates the remaining (residual) profit based on the relative value of each related party's "nonroutine" contributions.[519]

6.1[1][b][iv] "Commensurate with Income" Standard

In the case of the transfer (or license) of IP between related parties, Section 482 specifically allows the Service to adjust royalties "commensurate with the income attributable to the intangible."[520] In adding the "commensurate with income" standard, Congress noted a "recurrent problem" in transfer pricing "is the absence of comparable arm's length transactions between unrelated parties, and the inconsistent results of attempting to impose an arm's length concept in the absence of comparables."[521] Congress noted that the problem is "particularly acute in the case of transfers of high-profit potential intangibles."[522] So Congress was concerned that related parties often use allegedly "comparable" IP transfers to set royalties that do not reflect the actual income the transferred IP produces. By adopting the "commensurate with income" standard, Congress placed more emphasis on the income actually derived from intangibles (and away from "comparables"). In effect, the "commensurate with income" standard allows the Service to adjust royalties paid between related parties to reflect changing market conditions.[523] The Service can make adjustments in certain cases, even if the original royalty was reasonable at the time it was originally set.

Because Congress intended for the Service to make adjustments only for major market changes, the regulations provide exceptions where the Service cannot make periodic adjustments. The first exception is that the Service cannot adjust royalties that were based on an "exact comparable" under the CUT method (discussed above).[524] A second exception applies to royalties based on an "inexact comparable" under the CUT method or any other acceptable method (comparable profits or profit split methods). But the existence of an inexact comparable (or a comparable based on another method) is not an automatic bar to adjustment. Rather, the Service can generally make adjustments if the controlled taxpayer's aggregate profits actually earned (or cost savings realized) are (1) not less than 80 percent

---

[518] Treas. Reg. § 1.482-6(c)(3)(i)(A).

[519] Treas. Reg. § 1.482-6(c)(3)(i)(B).

[520] I.R.C. § 482.

[521] H.R. Rpt. 99-426 at 423-24 (Dec. 7, 1985).

[522] *Id.* at 424.

[523] Treas. Reg. § 1.482-4(f)(2)(i).

[524] Treas. Reg. § 1.482-4(f)(2)(ii)(A).

nor (2) more than 120 percent of the prospective profits (or cost savings) that were originally foreseeable.[525]

> **Problem 6.5**: Assume the same facts as **Problem 6.4**. Assume that USCo licensed Zymbol to Swiss Co. in Year 1. The Service later audits USCo's income tax return for Year 5 and must determine if the royalties Swiss Co. paid to USCo meet the "commensurate with income" standard. Swiss Co.'s projected and actual profits attributable to Zymbol sales are as follows:

Tax Year	Profit Projections (in millions USD)	Actual Profits (in millions USD)
Year 1	200	250
Year 2	250	500
Year 3	500	800
Year 4	350	700
Year 5	100	600
Total	1,400	2,850

> If USCo's license of Zymbol to Austria Co. can be used as an exact comparable to USCo's license of Zymbol to Swiss Co., can the Service adjust the five percent royalty Swiss Co. paid to USCo to meet the "commensurate with income" standard? How would your answer change if the USCo-Austria Co. license was an inexact comparable to the USCo-Swiss Co. license? What happens if Years 1 through 4 are closed under the statute of limitations?

This Chapter has demonstrated three basic ways to transfer existing IP offshore, including:

(1) an outright sale of "all significant rights" in the IP to a related foreign entity;
(2) a license of the IP to a related foreign entity; and
(3) a transfer of the IP to a related foreign subsidiary in a section 367(d) exchange.

In an outright sale and a license, the amount the foreign subsidiary pays for the IP must be "arm's length" and commensurate with the income from the transferred IP. A section 367(d) exchange applies the same standard, except that the foreign subsidiary is not actually

[525] Treas. Reg. § 1.482-4(f)(2)(ii)(B)(6).

required to pay royalties (section 367(d) deems royalties to be paid, whether actually made or not). Thus, in all three transfer methods noted above, the U.S. transferor must include arm's length royalties in its U.S. gross income (whether actually paid or not). But there may be non-tax reasons for choosing a license over an outright sale or a section 367(d) exchange. Generally, the U.S. transferor may want to retain ownership of the IP so it can maintain quality control over it.

Is there a way to get the best of both worlds? In other words, can a U.S. corporation transfer IP to a foreign subsidiary, maintain ownership over the transferred IP for quality control purposes, without a royalty (or deemed royalty) paid back to it? This is where *cost sharing arrangements* come into play. In addition to the three transfer methods noted above, a fourth method is a transfer pursuant to a cost sharing arrangement. For this reason, cost sharing arrangements are discussed below.

6.2 Cost Sharing Arrangements

A cost-sharing arrangement (CSA) is an agreement between parties (often related) to share the costs to develop IP that each party will exploit separately.[526] The parties must share costs and risks in proportion to their reasonably expected benefits from the developed IP.[527] A CSA "qualified" under the regulations is not treated as a partnership or joint venture.[528] For U.S. tax purposes, all parties to the CSA are deemed to own the IP developed pursuant to the CSA. Because all parties "own" the IP for tax purposes, no royalty must be paid between the related parties for its use. But from an IP law perspective, a U.S. parent can be the IP's exclusive legal owner and maintain quality control. So a multinational group can theoretically get the best of both worlds with a CSA by effectively transferring IP offshore without royalties paid back to the U.S. parent. The devil, of course, is in the details.

> **Problem 6.6**: USCo, a U.S. corporation, is a pharmaceutical developer and manufacturer. USCo's scientists have identified a compound that they believe inhibits STAT3 protein production in the human body. The STAT3 protein, when hyperactive, is thought to cause human cancer, particularly

---

[526] Treas. Reg. § 1.482-7T(b). Treasury issued temporary CSA regulations effective January 5, 2009 (due to expire on December 31, 2011). *See* 74 Fed. Reg. 340 (Jan. 5, 2009), *amended* 74 Fed. Reg. 9570 (Mar. 5, 2009). All references in this Chapter are made to these temporary regulations.

[527] Treas. Reg. § 1.482-7T(b)(1).

[528] Treas. Reg. § 1.482-7T(j)(2)(iii).

breast cancer. So USCo seeks to develop the compound into an approved cancer drug. Consider the tax consequences of the following:

(a) USCo incurs $100x in costs to develop the compound into an approved drug for sale. Assume USCo properly deducted these costs as section 174 research and experimentation expenditures. USCo markets the drug in the U.S. and its foreign branch conducts sales outside the U.S. Half of all drug sales occur in the U.S. and half in foreign countries (sold through the foreign branch). USCo's pre-tax profits (earned through its foreign branch) on its foreign sales are $1,000x. Assume USCo's U.S. effective tax rate is 35 percent. How much U.S. tax did USCo save by deducting its developmental costs and how much U.S. tax does it incur on its foreign profit?[529]

(b) Assume the facts of part (a), except USCo licenses the drug to its wholly-owned subsidiary, Euro Co., which is organized in a European country. Euro Co. then conducts foreign sales and earns a $1,000x pre-tax profit. Pursuant to the licensing agreement, Euro Co. pays $200x in royalties to USCo (assume these royalties are "arm's length"). Assume Euro Co. is subject to a 10 percent effective tax rate and its income is not "Subpart F" income to USCo. Describe the tax consequences to USCo and Euro Co. under this scenario and compare them to part (a).

(c) Assume the facts of parts (a) and (b), except very early in the compound's development, USCo enters into a CSA with Euro Co. to develop the compound into a marketable, approved drug. Because USCo and Euro Co. reasonably anticipate they would benefit equally from the compound's development, they agree to share costs equally. Accordingly, USCo and Euro Co. each incur $50x of the compound's development costs. Assume that Euro Co. deducts its share of development costs in its home country. Euro Co. earns $1,000x pre-tax profit on its sales and pays no royalty to

[529] Because USCo may deduct development costs years before earning profits on the drug, there is a strong time value of money component to this problem. For purposes of simplicity, ignore this time value of money component in this problem.

USCo. For purposes of simplicity, ignore any "buy in" payment Euro Co. may make to USCo. Describe the tax consequences to USCo and Euro Co. under this scenario and compare them to parts (a) and (b).

(d) Assume the same facts as part (c), except compound's development is a complete failure and leads to no marketable drug. How does this result compare to a scenario where there was no CSA and USCo undertook all costs to develop the compound?

Under a typical two-party[530] CSA, one party owns existing intangibles that are used under the CSA to develop new ones. In this case, the other party must compensate the first party for use of those existing intangibles through a "buy-in" payment.[531] For instance, in Problem 6.6(c), USCo and Euro Co. undoubtedly used some of USCo's existing intangibles to develop the cancer drug (after all, USCo's preliminary research led to the compound's initial discovery). So Euro Co. must compensate USCo for these existing intangibles with a buy-in payment. The question, of course, is how much?

Not surprisingly, the "how much" question is a contentious issue between multinationals and the Service. In computing buy-in payments, multinationals have the same tax savings incentive they do in transfer pricing. For instance, consider a CSA between a U.S. parent and its foreign subsidiary where the initial technology comes from the U.S. parent. The U.S. parent has an incentive to cause its foreign subsidiary's buy-in payment to be as low as possible. In this way, more profit is captured in the foreign subsidiary subject to low foreign rates, and U.S. tax is deferred indefinitely. Generally, buy-in payments will be lower early in an intangible's development and higher later on. For this reason, the earlier in an intangible's development a CSA is entered into, the better for the multinational group.

In the early 2000s, the Service audited numerous CSAs and determined that many multinationals undervalued buy-in payments.[532] According to the Service, the most abusive cases involve CSAs where the U.S. parent performs all research and development and

---

[530] A CSA may have multiple participants, each of which has existing intangibles to be used to develop new intangibles. For purposes of simplicity, a two-party CSA is discussed here.

[531] Treas. Reg. § 1.482-7T(b)(1)(ii). The temporary regulations refer to "buy in" payments as a "platform contribution transaction (PCT) payments" (this Chapter uses the colloquial term "buy in" payments for simplicity's sake).

[532] *See e.g.* FSA 200023014 (Feb. 29, 2000); FSA 200225009 (Mar. 7, 2002).

contributes all the existing intangibles and technology to the CSA. In these alleged abusive cases, the foreign entity only contributes the cash required to pay the CSA buy-in and to fund its proportional share of the intangible development costs. In many of these cases, the Service found the foreign entity earned profits from the CSA beyond the routine profits a typical cash investor would expect. These non-routine (extraordinary) profits, in the Service's view, should have been paid to the U.S. parent as a buy-in for its existing intangibles.

In response to these perceived abuses, the Service in 2007 labeled CSA buy-in payments a "Tier I" issue (the highest importance to the Service).[533] Treasury issued proposed regulations in 2005 and temporary regulations in 2009 to address, in large part, computation of buy-in payments.[534] These regulations are exhaustive and cannot be covered in great detail in this Chapter, but the regulations contain two very important aspects worth discussing briefly.

First, the temporary regulations define "existing intangibles"[535] very broadly as "any resource, capability, or right that a controlled participant has developed, maintained, or acquired externally to the intangible development activity (whether prior to or during the course of the CSA) that is reasonably anticipated to contribute to developing cost shared intangibles."[536] This definition is broader than the definition of "section 482 intangibles" contained in Treas. Reg. § 1.482-4(b)[537] and might arguably include assembled workforce, goodwill, and going concern value in certain cases. If assembled workforce, goodwill, and going concern value are "existing intangibles," buy-in payments would significantly increase.

---

[533] *Industry Director Directive #1 on Transfer of Intangibles Offshore/ §482 Cost Sharing Buy-in Payment*, LMSB-04-0307-027 (Apr. 5, 2007).

[534] *See* 70 Fed. Reg. 51116 (proposed regulations effective Aug. 29, 2005); 74 Fed. Reg. 340 (temporary regulations effective Jan. 5, 2009).

[535] Temporary regulations use the term "platform contribution" in place of "existing intangible." Treas. Reg. § 1.482-7T(c)(1).

[536] *Id.* Temporary regulations use the term "platform contributions" in place of "existing intangibles."

[537] Treas. Reg. § 1.482-4(b) defines an "intangible" as an asset that comprises any of the following items and has substantial value independent of the services of any individual, including (1) patents, inventions, formulae, processes, designs, patterns, or know-how; (2) copyrights and literary, musical, or artistic compositions; (3) trademarks, trade names, or brand names; (4) franchises, licenses, or contracts; (5) methods, programs, systems, procedures, campaigns, surveys, studies, forecasts, estimates, customer lists, or technical data; and (6) other similar items.

Second, the temporary regulations generally apply an "investor model" to computing "buy in" payments. Under this "investor model," each CSA party is generally expected to earn a return on its aggregate investment of cash, intangible property, and other resources in the CSA according to a risk-adjusted discount rate.[538] The "investor model" is really meant to limit the returns of a foreign entity that contributes only cash to CSA. In such case, the foreign entity earns only a discount rate on its cash contributions, with the bulk of non-routine profits allocated as a "buy-in" to the U.S. parent that contributed existing intangibles.

Buy-in payment computation was at issue in *Veritas Software Corp. v. Commissioner.*[539] In *Veritas*, a U.S. parent and its Irish subsidiary entered into a CSA to develop computer software. Because the U.S. parent contributed existing intangibles (mostly software) to the CSA, the Irish subsidiary made a $118 million buy-in payment. The U.S. parent computed the buy-in based on comparable licenses of the existing software to unrelated parties. The Service ultimately computed the buy-in at $1.675 billion based on many of the principles embodied in the 2009 temporary regulations (even though the tax years in issue predated the 2009 temporary regulations' effective date). In particular, the Service broadly defined existing intangibles (including assembled workforce[540]) and computed the buy-in payment based on methods similar to the investor model.

The Tax Court rejected the Service's computation and held for the U.S. parent. First, the Tax Court held that the Service improperly included assembled workforce as an existing intangible.[541] Second, the Tax Court criticized the Service's investor model computation method as "flimsy" and really "akin to a sale" of the entire U.S. parent's business.[542] At the time of this Chapter's writing, the impact of *Veritas* on the validity of the 2009 temporary regulations is unclear. Although the Service did not appeal *Veritas*, it did not acquiesce in the Tax Court's decision.[543]

---

[538] *See generally* Treas. Reg. § 1.482-7T(g)(2).

[539] 133 T.C. 297 (2009).

[540] The Service referred to "access to R&D team" and "access to marketing team" as existing intangibles subject to the buy-in. 133 T.C. at 316 & n. 22. This Chapter refers to these nebulous "intangible" rights simply as and "assembled workforce." It is also referred to as "workforce in place."

[541] *Id.* at 322-23. The Court held that workforce in place is not listed as a "section 482 intangible" as defined in Treas. Reg. § 1.482-4(b) and does not have "substantial value independent of the services of any individual." *Id.* at 323 n. 31.

[542] *Id.* at 315-16; 320-21.

[543] Action on Decision, 2010-49 (Dec. 6, 2010).

Another contentious issue between multinationals and the Service is whether stock-based compensation should be a shared cost under a CSA. To illustrate, suppose a U.S. parent and its foreign subsidiary enter a CSA to develop new technology. The U.S. parent's employees perform most of the research and development and are compensated, in part, with stock options. Should the foreign subsidiary have to share in this stock-based compensation as a shared cost? In *Xilinx, Inc. v. Commissioner*,[544] the Tax Court held that stock-based compensation is not a shared cost because unrelated parties typically do not share such costs. The Ninth Circuit initially reversed the Tax Court, but withdrew its opinion and affirmed the Tax Court's decision.[545] The tax years at issue in *Xilinx* predated changes in 2003 to the CSA regulations that now require related parties to share costs of stock-based compensation.

---

544 125 T.C. 37 (2005).

545 567 F.3d 482 (9th Cir. 2009), *opinion withdrawn*, 592 F.3d 1017 (2010), *rev'd*, 598 F.3d 1191 (2010).

Appendix A: An Intellectual Property Primer

Professor David C. Berry

Before exploring the tax consequences of acquiring, owning, or transferring legal rights falling in the broad class of intangible assets known as "intellectual property," a brief overview of intellectual property rights ("IPR") is in order. Each category of IPR alone could fill this casebook with statutes, cases, and commentary. The following sections provide only an overview of the four principal IPRs: Patents, Trade Secrets, Copyrights, and Trademarks.

At the outset, it is notable that each category of IPR is not exclusive of the other categories. One product of human creativity may include aspects protected by multiple IPRs. As a result, different aspects of the same product or process may be protected by different intellectual property principles, governed by different statutes or sources of law, featuring different legal requirements, and bestowing vastly different rights to the owner. This mosaic of intellectual property law creates challenging issues. The one common feature of all IPRs is that they allow the owner of the right to exercise some degree of control over the public use of an idea or expression of an idea that otherwise would be part of the "public domain."

A. The "Public Domain"

Creativity is impossible without a rich public domain. Nothing today, likely nothing since we tamed fire, is genuinely new: Culture, like science and technology, grows by accretion, each new creator building on the works of those who came before.

Alex Kozinski, U.S. Circuit Judge
Dissenting in *White v. Samsung Elec. Am., Inc.*, 989 F.2d 1512, 1513 (9th Cir. 1993)

INTERNATIONAL NEWS SERVICE v. ASSOCIATED PRESS

248 U.S. 215 (1918)

[Opinion of the Court omitted].

Mr. Justice Brandeis, dissenting:

[A]n essential element of individual property is the legal right to exclude others from enjoying it. If the property is private, the right of exclusion may be absolute; if the property is affected with a public interest, the right of exclusion is qualified. But the fact that a product of the mind has cost its producer money and labor, and has a value for which others are willing to pay, is not sufficient to ensure to it this legal attribute of property. The general rule of law is, that the noblest of human productions-knowledge, truths ascertained, conceptions, and ideas-become, after voluntary communication to others, free as the air to common use. Upon these incorporeal productions the attribute of property is continued after such communication only in certain classes of cases where public policy has seemed to demand it. These exceptions are confined to productions which, in some degree, involve creation, invention, or discovery. But by no means all such are endowed with this attribute of property. The creations which are recognized as property by the common law are literary, dramatic, musical, and other artistic creations; and these have also protection under the copyright statutes. The inventions and discoveries upon which this attribute of property is conferred only by statute, are the few comprised within the patent law. There are also many other cases in which courts interfere to prevent curtailment of plaintiff's enjoyment of incorporal productions; and in which the right to relief is often called a property right, but is such only in a special sense. In those cases, the plaintiff has no absolute right to the protection of his production; he has merely the qualified right to be protected as against the defendant's acts, because of the special relation in which the latter stands or the wrongful method or means employed in acquiring the knowledge or the manner in which it is used. Protection of this character is afforded where the suit is based upon breach of contract or of trust or upon unfair competition.

Notes:

1. **"Free As The Air."** Much artistic, scientific and commercial activity is the result of human creativity. When the originator of an idea discloses it to another person, the idea is available for use by any other person or entity unless it is protected by some legal device to

restrict that use. The body of ideas and information available for public use free of legal restraints is known as the "public domain." As Associate Justice Louis D. Brandeis observed in his dissent in the *International News Service* case, the general rule is that ideas in the public domain are "free as the air" for public use.

The originator of an idea can use several legal devices to prevent ideas from entering into the public domain. For example, an idea may be communicated under the terms of a confidentiality agreement, contractually limiting or prohibiting use or further disclosure by the recipient of the communications. Ideas may be protected by express or implied obligations to compensate the originator for use. *See, e.g., Nadel v. Play-By-Play Toys & Novelties, Inc.*, 208 F.3d 368 (2d Cir. 2000) (where plaintiff disclosed idea for new toy, recognizing claims to compensation on implied contract and *quantum meruit* theories). Some common law doctrines, including the "Hot News" doctrine recognized by the majority in *International News Service*, provide short-term protection for time-sensitive information to prevent competitors from free-riding on the owner's investment in collecting the information. *See, e.g., Nat'l Basketball Ass'n v. Motorola, Inc.*, 105 F.3d 841 (2d Cir. 1997) (rejecting the NBA's claim that use of Motorola's "SportsTrax" wireless score service violated the NBA's right to control information about games under the "Hot News" doctrine). Other restraint may arise from master-servant and fiduciary relationships.

2. **Loss of Intellectual Property Protection.** Although proprietary information that is protected by one or more IPR regimes is not part of the public domain, the loss of intellectual property protection usually results in loss of exclusivity. In other words, even once-protected information enters the public domain when the IPR protecting it lapse. *See, e.g., TrafFix Devices, Inc. v. Marketing Displays, Inc.*, 532 U.S. 23 (2001) (upon expiration of utility patent covering design for temporary outdoor signs, the design could not be protected under trademark or trade dress theories); *Dastar Corp. v. Twentieth Century Fox Film Corp.*, 539 U.S. 23 (2003) (following loss of copyright protection, author of television series could not bring claim under trademark law for lack of appropriate attribution when work was used in home video product).

3. **Unique Attributes Of Intellectual Property.** For practitioners familiar with the relatively predictable world of tangible property, including personal and real property, the intangible nature of intellectual property raises new issues. A sampling of the issues one might encounter include: (a) unlike tangible property, where possession implies some degree of title or ownership, the possessor of an idea does not result in any presumption of IP protection or ownership; (b) unlike tangible property, the use of intellectual property by another typically does not diminish the IPR owner's ability to use the idea or information;

(c) unlike tangible property, where possession by a competitor is typically quite apparent, IPR owners may be unaware that their ideas are being used by others without permission, and (d) unlike tangible property ,which is generally defined by a concrete, physical form, the extent and definition of intellectual property may be somewhat unclear and a subject of disagreement.

B. Patents

Next came the Patent laws. These began in England in 1624; and, in this country, with the adoption of our constitution. Before then, any man might instantly use what another had invented; so that the inventor had no special advantage from his own invention. The patent system changed this; secured to the inventor, for a limited time, the exclusive use of his invention; and thereby added the fuel of interest to the fire of genius, in the discovery and production of new and useful things.

Abraham Lincoln
Second Lecture on Discoveries and Inventions (1859).

BONITO BOATS, INC. v. THUNDER CRAFT BOATS, INC.
489 U.S. 141 (1989).

Justice O'CONNOR delivered the opinion of the Court.

We must decide today what limits the operation of the federal patent system places on the States' ability to offer substantial protection to utilitarian and design ideas which the patent laws leave otherwise unprotected. In *Interpart Corp. v. Italia*, 777 F.2d 678 (1985), the Court of Appeals for the Federal Circuit concluded that a California law prohibiting the use of the "direct molding process" to duplicate unpatented articles posed no threat to the policies behind the federal patent laws. In this case, the Florida Supreme Court came to a contrary conclusion. It struck down a Florida statute which prohibits the use of the direct molding process to duplicate unpatented boat hulls, finding that the protection offered by the Florida law conflicted with the balance struck by Congress in the federal patent statute between the encouragement of invention and free competition in unpatented ideas. 515 So.2d 220 (1987). We granted certiorari to resolve the conflict and we now affirm the judgment of the Florida Supreme Court.

I.

In September 1976, petitioner Bonito Boats, Inc. (Bonito), a Florida corporation, developed a hull design for a fiberglass recreational boat which it marketed under the trade name Bonito Boat Model 5VBR. Designing the boat hull required substantial effort on the part of Bonito. A set of engineering drawings was prepared, from which a hardwood model was created. The hardwood model was then sprayed with fiberglass to create a mold, which then served to produce the finished fiberglass boats for sale. The 5VBR was placed on the market sometime in September 1976. There is no indication in the record that a patent application was ever filed for protection of the utilitarian or design aspects of the hull, or for the process by which the hull was manufactured. The 5VBR was favorably received by the boating public, and "a broad interstate market" developed for its sale. *Ibid.*

In May 1983, after the Bonito 5VBR had been available to the public for over six years, the Florida Legislature enacted Fla.Stat. § 559.94 (1987). The statute makes "[i]t ... unlawful for any person to use the direct molding process to duplicate for the purpose of sale any manufactured vessel hull or component part of a vessel made by another without the written permission of that other person." § 559.94(2). The statute also makes it unlawful for a person to "knowingly sell a vessel hull or component part of a vessel duplicated in violation of subsection (2)." § 559.94(3). Damages, injunctive relief, and attorney's fees are made available to "[a]ny person who suffers injury or damage as the result of a violation" of the statute. § 559.94(4). The statute was made applicable to vessel hulls or component parts duplicated through the use of direct molding after July 1, 1983. § 559.94(5).

On December 21, 1984, Bonito filed this action in the Circuit Court of Orange County, Florida. The complaint alleged that respondent here, Thunder Craft Boats, Inc. (Thunder Craft), a Tennessee corporation, had violated the Florida statute by using the direct molding process to duplicate the Bonito 5VBR fiberglass hull, and had knowingly sold such duplicates in violation of the Florida statute. Bonito sought "a temporary and permanent injunction prohibiting [Thunder Craft] from continuing to unlawfully duplicate and sell Bonito Boat hulls or components," as well as an accounting of profits, treble damages, punitive damages, and attorney's fees. Respondent filed a motion to dismiss the complaint, arguing that under this Court's decisions in *Sears, Roebuck & Co. v. Stiffel Co.*, 376 U.S. 225, 84 S.Ct. 784, 11 L.Ed.2d 661 (1964), and *Compco Corp. v. Day-Brite Lighting, Inc.*, 376 U.S. 234, 84 S.Ct. 779, 11 L.Ed.2d 669 (1964), the Florida statute conflicted with federal patent law and was therefore invalid under the Supremacy Clause of the Federal Constitution. The trial court granted respondent's motion, *id.*, at 10-11, and a divided Court of Appeals affirmed the dismissal of petitioner's complaint. 487 So.2d 395 (1986).

On appeal, a sharply divided Florida Supreme Court agreed with the lower courts' conclusion that the Florida law impermissibly interfered with the scheme established by the federal patent laws. *See* 515 So.2d 220 (1987). The majority read our decisions in *Sears* and *Compco* for the proposition that "when an article is introduced into the public domain, only a patent can eliminate the inherent risk of competition and then but for a limited time." 515 So.2d, at 222. Relying on the Federal Circuit's decision in the *Interpart* case, the three dissenting judges argued that the Florida antidirect molding provision "does not prohibit the copying of an unpatented item. It prohibits one method of copying; the item remains in the public domain." 515 So.2d, at 223 (Shaw, J., dissenting).

II.

Article I, § 8, cl. 8, of the Constitution gives Congress the power "[t]o promote the Progress of Science and useful Arts, by securing for limited Times to Authors and Inventors the exclusive Right to their respective Writings and Discoveries." The Patent Clause itself reflects a balance between the need to encourage innovation and the avoidance of monopolies which stifle competition without any concomitant advance in the "Progress of Science and useful Arts." As we have noted in the past, the Clause contains both a grant of power and certain limitations upon the exercise of that power. Congress may not create patent monopolies of unlimited duration, nor may it "authorize the issuance of patents whose effects are to remove existent knowledge from the public domain, or to restrict free access to materials already available." *Graham v. John Deere Co. of Kansas City*, 383 U.S. 1, 6, 86 S.Ct. 684, 688, 15 L.Ed.2d 545 (1966).

From their inception, the federal patent laws have embodied a careful balance between the need to promote innovation and the recognition that imitation and refinement through imitation are both necessary to invention itself and the very lifeblood of a competitive economy. Soon after the adoption of the Constitution, the First Congress enacted the Patent Act of 1790, which allowed the grant of a limited monopoly of 14 years to any applicant that "hath ... invented or discovered any useful art, manufacture, ... or device, or any improvement therein not before known or used." 1 Stat. 109, 110. In addition to novelty, the 1790 Act required that the invention be "sufficiently useful and important" to merit the 14-year right of exclusion. *Ibid.* Section 2 of the Act required that the patentee deposit with the Secretary of State, a specification and if possible a model of the new invention, "which specification shall be so particular, and said models so exact, as not only to distinguish the invention or discovery from other things before known and used, but also to enable a workman or other person skilled in the art or manufacture ... to make, construct, or use the same, to the end that the public may have the full benefit thereof, after the expiration of the patent term." *Ibid.*

The first Patent Act established an agency known by self-designation as the "Commissioners for the promotion of Useful Arts," composed of the Secretary of State, the Secretary of the Department of War, and the Attorney General, any two of whom could grant a patent. Thomas Jefferson was the first Secretary of State, and the driving force behind early federal patent policy. For Jefferson, a central tenet of the patent system in a free market economy was that "a machine of which we were possessed, might be applied by every man to any use of which it is susceptible." 13 Writings of Thomas Jefferson 335 (Memorial ed. 1904). He viewed a grant of patent rights in an idea already disclosed to the public as akin to an ex post facto law, "obstruct[ing] others in the use of what they possessed before." *Id.*, at 326-327. Jefferson also played a large role in the drafting of our Nation's second Patent Act, which became law in 1793. The Patent Act of 1793 carried over the requirement that the subject of a patent application be "not known or used before the application." Ch. 11, 1 Stat. 318, 319. A defense to an infringement action was created where "the thing, thus secured by patent, was not originally discovered by the patentee, but had been in use, or had been described in some public work anterior to the supposed discovery of the patentee." *Id.*, at 322. Thus, from the outset, federal patent law has been about the difficult business "of drawing a line between the things which are worth to the public the embarrassment of an exclusive patent, and those which are not." 13 Writings of Thomas Jefferson, *supra*, at 335.

Today's patent statute is remarkably similar to the law as known to Jefferson in 1793. Protection is offered to "[w]hoever invents or discovers any new and useful process, machine, manufacture, or composition of matter, or any new and useful improvement thereof." 35 U.S.C. § 101. Since 1842, Congress has also made protection available for "any new, original and ornamental design for an article of manufacture." 35 U.S.C. § 171. To qualify for protection, a design must present an aesthetically pleasing appearance that is not dictated by function alone, and must satisfy the other criteria of patentability. The novelty requirement of patentability is presently expressed in 35 U.S.C. §§ 102(a) and (b), which provide:

"A person shall be entitled to a patent unless-

"(a) the invention was known or used by others in this country, or patented or described in a printed publication in this or a foreign country, before the invention thereof by the applicant for patent, or "(b) the invention was patented or described in a printed publication in this or a foreign country or in public use or on sale in this country more than one year prior to the date of application for patent in the United States...."

Sections 102(a) and (b) operate in tandem to exclude from consideration for patent protection knowledge that is already available to the public. They express a congressional determination that the creation of a monopoly in such information would not only serve no socially useful purpose, but would in fact injure the public by removing existing knowledge from public use. From the Patent Act of 1790 to the present day, the public sale of an unpatented article has acted as a complete bar to federal protection of the idea embodied in the article thus placed in public commerce.

In the case of *Pennock v. Dialogue*, 2 Pet. 1, 7 L.Ed. 327 (1829), Justice Story applied these principles under the patent law of 1800. The patentee had developed a new technique for the manufacture of rubber hose for the conveyance of air and fluids. The invention was reduced to practice in 1811, but letters patent were not sought and granted until 1818. In the interval, the patentee had licensed a third party to market the hose, and over 13,000 feet of the new product had been sold in the city of Philadelphia alone. The Court concluded that the patent was invalid due to the prior public sale, indicating that, "if [an inventor] suffers the thing he invented to go into public use, or to be publicly sold for use" "[h]is voluntary act or acquiescence in the public sale and use is an abandonment of his right." *Id.*, 2 Pet., at 23-24. The Court noted that under the common law of England, letters patent were unavailable for the protection of articles in public commerce at the time of the application, id., at 20, and that this same doctrine was immediately embodied in the first patent laws passed in this country. *Id.*, at 21-22.

As the holding of *Pennock* makes clear, the federal patent scheme creates a limited opportunity to obtain a property right in an idea. Once an inventor has decided to lift the veil of secrecy from his work, he must choose the protection of a federal patent or the dedication of his idea to the public at large. As Judge Learned Hand once put it: "[I]t is a condition upon the inventor's right to a patent that he shall not exploit his discovery competitively after it is ready for patenting; he must content himself with either secrecy or legal monopoly." *Metallizing Engineering Co. v. Kenyon Bearing & Auto Parts Co.*, 153 F.2d 516, 520 (2d Cir.), *cert. denied*, 328 U.S. 840, 66 S.Ct. 1016, 90 L.Ed. 1615 (1946).

In addition to the requirements of novelty and utility, the federal patent law has long required that an innovation not be anticipated by the prior art in the field. Even if a particular combination of elements is "novel" in the literal sense of the term, it will not qualify for federal patent protection if its contours are so traced by the existing technology in the field that the "improvement is the work of the skillful mechanic, not that of the inventor." *Hotchkiss v. Greenwood*, 11 How. 248, 267, 13 L.Ed. 683 (1851). In 1952, Congress codified this judicially developed requirement in 35 U.S.C. § 103, which refuses protection to new developments where "the differences between the subject matter sought to be patented and the prior art are such that the subject matter as a whole would have been obvious at the time the invention was made to a person of ordinary skill in the art to which said subject matter pertains." The nonobviousness requirement extends the field of unpatentable material beyond that which is known to the public under § 102, to include that which could readily be deduced from publicly available material by a person of ordinary skill in the pertinent field of endeavor. *See Graham*, 383 U.S., at 15, 86 S.Ct., at 692. Taken together, the novelty and nonobviousness requirements express a congressional determination that the purposes behind the Patent Clause are best served by free competition and exploitation of either that which is already available to the public or that which may be readily discerned from publicly available material. *See Aronson v. Quick Point Pencil Co.*, 440 U.S. 257, 262, 99 S.Ct. 1096, 1099, 59 L.Ed.2d 296 (1979) ("[T]he stringent requirements for patent protection seek to ensure that ideas in the public domain remain there for the use of the public").

The applicant whose invention satisfies the requirements of novelty, nonobviousness, and utility, and who is willing to reveal to the public the substance of his discovery and "the best mode ... of carrying out his invention," 35 U.S.C. § 112, is granted "the right to exclude others from making, using, or selling the invention throughout the United States," for a period of 17 years. 35 U.S.C. § 154. The federal patent system thus embodies a carefully crafted bargain for encouraging the creation and disclosure of new, useful, and nonobvious advances in technology and design in return for the exclusive right to practice the invention for a period of years. "[The inventor] may keep his invention secret and reap its fruits indefinitely. In consideration of its disclosure and the consequent benefit to the community, the patent is granted. An exclusive enjoyment is guaranteed him for seventeen years, but upon expiration of that period, the knowledge of the invention inures to the people, who are thus enabled without restriction to practice it and profit by its use." *United States v. Dubilier Condenser Corp.*, 289 U.S. 178, 186-187, 53 S.Ct. 554, 557, 77 L.Ed. 1114 (1933).

The attractiveness of such a bargain, and its effectiveness in inducing creative effort and disclosure of the results of that effort, depend almost entirely on a backdrop of free competition in the exploitation of unpatented designs and innovations. The novelty and nonobviousness requirements of patentability embody a congressional understanding, implicit in the Patent Clause itself, that free exploitation of ideas will be the rule, to which the protection of a federal patent is the exception. Moreover, the ultimate goal of the patent system is to bring new designs and technologies into the public domain through disclosure. State law protection for techniques and designs whose disclosure has already been induced by market rewards may conflict with the very purpose of the patent laws by decreasing the range of ideas available as the building blocks of further innovation. The offer of federal protection from competitive exploitation of intellectual property would be rendered meaningless in a world where substantially similar state law protections were readily available. To a limited extent, the federal patent laws must determine not only what is protected, but also what is free for all to use. *Cf. Arkansas Electric Cooperative Corp. v. Arkansas Public Service Comm'n*, 461 U.S. 375, 384, 103 S.Ct. 1905, 1912, 76 L.Ed.2d 1 (1983) ("[A] federal decision to forgo regulation in a given area may imply an authoritative federal determination that the area is best left un regulated, and in that event would have as much pre-emptive force as a decision to regulate") (emphasis in original).

Thus our past decisions have made clear that state regulation of intellectual property must yield to the extent that it clashes with the balance struck by Congress in our patent laws. The tension between the desire to freely exploit the full potential of our inventive resources and the need to create an incentive to deploy those resources is constant. Where it is clear how the patent laws strike that balance in a particular circumstance, that is not a judgment the States may second-guess. We have long held that after the expiration of a federal patent, the subject matter of the patent passes to the free use of the public as a matter of federal law. *See Coats v. Merrick Thread Co.*, 149 U.S. 562, 572, 13 S.Ct. 966, 969, 37 L.Ed. 847 (1893) ("[P]laintiffs' right to the use of the embossed periphery expired with their patent, and the public had the same right to make use of it as if it had never been patented"); *Kellogg Co. v. National Biscuit Co.*, 305 U.S. 111, 59 S.Ct. 109, 83 L.Ed. 73 (1938); *Singer Mfg. Co. v. June Mfg. Co.*, 163 U.S. 169, 16 S.Ct. 1002, 41 L.Ed. 118 (1896). Where the public has paid the congressionally mandated price for disclosure, the States may not render the exchange fruitless by offering patent-like protection to the subject matter of the expired patent. "It is self-evident that on the expiration of a patent the monopoly created by it ceases to exist, and the right to make the thing formerly covered by the patent becomes public property." *Singer, supra*, at 185, 16 S.Ct., at 1008.

In our decisions in *Sears, Roebuck & Co. v. Stiffel Co.*, 376 U.S. 225, 84 S.Ct. 784, 11 L.Ed.2d 661 (1964), and *Compco Corp. v. Day-Brite Lighting, Inc.*, 376 U.S. 234, 84 S.Ct. 779, 11 L.Ed.2d 669 (1964), we found that publicly known design and utilitarian ideas which were unprotected by patent occupied much the same position as the subject matter of an expired patent. . . .

At the heart of Sears and Compco is the conclusion that the efficient operation of the federal patent system depends upon substantially free trade in publicly known, unpatented design and utilitarian conceptions. In *Sears*, the state law offered "the equivalent of a patent monopoly," 376 U.S., at 233, 84 S.Ct., at 789, in the functional aspects of a product which had been placed in public commerce absent the protection of a valid patent. While, as noted above, our decisions since *Sears* have taken a decidedly less rigid view of the scope of federal pre-emption under the patent laws, *e.g., Kewane [Oil Co. v. Bicron Corp., 416 U.S. 470,* 479-480 (1974)], we believe that the *Sears* Court correctly concluded that the States may not offer patent-like protection to intellectual creations which would otherwise remain unprotected as a matter of federal law. Both the novelty and the nonobviousness requirements of federal patent law are grounded in the notion that concepts within the public grasp, or those so obvious that they readily could be, are the tools of creation available to all. They provide the baseline of free competition upon which the patent system's incentive to creative effort depends. A state law that substantially interferes with the enjoyment of an unpatented utilitarian or design conception which has been freely disclosed by its author to the public at large impermissibly contravenes the ultimate goal of public disclosure and use which is the centerpiece of federal patent policy. Moreover, through the creation of patent-like rights, the States could essentially redirect inventive efforts away from the careful criteria of patentability developed by Congress over the last 200 years. We understand this to be the reasoning at the core of our decisions in *Sears* and *Compco*, and we reaffirm that reasoning today.

III.

We believe that the Florida statute at issue in this case so substantially impedes the public use of the otherwise unprotected design and utilitarian ideas embodied in unpatented boat hulls as to run afoul of the teaching of our decisions in *Sears* and *Compco*. It is readily apparent that the Florida statute does not operate to prohibit "unfair competition" in the usual sense that the term is understood. The law of unfair competition has its roots in the common-law tort of deceit: its general concern is with protecting consumers from confusion as to source. While that concern may result in the creation of "quasi-property rights" in communicative symbols, the focus is on the protection of consumers, not the protection of producers as an incentive to product innovation. . . .

In contrast to the operation of unfair competition law, the Florida statute is aimed directly at preventing the exploitation of the design and utilitarian conceptions embodied in the product itself. The sparse legislative history surrounding its enactment indicates that it was intended to create an inducement for the improvement of boat hull designs. . . . To accomplish this goal, the Florida statute endows the original boat hull manufacturer with rights against the world, similar in scope and operation to the rights accorded a federal patentee. Like the patentee, the beneficiary of the Florida statute may prevent a competitor from "making" the product in what is evidently the most efficient manner available and from "selling" the product when it is produced in that fashion. Compare 35 U.S.C. § 154. The Florida scheme offers this protection for an unlimited number of years to all boat hulls and their component parts, without regard to their ornamental or technological merit. Protection is available for subject matter for which patent protection has been denied or has expired, as well as for designs which have been freely revealed to the consuming public by their creators.

In this case, the Bonito 5VBR fiberglass hull has been freely exposed to the public for a period in excess of six years. For purposes of federal law, it stands in the same stead as an item for which a patent has expired or been denied: it is unpatented and unpatentable. *See* 35 U.S.C. § 102(b). Whether because of a determination of unpatentability or other commercial concerns, petitioner chose to expose its hull design to the public in the marketplace, eschewing the bargain held out by the federal patent system of disclosure in exchange for exclusive use. Yet, the Florida statute allows petitioner to reassert a substantial property right in the idea, thereby constricting the spectrum of useful public knowledge. Moreover, it does so without the careful protections of high standards of innovation and limited monopoly contained in the federal scheme. We think it clear that such protection conflicts with the federal policy "that all ideas in general circulation be dedicated to the common good unless they are protected by a valid patent." *Lear, Inc. v. Adkins*, 395 U.S.[653, 668 (1969).]

That the Florida statute does not remove all means of reproduction and sale does not eliminate the conflict with the federal scheme. . . . In essence, the Florida law prohibits the entire public from engaging in a form of reverse engineering of a product in the public domain. This is clearly one of the rights vested in the federal patent holder, but has never been a part of state protection under the law of unfair competition or trade secrets. The duplication of boat hulls and their component parts may be an essential part of innovation in the field of hydrodynamic design. Variations as to size and combination of various elements may lead to significant advances in the field. Reverse engineering of chemical and mechanical articles in the public domain often leads to significant advances in technology. If Florida may prohibit this particular method of study and recomposition of an unpatented article, we fail to see the principle that would prohibit a State from banning the use of chromatography in the reconstitution of unpatented chemical compounds, or the use of robotics in the duplication of machinery in the public domain.

Moreover, as we noted in *Kewanee*, the competitive reality of reverse engineering may act as a spur to the inventor, creating an incentive to develop inventions that meet the rigorous requirements of patentability. 416 U.S., at 489-490, 94 S.Ct., at 1889-1890. The Florida statute substantially reduces this competitive incentive, thus eroding the general rule of free competition upon which the attractiveness of the federal patent bargain depends. . . .

The Florida scheme blurs this clear federal demarcation between public and private property. One of the fundamental purposes behind the Patent and Copyright Clauses of the Constitution was to promote national uniformity in the realm of intellectual property. *See* The Federalist No. 43, p. 309 (B. Wright ed. 1961). Since the Patent Act of 1800, Congress has lodged exclusive jurisdiction of actions "arising under" the patent laws in the federal courts, thus allowing for the development of a uniform body of law in resolving the constant tension between private right and public access. *See* 28 U.S.C. § 1338; *see also* Chisum, The Allocation of Jurisdiction Between State and Federal Courts in Patent Litigation, 46 Wash.L.Rev. 633, 636 (1971). Recently, Congress conferred exclusive jurisdiction of all patent appeals on the Court of Appeals for the Federal Circuit, in order to "provide nationwide uniformity in patent law." H.R.Rep. No. 97-312, p. 20 (1981). This purpose is frustrated by the Florida scheme, which renders the status of the design and utilitarian "ideas" embodied in the boat hulls it protects uncertain. Given the inherently ephemeral nature of property in ideas, and the great power such property has to cause harm to the competitive policies which underlay the federal patent laws, the demarcation of broad zones of public and private right is "the type of regulation that demands a uniform national rule." *Ray v. Atlantic Richfield Co.*, 435 U.S. 151, 179, 98 S.Ct. 988, 1005, 55 L.Ed.2d 179 (1978). Absent such a federal rule, each State could afford patent-like protection to particularly favored home industries, effectively insulating them from competition from outside the State. . . .

The Florida statute is aimed directly at the promotion of intellectual creation by substantially restricting the public's ability to exploit ideas that the patent system mandates shall be free for all to use. Like the interpretation of Illinois unfair competition law in *Sears* and *Compco*, the Florida statute represents a break with the tradition of peaceful co-existence between state market regulation and federal patent policy. The Florida law substantially restricts the public's ability to exploit an unpatented design in general circulation, raising the specter of state-created monopolies in a host of useful shapes and processes for which patent protection has been denied or is otherwise unobtainable. It thus enters a field of regulation which the patent laws have reserved to Congress. The patent statute's careful balance between public right and private monopoly to promote certain creative activity is a "scheme of federal regulation ... so pervasive as to make reasonable the inference that Congress left no room for the States to supplement it." *Rice v. Santa Fe Elevator Corp.*, 331 U.S. 218, 230, 67 S.Ct. 1146, 1152, 91 L.Ed. 1447 (1947).

Congress has considered extending various forms of limited protection to industrial design either through the copyright laws or by relaxing the restrictions on the availability of design patents. . . . and despite sustained criticism for a number of years, it has declined to alter the patent protections presently available for industrial design. . . . It is for Congress to determine if the present system of design and utility patents is ineffectual in promoting the useful arts in the context of industrial design. By offering patent-like protection for ideas deemed unprotected under the present federal scheme, the Florida statute conflicts with the "strong federal policy favoring free competition in ideas which do not merit patent protection." *Lear, Inc.*, 395 U.S., at 656, 89 S.Ct., at 1903. We therefore agree with the majority of the Florida Supreme Court that the Florida statute is preempted by the Supremacy Clause, and the judgment of that court is hereby affirmed.

It is so ordered.

Notes:

1. **Source of Law.** Patent law gives an inventor the right to exclude others from practicing his or her claimed invention, regardless of the specific means of implementation, for a limited term. As the Court in *Bonito Boats* observed, the United States patent system is based on a comprehensive scheme of federal law, administrative regulations, and courts. The Patent Act, 35 U.S.C. § 1, *et seq.* governs the granting and enforcement of patents. The various U.S. district courts have exclusive federal question jurisdiction over actions arising under the patent laws, including infringement actions and declaratory judgment actions seeking a determination that a patent is invalid or not infringed. 28 U.S.C. § 1338. The uniformity of judicial interpretations of the Patent Act is bolstered by the fact that one federal appeals court, the U.S. Court of Appeals for the Federal Circuit (known as the "CAFC"), has exclusive jurisdiction over appeals from patent cases from all district courts nationwide. 28 U.S.C. § 1295(a)(1). The CAFC also has jurisdiction over appeals from the U.S. International Trade Commission and administrative appeals from the U.S. Patent and Trademark Office ("USPTO"). As the *Bonito Boats* decision illustrates, state laws that provide patent-like rights are pre-empted.

2. **Examination.** Patents are issued by the USPTO to applicants for patent following an administrative review process known as "examination." During examination, a

government officer, known as an "examiner," reviews the application to determine whether the subject matter sought to be patented meets to statutory requirements for patentability set forth in the Patent Act. As the Court in *Bonito Boats* summarizes, the principal statutory requirements for patentability are eligible subject matter, 35 U.S.C. § 101, novelty, 35 U.S.C. § 102, nonobviousness, 35 U.S.C. § 103(a), utility, 35 U.S.C. § 101, and an adequate disclosure of the invention, 35 U.S.C. § 112, 1st par. Upon allowance of an application by the examiner, and payment of applicable fees, the USPTO issues the patent, and the patentee's right to exclude others from practicing the claims subject matter becomes effective. Examination is an *ex parte* process and may last many months. For Fiscal year 2009, the average total pendency period for patents was 34.6 months. USPTO, Performance and Accountability Report Fiscal Year 2009.

3. **USPTO Volume and Fees.** The USPTO processes a huge number of patent applications each year. During Fiscal year 2009, a total of 485,500 U.S. national patent applications were filed with the USPTO, and 190,121 patents were issued. The Patent Office is fully supported by user fees and substantial fees are required to pursue a patent. As of 2010, the filing fee for a basic utility application was $330; the search fee was $540; the examination fee was $220; and the issue fee was $1,510. Additional fees and surcharges are common. Following issuance, the patent owner must pay periodic maintenance fees to keep the patent in effect for its full term. As of 2010, the maintenance fee due at 3.5 years after issue was $980; the fee due at 7.5 years was $2,480; the final maintenance fee due at 11.5 years after issue was $4,110.

4. **Patent Term.** Patents provide a right to exclude others from practicing the claimed subject matter in the United States for a specific term. As the *Bonito Court* noted, the basic patent term for patents issued from applications filed prior to June 4, 1993 is 17 years from the date of issue. For applications filed on or after June 4, 1993, however, the patent term is the longer of 20 years from the application date or 17 years from the date of issue. Therefore, for most patents filed today, the patent term is 20 years from the application date. Because the average examination period is approximately three years, the net patent term from date of issue remains about 17 years on average. The Patent Act provides for adjustment or extension of patent term in limited situations, such as when unusual USPTO delays during examination delay issuance of the patent, 35 U.S.C. § 154(b), or when the owner of a patent covering a new drug product regulated by the U.S. Food and Drug Administration cannot market a product covered by the patent for part of the term due to FDA delay in granting approval. 35 U.S.C. § 155A.

5. **Eligible Subject Matter**. Utility patents are available only for "any new and useful process, machine, manufacture, or composition of matter, or any new and useful improvement thereof," so long as the other requirements of the Patent Act are satisfied. 35 U.S.C. § 101. The Supreme Court has noted that the legislative history of the current Patent Act, enacted in 1952, suggests that Congress intended it to cover both known and future, unforeseen areas of invention, and that it covers "anything under the sun that is made by man." *Diamond v. Chakrabarty*, 447 U.S. 303, 309 (1980), *quoting* S.Rep.No.1979, 82d Cong., 2d Sess., 5 (1952); H.R.Rep.No.1923, 82d Cong., 2d Sess., 6 (1952). However, patents are not available for laws of nature, physical phenomena, and abstract ideas. In a series of cases, the courts have recognized patent eligibility for several areas of technology that Congress likely did not foresee when passing the Patent Act in 1952. *See Chakrabarty*, 447 U.S. at 309-10 (concluding that living bacteria organisms modified by introducing plasmids providing a separate hydrocarbon degradative pathway was a "manufacture" and "composition of matter"); *Diamond v. Diehr*, 450 U.S. 175 (1981)(holding that a computerized process for curing rubber was eligible subject matter). Most recently, in *Bilski v. Kappos*, ___ U.S. ___, 130 S. Ct. 3218 (2010), the Court rejected a rigid test adopted by the Federal Circuit as the sole test for patent eligibility of process inventions. Under that test, process inventions were limited to those tied to a particular machine or resulting in a physical transformation. The *Bilski* Court held that the invention at issue, a process for hedging risk in commodity markets, was not eligible for patenting because it was merely an "abstract idea." Although it observed that the "Machine-or-Transformation" test was an important clue in determining eligibility, it was not a rigid requirement. The Court left to the Federal Circuit the task of developing eligibility guidelines to be applied in future cases.

6. **Novelty**. One important requirement for patentability is that the invention claimed in a patent must be novel. A determination of novelty requires a application of a set of detailed rules set forth in 35 U.S.C. § 102. For example, § 102(b) requires that the claimed invention not be publicly known or used in the United States, subject to a commercial offer for sale in the United States, or patented or disclosed in a printed publication anywhere in the world, more than one year before the effective filing date of the U.S. application leading to the patent. *See, e.g., Lough v. Brunswick Corp.*, 86 F.3d 1113 (Fed. Cir. 1996) (public use of invention more than one year prior to filing date created statutory bar to patentability). In addition, 35 U.S.C. § 102(a) creates a separate requirement that a claimed invention not be publicly known or used in the United States, or patented or disclosed in a printed publication anywhere in the world, prior to the date of invention.

7. **Nonobviousness.** A critical statutory requirement for patentability, and the most common reason for rejection of a patent application during examination, is that the claimed

invention must not have been obvious to a person ordinarily skilled in the relevant art at the time the invention was made. *See Graham v. John Deere Co. of Kansas City*, 383 U.S. 1 (1966). In order to determine obviousness, the USPTO must determine the scope and content of the "prior art," including public references and disclosures publicly accessible prior to the invention date, and compare the state of the prior art to the invention sought to be patented. In assessing whether a person of ordinary skill in the art would consider the invention obvious, the USPTO must consider the ordinary amount to creativity in the art. In a recent case, *KSR Int'l Co. v. Teleflex Inc.*, 550 U.S. 398 (2007), the Supreme Court rejected restrictive rules limiting the use of prior art to establish the obviousness of claimed inventions. As a result, the USPTO has greater latitude in rejecting applications for obviousness, and the courts are more likely to invalidate issued patents.

8. Disclosure. Another requirement for patentability is that the application for patent must disclose the invention in sufficient detail so that a person of ordinary skill in the art could make and use the invention without undue experimentation. *See, e.g., Hybritech Inc. v. Monoclonal Antibodies, Inc.*, 802 F.2d 1367 (Fed. Cir. 1986). In part, this disclosure of technology to the USPTO, which in most instances is later published, is the "*quid pro quo*" for the government's grant of patent rights to the applicant. *See Kewanee Oil Co. v. Bicron Corp.*, 416 U.S. 470, 484 (1974). In addition to enabling disclosure, the application must disclose the preferred mode of practicing the invention contemplated by the inventor as of the application filing date. *See Spectra-Physics, Inc. v. Coherent, Inc.*, 827 F.2d 1524 (Fed. Cir. 1987) (contrasting separate, but related, requirements of enablement and "best mode").

9. Inventorship and Priority. In the United States, patents are issued to the inventors of the claimed subject matter. An inventor is a person who mentally conceives part of at least one claimed invention in a patent. Often, patents identify multiple joint inventors. A joint inventor both must have conceived part of the invention and participated in a collaboration with the other inventors. *Kimberly-Clark Corp. v. Procter & Gamble Distrib. Co.*, 973 F.2d 911, 917 (Fed.Cir.1992). Occasionally, two applicants seek a patent on the same invention concurrently. At the time of this writing, the Patent Act awards priority in such instances to the inventor who first completed the invention process, by conceiving the claimed invention and reducing it to practice. 35 U.S.C. § 102(g)(2). The United States is the only country with a patent system featuring a "first-to-invent" priority system. Legislation to convert the U.S. patent system to a "first-to-file" system has been introduced into Congress. *See* Patent Reform Act of 2011, SB 33 (112th Cong.).

10. Ownership and Assignment. In the first instance, patent rights are intangible property co-owned by the named inventors. Many corporations have adopted a blanket policy requiring technical employees to execute "invention assignment" agreements, in which employees agree to assign their rights in any patents issued based on their work as an employee to the corporation. Each joint inventor or co-owner a patent has a separate right to practice, license, of assign their interest in the entire patent, even if the joint inventor's contribution was limited to only one claimed invention in a patent with many claims. *See, e.g., Ethicon, Inc. v. U.S. Surgical Corp.*, 135 F.3d 1456 (Fed. Cir. 1998) (omitted joint inventor of selected claims in patent had right to grant retroactive license to accused infringer without permission of other inventor). Moreover, in the absence of an agreement providing otherwise, each co-owner has the right to exploit their interest in the patent without accounting to the other owners. *Id.* Once issued by the USPTO, the transfer of interests in patents if largely governed by state property law. For example, state law governs the grant of security interests in patents. *See, e.g., In re Cybernetic Services, Inc.*, 252 F.3d 1039 (9th Cir. 2001) (perfection of security interest in patents governed by state version of Uniform Commercial Code).

11. Shop Rights. Even if an employer does not obtain an assignment of an employee's patent, it may receive an implied, non-transferrable, license to practice the invention under a common law doctrine known as "shop rights." *See McElmurry v. Arkansas Power & Light Co.*, 995 F.2d 1576, 1582 (Fed. Cir. 1993) (employer's shop rights in an invention depends of totality of circumstances, including whether employer provided wages, materials, tools and a work place).

12. Territoriality of Right. Patents provide a right to exclude only in the jurisdiction that issued the patent. As a result, U.S. patents only exclude the use of a patented invention in the United States. *See NTP, Inc. v. Research In Motion, Ltd.*, 418 F.3d 1282 (Fed. Cir. 2005) (considering whether wireless messaging system infringes U.S. patent when computer servers were located in Canada). Companies that compete in global markets generally obtain non-U.S. patent protection by filing counterpart applications in other commercially significant jurisdictions, including the European Union, South Korea, Japan, Canada, China and other industrialized countries. Although the Patent Cooperation Treaty provides for the filing of a single international patent application, that application subsequently must be nationalized to obtain separate patents in each jurisdiction.

13. Infringement. A patentee has the right to enforce a patent by filing an infringement action in a federal district court against any person or entity that makes, uses, offers for sale, sells, or imports into the United states a product or process covered by the patent. 35 U.S.C. § 271(a). Patent infringement is a strict liability offense, and an infringer is liable even if it was not aware of the patent. The Patent Act also provide liability for vicarious liability, such as for contributory infringement, 35 U.S.C. § 271(c), and active inducement of infringement, 35 U.S.C. § 271(b). If a patentee proves that a defendant is liable for infringing a valid patent claim, the patentee may be awarded damages, including lost profits, but not less than a reasonable royalty. 35 U.S.C. § 284. In addition, if the patentee can demonstrate irreparable harm, the lack of an adequate legal remedy, a favorable balance of the equities and public interest, court may grant a permanent injunction preventing the defendant from infringing the patent for the remainder of its term. *eBay Inc. v. MercExchange, L.L.C.*, 547 U.S. 388 (2006).

C. Trade Secrets

> Three may keep a secret, if two of them are dead.
> *Benjamin Franklin*

> He who trusts secrets to a servant makes him his master.
> *John Dryden*

LEARNING CURVE TOYS, INC. v. PLAYWOOD TOYS, INC.

342 F.3d 714 (7th Cir. 2003)

RIPPLE, Circuit Judge.

PlayWood Toys, Inc. ("PlayWood") obtained a jury verdict against Learning Curve Toys, Inc. and its representatives, Roy Wilson, Harry Abraham and John Lee (collectively, "Learning Curve"), for misappropriation of a trade secret in a realistic looking and sounding toy railroad track under the Illinois Trade Secrets Act, 765 ILCS § 1065/1 *et seq.* The jury awarded PlayWood a royalty of "8% for a license that would have been negotiated [absent the misappropriation] to last for the lifetime of the product." R.194. Although there was substantial evidence of misappropriation before the jury, the district court did not enter judgment on the jury's verdict. Instead, it granted judgment as a matter of law in favor of Learning Curve, holding that PlayWood did not have a protectable trade secret in the toy railroad track. PlayWood appealed. For the reasons set forth in the following opinion, we reverse the judgment of the district court and reinstate the jury's verdict. . . .

I

BACKGROUND

A. Facts

In 1992, Robert Clausi and his brother-in-law, Scott Moore, began creating prototypes of wooden toys under the name PlayWood Toys, Inc., a Canadian corporation. Clausi was the sole toy designer and Moore was the sole officer and director of PlayWood. Neither Clausi nor Moore had prior experience in the toy industry, but Clausi had "always been a bit of a doodler and designer," Trial Tr. at 58, and the two men desired to "create high-quality hardwood maple toys for the independent toy market," *id.* at 241. As a newly formed corporation, PlayWood did not own a facility in which it could produce toys. Instead, it worked in conjunction with Mario Borsato, who owned a wood-working facility. Subject to a written confidentiality agreement with PlayWood, Borsato manufactured prototypes for PlayWood based on Clausi's design specifications.

PlayWood's first attempt to market publicly its toys was at the Toronto Toy Fair on January 31, 1992. PlayWood received favorable reviews from many of the toy retailers in attendance; PlayWood also learned that the best way to get recognition for its toys was to attend the New York Toy Fair ("Toy Fair") the following month. Based on this information, Clausi and Moore secured a position at the Toy Fair in order to display PlayWood's prototypes. It was during this Toy Fair that Clausi and Moore first encountered Learning Curve representatives Roy Wilson, Harry Abraham and John Lee.

On the morning of February 12, 1993, the first day of the Toy Fair, Roy Wilson stopped at PlayWood's booth and engaged Clausi and Moore in conversation. Wilson identified himself as Learning Curve's toy designer and explained that his company had a license from the Britt Allcroft Company to develop Thomas the Tank Engine & Friends ™ (hereinafter "Thomas") trains and accessories. Wilson commented that he was impressed with the look and quality of PlayWood's prototypes and raised the possibility of working together under a custom manufacturing contract to produce Learning Curve's line of Thomas products. Clausi and Moore responded that such an arrangement would be of great interest to PlayWood. Later that same day, Harry Abraham, Learning Curve's vice president, and John Lee, Learning Curve's president, also stopped by PlayWood's booth. They too commented on the quality of PlayWood's prototypes and indicated that PlayWood might be a good candidate for a manufacturing contract with Learning Curve.

Clausi and Moore continued to have discussions with Learning Curve's representatives over the remaining days of the Toy Fair, which ended on February 14. During these discussions, Lee indicated that he would like two of his people, Abraham and Wilson, to visit PlayWood in Toronto the day after the Toy Fair ended in order to determine whether the two parties could work out a manufacturing arrangement for some or all of Learning Curve's wooden toys. Clausi, feeling a little overwhelmed by the suggestion, requested that their visit be postponed a few days so that he could better acquaint himself with Learning Curve's products. The parties ultimately agreed that Abraham and Wilson would visit PlayWood at Borsato's facility on February 18, 1993, four days after the conclusion of the Toy Fair. Clausi spent the next several days after the Toy Fair researching Learning Curve's products and considering how PlayWood could produce Learning Curve's trains and track.

On February 18, 1993, Abraham and Wilson visited PlayWood in Toronto as planned. The meeting began with a tour of Borsato's woodworking facility, where the prototypes on display at the Toy Fair had been made. After the tour, the parties went to the conference room at Borsato's facility. At this point, according to Clausi and Moore, the parties agreed to make their ensuing discussion confidential. Clausi testified:

After we sat down in the board room, Harry [Abraham of Learning Curve] immediately said: "Look, we're going to disclose confidential information to you guys, and we're going to disclose some designs that Roy [Wilson of Learning Curve] has that are pretty confidential. If Brio were to get their hands on them, then we wouldn't like that. And we're going to do it under the basis of a confidential understanding."

And I said: "I also have some things, some ideas on how to produce the track and produce the trains now that I've had a chance to look at them for the last couple of days, and I think they're confidential as well. So if we're both okay with that, we should continue." So we did.

Trial Tr. at 76-77.

Immediately after the parties agreed to keep their discussion confidential, Wilson, at Abraham's direction, showed Clausi and Moore drawings of various Thomas characters and provided information on the projected volume of each of the products. Clausi testified that he considered the documents disclosed by Learning Curve during the meeting confidential because they included information on products not yet released to the public, as well as Learning Curve's projected volumes, costs and profit margins for various products. After viewing Wilson's various drawings, the parties discussed PlayWood's ideas on how to manufacture Learning Curve's trains. Clausi suggested that they might use a CNC machine, which he defined as a computer numerically controlled drill that carves in three dimensions, to create Learning Curve's trains out of a single piece of wood (as opposed to piecing together separate pieces of wood).

The parties' discussion eventually moved away from train production and focused on track design. Wilson showed Clausi and Moore drawings of Learning Curve's track and provided samples of their current product. At this point, Abraham confided to Clausi and Moore that track had posed "a bit of a problem for Learning Curve." Trial Tr. at 85. Abraham explained that sales were terrific for Learning Curve's Thomas trains, but that sales were abysmal for its track. Abraham attributed the lack of sales to the fact that Learning Curve's track was virtually identical to that of its competitor, Brio, which had the lion's share of the track market. Because there was "no differentiation" between the two brands of track, Learning Curve's track was not even displayed in many of the toy stores that carried Learning Curve's products. Id. Learning Curve had worked unsuccessfully for several months attempting to differentiate its track from that of Brio.

After detailing the problems with Learning Curve's existing track, Abraham inquired of Clausi whether "there was a way to differentiate" its track from Brio's track. Trial Tr. at 86. Clausi immediately responded that he "had had a chance to look at the track and get a feel for it [over] the last few days" and that his "thoughts were that if the track were more realistic and more functional, that kids would enjoy playing with it more and it would give the retailer a reason to carry the product, especially if it looked different than the Brio track." *Id.* at 87. Clausi further explained that, if the track "made noise and [ ] looked like real train tracks, that the stores wouldn't have any problem, and the Thomas the Tank line, product line would have [ ] its own different track" and could "effectively compete with Brio." *Id.* Abraham and Wilson indicated that they were "intrigued" by Clausi's idea and asked him what he meant by "making noise." *Id.*

Clausi decided to show Abraham and Wilson exactly what he meant. Clausi took a piece of Learning Curve's existing track from the table, drew some lines across the track (about every three-quarters of an inch), and stated: "We can go ahead and machine grooves right across the upper section ..., which would look like railway tracks, and down below machine little indentations as well so that it would look more like or sound more like real track. You would roll along and bumpity-bumpity as you go along." Trial Tr. at 255. Clausi then called Borsato into the conference room and asked him to cut grooves into the wood "about a quarter of an inch deep from the top surface." *Id.* at 88. Borsato left the room, complied with Clausi's request, and returned with the cut track three or four minutes later. Clausi ran a train back and forth over the cut piece of track. The track looked more realistic than before, but it did not make noise because the grooves were not deep enough. Accordingly, Clausi instructed Borsato to cut the grooves "just a little bit deeper so that they go through the rails." *Id.* Borsato complied with Clausi's request once again and returned a few minutes later with the cut piece of track. Clausi proceeded to run a train back and forth over the track. This time the track made a "clickety-clack" sound, but the train did not run smoothly over the track because the grooves were cut "a little bit too deep." *Id.* at 258. Based on the sound produced by the track, Clausi told Abraham and Moore that if PlayWood procured a contract with Learning Curve to produce the track, they could call it "Clickety-Clack Track." *Id.* at 89.

Both Abraham and Wilson indicated that Clausi's concept of cutting grooves into the track to produce a clacking sound was a novel concept. Thereafter, Wilson and Clausi began to discuss how they could improve the idea to make the train run more smoothly on the track, but Abraham interrupted them and stated: "No, focus. You guys have to get the contract for the basic product first, and then we can talk about new products, because ... it takes [our licensor] a long time to approve new products and new designs." Trial Tr. at 89.

The meeting ended shortly thereafter without further discussion about Clausi's concept for the noise-producing track. Before he left, Wilson asked Clausi if he could take the piece of track that Borsato had cut with him while the parties continued their discussions. Clausi gave Wilson the piece of track without hesitation. The piece of track was the only item that Abraham and Wilson took from the meeting. Clausi and Moore did not ask Wilson for a receipt for the cut track, nor did they seek a written confidentiality agreement to protect PlayWood's alleged trade secret. After the meeting, Clausi amended PlayWood's confidentiality agreement with Borsato to ensure that materials discussed during the meeting would remain confidential. Clausi also stamped many of the documents that he received from Learning Curve during the meeting as confidential because they included information on products not yet released to the public. PlayWood never disclosed the contents of Learning Curve's documents to anyone.

During March of 1993, PlayWood and Learning Curve met on three separate occasions to discuss further the possibility of PlayWood manufacturing Learning Curve's Thomas products. At one of the meetings, and at Learning Curve's request, PlayWood submitted a manufacturing proposal for the Thomas products. Learning Curve rejected PlayWood's proposal. Learning Curve told Clausi that its licensor wanted the Thomas products to be made in the United States.

Thereafter, PlayWood had no contact with Learning Curve until late October of 1993, when Abraham contacted Clausi to discuss another possible manufacturing contract because Learning Curve's secondary supplier was not providing enough product. Again, PlayWood submitted a manufacturing proposal at Learning Curve's request, but it too was rejected. Learning Curve later stated that its new business partner had decided to manufacture the product in China.

Clausi and Moore continued to work on PlayWood's toy concepts. After the 1994 New York Toy Fair, which was not particularly successful for PlayWood, Clausi and Moore began to focus their efforts on refining PlayWood's concept for the noise-producing track. During this time, Clausi and Moore made no attempt to license or sell the concept to other toy companies because they believed that PlayWood still had "an opportunity to get in the door" with Learning Curve if they could perfect the concept and also because they believed that they were bound by a confidentiality agreement. Trial Tr. at 267.

In December of 1994, while shopping for additional track with which to experiment, Moore discovered that Learning Curve was selling noise-producing track under the name "Clickety-Clack Track." Like the piece of track that Clausi had Borsato cut during PlayWood's February 18, 1993 meeting with Learning Curve, Clickety-Clack Track TM has parallel grooves cut into the wood, which cause a "clacking" sound as train wheels roll over the grooves. Learning Curve was promoting the new track as

> the first significant innovation in track design since the inception of wooden train systems.... It is quite simply the newest and most exciting development to come along recently in the wooden train industry, and it's sure to cause a sensation in the marketplace.... [I]t brings that sound and feel of the real thing to a child's world of make-believe without bells, whistles, electronic sound chips or moving parts.

PlayWood's Tr. Ex.71.

Moore was "stunned" when he saw the track because he believed that Learning Curve had stolen PlayWood's concept. Trial Tr. at 268. He testified: "This was our idea. This is what we've been working on even up to that day to go back to [Learning Curve] as an opportunity to get in the door, and there it is on the shelf." *Id.* Moore purchased a package of Clickety-Clack Track TM and showed it to Clausi. Clausi testified that he was disappointed when he saw the track because he believed that Learning Curve had taken PlayWood's name and design concept "almost exactly as per [their] conversation" on February 18, 1993. Trial Tr. at 103.

PlayWood promptly wrote a cease and desist letter to Learning Curve. The letter accused Learning Curve of stealing PlayWood's concept for the noise-producing track that it disclosed to Learning Curve "in confidence in the context of a manufacturing proposal." PlayWood's Tr. Ex.66 at 1. Learning Curve responded by seeking a declaratory judgment that it owned the concept.

Previously, on March 16, 1994, Learning Curve had applied for a patent on the noise-producing track. The patent, which was obtained on October 3, 1995, claims the addition of parallel impressions or grooves in the rails, which cause a "clacking" sound to be emitted as train wheels roll over them. The patent identifies Roy Wilson of Learning Curve as the inventor.

Clickety-Clack Track ™ provided an enormous boost to Learning Curve's sales. Learning Curve had $20 million in track sales by the first quarter of 2000, and $40 million for combined track and accessory sales.

B. District Court Proceedings

[P]layWood's claim for trade secret misappropriation proceeded to trial. The jury returned a verdict in favor of PlayWood. The trial court declined to enter judgment on the verdict[.] . . . Specifically, the court determined that PlayWood did not have a trade secret in its concept for noise-producing toy railroad track under Illinois law because: (1) PlayWood did not demonstrate that its concept was unknown in the industry; (2) PlayWood's concept could have been easily acquired or duplicated through proper means; (3) PlayWood failed to guard the secrecy of its concept; (4) PlayWood's concept had no economic value; and (5) PlayWood expended no time, effort or money to develop the concept[.]

II

DISCUSSION

A. Trade Secret Status

. . .

The parties agree that their dispute is governed by the Illinois Trade Secrets Act ("Act"), 765 ILCS § 1065/1 *et seq*. To prevail on a claim for misappropriation of a trade secret under the Act, the plaintiff must demonstrate that the information at issue was a trade secret, that it was misappropriated and that it was used in the defendant's business. *See Composite Marine Propellers, Inc. v. Van Der Woude*, 962 F.2d 1263, 1265-66 (7th Cir.1992) (*per curiam*); *Southwest Whey, Inc. v. Nutrition 101, Inc.*, 117 F.Supp.2d 770, 775-76 (N.D.Ill.2000); *Magellan Int'l. Corp. v. Salzgitter Handel GmbH.*, 76 F.Supp.2d 919, 926 (N.D.Ill.1999). The issue currently before us is whether there was legally sufficient evidence for the jury to find that PlayWood had a trade secret in its concept for the noise-producing toy railroad track that it revealed to Learning Curve on February 18, 1993.

The Act defines a trade secret as:

> [I]nformation, including but not limited to, technical or non-technical data, a formula, pattern, compilation, program, device, method, technique, drawing, process, financial data, or list of actual or potential customers or suppliers, that:
>
> > (1) is sufficiently secret to derive economic value, actual or potential, from not being generally known to other persons who can obtain economic value from its disclosure or use; and
> > (2) is the subject of efforts that are reasonable under the circumstances to maintain its secrecy or confidentiality.

765 ILCS § 1065/2(d). Both of the Act's statutory requirements focus fundamentally on the secrecy of the information sought to be protected. *See Mangren Research & Dev. Corp. v. Nat'l Chem. Co., Inc.*, 87 F.3d 937, 942 (7th Cir.1996)[.] However, the requirements emphasize different aspects of secrecy. The first requirement, that the information be sufficiently secret to impart economic value because of its relative secrecy, "precludes trade secret protection for information generally known or understood within an industry even if

not to the public at large." . . . The second requirement, that the plaintiff take reasonable efforts to maintain the secrecy of the information, prevents a plaintiff who takes no affirmative measures to prevent others from using its proprietary information from obtaining trade secret protection. *See Jackson v. Hammer*, 274 Ill.App.3d 59, 210 Ill.Dec. 614, 653 N.E.2d 809, 816 (1995) ("[T]he Act requires a plaintiff to take 'affirmative measures' to prevent others from using information.").

Although the Act explicitly defines a trade secret in terms of these two requirements, Illinois courts frequently refer to six common law factors (which are derived from § 757 of the Restatement (First) of Torts) in determining whether a trade secret exists: (1) the extent to which the information is known outside of the plaintiff's business; (2) the extent to which the information is known by employees and others involved in the plaintiff's business; (3) the extent of measures taken by the plaintiff to guard the secrecy of the information; (4) the value of the information to the plaintiff's business and to its competitors; (5) the amount of time, effort and money expended by the plaintiff in developing the information; and (6) the ease or difficulty with which the information could be properly acquired or duplicated by others. *See Delta Med. Sys. v. Mid-America Med. Sys., Inc.*, 331 Ill.App.3d 777, 265 Ill.Dec. 397, 772 N.E.2d 768, 780 (2002)[.]

Contrary to Learning Curve's contention, we do not construe the foregoing factors as a six-part test, in which the absence of evidence on any single factor necessarily precludes a finding of trade secret protection. Instead, we interpret the common law factors as instructive guidelines for ascertaining whether a trade secret exists under the Act. The language of the Act itself makes no reference to these factors as independent requirements for trade secret status, and Illinois case law imposes no such requirement that each factor weigh in favor of the plaintiff. *See ILG Indus., Inc. v. Scott*, 49 Ill.2d 88, 273 N.E.2d 393, 396 (1971) ("An exact definition of a trade secret, applicable to all situations, is not possible. Some factors to be considered in determining whether given information is one's trade secret are [the six factors enumerated in the Restatement].") (internal quotation marks omitted). In this respect, Illinois law is compatible with the approach in other states. Courts from other jurisdictions, as well as legal scholars, have noted that the Restatement factors are not to be applied as a list of requisite elements. . . .

The existence of a trade secret ordinarily is a question of fact. As aptly observed by our colleagues on the Fifth Circuit, a trade secret "is one of the most elusive and difficult concepts in the law to define." *Lear Siegler, Inc. v. Ark-Ell Springs, Inc.*, 569 F.2d 286, 288 (5th Cir.1978). In many cases, the existence of a trade secret is not obvious; it requires an *ad hoc* evaluation of all the surrounding circumstances. For this reason, the question of whether certain information constitutes a trade secret ordinarily is best "resolved by a fact finder after full presentation of evidence from each side." *Id.* at 289. We do not believe that the district court was sufficiently mindful of these principles. The district court, in effect, treated the Restatement factors as requisite elements and substituted its judgment for that of the jury. PlayWood presented sufficient evidence for the jury reasonably to conclude that the Restatement factors weighed in PlayWood's favor.

1. Extent to which PlayWood's concept for noise-producing toy railroad track was known outside of PlayWood's business

PlayWood presented substantial evidence from which the jury could have determined that PlayWood's concept for noise-producing toy railroad track was not generally known outside of Playwood's business. It was undisputed at trial that no similar track was on the market until Learning Curve launched Clickety-Clack Track ™ in late 1994, more than a year after PlayWood first conceived of the concept. Of course, as Learning Curve correctly points out, "[m]erely being the first or only one to use particular information does not in and of itself transform otherwise general knowledge into a trade secret." *George S. May Int'l*, 195 Ill.Dec. 183, 628 N.E.2d at 654. "If it did, the first person to use the information, no matter how ordinary or well known, would be able to appropriate it to his own use under the guise of a trade secret." *Serv. Ctrs.*, 129 Ill.Dec. 367, 535 N.E.2d at 1137. However, in this case, there was additional evidence from which the jury could have determined that PlayWood's concept was not generally known within the industry.

First, there was substantial testimony that Learning Curve had attempted to differentiate its track from that of its competitors for several months, but that it had been unable to do so successfully.

Furthermore, PlayWood's expert witness, Michael Kennedy, testified that PlayWood's concept, as embodied in Clickety-Clack Track ™, was unique and permitted "its seller to differentiate itself from a host of competitors who [were] making a generic product." Trial Tr. at 518. Kennedy explained that the look, sound and feel of the track made it distinct from other toy railroad track: "[W]hen a child runs a train across this track, he can feel it hitting those little impressions. And when you're talking about young children [,] having the idea that they can see something that they couldn't see before, feel something that they couldn't feel before, hear something that they couldn't hear before, that is what differentiates this toy from its other competitors." *Id.* at 489.

Finally, PlayWood presented evidence that Learning Curve sought and obtained a patent on the noise-producing track. It goes without saying that the requirements for patent and trade secret protection are not synonymous. Unlike "a patentable invention, a trade secret need not be novel or unobvious." 2 Rudolf Callmann, The Law of Unfair Competition, Trademarks and Monopolies § 14.15, at 14-124 (4th ed.2003). "The idea need not be complicated; it may be intrinsically simple and nevertheless qualify as a secret, unless it is common knowledge and, therefore, within the public domain." *Forest Labs., Inc. v. Pillsbury Co.*, 452 F.2d 621, 624 (7th Cir.1971) (internal quotation marks omitted). However, it is commonly understood that "[i]f an invention has sufficient novelty to be entitled to patent protection, it may be said *a fortiori* to be entitled to protection as a trade secret." 1 Roger M. Milgrim, Milgrim on Trade Secrets § 1.08[1], at 1-353 (2002) (internal footnotes omitted). In light of this evidence, we cannot accept Learning Curve's argument that no rational jury could have found that PlayWood's concept was unknown outside of its business.

2. Extent to which PlayWood's concept was known to employees and others involved in PlayWood's business

The district court did not address the extent to which PlayWood's concept was known to employees and others involved in PlayWood's business. However, we agree with PlayWood that the evidence was sufficient to establish that its concept for noise-producing track was known only by key individuals in its business.

At the outset, we note briefly that PlayWood was a small business, consisting only of Clausi and Moore. Illinois courts have recognized on several occasions that the expectations for ensuring secrecy are different for small companies than for large companies. *See Jackson*, 210 Ill.Dec. 614, 653 N.E.2d at 815 ("[T]he determination of what steps are reasonably necessary to protect information is different for a large company than for a small one.")[. . .] Apart from Clausi (PlayWood's sole toy designer and the person who conceived of the concept for noise-producing track) and Moore (PlayWood's sole officer and director), the only person who knew about the concept was Borsato, the person who physically produced PlayWood's prototype at Clausi's direction. The concept was disclosed to Borsato in order for PlayWood to develop fully its trade secret. *See* 1 Roger M. Milgrim, Milgrim on Trade Secrets § 1.04, at 1-173 (2002) ("A trade secret does not lose its character by being confidentially disclosed to agents or servants, without whose assistance it could not be made of any value.") (internal quotation marks omitted). Moreover, Borsato's actions were governed by a written confidentiality agreement with PlayWood. Indeed, as an extra precaution, Clausi even amended PlayWood's confidentiality agreement with Borsato immediately after the February 18, 1993, meeting to ensure that materials discussed during the meeting would remain confidential. From this evidence, the jury reasonably could have determined that this factor also weighed in favor of PlayWood.

3. Measures taken by PlayWood to guard the secrecy of its concept

There also was sufficient evidence for the jury to determine that PlayWood took reasonable precautions to guard the secrecy of its concept. The Act requires the trade secret owner to take actions that are "reasonable under the circumstances to maintain [the] secrecy or confidentiality" of its trade secret; it does not require perfection. 765 ILCS § 1065/2(d)(2). Whether the measures taken by a trade secret owner are sufficient to satisfy the Act's reasonableness standard ordinarily is a question of fact for the jury. Indeed, we previously have recognized that "only in an extreme case can what is a 'reasonable' precaution be determined [as a matter of law], because the answer depends on a balancing of costs and benefits that will vary from case to case." *Rockwell Graphic Sys., Inc. v. DEV Indus., Inc.*, 925 F.2d 174, 179 (7th Cir.1991).

Here, the jury was instructed that it must find "by a preponderance of the evidence that PlayWood's trade secrets were given to Learning Curve as a result of a confidential relationship between the parties." Trial Tr. at 1449. By returning a verdict in favor of PlayWood, the jury necessarily found that Learning Curve was bound to PlayWood by a pledge of confidentiality. The jury's determination is amply supported by the evidence. Both Clausi and Moore testified that they entered into an oral confidentiality agreement with Abraham and Wilson before beginning their discussion on February 18, 1993. In particular, Clausi testified that he told Abraham and Wilson: "I also have some things, some ideas on how to produce the track and produce the trains now that I've had a chance to look at them for the last couple of days, and I think they're confidential as well. So if we're both okay with that, we should continue." Trial Tr. at 77. In addition to this testimony, the jury heard that Learning Curve had disclosed substantial information to PlayWood during the February 18th meeting, including projected volumes, costs and profit margins for various products, as well as drawings for toys not yet released to the public. The jury could have inferred that Learning Curve would not have disclosed such information in the absence of a confidentiality agreement. Finally, the jury also heard (from several of Learning Curve's former business associates) that Learning Curve routinely entered into oral confidentiality agreements like the one with PlayWood.

PlayWood might have done more to protect its secret. As Learning Curve points out, PlayWood gave its only prototype of the noise-producing track to Wilson without first obtaining a receipt or written confidentiality agreement from Learning Curve-a decision that proved unwise in hindsight. Nevertheless, we believe that the jury was entitled to conclude that PlayWood's reliance on the oral confidentiality agreement was reasonable under the circumstances of this case.[4] First, it is well established that "[t]he formation of a confidential relationship imposes upon the disclosee the duty to maintain the information received in the utmost secrecy" and that "the unprivileged use or disclosure of another's trade secret becomes the basis for an action in tort." *Burten v. Milton Bradley Co.*, 763 F.2d 461, 463 (1st Cir.1985). Second, both Clausi and Moore testified that they believed PlayWood had a realistic chance to "get in the door" with Learning Curve and to produce the concept as part of Learning Curve's line of Thomas products. Clausi and Moore did not anticipate that Learning Curve would violate the oral confidentiality agreement and utilize PlayWood's concept without permission; rather, they believed in good faith that they "were going to do business one day again with Learning Curve with respect to the design concept." Trial Tr. at 236-37. Finally, we believe that, as part of the reasonableness inquiry, the jury could have considered the size and sophistication of the parties, as well as the relevant industry. Both PlayWood and Learning Curve were small toy companies, and PlayWood was the smaller and less experienced of the two. Viewing the evidence in the light most favorable to PlayWood, as we must, we conclude that there was sufficient evidence for the jury to determine that PlayWood took reasonable measures to protect the secrecy of its concept.

4. Value of the concept to PlayWood and to its competitors

There was substantial evidence from which the jury could have determined that PlayWood's concept had value both to PlayWood and to its competitors. It was undisputed at trial that Learning Curve's sales skyrocketed after it began to sell Clickety-Clack Track ™. In addition, PlayWood's expert witness, Michael Kennedy, testified that PlayWood's concept for noise-producing track had tremendous value. Kennedy testified that the "cross-cuts and changes in the [track's] surface" imparted value to its seller by causing the track to "look different, feel different and sound different than generic track." Trial Tr. at 504. Kennedy further testified that, in his opinion, the track would have commanded a premium royalty under a negotiated license agreement because the "invention allows its seller to differentiate itself from a host of competitors who are making a generic product with whom it is

---

[4] We iterate that the proper inquiry is not whether, in our independent judgment, we believe that PlayWood took reasonable precautions to maintain the secrecy of its concept; rather, the issue is whether PlayWood's "failure to do more was so plain a breach of the obligation of a trade secret owner to make reasonable efforts to maintain secrecy as to justify" overturning the jury verdict in its favor[.]

competing in a way that is proprietary and exclusive, and it gives [the seller] a significant edge over [its] competition." *Id.* at 518-19.

Despite this evidence, the district court concluded that PlayWood's concept had no economic value. The court's conclusion was based, in part, on the fact that PlayWood's prototype did not work perfectly; as noted by the court, the first set of cuts were too shallow to produce sound and the second set of cuts were too deep to permit the train to roll smoothly across the track. In the district court's view, even if the concept of cutting grooves into the wooden track in order to produce noise originated with Clausi, the concept lacked value until it was refined, developed and manufactured by Learning Curve.

We cannot accept the district court's conclusion because it is belied by the evidence. At trial, Kennedy was asked whether, in his opinion, the fact that PlayWood's prototype did not work perfectly affected the value of PlayWood's concept, and he testified that it did not. *See* Trial Tr. at 578. Kennedy testified that he would assign the same value to PlayWood's concept as it was conceived on February 18, 1993, as he would the finished product that became known as Clickety-Clack Track ™ because, at that time, he would have known "that most of the design [had] already been done and that [he] just need[ed] to go a little bit further to make it really lovely." *Id.* at 578. Kennedy further testified that it was standard practice in the industry for a license to be negotiated based on a prototype (much like the one PlayWood disclosed to Learning Curve) rather than a finished product and that the license generally would cover the prototypical design, as well as any enhancements or improvements of that design. *See* Trial Tr. at 500-01. Based on this testimony, we cannot accept the district court's conclusion that PlayWood's concept possessed no economic value.

It is irrelevant under Illinois law that PlayWood did not actually use the concept in its business. "[T]he proper criterion is not 'actual use' but whether the trade secret is 'of value' to the company." *Syntex Ophthalmics, Inc. v. Tsuetaki*, 701 F.2d 677, 683 (7th Cir.1983).[6]

---

[6] Both the Uniform Trade Secrets Act and the Restatement (Third) of Unfair Competition expressly reject prior use by the person asserting rights in the information as a prerequisite to trade secret protection. See Unif. Trade Secrets Act § 1 cmt. (1990) ("The broader definition in the proposed Act extends protection to a plaintiff who has not yet had an opportunity or acquired the means to put a trade secret to use."); Restatement (Third) of Unfair Competition § 39 cmt. e (1995) ("Use by the person asserting rights in the information is not a prerequisite to protection under the rule stated in this Section," in part, because such a "requirement can deny protection during periods of research and development and is particularly burdensome for innovators who do not possess the capability to exploit their innovations.").

Kennedy's testimony was more than sufficient to permit the jury to conclude that the concept was "of value" to PlayWood. It is equally irrelevant that PlayWood did not seek to patent its concept. So long as the concept remains a secret, *i.e.*, outside of the public domain, there is no need for patent protection. Professor Milgrim makes this point well: "Since every inventor has the right to keep his invention secret, one who has made a patentable invention has the option to maintain it in secrecy, relying upon protection accorded to a trade secret rather than upon the rights which accrue by a patent grant." 1 Roger M. Milgrim, Milgrim on Trade Secrets § 1.08[1], at 1-353 (2002). It was up to PlayWood, not the district court, to determine when and how the concept should have been disclosed to the public.

5. Amount of time, effort and money expended by PlayWood in developing its concept

PlayWood expended very little time and money developing its concept; by Clausi's own account, the cost to PlayWood was less than one dollar and the time spent was less than one-half hour. The district court determined that "[s]uch an insignificant investment is ... insufficient as a matter of Illinois law to establish the status of a 'trade secret.' " R.202 at 16. We believe that the district court gave too much weight to the time, effort and expense of developing the track.

Although Illinois courts commonly look to the Restatement factors for guidance in determining whether a trade secret exists, as we have noted earlier, the requisite statutory inquiries under Illinois law are (1) whether the information "is sufficiently secret to derive economic value, actual or potential, from not being generally known to other persons who can obtain economic value from its disclosure or use;" and (2) whether the information "is the subject of efforts that are reasonable under the circumstances to maintain its secrecy or confidentiality." 765 ILCS § 1065/2(d). A significant expenditure of time and/or money in the production of information may provide evidence of value, which is relevant to the first inquiry above. However, we do not understand Illinois law to require such an expenditure in all cases.

As pointed out by the district court, several Illinois cases have emphasized the importance of developmental costs. However, notably, none of those cases concerned the sort of innovative and creative concept that we have in this case. Indeed, several of the cases in Illinois that emphasize developmental costs concern compilations of data, such as customer lists. In that context, it makes sense to require the expenditure of significant time and money because there is nothing original or creative about the alleged trade secret. Given enough time and money, we presume that the plaintiff's competitors could compile a similar list.

Here, by contrast, we are dealing with a new toy design that has been promoted as "the first significant innovation in track design since the inception of wooden train systems." PlayWood's Tr. Ex.71. Toy designers, like many artistic individuals, have intuitive flashes of creativity. Often, that intuitive flash is, in reality, the product of earlier thought and practice in an artistic craft. We fail to see how the value of PlayWood's concept would differ in any respect had Clausi spent several months and several thousand dollars creating the noise-producing track. Accordingly, we conclude that PlayWood's lack of proof on this factor does not preclude the existence of a trade secret.

6. Ease or difficulty with which PlayWood's concept could have been properly acquired or duplicated by others

Finally, we also believe that there was sufficient evidence for the jury to determine that PlayWood's concept could not have been easily acquired or duplicated through proper means. PlayWood's expert witness, Michael Kennedy, testified: "This is a fairly simple product if you look at it. But the truth is that because it delivers feeling and sound as well as appearance, it isn't so simple as it first appears. It's a little more elegant, actually, than you might think." Trial Tr. at 504. In addition to Kennedy's testimony, the jury heard that Learning Curve had spent months attempting to differentiate its track from Brio's before Clausi disclosed PlayWood's concept of noise-producing track. From this evidence, the jury could have inferred that, if PlayWood's concept really was obvious, Learning Curve would have thought of it earlier.

Despite this evidence, the district court concluded that PlayWood's concept was not a trade secret because it could have been easily duplicated, stating that "[h]ad PlayWood succeeded in producing and marketing [the] notched track, the appearance of the track product itself would have fully revealed the concept PlayWood now claims as a secret." R.202 at 5-6. Of course, the district court was correct in one sense; PlayWood's own expert recognized that, in the absence of patent or copyright protection, the track could have been reverse engineered just by looking at it. See Trial Tr. at 562. However, the district court failed to appreciate the fact that PlayWood's concept was not publicly available. As Professor Milgrim states: "A potent distinction exists between a trade secret which will be disclosed if and when the product in which it is embodied is placed on sale, and a 'trade secret' embodied in a product which has been placed on sale, which product admits of discovery of the 'secret' upon inspection, analysis, or reverse engineering." 1 Roger M. Milgrim, Milgrim on Trade Secrets § 1.05[4], at 1-228 (2002). "Until disclosed by sale the trade secret should be entitled to protection." *Id.*; *see also* 2 Rudolf Callmann, The Law of Unfair Competition, Trademarks and Monopolies § 14.15, at 14-123 (4th ed. 2003) ("The fact that a secret is easy to duplicate after it becomes known does not militate against its being a trade secret prior to that time."). Reverse engineering can defeat a trade secret claim, but only if the product could have been properly acquired by others, as is the case when the product is publicly sold. Here, PlayWood disclosed its concept to Learning Curve (and Learning Curve alone) in the context of a confidential relationship; Learning Curve had no legal authority to reverse engineer the prototype that it received in confidence. *See Laff v. John O. Butler Co.*, 64 Ill.App.3d 603, 21 Ill.Dec. 314, 381 N.E.2d 423, 433 (1978) ("[A] trade secret is open to anyone, not bound by a confidential relationship or a contract with the secret's owner, who can discover the secret through lawful means."). Accordingly, we must conclude that the jury was entitled to determine that PlayWood's concept could not easily have been acquired or duplicated through proper means.

Conclusion

For the foregoing reasons, the judgment of the district court is reversed, and the jury's verdict is reinstated. The case is remanded to the district court for a jury trial on exemplary damages and for consideration of attorneys' fees by the court. PlayWood may recover its costs in this court.

REVERSED AND REMANDED.

Notes:

1. Source of Law. Trade secret law protects qualified proprietary information from being used or disclosed after misappropriation by improper means. Although the law of trade secrets originated as a common law doctrine, most states have enacted statutory provisions protecting trade secrets from misappropriation. The most common statute in the Uniform Trade Secrets Act ("UTSA"), promulgated by the National Conference of Commissioners on Uniform State Laws. At least 45 states plus the District of Columbia have enacted some form of the UTSA. In addition, two states – Alabama and Massachusetts – have enacted a trade secrets statute not directly based on the UTSA. Only New York, New Jersey and Texas have not enacted legislation. In those jurisdictions, trade secret protection exists as a matter of common law. At the federal level, the Economic Espionage Act of 1996, 18 U.S.C. §§ 1831-39, creates criminal liability for the theft of trade secrets. The Supreme Court has held that state trade secrets laws are not preempted by the federal patent Act, because the state and federal laws provide different protections and advance different policies. *Kewanee Oil Co. v. Bicron Corp.*, 416 U.S. 470 (1974).

2. Information Potentially Protectable As Trade Secret. Trade secret law offers potential protection to the broad range of information. Under the UTSA, a trade secret is "information, including a formula, pattern, compilation, program, device, method, technique, or process[.]" UTSA § 1(4). Trade secrets may protect recipes, formulae, and other technical information. *See, e.g., Peggy Lawton Kitchens, Inc. v. Hogan*, 18 Mass. App. 937, 466 N.E.2d 138 (1984) (secret recipe for chocolate chip cookies); *Triple Tee Golf, Inc. v. Nike, Inc.*, 485 F.3d 253 (5th Cir. 2007)(designs for post-sale adjustable golf clubs). Competitive business information, including customer data, pricing or marketing strategies, and product development plans are also potentially protectable as trade secrets. Customer lists and databases are not protectable, however, if they simply compile data readily available in industry directories or other public sources. *See Leo Silfen, Inc., v. Cream*, 29 N.Y.2d 387, 392-93 (1972) ("where the customers are not known in the trade or are discoverable only by extraordinary efforts courts have not hesitated to protect customer lists and files as trade secrets. This is especially so where the customers' patronage had been secured by years of effort and advertising effected by the expenditure of substantial time and money.") Information may be protected as a trade secret even if it does not qualify for patent protection. For example, a technology may be not generally known in the industry and not readily ascertainable, and thus potentially protectable as a trade secret, even if it does not meet the technical requirement for novelty under the Patent Act. *See* 35 U.S.C. § 102(a) and (b).

3 "Improper Means" and Reverse Engineering. The UTSA establishes a cause of action for misappropriation of a trade secret. In general, misappropriation occurs when a person acquires, uses or discloses a trade secret through "improper means." The UTSA defines "improper means" as including "theft, bribery, misrepresentation, breach or inducement of a breach of a duty to maintain secrecy, or espionage through electronic or other means[.]" UTSA § 1(1). In addition to unlawful acts, some courts have found misappropriation where a defendant obtains a trade secret through conduct which violates acceptable standards for commercial competition. *See, e.g., E.I. DuPont deNemours & Co. v. Christopher*, 431 F.2d 1012 (5th Cir. 1970) (aerial photography of factory construction site was misappropriation under Texas law, "devotion to free wheeling industrial competition must not force us into accepting the law of the jungle as the standard morality expected in our commercial relations"). On the other hand, improper means does not include the reverse-engineering of a competitor's product to identify its secrets, at least in the absence of a contractual obligation or other legal requirement not to do so. As a result, trade secret law provides the owner of the secret with no protection against competitors' attempts to reverse-engineer commercial products. In fact, as noted by the court in *Learning Curve*, a trade secret which is readily apparent from the inspection of a product loses its protection as a trade secret when the product is marketed to the public. The trade secret is still protectable, however, during the product planning and development process.

4. **"Escaped" Employees.** Although some trade secret cases involve facts suggesting corporate espionage, the majority of lawsuits result from more mundane disputes between employers and their former employees. In many of these cases, trusted employees who are privy to proprietary information about the employer's business operations, customers, or product development plans resign to join a competitor or to start a rival company. In those cases, the ability of the former employee to establish that it implemented reasonable safeguard to protect its confidential information may depend on whether the "escaped" employee signed a non-disclosure agreement ("NDA") as part of a company-wide policy and practice of securing NDAs from employees.

5. **Indefinite Term.** Unlike a patent, which has a fixed statutory term, a trade secret may remain viable for many years. Trade secret rights continue until one of the legal requirements for trade secret status lapses. For example, a company may lose its ability to protect trade secrets if it discontinues reasonable practices designed to safeguard the confidentiality of its trade secrets. In addition, a trade secret is lost if the information becomes generally known in the industry, even if the disclosure is not the fault of the trade secret owner. *See, e.g., DVD Copy Control Ass'n v. Bunner*, 10 Cal. App. 4th 241 (Cal. App. 2004) (denying injunctive relief when trade secret, DeCSS program allowing copying of copy-protected DVDs, was posted and "quickly and widely republished" on the internet).

6. **Right To Injunctive Relief.** The UTSA authorizes courts to grant equitable relief to enjoin actual or "threatened" misappropriation of a plaintiff's trade secrets. In addition, several jurisdictions recognize the right to an injunction to prevent the "inevitable disclosure" of trade secrets. *See PepsiCo, Inc. v. Redmond*, 54 F.3d 1262 (7th Cir. 1995). The "inevitable disclosure" doctrine has been limited to situations in which an employee has left an employer to take a new position with a direct competitor, and where he or she had highly proprietary information that would be essential to fulfilling the responsibilities of the new position. Some jurisdictions have recently declined to recognize the inevitable disclosure doctrine where the former employee did not secure a restrictive covenant of noncompetition from the employee, or where public policy strongly disfavors restraints on competition. These courts reason that the former employer should not be allowed to stretch trade secret law to block the former employee's new position when it did not compensate the employee for an express promise not to work for a competitor. *See, e.g., Whyte v. Schlage Lock Co.*, 125 Cal. Rptr. 277 (Cal. Ct. App. 2002) (inevitable disclosure doctrine

inconsistent with strong California public policy against restraints on employment); *Del Monte Fresh Produce Co. v. Dole Food Co., Inc.*, 148 F. Supp.2d 1326 (S.D. Fla. 2001) ("Absent evidence of actual or threatened misappropriation, a court should not allow a plaintiff to use inevitable disclosure as an after-the-fact noncompete agreement").

7. Duration of Injunction Barring Use or Disclosure of Trade Secret. In many cases, a plaintiff bringing an action for misappropriation of trade secrets is primarily interested in obtaining interlocutory injunctive relief to prevent the imminent disclosure or use of its trade secrets. In most cases, however, any injunctive relief is limited to the time it would have taken the defendant to independently develop the trade secret, or obtain it through reverse-engineering or other lawful means. *See K-2 Ski Co v. Head Ski Co.*, 506 F.2d 471 (9th Cir. 1974) (proper length for permanent injunction is the length of time to reverse–engineer or independently develop secrets, less the time that defendant was subject to preliminary injunction).

D. Copyrights

SONY CORP. OF AMERICA v. UNIVERSAL CITY STUDIOS, INC.

464 U.S. 417 (1984)

Justice STEVENS delivered the opinion of the Court.

Petitioners manufacture and sell home video tape recorders. Respondents own the copyrights on some of the television programs that are broadcast on the public airwaves. Some members of the general public use video tape recorders sold by petitioners to record some of these broadcasts, as well as a large number of other broadcasts. The question presented is whether the sale of petitioners' copying equipment to the general public violates any of the rights conferred upon respondents by the Copyright Act.

Respondents commenced this copyright infringement action against petitioners in the United States District Court for the Central District of California in 1976. Respondents alleged that some individuals had used Betamax video tape recorders (VTR's) to record some of respondents' copyrighted works which had been exhibited on commercially sponsored television and contended that these individuals had thereby infringed respondents' copyrights. Respondents further maintained that petitioners were liable for the copyright infringement allegedly committed by Betamax consumers because of petitioners' marketing of the Betamax VTR's. Respondents sought no relief against any Betamax consumer.

Instead, they sought money damages and an equitable accounting of profits from petitioners, as well as an injunction against the manufacture and marketing of Betamax VTR's.

After a lengthy trial, the District Court denied respondents all the relief they sought and entered judgment for petitioners. 480 F.Supp. 429 (1979). The United States Court of Appeals for the Ninth Circuit reversed the District Court's judgment on respondent's copyright claim, holding petitioners liable for contributory infringement and ordering the District Court to fashion appropriate relief. 659 F.2d 963 (1981). . . . We now reverse.

An explanation of our rejection of respondents' unprecedented attempt to impose copyright liability upon the distributors of copying equipment requires a quite detailed recitation of the findings of the District Court. In summary, those findings reveal that the average member of the public uses a VTR principally to record a program he cannot view as it is being televised and then to watch it once at a later time. This practice, known as "time-shifting," enlarges the television viewing audience. For that reason, a significant amount of television programming may be used in this manner without objection from the owners of the copyrights on the programs. For the same reason, even the two respondents in this case, who do assert objections to time-shifting in this litigation, were unable to prove that the practice has impaired the commercial value of their copyrights or has created any likelihood of future harm. Given these findings, there is no basis in the Copyright Act upon which respondents can hold petitioners liable for distributing VTR's to the general public. The Court of Appeals' holding that respondents are entitled to enjoin the distribution of VTR's, to collect royalties on the sale of such equipment, or to obtain other relief, if affirmed, would enlarge the scope of respondents' statutory monopolies to encompass control over an article of commerce that is not the subject of copyright protection. Such an expansion of the copyright privilege is beyond the limits of the grants authorized by Congress.

I

The two respondents in this action, Universal Studios, Inc. and Walt Disney Productions, produce and hold the copyrights on a substantial number of motion pictures and other audiovisual works. In the current marketplace, they can exploit their rights in these works in a number of ways: by authorizing theatrical exhibitions, by licensing limited showings on cable and network television, by selling syndication rights for repeated airings on local television stations, and by marketing programs on prerecorded videotapes or videodiscs. Some works are suitable for exploitation through all of these avenues, while the market for other works is more limited.

Petitioner Sony manufactures millions of Betamax video tape recorders and markets these devices through numerous retail establishments, some of which are also petitioners in this action. Sony's Betamax VTR is a mechanism consisting of three basic components: (1) a tuner, which receives electromagnetic signals transmitted over the television band of the public airwaves and separates them into audio and visual signals; (2) a recorder, which records such signals on a magnetic tape; and (3) an adapter, which converts the audio and visual signals on the tape into a composite signal that can be received by a television set.

Several capabilities of the machine are noteworthy. The separate tuner in the Betamax enables it to record a broadcast off one station while the television set is tuned to another channel, permitting the viewer, for example, to watch two simultaneous news broadcasts by watching one "live" and recording the other for later viewing. Tapes may be reused, and programs that have been recorded may be erased either before or after viewing. A timer in the Betamax can be used to activate and deactivate the equipment at predetermined times, enabling an intended viewer to record programs that are transmitted when he or she is not at home. Thus a person may watch a program at home in the evening even though it was broadcast while the viewer was at work during the afternoon. The Betamax is also equipped with a pause button and a fast-forward control. The pause button, when depressed, deactivates the recorder until it is released, thus enabling a viewer to omit a commercial advertisement from the recording, provided, of course, that the viewer is present when the program is recorded. The fast forward control enables the viewer of a previously recorded program to run the tape rapidly when a segment he or she does not desire to see is being played back on the television screen.

The respondents and Sony both conducted surveys of the way the Betamax machine was used by several hundred owners during a sample period in 1978. Although there were some differences in the surveys, they both showed that the primary use of the machine for most owners was "time-shifting,"-the practice of recording a program to view it once at a later time, and thereafter erasing it. Time-shifting enables viewers to see programs they otherwise would miss because they are not at home, are occupied with other tasks, or are viewing a program on another station at the time of a broadcast that they desire to watch. Both surveys also showed, however, that a substantial number of interviewees had accumulated libraries of tapes. Sony's survey indicated that over 80% of the interviewees watched at least as much regular television as they had before owning a Betamax. Respondents offered no evidence of decreased television viewing by Betamax owners.

[Discussion of District Court and Appeals Court decisions omitted]

II

Article I, Sec. 8 of the Constitution provides that:

> "The Congress shall have Power ... to Promote the Progress of Science and useful Arts, by securing for limited Times to Authors and Inventors the exclusive Right to their respective Writings and Discoveries."

The monopoly privileges that Congress may authorize are neither unlimited nor primarily designed to provide a special private benefit. Rather, the limited grant is a means by which an important public purpose may be achieved. It is intended to motivate the creative activity of authors and inventors by the provision of a special reward, and to allow the public access to the products of their genius after the limited period of exclusive control has expired.

"The copyright law, like the patent statute, makes reward to the owner a secondary consideration. In *Fox Film Corp. v. Doyal,* 286 U.S. 123, 127 [52 S.Ct. 546, 547, 76 L.Ed. 1010], Chief Justice Hughes spoke as follows respecting the copyright monopoly granted by Congress, 'The sole interest of the United States and the primary object in conferring the monopoly lie in the general benefits derived by the public from the labors of authors.' It is said that reward to the author or artist serves to induce release to the public of the products of his creative genius." *United States v. Paramount Pictures,* 334 U.S. 131, 158, 68 S.Ct. 915, 929, 92 L.Ed. 1260.

As the text of the Constitution makes plain, it is Congress that has been assigned the task of defining the scope of the limited monopoly that should be granted to authors or to inventors in order to give the public appropriate access to their work product. Because this task involves a difficult balance between the interests of authors and inventors in the control and exploitation of their writings and discoveries on the one hand, and society's competing interest in the free flow of ideas, information, and commerce on the other hand, our patent and copyright statutes have been amended repeatedly.

From its beginning, the law of copyright has developed in response to significant changes in technology. Indeed, it was the invention of a new form of copying equipment-the printing press-that gave rise to the original need for copyright protection. Repeatedly, as new developments have occurred in this country, it has been the Congress that has fashioned the new rules that new technology made necessary. Thus, long before the enactment of the Copyright Act of 1909, 35 Stat. 1075, it was settled that the protection given to copyrights is wholly statutory. *Wheaton v. Peters,* 33 U.S. (8 Peters) 591, 661-662, 8 L.Ed. 1055 (1834). The remedies for infringement "are only those prescribed by Congress." *Thompson v. Hubbard,* 131 U.S. 123, 151, 9 S.Ct. 710, 720, 33 L.Ed. 76 (1889).

The judiciary's reluctance to expand the protections afforded by the copyright without explicit legislative guidance is a recurring theme. See, e.g., *Teleprompter Corp. v. CBS,* 415 U.S. 394, 94 S.Ct. 1129, 39 L.Ed.2d 415 (1974); *Fortnightly Corp. v. United Artists,* 392 U.S. 390, 88 S.Ct. 2084, 20 L.Ed.2d 1176 (1968); *White-Smith Music Publishing Co. v. Apollo Co.,* 209 U.S. 1, 28 S.Ct. 319, 52 L.Ed. 655 (1908); *Williams and Wilkins v. United States,* 487 F.2d 1345, 203 Ct.Cl. 74 (1973), affirmed by an equally divided court, 420 U.S. 376, 95 S.Ct. 1344, 43 L.Ed.2d 264 (1975). Sound policy, as well as history, supports our consistent deference to Congress when major technological innovations alter the market for copyrighted materials. Congress has the constitutional authority and the institutional ability to accommodate fully the varied permutations of competing interests that are inevitably implicated by such new technology.

In a case like this, in which Congress has not plainly marked our course, we must be circumspect in construing the scope of rights created by a legislative enactment which never contemplated such a calculus of interests. In doing so, we are guided by Justice Stewart's exposition of the correct approach to ambiguities in the law of copyright:

"The limited scope of the copyright holder's statutory monopoly, like the limited copyright duration required by the Constitution, reflects a balance of competing claims upon the public interest: Creative work is to be encouraged and rewarded, but private motivation must ultimately serve the cause of promoting broad public availability of literature, music, and the other arts. The immediate effect of our copyright law is to secure a fair return for an 'author's' creative labor. But the ultimate aim is, by this incentive, to stimulate artistic creativity for the general public good. 'The sole interest of the United States and the primary object in conferring the monopoly,' this Court has said, 'lie in the general benefits derived by the public from the labors of authors.' *Fox Film Corp. v. Doyal,* 286 U.S. 123, 127 [52 S.Ct. 546, 547, 76 L.Ed. 1010]. See *Kendall v. Winsor,* 21 How. 322, 327-328 [16 L.Ed. 165]; *Grant v. Raymond,* 6 Pet. 218, 241-242 [8 L.Ed. 376]. When technological change has rendered its literal terms ambiguous, the Copyright Act must be construed in light of this basic purpose." *Twentieth Century Music Corp. v. Aiken,* 422 U.S. 151, 156, 95 S.Ct. 2040, 2043, 45 L.Ed.2d 84 (footnotes omitted).

Copyright protection "subsists ... in original works of authorship fixed in any tangible medium of expression." 17 U.S.C. § 102(a). This protection has never accorded the copyright owner complete control over all possible uses of his work. Rather, the Copyright Act grants the copyright holder "exclusive" rights to use and to authorize the use of his work in five qualified ways, including reproduction of the copyrighted work in copies. *Id.,* § 106. All reproductions of the work, however, are not within the exclusive domain of the copyright owner; some are in the public domain. Any individual may reproduce a copyrighted work for a "fair use;" the copyright owner does not possess the exclusive right to such a use. Compare *id.,* § 106 with *id.,* § 107.

"Anyone who violates any of the exclusive rights of the copyright owner," that is, anyone who trespasses into his exclusive domain by using or authorizing the use of the copyrighted work in one of the five ways set forth in the statute, "is an infringer of the copyright." *Id.,* § 501(a). Conversely, anyone who is authorized by the copyright owner to use the copyrighted work in a way specified in the statute or who makes a fair use of the work is not an infringer of the copyright with respect to such use.

The Copyright Act provides the owner of a copyright with a potent arsenal of remedies against an infringer of his work, including an injunction to restrain the infringer from violating his rights, the impoundment and destruction of all reproductions of his work made in violation of his rights, a recovery of his actual damages and any additional profits realized by the infringer or a recovery of statutory damages, and attorneys fees. *Id.,* §§ 502-505.15.

The two respondents in this case do not seek relief against the Betamax users who have allegedly infringed their copyrights. Moreover, this is not a class action on behalf of all copyright owners who license their works for television broadcast, and respondents have no right to invoke whatever rights other copyright holders may have to bring infringement actions based on Betamax copying of their works. As was made clear by their own evidence, the copying of the respondents' programs represents a small portion of the total use of VTR's. It is, however, the taping of respondents own copyrighted programs that provides them with standing to charge Sony with contributory infringement. To prevail, they have the burden of proving that users of the Betamax have infringed their copyrights and that Sony should be held responsible for that infringement.

III

The Copyright Act does not expressly render anyone liable for infringement committed by another. In contrast, the Patent Act expressly brands anyone who "actively induces infringement of a patent" as an infringer, 35 U.S.C. § 271(b), and further imposes liability on certain individuals labeled "contributory" infringers, *id.,* § 271(c). The absence of such express language in the copyright statute does not preclude the imposition of liability for copyright infringements on certain parties who have not themselves engaged in the infringing activity. For vicarious liability is imposed in virtually all areas of the law, and the concept of contributory infringement is merely a species of the broader problem of identifying the circumstances in which it is just to hold one individual accountable for the actions of another.

Such circumstances were plainly present in *Kalem Co. v. Harper Brothers,* 222 U.S. 55, 32 S.Ct. 20, 56 L.Ed. 92 (1911), the copyright decision of this Court on which respondents place their principal reliance. In *Kalem,* the Court held that the producer of an unauthorized film dramatization of the copyrighted book *Ben Hur* was liable for his sale of the motion picture to jobbers, who in turn arranged for the commercial exhibition of the film. Justice Holmes, writing for the Court, explained:

"The defendant not only expected but invoked by advertisement the use of its films for dramatic reproduction of the story. That was the most conspicuous purpose for which they could be used, and the one for which especially they were made. If the defendant did not contribute to the infringement it is impossible to do so except by taking part in the final act. It is liable on principles recognized in every part of the law." 222 U.S., at 63, 32 S.Ct., at 22.

. . .

If vicarious liability is to be imposed on petitioners in this case, it must rest on the fact that they have sold equipment with constructive knowledge of the fact that their customers may use that equipment to make unauthorized copies of copyrighted material. There is no precedent in the law of copyright for the imposition of vicarious liability on such a theory. The closest analogy is provided by the patent law cases to which it is appropriate to refer because of the historic kinship between patent law and copyright law.19

. . ..

We recognize there are substantial differences between the patent and copyright laws. But in both areas the contributory infringement doctrine is grounded on the recognition that adequate protection of a monopoly may require the courts to look beyond actual duplication of a device or publication to the products or activities that make such duplication possible. The staple article of commerce doctrine must strike a balance between a copyright holder's legitimate demand for effective-not merely symbolic-protection of the statutory monopoly, and the rights of others freely to engage in substantially unrelated areas of commerce. Accordingly, the sale of copying equipment, like the sale of other articles of commerce, does not constitute contributory infringement if the product is widely used for legitimate, unobjectionable purposes. Indeed, it need merely be capable of substantial noninfringing uses.

IV

The question is thus whether the Betamax is capable of commercially significant noninfringing uses. In order to resolve that question, we need not explore *all* the different potential uses of the machine and determine whether or not they would constitute infringement. Rather, we need only consider whether on the basis of the facts as found by the district court a significant number of them would be non-infringing. Moreover, in order to resolve this case we need not give precise content to the question of how much use is commercially significant. For one potential use of the Betamax plainly satisfies this standard, however it is understood: private, noncommercial time-shifting in the home. It does so both (A) because respondents have no right to prevent other copyright holders from authorizing it for their programs, and (B) because the District Court's factual findings reveal that even the unauthorized home time-shifting of respondents' programs is legitimate fair use.

A. *Authorized Time Shifting*

Each of the respondents owns a large inventory of valuable copyrights, but in the total spectrum of television programming their combined market share is small. The exact percentage is not specified, but it is well below 10%. If they were to prevail, the outcome of this litigation would have a significant impact on both the producers and the viewers of the remaining 90% of the programming in the Nation. No doubt, many other producers share respondents' concern about the possible consequences of unrestricted copying. Nevertheless the findings of the District Court make it clear that time-shifting may enlarge the total viewing audience and that many producers are willing to allow private time-shifting to continue, at least for an experimental time period.

The District Court found:

"Even if it were deemed that home-use recording of copyrighted material constituted infringement, the Betamax could still legally be used to record noncopyrighted material or material whose owners consented to the copying. An injunction would deprive the public of the ability to use the Betamax for this noninfringing off-the-air recording.

"Defendants introduced considerable testimony at trial about the potential for such copying of sports, religious, educational and other programming. This included testimony from representatives of the Offices of the Commissioners of the National Football, Basketball, Baseball and Hockey Leagues and Associations, the Executive Director of National Religious Broadcasters and various educational communications agencies. Plaintiffs attack the weight of the testimony offered and also contend that an injunction is warranted because infringing uses outweigh noninfringing uses."

"Whatever the future percentage of legal versus illegal home-use recording might be, an injunction which seeks to deprive the public of the very tool or article of commerce capable of some noninfringing use would be an extremely harsh remedy, as well as one unprecedented in copyright law." 480 F.Supp., at 468.

Although the District Court made these statements in the context of considering the propriety of injunctive relief, the statements constitute a finding that the evidence concerning "sports, religious, educational, and other programming" was sufficient to establish a significant quantity of broadcasting whose copying is now authorized, and a significant potential for future authorized copying. That finding is amply supported by the record. In addition to the religious and sports officials identified explicitly by the District Court, two items in the record deserve specific mention.

First is the testimony of John Kenaston, the station manager of Channel 58, an educational station in Los Angeles affiliated with the Public Broadcasting Service. He explained and authenticated the station's published guide to its programs. For each program, the guide tells whether unlimited home taping is authorized, home taping is authorized subject to certain restrictions (such as erasure within seven days), or home taping is not authorized at all. The Spring 1978 edition of the guide described 107 programs. Sixty-two of those programs or

58% authorize some home taping. Twenty-one of them or almost 20% authorize unrestricted home taping.

Second is the testimony of Fred Rogers, president of the corporation that produces and owns the copyright on *Mr. Rogers' Neighborhood.* The program is carried by more public television stations than any other program. Its audience numbers over 3,000,000 families a day. He testified that he had absolutely no objection to home taping for noncommercial use and expressed the opinion that it is a real service to families to be able to record children's programs and to show them at appropriate times.

If there are millions of owners of VTR's who make copies of televised sports events, religious broadcasts, and educational programs such as *Mister Rogers' Neighborhood,* and if the proprietors of those programs welcome the practice, the business of supplying the equipment that makes such copying feasible should not be stifled simply because the equipment is used by some individuals to make unauthorized reproductions of respondents' works. The respondents do not represent a class composed of all copyright holders. Yet a finding of contributory infringement would inevitably frustrate the interests of broadcasters in reaching the portion of their audience that is available only through time-shifting.

Of course, the fact that other copyright holders may welcome the practice of time-shifting does not mean that respondents should be deemed to have granted a license to copy their programs. Third party conduct would be wholly irrelevant in an action for direct infringement of respondents' copyrights. But in an action for *contributory* infringement against the seller of copying equipment, the copyright holder may not prevail unless the relief that he seeks affects only his programs, or unless he speaks for virtually all copyright holders with an interest in the outcome. In this case, the record makes it perfectly clear that there are many important producers of national and local television programs who find nothing objectionable about the enlargement in the size of the television audience that results from the practice of time-shifting for private home use. The seller of the equipment that expands those producers' audiences cannot be a contributory infringer if, as is true in this case, it has had no direct involvement with any infringing activity.

B. *Unauthorized Time-Shifting*

Even unauthorized uses of a copyrighted work are not necessarily infringing. An unlicensed use of the copyright is not an infringement unless it conflicts with one of the specific exclusive rights conferred by the copyright statute. *Twentieth Century Music Corp. v. Aiken,* 422 U.S. 151, 154-155, 95 S.Ct. 2040, 2043, 45 L.Ed.2d 84. Moreover, the definition of exclusive rights in § 106 of the present Act is prefaced by the words "subject to sections 107 through 118." Those sections describe a variety of uses of copyrighted material that "are not infringements of copyright notwithstanding the provisions of § 106." The most pertinent in this case is § 107, the legislative endorsement of the doctrine of "fair use."

That section identifies various factors that enable a Court to apply an "equitable rule of reason" analysis to particular claims of infringement. Although not conclusive, the first factor requires that "the commercial or nonprofit character of an activity" be weighed in any fair use decision. If the Betamax were used to make copies for a commercial or profit-making purpose, such use would presumptively be unfair. The contrary presumption is appropriate here, however, because the District Court's findings plainly establish that time-shifting for private home use must be characterized as a noncommercial, nonprofit activity. Moreover, when one considers the nature of a televised copyrighted audiovisual work, see 17 U.S.C. § 107(2), and that timeshifting merely enables a viewer to see such a work which he had been invited to witness in its entirety free of charge, the fact that the entire work is reproduced, see *id.*, at § 107(3), does not have its ordinary effect of militating against a finding of fair use.

This is not, however, the end of the inquiry because Congress has also directed us to consider "the effect of the use upon the potential market for or value of the copyrighted work." *Id.*, at § 107(4). The purpose of copyright is to create incentives for creative effort. Even copying for noncommercial purposes may impair the copyright holder's ability to obtain the rewards that Congress intended him to have. But a use that has no demonstrable effect upon the potential market for, or the value of, the copyrighted work need not be prohibited in order to protect the author's incentive to create. The prohibition of such noncommercial uses would merely inhibit access to ideas without any countervailing benefit.

Thus, although every commercial use of copyrighted material is presumptively an unfair exploitation of the monopoly privilege that belongs to the owner of the copyright, noncommercial uses are a different matter. A challenge to a noncommercial use of a copyrighted work requires proof either that the particular use is harmful, or that if it should become widespread, it would adversely affect the potential market for the copyrighted work. Actual present harm need not be shown; such a requirement would leave the copyright holder with no defense against predictable damage. Nor is it necessary to show with certainty that future harm will result. What is necessary is a showing by a preponderance of the evidence that *some* meaningful likelihood of future harm exists. If the intended use is for commercial gain, that likelihood may be presumed. But if it is for a noncommercial purpose, the likelihood must be demonstrated.

In this case, respondents failed to carry their burden with regard to home time-shifting.

[Discussion of District Court Record omitted]

When these factors are all weighed in the "equitable rule of reason" balance, we must conclude that this record amply supports the District Court's conclusion that home time-shifting is fair use. In light of the findings of the District Court regarding the state of the empirical data, it is clear that the Court of Appeals erred in holding that the statute as presently written bars such conduct.

In summary, the record and findings of the District Court lead us to two conclusions. First, Sony demonstrated a significant likelihood that substantial numbers of copyright holders who license their works for broadcast on free television would not object to having their broadcasts time-shifted by private viewers. And second, respondents failed to demonstrate that time-shifting would cause any likelihood of nonminimal harm to the potential market for, or the value of, their copyrighted works. The Betamax is, therefore, capable of substantial noninfringing uses. Sony's sale of such equipment to the general public does not constitute contributory infringement of respondent's copyrights.

V

"The direction of Art. I is that *Congress* shall have the power to promote the progress of science and the useful arts. When, as here, the Constitution is permissive, the sign of how far Congress has chosen to go can come only from Congress." *Deepsouth Packing Co. v. Laitram Corp.,* 406 U.S. 518, 530, 92 S.Ct. 1700, 1707, 32 L.Ed.2d 273 (1972).

One may search the Copyright Act in vain for any sign that the elected representatives of the millions of people who watch television every day have made it unlawful to copy a program for later viewing at home, or have enacted a flat prohibition against the sale of machines that make such copying possible.

It may well be that Congress will take a fresh look at this new technology, just as it so often has examined other innovations in the past. But it is not our job to apply laws that have not yet been written. Applying the copyright statute, as it now reads, to the facts as they have been developed in this case, the judgment of the Court of Appeals must be reversed.

Notes:

1. **Source of Law.** Copyright protects original expressions of ideas that are fixed in a tangible medium. Unlike patents or trade secrets, copyright does not protect the idea itself, but only a specific expression of the idea. Protection is provided by the federal Copyright Act, 17 U.S.C. § 101, *et. seq*, enacted in 1976.

2. **Description of Protected Works.** Copyright extends to a wide range of works of authorship, including literary works, musical works, dramatic works, pantomimes and choreographic works, graphic and sculptural works, motion pictures and audiovisual works, sound recordings, and architectural works.

3. **Creation of Copyright.** Under the current Copyright Act, the authors rights begin at the instant an original work is fixed. Registration of the work is optional, although an owner must register the copyright prior to commencing a suit to enforce the copyright. See 17 U.S.C. §411(a), *Reed Elsevier, Inc. v. Muchnick*, ___ U.S. ___, 130 S. Ct. 1237 (2010) (registration under § 411(a) is a pre-condition to filing suit, but is not a jurisdictional requirement).

4. **Copyright Term.** A copyright gives the owner the exclusive right to the reproduction, adaptation, distribution, public performance, and public display of the work, subject to many limitations built into the Copyright Act. 17 U.S.C. § 106. That right lasts for the copyright term, which currently is the life of the author plus 70 years or, in the case of "works made for hire," the longer of 120 years from creation or 95 years from first publication. 17 U.S.C. § 301. As a result of the 1998 Sonny Bono Copyright Term Extension Act, copyright owners enjoy a fixed term much longer than that available under the Patent Act.

5. **Ownership**. A copyright typically is owned by the author of the work. In cases of joint work, the multiple authors become co-owners of the copyright. In cases in which an employee (or a non-employee creating a work in a handful of specific categories) creates a work in the course of his or her employment, the employer owns the copyright as a "work made for hire." *See* 17 U.S.C. § 101.

6. **Fair Use.** As illustrated in the *Sony* case, a copyright owner's ability to control the use of the work is more restricted than a patent owner's right to exclude others from practicing a claimed invention. The Copyright Act strikes a careful balance between the rights of authors and the rights of the public, which retains some right to use copyrighted

work. An important public right is the ability to make "fair use" of the copyrighted work. Whether a use is protected as fair use, 17 U.S.C. § 107, depends on a number of factors, including the purpose and character of the use, the amount and substantiality of the portion of the work used, and the effect the use has on the potential market for the work. *See Harper & Row Publishers, Inc. v. Nation Enterprises*, 471 U.S. 539 (1985).

E. Trademarks

The fourth major intellectual property right is the law of trademark. In the modern commercial marketplace, competing suppliers of goods and services invest enormous resources in developing brands and creating consumer recognition and goodwill associated with those brands. The law of trademark seeks to protect that investment by prohibiting competitors from using similar words, marks or symbols in a way that is likely to create confusion about the source or sponsorship of a good or service.

ABERCROMBIE & FITCH CO. v. HUNTING WORLD, INC.

537 F.2d 4, 189 U.S.P.Q. 769 (2d Cir 1976)

FRIENDLY, Circuit Judge:

This action in the District Court for the Southern District of New York by Abercrombie & Fitch Company (A&F), owner of well-known stores at Madison Avenue and 45th Street in New York City and seven places in other states against Hunting World, Incorporated (HW), operator of a competing store on East 53rd Street, is for infringement of some of A&F's registered trademarks using the word 'Safari'. It has had a long and, for A&F, an unhappy history. On this appeal from a judgment which not only dismissed the complaint but canceled all of A&F's 'Safari' registrations, including several that were not in suit, we relieve A&F of some of its unhappiness but not of all.

I.

The complaint, filed in January, 1970, after describing the general nature of A&F's business, reflecting its motto, "The Greatest Sporting Goods Store in the World," alleged as follows: For many years A&F has used the mark 'Safari' on articles "exclusively offered and sold by it." Since 1936 it has used the mark on a variety of men's and women's outer garments. Its United States trademark registrations include:

Trademark	Number	Issued	Goods
Safari	358,781	7/26/38	Men's and Women's outer garments, including hats.
Safari Mills	125,531	5/20/19	Cotton Piece goods.
Safari	652,098	9/24/57	Men's and Women's outer garments, including shoes.
Safari	703,279	8/23/60	Woven cloth, sporting goods, apparel, etc.

A&F has spent large sums of money in advertising and promoting products identified with its mark 'Safari' and in policing its right in the mark, including the successful conduct of trademark infringement suits. HW, the complaint continued, has engaged in the retail marketing of sporting apparel including hats and shoes, some identified by use of 'Safari' alone or by expressions such as 'Minisafari' and 'Safariland'. Continuation of HW's acts would confuse and deceive the public and impair "the distinct and unique quality of the plaintiff's trademark." A&F sought an injunction against infringement and an accounting for damages and profits.

HW filed an answer and counterclaim. This alleged, inter alia, that "the word 'safari' is an ordinary, common, descriptive, geographic, and generic word" which "is commonly used and understood by the public to mean and refer to a journey or expedition, especially for hunting or exploring in East Africa, and to the hunters, guides, men, animals, and equipment forming such an expedition" and is not subject to exclusive appropriation as a trademark. HW sought cancellation of all of A&F's registrations using the word 'Safari' on the ground that A&F had fraudulently failed to disclose the true nature of the term to the Patent Office.

HW having moved for summary judgment, Judge Lasker granted this only in part, 327 F.Supp. 657 (S.D.N.Y.1971). He held, 327 F.Supp. at 662, that:

> Although "safari" is a generic word, a genuine issue of fact exists as to whether the plaintiff has created a secondary meaning in its use of the word

> "identifying the source" and showing that "purchasers are moved to buy it because of its source."

On the other hand, he concluded that A&F had no right to prevent HW from using the word 'Safari' to describe its business as distinguished from use in the sale of a particular product[3] a conclusion we do not understand to be disputed; that HW had not infringed A&F's registered mark using the word 'Safari' under its brand name on a "classical safari hat" or in advertising this as "The Hat for Safari" since such use was purely descriptive, 327 F.Supp. at 664; that HW had also not infringed by using the term 'Minisafari' as a name for its narrower brimmed safari hats, and that HW was entitled to use the word 'Safariland' as the description of an area within its shop and as the name of a corporation engaged in the wholesale distribution of products imported from East Africa by an affiliate, Lee Expeditions, Ltd., and in the "Safariland News," a newsletter issued by HW and Lee Expeditions, 327 F.Supp. at 664-65. With respect to shoes he concluded that both parties had used the word 'Safari' in a fanciful rather than a descriptive sense and hence that plaintiff might have a valid infringement claim it could establish a secondary meaning, 327 F.Supp. at 665.

On A&F's appeal this court reversed and remanded for trial, 461 F.2d 1040 (2 Cir. 1972). Most of Judge Thomsen's opinion for the court concerned the issue of appealability, as did most of Judge Timbers' concurring opinion and all of Judge Feinberg's dissent. Intimating no opinion on the ultimate merits, this court concluded "that genuine issues of fact exist which made it improper to enter a summary judgment finally denying even in part the injunctive relief sought by plaintiff."

Judge Ryan, before whom the action was tried on remand, ruled broadly in HW's favor. He found there was frequent use of the word 'Safari' in connection with wearing apparel, that A&F's policing efforts thus had evidently been unsuccessful, and that A&F had itself used the term in a descriptive sense not covered by its registration, e. g., in urging customers to make a "Christmas Gift Safari" to the A&F store. After referring to statements by Judge Lasker that 'Safari' was a "weak" mark, 327 F.Supp. at 663, the judge found the mark to be invalid. 'Safari,' the court held, "is merely descriptive and does not serve to distinguish plaintiff's goods as listed on the registration from anybody else's"; while such terms are afforded protection by the Lanham Act if they come to identify the company merchandising the product, rather than the product itself, A&F had failed to establish that this had become

[3] He noted that HW had grown "from the operation of a company which actually organizes safaris and has common officers with that company," 327 F.Supp. at 663.

the situation with respect to 'Safari'. The opinion did not discuss A&F's assertion that some of its marks had become incontestable under § 15 of the Lanham Act, 15 U.S.C. § 1065. The court entered a judgment which dismissed the complaint and canceled not only the four registered trademarks in suit but all A&F's other registered 'Safari' trademarks. A&F has appealed.

II.

It will be useful at the outset to restate some basic principles of trademark law, which, although they should be familiar, tend to become lost in a welter of adjectives.

The cases, and in some instances the Lanham Act, identify four different categories of terms with respect to trademark protection. Arrayed in an ascending order which roughly reflects their eligibility to trademark status and the degree of protection accorded, these classes are (1) generic, (2) descriptive, (3) suggestive, and (4) arbitrary or fanciful. The lines of demarcation, however, are not always bright. Moreover, the difficulties are compounded because a term that is in one category for a particular product may be in quite a different one for another,[6] because a term may shift from one category to another in light of differences in usage through time,[7] because a term may have one meaning to one group of users and a different one to others, and because the same term may be put to different uses with respect to a single product. In various ways, all of these complications are involved in the instant case.

A generic term is one that refers, or has come to be understood as referring, to the genus of which the particular product is a species. At common law neither those terms which were generic nor those which were merely descriptive could become valid trademarks. The same was true under the Trademark Act of 1905, except for marks which had been the subject of exclusive use for ten years prior to its enactment. While, as we shall see, p. -- infra, the Lanham Act makes an important exception with respect to those merely descriptive terms which have acquired secondary meaning, *see* § 2(f), 15 U.S.C. § 1052(f), it offers no such exception for generic marks. The Act provides for the cancellation of a registered mark if at any time it "becomes the common descriptive name of an article or substance," § 14(c). This means that even proof of secondary meaning, by virtue of which some "merely descriptive"

---

[6] To take a familiar example "Ivory" would be generic when used to describe a product made from the tusks of elephants but arbitrary as applied to soap.

[7] *See, e. g., Haughton Elevator Co. v. Seeberger*, 85 U.S.P.Q. 80 (1950), in which the coined word 'Escalator', originally fanciful, or at the very least suggestive, was held to have become generic.

marks may be registered, cannot transform a generic term into a subject for trademark. As explained in *J. Kohnstam, Ltd. v. Louis Marx and Company*, 280 F.2d 437, 440, 47 CCPA 1080 (1960), no matter how much money and effort the user of a generic term has poured into promoting the sale of its merchandise and what success it has achieved in securing public identification, it cannot deprive competing manufacturers of the product of the right to call an article by its name.

The term which is descriptive but not generic stands on a better basis. Although § 2(e) of the Lanham Act, 15 U.S.C. § 1052, forbids the registration of a mark which, when applied to the goods of the applicant, is "merely descriptive," § 2(f) removes a considerable part of the sting by providing that "except as expressly excluded in paragraphs (a)-(d) of this section, nothing in this chapter shall prevent the registration of a mark used by the applicant which has become distinctive of the applicant's goods in commerce" and that the Commissioner may accept, as prima facie evidence that the mark has become distinctive, proof of substantially exclusive and continuous use of the mark applied to the applicant's goods for five years preceding the application. As indicated in the cases cited in the discussion of the unregistrability of generic terms, "common descriptive name," as used in §§ 14(c) and 15(4), refers to generic terms applied to products and not to terms that are "merely descriptive." In the former case any claim to an exclusive right must be denied since this in effect would confer a monopoly not only of the mark but of the product by rendering a competitor unable effectively to name what it was endeavoring to sell. In the latter case the law strikes the balance, with respect to registration, between the hardships to a competitor in hampering the use of an appropriate word and those to the owner who, having invested money and energy to endow a word with the good will adhering to his enterprise, would be deprived of the fruits of his efforts.

The category of "suggestive" marks was spawned by the felt need to accord protection to marks that were neither exactly descriptive on the one hand nor truly fanciful on the other a need that was particularly acute because of the bar in the Trademark Act of 1905, 33 Stat. 724, 726, (with an exceedingly limited exception noted above) on the registration of merely descriptive marks regardless of proof of secondary meaning. *See Orange Crush Co. v. California Crushed Fruit Co.*, 54 U.S.App.D.C. 313, 297 F. 892 (1924). Having created the category the courts have had great difficulty in defining it. Judge Learned Hand made the not very helpful statement:

> It is quite impossible to get any rule out of the cases beyond this: That the validity of the mark ends where suggestion ends and description begins.

Franklin Knitting Mills, Inc. v. Fashionit Sweater Mills, Inc., 297 F. 247, 248 (2 Cir. 1923), aff'd per curiam, 4 F.2d 1018 (2 Cir. 1925)[.] Another court has observed, somewhat more usefully, that:

> A term is suggestive if it requires imagination, thought and perception to reach a conclusion as to the nature of goods. A term is descriptive if it forthwith conveys an immediate idea of the ingredients, qualities or characteristics of the goods.

Stix Products, Inc. v. United Merchants & Manufacturers Inc., 295 F.Supp. 479, 488 (S.D.N.Y.1968) a formulation deriving from *General Shoe Corp. v. Rosen*, 111 F.2d 95, 98 (4 Cir. 1940). Also useful is the approach taken by this court in *Aluminum Fabricating Co. of Pittsburgh v. Season-All Window Corp.*, 259 F.2d 314 (2 Cir. 1958), that the reason for restricting the protection accorded descriptive terms, namely the undesirability of preventing an entrant from using a descriptive term for his product, is much less forceful when the trademark is a suggestive word since, as Judge Lumbard wrote, 259 F.2d at 317:

> The English language has a wealth of synonyms and related words with which to describe the qualities which manufacturers may wish to claim for their products and the ingenuity of the public relations profession supplies new words and slogans as they are needed.

If a term is suggestive, it is entitled to registration without proof of secondary meaning. Moreover, as held in the Season-All case, the decision of the Patent Office to register a mark without requiring proof of secondary meaning affords a rebuttable presumption that the mark is suggestive or arbitrary or fanciful rather than merely descriptive.

It need hardly be added that fanciful or arbitrary terms enjoy all the rights accorded to suggestive terms as marks without the need of debating whether the term is "merely descriptive" and with ease of establishing infringement.

In the light of these principles we must proceed to a decision of this case.

III.

We turn first to an analysis of A&F's trademarks to determine the scope of protection to which they are entitled. We have reached the following conclusions: (1) applied to specific types of clothing 'safari' has become a generic term and 'minisafari' may be used for a smaller brim hat; (2) 'safari' has not, however, become a generic term for boots or shoes; it is either "suggestive" or "merely descriptive" and is a valid trademark even if " merely descriptive" since it has become incontestable under the Lanham Act; but (3) in light of the justified finding below that 'Camel Safari,' 'Hippo Safari' and 'Safari Chukka' were devoted by HW to a purely descriptive use on its boots, HW has a defense against a charge of infringement with respect to these on the basis of "fair use." We now discuss how we have reached these conclusions.

It is common ground that A&F could not apply 'Safari' as a trademark for an expedition into the African wilderness. This would be a clear example of the use of 'Safari' as a generic term. What is perhaps less obvious is that a word may have more than one generic use. The word 'Safari' has become part of a family of generic terms which, although deriving no doubt from the original use of the word and reminiscent of its milieu, have come to be understood not as having to do with hunting in Africa, but as terms within the language referring to contemporary American fashion apparel. These terms name the components of the safari outfit well-known to the clothing industry and its customers: the 'Safari hat', a broad flat-brimmed hat with a single, large band; the 'Safari jacket', a belted bush jacket with patch pockets and a buttoned shoulder loop; when the jacket is accompanied by pants, the combination is called the 'Safari suit'. Typically these items are khaki-colored.

This outfit, and its components, were doubtless what Judge Ryan had in mind when he found that "the word 'safari' in connection with wearing apparel is widely used by the general public and people in the trade." The record abundantly supports the conclusion that many stores have advertised these items despite A&F's attempts to police its mark. In contrast, a search of the voluminous exhibits fails to disclose a single example of the use of 'Safari', by anyone other than A&F and HW, on merchandise for which A&F has registered 'Safari' except for the safari outfit and its components as described above.

What has been thus far established suffices to support the dismissal of the complaint with respect to many of the uses of 'Safari' by HW. Describing a publication as a "Safariland Newsletter", containing bulletins as to safari activity in Africa, was clearly a generic use which is nonenjoinable, *see CES Publishing Co. v. St. Regis Publications, Inc.*, supra. A&F also was not entitled to an injunction against HW's use of the word in advertising goods of the kind included in the safari outfit as described above. And if HW may advertise a hat of the kind worn on safaris as a safari hat, it may also advertise a similar hat with a smaller brim as a minisafari. Although the issue may be somewhat closer, the principle against giving trademark protection to a generic term also sustains the denial of an injunction against

HW's use of 'Safariland' as a name of a portion of its store devoted at least in part to the sale of clothing as to which the term 'Safari' has become generic.

A&F stands on stronger ground with respect to HW's use of 'Camel Safari', 'Hippo Safari' and Chukka 'Safari' as names for boots imported from Africa. As already indicated, there is no evidence that 'Safari' has become a generic term for boots. Since, as will appear, A&F's registration of 'Safari' for use on its shoes has become incontestable, it is immaterial (save for HW's contention of fraud which is later rejected) whether A&F's use of 'Safari' for boots was suggestive or "merely descriptive."

HW contends, however, that even if 'Safari' is a valid trademark for boots, it is entitled to the defense of "fair use" within § 33(b)(4) of the Lanham Act, 15 U.S.C. § 1115(b)(4). That section offers such a defense even as against marks that have become incontestable when the term charged to be an infringement is not used as a trademark "and is used fairly and in good faith only to describe to users the goods and services of such party, or their geographic origin."

Here, Lee Expeditions, Ltd., the parent company of HW, has been primarily engaged in arranging safaris to Africa since 1959; Robert Lee, the president of both companies, is the author of a book published in 1959 entitled "Safari Today The Modern Safari Handbook" and has, since 1961, booked persons on safaris as well as purchased safari clothing in Africa for resale in America. These facts suffice to establish, absent a contrary showing, that defendant's use of 'Safari' with respect to boots was made in the context of hunting and traveling expeditions and not as an attempt to garner A&F's good will. The district court here found the HW's use of 'Camel Safari', 'Hippo Safari', and 'Safari Chukka' as names for various boots imported from Africa constituted "a purely descriptive use to apprise the public of the type of product by referring to its origin and use." The court properly followed the course sanctioned by this court in *Venetianaire Corp. of America v. A&P Import Co.*, 429 F.2d 1079, 1081-82 (1970), by focusing on the "use of words, not on their nature or meaning in the abstract" (emphasis in original). When a plaintiff has chosen a mark with some descriptive qualities, he cannot altogether exclude some kinds of competing uses even when the mark is properly on the register[.] We do not have here a situation similar to those in *Venetianaire*, supra, and *Feathercombs, Inc. v. Solo Products Corp.*, 306 F.2d 251 (2 Cir. 1962), in both of which we rejected "fair use" defenses, wherein an assertedly descriptive use was found to have been in a trademark sense. It is significant that HW did not use 'Safari' alone on its shoes, as it would doubtless have done if confusion had been intended.

We thus hold that the district court was correct in dismissing the complaint.

IV.

We find much greater difficulty in the court's broad invalidation of A&F's trademark registrations. Section 37 of the Lanham Act, 15 U.S.C. § 1119, provides authority for the court to cancel those registrations of any party to an action involving a registered mark. The cases cited above, p. --, establish that when a term becomes the generic name of the product to which it is applied, grounds for cancellation exist. The relevant registrations of that sort are Nos. 358,781 and 703,279[.]

There remain eight other registrations and those terms not pared from No. 703,279. Three of these registrations, Nos. 652,098, 768,332 and 770,336, and the non-generic portions of No. 703,279 appear to have become incontestable by virtue of the filing of affidavits under § 15(3), of five years continuous use. There is nothing to suggest that the uses included in these registrations, except the uses described above with respect to 703,279 are the common descriptive names of either current fashion styles or African expeditions. The generic term for A&F's 'safari cloth Bermuda shorts', for example, is 'Bermuda shorts', not 'safari'; indeed one would suppose this garment to be almost ideally unsuited for the forest or the jungle and there is no evidence that it has entered into the family for which 'Safari' has become a generic adjective. The same analysis holds for luggage, portable grills, and the rest of the suburban paraphernalia, from swimtrunks and raincoats to belts and scarves, included in these registrations. HW alleged that these registrations were procured by fraud, a claim which, if successful, would deny incontestability to A&F's marks, see § 14(c), 15 U.S.C. § 1064(c). But these allegations seem to have meant no more than that HW believed the terms to be merely descriptive and hence unregistrable, and that the Patent Office must have been duped into registering them in the first place without proof of secondary meaning. However, we regard these terms as suggestive rather than "merely descriptive." Moreover, even if they were the latter, assuming that the person filing the applications made the required allegation that "no other person, firm, corporation, or association, to the best of his knowledge and belief, has the right to use such mark in commerce either in the identical form thereof or in such near resemblance thereto as might be calculated to deceive," see § 1(a)(1), 15 U.S.C. § 1051(a)(1), there is nothing to show that such statements were knowingly false when made. The scheme of the Lanham Act forbids a denial of incontestability to a "merely descriptive" mark which would otherwise have become incontestable under § 14 on the basis of a mere allegation of fraud in obtaining registration, without supporting proof.

We hold also that the registrations which have not become incontestable should not have been canceled. 'Safari' as applied to ice chests, axes, tents and smoking tobacco does not describe such items. Rather it is a way of conveying to affluent patrons of A&F a romantic notion of high style, coupled with an attractive foreign allusion. As such, these uses fit what was said many years ago in upholding 'Ideal' as a mark for hair brushes:

> The word "Ideal" has no application to hair brushes, except as we arbitrarily apply it, and the word is in no sense indicative or descriptive of the qualities or characteristics or merits of the brush except that it meets the very highest ideal, mental conception, of what a hair brush should be.

Hughes v. Alfred H. Smith Co., 205 F. 302, 309 (S.D.N.Y.), aff'd. per curiam, 209 F. 37 (2 Cir. 1913). It is even wider of the mark to say that 'Safari Mills' "describes" cotton piece goods. Such uses fit into the category of suggestive marks. We need not now decide how valuable they may prove to be; it suffices here that they should not have been canceled.

In sum, we conclude that cancellation should have been directed only with respect to No. 358,781 and portions of No. 703,279 and the New York registration. With respect to the remaining registrations A&F will have the benefits accorded by § 7(b) that registration shall be "prima facie evidence of the validity of the registration . . . and of (the) registrant's exclusive right to use the mark in commerce," 15 U.S.C. § 1057(b). This means "not only that the burden of going forward is upon the contestant of the registration but that there is a strong presumption of validity so that the party claiming invalidity has the burden of proof (and) must put something more into the scales than the registrant." *Aluminum Fabricating Co. of Pittsburgh v. Season-All Window Corp.*, 259 F.2d 314, 316 (2 Cir. 1958). In the case of registrations that have become incontestable A&F will have the further benefit accorded by § 33(a), 15 U.S.C. § 1115(a), subject to the limitations contained therein and in § 33(b), 15 U.S.C. § 1115(b). Whether all this will suffice for a victory will depend on the facts in each case.

So much of the judgment as dismissed the complaint is affirmed; so much of the judgment as directed cancellation of the registrations is affirmed in part and reversed in part, and the cause is remanded for the entry of a new judgment consistent with this opinion. No costs.

Notes:

1. **Source of Law**. Trademark law protects marks which consumers associate with the source or sponsorship of products or services from use likely to cause confusion. Trademarks exist under both federal and state law. The federal Lanham Act, 15 U.S.C. §

1051, *et seq.*, protects trademarks based on a nationwide registration system. In addition, all 50 states provide protection for trademarks under state registration systems, common law or as part of statutes governing unfair business practices. *See, e.g.*, Cal. Bus. & Prof. Code §§ 14200- 14342.

2. **Registration.** In the United States, trademarks can be obtained either under state law or under the federal Lanham Act. Under state law, one can typically acquire common law rights by affixing a word, symbol or other device to a good or product or in advertising associated with a good or service. Once established, state trademark rights allow the first user of the mark to preclude infringing use in the marketplace. In addition, an owner can obtain federal rights under the Lanham Act by registering a trademark with the U.S. Patent and Trademark Office. In order to obtain a federal registration, the applicant must establish that the mark was be the subject of a "bona fide use . . . in the ordinary course of trade, and not made merely to reserve a right in a mark." 15 U.S.C. § 1127.

3. **Strength of Trademarks.** Trademarks are categorized according to their distinctiveness.

- Marks the merely describe an associated product or service are known as "descriptive" marks. Descriptive marks cannot be protected as trademarks unless they have acquired distinctiveness through use by becoming associated with a particular source through usage. Examples of descriptive marks include FROSTED MINI WHEATS (cereal), HOLIDAY INN (hotel), and BUDGET CAR RENTAL (car rental agency).

- "Suggestive" marks are stronger than descriptive marks, and are considered to be inherently distinctive. Suggestive marks relate to some characteristic of the associated good or service, but require the consumer to use their imagination to interpret the mark with the characteristic. Examples of suggestive marks include WHIRLPOOL (washing machines), GREYHOUND (bus service), MICROSOFT (PC software), and COPPERTONE (tanning lotion).

- "Arbitrary" marks are even stronger trademarks. Arbitrary marks are recognized words, but do not reflect a characteristic of the associated good or service. Example of arbitrary marks include APPLE (personal electronics), DIAL (soap), and SATURN (automobiles).

- "Fanciful" marks are the strongest trademarks. Fanciful marks are generally made-up words that have no meaning apart identifying the associated good or services. Examples of fanciful marks include GOOGLE (search engine), KODAK (photography supplies), PENTIUM (PC microprocessors), and XEROX (image processing).

4. "Genericness." If a mark loses its ability to indicate the source or sponsorship of a product or service, and becomes a general name for a category of product, it loses its status as a trademark. Several words in our vocabulary started as trademarks, but overtime fell victiom to "genericide," including ASPIRIN, THERMOS, TRAMPOLINE, ESCALATOR, and CELLOPHANE. Generic terms have no inherent or acquired distinctiveness.

Internal Revenue Code – Selected Sections

(Effective as of January 1, 2011)

I.R.C. § 41: Credit for increasing research activities.

(a) General rule. For purposes of section 38, the research credit determined under this section for the taxable year shall be an amount equal to the sum of—

(1) 20 percent of the excess (if any) of—

(A) the qualified research expenses for the taxable year, over

(B) the base amount,

(2) 20 percent of the basic research payments determined under subsection (e)(1)(A), and

(3) 20 percent of the amounts paid or incurred by the taxpayer in carrying on any trade or business of the taxpayer during the taxable year (including as contributions) to an energy research consortium for energy research.

(b) Qualified research expenses. For purposes of this section—

(1) Qualified research expenses. The term "qualified research expenses" means the sum of the following amounts which are paid or incurred by the taxpayer during the taxable year in carrying on any trade or business of the taxpayer—

(A) in-house research expenses, and

(B) contract research expenses.

(2) In-house research expenses.

(A) *In general*. The term "in- house research expenses" means—

(i) any wages paid or incurred to an employee for qualified services performed by such employee,

(ii) any amount paid or incurred for supplies used in the conduct of qualified research, and

(iii) under regulations prescribed by the Secretary, any amount paid or incurred to another person for the right to use computers in the conduct of qualified research.

Clause (iii) shall not apply to any amount to the extent that the taxpayer (or any person with whom the taxpayer must aggregate expenditures under subsection (f)(1)) receives or accrues any amount from any other person for the right to use substantially identical personal property.

(B) *Qualified services.* The term "qualified services" means services consisting of—

(i) engaging in qualified research, or

(ii) engaging in the direct supervision or direct support of research activities which constitute qualified research.

If substantially all of the services performed by an individual for the taxpayer during the taxable year consists of services meeting the requirements of clause (i) or (ii), the term "qualified services" means all of the services performed by such individual for the taxpayer during the taxable year.

(C) *Supplies.* The term "supplies" means any tangible property other than—

(i) land or improvements to land, and

(ii) property of a character subject to the allowance for depreciation.

(D) *Wages.*

(i) *In general.* The term "wages" has the meaning given such term by section 3401(a)

(ii) *Self-employed individuals and owner-employees.* In the case of an employee (within the meaning of section 401(c)(1), the term "wages" includes the earned income (as defined in section 401(c)(2) of such employee.

(iii) *Exclusion for wages to which work opportunity credit applies.* The term "wages" shall not include any amount taken into account in determining the work opportunity credit under section 51(a).

(3) Contract research expenses.

(A) *In general.* The term "contract research expenses" means 65 percent of any amount paid or incurred by the taxpayer to any person (other than an employee of the taxpayer) for qualified research.

(B) *Prepaid amounts.* If any contract research expenses paid or incurred during any taxable year are attributable to qualified research to be conducted after the close of such taxable year, such amount shall be treated as paid or incurred during the period during which the qualified research is conducted.

(C) *Amounts paid to certain research consortia.*

(i) *In general.* Subparagraph (A) shall be applied by substituting "75 percent" for "65 percent" with respect to amounts paid or incurred by the taxpayer to a qualified research consortium for qualified research on behalf of the taxpayer and 1 or more unrelated taxpayers. For purposes of the preceding sentence, all persons treated as a single employer under subsection (a) or (b) of section 52 shall be treated as related taxpayers.

(ii) *Qualified research consortium.* The term "qualified research consortium" means any organization which—

(I) is described in section 501(c)(3) or 501(c)(6) and is exempt from tax under section 501(a),

(II) is organized and operated primarily to conduct scientific research, and

(III) is not a private foundation.

* * *

(d) Qualified research defined. For purposes of this section—

(1) In general. The term "qualified research" means research—

(A) with respect to which expenditures may be treated as expenses under section 174,

(B) which is undertaken for the purpose of discovering information—

(i) which is technological in nature, and

(ii) the application of which is intended to be useful in the development of a new or improved business component of the taxpayer, and

(C) substantially all of the activities of which constitute elements of a process of experimentation for a purpose described in paragraph (3).

Such term does not include any activity described in paragraph (4).

(2) Tests to be applied separately to each business component. For purposes of this subsection—

(A) *In general.* Paragraph (1) shall be applied separately with respect to each business component of the taxpayer.

(B) *Business component defined.* The term "business component" means any product, process, computer software, technique, formula, or invention which is to be—

(i) held for sale, lease, or license, or

(ii) used by the taxpayer in a trade or business of the taxpayer.

(C) *Special rule for production processes.* Any plant process, machinery, or technique for commercial production of a business component shall be treated as a separate business component (and not as part of the business component being produced).

(3) Purposes for which research may qualify for credit. For purposes of paragraph (1)(C)—

(A) *In general.* Research shall be treated as conducted for a purpose described in this paragraph if it relates to—

(i) a new or improved function,

(ii) performance, or

(iii) reliability or quality.

(B) *Certain purposes not qualified.* Research shall in no event be treated as conducted for a purpose described in this paragraph if it relates to style, taste, cosmetic, or seasonal design factors.

(4) Activities for which credit not allowed. The term "qualified research" shall not include any of the following:

(A) *Research after commercial production.* Any research conducted after the beginning of commercial production of the business component.

(B) *Adaptation of existing business components.* Any research related to the adaptation of an existing business component to a particular customer's requirement or need.

(C) *Duplication of existing business component.* Any research related to the reproduction of an existing business component (in whole or in part) from a physical examination of the business component itself or from plans, blueprints, detailed specifications, or publicly available information with respect to such business component.

(D) *Surveys, studies, etc.* Any—

(i) efficiency survey,

(ii) activity relating to management function or technique,

(iii) market research, testing, or development (including advertising or promotions),

(iv) routine data collection, or

(v) routine or ordinary testing or inspection for quality control.

(E) *Computer software.* Except to the extent provided in regulations, any research with respect to computer software which is developed by (or for the benefit of) the taxpayer primarily for internal use by the taxpayer, other than for use in—

(i) an activity which constitutes qualified research (determined with regard to this subparagraph), or

(ii) a production process with respect to which the requirements of paragraph (1) are met.

(F) *Foreign research.* Any research conducted outside the United States, the Commonwealth of Puerto Rico, or any possession of the United States.

(G) *Social sciences, etc.* Any research in the social sciences, arts, or humanities.

(H) *Funded research.* Any research to the extent funded by any grant, contract, or otherwise by another person (or governmental entity).

* * *

I.R.C. § 61. Gross income defined.

(a) General definition. Except as otherwise provided in this subtitle, gross income means all income from whatever source derived, including (but not limited to) the following items:

(1) Compensation for services, including fees, commissions, fringe benefits, and similar items;

(2) Gross income derived from business;

(3) Gains derived from dealings in property;

(4) Interest;

(5) Rents;

(6) Royalties;

(7) Dividends;

(8) Alimony and separate maintenance payments;

(9) Annuities;

(10) Income from life insurance and endowment contracts;

(11) Pensions;

(12) Income from discharge of indebtedness;

(13) Distributive share of partnership gross income;

(14) Income in respect of a decedent; and

(15) Income from an interest in an estate or trust.

I.R.C. § 162. Trade or business expenses.

(a) In general. There shall be allowed as a deduction all the ordinary and necessary expenses paid or incurred during the taxable year in carrying on any trade or business, including—

(1) a reasonable allowance for salaries or other compensation for personal services actually rendered;

(2) traveling expenses (including amounts expended for meals and lodging other than amounts which are lavish or extravagant under the circumstances) while away from home in the pursuit of a trade or business; and

(3) rentals or other payments required to be made as a condition to the continued use or possession, for purposes of the trade or business, of property to which the taxpayer has not taken or is not taking title or in which he has no equity.

* * *

I.R.C. § 165. Losses.

(a) General rule. There shall be allowed as a deduction any loss sustained during the taxable year and not compensated for by insurance or otherwise.

(b) Amount of deduction. For purposes of subsection (a), the basis for determining the amount of the deduction for any loss shall be the adjusted basis provided in section 1011 for determining the loss from the sale or other disposition of property.

(c) Limitation on losses of individuals. In the case of an individual, the deduction under subsection (a) shall be limited to

(1) losses incurred in a trade or business;

(2) losses incurred in any transaction entered into for profit, though not connected with a trade or business; and

(3) except as provided in subsection (h), losses of property not connected with a trade or business or a transaction entered into for profit, if such losses arise from fire, storm, shipwreck, or other casualty, or from theft.

* * *

(f) Capital losses. Losses from sales or exchanges of capital assets shall be allowed only to the extent allowed in sections 1211 and 1212.

* * *

I.R.C. § 167. Depreciation.

(a) General rule. There shall be allowed as a depreciation deduction a reasonable allowance for the exhaustion, wear and tear (including a reasonable allowance for obsolescence)—

(1) of property used in the trade or business, or

(2) of property held for the production of income.

* * *

(f) Treatment of certain property excluded from section 197.

(1) Computer software.

(A) *In general.* If a depreciation deduction is allowable under subsection (a) with respect to any computer software, such deduction shall be computed by using the straight line method and a useful life of 36 months.

(B) *Computer software.* For purposes of this section, the term "computer software" has the meaning given to such term by section 197(e)(3)(B); except that such term shall not include any such software which is an amortizable section 197 intangible.

(C) *Tax-exempt use property subject to lease.* In the case of computer software which would be tax-exempt use property as defined in subsection (h) of section 168 if such section applied to computer software, the useful life under subparagraph (A) shall not be less than 125 percent of the lease term (within the meaning of section 168(i)(3)).

(2) Certain interests or rights acquired separately. If a depreciation deduction is allowable under subsection (a) with respect to any property described in subparagraph (B), (C), or (D) of section 197(e)(4), such deduction shall be computed in accordance with regulations prescribed by the Secretary. If such property would be tax-exempt use property as defined in subsection (h) of section 168 if such section applied to such property, the useful life under such regulations shall not be less than 125 percent of the lease term (within the meaning of section 168(i)(3)).

* * *

(g) Depreciation under income forecast method.

(1) In general. If the depreciation deduction allowable under this section to any taxpayer with respect to any property is determined under the income forecast method or any similar method—

(A) the income from the property to be taken into account in determining the depreciation deduction under such method shall be equal to the amount of income earned in connection with the property before the close of the 10th taxable year following the taxable year in which the property was placed in service,

(B) the adjusted basis of the property shall only include amounts with respect to which the requirements of section 461(h) are satisfied,

(C) the depreciation deduction under such method for the 10th taxable year beginning after the taxable year in which the property was placed in service shall be equal to the adjusted basis of such property as of the beginning of such 10th taxable year, and

(D) such taxpayer shall pay (or be entitled to receive) interest computed under the look-back method of paragraph (2) for any recomputation year.

(2) Look-back method. The interest computed under the look-back method of this paragraph for any recomputation year shall be determined by—

(A) first determining the depreciation deductions under this section with respect to such property which would have been allowable for prior taxable years if the determination of the amounts so allowable had been made on the basis of the sum of the following (instead of the estimated income from such property)—

(i) the actual income earned in connection with such property for periods before the close of the recomputation year, and

(ii) an estimate of the future income to be earned in connection with such property for periods after the recomputation year and before the close of the 10th taxable year following the taxable year in which the property was placed in service,

(B) second, determining (solely for purposes of computing such interest) the overpayment or underpayment of tax for each such prior taxable year which would result solely from the application of subparagraph (A), and

(C) then using the adjusted overpayment rate (as defined in section 460(b)(7), compounded daily, on the overpayment or underpayment determined under subparagraph (B).

For purposes of the preceding sentence, any cost incurred after the property is placed in service (which is not treated as a separate property under paragraph (5)) shall be taken into account by discounting (using the Federal mid-term rate determined under section 1274(d) as of the time such cost is incurred) such cost to its value as of the date the property is placed in service. The taxpayer may elect with respect to any property to have the preceding sentence not apply to such property.

(3) Exception from look-back method. Paragraph (1)(D) shall not apply with respect to any property which had a cost basis of $100,000 or less.

(4) Recomputation year. For purposes of this subsection, except as provided in regulations, the term "recomputation year" means, with respect to any property, the 3d and the 10th taxable years beginning after the taxable year in which the property was placed in service, unless the actual income earned in connection with the property for the period before the close of such 3d or 10th taxable year is within 10 percent of the income earned in connection with the property for such period which was taken into account under paragraph (1)(A).

(5) Special rules.

(A) *Certain costs treated as separate property.* For purposes of this subsection, the following costs shall be treated as separate properties:

(i) Any costs incurred with respect to any property after the 10th taxable year beginning after the taxable year in which the property was placed in service.

(ii) Any costs incurred after the property is placed in service and before the close of such 10th taxable year if such costs are significant and give rise to a significant increase in the income from the property which was not included in the estimated income from the property.

(B) *Syndication income from television series.* In the case of property which is 1 or more episodes in a television series, income from syndicating such series shall not be required to be taken into account under this subsection before the earlier of—

(i) the 4th taxable year beginning after the date the first episode in such series is placed in service, or

(ii) the earliest taxable year in which the taxpayer has an arrangement relating to the future syndication of such series.

(C) *Special rules for financial exploitation of characters, etc.* For purposes of this subsection, in the case of television and motion picture films, the income from the property shall include income from the exploitation of characters, designs, scripts, scores, and other incidental income associated with such films, but only to the extent that such income is earned in connection with the ultimate use of such items by, or the ultimate sale of merchandise to, persons who are not related persons (within the meaning of section 267(b)) to the taxpayer.

(D) *Collection of interest.* For purposes of subtitle F (other than sections 6654 and 6655), any interest required to be paid by the taxpayer under paragraph (1) for any recomputation year shall be treated as an increase in the tax imposed by this chapter for such year.

(E) *Treatment of distribution costs.* For purposes of this subsection, the income with respect to any property shall be the taxpayer's gross income from such property.

(F) *Determinations.* For purposes of paragraph (2), determinations of the amount of income earned in connection with any property shall be made in the same manner as for purposes of applying the income forecast method;

except that any income from the disposition of such property shall be taken into account.

(G) *Treatment of pass-thru entities.* Rules similar to the rules of section 460(b)(4) shall apply for purposes of this subsection.

(6) Limitation on property for which income forecast method may be used. The depreciation deduction allowable under this section may be determined under the income forecast method or any similar method only with respect to—

(A) property described in paragraph (3) or (4) of section 168(f),

(B) copyrights,

(C) books,

(D) patents, and

(E) other property specified in regulations.

Such methods may not be used with respect to any amortizable section 197 intangible (as defined in section 197(c)).

(7) Treatment of participations and residuals.

(A) *In general.* For purposes of determining the depreciation deduction allowable with respect to a property under this subsection, the taxpayer may include participations and residuals with respect to such property in the adjusted basis of such property for the taxable year in which the property is placed in service, but only to the extent that such participations and residuals relate to income estimated (for purposes of this subsection) to be earned in connection with the property before the close of the 10th taxable year referred to in paragraph (1)(A).

(B) *Participations and residuals.* For purposes of this paragraph, the term "participations and residuals" means, with respect to any property, costs the amount of which by contract varies with the amount of income earned in connection with such property.

(C) *Special rules relating to recomputation years.* If the adjusted basis of any property is determined under this paragraph, paragraph (4) shall be applied by substituting "for each taxable year in such period" for "for such period."

(D) *Other special rules.*

(i) Participations and residuals. Notwithstanding subparagraph (A), the taxpayer may exclude participations and residuals from the adjusted basis of such property and deduct such participations and residuals in the taxable year that such participations and residuals are paid.

(ii) Coordination with other rules. Deductions computed in accordance with this paragraph shall be allowable notwithstanding paragraph (1)(B), section 263, 263A, 404, 419, or 461(h).

(E) *Authority to make adjustments.* The Secretary shall prescribe appropriate adjustments to the basis of property and to the look-back method for the additional amounts allowable as a deduction solely by reason of this paragraph.

(8) Special rules for certain musical works and copyrights.

(A) *In general.* If an election is in effect under this paragraph for any taxable year, then, notwithstanding paragraph (1), any expense which—

(i) is paid or incurred by the taxpayer in creating or acquiring any applicable musical property placed in service during the taxable year, and

(ii) is otherwise properly chargeable to capital account,

shall be amortized ratably over the 5-year period beginning with the month in which the property was placed in service. The preceding sentence shall not apply to any expense which, without regard to this paragraph, would not be allowable as a deduction.

(B) *Exclusive method.* Except as provided in this paragraph, no depreciation or amortization deduction shall be allowed with respect to any expense to which subparagraph (A) applies.

(C) *Applicable musical property.* For purposes of this paragraph—

(i) In general. The term "applicable musical property" means any musical composition (including any accompanying words), or any copyright with respect to a musical composition, which is property to which this subsection applies without regard to this paragraph.

(ii) Exceptions. Such term shall not include any property—

(I) with respect to which expenses are treated as qualified creative expenses to which section 263A(h) applies,

(II) to which a simplified procedure established under section 263A(i)(2) applies, or

(III) which is an amortizable section 197 intangible (as defined in section 197(c)).

(D) *Election.* An election under this paragraph shall be made at such time and in such form as the Secretary may prescribe and shall apply to all applicable musical property placed in service during the taxable year for which the election applies.

(E) *Termination.* An election may not be made under this paragraph for any taxable year beginning after December 31, 2010.

* * *

I.R.C. § 174. Research and experimental expenditures.

(a) Treatment as expenses.

(1) In general. A taxpayer may treat research or experimental expenditures which are paid or incurred by him during the taxable year in connection with his trade or business as expenses which are not chargeable to capital account. The expenditures so treated shall be allowed as a deduction.

(2) When method may be adopted.

(A) *Without consent.* A taxpayer may, without the consent of the Secretary, adopt the method provided in this subsection for his first taxable year—

(i) which begins after December 31, 1953, and ends after August 16, 1954, and

(ii) for which expenditures described in paragraph (1) are paid or incurred.

(B) *With consent.* A taxpayer may, with the consent of the Secretary, adopt at any time the method provided in this subsection.

(3) Scope. The method adopted under this subsection shall apply to all expenditures described in paragraph (1). The method adopted shall be adhered to in computing taxable income for the taxable year and for all subsequent taxable years unless, with the approval of the Secretary, a change to a different method is authorized with respect to part or all of such expenditures.

(b) Amortization of certain research and experimental expenditures.

(1) In general. At the election of the taxpayer, made in accordance with regulations prescribed by the Secretary, research or experimental expenditures which are—

(A) paid or incurred by the taxpayer in connection with his trade or business,

(B) not treated as expenses under subsection (a), and

(C) chargeable to capital account but not chargeable to property of a character which is subject to the allowance under section 167 (relating to allowance for depreciation, etc.) or section 611 (relating to allowance for depletion), may be treated as deferred expenses. In computing taxable income, such deferred expenses shall be allowed as a deduction ratably over such period of not less than 60 months as may be selected by the taxpayer (beginning with the month in which the taxpayer first realizes benefits from such expenditures). Such deferred expenses are expenditures properly chargeable to capital account for purposes of section 1016(a)(1) (relating to adjustments to basis of property).

(2) Time for and scope of election. The election provided by paragraph (1) may be made for any taxable year beginning after December 31, 1953, but only if made not later than the time prescribed by law for filing the return for such taxable year (including extensions thereof). The method so elected, and the period selected by the taxpayer, shall be adhered to in computing taxable income for the taxable year for which the election is made and for all subsequent taxable years unless, with the approval of the Secretary, a change to a different method (or to a different period) is authorized with respect to part or all of such expenditures. The election shall not apply to any expenditure paid or incurred during any taxable year before the taxable year for which the taxpayer makes the election.

(c) Land and other property. This section shall not apply to any expenditure for the acquisition or improvement of land, or for the acquisition or improvement of property to be used in connection with the research or experimentation and of a character which is subject to the allowance under section 167 (relating to allowance for depreciation, etc.) or section 611 (relating to allowance for depletion); but for purposes of this section allowances under section 167, and allowances under section 611, shall be considered as expenditures.

(d) Exploration expenditures. This section shall not apply to any expenditure paid or incurred for the purpose of ascertaining the existence, location, extent, or quality of any deposit of ore or other mineral (including oil and gas).

(e) Only reasonable research expenditures eligible. This section shall apply to a research or experimental expenditure only to the extent that the amount thereof is reasonable under the circumstances.

(f) Cross References.

(1) For adjustments to basis of property for amounts allowed as deductions as deferred expenses under subsection (b), see section 1016(a)(14).

(2) For election of 10-year amortization of expenditures allowable as a deduction under subsection (a), see section 59(e).

I.R.C. § 195. Start-up expenditures.

(a) Capitalization of expenditures. Except as otherwise provided in this section, no deduction shall be allowed for start-up expenditures.

(b) Election to deduct.

(1) Allowance of deduction. If a taxpayer elects the application of this subsection with respect to any start-up expenditures—

(A) the taxpayer shall be allowed a deduction for the taxable year in which the active trade or business begins in an amount equal to the lesser of—

(i) the amount of start-up expenditures with respect to the active trade or business, or

(ii) $5,000, reduced (but not below zero) by the amount by which such start-up expenditures exceed $50,000, and

(B) the remainder of such start-up expenditures shall be allowed as a deduction ratably over the 180-month period beginning with the month in which the active trade or business begins.

(2) Dispositions before close of amortization period. In any case in which a trade or business is completely disposed of by the taxpayer before the end of the period to which paragraph (1) applies, any deferred expenses attributable to such trade or business which were not allowed as a deduction by reason of this section may be deducted to the extent allowable under section 165.

* * *

(c) Definitions. For purposes of this section—

(1) Start-up expenditures. The term "start-up expenditure" means any amount—

(A) paid or incurred in connection with—

(i) investigating the creation or acquisition of an active trade or business, or

(ii) creating an active trade or business, or

(iii) any activity engaged in for profit and for the production of income before the day on which the active trade or business begins, in anticipation of such activity becoming an active trade or business, and

(B) which, if paid or incurred in connection with the operation of an existing active trade or business (in the same field as the trade or business referred to in subparagraph (A)), would be allowable as a deduction for the taxable year in which paid or incurred.

The term "start-up expenditure" does not include any amount with respect to which a deduction is allowable under section 163(a), 164, or 174.

(2) Beginning of trade or business.

(A) *In general.* Except as provided in subparagraph (B), the determination of when an active trade or business begins shall be made in accordance with such regulations as the Secretary may prescribe.

(B) *Acquired trade or business.* An acquired active trade or business shall be treated as beginning when the taxpayer acquires it.

(d) Election.

(1) Time for making election. An election under subsection (b) shall be made not later than the time prescribed by law for filing the return for the taxable year in which the trade or business begins (including extensions thereof).

(2) Scope of election. The period selected under subsection (b) shall be adhered to in computing taxable income for the taxable year for which the election is made and all subsequent taxable years.

I.R.C. § 197. Amortization of goodwill and certain other intangibles.

(a) General rule. A taxpayer shall be entitled to an amortization deduction with respect to any amortizable section 197 intangible. The amount of such deduction shall be determined by amortizing the adjusted basis (for purposes of determining gain) of such intangible ratably over the 15-year period beginning with the month in which such intangible was acquired.

(b) No other depreciation or amortization deduction allowable. Except as provided in subsection (a), no depreciation or amortization deduction shall be allowable with respect to any amortizable section 197 intangible.

(c) Amortizable section 197 intangible. For purposes of this section—

(1) In general. Except as otherwise provided in this section, the term "amortizable section 197 intangible" means any section 197 intangible—

(A) which is acquired by the taxpayer after the date of the enactment of this section, and

(B) which is held in connection with the conduct of a trade or business or an activity described in section 212.

(2) Exclusion of self-created intangibles, etc. The term "amortizable section 197 intangible" shall not include any section 197 intangible—

(A) which is not described in subparagraph (D), (E), or (F) of subsection (d)(1), and

(B) which is created by the taxpayer.

This paragraph shall not apply if the intangible is created in connection with a transaction (or series of related transactions) involving the acquisition of assets constituting a trade or business or substantial portion thereof.

(3) Anti-churning rules. For exclusion of intangibles acquired in certain transactions, see subsection (f)(9).

(d) Section 197 intangible. For purposes of this section—

(1) In general. Except as otherwise provided in this section, the term "section 197 intangible" means—

(A) goodwill,

(B) going concern value,

(C) any of the following intangible items:

(i) workforce in place including its composition and terms and conditions (contractual or otherwise) of its employment,

(ii) business books and records, operating systems, or any other information base (including lists or other information with respect to current or prospective customers),

(iii) any patent, copyright, formula, process, design, pattern, knowhow, format, or other similar item,

(iv) any customer-based intangible,

(v) any supplier-based intangible, and

(vi) any other similar item,

(D) any license, permit, or other right granted by a governmental unit or an agency or instrumentality thereof,

(E) any covenant not to compete (or other arrangement to the extent such arrangement has substantially the same effect as a covenant not to compete) entered into in connection with an acquisition (directly or indirectly) of an interest in a trade or business or substantial portion thereof, and

(F) any franchise, trademark, or trade name.

(2) Customer-based intangible.

(A) *In general*. The term "customer-based intangible" means—

(i) composition of market,

(ii) market share, and

(iii) any other value resulting from future provision of goods or services pursuant to relationships (contractual or otherwise) in the ordinary course of business with customers.

(B) *Special rule for financial institutions.* In the case of a financial institution, the term "customer-based intangible" includes deposit base and similar items.

(3) Supplier-based intangible. The term "supplier-based intangible" means any value resulting from future acquisitions of goods or services pursuant to relationships (contractual or otherwise) in the ordinary course of business with suppliers of goods or services to be used or sold by the taxpayer.

(e) Exceptions. For purposes of this section, the term "section 197 intangible" shall not include any of the following:

(1) Financial interests. Any interest—

(A) in a corporation, partnership, trust, or estate, or

(B) under an existing futures contract, foreign currency contract, notional principal contract, or other similar financial contract.

(2) Land. Any interest in land.

(3) Computer software.

(A) *In general.* Any—

(i) computer software which is readily available for purchase by the general public, is subject to a nonexclusive license, and has not been substantially modified, and

(ii) other computer software which is not acquired in a transaction (or series of related transactions) involving the acquisition of assets constituting a trade or business or substantial portion thereof.

(B) *Computer software defined.* For purposes of subparagraph (A), the term "computer software" means any program designed to cause a computer to perform a desired function. Such term shall not include any data base or similar item unless the data base or item is in the public domain and is incidental to the operation of otherwise qualifying computer software.

(4) Certain interests or rights acquired separately. Any of the following not acquired in a transaction (or series of related transactions) involving the acquisition of assets constituting a trade business or substantial portion thereof:

(A) Any interest in a film, sound recording, video tape, book, or similar property.

(B) Any right to receive tangible property or services under a contract or granted by a governmental unit or agency or instrumentality thereof.

(C) Any interest in a patent or copyright.

(D) To the extent provided in regulations, any right under a contract (or granted by a governmental unit or an agency or instrumentality thereof) if such right—

(i) has a fixed duration of less than 15 years, or

(ii) is fixed as to amount and, without regard to this section, would be recoverable under a method similar to the unit-of-production method.

(5) Interests under leases and debt instruments. Any interest under—

(A) an existing lease of tangible property, or

(B) except as provided in subsection (d)(2)(B), any existing indebtedness.

(6) Mortgage servicing. Any right to service indebtedness which is secured by residential real property unless such right is acquired in a transaction (or series of related transactions) involving the acquisition of assets (other than rights described in this paragraph) constituting a trade or business or substantial portion thereof.

(7) Certain transaction costs. Any fees for professional services, and any transaction costs, incurred by parties to a transaction with respect to which any portion of the gain or loss is not recognized under part III of subchapter C.

(f) Special rules.

(1) Treatment of certain dispositions, etc.

(A) *In general*. If there is a disposition of any amortizable section 197 intangible acquired in a transaction or series of related transactions (or any such intangible becomes worthless) and one or more other amortizable section 197 intangibles acquired in such transaction or series of related transactions are retained—

(i) no loss shall be recognized by reason of such disposition (or such worthlessness), and

(ii) appropriate adjustments to the adjusted bases of such retained intangibles shall be made for any loss not recognized under clause (i).

(B) *Special rule for covenants not to compete*. In the case of any section 197 intangible which is a covenant not to compete (or other arrangement) described in subsection (d)(1)(E), in no event shall such covenant or other arrangement be treated as disposed of (or becoming worthless) before the disposition of the entire interest described in such subsection in connection with which such covenant (or other arrangement) was entered into.

(C) *Special rule.* All persons treated as a single taxpayer under section 41(f)(1) shall be so treated for purposes of this paragraph.

(2) Treatment of certain transfers.

(A) *In general.* In the case of any section 197 intangible transferred in a transaction described in subparagraph (B), the transferee shall be treated as the transferor for purposes of applying this section with respect to so much of the adjusted basis in the hands of the transferee as does not exceed the adjusted basis in the hands of the transferor.

(B) *Transactions covered.* The transactions described in this subparagraph are—

(i) any transaction described in section 332, 351, 361, 721, 731, 1031, or 1033, and

(ii) any transaction between members of the same affiliated group during any taxable year for which a consolidated return is made by such group.

(3) Treatment of amounts paid pursuant to covenants not to compete, etc. Any amount paid or incurred pursuant to a covenant or arrangement referred to in subsection (d)(1)(E) shall be treated as an amount chargeable to capital account.

(4) Treatment of franchises, etc.

(A) Franchise. The term "franchise" has the meaning given to such term by section 1253(b)(1).

(B) Treatment of renewals. Any renewal of a franchise, trademark, or trade name (or of a license, a permit, or other right referred to in subsection (d)(1)(D)) shall be treated as an acquisition. The preceding sentence shall only apply with respect to costs incurred in connection with such renewal.

(C) Certain amounts not taken into account. Any amount to which section 1253(d)(1) applies shall not be taken into account under this section.

* * *

(7) Treatment as depreciable. For purposes of this chapter, any amortizable section 197 intangible shall be treated as property which is of a character subject to the allowance for depreciation provided in section 167.

* * *

(g) Regulations. The Secretary shall prescribe such regulations as may be appropriate to carry out the purposes of this section, including such regulations as may be appropriate to prevent avoidance of the purposes of this section through related persons or otherwise.

I.R.C. § 262. Personal, living, and family expenses.

(a) General rule. Except as otherwise expressly provided in this chapter, no deduction shall be allowed for personal, living, or family expenses.

* * *

I.R.C. § 263. Capital expenditures.

(a) General rule. No deduction shall be allowed for—

(1) Any amount paid out for new buildings or for permanent improvements or betterments made to increase the value of any property or estate. This paragraph shall not apply to—

* * *

(B) research and experimental expenditures deductible under section 174,

* * *

(2) Any amount expended in restoring property or in making good the exhaustion thereof for which an allowance is or has been made.

* * *

I.R.C. § 263A. Capitalization and inclusion in inventory costs of certain expenses.

(a) Nondeductibility of certain direct and indirect costs.

(1) In general. In the case of any property to which this section applies, any costs described in paragraph (2)—

(A) in the case of property which is inventory in the hands of the taxpayer, shall be included in inventory costs, and

(B) in the case of any other property, shall be capitalized.

(2) Allocable costs. The costs described in this paragraph with respect to any property are—

(A) the direct costs of such property, and

(B) such property's proper share of those indirect costs (including taxes) part or all of which are allocable to such property.

Any cost which (but for this subsection) could not be taken into account in computing taxable income for any taxable year shall not be treated as a cost described in this paragraph.

(b) Property to which section applies. Except as otherwise provided in this section, this section shall apply to—

(1) Property produced by taxpayer. Real or tangible personal property produced by the taxpayer.

(2) Property acquired for resale.

(A) *In general.* Real or personal property described in section 1221(a)(1) which is acquired by the taxpayer for resale.

(B) *Exception for taxpayer with gross receipts of $10,000,000 or less.* Subparagraph (A) shall not apply to any personal property acquired during any taxable year by the taxpayer for resale if the average annual gross receipts of the taxpayer (or any predecessor) for the 3-taxable year period ending with the taxable year preceding such taxable year do not exceed $10,000,000.

(C) *Aggregation rules, etc.* For purposes of subparagraph (B), rules similar to the rules of paragraphs (2) and (3) of section 448(c) shall apply.

For purposes of paragraph (1), the term "tangible personal property" shall include a film, sound recording, video tape, book, or similar property.

* * *

(h) Exemption for free lance authors, photographers, and artists.

(1) In general. Nothing in this section shall require the capitalization of any qualified creative expense.

(2) Qualified creative expense. For purposes of this subsection, the term "qualified creative expense" means any expense—

(A) which is paid or incurred by an individual in the trade or business of such individual (other than as an employee) of being a writer, photographer, or artist, and

(B) which, without regard to this section, would be allowable as a deduction for the taxable year.

Such term does not include any expense related to printing, photographic plates, motion picture films, video tapes, or similar items.

(3) Definitions. For purposes of this subsection—

(A) *Writer.* The term "writer" means any individual if the personal efforts of such individual create (or may reasonably be expected to create) a literary manuscript, musical composition (including any accompanying words), or dance score.

(B) *Photographer.* The term "photographer" means any individual if the personal efforts of such individual create (or may reasonably be expected to create) a photograph or photographic negative or transparency.

(C) *Artist.*—

(i) *In general.* The term "artist" means any individual if the personal efforts of such individual create (or may reasonably be expected to create) a picture, painting, sculpture, statue, etching, drawing, cartoon, graphic design, or original print edition.

(ii) *Criteria.* In determining whether any expense is paid or incurred in the trade or business of being an artist, the following criteria shall be taken into account:

(I) The originality and uniqueness of the item created (or to be created).

(II) The predominance of aesthetic value over utilitarian value of the item created (or to be created).

(D) *Treatment of certain corporations.*

(i) *In general.* If—

(I) substantially all of the stock of a corporation is owned by a qualified employee-owner and members of his family (as defined in section 267(c)(4)), and

(II) the principal activity of such corporation is performance of personal services directly related to the activities of the qualified employee-owner and such services are substantially performed by the qualified employee-owner,

this subsection shall apply to any expense of such corporation which directly relates to the activities of such employee-owner in the same manner as if such expense were incurred by such employee-owner.

(ii) *Qualified employee-owner.* For purposes of this subparagraph, the term "qualified employee-owner" means any individual who is an employee-owner of the corporation (as defined in section 269A(b)(2)) and who is a writer, photographer, or artist.

* * *

I.R.C. § 351. Transfer to corporation controlled by transferor.

(a) General rule. No gain or loss shall be recognized if property is transferred to a corporation by one or more persons solely in exchange for stock in such corporation and immediately after the exchange such person or persons are in control (as defined in section 368(c)) of the corporation.

* * *

I.R.C. § 361. Nonrecognition of gain or loss to corporations; treatment of distributions.

(a) General rule. No gain or loss shall be recognized to a corporation if such corporation is a party to a reorganization and exchanges property, in pursuance of the plan of reorganization, solely for stock or securities in another corporation a party to the reorganization.

* * *

I.R.C. § 367. Foreign corporations.

(a) Transfers of property from the United States.

(1) General rule. If, in connection with any exchange described in section 332, 351, 354, 356, or 361, a United States person transfers property to a foreign corporation, such foreign corporation shall not, for purposes of determining the extent to which gain shall be recognized on such transfer, be considered to be a corporation.

* * *

(d) Special rules relating to transfers of intangibles.

(1) In general. Except as provided in regulations prescribed by the Secretary, if a United States person transfers any intangible property (within the meaning of section 936(h)(3)(B)) to a foreign corporation in an exchange described in section 351 or 361—

(A) subsection (a) shall not apply to the transfer of such property, and

(B) the provisions of this subsection shall apply to such transfer.

(2) Transfer of intangibles treated as transfer pursuant to sale of contingent payments.

(A) *In general.* If paragraph (1) applies to any transfer, the United States person transferring such property shall be treated as—

(i) having sold such property in exchange for payments which are contingent upon the productivity, use, or disposition of such property, and

(ii) receiving amounts which reasonably reflect the amounts which would have been received—

(I) annually in the form of such payments over the useful life of such property, or

(II) in the case of a disposition following such transfer (whether direct or indirect), at the time of the disposition.

The amounts taken into account under clause (ii) shall be commensurate with the income attributable to the intangible.

(B) *Effect on earnings and profits*. For purposes of this chapter, the earnings and profits of a foreign corporation to which the intangible property was transferred shall be reduced by the amount required to be included in the income of the transferor of the intangible property under subparagraph (A)(ii).

(C) *Amounts received treated as ordinary income*. For purposes of this chapter, any amount included in gross income by reason of this subsection shall be treated as ordinary income. For purposes of applying section 904(d), any such amount shall be treated in the same manner as if such amount were a royalty.

(3) Regulations relating to transfers of intangibles to partnerships. The Secretary may provide by regulations that the rules of paragraph (2) also apply to the transfer of intangible property by a United States person to a partnership in circumstances consistent with the purposes of this subsection.

I.R.C. § 368. Definitions relating to corporate reorganizations.

(a) Reorganization.

(1) In general. For purposes of parts I and II and this part, the term "reorganization" means—

(A) a statutory merger or consolidation;

(B) the acquisition by one corporation, in exchange solely for all or a part of its voting stock (or in exchange solely for all or a part of the voting stock of a corporation which is in control of the acquiring corporation), of stock of another corporation if, immediately after the acquisition, the acquiring corporation has control of such other corporation (whether or not such acquiring corporation had control immediately before the acquisition);

(C) the acquisition by one corporation, in exchange solely for all or a part of its voting stock (or in exchange solely for all or a part of the voting stock of a corporation which is in control of the acquiring corporation), of substantially all of the properties of another corporation, but in determining whether the exchange is solely for stock the assumption by the acquiring corporation of a liability of the other shall be disregarded;

(D) a transfer by a corporation of all or a part of its assets to another corporation if immediately after the transfer the transferor, or one or more of its shareholders (including persons who were shareholders immediately before the transfer), or any combination thereof, is in control of the corporation to which the assets are transferred; but only if, in pursuance of the plan, stock or securities of the corporation to which the assets are transferred are distributed in a transaction which qualifies under section 354, 355, or 356;

(E) a recapitalization;

(F) a mere change in identity, form, or place of organization of one corporation, however effected; or

(G) a transfer by a corporation of all or part of its assets to another corporation in a title 11 or similar case; but only if, in pursuance of the plan, stock or securities of the corporation to which the assets are transferred are distributed in a transaction which qualifies under section 354, 355, or 356.

* * *

(b) Party to a reorganization. For purposes of this part, the term "a party to a reorganization" includes—

(1) a corporation resulting from a reorganization, and

(2) both corporations, in the case of a reorganization resulting from the acquisition by one corporation of stock or properties of another.

* * *

(c) Control defined. For purposes of part I (other than section 304), part II, this part, and part V, the term "control" means the ownership of stock possessing at least 80 percent of the total combined voting power of all classes of stock entitled to vote and at least 80 percent of the total number of shares of all other classes of stock of the corporation.

I.R.C. § 453. Installment method.

(a) General rule. Except as otherwise provided in this section, income from an installment sale shall be taken into account for purposes of this title under the installment method.

(b) Installment sale defined. For purposes of this section—

(1) In general. The term "installment sale" means a disposition of property where at least 1 payment is to be received after the close of the taxable year in which the disposition occurs.

(2) Exceptions. The term "installment sale" does not include—

(A) *Dealer dispositions.* Any dealer disposition (as defined in subsection (l)).

(B) *Inventories of personal property.* A disposition of personal property of a kind which is required to be included in the inventory of the taxpayer if on hand at the close of the taxable year.

(c) Installment method defined. For purposes of this section, the term "installment method" means a method under which the income recognized for any taxable year from a disposition is that proportion of the payments received in that year which the gross profit (realized or to be realized when payment is completed) bears to the total contract price.

(d) Election out.

(1) In general. Subsection (a) shall not apply to any disposition if the taxpayer elects to have subsection (a) not apply to such disposition.

(2) Time and manner for making election. Except as otherwise provided by regulations, an election under paragraph (1) with respect to a disposition may be made only on or before the due date prescribed by law (including extensions) for filing the taxpayer's return of the tax imposed by this chapter for the taxable year in which the disposition occurs. Such an election shall be made in the manner prescribed by regulations.

(3) Election revocable only with consent. An election under paragraph (1) with respect to any disposition may be revoked only with the consent of the Secretary.

* * *

(i) Recognition of recapture income in year of disposition.

(1) In general. In the case of any installment sale of property to which subsection (a) applies—

(A) notwithstanding subsection (a), any recapture income shall be recognized in the year of the disposition, and

(B) any gain in excess of the recapture income shall be taken into account under the installment method.

(2) Recapture income. For purposes of paragraph (1), the term "recapture income" means, with respect to any installment sale, the aggregate amount which would be treated as ordinary income under section 1245 or 1250 (or so much of section 751 as relates to section 1245 or 1250) for the taxable year of the disposition if all payments to be received were received in the taxable year of disposition.

(j) Regulations.

(1) In general. The Secretary shall prescribe such regulations as may be necessary or appropriate to carry out the provisions of this section.

(2) Selling price not readily ascertainable. The regulations prescribed under paragraph (1) shall include regulations providing for ratable basis recovery in transactions where the gross profit or the total contract price (or both) cannot be readily ascertained.

* * *

I.R.C. § 482. Allocation of income and deductions among taxpayers.

In any case of two or more organizations, trades, or businesses (whether or not incorporated, whether or not organized in the United States, and whether or not affiliated) owned or controlled directly or indirectly by the same interests, the Secretary may distribute, apportion, or allocate gross income, deductions, credits, or allowances between or among such organizations, trades, or businesses, if he determines that such distribution, apportionment, or allocation is necessary in order to prevent evasion of taxes or clearly to reflect the income of any of such organizations, trades, or businesses. In the case of any transfer (or license) of intangible property (within the meaning of section 936(h)(3)(B)), the income with respect to such transfer or license shall be commensurate with the income attributable to the intangible.

I.R.C. § 936. Puerto Rico and possession tax credit.

* * *

(h) Tax treatment of intangible property income.

* * *

(3) Intangible property income. For purposes of this subsection—

* * *

(B) *Intangible property.* The term "intangible property" means any—

(i) patent, invention, formula, process, design, pattern, or know-how;

(ii) copyright, literary, musical, or artistic composition;

(iii) trademark, trade name, or brand name;

(iv) franchise, license, or contract;

(v) method, program, system, procedure, campaign, survey, study, forecast, estimate, customer list, or technical data; or

(vi) any similar item,

which has substantial value independent of the services of any individual.

* * *

I.R.C. § 951. Amounts included in gross income of United States shareholders.

(a) Amounts included.

(1) In general. If a foreign corporation is a controlled foreign corporation for an uninterrupted period of 30 days or more during any taxable year, every person who is a United States shareholder (as defined in subsection (b)) of such corporation and who owns (within the meaning of section 958(a)) stock in such corporation on the last day, in such year, on which such corporation is a controlled foreign corporation shall include in his gross income, for his taxable year in which or with which such taxable year of the corporation ends—

(A) the sum of—

(i) his pro rata share (determined under paragraph (2)) of the corporation's subpart F income for such year,

* * *

(2) Pro rata share of subpart F income. The pro rata share referred to in paragraph (1)(A)(i) in the case of any United States shareholder is the amount—

(A) which would have been distributed with respect to the stock which such shareholder owns (within the meaning of section 958(a)) in such corporation if on the last day, in its taxable year, on which the corporation is a controlled foreign corporation it had distributed pro rata to its shareholders an amount (i) which bears the same ratio to its subpart F income for the taxable year, as (ii) the part of such year during which the corporation is a controlled foreign corporation bears to the entire year, reduced by

(B) the amount of distributions received by any other person during such year as a dividend with respect to such stock, but only to the extent of the dividend which would have been received if the distribution by the corporation had been the amount (i) which bears the same ratio to the subpart F income of such corporation for the taxable year, as (ii) the part of such year during which such shareholder did not own (within the meaning of section 958(a)) such stock bears to the entire year.

For purposes of subparagraph (B), any gain included in the gross income of any person as a dividend under section 1248 shall be treated as a distribution received by such person with respect to the stock involved.

(3) Limitation on pro rata share of previously excluded subpart F income withdrawn from investment. For purposes of paragraph (1)(A)(iii), the pro rata share of any United States shareholder of the previously excluded subpart F income of a controlled foreign corporation withdrawn from investment in foreign base company shipping operations shall not exceed an amount—

(A) which bears the same ratio to his pro rata share of such income withdrawn (as determined under section 955(a)(3)) for the taxable year, as

(B) the part of such year during which the corporation is a controlled foreign corporation bears to the entire year.

(b) United States shareholder defined. For purposes of this subpart, the term "United States shareholder" means, with respect to any foreign corporation, a United States person (as defined in section 957(c)) who owns (within the meaning of section 958(a)), or is considered as owning by applying the rules of ownership of section 958(b), 10 percent or more of the total combined voting power of all classes of stock entitled to vote of such foreign corporation.

* * *

I.R.C. § 952. Subpart F income defined.

(a) In general. For purposes of this subpart, the term "subpart F income" means, in the case of any controlled foreign corporation, the sum of—

* * *

(2) the foreign base company income (as determined under section 954),

* * *

I.R.C. § 954. Foreign base company income.

(a) Foreign base company income. For purposes of section 952(a)(2), the term "foreign base company income" means for any taxable year the sum of—

(1) the foreign personal holding company income for the taxable year (determined under subsection (c) and reduced as provided in subsection (b)(5)),

(2) the foreign base company sales income for the taxable year (determined under subsection (d) and reduced as provided in subsection (b)(5)),

(3) the foreign base company services income for the taxable year (determined under subsection (e) and reduced as provided in subsection (b)(5)),

(4) [Deleted]

(5) the foreign base company oil related income for the taxable year (determined under subsection (g) and reduced as provided in subsection (b)(5)).

(b) Exclusions and special rules.

(1), (2) [Repealed]

(3) De minimis, etc., rules. For purposes of subsection (a) and section 953—

(A) *De minimis rule.* If the sum of foreign base company income (determined without regard to paragraph (5)) and the gross insurance income for the taxable year is less than the lesser of—

(i) 5 percent of gross income, or

(ii) $1,000,000,

no part of the gross income for the taxable year shall be treated as foreign base company income or insurance income.

* * *

(5) Deductions to be taken into account. For purposes of subsection (a), the foreign personal holding company income, the foreign base company sales income, the foreign base company services income, and the foreign base company oil related income shall be reduced, under regulations prescribed by the Secretary, so as to take into account deductions (including taxes) properly allocable to such income. Except to the extent provided in regulations prescribed by the Secretary, any interest which is paid or accrued by the controlled foreign corporation to any United States shareholder in such corporation (or any controlled foreign corporation related to such a shareholder) shall be allocated first to foreign personal holding company income which is passive income (within the meaning of section 904(d)(2)) of such corporation to the extent thereof. The Secretary may, by regulations, provide that the preceding sentence shall apply also to interest paid or accrued to other persons.

* * *

(c) Foreign personal holding company income.

(1) In general. For purposes of subsection (a)(1), the term "foreign personal holding company income" means the portion of the gross income which consists of:

(A) *Dividends, etc.* Dividends, interest, royalties, rents, and annuities.

(B) *Certain property transactions.* The excess of gains over losses from the sale or exchange of property—

(i) which gives rise to income described in subparagraph (A) (after application of paragraph (2)(A) other than property which gives rise to income not treated as foreign personal holding company income by reason of subsection (h) or (i) for the taxable year,

(ii) which is an interest in a trust, partnership, or REMIC, or

(iii) which does not give rise to any income.

* * *

(2) Exception for certain amounts.

(A) *Rents and royalties derived in active business.* Foreign personal holding company income shall not include rents and royalties which are derived in the active conduct of a trade or business and which are received from a person other than a related person (within the meaning of subsection (d)(3)). For purposes of the preceding sentence, rents derived from leasing an aircraft or vessel in foreign commerce shall not fail to be treated as derived in the active conduct of a trade or business if, as determined under regulations prescribed by the Secretary, the active leasing expenses are not less than 10 percent of the profit on the lease.

* * *

(d) Foreign base company sales income.

(1) In general. For purposes of subsection (a)(2), the term "foreign base company sales income" means income (whether in the form of profits, commissions, fees, or otherwise) derived in connection with the purchase of personal property from a related person and its sale to any person, the sale of personal property to any person on behalf of a related person, the purchase of personal property from any person and its sale to a related person, or the purchase of personal property from any person on behalf of a related person where—

(A) the property which is purchased (or in the case of property sold on behalf of a related person, the property which is sold) is manufactured, produced, grown, or extracted outside the country under the laws of which the controlled foreign corporation is created or organized, and

(B) the property is sold for use, consumption, or disposition outside such foreign country, or, in the case of property purchased on behalf of a related person, is purchased for use, consumption, or disposition outside such foreign country.

For purposes of this subsection, personal property does not include agricultural commodities which are not grown in the United States in commercially marketable quantities.

* * *

(3) Related person defined. For purposes of this section, a person is a related person with respect to a controlled foreign corporation, if—

(A) such person is an individual, corporation, partnership, trust, or estate which controls, or is controlled by, the controlled foreign corporation, or

(B) such person is a corporation, partnership, trust, or estate which is controlled by the same person or persons which control the controlled foreign corporation.

For purposes of the preceding sentence, control means, with respect to a corporation, the ownership, directly or indirectly, of stock possessing more than 50 percent of the total voting power of all classes of stock entitled to vote or of the total value of stock of such corporation. In the case of a partnership, trust, or estate, control means the ownership, directly or indirectly, of more than 50 percent (by value) of the beneficial interests in such partnership, trust, or estate. For purposes of this paragraph, rules similar to the rules of section 958 shall apply.

(e) Foreign base company services income.

(1) In general. For purposes of subsection (a)(3), the term "foreign base company services income" means income (whether in the form of compensation, commissions, fees, or otherwise) derived in connection with the performance of technical, managerial, engineering, architectural, scientific, skilled, industrial, commercial, or like services which—

(A) are performed for or on behalf of any related person (within the meaning of subsection (d)(3), and

(B) are performed outside the country under the laws of which the controlled foreign corporation is created or organized.

(2) Exception. Paragraph (1) shall not apply to income derived in connection with the performance of services which are directly related to—

(A) the sale or exchange by the controlled foreign corporation of property manufactured, produced, grown, or extracted by it and which are performed before the time of the sale or exchange, or

(B) an offer or effort to sell or exchange such property.

Paragraph (1) shall also not apply to income which is exempt insurance income (as defined in section 953(e)) or which is not treated as foreign personal holding income by reason of subsection (c)(2)(C)(ii), (h), or (i).

I.R.C. § 957. Controlled foreign corporations; United States persons.

(a) General rule. For purposes of this subpart, the term 'controlled foreign corporation' means any foreign corporation if more than 50 percent of—

(1) the total combined voting power of all classes of stock of such corporation entitled to vote, or

(2) the total value of the stock of such corporation,

is owned (within the meaning of section 958(a)), or is considered as owned by applying the rules of ownership of section 958(b), by United States shareholders on any day during the taxable year of such foreign corporation.

* * *

(c) United States person. For purposes of this subpart, the term 'United States person' has the meaning assigned to it by section 7701(a)(30) except that—

(1) with respect to a corporation organized under the laws of the Commonwealth of Puerto Rico, such term does not include an individual who is a bona fide resident of Puerto Rico, if a dividend received by such individual during the taxable year from such corporation would, for purposes of section 933(1), be treated as income derived from sources within Puerto Rico, and

(2) with respect to a corporation organized under the laws of Guam, American Samoa, or the Northern Mariana Islands—

(A) 80 percent or more of the gross income of which for the 3-year period ending at the close of the taxable year (or for such part of such period as such corporation or any predecessor has been in existence) was derived from sources within such a possession or was effectively connected with the conduct of a trade or business in such a possession, and(B) 50 percent or more of the gross income of which for such period (or part) was derived from the active conduct of a trade or business within such a possession,

such term does not include an individual who is a bona fide resident of Guam, American Samoa, or the Northern Mariana Islands.

For purposes of subparagraphs (A) and (B) of paragraph (2), the determination as to whether income was derived from the active conduct of a trade or business within a possession shall be made under regulations prescribed by the Secretary.

I.R.C. § 958. Rules for determining stock ownership.

(a) Direct and indirect ownership.

(1) General rule. For purposes of this subpart (other than section 960(a)(1)), stock owned means—

(A) stock owned directly, and

(B) stock owned with the application of paragraph (2).

(2) Stock ownership through foreign entities. For purposes of subparagraph (B) of paragraph (1), stock owned, directly or indirectly, by or for a foreign corporation, foreign partnership, or foreign trust or foreign estate (within the meaning of section 7701(a)(31)) shall be considered as being owned proportionately by its shareholders, partners, or beneficiaries. Stock considered to be owned by a person by reason of the application of the preceding sentence shall, for purposes of applying such sentence, be treated as actually owned by such person.

(3) Special rule for mutual insurance companies. For purposes of applying paragraph (1) in the case of a foreign mutual insurance company, the term 'stock' shall include any certificate entitling the holder to voting power in the corporation.

(b) Constructive ownership. For purposes of sections 951(b), 954(d)(3), 956(c)(2), and 957, section 318(a) (relating to constructive ownership of stock) shall apply to the extent that the effect is to treat any United States person as a United States shareholder within the meaning of section 951(b), to treat a person as a related person within the meaning of section 954(d)(3), to treat the stock of a domestic corporation as owned by a United States shareholder of the controlled foreign corporation for purposes of section 956(c)(2), or to treat a foreign corporation as a controlled foreign corporation under section 957, except that—

(1) In applying paragraph (1)(A) of section 318(a), stock owned by a nonresident alien individual (other than a foreign trust or foreign estate) shall not be considered as owned by a citizen or by a resident alien individual.

(2) In applying subparagraphs (A), (B), and (C) of section 318(a)(2), if a partnership, estate, trust, or corporation owns, directly or indirectly, more than 50 percent of the total combined voting power of all classes of stock entitled to vote of a corporation, it shall be considered as owning all the stock entitled to vote.

(3) In applying subparagraph (C) of section 318(a)(2), the phrase '10 percent' shall be substituted for the phrase '50 percent' used in subparagraph (C).

(4) Subparagraphs (A), (B), and (C) of section 318(a)(3) shall not be applied so as to consider a United States person as owning stock which is owned by a person who is not a United States person.

Paragraphs (1) and (4) shall not apply for purposes of section 956(c)(2) to treat stock of a domestic corporation as not owned by a United States shareholder.

I.R.C. § 1001. Determination of amount of and recognition of gain or loss.

(a) Computation of gain or loss. The gain from the sale or other disposition of property shall be the excess of the amount realized therefrom over the adjusted basis provided in section 1011 for determining gain, and the loss shall be the excess of the adjusted basis provided in such section for determining loss over the amount realized.

(b) Amount realized. The amount realized from the sale or other disposition of property shall be the sum of any money received plus the fair market value of the property (other than money) received. In determining the amount realized—

(1) there shall not be taken into account any amount received as reimbursement for real property taxes which are treated under section 164(d) as imposed on the purchaser, and

(2) there shall be taken into account amounts representing real property taxes which are treated under section 164(das imposed on the taxpayer if such taxes are to be paid by the purchaser.

(c) Recognition of gain or loss. Except as otherwise provided in this subtitle, the entire amount of the gain or loss, determined under this section, on the sale or exchange of property shall be recognized.

(d) Installment sales. Nothing in this section shall be construed to prevent (in the case of property sold under contract providing for payment in installments) the taxation of that portion of any installment payment representing gain or profit in the year in which such payment is received.

* * *

I.R.C. § 1012. Basis of property--cost.

(a) In general. The basis of property shall be the cost of such property, except as otherwise provided in this subchapter and subchapters C (relating to corporate distributions and adjustments), K (relating to partners and partnerships), and P (relating to capital gains and losses).

* * *

I.R.C. § 1016. Adjustments to basis.

(a) General rule. Proper adjustment in respect of the property shall in all cases be made—

(1) for expenditures, receipts, losses, or other items, properly chargeable to capital account, but no such adjustment shall be made—

(A) for taxes or other carrying charges described in section 266, or

(B) for expenditures described in section 173 (relating to circulation expenditures),

for which deductions have been taken by the taxpayer in determining taxable income for the taxable year or prior taxable years;

(2) in respect of any period since February 28, 1913, for exhaustion, wear and tear, obsolescence, amortization, and depletion, to the extent of the amount—

(A) allowed as deductions in computing taxable income under this subtitle or prior income tax laws, and

(B) resulting (by reason of the deductions so allowed) in a reduction for any taxable year of the taxpayer's taxes under this subtitle (other than chapter 2, relating to tax on self-employment income), or prior income, war-profits, or excess-profits tax laws,

but not less than the amount allowable under this subtitle or prior income tax laws. Where no method has been adopted under section 167 (relating to depreciation deduction), the amount allowable shall be determined under the straight line method. Subparagraph (B) of this paragraph shall not apply in respect of any period since February 28, 1913, and before January 1, 1952, unless an election has been made under section 1020 (as in effect before the date of the enactment of the Tax Reform Act of 1976). Where for any taxable year before the taxable year 1932 the depletion allowance was based on discovery value or a percentage of income, then the adjustment for depletion for such year shall be based on the depletion which would have been allowable for such year if computed without reference to discovery value or a percentage of income;

* * *

(14) for amounts allowed as deductions as deferred expenses under section 174(b)(1) (relating to research and experimental expenditures) and resulting in a reduction of the taxpayers' taxes under this subtitle, but not less than the amounts allowable under such section for the taxable year and prior years;

* * *

I.R.C. § 1060. Special allocation rules for certain asset acquisitions.

(a) General rule. In the case of any applicable asset acquisition, for purposes of determining both—

(1) the transferee's basis in such assets, and

(2) the gain or loss of the transferor with respect to such acquisition,

the consideration received for such assets shall be allocated among such assets acquired in such acquisition in the same manner as amounts are allocated to assets under section 338(b)(5). If in connection with an applicable asset acquisition, the transferee and transferor agree in writing as to the allocation of any consideration, or as to the fair market value of any of the assets, such agreement shall be binding on both the transferee and transferor unless the Secretary determines that such allocation (or fair market value) is not appropriate.

* * *

(c) Applicable asset acquisition. For purposes of this section, the term "applicable asset acquisition" means any transfer (whether directly or indirectly)—

(1) of assets which constitute a trade or business, and

(2) with respect to which the transferee's basis in such assets is determined wholly by reference to the consideration paid for such assets.

A transfer shall not be treated as failing to be an applicable asset acquisition merely because section 1031 applies to a portion of the assets transferred.

I.R.C. § 1201. Alternative tax for corporations.

(a) General rule. If for any taxable year a corporation has a net capital gain and any rate of tax imposed by section 11, 511, or 831(a) or (b) (whichever is applicable) exceeds 35 percent (determined without regard to the last 2 sentences of section 11(b)(1)), then, in lieu of any such tax, there is hereby imposed a tax (if such tax is less than the tax imposed by such sections) which shall consist of the sum of—

(1) a tax computed on the taxable income reduced by the amount of the net capital gain, at the rates and in the manner as if this subsection had not been enacted, plus

(2) a tax of 35 percent of the net capital gain (or, if less, taxable income).

* * *

I.R.C. § 1211. Limitation on capital losses.

(a) Corporations. In the case of a corporation, losses from sales or exchanges of capital assets shall be allowed only to the extent of gains from such sales or exchanges.

(b) Other taxpayers. In the case of a taxpayer other than a corporation, losses from sales or exchanges of capital assets shall be allowed only to the extent of the gains from such sales or exchanges, plus (if such losses exceed such gains) the lower of—

(1) $3,000 ($1,500 in the case of a married individual filing a separate return), or

(2) the excess of such losses over such gains.

I.R.C. § 1212. Capital loss carrybacks and carryovers.

(a) Corporations.

(1) In general. If a corporation has a net capital loss for any taxable year (hereinafter in this paragraph referred to as the "loss year"), the amount thereof shall be—

(A) a capital loss carryback to each of the 3 taxable years preceding the loss year, but only to the extent—

(i) such loss is not attributable to a foreign expropriation capital loss, and

(ii) the carryback of such loss does not increase or produce a net operating loss (as defined in section 172(c)) for the taxable year to which it is being carried back;

(B) except as provided in subparagraph (C), a capital loss carryover to each of the 5 taxable years succeeding the loss year; and

(C) a capital loss carryover to each of the 10 taxable years succeeding the loss year, but only to the extent such loss is attributable to a foreign expropriation loss,

and shall be treated as a short-term capital loss in each such taxable year. The entire amount of the net capital loss for any taxable year shall be carried to the earliest of the taxable years to which such loss may be carried, and the portion of such loss which shall be carried to each of the other taxable years to which such loss may be carried shall be the excess, if any, of such loss over the total of the capital gain net income for each of the prior taxable years to which such loss may be carried. For purposes of the preceding sentence, the capital gain net income for any such prior taxable year shall be computed without regard to the net capital loss for the loss year or for any taxable year thereafter. In the case of any net capital loss which cannot be carried back in full to a preceding taxable year by reason of clause (ii) of subparagraph (A), the capital gain net income for such prior taxable year shall in no case be treated as greater than the amount of such loss which can be carried back to such preceding taxable year upon the application of such clause (ii).

* * *

(b) Other taxpayers.

(1) In general. If a taxpayer other than a corporation has a net capital loss for any taxable year—

(A) the excess of the net short-term capital loss over the net long-term capital gain for such year shall be a short-term capital loss in the succeeding taxable year, and

(B) the excess of the net long-term capital loss over the net short-term capital gain for such year shall be a long-term capital loss in the succeeding taxable year.

(2) Treatment of amounts allowed under section 1211(b)(1) or (2).

(A) *In general.* For purposes of determining the excess referred to in subparagraph (A) or (B) of paragraph (1), there shall be treated as a short-term capital gain in the taxable year an amount equal to the lesser of—

(i) the amount allowed for the taxable year under paragraph (1) or (2) of section 1211(b), or

(ii) the adjusted taxable income for such taxable year.

(B) *Adjusted taxable income.* For purposes of subparagraph (A), the term "adjusted taxable income" means taxable income increased by the sum of—

(i) the amount allowed for the taxable year under paragraph (1) or (2) of section 1211(b), and

(ii) the deduction allowed for such year under section 151 or any deduction in lieu thereof.

For purposes of the preceding sentence, any excess of the deductions allowed for the taxable year over the gross income for such year shall be taken into account as negative taxable income.

* * *

I.R.C. § 1221. Capital asset defined.

(a) In general. For purposes of this subtitle, the term "capital asset" means property held by the taxpayer (whether or not connected with his trade or business), but does not include—

(1) stock in trade of the taxpayer or other property of a kind which would properly be included in the inventory of the taxpayer if on hand at the close of the taxable year, or property held by the taxpayer primarily for sale to customers in the ordinary course of his trade or business;

(2) property, used in his trade or business, of a character which is subject to the allowance for depreciation provided in section 167, or real property used in his trade or business;

(3) a copyright, a literary, musical, or artistic composition, a letter or memorandum, or similar property, held by—

(A) a taxpayer whose personal efforts created such property,

(B) in the case of a letter, memorandum, or similar property, a taxpayer for whom such property was prepared or produced, or

(C) a taxpayer in whose hands the basis of such property is determined, for purposes of determining gain from a sale or exchange, in whole or part by reference to the basis of such property in the hands of a taxpayer described in subparagraph (A) or (B);

(4) accounts or notes receivable acquired in the ordinary course of trade or business for services rendered or from the sale of property described in paragraph (1);

* * *

I.R.C. § 1222. Other terms relating to capital gains and losses.

For purposes of this subtitle—

(1) Short-term capital gain. The term "short-term capital gain" means gain from the sale or exchange of a capital asset held for not more than 1 year, if and to the extent such gain is taken into account in computing gross income.

(2) Short-term capital loss. The term "short-term capital loss" means loss from the sale or exchange of a capital asset held for not more than 1 year, if and to the extent that such loss is taken into account in computing taxable income.

(3) Long-term capital gain. The term "long-term capital gain" means gain from the sale or exchange of a capital asset held for more than 1 year, if and to the extent such gain is taken into account in computing gross income.

(4) Long-term capital loss. The term "long-term capital loss" means loss from the sale or exchange of a capital asset held for more than 1 year, if and to the extent that such loss is taken into account in computing taxable income.

(5) Net short-term capital gain. The term "net short-term capital gain" means the excess of short-term capital gains for the taxable year over the short-term capital losses for such year.

(6) Net short-term capital loss. The term "net short-term capital loss" means the excess of short-term capital losses for the taxable year over the short-term capital gains for such year.

(7) Net long-term capital gain. The term "net long-term capital gain" means the excess of long-term capital gains for the taxable year over the long-term capital losses for such year.

(8) Net long-term capital loss. The term "net long-term capital loss" means the excess of long-term capital losses for the taxable year over the long-term capital gains for such year.

(9) Capital gain net income. The term "capital gain net income" means the excess of the gains from sales or exchanges of capital assets over the losses from such sales or exchanges.

(10) Net capital loss. The term "net capital loss" means the excess of the losses from sales or exchanges of capital assets over the sum allowed under section 1211. In the case of a corporation, for the purpose of determining losses under this paragraph, amounts which are short-term capital losses under section 1212(a)(1) shall be excluded.

(11) Net capital gain. The term "net capital gain" means the excess of the net long-term capital gain for the taxable year over the net short-term capital loss for such year.

For purposes of this subtitle, in the case of futures transactions in any commodity subject to the rules of a board of trade or commodity exchange, the length of the holding period taken into account under this section or under any other section amended by section 1402 of the Tax Reform Act of 1976 shall be determined without regard to the amendments made by subsections (a) and (b) of such section 1402.

I.R.C. § 1223. Holding period of property.

For purposes of this subtitle—

(1) In determining the period for which the taxpayer has held property received in an exchange, there shall be included the period for which he held the property exchanged if, under this chapter, the property has, for the purpose of determining gain or loss from a sale or exchange, the same basis in whole or in part in his hands as the property exchanged, and, in the case of such exchanges after March 1, 1954, the property exchanged at the time of such exchange was a capital asset as defined in section 1221 or property described in section 1231. For purposes of this paragraph—

(A) an involuntary conversion described in section 1033 shall be considered an exchange of the property converted for the property acquired, and

(B) a distribution to which section 355 (or so much of section 356 as relates to section 355) applies shall be treated as an exchange.

(2) In determining the period for which the taxpayer has held property however acquired there shall be included the period for which such property was held by any other person, if under this chapter such property has, for the purpose of determining gain or loss from a sale or exchange, the same basis in whole or in part in his hands as it would have in the hands of such other person.

* * *

I.R.C. § 1231. Property used in the trade or business and involuntary conversions.

(a) General rule.

(1) Gains exceed losses. If—

(A) the section 1231 gains for any taxable year, exceed

(B) the section 1231 losses for such taxable year,

such gains and losses shall be treated as long-term capital gains or long-term capital losses, as the case may be.

(2) Gains do not exceed losses. If—

(A) the section 1231 gains for any taxable year, do not exceed

(B) the section 1231 losses for such taxable year,

such gains and losses shall not be treated as gains and losses from sales or exchanges of capital assets.

(3) Section 1231 gains and losses. For purposes of this subsection—

(A) *Section 1231 gain.* The term "section 1231 gain" means—

(i) any recognized gain on the sale or exchange of property used in the trade or business, and

(ii) any recognized gain from the compulsory or involuntary conversion (as a result of destruction in whole or in part, theft or seizure, or an exercise of the power of requisition or condemnation or the threat or imminence thereof) into other property or money of—

(I) property used in the trade or business, or

(II) any capital asset which is held for more than 1 year and is held in connection with a trade or business or a transaction entered into for profit.

(B) *Section 1231 loss*. The term "section 1231 loss" means any recognized loss from a sale or exchange or conversion described in subparagraph (A).

(4) Special rules. For purposes of this subsection—

(A) In determining under this subsection whether gains exceed losses—

(i) the section 1231 gains shall be included only if and to the extent taken into account in computing gross income, and

(ii) the section 1231 losses shall be included only if and to the extent taken into account in computing taxable income, except that section 1211 shall not apply.

(B) Losses (including losses not compensated for by insurance or otherwise) on the destruction, in whole or in part, theft or seizure, or requisition or condemnation of—

(i) property used in the trade or business, or

(ii) capital assets which are held for more than 1 year and are held in connection with a trade or business or a transaction entered into for profit,

shall be treated as losses from a compulsory or involuntary conversion.

(C) In the case of any involuntary conversion (subject to the provisions of this subsection but for this sentence) arising from fire, storm, shipwreck, or other casualty, or from theft, of any—

(i) property used in the trade or business, or

(ii) any capital asset which is held for more than 1 year and is held in connection with a trade or business or a transaction entered into for profit,

this subsection shall not apply to such conversion (whether resulting in gain or loss) if during the taxable year the recognized losses from such conversions exceed the recognized gains from such conversions.

(b) Definition of property used in the trade or business. For purposes of this section—

(1) General rule. The term "property used in the trade or business" means property used in the trade or business, of a character which is subject to the allowance for depreciation provided in section 167, held for more than 1 year, and real property used in the trade or business, held for more than 1 year, which is not—

(A) property of a kind which would properly be includible in the inventory of the taxpayer if on hand at the close of the taxable year,

(B) property held by the taxpayer primarily for sale to customers in the ordinary course of his trade or business,

(C) a copyright, a literary, musical, or artistic composition, a letter or memorandum, or similar property, held by a taxpayer described in paragraph (3) of section 1221(a), or

* * *

(c) Recapture of net ordinary losses.

(1) In general. The net section 1231 gain for any taxable year shall be treated as ordinary income to the extent such gain does not exceed the non-recaptured net section 1231 losses.

(2) Non-recaptured net section 1231 losses. For purposes of this subsection, the term "non-recaptured net section 1231 losses" means the excess of—

(A) the aggregate amount of the net section 1231 losses for the 5 most recent preceding taxable years beginning after December 31, 1981, over

(B) the portion of such losses taken into account under paragraph (1) for such preceding taxable years.

(3) Net section 1231 gain. For purposes of this subsection, the term "net section 1231 gain" means the excess of—

(A) the section 1231 gains, over

(B) the section 1231 losses.

(4) Net section 1231 loss. For purposes of this subsection, the term "net section 1231 loss" means the excess of—

(A) the section 1231 losses, over

(B) the section 1231 gains.

(5) Special rules. For purposes of determining the amount of the net section 1231 gain or loss for any taxable year, the rules of paragraph (4) of subsection (a) shall apply.

I.R.C. § 1235. Sale or exchange of patents.

(a) General. A transfer (other than by gift, inheritance, or devise) of property consisting of all substantial rights to a patent, or an undivided interest therein which includes a part of all such rights, by any holder shall be considered the sale or exchange of a capital asset held for more than 1 year, regardless of whether or not payments in consideration of such transfer are—

(1) payable periodically over a period generally coterminous with the transferee's use of the patent, or

(2) contingent on the productivity, use, or disposition of the property transferred.

(b) "Holder" defined. For purposes of this section, the term "holder" means—

(1) any individual whose efforts created such property, or

(2) any other individual who has acquired his interest in such property in exchange for consideration in money or money's worth paid to such creator prior to actual reduction to practice of the invention covered by the patent, if such individual is neither—

(A) the employer of such creator, nor

(B) related to such creator (within the meaning of subsection (d)).

(c) Effective date. This section shall be applicable with regard to any amounts received, or payments made, pursuant to a transfer described in subsection (a) in any taxable year to which this subtitle applies, regardless of the taxable year in which such transfer occurred.

(d) Related persons. Subsection (a) shall not apply to any transfer, directly or indirectly, between persons specified within any one of the paragraphs of section 267(b) or persons described in section 707(b); except that, in applying section 267(b) and (c) and section 707(b) for purposes of this section—

(1) the phrase "25 percent or more" shall be substituted for the phrase "more than 50 percent" each place it appears in section 267(b) or 707(b), and

(2) paragraph (4) of section 267(c) shall be treated as providing that the family of an individual shall include only his spouse, ancestors, and lineal descendants.

(e) Cross reference. For special rule relating to nonresident aliens, see section 871(a).

I.R.C. § 1239. Gain from sale of depreciable property between certain related taxpayers.

(a) Treatment of gain as ordinary income. In the case of a sale or exchange of property, directly or indirectly, between related persons, any gain recognized to the transferor shall be treated as ordinary income if such property is, in the hands of the transferee, of a character which is subject to the allowance for depreciation provided in section 167.

(b) Related persons. For purposes of subsection (a), the term "related persons" means—

(1) a person and all entities which are controlled entities with respect to such person,

(2) a taxpayer and any trust in which such taxpayer (or his spouse) is a beneficiary, unless such beneficiary's interest in the trust is a remote contingent interest (within the meaning of section 318(a)(3)(B)(i)), and

(3) except in the case of a sale or exchange in satisfaction of a pecuniary bequest, an executor of an estate and a beneficiary of such estate.

(c) Controlled entity defined.

(1) General rule. For purposes of this section, the term "controlled entity" means, with respect to any person—

(A) a corporation more than 50 percent of the value of the outstanding stock of which is owned (directly or indirectly) by or for such person,

(B) a partnership more than 50 percent of the capital interest or profits interest in which is owned (directly or indirectly) by or for such person, and

(C) any entity which is a related person to such person under paragraph (3), (10), (11), or (12) of section 267(b).

(2) Constructive ownership. For purposes of this section, ownership shall be determined in accordance with rules similar to the rules under section 267(c) (other than paragraph (3) thereof).

* * *

(e) Patent applications treated as depreciable property. For purposes of this section, a patent application shall be treated as property which, in the hands of the transferee, is of a character which is subject to the allowance for depreciation provided in section 167.

I.R.C. § 1245. Gain from dispositions of certain depreciable property.

(a) General rule.

(1) Ordinary income. Except as otherwise provided in this section, if section 1245 property is disposed of the amount by which the lower of—

(A) the recomputed basis of the property, or

(B) (i) in the case of a sale, exchange, or involuntary conversion, the amount realized, or (ii) in the case of any other disposition, the fair market value of such property,

exceeds the adjusted basis of such property shall be treated as ordinary income. Such gain shall be recognized notwithstanding any other provision of this subtitle.

(2) Recomputed basis. For purposes of this section—

(A) In general. The term "recomputed basis" means, with respect to any property, its adjusted basis recomputed by adding thereto all adjustments reflected in such adjusted basis on account of deductions (whether in respect of the same or other property) allowed or allowable to the taxpayer or to any other person for depreciation or amortization.

(B) Taxpayer may establish amount allowed. For purposes of subparagraph (A), if the taxpayer can establish by adequate records or other sufficient evidence that the amount allowed for depreciation or amortization for any period was less than the amount allowable, the amount added for such period shall be the amount allowed.

(C) Certain deductions treated as amortization. Any deduction allowable under section 179, 179A, 179B, 179C, 179D, 179E, 181, 190, 193, or 194 shall be treated as if it were a deduction allowable for amortization.

(3) Section 1245 property. For purposes of this section, the term "section 1245 property" means any property which is or has been property of a character subject to the allowance for depreciation provided in section 167 and is either—

(A) personal property,

(B) other property (not including a building or its structural components) but only if such other property is tangible and has an adjusted basis in which there are reflected adjustments described in paragraph (2) for a period in which such property (or other property)—

(i) was used as an integral part of manufacturing, production, or extraction or of furnishing transportation, communications, electrical energy, gas, water, or sewage disposal services,

(ii) constituted a research facility used in connection with any of the activities referred to in clause (i), or

(iii) constituted a facility used in connection with any of the activities referred to in clause (i) for the bulk storage of fungible commodities (including commodities in a liquid or gaseous state),

(C) so much of any real property (other than any property described in subparagraph (B)) which has an adjusted basis in which there are reflected adjustments for amortization under section 169, 179, 179A, 179B, 179C, 179D, 179E, 185, 188 (as in effect before its repeal by the Revenue Reconciliation Act of 1990), 190, 193, or 194,

(D) a single purpose agricultural or horticultural structure (as defined in section 168(i)(13)),

(E) a storage facility (not including a building or its structural components) used in connection with the distribution of petroleum or any primary product of petroleum, or

(F) any railroad grading or tunnel bore (as defined in section 168(e)(4)).

(b) Exceptions and limitations.

(1) Gifts. Subsection (a) shall not apply to a disposition by gift.

(2) Transfers at death. Except as provided in section 691 (relating to income in respect of a decedent), subsection (a) shall not apply to a transfer at death.

(3) Certain tax-free transactions. If the basis of property in the hands of a transferee is determined by reference to its basis in the hands of the transferor by reason of the application of section 332, 351, 361, 721, or 731, then the amount of gain taken into account by the transferor under subsection (a)(1) shall not exceed the amount of gain recognized to the transferor on the transfer of such property (determined without regard to this section). Except as provided in paragraph (6), this paragraph shall not apply to a disposition to an organization (other than a cooperative described in section 521) which is exempt from the tax imposed by this chapter.

(4) Like kind exchanges; involuntary conversions, etc. If property is disposed of and gain (determined without regard to this section) is not recognized in whole or in part under section 1031 or 1033, then the amount of gain taken into account by the transferor under subsection (a)(1) shall not exceed the sum of—

(A) the amount of gain recognized on such disposition (determined without regard to this section), plus

(B) the fair market value of property acquired which is not section 1245 property and which is not taken into account under subparagraph (A).

* * *

(8) Disposition of amortizable section 197 intangibles.

(A) *In general.* If a taxpayer disposes of more than 1 amortizable section 197 intangible (as defined in section 197(c)) in a transaction or a series of related transactions, all such amortizable 197 intangibles shall be treated as 1 section 1245 property for purposes of this section.

(B) *Exception.* Subparagraph (A) shall not apply to any amortizable section 197 intangible (as so defined) with respect to which the adjusted basis exceeds the fair market value.

(c) Adjustments to basis. The Secretary shall prescribe such regulations as he may deem necessary to provide for adjustments to the basis of property to reflect gain recognized under subsection (a).

(d) Application of section. This section shall apply notwithstanding any other provision of this subtitle.

I.R.C. § 1253. Transfers of franchises, trademarks, and trade names.

(a) General rule. A transfer of a franchise, trademark, or trade name shall not be treated as a sale or exchange of a capital asset if the transferor retains any significant power, right, or continuing interest with respect to the subject matter of the franchise, trademark, or trade name.

(b) Definitions. For purposes of this section—

(1) Franchise. The term "franchise" includes an agreement which gives one of the parties to the agreement the right to distribute, sell, or provide goods, services, or facilities, within a specified area.

(2) Significant power, right, or continuing interest. The term "significant power, right, or continuing interest" includes, but is not limited to, the following rights with respect to the interest transferred:

(A) A right to disapprove any assignment of such interest, or any part thereof.

(B) A right to terminate at will.

(C) A right to prescribe the standards of quality of products used or sold, or of services furnished, and of the equipment and facilities used to promote such products or services.

(D) A right to require that the transferee sell or advertise only products or services of the transferor.

(E) A right to require that the transferee purchase substantially all of his supplies and equipment from the transferor.

(F) A right to payments contingent on the productivity, use, or disposition of the subject matter of the interest transferred, if such payments constitute a substantial element under the transfer agreement.

(3) Transfer. The term "transfer" includes the renewal of a franchise, trademark, or trade name.

(c) Treatment of contingent payments by transferor. Amounts received or accrued on account of a transfer, sale, or other disposition of a franchise, trademark, or trade name which are contingent on the productivity, use, or disposition of the franchise, trademark, or trade name transferred shall be treated as amounts received or accrued from the sale or other disposition of property which is not a capital asset.

(d) Treatment of payments by transferee.

(1) Contingent serial payments.

(A) In general. Any amount described in subparagraph (B) which is paid or incurred during the taxable year on account of a transfer, sale, or other disposition of a franchise, trademark, or trade name shall be allowed as a deduction under section 162(a) (relating to trade or business expenses).

(B) Amounts to which paragraph applies. An amount is described in this subparagraph if it—

(i) is contingent on the productivity, use, or disposition of the franchise, trademark, or trade name, and

(ii) is paid as part of a series of payments—

(I) which are payable not less frequently than annually throughout the entire term of the transfer agreement, and

(II) which are substantially equal in amount (or payable under a fixed formula).

(2) Other payments. Any amount paid or incurred on account of a transfer, sale, or other disposition of a franchise, trademark, or trade name to which paragraph (1) does not apply shall be treated as an amount chargeable to capital account.

(3) Renewals, etc. For purposes of determining the term of a transfer agreement under this section, there shall be taken into account all renewal options (and any other period for which the parties reasonably expect the agreement to be renewed).

I.R.C. § 7701. Definitions.

(a) When used in this title, where not otherwise distinctly expressed or manifestly incompatible with the intent thereof—

* * *

(30) United States person. The term "United States person" means—

(A) a citizen or resident of the United States,

(B) a domestic partnership,

(C) a domestic corporation,

(D) any estate (other than a foreign estate, within the meaning of paragraph (31)), and

(E) any trust if—

(i) a court within the United States is able to exercise primary supervision over the administration of the trust, and

(ii) one or more United States persons have the authority to control all substantial decisions of the trust.

Treasury Regulations – Selected Sections

(Effective as of January 1, 2011)

Treas. Reg. § 1.41-4. Qualified research for expenditures paid or incurred in taxable years ending on or after December 31, 2003.

(a) Qualified research—

(1) General rule. Research activities related to the development or improvement of a business component constitute qualified research only if the research activities meet all of the requirements of section 41(d)(1) and this section, and are not otherwise excluded under section 41(d)(3)(B) or (d)(4), or this section.

(2) Requirements of section 41(d)(1). Research constitutes qualified research only if it is research—

(i) With respect to which expenditures may be treated as expenses under section 174, see § 1.174-2;

(ii) That is undertaken for the purpose of discovering information that is technological in nature, and the application of which is intended to be useful in the development of a new or improved business component of the taxpayer; and

(iii) Substantially all of the activities of which constitute elements of a process of experimentation that relates to a qualified purpose.

(3) Undertaken for the purpose of discovering information—

(i) *In general*. For purposes of section 41(d) and this section, research must be undertaken for the purpose of discovering information that is technological in nature. Research is undertaken for the purpose of discovering information if it is intended to eliminate uncertainty concerning the development or improvement of a business component. Uncertainty exists if the information available to the taxpayer does not establish the capability or method for developing or improving the business component, or the appropriate design of the business component.

(ii) *Application of the discovering information requirement*. A determination that research is undertaken for the purpose of discovering information that is technological in nature does not require the taxpayer be seeking to obtain information that exceeds, expands or refines the common knowledge of skilled professionals in the particular field of science or engineering in which the taxpayer is performing the research. In addition, a determination that research is undertaken for the purpose of discovering information that is technological in nature does not require that the taxpayer succeed in developing a new or improved business component.

(iii) *Patent safe harbor.* For purposes of section 41(d) and paragraph (a)(3)(i) of this section, the issuance of a patent by the Patent and Trademark Office under the provisions of 35 U.S.C. 151 (other than a patent for design issued under the provisions of 35 U.S.C. 171) is conclusive evidence that a taxpayer has discovered information that is technological in nature that is intended to eliminate uncertainty concerning the development or improvement of a business component. However, the issuance of such a patent is not a precondition for credit availability.

(4) Technological in nature. For purposes of section 41(d) and this section, information is technological in nature if the process of experimentation used to discover such information fundamentally relies on principles of the physical or biological sciences, engineering, or computer science. A taxpayer may employ existing technologies and may rely on existing principles of the physical or biological sciences, engineering, or computer science to satisfy this requirement.

(5) Process of experimentation –

(i) *In general.* For purposes of section 41(d) and this section, a process of experimentation is a process designed to evaluate one or more alternatives to achieve a result where the capability or the method of achieving that result, or the appropriate design of that result, is uncertain as of the beginning of the taxpayer's research activities. A process of experimentation must fundamentally rely on the principles of the physical or biological sciences, engineering, or computer science and involves the identification of uncertainty concerning the development or improvement of a business component, the identification of one or more alternatives intended to eliminate that uncertainty, and the identification and the conduct of a process of evaluating the alternatives (through, for example, modeling, simulation, or a systematic trial and error methodology). A process of experimentation must be an evaluative process and generally should be capable of evaluating more than one alternative. A taxpayer may undertake a process of experimentation if there is no uncertainty concerning the taxpayer's capability or method of achieving the desired result so long as the appropriate design of the desired result is uncertain as of the beginning of the taxpayer's research activities. Uncertainty concerning the development or improvement of the business component (e.g., its appropriate design) does not establish that all activities undertaken to achieve that new or improved business component constitute a process of experimentation.

(ii) *Qualified purpose*. For purposes of section 41(d) and this section, a process of experimentation is undertaken for a qualified purpose if it relates to a new or improved function, performance, reliability or quality of the business component. Research will not be treated as conducted for a qualified purpose if it relates to style, taste, cosmetic, or seasonal design factors.

(6) Substantially all requirement. In order for activities to constitute qualified research under section 41(d)(1), substantially all of the activities must constitute elements of a process of experimentation that relates to a qualified purpose. The substantially all requirement of section 41(d)(1)(C) and paragraph (a)(2)(iii) of this section is satisfied only if 80 percent or more of a taxpayer's research activities, measured on a cost or other consistently applied reasonable basis (and without regard to section 1.41-2(d)(2)), constitute elements of a process of experimentation for a purpose described in section 41(d)(3). Accordingly, if 80 percent (or more) of a taxpayer's research activities with respect to a business component constitute elements of a process of experimentation for a purpose described in section 41(d)(3), the substantially all requirement is satisfied even if the remaining 20 percent (or less) of a taxpayer's research activities with respect to the business component do not constitute elements of a process of experimentation for a purpose described in section 41(d)(3), so long as these remaining research activities satisfy the requirements of section 41(d)(1)(A) and are not otherwise excluded under section 41(d)(4). The substantially all requirement is applied separately to each business component.

(7) Use of computers and information technology. The employment of computers or information technology, or the reliance on principles of computer science or information technology to store, collect, manipulate, translate, disseminate, produce, distribute, or process data or information, and similar uses of computers and information technology does not itself establish that qualified research has been undertaken.

* * *

Prop. Reg. § 1.41-4. Qualified research for expenditures paid or incurred in taxable years ending on or after December 26, 2001.

* * *

(c)(6) Internal use software for taxable years beginning on or after December 31, 1985.

(i) *General rule.* Research with respect to computer software that is developed by (or for the benefit of) the taxpayer primarily for the taxpayer's internal use is eligible for the research credit only if the software satisfies the requirements of paragraph (c)(6)(ii) of this section.

(ii) *Requirements.* The requirements of this paragraph (c)(6)(ii) are—

(A) The software satisfies the requirements of section 41(d)(1);

(B) The software is not otherwise excluded under section 41(d)(4) (other than section 41(d)(4)(E)); and

(C) One of the following conditions is met—

(1) The taxpayer develops the software for use in an activity that constitutes qualified research (other than the development of the internal-use software itself);

(2) The taxpayer develops the software for use in a production process that satisfies the requirements of section 41(d)(1);

(3) The taxpayer develops the software for use in providing computer services to customers; or

(4) The software satisfies the high threshold of innovation test of paragraph (c)(6)(vi) of this section.

(iii) *Computer software and hardware developed as a single product.* This paragraph (c)(6) does not apply to the development costs of a new or improved package of computer software and hardware developed together by the taxpayer as a single product (or to the costs to modify an acquired computer software and hardware package), of which the software is an integral part, that is used directly by the taxpayer in providing services in its trade or business to customers. In these cases, eligibility for the research credit is to be determined by examining the combined software-hardware product as a single product.

(iv) *Primarily for internal use.* Unless computer software is developed to be commercially sold, leased, licensed, or otherwise marketed, for separately stated consideration to unrelated third parties, computer software is presumed developed by (or for the benefit of) the taxpayer primarily for the taxpayer's internal use. For example, the computer software may serve general and administrative functions of the taxpayer, or may be used in providing a noncomputer service. General and administrative functions include, but are not limited to, functions such as payroll, bookkeeping, financial management, financial reporting, personnel management, sales and marketing, fixed asset accounting, inventory management and cost accounting. Computer software that is developed to be commercially sold, leased, licensed or otherwise marketed, for separately stated consideration to unrelated third parties is not developed primarily for the taxpayer's internal use. The requirements of this paragraph (c)(6) apply to computer software that is developed primarily for the taxpayer's internal use even though the taxpayer subsequently sells, leases, licenses, or otherwise markets the computer software for separately stated consideration to unrelated third parties.

(v) *Software used in the provision of services.*

(A) *Computer services.* For purposes of this section, a computer service is a service offered by a taxpayer to customers who conduct business with the taxpayer primarily for the use of the taxpayer's computer or software technology. A taxpayer does not provide a computer service merely because customers interact with the taxpayer's software.

(B) *Noncomputer services.* For purposes of this section, a noncomputer service is a service offered by a taxpayer to customers who conduct business with the taxpayer primarily to obtain a service other than a computer service, even if such other service is enabled, supported, or facilitated by computer or software technology.

(vi) *High threshold of innovation test.* Computer software satisfies this paragraph (c)(6)(vi) only if the taxpayer can establish that—

(A) The software is innovative in that the software is intended to be unique or novel and is intended to differ in a significant and inventive way from prior software implementations or methods;

(B) The software development involves significant economic risk in that the taxpayer commits substantial resources to the development and there is substantial uncertainty, because of technical risk, that such resources would be recovered within a reasonable period; and

(C) The software is not commercially available for use by the taxpayer in that the software cannot be purchased, leased, or licensed and used for the intended purpose without modifications that would satisfy the requirements of paragraphs (c)(6)(vi)(A) and (B) of this section.

(vii) *Application of high threshold of innovation test*. The costs of developing internal use software are eligible for the research credit only if the software satisfies the high threshold of innovation test of paragraph (c)(6)(vi) of this section. This test takes into account only the results attributable to the development of the new or improved software independent of the effect of any modifications to related hardware or other software.

* * *

Treas. Reg. § 1.61-6. Gains derived from dealings in property.

(a) In general. Gain realized on the sale or exchange of property is included in gross income, unless excluded by law. For this purpose property includes tangible items, such as a building, and intangible items, such as goodwill. Generally, the gain is the excess of the amount realized over the unrecovered cost or other basis for the property sold or exchanged. The specific rules for computing the amount of gain or loss are contained in section 1001 and the regulations thereunder. When a part of a larger property is sold, the cost or other basis of the entire property shall be equitably apportioned among the several parts, and the gain realized or loss sustained on the part of the entire property sold is the difference between the selling price and the cost or other basis allocated to such part. The sale of each part is treated as a separate transaction and gain or loss shall be computed separately on each part. Thus, gain or loss shall be determined at the time of sale of each part and not deferred until the entire property has been disposed of. This rule may be illustrated by the following examples:

Example (1). A, a dealer in real estate, acquires a 10-acre tract for $10,000, which he divides into 20 lots. The $10,000 cost must be equitably apportioned among the lots so that on the sale of each A can determine his taxable gain or deductible loss.

Example (2). B purchases for $25,000 property consisting of a used car lot and adjoining filling station. At the time, the fair market value of the filling station is $15,000 and the fair market value of the used car lot is $10,000. Five years later B sells the filling station for $20,000 at a time when $2,000 has been properly allowed as depreciation thereon. B's gain on this sale is $7,000, since $7,000 is the amount by which the selling price of the filling station exceeds the portion of the cost equitably allocable to the filling station at the time of purchase reduced by the depreciation properly allowed.

* * *

Treas. Reg. § 1.162-1. Business expenses.

(a) In general. Business expenses deductible from gross income include the ordinary and necessary expenditures directly connected with or pertaining to the taxpayer's trade or business, except items which are used as the basis for a deduction or a credit under provisions of law other than section 162. The cost of goods purchased for resale, with proper adjustment for opening and closing inventories, is deducted from gross sales in computing gross income. See paragraph (a) of § 1.161-3. Among the items included in business expenses are management expenses, commissions (but see section 263 and the regulations thereunder), labor, supplies, incidental repairs, operating expenses of automobiles used in the trade or business, traveling expenses while away from home solely in the pursuit of a trade or business (see § 1.162-2), advertising and other selling expenses, together with insurance premiums against fire, storm, theft, accident, or other similar losses in the case of a business, and rental for the use of business property. No such item shall be included in business expenses, however, to the extent that it is used by the taxpayer in computing the cost of property included in its inventory or used in determining the gain or loss basis of its plant, equipment, or other property. See section 1054 and the regulations thereunder. A deduction for an expense paid or incurred after December 30, 1969, which would otherwise be allowable under section 162 shall not be denied on the grounds that allowance of such deduction would frustrate a sharply defined public policy. See section 162(c), (f), and (g) and the regulations thereunder. The full amount of the allowable deduction for ordinary and necessary expenses in carrying on a business is deductible, even though such expenses exceed the gross income derived during the taxable year from such business. In the case of any sports program to which section 114 (relating to sports programs conducted for the American National Red Cross) applies, expenses described in section 114(a)(2) shall be allowable as deductions under section 162(a) only to the extent that such expenses exceed the amount excluded from gross income under section 114(a).

* * *

Treas. Reg. § 1.162-20. Expenditures attributable to lobbying, political campaigns, attempts to influence legislation, etc., and certain advertising.

(a) In general—

(1) Scope of section. This section contains rules governing the deductibility or nondeductibility of expenditures for lobbying purposes, for the promotion or defeat of legislation, for political campaign purposes (including the support of or opposition to any candidate for public office) or for carrying on propaganda (including advertising) related to any of the foregoing purposes. For rules applicable to such expenditures in respect of taxable years beginning before January 1, 1963, and for taxable years beginning after December 31, 1962, see paragraphs (b) and (c), respectively, of this section. This section also deals with expenditures for institutional or "good will" advertising.

(2) Institutional or "good will" advertising. Expenditures for institutional or "good will" advertising which keeps the taxpayer's name before the public are generally deductible as ordinary and necessary business expenses provided the expenditures are related to the patronage the taxpayer might reasonably expect in the future. For example, a deduction will ordinarily be allowed for the cost of advertising which keeps the taxpayer's name before the public in connection with encouraging contributions to such organizations as the Red Cross, the purchase of United States Savings Bonds, or participation in similar causes. In like fashion, expenditures for advertising which presents views on economic, financial, social, or other subjects of a general nature, but which does not involve any of the activities specified in paragraph (b) or (c) of this section for which a deduction is not allowable, are deductible if they otherwise meet the requirements of the regulations under section 162.

* * *

Treas. Reg. § 1.167(a)-3. Intangibles.

(a) In general. If an intangible asset is known from experience or other factors to be of use in the business or in the production of income for only a limited period, the length of which can be estimated with reasonable accuracy, such an intangible asset may be the subject of a depreciation allowance. Examples are patents and copyrights. An intangible asset, the useful life of which is not limited, is not subject to the allowance for depreciation. No allowance will be permitted merely because, in the unsupported opinion of the taxpayer, the intangible asset has a limited useful life. No deduction for depreciation is allowable with respect to goodwill. For rules with respect to organizational expenditures, see section 248 and the regulations thereunder. For rules with respect to trademark and trade name expenditures, see section 177 and the regulations thereunder. See sections 197 and 167(f) and, to the extent applicable, §§ 1.197-2 and 1.167(a)-14 for amortization of goodwill and certain other intangibles acquired after August 10, 1993, or after July 25, 1991, if a valid retroactive election under § 1.197-1T has been made.

(b) Safe harbor amortization for certain intangible assets—

(1) Useful life. Solely for purposes of determining the depreciation allowance referred to in paragraph (a) of this section, a taxpayer may treat an intangible asset as having a useful life equal to 15 years unless—

(i) An amortization period or useful life for the intangible asset is specifically prescribed or prohibited by the Internal Revenue Code, the regulations thereunder (other than by this paragraph (b)), or other published guidance in the Internal Revenue Bulletin (see § 601.601(d)(2) of this chapter);

(ii) The intangible asset is described in § 1.263(a)-4(c) (relating to intangibles acquired from another person) or § 1.263(a)-4(d)(2) (relating to created financial interests);

(iii) The intangible asset has a useful life the length of which can be estimated with reasonable accuracy; or

(iv) The intangible asset is described in § 1.263(a)-4(d)(8) (relating to certain benefits arising from the provision, production, or improvement of real property), in which case the taxpayer may treat the intangible asset as having a useful life equal to 25 years solely for purposes of determining the depreciation allowance referred to in paragraph (a) of this section.

(2) Applicability to acquisitions of a trade or business, changes in the capital structure of a business entity, and certain other transactions. The safe harbor useful life provided by paragraph (b)(1) of this section does not apply to an amount required to be capitalized by § 1.263(a)-5 (relating to amounts paid to facilitate an acquisition of a trade or business, a change in the capital structure of a business entity, and certain other transactions).

(3) Depreciation method. A taxpayer that determines its depreciation allowance for an intangible asset using the 15-year useful life prescribed by paragraph (b)(1) of this section (or the 25-year useful life in the case of an intangible asset described in § 1.263(a)-4(d)(8)) must determine the allowance by amortizing the basis of the intangible asset (as determined under section 167(c) and without regard to salvage value) ratably over the useful life beginning on the first day of the month in which the intangible asset is placed in service by the taxpayer. The intangible asset is not eligible for amortization in the month of disposition.

(4) Effective date. This paragraph (b) applies to intangible assets created on or after December 31, 2003.

Treas. Reg. § 1.167(a)-14. Treatment of certain intangible property excluded from section 197.

(a) Overview. This section provides rules for the amortization of certain intangibles that are excluded from section 197 (relating to the amortization of goodwill and certain other intangibles). These excluded intangibles are specifically described in § 1.197-2(c) (4), (6), (7), (11), and (13) and include certain computer software and certain other separately acquired rights, such as rights to receive tangible property or services, patents and copyrights, certain mortgage servicing rights, and rights of fixed duration or amount. Intangibles for which an amortization amount is determined under section 167(f) and intangibles otherwise excluded from section 197 are amortizable only if they qualify as property subject to the allowance for depreciation under section 167(a).

(b) Computer software—

(1) In general. The amount of the deduction for computer software described in section 167(f)(1) and § 1.197-2(c)(4) is determined by amortizing the cost or other basis of the computer software using the straight line method described in § 1.167(b)-1 (except that its salvage value is treated as zero) and an amortization period of 36 months beginning on the first day of the month that the computer software is placed in service. Before determining the amortization deduction allowable under this paragraph (b), the cost or other basis of computer software that is section 179 property, as defined in section 179(d)(1)(A)(ii), must be reduced for any portion of the basis the taxpayer properly elects to treat as an expense under section 179. In addition, the cost or other basis of computer software that is qualified property under section 168(k)(2) or § 1.168(k)-1, 50-percent bonus depreciation property under section 168(k)(4) or § 1.168(k)-1, or qualified New York Liberty Zone property under section 1400L(b) or § 1.1400L(b)-1, must be reduced by the amount of the additional first year depreciation deduction allowed or allowable, whichever is greater, under section 168(k) or section 1400L(b) for the computer software. If costs for developing computer software that the taxpayer properly elects to defer under section 174(b) result in the development of property subject to the allowance for depreciation under section 167, the rules of this paragraph (b) will apply to the unrecovered costs. In addition, this paragraph (b) applies to the cost of separately acquired computer software if the cost to acquire the software is separately stated and the cost is required to be capitalized under section 263(a).

(2) Exceptions. Paragraph (b)(1) of this section does not apply to the cost of computer software properly and consistently taken into account under § 1.162-11. The cost of acquiring an interest in computer software that is included, without being separately stated, in the cost of the hardware or other tangible property is treated as part of the cost of the hardware or other tangible property that is capitalized and depreciated under other applicable sections of the Internal Revenue Code.

(3) Additional rules. Rules similar to those in § 1.197-2 (f)(1)(iii), (f)(1)(iv), and (f)(2) (relating to the computation of amortization deductions and the treatment of contingent amounts) apply for purposes of this paragraph (b).

(c) Certain interests or rights not acquired as part of a purchase of a trade or business—

(1) Certain rights to receive tangible property or services. The amount of the deduction for a right (other than a right acquired as part of a purchase of a trade or business) to receive tangible property or services under a contract or from a governmental unit (as specified in section 167(f)(2) and § 1.197-2(c)(6)) is determined as follows:

(i) *Amortization of fixed amounts*. The basis of a right to receive a fixed amount of tangible property or services is amortized for each taxable year by multiplying the basis of the right by a fraction, the numerator of which is the amount of tangible property or services received during the taxable year and the denominator of which is the total amount of tangible property or services received or to be received under the terms of the contract or governmental grant. For example, if a taxpayer acquires a favorable contract right to receive a fixed amount of raw materials during an unspecified period, the taxpayer must amortize the cost of acquiring the contract right by multiplying the total cost by a fraction, the numerator of which is the amount of raw materials received under the contract during the taxable year and the denominator of which is the total amount of raw materials received or to be received under the contract.

(ii) *Amortization of unspecified amount over fixed period*. The cost or other basis of a right to receive an unspecified amount of tangible property or services over a fixed period is amortized ratably over the period of the right. (See paragraph (c)(3) of this section regarding renewals).

(iii) *Amortization in other cases*. [Reserved]

(2) Rights of fixed duration or amount. The amount of the deduction for a right (other than a right acquired as part of a purchase of a trade or business) of fixed duration or amount received under a contract or granted by a governmental unit (specified in section 167(f)(2) and § 1.197-2(c)(13)) and not covered by paragraph (c)(1) of this section is determined as follows:

(i) *Rights to a fixed amount.* The basis of a right to a fixed amount is amortized for each taxable year by multiplying the basis by a fraction, the numerator of which is the amount received during the taxable year and the denominator of which is the total amount received or to be received under the terms of the contract or governmental grant.

(ii) *Rights to an unspecified amount over fixed duration of less than 15 years.* The basis of a right to an unspecified amount over a fixed duration of less than 15 years is amortized ratably over the period of the right.

(3) Application of renewals.

(i) For purposes of paragraphs (c) (1) and (2) of this section, the duration of a right under a contract (or granted by a governmental unit) includes any renewal period if, based on all of the facts and circumstances in existence at any time during the taxable year in which the right is acquired, the facts clearly indicate a reasonable expectancy of renewal.

(ii) The mere fact that a taxpayer will have the opportunity to renew a contract right or other right on the same terms as are available to others, in a competitive auction or similar process that is designed to reflect fair market value and in which the taxpayer is not contractually advantaged, will generally not be taken into account in determining the duration of such right provided that the bidding produces a fair market value price comparable to the price that would be obtained if the rights were purchased immediately after renewal from a person (other than the person granting the renewal) in an arm's-length transaction.

(iii) The cost of a renewal not included in the terms of the contract or governmental grant is treated as the acquisition of a separate intangible asset.

(4) Patents and copyrights. If the purchase price of a interest (other than an interest acquired as part of a purchase of a trade or business) in a patent or copyright described in section 167(f)(2) and § 1.197-2(c)(7) is payable on at least an annual basis as either a fixed amount per use or a fixed percentage of the revenue derived from the use of the patent or copyright, the depreciation deduction for a taxable year is equal to the amount of the purchase price paid or incurred during the year. Otherwise, the basis of such patent or copyright (or an interest therein) is depreciated either ratably over its remaining useful life or under section 167(g) (income forecast method). If a patent or copyright becomes valueless in any year before its legal expiration, the adjusted basis may be deducted in that year.

(5) Additional rules. The period of amortization under paragraphs (c) (1) through (4) of this section begins when the intangible is placed in service, and rules similar to those in § 1.197-2(f)(2) apply for purposes of this paragraph (c).

* * *

Treas. Reg. § 1.167(b)-1. Straight line method.

(a) In general. Under the straight line method the cost or other basis of the property less its estimated salvage value is deductible in equal annual amounts over the period of the estimated useful life of the property. The allowance for depreciation for the taxable year is determined by dividing the adjusted basis of the property at the beginning of the taxable year, less salvage value, by the remaining useful life of the property at such time. For convenience, the allowance so determined may be reduced to a percentage or fraction. The straight line method may be used in determining a reasonable allowance for depreciation for any property which is subject to depreciation under section 167 and it shall be used in all cases where the taxpayer has not adopted a different acceptable method with respect to such property.

* * *

Prop. Reg. § 1.167(n)-1. Income forecast method.

(a) Overview. This section and Secs. 1.167(n)-2 through 1.167(n)-7 provide rules for computing depreciation allowances under section 167 for property depreciated using the income forecast method. Because the income forecast method is only appropriate for property with unique income earning characteristics, only property specified in §1.167(n)-5 may be depreciated under the income forecast method. A taxpayer using the income forecast method generally computes depreciation allowances each year based upon the ratio of current year income to forecasted total income from the property as described in §1.167(n)-4. Current year income and forecasted total income are determined in accordance with the provisions of §1.167(n)-3. In addition, a taxpayer must determine depreciable basis for income forecast property in accordance with the basis rules of §1.167(n)-2. Property depreciated under the income forecast method generally is subject to the look-back rules of §1.167(n)-6 whereby taxpayers must determine the amount of interest owed on any hypothetical underpayment of tax, or due on any hypothetical overpayment of tax, attributable to the use of estimated income in the computation of income forecast depreciation. Under these rules, look-back computations must be performed in specified recomputation years, which are generally the 3rd and 10th taxable years after the taxable year that the property is placed in service.

* * *

Prop. Reg. § 1.167(n)-2. Basis.

(a) Depreciable basis.

(1) In general. The basis upon which the allowance for depreciation is computed with respect to income forecast property is the basis of the income forecast property for purposes of section 1011 without regard to the adjustments described in section 1016(a)(2) and (3).

(2) Timing of basis determinations and redeterminations. Costs paid or incurred in or after the taxable year in which the income forecast property is placed in service are taken into account in accordance with a taxpayer's method of accounting in redetermining the basis of income forecast property in the taxable year paid or incurred (i.e., when all events have occurred that establish the fact of the liability, the amount of the liability can be determined with reasonable accuracy, and economic performance has occurred with respect to the liability). See §1.446-1(c)(1)(i) and (ii), 1.461-1(a)(1) and (2), and 1.263A-1(c). Accordingly, contingent payments may not be included in the basis of income forecast property when the property is placed in service, but are included in the basis of income forecast property in the taxable year in which they are paid or incurred, even if the forecasted total income used in the computation of income forecast depreciation allowances is sufficient to indicate that the contingency will be satisfied.

(3) Separate property. Certain amounts paid or incurred in taxable years after income forecast property is placed in service are treated as separate property for purposes of computing depreciation allowances under the income forecast method. See §1.167(n)-5(c).

(b) Basis redeterminations. If an amount required to be capitalized into the basis of income forecast property is paid or incurred after the income forecast property is placed in service, and if the amount required to be capitalized is not treated as separate property in accordance with §1.167(n)-5(c), the basis of the income forecast property is redetermined and the amount required to be capitalized is the basis redetermination amount. The redetermined basis of the income forecast property is the depreciable basis of the income forecast property increased by the basis redetermination amount. In the year basis is redetermined (and in subsequent taxable years), the redetermined basis must be used to determine depreciation under the income forecast method. An additional allowance for depreciation under the income forecast method is allowed in the taxable year the basis of certain income forecast property is redetermined. See §1.167(n)- 4(c).

(c) Unrecovered depreciable basis. For any taxable year, the unrecovered depreciable basis of an income forecast property is the depreciable basis of the property less the adjustments described in section 1016(a)(2) and (3).

(d) Example. The provisions of §1.167(n)-2 are illustrated by the following example:

Example. (i) Studio contracts with Actor to star in a motion picture film to be produced by Studio. Both Studio and Actor are calendar year taxpayers; Studio is an accrual basis taxpayer and Actor is a cash basis taxpayer. As compensation for Actor's services, the contract guarantees Actor a payment of five percent of the gross income from the film, beginning after the film has earned a total gross income (net of distribution costs) of $100x. Studio estimates that the film will earn a total gross income of $160x by the end of the 10th taxable year following the taxable year that the film is placed in service. The film is placed in service and earns $65x of gross income in year one, $30x in year two, and $25x in year three. Because the income from the film does not exceed $100x in either year one or year two, Studio pays nothing under the contract to Actor in years one and two. In year three, the cumulative income from the film reaches $120x, which exceeds the $100x threshold by $20x. Based on this excess, Studio calculates that it owes Actor $1x, calculated by multiplying $20x by Actor's contractual percentage of five percent. Studio pays $1x to Actor 20 days after the end of year three.

(ii) Studio may not include the $1x paid to Actor in the basis of the film in years one or two because Studio does not have a fixed liability to pay Actor any amount under the contract in years one and two. Furthermore, while Studio does have a fixed liability to pay Actor $1x in year three, the requirements of section 404 are not met in year three and Studio thus may not include the $1x in the basis of the film in year three. In year four, when section 404 is satisfied, Studio incurs the $1x in accordance with §1.263A-1(c) and increases its basis in the film. The $1x is treated as a basis redetermination amount under §1.167(n)-2(b) in year four.

Prop. Reg. § 1.167(n)-3. Income from the property.

(a) Current year income.

(1) In general. Current year income is the income from an income forecast property for the current year (less the distribution costs of the income forecast property for such year), determined in accordance with the taxpayer's method of accounting. All income earned in connection with the income forecast property is included in current year income, except as provided in paragraph (d) of this section. In the case of a film, television show, or similar property, such income includes, but is not limited to—

(i) Income from foreign and domestic theatrical, television, and other releases and syndications;

(ii) Income from releases, sales, rentals, and syndications of video tape, DVD, and other media; and

(iii) Incidental income associated with the property, such as income from the financial exploitation of characters, designs, titles, scripts, and scores, but only to the extent that such incidental income is earned in connection with the ultimate use of such items by, or the ultimate sale of merchandise to, persons who are not related to the taxpayer (within the meaning of section 267(b)).

(2) Special rule for advance payments. In the year that income forecast property is placed in service, current year income for an income forecast property includes income included in gross income for any prior taxable year in connection with the property. This paragraph applies separately to any cost treated as separate property under §1.167(n)-5(c).

(b) Forecasted total income. Forecasted total income is the sum of current year income for the year that income forecast property is placed in service, plus all income from the income forecast property that the taxpayer reasonably believes will be includible in current year income in subsequent taxable years (as adjusted for distribution costs) up to and including the 10th taxable year after the year in which the income forecast property is placed in service. Forecasted total income is based on the conditions known to exist at the end of the taxable year for which the income forecast property is placed in service.

(c) Revised forecasted total income. If information is discovered in a taxable year following the year in which income forecast property is placed in service that indicates that forecasted total income is inaccurate, a taxpayer must compute revised forecasted total income for the taxable year. Revised forecasted total income is based on the conditions known to exist at the end of the taxable year for which the revised forecast is being made. Revised forecasted total income for the taxable year is the sum of current year income for the taxable year and all prior taxable years, plus all income from the income forecast property that the taxpayer reasonably believes will be includible in current year income in taxable years after the current taxable year up to and including the 10th taxable year after the year in which the income forecast property is placed in service. Where a taxpayer computes revised forecasted total income in accordance with this §1.167(n)-3(c), see §1.167(n)-4(b) for the computation of the allowance for income forecast depreciation.

(d) Special rules.

(1) Disposition of the property. In computing the depreciation allowance for an income forecast property, income from the sale or other disposition of income forecast property is not included in current year income. However, if the income forecast property is disposed of prior to the end of the 10th taxable year following the taxable year in which the property is placed in service, income from the sale or other disposition of income forecast property is taken into account in calculating revised forecasted total income both for purposes of calculating the allowance for depreciation in the year of disposition and for purposes of applying look-back. See §1.167(n)-4(d)(3) and §1.167(n)-6(c)(2).

(2) Syndication income from television series.

(i) In the case of a television series produced for distribution on television networks, current year income and forecasted total income (or, if applicable, revised forecasted total income) used in the computation of the depreciation allowance for such property under §1.167(n)-4 need not include income from syndication of the television series before the earlier of—

(A) The fourth taxable year beginning after the date the first episode in the series is placed in service; or

(B) The earliest taxable year in which the taxpayer has an arrangement relating to the syndication of the series.

(ii) For purposes of this paragraph (d)(2), an arrangement relating to syndication of a series of television shows means any arrangement other than the first run exhibition agreement. For example, an arrangement for exhibition of a television series by individual television stations is an arrangement for syndication if it results in an exhibition of one or more episodes of the series beginning after one or more episodes of the series have been exhibited on a television network. A first run exhibition agreement is an agreement under which any episode (including a pilot episode) of a television series is first placed in service within a particular market.

(3) Apportionment of income in certain circumstances. When income from a particular source relates to more than one income forecast property the taxpayer must make a reasonable allocation of the income among those properties based on all relevant factors. Situations where allocation is necessary include income generated by a syndication arrangement involving more than one income forecast property, incidental income described in paragraph (a)(1)(iii) of this section that relates to more than one motion picture, and income associated with income forecast property when expenditures relating to the property have given rise to separate property as defined in §1.167(n)-5(c). For example, when a taxpayer sells or licenses merchandise that features the likeness of a character that has appeared in more than one film, relevant factors might include merchandise sales figures prior to the release of the subsequent film, specific identification of certain merchandise with one particular film, and the taxpayer's prior experience with similar situations.

(4) Examples. The provisions of this section are illustrated by the following examples:

Example (1). FTC C produces a motion picture film featuring the adventures of a fictional character. C sells merchandise using the character's image, enters into licensing agreements with unrelated parties for the use of the image, and uses the image to promote a ride at an amusement park that is wholly owned by C. Pursuant to paragraph (a)(1) of this section, income from the sales of merchandise by C to consumers and income from the licensing agreements are included in current year income. No portion of the admission fees for the amusement park is included in current year income because the amusement part is wholly owned by C.

Example (2). FTC Assume the same facts as in Example 1. C forecasts that the cumulative amount of current year income it will earn (net of distribution costs) from the year it places the motion picture film in service through the end of the 7th taxable year thereafter to be $345x. C also forecasts that the motion picture film will earn current year income of $155x from the beginning of the 8th taxable year through the end of the 10th taxable year after the year the income forecast property is placed in service. C anticipates the sale of the motion picture film at the end of the 7th taxable year after the year the property is placed in service and in fact sells the motion picture film for $200x on the last day of the 7th taxable year after the year the property is placed in service. C's computations of forecasted total income must reflect the fact that C forecasts that $500x will be earned by the motion picture film through the end of the 10th taxable year after the year the property is placed in service ($345x from the year the film is placed in service through the end of the 7th taxable year after the taxable year that the property was placed in service, plus $155x C forecasts from the beginning of the 8th taxable year through the end of the 10th taxable year after the year the property is placed in service). Even though C only expects to earn $345x prior to the sale of the film, C may not use $345x as forecasted total income in computing its depreciation allowance under the income forecast method. Similarly, C may not use the combination of the amounts it expects to earn prior to the sale ($345x) plus the anticipated sales proceeds ($200x) or $545x as forecasted total income, except when computing its depreciation allowance for the 7th taxable year after the year in which the income forecast property was placed in service and for purposes of computing look-back interest.

Prop. Reg. § 1.167(n)-4. Computation of depreciation using the income forecast method.

(a) Computation of depreciation allowance. Generally, the depreciation allowance for an income forecast property for a given taxable year is computed by multiplying the depreciable or redetermined basis of the property (as defined in §1.167(n)-2) by a fraction, the numerator of which is current year income (as defined in §1.167(n)-3(a)) and the denominator of which is forecasted total income (as defined in §1.167(n)-3(b)).

(b) Revised computation.

(1) Change in estimated income. The depreciation allowance for an income forecast property for any taxable year following the year in which income forecast property is placed in service may be computed using the computation provided in this paragraph (b)(1) if revised forecasted total income differs from forecasted total income. Thus, for example, a taxpayer using the income forecast method for a motion picture may revise upward the forecast of total income from the motion picture (to arrive at revised forecasted total income) in a taxable year wherein the taxpayer discovers that the motion picture is more popular than originally expected, and may thereafter use the revised computation to compute the allowance for income forecast depreciation for the motion picture. Under the revised computation, the unrecovered depreciable basis of the income forecast property (as defined in §1.167(n)-2(c)) is multiplied by a fraction, the numerator of which is current year

income and the denominator of which is obtained by subtracting from revised forecasted total income the amounts of current year income from prior taxable years.
(2) Requirement to use the revised computation. The revised computation described in paragraph (b)(1) of this section must be used in any taxable year following the year in which income forecast property is placed in service if forecasted total income (as defined in §1.167(n)-3(b)) (or, if applicable, revised forecasted total income (as defined in §1.167(n)-3(c)) in the immediately preceding taxable year is either—

(i) Less than 90 percent of revised forecasted total income for the taxable year; or

(ii) Greater than 110 percent of revised forecasted total income for the taxable year.

(c) Basis redeterminations.

(1) Calculation of depreciation allowance. An additional depreciation allowance is available under this paragraph in the taxable year that basis is redetermined under §1.167(n)-2(b) when that taxable year is subsequent to the taxable year in which income forecast property is placed in service, but prior to the 10th taxable year following the taxable year in which the property is placed in service. The additional depreciation allowance is that portion of the basis redetermination amount that would have been recovered through depreciation allowances in prior taxable years if the basis redetermination amount had been included in depreciable basis in the taxable year that the property was placed in service. This §1.167(n)-4(c) does not apply to property treated as a single income forecast property pursuant to §1.167(n)-5(d)(1) through (4).

(2) Example. The provisions of paragraph (c)(1) of this section are illustrated by the following example:

Example. D, an accrual basis movie producer, enters into a contract with E, an author, under which D will make a film based on E's book. E performs no services for D, but merely permits D to use the book as a basis for D's film. D pays E a fixed dollar amount upon entry into the agreement and promises to pay E a contingent payment of five percent of D's income from the film, beginning after the film has earned $100,000 (net of distribution costs). D estimates that forecasted total income from the film will be $200,000. The film earns $65,000 of current year income in year one, $30,000 in year two, and $25,000 in year three. D takes allowances for depreciation in year one ($65,000 divided by $200,000, multiplied by the basis of the film) and year two ($30,000 divided by $200,000, multiplied by the basis of the film). In year three, D's liability to E becomes fixed and D pays E $1,000. The $1,000 incurred by D is a basis redetermination amount that increases the basis of the film for purposes of computing D's depreciation allowance for the film for year three. In addition to the year three allowance based on current year income ($25,000 divided by $200,000 multiplied by the basis of the film, which includes for year three the $1,000 basis redetermination amount), D is entitled to an additional allowance for depreciation for year three under paragraph (c)(1). This additional allowance is $475, the sum of the allowance of $325 that would have been allowed in year one ($65,000 divided by $200,000, multiplied by the $1,000 payment to E) and the allowance of $150 that would have been allowed in year two ($30,000 divided by $200,000, multiplied by $1,000) if the $1,000 had been included in basis in the year that the film was placed in service.

(d) Special rules.

(1) Final year depreciation. Except as provided in paragraphs (d)(2) and (3) of this section, a taxpayer may deduct as a depreciation allowance the remaining depreciable basis of income forecast property depreciated under the income forecast method in the earlier of—

(i) The year in which the taxpayer reasonably believes, based on the conditions known to exist at the end of the taxable year, that no income from the income forecast property will be included in current year income in any subsequent taxable year up to and including the 10th taxable year following the taxable year the income forecast property is placed in service; or

(ii) The 10th taxable year following the taxable year the income forecast property is placed in service.

(2) Certain basis redeterminations. A taxpayer may deduct as a depreciation allowance the amount of any basis redetermination that occurs in a taxable year in which the taxpayer reasonably believes, based on the conditions known to exist at the end of the taxable year, that no income from the income forecast property will be included in current year income in any subsequent taxable year. In addition, a taxpayer may deduct as a depreciation allowance the amount of any basis redetermination that occurs in a taxable year following a taxable year in which a deduction is allowable under paragraph (d)(1) of this section.

(3) Disposition of property. Paragraph (d)(1) of this section does not apply to income forecast property that is sold or otherwise disposed of before the end of the 10th taxable year following the taxable year that the property is placed in service. In the case of such a disposition, the allowance for depreciation in the year of disposition is calculated by multiplying the depreciable basis (or, if applicable, the redetermined basis) of the property by a fraction, the numerator of which is current year income and the denominator of which is the sum of the amount realized on the

disposition of the property plus all amounts included in current year income in the year of disposition and in taxable years prior to the year of disposition.

(4) Separate property. The deductions provided in paragraphs (d)(1) and (2) of this section apply separately to property that is treated as separate property under §1.167(n)-5(c).

(e) Examples. The provisions of this section are illustrated by the following examples:

Example (1). FTC F places in service income forecast property with a depreciable basis of $100x, and estimates that forecasted total income from the property will be $200x. In taxable year one, current year income is $80x. The depreciation allowance for year one is $40x, computed by multiplying the depreciable basis of the property of $100x by the fraction obtained by dividing current year income of $80x by forecasted total income of $200x.

Example (2). FTC Assume the same facts as in Example 1. In year two, F's current year income is $40x. In addition, F computes revised forecasted total income to be $176x. F is required to compute its depreciation allowance for this property using the revised computation of paragraph (b)(1) of this section because forecasted total income in year one of $200x is greater than 110 percent of revised forecasted total income in year two (110 percent of $176x = $193.6x). The depreciation allowance for taxable year two computed under the revised computation is $25x, computed by multiplying the unrecovered depreciable basis of $60x by the fraction obtained by dividing current year income of $40x by $96x (revised forecasted total income of $176x less current year income from prior taxable years of $80x).

Example (3). FTC Assume the same facts as in Example 2. Because F used the revised computation in year two, the revised computation applies in year three. In year three, F's current year income is $32x. The depreciation allowance for year three computed under the revised computation is $20x, computed by multiplying the unrecovered depreciable basis of $60x by the fraction obtained by dividing current year income of $32x by $96x (revised forecasted total income of $176x less current year income from taxable years prior to the change in estimate taxable year of $80x).

Prop. Reg. § 1.167(n)-5. Property for which the income forecast method may be used.

(a) In general. The depreciation allowance under §1.167(n)-4 may be computed under the income forecast method only with respect to eligible property. Eligible property is limited to an interest (including interests involving limited rights in property) in the following property—

(1) Property described in section 168(f)(3) and (4);

(2) Copyrights;

(3) Books;

(4) Patents;

(5) Theatrical productions; and

(6) Other property as designated in published guidance by the Commissioner.

(b) Specific exclusions. The income forecast method does not apply to any amortizable section 197 intangible (as defined in section 197(c) and §1.197-2(d)).
* * *

Prop. Reg. § 1.167(n)-6. Look-back method.

(a) Application of the look-back method. If a taxpayer claims a depreciation deduction under the income forecast method for any eligible income forecast property, such taxpayer is required to pay (or is entitled to receive) interest computed as described in this paragraph for any year to which the look-back method applies (a recomputation year). The look-back method generally must be applied when income forecast property is disposed of or ceases to generate income. Further, the look-back method generally applies in the 3rd and 10th taxable years following the year in which income forecast property is placed in service. Under the look-back method, taxpayers must pay interest on deductions accelerated by the underestimation of either forecasted total income or revised forecasted total income from income forecast property. Conversely, taxpayers are entitled to receive interest on deductions delayed by the overestimation of either forecasted total income or revised forecasted total income from income forecast property. If either forecasted total income or revised forecasted total income are overestimated or underestimated, interest may arise from basis redeterminations. The computation of adjusted tax liability as part of the look-back method is hypothetical; application of the look-back method does not require a taxpayer to adjust tax liability as reported on the taxpayer's tax returns, on an amended return, or as adjusted on examination for prior years.
* * *

(e) Recomputation year.

(1) In general. Except as provided in this paragraph (e), the term recomputation year means, with respect to any income forecast property—

(i) The earlier of—

(A) The year the income from the income forecast property ceases with respect to the taxpayer (and with respect to any person who would be treated as a single taxpayer with the taxpayer under rules similar to those in section 41(f)(1)); or

(B) The 3rd taxable year beginning after the taxable year in which the income forecast property was placed in service; and

(ii) The earlier of—

(A) The year the income from the income forecast property ceases with respect to the taxpayer (and with respect to any person who would be treated as a single taxpayer with the taxpayer under rules similar to those in section 41(f)(1)); or

(B) The 10th taxable year following the taxable year the income forecast property is placed in service.

(2) Look-back method inapplicable in certain de minimis cases.

(i) *De minimis difference between actual and forecasted income*. A taxable year described in paragraph (e)(1) of this section is not a recomputation year if forecasted total income (as defined in §1.167(n)-3(b)) or, where applicable, revised forecasted total income (as defined in §1.167(n)-3(c)), for each preceding taxable years is—

(A) Greater than 90 percent of revised forecasted total income for the taxable year that would otherwise be a recomputation year; and

(B) Less than 110 percent of revised forecasted total income for the taxable year that would otherwise be a recomputation year.

(ii) *Application of the de minimis rule where the look-back method was previously applied*. For purposes of applying paragraph (e)(2)(i) of this section in any taxable year after a taxable year in which the look-back method has previously been applied, revised forecasted total income for the year the look-back method was applied, forecasted total income for the year the income forecast property was placed in service, and revised forecasted total income for all taxable years preceding the taxable year in which the look-back method was previously applied are deemed to be equal to the amount of revised forecasted total income that was used for purposes of applying the look-back method in the most recent taxable year for which the look-back method was applied.

(f) De minimis basis exception. The look-back method does not apply to any income forecast property with an adjusted basis, determined in accordance with section 1011 but without regard to the adjustments described in section 1016(a)(2) and (3), as of the close of any year that would otherwise be a recomputation year of $100,000 or less.

Treas. Reg. § 1.174-1. Research and experimental expenditures; in general.

Section 174 provides two methods for treating research or experimental expenditures paid or incurred by the taxpayer in connection with his trade or business. These expenditures may be treated as expenses not chargeable to capital account and deducted in the year in which they are paid or incurred (see § 1.174-3), or they may be deferred and amortized (see § 1.174-4). Research or experimental expenditures which are neither treated as expenses nor deferred and amortized under section 174 must be charged to capital account. The expenditures to which section 174 applies may relate either to a general research program or to a particular project. See § 1.174-2 for the definition of research and experimental expenditures. The term "paid or incurred", as used in section 174 and in §§ 1.174-1 to 1.174-4, inclusive, is to be construed according to the method of accounting used by the taxpayer in computing taxable income. See section 7701(a)(25).

Treas. Reg. § 1.174-2. Definition of research and experimental expenditures.

(a) In general.

> **(1)** The term research or experimental expenditures, as used in section 174, means expenditures incurred in connection with the taxpayer's trade or business which represent research and development costs in the experimental or laboratory sense. The term generally includes all such costs incident to the development or improvement of a product. The term includes the costs of obtaining a patent, such as attorneys' fees expended in making and perfecting a patent application. Expenditures represent research and development costs in the experimental or laboratory sense if they are for activities intended to discover information that would eliminate uncertainty concerning the development or improvement of a product. Uncertainty exists if the information available to the taxpayer does not establish the capability or method for developing or improving the product or the appropriate design of the product. Whether expenditures qualify as research or experimental expenditures depends on the nature of the activity to which the expenditures relate, not the nature of the product or improvement being developed or the level of technological advancement the product or improvement represents.
>
> **(2)** For purposes of this section, the term product includes any pilot model, process, formula, invention, technique, patent, or similar property, and includes products to

be used by the taxpayer in its trade or business as well as products to be held for sale, lease, or license.

(3) The term research or experimental expenditures does not include expenditures for—

(i) The ordinary testing or inspection of materials or products for quality control (quality control testing);

(ii) Efficiency surveys;

(iii) Management studies;

(iv) Consumer surveys;

(v) Advertising or promotions;

(vi) The acquisition of another's patent, model, production or process; or

(vii) Research in connection with literary, historical, or similar projects.

(4) For purposes of paragraph (a)(3)(i) of this section, testing or inspection to determine whether particular units of materials or products conform to specified parameters is quality control testing. However, quality control testing does not include testing to determine if the design of the product is appropriate.

(5) See section 263A and the regulations thereunder for cost capitalization rules which apply to expenditures paid or incurred for research in connection with literary, historical, or similar projects involving the production of property, including the production of films, sound recordings, video tapes, books, or similar properties.

(6) Section 174 applies to a research or experimental expenditure only to the extent that the amount of the expenditure is reasonable under the circumstances. In general, the amount of an expenditure for research or experimental activities is reasonable if the amount would ordinarily be paid for like activities by like enterprises under like circumstances. Amounts supposedly paid for research that are not reasonable under the circumstances may be characterized as disguised dividends, gifts, loans, or similar payments. The reasonableness requirement of this paragraph (a)(6) does not apply to the reasonableness of the type or nature of the activities themselves.

(7) This paragraph (a) applies to taxable years beginning after October 3, 1994.

(8) The provisions of this section apply not only to costs paid or incurred by the taxpayer for research or experimentation undertaken directly by him but also to expenditures paid or incurred for research or experimentation carried on in his behalf by another person or organization (such as a research institute, foundation, engineering company, or similar contractor). However, any expenditures for research or experimentation carried on in the taxpayer's behalf by another person are not expenditures to which section 174 relates, to the extent that they represent expenditures for the acquisition or improvement of land or depreciable property, used in connection with the research or experimentation, to which the taxpayer acquires rights of ownership.

(9) The application of subparagraph (2) of this paragraph may be illustrated by the following examples:

Example 1. A engages B to undertake research and experimental work in order to create a particular product. B will be paid annually a fixed sum plus an amount equivalent to his actual expenditures. In 1957, A pays to B in respect of the project the sum of $150,000 of which $25,000 represents an addition to B's laboratory and the balance represents charges for research and experimentation on the project. It is agreed between the parties that A will absorb the entire cost of this addition to B's laboratory which will be retained by B. A may treat the entire $150,000 as expenditures under section 174.

Example 2. X Corporation, a manufacturer of explosives, contracts with the Y research organization to attempt through research and experimentation the creation of a new process for making certain explosives. Because of the danger involved in such an undertaking, Y is compelled to acquire an isolated tract of land on which to conduct the research and experimentation. It is agreed that upon completion of the project Y will transfer this tract, including any improvements thereon, to X. Section 174 [26 USCS § 174] does not apply to the amount paid to Y representing the costs of the tract of land and improvements.

(b) Certain expenditures with respect to land and other property.

(1) Expenditures by the taxpayer for the acquisition or improvement of land, or for the acquisition or improvement of property which is subject to an allowance for depreciation under section 167 or depletion under section 611, are not deductible under section 174, irrespective of the fact that the property or improvements may be used by the taxpayer in connection with research or experimentation. However, allowances for depreciation or depletion of property are considered as research or experimental expenditures, for purposes of section 174, to the extent that the property to which the allowances relate is used in connection with research or experimentation. If any part of the cost of acquisition or improvement of depreciable property is attributable to research or experimentation (whether made by the taxpayer or another), see subparagraphs (2), (3), and (4) of this paragraph.

(2) Expenditures for research or experimentation which result, as an end product of the research or experimentation, in depreciable property to be used in the taxpayer's trade or business may, subject to the limitations of subparagraph (4) of this paragraph, be allowable as a current expense deduction under section 174(a). Such expenditures cannot be amortized under section 174(b) except to the extent provided in paragraph (a)(4) of § 1.174-4.

(3) If expenditures for research or experimentation are incurred in connection with the construction or manufacture of depreciable property by another, they are deductible under section 174(a) only if made upon the taxpayer's order and at his risk. No deduction will be allowed (i) if the taxpayer purchases another's product under a performance guarantee (whether express, implied, or imposed by local law) unless the guarantee is limited, to engineering specifications or otherwise, in such a way that economic utility is not taken into account; or (ii) for any part of the purchase price of a product in regular production. For example, if a taxpayer orders a specially-built automatic milling machine under a guarantee that the machine will be capable of producing a given number of units per hour, no portion of the expenditure is deductible since none of it is made at the taxpayer's risk. Similarly, no deductible expense is incurred if a taxpayer enters into a contract for the construction of a new type of chemical processing plant under a turn-key contract guaranteeing a given annual production and a given consumption of raw material and fuel per unit. On the other hand, if the contract contained no guarantee of quality of production and of quantity of units in relation to consumption of raw material and fuel, and if real doubt existed as to the capabilities of the process, expenses for research or experimentation under the contract are at the taxpayer's risk and are deductible under section 174(a). However, see subparagraph (4) of this paragraph.

(4) The deductions referred to in subparagraphs (2) and (3) of this paragraph for expenditures in connection with the acquisition or production of depreciable property to be used in the taxpayer's trade or business are limited to amounts expended for research or experimentation. For the purpose of the preceding sentence, amounts expended for research or experimentation do not include the costs of the component materials of the depreciable property, the costs of labor or other elements involved in its construction and installation, or costs attributable to the acquisition or improvement of the property. For example, a taxpayer undertakes to develop a new machine for use in his business. He expends $30,000 on the project of which $10,000 represents the actual costs of material, labor, etc., to construct the machine, and $20,000 represents research costs which are not attributable to the machine itself. Under section 174(a) the taxpayer would be permitted to deduct the $20,000 as expenses not chargeable to capital account, but the $10,000 must be charged to the asset account (the machine).

(c) Exploration expenditures. The provisions of section 174 are not applicable to any expenditures paid or incurred for the purpose of ascertaining the existence, location, extent, or quality of any deposit of ore, oil, gas or other mineral. See sections 617 and 263.

Treas. Reg. § 1.197-2. Amortization of goodwill and certain other intangibles.

(a) Overview—

(1) In general. Section 197 allows an amortization deduction for the capitalized costs of an amortizable section 197 intangible and prohibits any other depreciation or amortization with respect to that property. Paragraphs (b), (c), and (e) of this section provide rules and definitions for determining whether property is a section 197 intangible, and paragraphs (d) and (e) of this section provide rules and definitions for determining whether a section 197 intangible is an amortizable section 197 intangible. The amortization deduction under section 197 is determined by amortizing basis ratably over a 15-year period under the rules of paragraph (f) of this section. Section 197 also includes various special rules pertaining to the disposition of amortizable section 197 intangibles, nonrecognition transactions, anti-churning rules, and anti-abuse rules. Rules relating to these provisions are contained in paragraphs (g), (h), and (j) of this section. Examples demonstrating the application of these provisions are contained in paragraph (k) of this section. The effective date of the rules in this section is contained in paragraph (l) of this section.

(2) Section 167(f) property. Section 167(f) prescribes rules for computing the depreciation deduction for certain property to which section 197 does not apply. See § 1.167(a)-14 for rules under section 167(f) and paragraphs (c)(4), (6), (7), (11), and (13) of this section for a description of the property subject to section 167(f).

(3) Amounts otherwise deductible. Section 197 does not apply to amounts that are not chargeable to capital account under paragraph (f)(3) (relating to basis determinations for covenants not to compete and certain contracts for the use of section 197 intangibles) of this section and are otherwise currently deductible. For this purpose, an amount described in § 1.162-11 is not currently deductible if, without regard to § 1.162-11, such amount is properly chargeable to capital account.

(b) Section 197 intangibles; in general. Except as otherwise provided in paragraph (c) of this section, the term section 197 intangible means any property described in section 197(d)(1). The following rules and definitions provide guidance concerning property that is a section 197 intangible unless an exception applies:

(1) Goodwill. Section 197 intangibles include goodwill. Goodwill is the value of a trade or business attributable to the expectancy of continued customer patronage. This expectancy may be due to the name or reputation of a trade or business or any other factor.

(2) Going concern value. Section 197 intangibles include going concern value. Going concern value is the additional value that attaches to property by reason of its existence as an integral part of an ongoing business activity. Going concern value includes the value attributable to the ability of a trade or business (or a part of a trade or business) to continue functioning or generating income without interruption notwithstanding a change in ownership, but does not include any of the intangibles described in any other provision of this paragraph (b). It also includes the value that is attributable to the immediate use or availability of an acquired trade or business, such as, for example, the use of the revenues or net earnings that otherwise would not be received during any period if the acquired trade or business were not available or operational.

(3) Workforce in place. Section 197 intangibles include workforce in place. Workforce in place (sometimes referred to as agency force or assembled workforce) includes the composition of a workforce (for example, the experience, education, or training of a workforce), the terms and conditions of employment whether contractual or otherwise, and any other value placed on employees or any of their attributes. Thus, the amount paid or incurred for workforce in place includes, for example, any portion of the purchase price of an acquired trade or business attributable to the existence of a highly-skilled workforce, an existing employment contract (or contracts), or a relationship with employees or consultants (including, but not limited to, any key employee contract or relationship). Workforce in place does not include any covenant not to compete or other similar arrangement described in paragraph (b)(9) of this section.

(4) Information base. Section 197 intangibles include any information base, including a customer-related information base. For this purpose, an information base includes business books and records, operating systems, and any other information base (regardless of the method of recording the information) and a customer-related information base is any information base that includes lists or other information with respect to current or prospective customers. Thus, the amount paid or incurred for information base includes, for example, any portion of the purchase price of an acquired trade or business attributable to the intangible value of technical manuals, training manuals or programs, data files, and accounting or inventory control systems. Other examples include the cost of acquiring customer lists, subscription lists, insurance expirations, patient or client files, or lists of newspaper, magazine, radio, or television advertisers.

(5) Know-how, etc. Section 197 intangibles include any patent, copyright, formula, process, design, pattern, know-how, format, package design, computer software (as defined in paragraph (c)(4)(iv) of this section), or interest in a film, sound recording, video tape, book, or other similar property. (See, however, the exceptions in paragraph (c) of this section.)

(6) Customer-based intangibles. Section 197 intangibles include any customer-based intangible. A customer-based intangible is any composition of market, market share, or other value resulting from the future provision of goods or services pursuant to contractual or other relationships in the ordinary course of business with customers. Thus, the amount paid or incurred for customer-based intangibles includes, for example, any portion of the purchase price of an acquired trade or business attributable to the existence of a customer base, a circulation base, an undeveloped market or market growth, insurance in force, the existence of a qualification to supply goods or services to a particular customer, a mortgage servicing contract (as defined in paragraph (c)(11) of this section), an investment management contract, or other relationship with customers involving the future provision of goods or services. (See, however, the exceptions in paragraph (c) of this section.) In addition, customer-based intangibles include the deposit base and any similar asset of a financial institution. Thus, the amount paid or incurred for customer-based intangibles also includes any portion of the purchase price of an acquired financial institution attributable to the value represented by existing checking accounts, savings accounts, escrow accounts, and other similar items of the financial institution. However, any portion of the purchase price of an acquired trade or business attributable to accounts receivable or other similar rights to income for goods or services provided to customers prior to the acquisition of a trade or business is not an amount paid or incurred for a customer-based intangible.

(7) Supplier-based intangibles. Section 197 intangibles include any supplier-based intangible. A supplier-based intangible is the value resulting from the future acquisition, pursuant to contractual or other relationships with suppliers in the ordinary course of business, of goods or services that will be sold or used by the taxpayer. Thus, the amount paid or incurred for supplier-based intangibles includes, for example, any portion of the purchase price of an acquired trade or business attributable to the existence of a favorable relationship with persons providing distribution services (such as favorable shelf or display space at a retail outlet), the existence of a favorable credit rating, or the existence of favorable supply contracts. The amount paid or incurred for supplier-based intangibles does not include any amount required to be paid for the goods or services themselves pursuant to the terms of the agreement or other relationship. In addition, see the exceptions in paragraph (c) of this section, including the exception in paragraph (c)(6) of this section for certain rights to receive tangible property or services from another person.

(8) Licenses, permits, and other rights granted by governmental units. Section 197 intangibles include any license, permit, or other right granted by a governmental unit (including, for purposes of section 197, an agency or instrumentality thereof) even if the right is granted for an indefinite period or is reasonably expected to be renewed for an indefinite period. These rights include, for example, a liquor license, a taxi-cab medallion (or license), an airport landing or takeoff right (sometimes referred to as a slot), a regulated airline route, or a television or radio broadcasting license. The issuance or renewal of a license, permit, or other right granted by a governmental unit is considered an acquisition of the license, permit, or other right. (See, however, the exceptions in paragraph (c) of this section, including the exceptions in paragraph (c)(3) of this section for an interest in land, paragraph (c)(6) of this section for certain rights to receive tangible property or services, paragraph (c)(8) of this section for an interest under a lease of tangible property, and paragraph (c)(13) of this section for certain rights granted by a governmental unit. See paragraph (b)(10) of this section for the treatment of franchises.)

(9) Covenants not to compete and other similar arrangements. Section 197 intangibles include any covenant not to compete, or agreement having substantially the same effect, entered into in connection with the direct or indirect acquisition of an interest in a trade or business or a substantial portion thereof. For purposes of this paragraph (b)(9), an acquisition may be made in the form of an asset acquisition (including a qualified stock purchase that is treated as a purchase of assets under section 338), a stock acquisition or redemption, and the acquisition or redemption of a partnership interest. An agreement requiring the performance of services for the acquiring taxpayer or the provision of property or its use to the acquiring taxpayer does not have substantially the same effect as a covenant not to compete to the extent that the amount paid under the agreement represents reasonable compensation for the services actually rendered or for the property or use of the property actually provided.

(10) Franchises, trademarks, and trade names.

(i) Section 197 intangibles include any franchise, trademark, or trade name. The term franchise has the meaning given in section 1253(b)(1) and includes any agreement that provides one of the parties to the agreement with the right to distribute, sell, or provide goods, services, or facilities, within a specified area. The term trademark includes any word, name, symbol, or device, or any combination thereof, adopted and used to identify goods or services and distinguish them from those provided by others. The term trade name includes any name used to identify or designate a particular trade or business or the name or title used by a person or organization engaged in a trade or business. A license, permit, or other right granted by a governmental unit is a franchise if it otherwise meets the definition of a franchise. A trademark or trade name includes any trademark or trade name arising under statute or applicable common law, and any similar right granted by contract. The renewal of a franchise, trademark, or trade name is treated as an acquisition of the franchise, trademark, or trade name.

(ii) Notwithstanding the definitions provided in paragraph (b)(10)(i) of this section, any amount that is paid or incurred on account of a transfer, sale, or other disposition of a franchise, trademark, or trade name and that is subject to section 1253(d)(1) is not included in the basis of a section 197 intangible. (See paragraph (g)(6) of this section.)

(11) Contracts for the use of, and term interests in, section 197 intangibles. Section 197 intangibles include any right under a license, contract, or other arrangement providing for the use of property that would be a section 197 intangible under any provision of this paragraph (b) (including this paragraph (b)(11)) after giving effect to all of the exceptions provided in paragraph (c) of this section. Section 197 intangibles also include any term interest (whether outright or in trust) in such property.

(12) Other similar items. Section 197 intangibles include any other intangible property that is similar in all material respects to the property specifically described in section 197(d)(1)(C)(i) through (v) and paragraphs (b)(3) through (7) of this section. (See paragraph (g)(5) of this section for special rules regarding certain reinsurance transactions.)

(c) Section 197 intangibles; exceptions. The term section 197 intangible does not include property described in section 197(e). The following rules and definitions provide guidance concerning property to which the exceptions apply:

* * *

(4) Certain computer software—

(i) *Publicly available*. Section 197 intangibles do not include any interest in computer software that is (or has been) readily available to the general public on similar terms, is subject to a nonexclusive license, and has not been substantially modified. Computer software will be treated as readily available to the general public if the software may be obtained on substantially the same terms by a significant number of persons that would reasonably be expected to use the software. This requirement can be met even though the software is not available through a system of retail distribution. Computer software will not be considered to have been substantially modified if the cost of all modifications to the version of the software that is readily available to the general public does not exceed the greater of 25 percent of the price at which the unmodified version of the software is readily available to the general public or $2,000. For the purpose of determining whether computer software has been substantially modified—

(A) Integrated programs acquired in a package from a single source are treated as a single computer program; and

(B) Any cost incurred to install the computer software on a system is not treated as a cost of the software. However, the costs for customization, such as tailoring to a user's specifications (other than embedded programming options) are costs of modifying the software.

(ii) *Not acquired as part of trade or business.* Section 197 intangibles do not include an interest in computer software that is not acquired as part of a purchase of a trade or business.

(iii) *Other exceptions.* For other exceptions applicable to computer software, see paragraph (a)(3) of this section (relating to otherwise deductible amounts) and paragraph (g)(7) of this section (relating to amounts properly taken into account in determining the cost of property that is not a section 197 intangible).

(iv) *Computer software defined.* For purposes of this section, computer software is any program or routine (that is, any sequence of machine-readable code) that is designed to cause a computer to perform a desired function or set of functions, and the documentation required to describe and maintain that program or routine. It includes all forms and media in which the software is contained, whether written, magnetic, or otherwise. Computer programs of all classes, for example, operating systems, executive systems, monitors, compilers and translators, assembly routines, and utility programs as well as application programs, are included. Computer software also includes any incidental and ancillary rights that are necessary to effect the acquisition of the title to, the ownership of, or the right to use the computer software, and that are used only in connection with that specific computer software. Such incidental and ancillary rights are not included in the definition of trademark or trade name under paragraph (b)(10)(i) of this section. For example, a trademark or trade name that is ancillary to the ownership or use of a specific computer software program in the taxpayer's trade or business and is not acquired for the purpose of marketing the computer software is included in the definition of computer software and is not included in the definition of trademark or trade name. Computer software does not include any data or information base described in paragraph (b)(4) of this section unless the data base or item is in the public domain and is incidental to a computer program. For this purpose, a copy-righted or proprietary data or information base is treated as in the public domain if its availability through the computer program does not contribute significantly to the cost of the program. For example, if a word-processing program includes a dictionary feature used to spell-check a document or any portion thereof, the entire program (including the dictionary feature) is computer software regardless of the form in which the feature is maintained or stored.

(5) Certain interests in films, sound recordings, video tapes, books, or other similar property. Section 197 intangibles do not include any interest (including an interest as a licensee) in a film, sound recording, video tape, book, or other similar property (such as the right to broadcast or transmit a live event) if the interest is not acquired as part of a purchase of a trade or business. A film, sound recording, video tape, book, or other similar property includes any incidental and ancillary rights (such as a trademark or trade name) that are necessary to effect the acquisition of title to, the ownership of, or the right to use the property and are used only in connection with that property. Such incidental and ancillary rights are not included in the definition of trademark or trade name under paragraph (b)(10)(i) of this section. For purposes of this paragraph (c)(5), computer software (as defined in paragraph (c)(4)(iv) of this section) is not treated as other property similar to a film, sound recording, video tape, or book. (See section 167 for amortization of excluded intangible property or interests.)

* * *

(7) Certain interests in patents or copyrights. Section 197 intangibles do not include any interest (including an interest as a licensee) in a patent, patent application, or copyright that is not acquired as part of a purchase of a trade or business. A patent or copyright includes any incidental and ancillary rights (such as a trademark or trade name) that are necessary to effect the acquisition of title to, the ownership of, or the right to use the property and are used only in connection with that property. Such incidental and ancillary rights are not included in the definition of trademark or trade name under paragraph (b)(10)(i) of this section. (See § 1.167(a)-14(c)(4) for applicable rules.)

* * *

(d) Amortizable section 197 intangibles—

(1) Definition. Except as otherwise provided in this paragraph (d), the term amortizable section 197 intangible means any section 197 intangible acquired after August 10, 1993 (or after July 25, 1991, if a valid retroactive election under § 1.197-1T has been made), and held in connection with the conduct of a trade or business or an activity described in section 212.

(2) Exception for self-created intangibles—

(i) *In general.* Except as provided in paragraph (d)(2)(iii) of this section, amortizable section 197 intangibles do not include any section 197 intangible created by the taxpayer (a self-created intangible).

(ii) *Created by the taxpayer—*

(A) *Defined.* A section 197 intangible is created by the taxpayer to the extent the taxpayer makes payments or otherwise incurs costs for its creation, production, development, or improvement, whether the actual work is performed by the taxpayer or by another person under a contract with the taxpayer entered into before the contracted creation, production, development, or improvement occurs. For example, a technological process developed specifically for a taxpayer under an arrangement with another person pursuant to which the taxpayer retains all rights to the process is created by the taxpayer.

(B) *Contracts for the use of intangibles.* A section 197 intangible is not a self-created intangible to the extent that it results from the entry into (or renewal of) a contract for the use of an existing section 197 intangible. Thus, for example, the exception for self-created intangibles does not apply to capitalized costs, such as legal and other professional fees, incurred by a licensee in connection with the entry into (or renewal of) a contract for the use of know-how or similar property.

(C) *Improvements and modifications.* If an existing section 197 intangible is improved or otherwise modified by the taxpayer or by another person under a contract with the taxpayer, the existing intangible and the capitalized costs (if any) of the improvements or other modifications are each treated as a separate section 197 intangible for purposes of this paragraph (d).

(iii) *Exceptions.*

(A) The exception for self-created intangibles does not apply to any section 197 intangible described in section 197(d)(1)(D) (relating to licenses, permits or other rights granted by a governmental unit), 197(d)(1)(E) (relating to covenants not to compete), or 197(d)(1)(F) (relating to franchises, trademarks, and trade names). Thus, for example, capitalized costs incurred in the development, registration, or defense of a trademark or trade name do not qualify for the exception and are amortized over 15 years under section 197.

(B) The exception for self-created intangibles does not apply to any section 197 intangible created in connection with the purchase of a trade or business (as defined in paragraph (e) of this section).

(C) If a taxpayer disposes of a self-created intangible and subsequently reacquires the intangible in an acquisition described in paragraph (h)(5)(ii) of this section, the exception for self-created intangibles does not apply to the reacquired intangible.

* * *

(e) Purchase of a trade or business. Several of the exceptions in section 197 apply only to property that is not acquired in (or created in connection with) a transaction or series of related transactions involving the acquisition of assets constituting a trade or business or a substantial portion thereof. Property acquired in (or created in connection with) such a transaction or series of related transactions is referred to in this section as property acquired as part of (or created in connection with) a purchase of a trade or business. For purposes of section 197 and this section, the applicability of the limitation is determined under the following rules:

(1) Goodwill or going concern value. An asset or group of assets constitutes a trade or business or a substantial portion thereof if their use would constitute a trade or business under section 1060 (that is, if goodwill or going concern value could under any circumstances attach to the assets). See § 1.1060-1(b)(2). For this purpose, all the facts and circumstances, including any employee relationships that continue (or covenants not to compete that are entered into) as part of the transfer of the assets, are taken into account in determining whether goodwill or going concern value could attach to the assets.

(2) Franchise, trademark, or trade name—

(i) *In general*. The acquisition of a franchise, trademark, or trade name constitutes the acquisition of a trade or business or a substantial portion thereof.

(ii) *Exceptions*. For purposes of this paragraph (e)(2)—

(A) A trademark or trade name is disregarded if it is included in computer software under paragraph (c)(4) of this section or in an interest in a film, sound recording, video tape, book, or other similar property under paragraph (c)(5) of this section;

(B) A franchise, trademark, or trade name is disregarded if its value is nominal or the taxpayer irrevocably disposes of it immediately after its acquisition; and

(C) The acquisition of a right or interest in a trademark or trade name is disregarded if the grant of the right or interest is not, under the principles of section 1253, a transfer of all substantial rights to such property or of an undivided interest in all substantial rights to such property.

* * *

(4) Substantial portion. The determination of whether acquired assets constitute a substantial portion of a trade or business is to be based on all of the facts and circumstances, including the nature and the amount of the assets acquired as well as the nature and amount of the assets retained by the transferor. The value of the assets acquired relative to the value of the assets retained by the transferor is not determinative of whether the acquired assets constitute a substantial portion of a trade or business.

(f) Computation of amortization deduction—

(1) In general. Except as provided in paragraph (f)(2) of this section, the amortization deduction allowable under section 197(a) is computed as follows:

(i) The basis of an amortizable section 197 intangible is amortized ratably over the 15-year period beginning on the later of—

(A) The first day of the month in which the property is acquired; or

(B) In the case of property held in connection with the conduct of a trade or business or in an activity described in section 212, the first day of the month in which the conduct of the trade or business or the activity begins.

(ii) Except as otherwise provided in this section, basis is determined under section 1011 and salvage value is disregarded.

(iii) Property is not eligible for amortization in the month of disposition.

(iv) The amortization deduction for a short taxable year is based on the number of months in the short taxable year.

(2) Treatment of contingent amounts—

(i) *Amounts added to basis during 15-year period.* Any amount that is properly included in the basis of an amortizable section 197 intangible after the first month of the 15-year period described in paragraph (f)(1)(i) of this section and before the expiration of that period is amortized ratably over the remainder of the 15-year period. For this purpose, the remainder of the 15-year period begins on the first day of the month in which the basis increase occurs.

(ii) *Amounts becoming fixed after expiration of 15-year period.* Any amount that is not properly included in the basis of an amortizable section 197 intangible until after the expiration of the 15-year period described in paragraph (f)(1)(i) of this section is amortized in full immediately upon the inclusion of the amount in the basis of the intangible.

(iii) *Rules for including amounts in basis.* See §§ 1.1275-4(c)(4) and 1.483-4(a) for rules governing the extent to which contingent amounts payable under a debt instrument given in consideration for the sale or exchange of an amortizable section 197 intangible are treated as payments of principal and the time at which the amount treated as principal is included in basis. See § 1.461-1(a)(1) and (2) for rules governing the time at which other contingent amounts are taken into account in determining the basis of an amortizable section 197 intangible.

(3) Basis determinations for certain assets—

(i) *Covenants not to compete.* In the case of a covenant not to compete or other similar arrangement described in paragraph (b)(9) of this section (a covenant), the amount chargeable to capital account includes, except as provided in this paragraph (f)(3), all amounts that are required to be paid pursuant to the covenant, whether or not any such amount would be deductible under section 162 if the covenant were not a section 197 intangible.

(ii) *Contracts for the use of section 197 intangibles; acquired as part of a trade or business—*

(A) *In general.* Except as provided in this paragraph (f)(3), any amount paid or incurred by the transferee on account of the transfer of a right or term interest described in paragraph (b)(11) of this section (relating to contracts for the use of, and term interests in, section 197 intangibles) by the owner of the property to which such right or interest relates and as part of a purchase of a trade or business is chargeable to capital account, whether or not such amount would be deductible under section 162 if the property were not a section 197 intangible.

(B) *Know-how and certain information base.* The amount chargeable to capital account with respect to a right or term interest described in paragraph (b)(11) of this section is determined without regard to the rule in paragraph (f)(3)(ii)(A) of this section if the right or interest relates to property (other than a customer-related information base) described in paragraph (b)(4) or (5) of this section and the acquiring taxpayer establishes that—

(1) The transfer of the right or interest is not, under the principles of section 1235, a transfer of all substantial rights to such property or of an undivided interest in all substantial rights to such property; and

(2) The right or interest was transferred for an arm's-length consideration.

(iii) *Contracts for the use of section 197 intangibles; not acquired as part of a trade or business.* The transfer of a right or term interest described in paragraph (b)(11) of this section by the owner of the property to which such right or interest relates but not as part of a purchase of a trade or business will be closely scrutinized under the principles of section 1235 for purposes of determining whether the transfer is a sale or exchange and, accordingly, whether amounts paid on account of the transfer are chargeable to capital account. If under the principles of section 1235 the transaction is not a sale or exchange, amounts paid on account of the transfer are not chargeable to capital account under this paragraph (f)(3).

(iv) *Applicable rules—*

(A) *Franchises, trade-marks, and trade names.* For purposes of this paragraph (f)(3), section 197 intangibles described in paragraph (b)(11) of this section do not include any property that is also described in paragraph (b)(10) of this section (relating to franchises, trademarks, and trade names).

* * *

Treas. Reg. § 1.263(a)-4. Amounts paid to acquire or create intangibles.

(a) Overview. This section provides rules for applying section 263(a) to amounts paid to acquire or create intangibles. Except to the extent provided in paragraph (d)(8) of this section, the rules provided by this section do not apply to amounts paid to acquire or create tangible assets. Paragraph (b) of this section provides a general principle of capitalization. Paragraphs (c) and (d) of this section identify intangibles for which capitalization is specifically required under the general principle. Paragraph (e) of this section provides rules for determining the extent to which taxpayers must capitalize transaction costs. Paragraph (f) of this section provides a 12-month rule intended to simplify the application of the general principle to certain payments that create benefits of a brief duration. . . .

(b) Capitalization with respect to intangibles—

(1) In general. Except as otherwise provided in this section, a taxpayer must capitalize—

(i) An amount paid to acquire an intangible (see paragraph (c) of this section);

(ii) An amount paid to create an intangible described in paragraph (d) of this section;

(iii) An amount paid to create or enhance a separate and distinct intangible asset within the meaning of paragraph (b)(3) of this section;

(iv) An amount paid to create or enhance a future benefit identified in published guidance in the Federal Register or in the Internal Revenue Bulletin (see § 601.601(d)(2)(ii) of this chapter) as an intangible for which capitalization is required under this section; and

(v) An amount paid to facilitate (within the meaning of paragraph (e)(1) of this section) an acquisition or creation of an intangible described in paragraph (b)(1)(i), (ii), (iii) or (iv) of this section.

(2) Published guidance. Any published guidance identifying a future benefit as an intangible for which capitalization is required under paragraph (b)(1)(iv) of this section applies only to amounts paid on or after the date of publication of the guidance.

(3) Separate and distinct intangible asset—

(i) *Definition*. The term separate and distinct intangible asset means a property interest of ascertainable and measurable value in money's worth that is subject to protection under applicable State, Federal or foreign law and the possession and control of which is intrinsically capable of being sold, transferred or pledged (ignoring any restrictions imposed on assignability) separate and apart from a trade or business. In addition, for purposes of this section, a fund (or similar account) is treated as a separate and distinct intangible asset of the taxpayer if amounts in the fund (or account) may revert to the taxpayer. The determination of whether a payment creates a separate and distinct intangible asset is made based on all of the facts and circumstances existing during the taxable year in which the payment is made.

(ii) *Creation or termination of contract rights.* Amounts paid to another party to create, originate, enter into, renew or renegotiate an agreement with that party that produces rights or benefits for the taxpayer (and amounts paid to facilitate the creation, origination, enhancement, renewal or renegotiation of such an agreement) are treated as amounts that do not create (or facilitate the creation of) a separate and distinct intangible asset within the meaning of this paragraph (b)(3). Further, amounts paid to another party to terminate (or facilitate the termination of) an agreement with that party are treated as amounts that do not create a separate and distinct intangible asset within the meaning of this paragraph (b)(3). See paragraphs (d)(2), (d)(6), and (d)(7) of this section for rules that specifically require capitalization of amounts paid to create or terminate certain agreements.

(iii) *Amounts paid in performing services.* Amounts paid in performing services under an agreement are treated as amounts that do not create a separate and distinct intangible asset within the meaning of this paragraph (b)(3), regardless of whether the amounts result in the creation of an income stream under the agreement.

(iv) *Creation of computer software.* Except as otherwise provided in the Internal Revenue Code, the regulations thereunder, or other published guidance in the Federal Register or in the Internal Revenue Bulletin (see § 601.601(d)(2)(ii) of this chapter), amounts paid to develop computer software are treated as amounts that do not create a separate and distinct intangible asset within the meaning of this paragraph (b)(3).

(v) *Creation of package design.* Amounts paid to develop a package design are treated as amounts that do not create a separate and distinct intangible asset within the meaning of this paragraph (b)(3). For purposes of this section, the term package design means the specific graphic arrangement or design of shapes, colors, words, pictures, lettering, and other elements on a given product package, or the design of a container with respect to its shape or function.

* * *

(c) Acquired intangibles—

(1) In general. A taxpayer must capitalize amounts paid to another party to acquire any intangible from that party in a purchase or similar transaction. Examples of intangibles within the scope of this paragraph (c) include, but are not limited to, the following (if acquired from another party in a purchase or similar transaction):

(i) An ownership interest in a corporation, partnership, trust, estate, limited liability company, or other entity.

(ii) A debt instrument, deposit, stripped bond, stripped coupon (including a servicing right treated for federal income tax purposes as a stripped coupon), regular interest in a REMIC or FASIT, or any other intangible treated as debt for federal income tax purposes.

(iii) A financial instrument. . . .

(iv) An endowment contract, annuity contract, or insurance contract.

(v) Non-functional currency.

(vi) A lease.

(vii) A patent or copyright.

(viii) A franchise, trademark or tradename (as defined in § 1.197-2(b)(10)).

(ix) An assembled workforce (as defined in § 1.197-2(b)(3)).

(x) Goodwill (as defined in § 1.197-2(b)(1)) or going concern value (as defined in § 1.197-2(b)(2)).

(xi) A customer list.

(xii) A servicing right (for example, a mortgage servicing right that is not treated for Federal income tax purposes as a stripped coupon).

(xiii) A customer-based intangible (as defined in § 1.197-2(b)(6)) or supplier-based intangible (as defined in § 1.197-2(b)(7)).

(xiv) Computer software.

(xv) An agreement providing either party the right to use, possess or sell an intangible described in paragraphs (c)(1)(i) through (v) of this section.

(2) Readily available software. An amount paid to obtain a nonexclusive license for software that is (or has been) readily available to the general public on similar terms and has not been substantially modified (within the meaning of § 1.197-2(c)(4)) is treated for purposes of this paragraph (c) as an amount paid to another party to acquire an intangible from that party in a purchase or similar transaction.

(3) Intangibles acquired from an employee. Amounts paid to an employee to acquire an intangible from that employee are not required to be capitalized under this section if the amounts are includible in the employee's income in connection with the performance of services under section 61 or 83. For purposes of this section, whether an individual is an employee is determined in accordance with the rules contained in section 3401(c) and the regulations thereunder.

(4) Examples. The following examples illustrate the rules of this paragraph (c):

* * *

Example 4. *Customer list*. N corporation, a retailer, sells its products through its catalog and mail order system. N purchases a customer list from R corporation. N pays R $100,000 in exchange for the customer list. The $100,000 paid to R constitutes an amount paid to acquire an intangible from R and must be capitalized.

Example 5. *Goodwill*. Z corporation pays W corporation $10,000,000 to purchase all of the assets of W in a transaction that constitutes an applicable asset acquisition under section 1060(c). Of the $10,000,000 consideration paid in the transaction, $9,000,000 is allocable to tangible assets purchased from W and $1,000,000 is allocable to goodwill. The $1,000,000 allocable to goodwill constitutes an amount paid to W to acquire an intangible from W and must be capitalized.

(d) Created intangibles—

(1) In general. Except as provided in paragraph (f) of this section (relating to the 12-month rule), a taxpayer must capitalize amounts paid to create an intangible described in this paragraph (d). The determination of whether an amount is paid to create an intangible described in this paragraph (d) is to be made based on all of the facts and circumstances, disregarding distinctions between the labels used in this paragraph (d) to describe the intangible and the labels used by the taxpayer and other parties to the transaction.

* * *

(3) Prepaid expenses—

(i) *In general*. A taxpayer must capitalize prepaid expenses.

(ii) *Examples*. The following examples illustrate the rules of this paragraph (d)(3):

Example 1. *Prepaid insurance*. N corporation, an accrual method taxpayer, pays $10,000 to an insurer to obtain three years of coverage under a property and casualty insurance policy. The $10,000 is a prepaid expense and must be capitalized under this paragraph (d)(3). Paragraph (d)(2) of this section does not apply to the payment because the policy has no cash value.

Example 2. *Prepaid rent*. X corporation, a cash method taxpayer, enters into a 24-month lease of office space. At the time of the lease signing, X prepays $240,000. No other amounts are due under the lease. The $240,000 is a prepaid expense and must be capitalized under this paragraph (d)(3).

(4) Certain memberships and privileges—

(i) *In general.* A taxpayer must capitalize amounts paid to an organization to obtain, renew, renegotiate, or upgrade a membership or privilege from that organization. A taxpayer is not required to capitalize under this paragraph (d)(4) an amount paid to obtain, renew, renegotiate or upgrade certification of the taxpayer's products, services, or business processes.

(ii) *Examples.* The following examples illustrate the rules of this paragraph (d)(4):

Example 1. *Hospital privilege.* B, a physician, pays $10,000 to Y corporation to obtain lifetime staff privileges at a hospital operated by Y. B must capitalize the $10,000 payment under this paragraph (d)(4).

Example 2. *Initiation fee.* X corporation pays a $50,000 initiation fee to obtain membership in a trade association. X must capitalize the $50,000 payment under this paragraph (d)(4).

Example 3. *Product rating.* V corporation, an automobile manufacturer, pays W corporation, a national quality ratings association, $100,000 to conduct a study and provide a rating of the quality and safety of a line of V's automobiles. V's payment is an amount paid to obtain a certification of V's product and is not required to be capitalized under this paragraph (d)(4).

Example 4. *Business process certification.* Z corporation, a manufacturer, seeks to obtain a certification that its quality control standards meet a series of international standards known as ISO 9000. Z pays $50,000 to an independent registrar to obtain a certification from the registrar that Z's quality management system conforms to the ISO 9000 standard. Z's payment is an amount paid to obtain a certification of Z's business processes and is not required to be capitalized under this paragraph (d)(4).

(5) Certain rights obtained from a governmental agency—

(i) *In general.* A taxpayer must capitalize amounts paid to a governmental agency to obtain, renew, renegotiate, or upgrade its rights under a trademark, trade name, copyright, license, permit, franchise, or other similar right granted by that governmental agency.

(ii) *Examples*. The following examples illustrate the rules of this paragraph (d)(5):

Example 1. *Business license*. X corporation pays $15,000 to state Y to obtain a business license that is valid indefinitely. Under this paragraph (d)(5), the amount paid to state Y is an amount paid to a government agency for a right granted by that agency. Accordingly, X must capitalize the $15,000 payment.

Example 2. *Bar admission*. A, an individual, pays $1,000 to an agency of state Z to obtain a license to practice law in state Z that is valid indefinitely, provided A adheres to the requirements governing the practice of law in state Z. Under this paragraph (d)(5), the amount paid to state Z is an amount paid to a government agency for a right granted by that agency. Accordingly, A must capitalize the $1,000 payment.

(6) Certain contract rights—

(i) *In general*. Except as otherwise provided in this paragraph (d)(6), a taxpayer must capitalize amounts paid to another party to create, originate, enter into, renew or renegotiate with that party—

(A) An agreement providing the taxpayer the right to use tangible or intangible property or the right to be compensated for the use of tangible or intangible property;

(B) An agreement providing the taxpayer the right to provide or to receive services (or the right to be compensated for services regardless of whether the taxpayer provides such services);

(C) A covenant not to compete or an agreement having substantially the same effect as a covenant not to compete (except, in the case of an agreement that requires the performance of services, to the extent that the amount represents reasonable compensation for services actually rendered);

(D) An agreement not to acquire additional ownership interests in the taxpayer; or

(E) An agreement providing the taxpayer (as the covered party) with an annuity, an endowment, or insurance coverage.

(ii) *Amounts paid to create, originate, enter into, renew or renegotiate*. An amount paid to another party is not paid to create, originate, enter into, renew or renegotiate an agreement with that party if the payment is made with the mere hope or expectation of developing or maintaining a business relationship with that party and is not contingent on the origination, renewal or renegotiation of an agreement with that party.

(iii) *Renegotiate*. A taxpayer is treated as renegotiating an agreement if the terms of the agreement are modified. A taxpayer also is treated as renegotiating an agreement if the taxpayer enters into a new agreement with the same party (or substantially the same parties) to a terminated agreement, the taxpayer could not cancel the terminated agreement without the consent of the other party (or parties), and the other party (or parties) would not have consented to the cancellation unless the taxpayer entered into the new agreement. A taxpayer is treated as unable to cancel an agreement without the consent of the other party (or parties) if, under the terms of the agreement, the taxpayer is subject to a termination penalty and the other party (or parties) to the agreement modifies the terms of the penalty.

(iv) *Right*. An agreement does not provide the taxpayer a right to use property or to provide or receive services if the agreement may be terminated at will by the other party (or parties) to the agreement before the end of the period prescribed by paragraph (f)(1) of this section. An agreement is not terminable at will if the other party (or parties) to the agreement is economically compelled not to terminate the agreement until the end of the period prescribed by paragraph (f)(1) of this section. All of the facts and circumstances will be considered in determining whether the other party (or parties) to an agreement is economically compelled not to terminate the agreement. An agreement also does not provide the taxpayer the right to provide services if the agreement merely provides that the taxpayer will stand ready to provide services if requested, but places no obligation on another person to request or pay for the taxpayer's services.

(v) *De minimis amounts*. A taxpayer is not required to capitalize amounts paid to another party (or parties) to create, originate, enter into, renew or renegotiate with that party (or those parties) an agreement described in paragraph (d)(6)(i) of this section if the aggregate of all amounts paid to that party (or those parties) with respect to the agreement does not exceed $5,000. If the aggregate of all amounts paid to the other party (or parties) with respect to that agreement exceeds $5,000, then all amounts must be capitalized. For purposes of this paragraph (d)(6), an amount paid in the form of property is valued at its fair market value at the time of the payment. In general, a taxpayer must determine whether the rules of this paragraph (d)(6)(v) apply by accounting for the specific amounts paid with respect to each agreement. However, a taxpayer that reasonably expects to create, originate, enter into, renew or renegotiate at least 25 similar agreements during the taxable year may establish a pool of agreements for purposes of determining the amounts paid with respect to the agreements in the pool. Under this pooling method, the amount paid with respect to each agreement included in the pool is equal to the average amount paid with respect to all agreements included in the pool. A taxpayer computes the average amount paid with respect to all agreements included in the pool by dividing the sum of all amounts paid with respect to all agreements included in the pool by the number of agreements included in the pool. See paragraph (h) of this section for additional rules relating to pooling.

* * *

(vii) *Examples.* The following examples illustrate the rules of this paragraph (d)(6):

* * *

Example 6. *Covenant not to compete.* R corporation enters into an agreement with A, an individual, that prohibits A from competing with R for a period of three years. To encourage A to enter into the agreement, R agrees to pay A $100,000 upon the signing of the agreement. R's payment is an amount paid to another party to enter into a covenant not to compete. Because the $100,000 payment exceeds $5,000, no portion of the amount paid to A is de minimis for purposes of paragraph (d)(6)(v) of this section. Under paragraph (d)(6)(i)(C) of this section, R must capitalize the entire $100,000 payment.

* * *

(7) Certain contract terminations—

(i) *In general.* A taxpayer must capitalize amounts paid to another party to terminate—

(A) A lease of real or tangible personal property between the taxpayer (as lessor) and that party (as lessee);

(B) An agreement that grants that party the exclusive right to acquire or use the taxpayer's property or services or to conduct the taxpayer's business (other than an intangible described in paragraph (c)(1)(i) through (iv) of this section or a financial interest described in paragraph (d)(2) of this section); or

(C) An agreement that prohibits the taxpayer from competing with that party or from acquiring property or services from a competitor of that party.

* * *

(iii) *Examples.* The following examples illustrate the rules of this paragraph (d)(7):

* * *

Example 3. *Termination of covenant not to compete.* On February 1, 2005, Y corporation enters into a covenant not to compete with Z corporation that prohibits Y from competing with Z in city V for a period of 5 years. On January 31, 2007, Y pays Z $1,000,000 in exchange for Z's agreement to terminate the covenant not to compete. Y's payment to terminate the covenant not to compete with Z constitutes a payment to terminate an agreement that prohibits Y from competing with Z, as described in paragraph (d)(7)(i)(C) of this section. Accordingly, Y must capitalize its $1,000,000 payment to Z.

* * *

(9) Defense or perfection of title to intangible property—

(i) *In general.* A taxpayer must capitalize amounts paid to another party to defend or perfect title to intangible property if that other party challenges the taxpayer's title to the intangible property.

(ii) *Certain break-up fees.* Paragraph (d)(9)(i) of this section does not apply to the termination of a transaction described in § 1.263(a)-5(a) (relating to an acquisition of a trade or business, a change in the capital structure of a business entity, and certain other transactions). See § 1.263(a)-5 for rules governing the treatment of amounts paid to terminate a transaction to which that section applies. Paragraph (d)(9)(i) of this section also does not apply to an amount paid to another party to terminate an agreement that grants that party the right to purchase the taxpayer's intangible property.

(iii) *Example.* The following example illustrates the rules of this paragraph (d)(9):

Example. *Defense of title.* R corporation claims to own an exclusive patent on a particular technology. U corporation brings a lawsuit against R, claiming that U is the true owner of the patent and that R stole the technology from U. The sole issue in the suit involves the validity of R's patent. R chooses to settle the suit by paying U $100,000 in exchange for U's release of all future claim to the patent. R's payment to U is an amount paid to defend or perfect title to intangible property under paragraph (d)(9) of this section and must be capitalized.

(e) Transaction costs—

(1) Scope of facilitate—

(i) *In general.* Except as otherwise provided in this section, an amount is paid to facilitate the acquisition or creation of an intangible (the transaction) if the amount is paid in the process of investigating or otherwise pursuing the transaction. Whether an amount is paid in the process of investigating or otherwise pursuing the transaction is determined based on all of the facts and circumstances. In determining whether an amount is paid to facilitate a transaction, the fact that the amount would (or would not) have been paid but for the transaction is relevant, but is not determinative. An amount paid to determine the value or price of an intangible is an amount paid in the process of investigating or otherwise pursuing the transaction.

(ii) *Treatment of termination payments.* An amount paid to terminate (or facilitate the termination of) an existing agreement does not facilitate the acquisition or creation of another agreement under this section. See paragraph (d)(6)(iii) of this section for the treatment of termination fees paid to the other party (or parties) of a renegotiated agreement.

(iii) *Special rule for contracts.* An amount is treated as not paid in the process of investigating or otherwise pursuing the creation of an agreement described in paragraph (d)(2) or (d)(6) of this section if the amount relates to activities performed before the earlier of the date the taxpayer begins preparing its bid for the agreement or the date the taxpayer begins discussing or negotiating the agreement with another party to the agreement.

(iv) *Borrowing costs.* An amount paid to facilitate a borrowing does not facilitate an acquisition or creation of an intangible described in paragraphs (b)(1)(i) through (iv) of this section. See §§ 1.263(a)-5 and 1.446-5 for the treatment of an amount paid to facilitate a borrowing.

* * *

(2) Coordination with paragraph (d) of this section. In the case of an amount paid to facilitate the creation of an intangible described in paragraph (d) of this section, the provisions of this paragraph (e) apply regardless of whether a payment described in paragraph (d) is made.

(3) Transaction. For purposes of this section, the term transaction means all of the factual elements comprising an acquisition or creation of an intangible and includes a series of steps carried out as part of a single plan. Thus, a transaction can involve more than one invoice and more than one intangible. For example, a purchase of intangibles under one purchase agreement constitutes a single transaction, notwithstanding the fact that the acquisition involves multiple intangibles and the amounts paid to facilitate the acquisition are capable of being allocated among the various intangibles acquired.

(4) Simplifying conventions—

(i) *In general.* For purposes of this section, employee compensation (within the meaning of paragraph (e)(4)(ii) of this section), overhead, and de minimis costs (within the meaning of paragraph (e)(4)(iii) of this section) are treated as amounts that do not facilitate the acquisition or creation of an intangible.

(ii) *Employee compensation—*

(A) *In general.* The term employee compensation means compensation (including salary, bonuses and commissions) paid to an employee of the taxpayer. For purposes of this section, whether an individual is an employee is determined in accordance with the rules contained in section 3401(c) and the regulations thereunder.

(B) *Certain amounts treated as employee compensation.* For purposes of this section, a guaranteed payment to a partner in a partnership is treated as employee compensation. For purposes of this section, annual compensation paid to a director of a corporation is treated as employee compensation. For example, an amount paid to a director of a corporation for attendance at a regular meeting of the board of directors (or committee thereof) is treated as employee compensation for purposes of this section. However, an amount paid to a director for attendance at a special meeting of the board of directors (or committee thereof) is not treated as employee compensation. An amount paid to a person that is not an employee of the taxpayer (including the employer of the individual who performs the services) is treated as employee compensation for purposes of this section only if the amount is paid for secretarial, clerical, or similar administrative support services. In the case of an affiliated group of corporations filing a consolidated Federal income tax return, a payment by one member of the group to a second member of the group for services performed by an employee of the second member is treated as employee compensation if the services provided by the employee are provided at a time during which both members are affiliated.

(iii) *De minimis costs*—

(A) *In general.* Except as provided in paragraph (e)(4)(iii)(B) of this section, the term de minimis costs means amounts (other than employee compensation and overhead) paid in the process of investigating or otherwise pursuing a transaction if, in the aggregate, the amounts do not exceed $5,000 (or such greater amount as may be set forth in published guidance). If the amounts exceed $5,000 (or such greater amount as may be set forth in published guidance), none of the amounts are de minimis costs within the meaning of this paragraph (e)(4)(iii)(A). For purposes of this paragraph (e)(4)(iii), an amount paid in the form of property is valued at its fair market value at the time of the payment. In determining the amount of transaction costs paid in the process of investigating or otherwise pursuing a transaction, a taxpayer generally must account for the specific costs paid with respect to each transaction. However, a taxpayer that reasonably expects to enter into at least 25 similar transactions during the taxable year may establish a pool of similar transactions for purposes of determining the amount of transaction costs paid in the process of investigating or otherwise pursuing the transactions in the pool. Under this pooling method, the amount of transaction costs paid in the process of investigating or otherwise pursuing each transaction included in the pool is equal to the average transaction costs paid in the process of investigating or otherwise pursuing all transactions included in the pool. A taxpayer computes the average transaction costs paid in the process of investigating or otherwise pursuing all transactions included in the pool by dividing the sum of all transaction costs paid in the process of investigating or otherwise pursuing all transactions included in the pool by the number of transactions included in the pool. See paragraph (h) of this section for additional rules relating to pooling.

(B) *Treatment of commissions.* The term de minimis costs does not include commissions paid to facilitate the acquisition of an intangible described in paragraphs (c)(1)(i) through (v) of this section or to facilitate the creation, origination, entrance into, renewal or renegotiation of an intangible described in paragraph (d)(2)(i) of this section.

(iv) *Election to capitalize.* A taxpayer may elect to treat employee compensation, overhead, or de minimis costs paid in the process of investigating or otherwise pursuing a transaction as amounts that facilitate the transaction. The election is made separately for each transaction and applies to employee compensation, overhead, or de minimis costs, or to any combination thereof. For example, a taxpayer may elect to treat overhead and de minimis costs, but not employee compensation, as amounts that facilitate the transaction. A taxpayer makes the election by treating the amounts to which the election applies as amounts that facilitate the transaction in the taxpayer's timely filed original Federal income tax return (including extensions) for the taxable year during which the amounts are paid. In the case of an affiliated group of corporations filing a consolidated return, the election is made separately with respect to each member of the group, and not with respect to the group as a whole. In the case of an S corporation or partnership, the election is made by the S corporation or by the partnership, and not by the shareholders or partners. An election made under this paragraph (e)(4)(iv) is revocable with respect to each taxable year for which made only with the consent of the Commissioner.

(5) *Examples*. The following examples illustrate the rules of this paragraph (e):

* * *

Example 6. *Costs that do not facilitate*. X corporation brings a legal action against Y corporation to recover lost profits resulting from Y's alleged infringement of X's copyright. Y does not challenge X's copyright, but argues that it did not infringe upon X's copyright. X pays its outside counsel $25,000 for legal services rendered in pursuing the suit against Y. Because X's title to its copyright is not in question, X's action against Y does not involve X's defense or perfection of title to intangible property. Thus, the amount paid to outside counsel does not facilitate the creation of an intangible described in paragraph (d)(9) of this section. Accordingly, X is not required to capitalize its $25,000 payment under this section.

* * *

(f) 12-month rule—

(1) In general. Except as otherwise provided in this paragraph (f), a taxpayer is not required to capitalize under this section amounts paid to create (or to facilitate the creation of) any right or benefit for the taxpayer that does not extend beyond the earlier of—

(i) 12 months after the first date on which the taxpayer realizes the right or benefit; or

(ii) The end of the taxable year following the taxable year in which the payment is made.

* * *

(5) Rights subject to renewal—

(i) *In general.* For purposes of paragraph (f)(1) of this section, the duration of a right includes any renewal period if all of the facts and circumstances in existence during the taxable year in which the right is created indicate a reasonable expectancy of renewal.

* * *

(8) **Examples**. The rules of this paragraph (f) are illustrated by the following examples, in which it is assumed (unless otherwise stated) that the taxpayer is a calendar year, accrual method taxpayer that does not have a short taxable year in any taxable year and has not made an election under paragraph (f)(7) of this section:

* * *

Example 5. *License.* (i) On July 1, 2005, R corporation pays $10,000 to state X to obtain a license to operate a business in state X for a period of 5 years. The terms of the license require R to pay state X an annual fee of $500 due on July 1, 2005, and each of the succeeding four years. R pays the $500 fee on July 1 as required by the license.

(ii) R's payment of $10,000 is an amount paid to a governmental agency for a license granted by that agency to which paragraph (d)(5) of this section applies. Because R's payment creates rights or benefits for R that extend beyond 12 months after the first date on which R realizes the rights or benefits attributable to the payment and beyond the end of 2006 (the taxable year following the taxable year in which the payment is made), the rules of this paragraph (f) do not apply to R's payment. Accordingly, R must capitalize the $10,000 payment.

(iii) R's payment of each $500 annual fee is a prepaid expense described in paragraph (d)(3) of this section. R is not required to capitalize the $500 fee in each taxable year. The rules of this paragraph (f) apply to each such payment because each payment provides a right or benefit to R that does not extend beyond 12 months after the first date on which R realizes the rights or benefits attributable to the payment and does not extend beyond the end of the taxable year following the taxable year in which the payment is made.

* * *

Treas. Reg. § 1.367(d)-1T. Transfers of intangible property to foreign corporations (temporary).

(a) Purpose and scope. This section provides rules under section 367(d) concerning transfers of intangible property by U.S. persons to foreign corporations pursuant to section 351 or 361. Paragraph (b) of this section specifies the transfers that are subject to section 367(d) and the rules of this section, while paragraph (c) provides rules concerning the consequences of such a transfer. In general, the U.S. transferor will be treated as receiving annual payments contingent on productivity or use of the transferred property, over the useful life of the property (regardless of whether such payments are in fact made by the transferee). . . .

(b) Intangible property subject to section 367(d). Section 367(d) and the rules of this section shall apply to the transfer of any intangible property, as defined in § 1.367(a)-1T(d)(5)(i). However, section 367(d) and the rules of this section shall not apply to the transfer of foreign goodwill or going concern value, as defined in § 1.367(a)-1T(d)(5)(iii). . . . Transfers of intangible property to foreign corporations pursuant to section 351 or 361 are subject to the rules of this section regardless of whether the property is to be used in the United States, in connection with goods to be sold or consumed in the United States, or in connection with a trade or business outside the United States.

(c) Deemed payments upon transfer of intangible property to foreign corporation—

(1) In general. If a U.S. person transfers intangible property that is subject to section 367(d) and the rules of this section to a foreign corporation in an exchange described in section 351 or 361, then such person shall be treated as having transferred that property in exchange for annual payments contingent on the productivity or use of the property. Such person shall, over the useful life of the property, annually include in gross income an amount that represents an appropriate arms-length charge for the use of the property. The appropriate charge shall be determined in accordance with the provisions of section 482 and regulations thereunder. See § 1.482-2(d). The amount of the deemed payment thus calculated shall be reduced by any royalty or other periodic payment made or accrued by the transferee to an unrelated person during that taxable year for the right to use the intangible property. Amounts so included in the transferor's income shall be treated as ordinary income from sources within the United States. For purposes of computing estimated tax payments, deemed payments under this paragraph (c) shall be treated as received by the transferor on the last day of its taxable year.

* * *

Treas. Reg. § 15a.453-1. Installment method reporting for sales of real property and casual sales of personal property.

(a) In general. Unless the taxpayer otherwise elects in the manner prescribed in paragraph (d)(3) of this section, income from a sale of real property or a casual sale of personal property, where any payment is to be received in a taxable year after the year of sale, is to be reported on the installment method.

(b) Installment sale defined—

(1) In general. The term "installment sale" means a disposition of property (except as provided in paragraph (b)(4) of this section) where at least one payment is to be received after the close of the taxable year in which the disposition occurs. The term "installment sale" includes dispositions from which payment is to be received in a lump sum in a taxable year subsequent to the year of sale. For purposes of this paragraph, the taxable year in which payments are to be received is to be determined without regard to section 453(e) (relating to related party sales), section (f)(3) (relating to the definition of a "payment") and section (g) [26 USCS § 453(e), (f)(3) and (g)] (relating to sales of depreciable property to a spouse or 80-percent-owned entity).

(2) Installment method defined—

(i) *In general.* Under the installment method, the amount of any payment which is income to the taxpayer is that portion of the installment payment received in that year which the gross profit realized or to be realized bears to the total contract price (the "gross profit ratio"). See paragraph (c) of this section for rules describing installment method reporting of contingent payment sales.

(ii) *Selling price defined.* The term "selling price" means the gross selling price without reduction to reflect any existing mortgage or other encumbrance on the property (whether assumed or taken subject to by the buyer) and, for installment sales in taxable years ending after October 19, 1980, without reduction to reflect any selling expenses. Neither interest, whether stated or unstated, nor original issue discount is considered to be a part of the selling price. See paragraph (c) of this section for rules describing installment method reporting of contingent payment sales.

(iii) *Contract price defined.* The term "contract price" means the total contract price equal to selling price reduced by that portion of any qualifying indebtedness (as defined in paragraph (b)(2)(iv) of this section), assumed or taken subject to by the buyer, which does not exceed the seller's basis in the property (adjusted, for installment sales in taxable years ending after October 19, 1980, to reflect commissions and other selling expenses as provided in paragraph (b)(2)(v) of this section). See paragraph (c) of this section for rules describing installment method reporting of contingent payment sales.

(iv) *Qualifying indebtedness*. The term "qualifying indebtedness" means a mortgage or other indebtedness encumbering the property and indebtedness, not secured by the property but incurred or assumed by the purchaser incident to the purchaser's acquisition, holding, or operation in the ordinary course of business or investment, of the property. The term "qualifying indebtedness" does not include an obligation of the taxpayer incurred incident to the disposition of the property (e.g., legal fees relating to the taxpayer's sale of the property) or an obligation functionally unrelated to the acquisition, holding, or operating of the property (e.g., the taxpayer's medical bill). Any obligation created subsequent to the taxpayer's acquisition of the property and incurred or assumed by the taxpayer or placed as an encumbrance on the property in contemplation of disposition of the property is not qualifying indebtedness if the arrangement results in accelerating recovery of the taxpayer's basis in the installment sale.

(v) *Gross profit defined.* The term "gross profit" means the selling price less the adjusted basis as defined in section 1011 and the regulations thereunder. For sales in taxable years ending after October 19, 1980, in the case of sales of real property by a person other than a dealer and casual sales of personal property, commissions and other selling expenses shall be added to basis for purposes of determining the proportion of payments which is gross profit attributable to the disposition. Such additions to basis will not be deemed to affect the taxpayer's holding period in the transferred property.

* * *

(c) Contingent payment sales—

(1) In general. Unless the taxpayer otherwise elects in the manner prescribed in paragraph (d)(3) of this section, contingent payment sales are to be reported on the installment method. As used in this section, the term "contingent payment sale" means a sale or other disposition of property in which the aggregate selling price cannot be determined by the close of the taxable year in which such sale or other disposition occurs.

The term "contingent payment sale" does not include transactions with respect to which the installment obligation represents, under applicable principles of tax law, a retained interest in the property which is the subject of the transaction, an interest in a joint venture or a partnership, an equity interest in a corporation or similar transactions, regardless of the existence of a stated maximum selling price or a fixed payment term. See paragraph (c)(8) of this section, describing the extent to which the regulations under section 385 apply to the determination of whether an installment obligation represents an equity interest in a corporation.

This paragraph prescribes the rules to be applied in allocating the taxpayer's basis (including selling expenses except for selling expenses of dealers in real estate) to payments received and to be received in a contingent payment sale. The rules are designed appropriately to distinguish contingent payment sales for which a maximum selling price is determinable, sales for which a maximum selling price is not determinable but the time over which payments will be received is determinable, and sales for which neither a maximum selling price nor a definite payment term is determinable. In addition, rules are prescribed under which, in appropriate circumstances, the taxpayer will be permitted to recover basis under an income forecast computation.

(2) Stated maximum selling price—

(i) *In general.*

(A) contingent payment sale will be treated as having a stated maximum selling price if, under the terms of the agreement, the maximum amount of sale proceeds that may be received by the taxpayer can be determined as of the end of the taxable year in which the sale or other disposition occurs. The stated maximum selling price shall be determined by assuming that all of the contingencies contemplated by the agreement are met or otherwise resolved in a manner that will maximize the selling price and accelerate payments to the earliest date or dates permitted under the agreement. Except as provided in paragraph (c)(2)(ii) and (7) of this section (relating to certain payment recomputations), the taxpayer's basis shall be allocated to payments received and to be received under a stated maximum selling price agreement by treating the stated maximum selling price as the selling price for purposes of paragraph (b) of this section. The stated maximum selling price, as initially determined, shall thereafter be treated as the selling price unless and until that maximum amount is reduced, whether pursuant to the terms of the original agreement, by subsequent amendment, by application of the payment recharacterization rule (discribed in paragraph (c)(2)(ii) of this section), or by a subsequent supervening event such as bankruptcy of the obligor. When the maximum amount is subsequently reduced, the gross profit ratio will be recomputed with respect to payments received in or after the taxable year in which an event requiring reduction occurs. If, however, application of the foregoing rules in a particular case would substantially and inappropriately accelerate or defer recovery of the taxpayer's basis, a special rule will apply. See paragraph (c)(7) of this section.

(B) The following examples illustrate the provisions of paragraph (c)(2)(i) of this section. In each example, it is assumed that application of the rules illustrated will not substantially and inappropriately defer or accelerate recovery of the taxpayer's basis.

Example (1). A sells all of the stock of X corporation to B for $100,000 payable at closing plus an amount equal to 5% of the net profits of X for each of the next nine years, the contingent payments to be made annually together with adequate stated interest. The agreement provides that the maximum amount A may receive, inclusive of the $100,000 down payment but exclusive of interest, shall be $2,000,000. A's basis in the stock of X inclusive of selling expenses, is $200,000. Selling price and contract price are considered to be $2,000,000. Gross profit is $1,800,000, and the gross profit ratio is 9/10 ($1,800,000/$2,000,000). Accordingly, of the $100,000 received by A in the year of sale, $90,000 is reportable as gain attributable to the sale and $10,000 is recovery of basis.

Example (2). C owns Blackacre which is encumbered by a long-standing mortgage of $100,000. On January 15, 1981, C sells Blackacre to D under the following payment arrangement: $100,000 in cash on closing; nine equal annual installment payments of $100,000 commencing January 15, 1982; and nine annual payments (the first to be made on March 30, 1982) equal to 5% of the gross annual rental receipts from Blackacre generated during the preceding calendar year. The agreement provides that each deferred payment shall be accompanied by a payment of interest calculated at the rate of 12% per annum and that the maximum amount payable to C under the agreement

> (exclusive of interest) shall be $2,100,000. The agreement also specifies that D will assume the long-standing mortgage. C's basis (inclusive of selling expenses) in Blackacre is $300,000. Accordingly, selling price is $2,100,000 and contract price is $2,000,000 (selling price of $2,100,000 less the $100,000 mortgage). The gross profit ratio is 9/10 (gross profit of $1,800,000 divided by $2,000,000 contract price). Of the $100,000 cash payment received by C in 1981, $90,000 is gain attributable to the sale of Blackacre and $10,000 is recovery of basis.

* * *

(3) Fixed period—

(i) *In general.* When a stated maximum selling price cannot be determined as of the close of the taxable year in which the sale or other disposition occurs, but the maximum period over which payments may be received under the contingent sale price agreement is fixed, the taxpayer's basis (inclusive of selling expenses) shall be allocated to the taxable years in which payment may be received under the agreement in equal annual increments. In making the allocation it is not relevant whether the buyer is required to pay adequate stated interest. However, if the terms of the agreement incorporate an arithmetic component that is not identical for all taxable years, basis shall be allocated among the taxable years to accord with that component unless, taking into account all of the payment terms of the agreement, it is inappropriate to presume that payments under the contract are likely to accord with the variable component. If in any taxable year no payment is received or the amount of payment received (exclusive of interest) is less than the basis allocated to that taxable year, no loss shall be allowed unless the taxable year is the final payment year under the agreement or unless it is otherwise determined in accordance with the rules generally applicable to worthless debts that the future payment obligation under the agreement has become worthless. When no loss is allowed, the unrecovered portion of basis allocated to the taxable year shall be carried forward to the next succeeding taxable year. If application of the foregoing rules to a particular case would substantially and inappropriately defer or accelerate recovery of the taxpayer's basis, a special rule will apply. See paragraph (c)(7) of this section.

* * *

(4) Neither stated maximum selling price nor fixed period. If the agreement neither specifies a maximum selling price nor limits payments to a fixed period, a question arises whether a sale realistically has occurred or whether, in economic effect, payments received under the agreement are in the nature of rent or royalty income. Arrangements of this sort will be closely scrutinized. If, taking into account all of the pertinent facts, including the nature of the property, the arrangement is determined to qualify as a sale, the taxpayer's basis (including selling expenses) shall be recovered in equal annual increments over a period of 15 years commencing with the date of sale. However, if in any taxable year no payment is received or the amount of payment received (exclusive of interest) is less than basis allocated to the year, no loss shall be allowed unless it is otherwise determined in accordance with the timing rules generally applicable to worthless debts that the future payment obligation under the agreement has become worthless; instead the excess basis shall be reallocated in level amounts over the balance of the 15 year term. Any basis not recovered at the end of the 15th year shall be carried forward to the next succeeding year, and to the extent unrecovered thereafter shall be carried forward from year to year until all basis has been recovered or the future payment obligation is determined to be worthless. The general rule requiring initial level allocation of basis over 15 years shall not apply if the taxpayer can establish to the satisfaction of the Internal Revenue Service that application of the general rule would substantially and inappropriately defer recovery of the taxpayer's basis. See paragraph (c)(7) of this section. If the Service determines that initially allocating basis in level amounts over the first 15 years will substantially and inappropriately accelerate recovery of the taxpayer's basis in early years of that 15-year term, the Service may require that basis be reallocated within the 15-year term but the Service will not require that basis initially be allocated over more than 15 years. See paragraph (c)(7) of this section.

* * *

(d) Election not to report an installment sale on the installment method—

(1) In general. An installment sale is to be reported on the installment method unless the taxpayer elects otherwise in accordance with the rules set forth in paragraph (d)(3) of this section.

(2) Treatment of an installment sale when a taxpayer elects not to report on the installment method—

(i) *In general.* A taxpayer who elects not to report an installment sale on the installment method must recognize gain on the sale in accordance with the taxpayer's method of accounting. The fair market value of an installment obligation shall be determined in accordance with paragraph (d)(2) (ii) and

(iii) of this section. In making such determination, any provision of contract or local law restricting the transferability of the installment obligation shall be disregarded. Receipt of an installment obligation shall be treated as a receipt of property, in an amount equal to the fair market value of the installment obligation, whether or not such obligation is the equivalent of cash. An installment obligation is considered to be property and is subject to valuation, as provided in paragraph (d)(2) (ii) and (iii) of this section, without regard to whether the obligation is embodied in a note, an executory contract, or any other instrument, or is an oral promise enforceable under local law.

* * *

(iii) *Contingent payment obligations.* Any installment obligation which is not a fixed amount obligation (as defined in paragraph (d)(2)(ii) of this section) is a contingent payment obligation. If an installment obligation contains both a fixed amount component and a contingent payment component, the fixed amount component shall be treated under the rules of paragraph (d)(2)(ii) of this section and the contingent amount component shall be treated under the rules of this (iii). The fair market value of a contingent payment obligation shall be determined by disregarding any restrictions on transfer imposed by agreement or under local law. The fair market value of a contingent payment obligation may be ascertained from, and in no event shall be considered to be less than, the fair market value of the property sold (less the amount of any other consideration received in the sale). Only in those rare and extraordinary cases involving sales for a contingent payment obligation in which the fair market value of the obligation (determinable under the preceding sentences) cannot reasonably be ascertained will the taxpayer be entitled to assert that the transaction is "open." Any such transaction will be carefully scrutinized to determine whether a sale in fact has taken place. A taxpayer using the cash receipts and disbursements method of accounting must report as an amount realized in the year of sale the fair market value of the contingent payment obligation. A taxpayer using the accrual method of accounting must report an amount realized in the year of sale determined in accordance with that method of accounting, but in no event less than the fair market value of the contingent payment obligation.

* * *

Treas. Reg. § 1.482-1. Allocation of income and deductions among taxpayers.

(a) In general—

(1) Purpose and scope. The purpose of section 482 is to ensure that taxpayers clearly reflect income attributable to controlled transactions and to prevent the avoidance of taxes with respect to such transactions. Section 482 places a controlled taxpayer on a tax parity with an uncontrolled taxpayer by determining the true taxable income of the controlled taxpayer. This section sets forth general principles and guidelines to be followed under section 482. . . .

(2) Authority to make allocations. The district director may make allocations between or among the members of a controlled group if a controlled taxpayer has not reported its true taxable income. In such case, the district director may allocate income, deductions, credits, allowances, basis, or any other item or element affecting taxable income (referred to as allocations). The appropriate allocation may take the form of an increase or decrease in any relevant amount.

* * *

(b) Arm's length standard—

(1) In general. In determining the true taxable income of a controlled taxpayer, the standard to be applied in every case is that of a taxpayer dealing at arm's length with an uncontrolled taxpayer. A controlled transaction meets the arm's length standard if the results of the transaction are consistent with the results that would have been realized if uncontrolled taxpayers had engaged in the same transaction under the same circumstances (arm's length result). However, because identical transactions can rarely be located, whether a transaction produces an arm's length result generally will be determined by reference to the results of comparable transactions under comparable circumstances. . . .

* * *

Treas. Reg. § 1.482-4. Methods to determine taxable income in connection with a transfer of intangible property.

(a) In general. The arm's length amount charged in a controlled transfer of intangible property must be determined under one of the four methods listed in this paragraph (a). Each of the methods must be applied in accordance with all of the provisions of § 1.482-1. . . . The arm's length consideration for the transfer of an intangible determined under this section must be commensurate with the income attributable to the intangible. See § 1.482-4(f)(2) (Periodic adjustments). The available methods are—

(1) The comparable uncontrolled transaction method, described in paragraph (c) of this section;

(2) The comparable profits method, described in § 1.482-5;

(3) The profit split method, described in § 1.482-6; and

(4) Unspecified methods described in paragraph (d) of this section.

(b) Definition of intangible. For purposes of section 482, an intangible is an asset that comprises any of the following items and has substantial value independent of the services of any individual—

(1) Patents, inventions, formulae, processes, designs, patterns, or know-how;

(2) Copyrights and literary, musical, or artistic compositions;

(3) Trademarks, trade names, or brand names;

(4) Franchises, licenses, or contracts;

(5) Methods, programs, systems, procedures, campaigns, surveys, studies, forecasts, estimates, customer lists, or technical data; and

(6) Other similar items. For purposes of section 482, an item is considered similar to those listed in paragraph (b)(1) through (5) of this section if it derives its value not from its physical attributes but from its intellectual content or other intangible properties.

(c) Comparable uncontrolled transaction method—

(1) In general. The comparable uncontrolled transaction method evaluates whether the amount charged for a controlled transfer of intangible property was arm's length by reference to the amount charged in a comparable uncontrolled transaction. The amount determined under this method may be adjusted as required by paragraph (f)(2) of this section (Periodic adjustments).

(2) Comparability and reliability considerations—

(i) *In general.* Whether results derived from applications of this method are the most reliable measure of an arm's length result is determined using the factors described under the best method rule in § 1.482-1(c). The application of these factors under the comparable uncontrolled transaction method is discussed in paragraphs (c)(2)(ii), (iii), and (iv) of this section.

(ii) *Reliability.* If an uncontrolled transaction involves the transfer of the same intangible under the same, or substantially the same, circumstances as the controlled transaction, the results derived from applying the comparable uncontrolled transaction method will generally be the most direct and reliable measure of the arm's length result for the controlled transfer of an intangible. Circumstances between the controlled and uncontrolled transactions will be considered substantially the same if there are at most only minor differences that have a definite and reasonably ascertainable effect on the amount charged and for which appropriate adjustments are made. If such uncontrolled transactions cannot be identified, uncontrolled transactions that involve the transfer of comparable intangibles under comparable circumstances may be used to apply this method, but the reliability of the analysis will be reduced.

(iii) *Comparability*—

(A) *In general.* The degree of comparability between controlled and uncontrolled transactions is determined by applying the comparability provisions of § 1.482-1(d). Although all of the factors described in § 1.482-1(d)(3) must be considered, specific factors may be particularly relevant to this method. In particular, the application of this method requires that the controlled and uncontrolled transactions involve either the same intangible property or comparable intangible property, as defined in paragraph (c)(2)(iii)(B)(1) of this section. In addition, because differences in contractual terms, or the economic conditions in which transactions take place, could materially affect the amount charged, comparability under this method also depends on similarity with respect to these factors, or adjustments to account for material differences in such circumstances.

(B) *Factors to be considered in determining comparability*—

(1) *Comparable intangible property.* In order for the intangible property involved in an uncontrolled transaction to be considered comparable to the intangible property involved in the controlled transaction, both intangibles must—

(i) Be used in connection with similar products or processes within the same general industry or market; and

(ii) Have similar profit potential. The profit potential of an intangible is most reliably measured by directly calculating the net present value of the benefits to be realized (based on prospective profits to be realized or costs to be saved) through the use or subsequent transfer of the intangible, considering the capital investment and start-up expenses required, the risks to be assumed, and other relevant considerations. The need to reliably measure profit potential increases in relation to both the total amount of potential profits and the potential rate of return on investment necessary to exploit the intangible. If the information necessary to directly calculate net present value of the benefits to be realized is unavailable, and the need to reliably measure profit potential is reduced because the potential profits are relatively small in terms of total amount and rate of return, comparison of profit potential may be based upon the factors referred to in paragraph (c)(2)(iii)(B)(2) of this section. See Example 3 of § 1.482-4(c)(4). Finally, the reliability of a measure of profit potential is affected by the extent to which the profit attributable to the intangible can be isolated from the profit attributable to other factors, such as functions performed and other resources employed.

(2) *Comparable circumstances.* In evaluating the comparability of the circumstances of the controlled and uncontrolled transactions, although all of the factors described in § 1.482-1(d)(3) must be considered, specific factors that may be particularly relevant to this method include the following—

(i) The terms of the transfer, including the exploitation rights granted in the intangible, the exclusive or nonexclusive character of any rights granted, any restrictions on use, or any limitations on the geographic area in which the rights may be exploited;

(ii) The stage of development of the intangible (including, where appropriate, necessary governmental approvals, authorizations, or licenses) in the market in which the intangible is to be used;

(iii) Rights to receive updates, revisions, or modifications of the intangible;

(iv) The uniqueness of the property and the period for which it remains unique, including the degree and duration of protection afforded to the property under the laws of the relevant countries;

(v) The duration of the license, contract, or other agreement, and any termination or renegotiation rights;

(vi) Any economic and product liability risks to be assumed by the transferee;

(vii) The existence and extent of any collateral transactions or ongoing business relationships between the transferee and transferor; and

(viii) The functions to be performed by the transferor and transferee, including any ancillary or subsidiary services.

(iv) *Data and assumptions*. The reliability of the results derived from the comparable uncontrolled transaction method is affected by the completeness and accuracy of the data used and the reliability of the assumptions made to apply this method. See § 1.482-1(c) (Best method rule).

(3) Arm's length range. See § 1.482-1(e)(2) for the determination of an arm's length range.

(4) Examples. The following examples illustrate the principles of this paragraph (c).

Example 1. (i) USpharm, a U.S. pharmaceutical company, develops a new drug Z that is a safe and effective treatment for the disease zeezee. USpharm has obtained patents covering drug Z in the United States and in various foreign countries. USpharm has also obtained the regulatory authorizations necessary to market drug Z in the United States and in foreign countries.

(ii) USpharm licenses its subsidiary in country X, Xpharm, to produce and sell drug Z in country X. At the same time, it licenses an unrelated company, Ydrug, to produce and sell drug Z in country Y, a neighboring country. Prior to licensing the drug, USpharm had obtained patent protection and regulatory approvals in both countries and both countries provide similar protection for intellectual property rights. Country X and country Y are similar countries in terms of population, per capita income and the incidence of disease zeezee. Consequently, drug Z is expected to sell in similar quantities and at similar prices in both countries. In addition, costs of producing and marketing drug Z in each country are expected to be approximately the same.

(iii) USpharm and Xpharm establish terms for the license of drug Z that are identical in every material respect, including royalty rate, to the terms established between USpharm and Ydrug. In this case the district director determines that the royalty rate established in the Ydrug license agreement is a reliable measure of the arm's length royalty rate for the Xpharm license agreement.

Example 2. The facts are the same as in Example 1, except that the incidence of the disease zeezee in Country Y is much higher than in Country X. In this case, the profit potential from exploitation of the right to make and sell drug Z is likely to be much higher in country Y than it is in Country X. Consequently, the Ydrug license agreement is unlikely to provide a reliable measure of the arm's length royalty rate for the Xpharm license.

* * *

Example 4. (i) USdrug, a U.S. pharmaceutical company, has developed a new drug, Nosplit, that is useful in treating migraine headaches and produces no significant side effects. Nosplit replaces another drug, Lessplit, that USdrug had previously produced and marketed as a treatment for migraine headaches. A number of other drugs for treating migraine headaches are already on the market, but Nosplit can be expected rapidly to dominate the worldwide market for such treatments and to command a premium price since all other treatments produce side effects. Thus, USdrug projects that extraordinary profits will be derived from Nosplit in the U.S. market and other markets.

(ii) USdrug licenses its newly established European subsidiary, Eurodrug, the rights to produce and market Nosplit in the European market. In setting the royalty rate for this license, USdrug considers the royalty that it established previously when it licensed the right to produce and market Lessplit in the European market to an unrelated European pharmaceutical company. In many respects the two license agreements are closely comparable. The drugs were licensed at the same stage in their development and the agreements conveyed identical rights to the licensees. Moreover, there appear to have been no significant changes in the European market for migraine headache treatments since Lessplit was licensed. However, at the time that Lessplit was licensed there were several other similar drugs already on the market to which Lessplit was not in all cases superior. Consequently, the projected and actual Lessplit profits were substantially less than the projected Nosplit profits. Thus, USdrug concludes that the profit potential of Lessplit is not similar to the profit potential of Nosplit, and the Lessplit license agreement consequently is not a comparable uncontrolled transaction for purposes of this paragraph (c) in spite of the other indicia of comparability between the two intangibles.

* * *

(f) Special rules for transfers of intangible property—

(1) Form of consideration. If a transferee of an intangible pays nominal or no consideration and the transferor has retained a substantial interest in the property, the arm's length consideration shall be in the form of a royalty, unless a different form is demonstrably more appropriate.

(2) Periodic adjustments—

(i) *General rule.* If an intangible is transferred under an arrangement that covers more than one year, the consideration charged in each taxable year may be adjusted to ensure that it is commensurate with the income attributable to the intangible. Adjustments made pursuant to this paragraph (f)(2) shall be consistent with the arm's length standard and the provisions of § 1.482-1. In determining whether to make such adjustments in the taxable year under examination, the district director may consider all relevant facts and circumstances throughout the period the intangible is used. The determination in an earlier year that the amount charged for an intangible was an arm's length amount will not preclude the district director in a subsequent taxable year from making an adjustment to the amount charged for the intangible in the subsequent year. A periodic adjustment under the commensurate with income requirement of section 482 may be made in a subsequent taxable year without regard to whether the taxable year of the original transfer remains open for statute of limitation purposes. For exceptions to this rule see paragraph (f)(2)(ii) of this section.

(ii) *Exceptions—*

(A) *Transactions involving the same intangible.* If the same intangible was transferred to an uncontrolled taxpayer under substantially the same circumstances as those of the controlled transaction; this transaction serves as the basis for the application of the comparable uncontrolled transaction method in the first taxable year in which substantial periodic consideration was required to be paid; and the amount paid in that year was an arm's length amount, then no allocation in a subsequent year will be made under paragraph (f)(2)(i) of this paragraph for a controlled transfer of intangible property.

(B) *Transactions involving comparable intangible.* If the arm's length result is derived from the application of the comparable uncontrolled transaction method based on the transfer of a comparable intangible under comparable circumstances to those of the controlled transaction, no allocation will be made under paragraph (f)(2)(i) of this section if each of the following facts is established—

(1) The controlled taxpayers entered into a written agreement (controlled agreement) that provided for an amount of consideration with respect to each taxable year subject to such agreement, such consideration was an arm's length amount for the first taxable year in which substantial periodic consideration was required to be paid under the agreement, and such agreement remained in effect for the taxable year under review;

(2) There is a written agreement setting forth the terms of the comparable uncontrolled transaction relied upon to establish the arm's length consideration (uncontrolled agreement), which contains no provisions that would permit any change to the amount of consideration, a renegotiation, or a termination of the agreement, in circumstances comparable to those of the controlled transaction in the taxable year under review (or that contains provisions permitting only specified, noncontingent, periodic changes to the amount of consideration);

(3) The controlled agreement is substantially similar to the uncontrolled agreement, with respect to the time period for which it is effective and the provisions described in paragraph (f)(2)(ii)(B)(2) of this section;

(4) The controlled agreement limits use of the intangible to a specified field or purpose in a manner that is consistent with industry practice and any such limitation in the uncontrolled agreement;

(5) There were no substantial changes in the functions performed by the controlled transferee after the controlled

agreement was executed, except changes required by events that were not foreseeable; and

(6) The aggregate profits actually earned or the aggregate cost savings actually realized by the controlled taxpayer from the exploitation of the intangible in the year under examination, and all past years, are not less than 80% nor more than 120% of the prospective profits or cost savings that were foreseeable when the comparability of the uncontrolled agreement was established under paragraph (c)(2) of this section.

* * *

(iii) *Examples*. The following examples illustrate this paragraph (f)(2).

Example 1. (i) USdrug, a U.S. pharmaceutical company, has developed a new drug, Nosplit, that is useful in treating migraine headaches and produces no significant side effects. A number of other drugs for treating migraine headaches are already on the market, but Nosplit can be expected rapidly to dominate the worldwide market for such treatments and to command a premium price since all other treatments produce side effects. Thus, USdrug projects that extraordinary profits will be derived from Nosplit in the U.S. and European markets.

(ii) USdrug licenses its newly established European subsidiary, Eurodrug, the rights to produce and market Nosplit for the European market for 5 years. In setting the royalty rate for this license, USdrug makes projections of the annual sales revenue and the annual profits to be derived from the exploitation of Nosplit by Eurodrug. Based on the projections, a royalty rate of 3.9% is established for the term of the license.

(iii) In Year 1, USdrug evaluates the royalty rate it received from Eurodrug. Given the high profit potential of Nosplit, USdrug is unable to locate any uncontrolled transactions dealing with licenses of comparable intangible property. USdrug therefore determines that the comparable uncontrolled transaction method will not provide a reliable measure of an arm's length royalty. However, applying the comparable profits method to Eurodrug, USdrug determines that a royalty rate of 3.9% will result in Eurodrug earning an arm's length return for its manufacturing and marketing functions.

(iv) In Year 5, the U.S. income tax return for USdrug is examined, and the district director must determine whether the royalty rate between USdrug and Eurodrug is commensurate with the income attributable to Nosplit. In making this determination, the district director considers whether any of the exceptions in § 1.482-4(f)(2)(ii) are applicable. In particular, the district director compares the profit projections attributable to Nosplit made by USdrug against the actual profits realized by Eurodrug. The projected and actual profits are as follows:

	Profit projections	**Actual profits**
Year 1	200	250
Year 2	250	300
Year 3	500	600
Year 4	350	200
Year 5	100	100
Total	1400	1450

(v) The total profits earned through Year 5 were not less than 80% nor more than 120% of the profits that were projected when the license was entered into. If the district director determines that the other requirements of § 1.482-4(f)(2)(ii)(C) were met, no adjustment will be made to the royalty rate between USdrug and Eurodrug for the license of Nosplit.

Example 2. (i) The facts are the same as in Example 1, except that Eurodrug's actual profits earned were much higher than the projected profits, as follows:

	Profit projections	**Actual profits**
Year 1	200	250
Year 2	250	500
Year 3	500	800
Year 4	350	700
Year 5	100	600
Total	1400	2850

(ii) In examining USdrug's tax return for Year 5, the district director considers the actual profits realized by Eurodrug in Year 5, and all past years. Accordingly, although Years 1 through 4 may be closed under the statute of limitations, for purposes of determining whether an adjustment should be made with respect to the royalty rate in Year 5 with respect to Nosplit, the district director aggregates the actual profits from those years with the profits of Year 5. However, the district director will make an adjustment, if any, only with respect to Year 5.

* * *

Treas. Reg. § 1.482-7T. Methods to determine taxable income in connection with a cost sharing arrangement (temporary).

(a) In general. The arm's length amount charged in a controlled transaction reasonably anticipated to contribute to developing intangibles pursuant to a cost sharing arrangement (CSA), as described in paragraph (b) of this section, must be determined under a method described in this section. Each method must be applied in accordance with the provisions of § 1.482-1, except as those provisions are modified in this section.

(1) RAB share method for cost sharing transactions (CSTs). See paragraph (b)(1)(i) of this section regarding the requirement that controlled participants, as defined in section (j)(1)(i) of this section, share intangible development costs (IDCs) in proportion to their shares of reasonably anticipated benefits (RAB shares) by entering into cost sharing transactions (CSTs).

(2) Methods for platform contribution transactions (PCTs). The arm's length amount charged in a platform contribution transaction (PCT) described in paragraph (b)(1)(ii) of this section must be determined under the method or methods applicable under the other section or sections of the section 482 regulations, as supplemented by paragraph (g) of this section. See § 1.482-1(b)(2)(ii) (Selection of category of method applicable to transaction), § 1.482-1T(b)(2)(iii) (Coordination of methods applicable to certain intangible development arrangements), and paragraph (g) of this section (Supplemental guidance on methods applicable to PCTs).

(3) Methods for other controlled transactions—

(i) *Contribution to a CSA by a controlled taxpayer that is not a controlled participant*. If a controlled taxpayer that is not a controlled participant contributes to developing a cost shared intangible, as defined in section (j)(1)(i) of this section, it must receive consideration from the controlled participants under the rules of § 1.482-4T(f)(4) (Contribution to the value of an intangible owned by another). Such consideration will be treated as an intangible development cost for purposes of paragraph (d) of this section.

(ii) *Transfer of interest in a cost shared intangible*. If at any time (during the term, or upon or after the termination, of a CSA) a controlled participant transfers an interest in a cost shared intangible to another controlled taxpayer, the controlled participant must receive an arm's length amount of consideration from the transferee under the rules of §§ 1.482-1 and 1.482-4 through 1.482-6 as supplemented by paragraph (f)(4) of this section regarding arm's length consideration for a change in participation. For this purpose, a capability variation described in paragraph (f)(3) of this section is considered to be a controlled transfer of interests in cost shared intangibles.

(iii) *Other controlled transactions in connection with a CSA*. Controlled transactions between controlled participants that are not PCTs or CSTs (for example, provision of a cross operating contribution, as defined in paragraph (j)(1)(i) of this section, or make-or-sell rights) require arm's length consideration from the latter controlled participant under the rules of §§ 1.482-1, 1.482-4 through 1.482-6, and 1.482-9T as supplemented by paragraph (g)(2)(iv) of this section.

(iv) *Controlled transactions in the absence of a CSA*. If a controlled transaction is reasonably anticipated to contribute to developing intangibles pursuant to an arrangement that is not a CSA described in paragraph (b)(1) or (5) of this section, whether the results of any such controlled transaction are consistent with an arm's length result must be determined under the applicable rules of the other sections of the regulations under section 482. For example, an arrangement for developing intangibles in which one controlled taxpayer's costs of developing the intangibles significantly exceeds its share of reasonably anticipated benefits from exploiting the developed intangibles would not in substance be a CSA, as described in paragraphs (b)(1)(i) through (iii) of this section or paragraph (b)(5)(i) of this section. In such a case, unless the rules of this section are applicable by reason of paragraph (b)(5) of this section, the arrangement must be analyzed under other applicable sections of regulations under section 482 to determine whether it achieves arm's length results, and if not, to determine any allocations by the Commissioner that are consistent with such other regulations under section 482. See §§ 1.482-1(b)(2)(ii) (Selection of category of method applicable to transaction) and 1.482-1T(b)(2)(iii) (Coordination of methods applicable to certain intangible development arrangements).

(4) Coordination with the arm's length standard. A CSA produces results that are consistent with an arm's length result within the meaning of § 1.482-(b)(1) if, and only if, each controlled participant's IDC share (as determined under paragraph (d)(4) of this section) equals its RAB share, each controlled participant compensates its RAB share of the value of all platform contributions by other controlled participants, and all other requirements of this section are satisfied.

(b) Cost sharing arrangement. A cost sharing arrangement is an arrangement by which controlled participants share the costs and risks of developing cost shared intangibles in proportion to their RAB shares. An arrangement is a CSA if and only if the requirements of paragraphs (b)(1) through (4) of this section are met.

(1) Substantive requirements—

(i) *CSTs*. All controlled participants must commit to, and in fact, engage in cost sharing transactions. In CSTs, the controlled participants make payments to each other (CST Payments) as appropriate, so that in each taxable year each controlled participant's IDC share is in proportion to its respective RAB share.

(ii) *PCTs*. All controlled participants must commit to, and in fact, engage in platform contributions transactions to the extent that there are platform contributions pursuant to paragraph (c) of this section. In a PCT, each other controlled participant (PCT Payor) is obligated to, and must in fact, make arm's length payments (PCT Payments) to each controlled participant (PCT Payee) that provides a platform contribution. For guidance on determining such arm's length obligation, see paragraph (g) of this section.

(iii) *Divisional interests*. Each controlled participant must receive a non-overlapping interest in the cost shared intangibles without further obligation to compensate another controlled participant for such interest.

* * *

(2) Administrative requirements. The CSA must meet the requirements of paragraph (k) of this section.

(3) Date of a PCT. The controlled participants must enter into a PCT as of the earliest date on or after the CSA is entered into on which a platform contribution is reasonably anticipated to contribute to developing cost shared intangibles.

(4) Divisional interests—

(i) *In general*. Pursuant to paragraph (b)(1)(iii) of this section, each controlled participant must receive a non-overlapping interest in the cost shared intangibles without further obligation to compensate another controlled participant for such interest. Each controlled participant must be entitled to the perpetual and exclusive right to the profits from transactions of any member of the controlled group that includes the controlled participant with uncontrolled taxpayers to the extent that such profits are attributable to such interest in the cost shared intangibles.

* * *

(c) Platform contributions—

(1) In general. A platform contribution is any resource, capability, or right that a controlled participant has developed, maintained, or acquired externally to the intangible development activity (whether prior to or during the course of the CSA) that is reasonably anticipated to contribute to developing cost shared intangibles. The determination whether a resource, capability, or right is reasonably anticipated to contribute to developing cost shared intangibles is ongoing and based on the best available information. Therefore, a resource, capability, or right reasonably determined not to be a platform contribution as of an earlier point in time, may be reasonably determined to be a platform contribution at a later point in time. The PCT obligation regarding a resource or capability or right once determined to be a platform contribution does not terminate merely because it may later be determined that such resource or capability or right has not contributed, and no longer is reasonably anticipated to contribute, to developing cost shared intangibles. Notwithstanding the other provisions of this paragraph (c), platform contributions do not include rights in land or depreciable tangible property, and do not include rights in other resources acquired by IDCs.

* * *

(j) Definitions and special rules—

(1) Definitions—

* * *

(iii) *Partnership.* A CSA, or an arrangement to which the Commissioner applies the rules of this section, will not be treated as a partnership to which the rules of subchapter K of the Internal Revenue Code apply. See § 301.7701-1(c) of this chapter.

Treas. Reg. § 1.1235-1. Sale or exchange of patents.

(a) General rule. Section 1235 provides that a transfer (other than by gift, inheritance, or devise) of all substantial rights to a patent, or of an undivided interest in all such rights to a patent, by a holder to a person other than a related person constitutes the sale or exchange of a capital asset held for more than 1 year (6 months for taxable years beginning before 1977; 9 months for taxable years beginning in 1977), whether or not payments therefor are:

(1) Payable periodically over a period generally coterminous with the transferee's use of the patent, or

(2) Contingent on the productivity, use, or disposition of the property transferred.

(b) Scope of section 1235. If a transfer is not one described in paragraph (a) of this section, section 1235 shall be disregarded in determining whether or not such transfer is the sale or exchange of a capital asset. For example, a transfer by a person other than a holder or a transfer by a holder to a related person is not governed by section 1235. The tax consequences of such transfers shall be determined under other provisions of the internal revenue laws.

(c) Special rules—

(1) Payments for infringement. If section 1235 applies to the transfer of all substantial rights to a patent (or an undivided interest therein), amounts received in settlement of, or as the award of damages in, a suit for compensatory damages for infringement of the patent shall be considered payments attributable to a transfer to which section 1235 applies to the extent that such amounts relate to the interest transferred. For taxable years beginning before January 1, 1964, see section 1304, as in effect before such date, and § 1.1304A-1 for treatment of compensatory damages for patent infringement.

(2) Payments to an employee. Payments received by an employee as compensation for services rendered as an employee under an employment contract requiring the employee to transfer to the employer the rights to any invention by such employee are not attributable to a transfer to which section 1235 applies. However, whether payments received by an employee from his employer (under an employment contract or otherwise) are attributable to the transfer by the employee of all substantial rights to a patent (or an undivided interest therein) or are compensation for services rendered the employer by the employee is a question of fact. In determining which is the case, consideration shall be given not only to all the facts and circumstances of the employment relationship but also to whether the amount of such payments depends upon the production, sale, or use by, or the value to, the employer of the patent rights transferred by the employee. If it is determined that payments are attributable to the transfer of patent rights, and all other requirements under section 1235 are met, such payments shall be treated as proceeds derived from the sale of a patent.

(3) Successive transfers. The applicability of section 1235 to transfers of undivided interest in patents, or to successive transfers of such rights, shall be determined separately with respect to each transfer. For example, X, who is a holder, and Y, who is not a holder, transfer their respective two-thirds and one-third undivided interests in a patent to Z. Assume the transfer by X qualifies under section 1235 and that X in a later transfer acquires all the rights with respect to Y's interest, including the rights to payments from Z. One-third of all the payments thereafter received by X from Z are not attributable to a transfer to which section 1235 applies.

(d) Payor's treatment of payments in a transfer under section 1235. Payments made by the transferee of patent rights pursuant to a transfer satisfying the requirements of section 1235 are payments of the purchase price for the patent rights and are not the payment of royalties.

* * *

Treas. Reg. § 1.1235-2 Definition of terms.

For the purposes of section 1235 and § 1.1235-1:

(a) Patent. The term patent means a patent granted under the provisions of Title 35 of the United States Code, or any foreign patent granting rights generally similar to those under a United States patent. It is not necessary that the patent or patent application for the invention be in existence if the requirements of section 1235 are otherwise met.

(b) All substantial rights to a patent.

(1) The term all substantial rights to a patent means all rights (whether or not then held by the grantor) which are of value at the time the rights to the patent (or an undivided interest therein) are transferred. The term all substantial rights to a patent does not include a grant of rights to a patent:

(i) Which is limited geographically within the country of issuance;

(ii) Which is limited in duration by the terms of the agreement to a period less than the remaining life of the patent;

(iii) Which grants rights to the grantee, in fields of use within trades or industries, which are less than all the rights covered by the patent, which exist and have value at the time of the grant; or

(iv) Which grants to the grantee less than all the claims or inventions covered by the patent which exist and have value at the time of the grant.

The circumstances of the whole transaction, rather than the particular terminology used in the instrument of transfer, shall be considered in determining whether or not all substantial rights to a patent are transferred in a transaction.

(2) Rights which are not considered substantial for purposes of section 1235 may be retained by the holder. Examples of such rights are:

(i) The retention by the transferor of legal title for the purpose of securing performance or payment by the transferee in a transaction involving transfer of an exclusive license to manufacture, use, and sell for the life of the patent;

(ii) The retention by the transferor of rights in the property which are not inconsistent with the passage of ownership, such as the retention of a security interest (such as a vendor's lien), or a reservation in the nature of a condition subsequent (such as a provision for forfeiture on account of nonperformance).

(3) Examples of rights which may or may not be substantial, depending upon the circumstances of the whole transaction in which rights to a patent are transferred, are:

(i) The retention by the transferor of an absolute right to prohibit sublicensing or subassignment by the transferee;

(ii) The failure to convey to the transferee the right to use or to sell the patent property.

(4) The retention of a right to terminate the transfer at will is the retention of a substantial right for the purposes of section 1235.

(c) Undivided interest. A person owns an undivided interest in all substantial rights to a patent when he owns the same fractional share of each and every substantial right to the patent. It does not include, for example, a right to the income from a patent, or a license limited geographically, or a license which covers some, but not all, of the valuable claims or uses covered by the patent. A transfer limited in duration by the terms of the instrument to a period less than the remaining life of the patent is not a transfer of an undivided interest in all substantial rights to a patent.

(d) Holder.

(1) The term holder means any individual:

(i) Whose efforts created the patent property and who would qualify as the original and first inventor, or joint inventor, within the meaning of title 35 U.S.C., or

(ii) Who has acquired his interest in the patent property in exchange for a consideration paid to the inventor in money or money's worth prior to the actual reduction of the invention to practice (see paragraph (e) of this section), provided that such individual was neither the employer of the inventor nor related to him (see paragraph (f) of this section). The requirement that such individual is neither the employer of the inventor nor related to him must be satisfied at the time when the substantive rights as to the interest to be acquired are determined, and at the time when the consideration in money or money's worth to be paid is definitely fixed. For example, if prior to the actual reduction to practice of an invention an individual who is neither the employer of the inventor nor related to him agrees to pay the inventor a sum of money definitely fixed as to amount in return for an undivided one-half interest in rights to a patent and at a later date, when such individual has become the employer of the inventor, he pays the definitely fixed sum of money pursuant to the earlier agreement, such individual will not be denied the status of a holder because of such employment relationship.

(2) Although a partnership cannot be a holder, each member of a partnership who is an individual may qualify as a holder as to his share of a patent owned by the partnership. For example, if an inventor who is a member of a partnership composed solely of individuals uses partnership property in the development of his invention with the understanding that the patent when issued will become partnership property, each of the inventor's partners during this period would qualify as a holder. If, in this example, the partnership were not composed solely of individuals, nevertheless, each of the individual partners' distributive shares of income attributable to the transfer of all substantial rights to the patent or an undivided interest therein, would be considered proceeds from the sale or exchange of a capital asset held for more than 1 year (6 months for taxable years beginning before 1977; 9 months for taxable years beginning in 1977).

(3) An individual may qualify as a holder whether or not he is in the business of making inventions or in the business of buying and selling patents.

(e) Actual reduction to practice. For the purposes of determining whether an individual is a holder under paragraph (d) of this section, the term actual reduction to practice has the same meaning as it does under section 102(g) of Title 35 of the United States Code. Generally, an invention is reduced to actual practice when it has been tested and operated successfully under operating conditions. This may occur either before or after application for a patent but cannot occur later than the earliest time that commercial exploitation of the invention occurs.

(f) Related person.

(1) The term related person means one whose relationship to another person at the time of the transfer is described in section 267(b), except that the term does not include a brother or sister, whether of the whole or the half blood. Thus, if a holder transfers all his substantial rights to a patent to his brother or sister, or both, such transfer is not to a related person.

(2) If, prior to September 3, 1958, a holder transferred all his substantial rights to a patent to a corporation in which he owned more than 50 percent in value of the outstanding stock, he is considered as having transferred such rights to a related person for the purpose of section 1235. On the other hand, if a holder, prior to September 3, 1958, transferred all his substantial rights to a patent to a corporation in which he owned 50 percent or less in value of the outstanding stock and his brother owned the remaining stock, he is not considered as having transferred such rights to a related person since the brother relationship is to be disregarded for purposes of section 1235.

(3) If, subsequent to September 2, 1958, a holder transfers all his substantial rights to a patent to a corporation in which he owns 25 percent or more in value of the outstanding stock, he is considered as transferring such rights to a related person for the purpose of section 1235. On the other hand if a holder, subsequent to September 2, 1958, transfers all his substantial rights to a patent to a corporation in which he owns less than 25 percent in value of the outstanding stock and his brother owns the remaining stock, he is not considered as transferring such rights to a related person since the brother relationship is to be disregarded for purposes of section 1235.

(4) If a relationship described in section 267(b) exists independently of family status, the brother-sister exception, described in subparagraphs (1), (2), and (3) of this paragraph, does not apply. Thus, if a holder transfers all his substantial rights to a patent to the fiduciary of a trust of which the holder is the grantor, the holder and the fiduciary are related persons for purposes of section 1235(d). (See section 267(b)(4)) The transfer, therefore, would not qualify under section 1235(a). This result obtains whether or not the fiduciary is the brother or sister of the holder since the disqualifying relationship exists because of the grantor-fiduciary status and not because of family status.

* * *

Uniform Division of Income for Tax Purposes Act

UDITPA § 1

As used in this Act, unless the context otherwise requires:

(a) "Business income" means income arising from transactions and activity in the regular course of the taxpayer's trade or business and includes income from tangible and intangible property if the acquisition, management, and disposition of the property constitute integral parts of the taxpayer's regular trade or business operations.

(b) "Commercial domicile" means the principal place from which the trade or business of the taxpayer is directed or managed.

(c) "Compensation" means wages, salaries, commissions and any other form of remuneration paid to employees for personal services.

* * *

(e) "Non-business income" means all income other than business income.

* * *

(g) "Sales" means all gross receipts of the taxpayer not allocated under sections 4 through 8 of this Act.

(h) "State" means any state of the United States, the District of Columbia, the Commonwealth of Puerto Rico, any territory or possession of the United States, and any foreign country or political subdivision thereof.

UDITPA § 4

Rents and royalties from real or tangible personal property, capital gains, interest, dividends, or patent or copyright royalties, to the extent that they constitute non-business income, shall be allocated as provided in sections 5 through 8 of this Act.

UDITPA § 5

(a) Net rents and royalties from real property located in this state are allocable to this state.

(b) Net rents and royalties from tangible personal property are allocable to this state:

(1) if and to the extent that the property is utilized in this state, or

(2) in their entirety if the taxpayer's commercial domicile is in this state and the taxpayer is not organized under the laws of or taxable in the state in which the property is utilized.

(c) The extent of utilization of tangible personal property in a state is determined by multiplying the rents and royalties by a fraction, the numerator of which is the number of days of physical location of the property in the state during the rental or royalty period in the taxable year and the denominator of which is the number of days of physical location of the property everywhere during all rental or royalty periods in the taxable year. If the physical location of the property during the rental or royalty period is unknown or unascertainable by the taxpayer, tangible personal property is utilized in the state in which the property was located at the time the rental or royalty payer obtained possession.

UDITPA § 6

(a) Capital gains and losses from sales of real property located in this state are allocable to this state.

(b) Capital gains and losses from sales of tangible personal property are allocable to this state if—

(1) the property had a situs in this state at the time of the sale, or

(2) the taxpayer's commercial domicile is in this state and the taxpayer is not taxable in the state in which the property had a situs.

(c) Capital gains and losses from sales of intangible personal property are allocable to this state if the taxpayer's commercial domicile is in this state.

UDITPA § 7

Interest and dividends are allocable to this state if the taxpayer's commercial domicile is in this state.

UDITPA § 8

(a) Patent and copyright royalties are allocable to this state:

(1) if and to the extent that the patent or copyright is utilized by the payer in this state, or

(2) if and to the extent that the patent or copyright is utilized by the payer in a state in which the taxpayer is not taxable and the taxpayer's commercial domicile is in this state.

(b) A patent is utilized in a state to the extent that it is employed in production, fabrication, manufacturing, or other processing in the state or to the extent that a patented product is produced in the state. If the basis of receipts from patent royalties does not permit allocation to states or if the accounting procedures do not reflect states of utilization, the patent is utilized in the state in which the taxpayer's commercial domicile is located.

(c) A copyright is utilized in a state to the extent that printing or other publication originates in the state. If the basis of receipts from copyright royalties does not permit allocation to states or if the accounting procedures do not reflect states of utilization, the copyright is utilized in the state in which the taxpayer's commercial domicile is located.

UDITPA § 9

All business income shall be apportioned to this state by multiplying the income by a fraction, the numerator of which is the property factor plus the payroll factor plus the sales factor, and the denominator of which is three.

UDITPA § 10

The property factor is a fraction, the numerator of which is the average value of the taxpayer's real and tangible personal property owned or rented and used in this state during the tax period and the denominator of which is the average value of all the taxpayer's real and tangible personal property owned or rented and used during the tax period.

UDITPA § 11

Property owned by the taxpayer is valued at its original cost. Property rented by the taxpayer is valued at eight times the net annual rental rate. Net annual rental rate is the annual rental rate paid by the taxpayer less any annual rental rate received by the taxpayer from sub-rentals.

> **Comment**: This section is admittedly arbitrary in using original cost rather than depreciated cost, and in valuing rented property as eight times the annual rental. This approach is justified because the act does not impose a tax, nor prescribe the depreciation allowable in computing the tax, but merely provides a basis for division of the taxable income among the several states. The use of original cost obviates any differences due to varying methods of depreciation, and has the advantage that the basic figure is readily ascertainable from the taxpayer's books. No method of valuing the property would probably be universally acceptable.

* * *

UDITPA § 12

The average value of property shall be determined by averaging the values at the beginning and ending of the tax period but the [tax administrator] may require the averaging of monthly values during the tax period of reasonably required to reflect properly the average value of the taxpayer's property.

UDITPA § 13

The payroll factor is a fraction, the numerator of which is the total amount paid in this state during the tax period by the taxpayer for compensation, and the denominator of which is the total compensation paid everywhere during the tax period.

UDITPA § 14

Compensation is paid in this state if:

(a) the individual's service is performed entirely within the state; or

(b) the individual's service is performed both within and without the state, but the service performed without the state is incidental to the individual's service within the state; or

(c) some of the service is performed in the state and (1) the base of operations or, if there is no base of operations, the place from which the service is directed or controlled is in the state, or (2) the base of operations or the place from which the service is directed or controlled is not in any state in which some part of the service is performed, but the individual's residence is in this state

---

UDITPA § 15

The sales factor is a fraction, the numerator of which is the total sales of the taxpayer in this state during the tax period, and the denominator of which is the total sales of the taxpayer everywhere during the tax period.

Comment: The sales to be included in the fraction are only the sales which produce business income. Sales which produce "capital gains" are under section 6 and are to be allocated rather than apportioned.

"Total sales" means "total net sales" after discounts and returns.

UDITPA § 16

Sales of tangible personal property are in this state if:

(a) the property is delivered or shipped to a purchaser, other than the United States government, within this state regardless of the f.o.b. point or other conditions of the sale; or

(b) the property is shipped from an office, store, warehouse, factory, or other place of storage in this state and (1) the purchaser is the United States government or (2) the taxpayer is not taxable in the state of the purchaser.

---

www.ingramcontent.com/pod-product-compliance
Lightning Source LLC
LaVergne TN
LVHW062243200926
848484LV00006B/1604
9781600421563